J.B. Harkin

FATHER OF CANADA'S NATIONAL PARKS

J.B. Harkin

FATHER OF CANADA'S NATIONAL PARKS

E.J. (Ted) Hart

UNIVERSITY OF ALBERTA PRESS, EDMONTON

Published by

The University of Alberta Press
Ring House 2
Edmonton, Alberta, Canada T6G 2E1

Library and Archives Canada Cataloguing in Publication

Hart, E.J. (Edward John), 1946–

J.B. Harkin : father of Canada's national parks / E.J. (Ted) Hart.
(Mountain cairns : a series on the history and culture of the Canadian Rockies)

Includes index.
ISBN 978-0-88864-512-8

1. Harkin, J. B. (James Bernard), 1875–1955. 2. National parks and reserves—Canada. 3. Wildlife conservation--Canada. 4. Canada. Dominion Parks Branch—Officials and employees—Biography. I. Title. II. Series: Mountain cairns

FC215.H37 2009 333.78092 C2009-902152-8

First edition, first printing, 2010.
Printed and bound in Canada by Kromar Printing, Winnipeg, Manitoba.
Copyediting and Proofreading by Jean Wilson.
Indexing by Adrian Mather.

The University of Alberta Press is committed to protecting our natural environment. As part of our efforts, this book is printed on Enviro Paper: it contains 100% post-consumer recycled fibres and is acid- and chlorine-free.

The University of Alberta Press gratefully acknowledges the support received for its publishing program from The Canada Council for the Arts. The University of Alberta Press also gratefully acknowledges the financial support of the Government of Canada through the Book Publishing Industry Development Program (BPIDP) and from the Alberta Foundation for the Arts for its publishing activities.

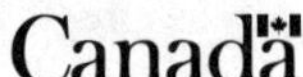

Canada Council for the Arts
Conseil des Arts du Canada

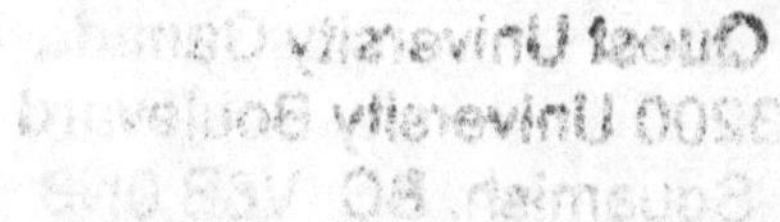

CONTENTS

ABBREVIATIONS

ELHF	Eleanor Luxton Historical Foundation
GA	Glenbow Archives
JYHS	Jasper Yellowhead Historical Society
LAC	Library and Archives Canada
PAA	Provincial Archives of Alberta
WMCR	Whyte Museum of the Canadian Rockies

Acknowledgements

THIS PROJECT WOULD not have been possible without the excellent interlibrary loan service provided by Library and Archives Canada that makes microfilm of government files available to researchers and which I relied on so heavily for access to the Dominion Parks Branch files (RG 84). I would like to thank those administering the program for their timely provision of this material and Elizabeth Kundert-Cameron and Lena Goon at the Whyte Museum of the Canadian Rockies, Library and Archives for accessing it and many other interlibrary loans for me.

I would also like to thank parks historian Jim Taylor, who read and commented on an early version of the manuscript, and two unknown (to me) peer reviewers who reviewed the manuscript for the University of Alberta Press and likewise made valuable suggestions. A subject as complex as Harkin required a strong grasp of Canada's park story and environmental history and the suggestions and information offered by these readers has, I believe, made the book much stronger. In the same vein, I would like to acknowledge the excellent editing carried out by Jean Wilson.

Finally, I would like to thank my wife Pat for persevering with me through the five years this project took to complete. Only the spouses and significant others of those bitten by the history bug can appreciate the patience and sacrifice required.

Introduction

ON THE BANFF-WINDERMERE Highway south of Kootenay Crossing is a small turn-out for a rather nondescript interpretive sign. It features a serious-looking young man looking the viewer straight in the eye, accompanied by an explanation for the naming of the peak standing in the distance behind. Time has not been kind to the Mount Harkin sign. Leaning and a little bit dilapidated, it is perhaps a fitting metaphor for the modern public's interest in its subject, James Bernard Harkin. For many years hailed as the visionary creator of Canada's unparalleled system of natural reserves with the sobriquet "Father of Canada's National Parks," more recently he has either been lost from public view or, equally disturbingly, has been viewed by environmental historians as somewhat less than praiseworthy. I hope to address these circumstances—to shine some light on this long-neglected individual so that Canadians can understand both Harkin and the world he functioned in, and by extension gain a better appreciation for their heritage of national parks and wildlife. For those with a deeper interest in environmental history I provide a framework to assist in a more informed debate about Harkin's proper place in the Canadian conservation movement.

Harkin certainly needs the exposure. About 1956 Mabel Williams, a long-time employee of the Dominion (later National) Parks Branch and author of a series of popular guide books it began producing in the 1920s, penned a biographical sketch in which she offered an assessment of Canada's national parks and their former head:

> In 1911 when Mr. Harkin took office not one person in 10,000 had ever heard the term [national park]. Today, they are accepted by the whole people. The amount of money they have brought into Canada would be difficult to calculate. They are our chief tourist attraction and draw hundreds of thousands of foreign visitors each year. To Canadians they are a source of pride and enjoyment. [They accept] their ordered loveliness; the delightful means provided for their enjoyment, without question, and least of all do they remember the man who was responsible, almost entirely for bringing them into creation, Jas. Bernard Harkin.[1]

After half a century, little has changed. While virtually every Canadian is aware of the natural and cultural heritage contained in our extensive system of national parks, not one in 10,000 would have heard of their "father." Given modern society's focus on issues of conservation, recreation, historic site preservation, and tourism, it seems strange that a man who played such a key role in establishing a legacy in these matters for future generations should be unknown. But perhaps not, for we are more accustomed to our heroes being actors, sports stars, generals, and scientists, not government bureaucrats. However, through a peculiar set of circumstances reflecting early twentieth-century history and society, the man who led the movement for conservation of Canada's national parks and wildlife was a civil servant—commissioner of

J.B. Harkin, "the father of Canada's national parks," 1947. Yousuf Karsh photograph.

Dominion Parks in the formative period of Canadian conservation between 1911 and 1936.

As a young historian and archivist in the early 1970s concentrating on Canada's mountain national parks, I came across Harkin's name frequently. It was apparent that he had not only played a key role in the events that occurred over an important period in Canadian Rockies history, but also to a great degree had controlled and orchestrated them. I also knew, as did any self-respecting student of national parks history, that Harkin's name was inextricably linked with creation of the *National Parks Act* of 1930, the *Magna Charta* of the modern Canadian parks system. Yet for information about him, there were only a few sources to which I could turn. One was an interesting little book entitled *Guardians of the Wild* published in 1936—the year Harkin retired—by the selfsame Mabel Williams, while living in London, England. The book was a somewhat romanticized, albeit very competent account of the Dominion Parks Branch and its work, and its pages left no doubt that Williams regarded her former superior as the key "guardian" in the parks story. But while summarizing the activities and accomplishments of Harkin and the branch, it failed to reveal his background, motivations, and beliefs or how they coalesced in the successes recounted. A second publication, appearing after Harkin's death in 1956 and entitled *The History and Meaning of the National Parks of Canada*, was again produced by Williams, although it appeared under Harkin's name as a collection of his writings and observations on his philosophy of national parks and their importance to the Canadian nation and mankind in general. While this revealing little tome certainly helped clarify his motivations and beliefs, at least those he had reflected upon in retirement, this work also lacked the background and context for the influences and events that spawned them.

In time, I found a few other clues. One which provided a "big picture" of the development of national parks during their formative period up to 1930 was Sylvia Van Kirk's groundbreaking thesis, "The Development of National Park Policy in Canada's National Parks, 1885 to 1930," submitted for her MA in history at the University of Alberta in 1969. In it there were frequent references to Harkin and his involvement in the major issues of the day, such as tourist promotion, industrial development, and forest and wildlife protection. Van Kirk interviewed Mabel Williams concerning these matters, but she had also used Harkin's numerous submissions appearing as part of the annual Department of the Interior reports. Apart from Van Kirk's work, which was never published, I found a few references to Harkin in "Wilderness and Man in North America" by Roderick Nash, assistant professor of history at the University of California, Santa Barbara, one of the first academics to engage in the emerging field of environmental history, presented at the seminal "The Canadian National Parks: Today and Tomorrow" conference at the University of Calgary in 1968. Nash was already being hailed for his work on the role of wilderness in American development with the recent publication of *Wilderness and the American Mind*; part of the thesis of his paper was an explanation of why wilderness appreciation (and hence conservation action) in Canada lagged two generations behind that in the United States. He placed part of the blame on Harkin for having too much concern for the economic and tourism value of Canada's parks and not enough for preserving their wilderness. He did, however, seem to admire the man, noting that he "personally had a clear conception of the aesthetic and spiritual value of wilderness," and stating that he "might have become the leader for a national wilderness crusade had his countrymen become more receptive to his ideas." Citing Harkin's recognition that there was need for a public voice for wilderness preservation, Nash mentioned that one had not appeared in Canada until several decades later, something I knew to be incorrect.[2] Another important paper presented at the conference, "The Doctrine of Usefulness: Natural Resource and National Parks Policy in Canada, 1887–1914" by University of Toronto history professor Robert Craig Brown, while not dealing directly with Harkin, provided an interesting point of view on the motivating influence for the Canadian parks he inherited in 1911, postulating that they were regarded as simply one more resource to be exploited in the realization of Prime Minister John A. Macdonald's famous "national policy."[3]

Although I doubted the accuracy of Nash's contentions regarding conservation in Canada, I had no way of confirming or denying them. In fact, it was becoming clear that the information necessary to properly understand Harkin and his work was simply not readily available, and the reason why was not too difficult to discern. As a bureaucrat, he could not publicly speak or write about government policy and, as an extremely private man, had apparently not left any papers that would shed light on his career. Fortunately, at this point I met a man who had insights that few others possessed, Fergus Lothian, himself an employee of the branch who had worked under Harkin and had gone on to a long career with Parks, retiring as assistant chief of the National Parks Service in 1968. Beginning in 1956, Parks administration had tried to have superintendents prepare histories of their parks, but by the 1960s it was apparent that the results were uneven and that much information on the system resided in Ottawa. As an authority on parks historical matters, Lothian had been contracted in 1969 to bring the disparate elements together and prepare a history of national parks development in Canada. Recognizing Harkin's key role, one of Lothian's first tasks had been to prepare a biographical sketch of his mentor, and in 1973 he presented a copy of it to my superior, Maryalice Stewart, for the Archives of the Canadian Rockies in Banff, my employer. It was at least part of the missing link, providing both a personal and official look at Harkin and his work and a few insights that added substance to the known facts. Later I realized I should have questioned Lothian further on his personal reminiscences of Harkin, but I missed the opportunity. Three years later this work helped form the basis for much of the background in his magnum opus, *A History of Canada's National Parks*, published by Parks Canada, a comprehensive although somewhat tedious, administrative overview of the Canadian parks system and each park, eventually comprising four volumes. While extremely valuable for documenting the history of Canada's parks, Lothian's work was not widely available and did not focus specifically on Harkin. Nevertheless, along with Williams's earlier efforts and Van Kirk's thesis, it still provides the primary background for today's historians. Virtually every writer who has dealt with aspects of Canadian parks and wildlife over the last three decades has used this rather limited information unequivocally and seemingly without much further investigation.

One who did so quite successfully was Janet Foster in her landmark work on wildlife preservation in Canada, originally done for her doctorate at York University in 1971 but later published by University of Toronto Press in 1978 as *Working For Wildlife: The Beginning of Preservation in Canada*. Foster's thesis was that unlike in the United States, where there had been a "crusade" for wildlife preservation, the beginning of wildlife consciousness in Canada resulted from "a small number of men in government service [who] recognized in the early twentieth century that wildlife was one of Canada's most valuable and most neglected resources and that some species were declining rapidly into extinction." These senior civil servants, she found, "used their influence to guide government policy along the lines of their personal beliefs and convictions."[4] Among these individuals—men such as Howard Douglas, superintendent of Rocky Mountains Park, Robert Campbell, director of the Forestry Branch, and Gordon Hewitt, Dominion entomologist in the Department of Agriculture—Harkin stood shoulder-to-shoulder, possessing "a clear and unfailing vision of what wilderness, parks and wildlife signified for the Canadian people in terms of both aesthetic and economic importance."[5] Foster concluded that he was fifty years ahead of his time. This was perhaps an exaggeration, but overall the picture she provided resonated with me; I was particularly impressed by her use of primary source materials on parks and wildlife matters that were becoming available in the treasure trove of government files housed at the Public Archives of Canada (now Library and Archives Canada). One of its few drawbacks was that it only took the story to 1922, ending with the first Dominion-provincial conference on wildlife, which, Foster indicated, "marks the end of the beginning in the story of wildlife conservation in Canada."[6]

Part of the importance of Foster's work was its influence in opening up the environmental history movement to Canadian topics, providing a beachhead on which others could build. In the thirty years since its appearance, work in this field has grown exponentially, and inevitably some of it has continued to touch on Harkin as a major protagonist in the story.[7] National parks and conservation historians such as Bill Waiser, Jim Taylor, PearlAnn Reichwein, Alan MacEachern, and John Sandlos have peeled back the layers that have obscured his place, and, not surprisingly, in the crucible of academic rigour where the accepted version is constantly being re-examined and reinterpreted, not all treatments have been positive. The first to take a serious tilt at Harkin was Leslie Bella, a political scientist with a strong social bent, in her 1987 critique of Canada's parks, which bore the revealing title *Parks for Profit*. Probing the longstanding relationship between preservation and development evident in Canadian parks policy, she picked up on

Brown's examination of natural resource utilization in national parks and extended it to more modern times. She found Harkin culpable of gross exploitation in his tourism policies, outlining in a chapter entitled "Autoparks" his role in developing automobile-based tourism and concluding that "Harkin had entrenched autotourism as the major purpose of Canada's national parks." Tellingly, in another chapter entitled "The First Conservation Movement," while correcting Nash's contentions about the appearance of public conservation action in Canada, she completely overlooked Harkin's role in fostering and promoting the Canadian National Parks Association in the early 1920s.[8]

Bella was joined by others who found Harkin wanting. One was historian Alan MacEachern, who at the 1994 meeting of the Canadian Historical Association delivered a paper on "Rationality and Rationalization in Canadian National Parks Predator Policy," in which he expressed a rather low opinion of Harkin, characterizing him as a mere mouthpiece for the scientists in his branch who were expressing concerns about its predator control policies but had no understanding of predator issues himself.[9] In his PhD research at Queen's University, he studied the establishment of national parks in Atlantic Canada, work that became his 2001 book *Natural Selections, National Parks in Atlantic Canada*, 1935–1970. Amplifying his earlier assessment of Harkin, he found him to be rather ineffectual and even redundant to the parks story. In his first chapter, "James Harkin and the National Parks Branch," MacEachern scolded those who had written previously about him and, likely referring to Foster's laudatory treatment, found that they had made him a "hero, if only by default." Reviewing, as I have, the lack of research material available on Harkin's background, MacEachern concluded that "we do not know enough about Harkin and as a result cannot know enough about the Parks Branch." Despite this impediment, or perhaps because of it, he had no hesitation in stating that writers "have made him ahead of his time rather than a product of it" and consequently "the Parks Branch becomes a mere backdrop to Harkin's work, and necessarily an ineffectual organization." In order to set the stage for his chosen topic, "rather than search out a way to prove Harkin's personal importance, it seems more sensible to study him as representative of the Parks Branch as a whole" and in doing so found that with no expertise in parks "Harkin relied on his staff to help draft policy, and so served as a conduit for the philosophy germinating within the Branch." While I could hardly agree with much of his opinion about Harkin, and in particular that he was merely a "conduit" in the organization, I found other of his arguments more in line with my own thinking, particularly his discussion of Harkin's approach to a central issue of parks, where MacEachern stated "his writings suggest a complex interest in both use and preservation, as well as a belief that these two were not necessarily contradictory."[10]

More recently, environmental historians have examined how government officials responsible for conservation extended their authority over remote areas, including national parks, and abrogated traditional rights of access by aboriginal and local peoples to game resources. This school is still very new, having begun in the work of Karl Jacoby, professor of history at Brown University, who in 2001 published the landmark *Crimes Against Nature: Squatters, Poachers, Thieves and the Hidden History of American Conservation*, focusing on the first U.S. parks, the Adirondacks, Yellowstone and the Grand Canyon. Jacoby believed that it was time for historians of the conservation movement to leave behind its "pantheon of conservation prophets," celebrated Americans such as John Muir, Gifford Pinchot, and Theodore Roosevelt, who laid the political and intellectual groundwork of the movement, and examine the responses of ordinary folk. This was necessary, he stated, because the traditional approach only provided one side of the picture: "Framed in this manner the history of conservation has become little more than a triumphant tale of the unfolding of an ever-more enlightened attitude toward the environment. The result has been a narrative drained of all moral complexity, its actors neatly compartmentalized into crusading heroes (conservationists) and small minded, selfish villains (conservation's opponents)."[11] His theme of a government-based technocratic approach negating a locally based "commons" was picked up in several recent works by Canadian historians. Ted Binnema in his 2006 article "'Let the Line be Drawn Now': Wilderness Conservation and the Exclusion of Aboriginal Peoples from Banff National Park" and Tina Loo in

States of Nature: Conserving Canada's Wildlife in Twentieth Century Canada published the same year both use this approach, and although neither mentioned Harkin specifically from this perspective it certainly would not be a stretch to have included him.[12] A fuller treatment is in John Sandlos's 2007 book *Hunters at the Margin: Native People and Wildlife Conservation in the Northwest Territories*, which examines a seventy-five-year period in the North beginning in the 1890s when "federal wildlife authorities assumed that state control over the region's Aboriginal hunters was the only way to save big game populations such as the caribou, the muskox, and the wood bison." Sandlos believes many authorities were contemptuous of aboriginal hunting practices, speaking of "wasteful" slaughters and "primordial bloodlust" in their hunts, and described them with strong racist overtones. He casts a wide net in identification of bureaucrats, naturalists, and biologists guilty of such practices, being particularly critical of Maxwell Graham, head of the Parks Branch's Animal Division, and O.S. Finnie, director of the Northwest Territories and Yukon Branch, but somewhat more measured in his discussion of Harkin. Several instances where his involvement is cited make him appear more sympathetic than his peers to the situation native people found themselves in, although this certainly did not absolve him in Sandlos's view. However, from my perspective, equally important is his observation in the introduction that Harkin and other senior conservationists were "adherents to many of the cultural and ideological influences that shaped the wider North American conservation movement," and that they were "both practical administrators and idealists, willing to combine the lofty aesthetic associated with an emerging wildlife ethic and the more practical language of the commercial promoter in order to inspire public support or political action."[13] This seems to indicate an acceptance that their failings, in particular their determination to make wildlife conservation a commercial enterprise and their neglect of native rights, must be viewed in light of the thinking and practices of the times and not entirely from our modern perspective, which seems to me to be too often the case.

The issues raised by these writers and the opinions of several other environmental historians will be dealt with in the pages that follow. In light of the paradigm shift in the assessment of Harkin that has taken place since the 1970s—where he has gone from being part of a pantheon of enlightened Canadian wildlife conservationists in Foster's view to one of a misanthropic group of bureaucrats intent on dispossessing native peoples in pursuit of a wildlife-based northern economy in the eyes of Sandlos—I almost feared to tread with what might be regarded as a more prosaic biography of the man. But, given the long interest I have had in the subject, the inability of several historians to find good background material and context on Harkin, as well as their sometimes, in my opinion, flawed assessments of him, I resolved to make an effort to correct some deficiencies and errors. Foster in her now three-decade-old work had decried the lack of biographies on her farsighted bureaucrat-conservationists and, because no one had stepped up to the plate, the field was still open.

My first effort in this direction appeared in a book I wrote as a result of my involvement in the Banff-Bow Valley Study of 1995–1996, where one recommendation to secure the ecological health of Banff National Park called for more emphasis on heritage tourism. Believing that there was insufficient information available for the public to fully understand what was meant by this concept, I wrote *The Place of Bows: Exploring the Heritage of the Banff-Bow Valley, Part I to 1930*. In a chapter entitled "Sanctuaries of the Original and the Wild," I explain how utilization of the parks' resources, and indeed the park as a resource itself, began to be changed to focus on a more preservationist ethic by the steadying hands of individuals such as Howard Douglas, Howard Sibbald, and Harkin. My interest piqued by the basic research I undertook, which brought my understanding of Harkin to a higher plane, I began a more in-depth inquiry in 2002, after completing *The Battle for Banff*, which took the Banff-Bow Valley heritage story to 1985. Seeking new sources where more detail about the life and times of Harkin could be found, I turned to the daunting task of reading the virtual mountain of Department of the Interior files dealing with Parks Branch matters over his period of service. Largely dry, tedious compilations focusing on mundane administrative matters concerning management of the parks, conservation of their wildlife, and marking of important historic sites, every so often their mining revealed a nugget of information on Harkin's beliefs, methods, and accomplishments. These discoveries were ultimately combined with information gleaned from other government department files, his voluminous submissions to the annual Department of the Interior report, what turned out to be a significant body of other reports and articles he produced during his period of service, and the assessments of the historians mentioned above, helping to sharpen the focus. Then, serendipitously, in one of those moments that any historian loves, a collection of Mabel Williams's papers, collected by Professor Robin Winks and containing correspondence with her mentor and notes for her work on the 1957 *Origin and History* book, arrived at the Whyte Museum Archives while I was working on the book, passed on by Library and Archives Canada after sitting in limbo in their vaults for many years after being deemed unsuitable for adding to their collections.

In undertaking my work I found that when Harkin began his quarter century as Commissioner of Dominion Parks, he faced some daunting obstacles. The Department of the Interior was highly competitive, and to insert himself into its extensive bureaucracy he needed to be creative, clever, and extremely hard-nosed. In particular, as we shall see, the forestry, irrigation, reclamation, and water power services regarded his branch, if not as an outright competitor then at the very least as an unwelcome interloper. As well, politicians of the time were at best not attuned to or at worst not interested in the idea of national parks, given their recent appearance and disparate nature, but rather were more focused on making the lands of the West the parks occupied pay through natural resource exploitation. Even after the creation of the Parks Branch in 1911, the overwhelming political expectation was that they would serve the progressive concepts that had been enunciated by the Canadian Commission of Conservation, which held that conservation activities should provide a form of sustainable development for the nation. Finally, the Canadian public had not for the most part even heard of national parks, and therefore had to be educated as to their benefits and potential and be convinced they could make a difference in their lives. As time went on, Harkin had to not only sell the populace on the need for parks but also to convince them to be prepared to fight for their protection.

I found that Harkin had used every means at his disposal and all the skills he had gained as a publicist and a secretary to two powerful and influential ministers of the Interior to push his agenda of creating and then sustaining a separate branch for national parks in an often hostile bureaucratic, political, social, and economic environment. He employed the income from tourism, the technological advantages of the automobile and its attendant roads and tourist facilities, the social mores of the times, based on the health-giving benefits of recreation and life in the outdoors, and just about any other argument he could muster to ensure success. Equally, my research revealed a man, though virtually invisible, who not only participated in but also led some of the most important conservation initiatives in Canadian history. In the process, Harkin left us with what is still today the key benchmark for national parks creation and protection, the *National Parks Act* of 1930. He turned out to be a very complex man, not only capable of using whatever was available to move his agenda forward but also exhibiting an ability to modify his outlook as the country and its citizens went through a period of rapid change. In this respect he was not a "visionary" in the manner of a Thoreau or a Muir whose conservation thinking transcended their time, but rather an "art of the possible" conservationist with an ability to make important strides in the face of the restrictive attitudes and conventions of his time.

In the final analysis, my investigations led me to some unexpected conclusions. The evidence suggested that Harkin was much more than a very high-functioning and successful bureaucrat who regarded his mandate as solely focusing on Canada's parks and wildlife. Instead, he saw himself as a representative of the Department of the Interior as a whole and equally responsible with other senior bureaucrats within its ranks to both protect Canada's public lands, in particular the large body of western lands under its control, and to undertake to produce income from them in line with the *raison d'être* of the department. Sometimes this meant that development had to be undertaken, even on important wilderness lands, so that parks could play their part in fulfilling departmental goals or gain political and public support, and sometimes it meant that their wildlife and waters had to be protected at all costs to retain Canada's natural heritage for future generations to enjoy. From this dichotomy was born the so-called "double mandate" of Canada's national parks—development and preservation—which often required compromises Harkin found entirely appropriate but which have bedeviled generations of parks administrators ever since. Indeed, I found that Harkin believed his work with the Department of the Interior helped ensure the well-being of the nation as a whole and that he possessed a national vision. Throughout his career he would recommend or participate in activities, both within and outside of his parks work, which he believed would be to the country's ultimate benefit, and this has sometimes led to a misunderstanding of his actions and motivations. But for me, this just made the man all the more interesting. Having set out to reveal a great builder and administrator of Canada's national park system and a champion for its wildlife, I instead discovered a great Canadian.[14]

ONE

Secretary Harkin

MUCH AS IS THE CASE with his entire personal life, information on James Bernard Harkin's early years is shrouded in time. We do know that he was born on January 30, 1875 at Vankleek Hill in eastern Ontario, the last of four sons and one daughter comprising the family of Dr. William Harkin and his wife Elizabeth (McDonnell). William Harkin hailed from nearby West Hawkesbury, a mixed United Empire Loyalist and French-Canadian district, where he had been born to Irish Protestant immigrants in 1831, receiving his early education there and eventually becoming a schoolteacher in Vankleek Hill. Later, he went on to study medicine at McGill University, and after returning home to set up his practice and marry his Scots-born Roman Catholic bride, he became one of the area's foremost citizens.

Given their mixed heritage, the Harkin children possessed keen minds and a strong work ethic, but differing viewpoints. The oldest son would become a priest and the only girl would also follow her mother's devout Catholic outlook; the other three boys—one becoming a physician like his father, one achieving a reputation as a noted journalist and political biographer, and the third destined to be "the father of Canada's national parks"—would be far less motivated by religious concerns.[1] However, all family members had a common outlook when it came to politics, for the same year that James was born Dr. Harkin's admiration for the Conservative Party had led him to successfully contest a seat in the Legislative Assembly for the constituency of Prescott. While few details about his political career are known, it is clear that despite his Irish background he was somewhat successful in bridging the gap between the "two solitudes" of the constituency's French and English electors, a not inconsiderable feat perhaps related to his wife's membership in the Catholic Church. Local Conservative Party operative John Hamilton, who had sponsored a petition to the assembly to divide Prescott Township along ethnic lines because of an increasing French-Canadian presence, complained to Prime Minister Sir John A. Macdonald in January 1876 that Harkin, who, he claimed, was "largely indebted to French Rolls for his election," had successfully blocked the action. In doing so, he created a bitter enemy, one who perhaps affected his ambition to serve in the House of Commons. In May 1877 Hamilton again wrote Macdonald and reported, "I think the County of Prescott will be sure to be lost unless something is done to prevent Dr. Harkin's running for the Commons—unquestionably under no possible circumstances shall I support him and I shall do my utmost with my friends to prevent his election."[2]

In a heated contest the following April the doctor failed to gain the nomination by just two votes, but as a loyal party man agreed to support the successful candidate. In writing directly to Sir John on April 12, 1878, he voiced his fear about the discontent of the French Canadians with the outcome, worrying that they might nominate their own independent Conservative candidate, and after promising to speak with "the principal objectors," requested, "If you can give me any advice or assistance in settling the matter, I shall be very glad of it."[3] None was forthcoming, but in spite of the setback of the Prescott nomination, it did not deter Dr. Harkin from his provincial efforts, and he again won the seat at Queen's Park in the 1879 election. Perhaps preparing for another attempt at the Commons, tragedy struck in 1881 when he had a heart attack while speaking in the Assembly; he died a few hours later.

While by no means destitute, with her daughter Minnie and her youngest son still at home, Elizabeth Harkin increasingly came to rely for support on her brother-in-law James Harkin, one of the most prosperous farmers in the district. Young James, already known to his friends as "Bunny," likely due to his diminutive stature, worked on his uncle's farm when not in school, but particularly looked forward to the weekend visits of his brother, William, a political journalist for the *Ottawa Journal*. William carefully followed the debates in the House from his seat in the Parliamentary Press Gallery, but was particularly enthralled with the West, having covered the Riel Rebellion as a special correspondent, an assignment that had gained him stature in the eyes of the newspaper-buying public as well as those of his younger brother. On a visit home in the spring of 1887 he perhaps told Bunny about another western story he was covering that had all parliamentarians' attention. A bill, known as the *Rocky Mountains Park Act*, was being debated that would see a 260-square-mile block of land around the hot springs near the tiny railway siding of Banff become Canada's first official national park. He would have explained that some of the land had initially been set aside as a "hot springs reserve" by order-in-council in November 1885 after Macdonald's government had become concerned that private interests were vying to develop the recently-discovered springs for their personal commercial advantage.[4] Because, as Superintendent of Mines William Pearce pointed out, there were no regulations under which title to the springs could be registered, as they constituted neither mineral nor agricultural lands, the government thought it was advisable to reserve the area so that proper control of the lands surrounding the springs could be vested in the Crown. The following summer, Pearce, the senior government official in the area (and a man who ultimately played a significant role in Harkin's career), had been directed to hold a public inquiry into the several claims of discovery, and once his report had been accepted and compensation awarded the way had been cleared for further Dominion government decisions concerning the springs' ultimate use.

William noted that the proposed legislation did not represent the declaration of any high-minded principle concerning protection of the waters and their surrounding mountain scenery for their intrinsic value, as had occurred in the United States in creating North America's first national park at Yellowstone in 1872. Rather, it was more in line with the prime minister's thinking about all the lands of the newly opened West—they should be utilized for their resources to help recoup the costs of building the railway and ensure the financial future of the nation distinct from the United States. Macdonald voiced this thinking in a speech during the debate:

> I do not suppose in any portion of the world there can be found a spot, taken together, which combines so many attractions and which promises in as great a degree not only large pecuniary advantage to the Dominion, but much prestige to the whole country by attracting the population, not only on this continent, but of Europe to this place. It has all the qualifications necessary to make it a place of great resort....There is beautiful scenery, there are curative properties of the water, there is a genial climate, there is prairie sport and there is mountain sport; and I have no doubt that it will become a great watering-place and that there will be a large town on the south side of the Bow River where the Government have laid out a town plot.[5]

This doctrine, known as the "national policy," had been extensively reported on by William and other newspapermen. All resources, particularly timber and minerals, were to be exploited along with the scenery in the new park. It was a point of view shared by the CPR, which likewise wanted to capitalize on its investment, resulting in the railway's support for park reservations and General Manager William Cornelius Van Horne's famous mountain rallying cry, "If we can't export the scenery, we'll import the tourists." This, William's newspaper instincts told him, would make the relationship between the Canadian government and the railway a very cozy one in Rocky Mountains Park, as well as at other mountain reserves in British Columbia around Mount Stephen at the mouth of the Yoho Valley and at Rogers Pass in the Selkirks, set aside by order-in-council in October 1886. With the decision to build bathhouses and pools at Banff's Cave and Basin springs, to upgrade carriage roads in the new townsite nearby, and to lease out lots to the people of distinction Macdonald hoped to attract, it was apparent to all parties that the government was prepared to invest at least some resources to provide tourist amenities and attractions. At the same time, the CPR had begun construction of what Van Horne described as "the finest hotel on the North American continent," the Banff Springs, above the confluence of the Bow and Spray rivers, indicating that the CPR was intent on providing a high level of accommodation and services.

While undoubtedly fascinated listening to his brother discuss such matters around the family table, at twelve years old much of it was likely beyond Bunny's understanding. Circumstances dictated that he had to continue to work while attending school and during his high school years he lived with the family of his doctor brother in Marquette, Michigan. He was a quick learner, but as the tenor of the times required that boys of his age not bound for university were not to spend an undue amount of time getting book learning and with the continuing need to help support his mother and sister, he soon had to consider a career.[6] For some time he had known that he wanted to follow in William's footsteps, and in 1892, at the tender age of seventeen, a position as cub reporter was secured with the *Montreal Herald*, likely through his influence. He proved to be a capable writer with a knack for reporting, soon leading to William finding him employment with his own paper, one of the nation's leading Conservative dailies. There he fell under the tutelage of the *Journal*'s editor and proprietor P.D. Ross, a man known as a tough taskmaster but one who taught his staff to write with precision and accuracy and inspired them to emulate his own mental alertness. Young Harkin's intelligence and voracity for work did not escape his notice; he was quickly promoted to the position of city editor with his own seat in the Parliamentary Press Gallery, undoubtedly benefiting from his more experienced brother's advice on current political machinations.

Using this to his advantage, he gained important insights into the workings of government and the political issues of the day. In 1896, with Macdonald dead and the Conservative Party in disarray, he watched as Sir Charles Tupper was soundly beaten in the election by the skilful Quebec leader of the resurgent Liberal Party, Wilfrid Laurier. Indeed, Election Day, June 23, was a memorable one in his newspaper career as the *Journal* had a special link with Canadian Pacific Telegraph Services that put it in a position to be the focus of the city's election reporting activities. The paper set up a "limelight apparatus," operated by W.J. Topley, one of Ottawa's leading photographers, to project the results on a large screen hung on the side of the Russell House hotel opposite the paper's Elgin Street premises. With the long June evening initially making the projection ineffective, until 8:30 p.m. he and his colleagues had to, by turns, shout out the results from the upstairs office window to the excited throng in the street below.[7] Later a strong advocate for the preservation of Canadian history, Harkin could little realize he was participating in what would prove to be one of its defining moments.

Although a Conservative organ, the *Journal* did not support the party in the 1896 election, stating its intention to "strike for cleaner politics from the word go." This would mean giving the new government a chance to prove itself, and Harkin was tasked with paying close attention to how it went about its business. Despite his own partisan background, he was particularly struck by Laurier's effectiveness in using the art of compromise to begin to heal political wounds. As well, he was impressed with some of the government's first acts, as the election signalled the beginning of an unprecedented period of growth and prosperity for Canada. In particular he was attracted to the activities of Clifford Sifton, the brilliant Manitoba lawyer who had formerly served in that province's government as attorney general and who Laurier had appointed minister of the Interior and superintendent of Indian Affairs.

Sifton was highly energetic, a strong Canadian nationalist, and a believer in the role of government in national development, making his greatest mark in fostering increased immigration with the intention of populating the West with productive agrarian settlers. But his responsibilities at Interior were much broader, embodying almost everything that happened on western lands under Dominion control after passing from the ownership of the Hudson's Bay Company in 1870, including lands administration, land and topographic surveys, administration of the Yukon and North-West Territories, water power and irrigation, forestry, parks, and immigration as well as Indian affairs. Over the next few years, embracing his brother's keen interest in the West, editor Harkin watched these activities and duly reported the minister's struggles with administration of the Yukon, his work at settling eastern European immigrants on prairie lands despite the complaints of those of British stock, his attempts at fostering improved transportation infrastructure for the movement of western grain, and his success in establishing a new branch to protect the forests of the eastern slopes and British Columbia.

As the most senior Liberal in western Canada, Sifton was also responsible for ensuring solid party support throughout the region. To assist his political goals, he acquired the *Manitoba Free Press* in 1897 with the intention that it would become both a viable business and a strong Liberal voice and agent for spreading his message to a wide western readership. His position also required him to pay close attention to the political details of each constituency in Manitoba, the North-West Territories, and British Columbia, including attending to the all-important matter of patronage appointments to public positions both to ensure and reward party loyalty. In 1901, after a difficult but successful campaign in the 1900 Dominion election, he decided he needed a "political secretary" to assist his private secretary, A.P. Collier. Seeking a recommendation from his newspaper friend P.D. Ross, who understood Ottawa, he was directed to the *Journal*'s city editor, young Jim Harkin, as the only man he knew who had the necessary qualifications, background, and intelligence for such a sensitive post. Sifton offered him the position, making for a difficult decision given the Conservative

Clifford Sifton, 1910. W.J. Topley photograph. Sifton was Harkin's minister and mentor during his early career as secretary to the minister of the Interior. [LAC, PA-025966]

loyalty that was such an important part of Harkin's heritage. But undoubtedly feeling continuing responsibility for his family, recognizing the security of the position as compared to the uncertainties of a newspaper career, and having watched for five years the decisive way in which the minister dealt with his challenges, he accepted. After passing his civil service qualifying examination, James Bernard Harkin went on government service at the age of twenty-six as a second-class clerk in the Department of Indian Affairs on December 2, 1901 at a salary of

$1,100 per annum. As head of Indian Affairs, Sifton was eligible for a second secretary in addition to Collier, who was employed under his Interior mandate, and Harkin was also awarded further compensation of $300 as "Private Secretary of Superintendent General of Indian Affairs."[8] It was the beginning of a thirty-five-year career of excellence in Canada's service.

When Harkin accepted Sifton's offer, there were several currents of thought affecting how people perceived the vast agricultural and wilderness lands that were Interior's responsibility. He would have been aware of these, given that they were most often discussed in the periodicals and newspapers of the day. In fact, he was not only conscious of them, but also greatly influenced by the new thinking they implied. These concepts were based on the belief that by the mid-1890s many Canadians no longer thought of nature simply as something that provided endless resources for their personal use or to be feared and beaten back. Rather, it had limits and more positive humanizing elements. According to historian George Altmeyer, this new positive perception "involved the ideas of Nature as a Benevolent Mother capable of soothing city-worn nerves and restoring health, of rejuvenating a physically deteriorating race and of teaching lessons no book learning could give; as a Limited Storehouse whosc treasures must be treated with greater respect; and as a Temple where one could again find and communicate with the Deity."[9]

The first idea—nature as a benevolent mother—had its origins in the economic success and national transformation achieved by the very government for whom Harkin now worked. At the time, the future of Canada looked incredibly bright, Laurier himself pronouncing in a speech that "the twentieth century shall be the century of Canada." Yet in an age of rapid industrialization and urbanization (in the decade after 1901 Canada's urban population increased 62 per cent), the newspapers were full of articles with headlines such as "Worry: The Disease of the Age." According to one of the theory's foremost proponents, "Worry was the price for the advancement of civilization; each successive step intensified the type and tempo of the struggle for existence, culminating in the present society whose chief malady was stress."

Its main cause was city life—artificial, monotonous, isolated, and basically unhealthy—leading Professor Adam Shortt of Queen's University to advise in an 1898 article in *Canadian Magazine* that Canadians could be bettered by an "improvement in the whole physical setting of our social life, involving the relations of man and nature." This "back to nature" idea was picked up by several other writers, one of whom, J.W. Dafoe, Harkin knew as a former editor at the *Journal* and, beginning in 1901, at Sifton's *Free Press*. In 1899 Dafoe wrote in *Rod and Gun*, "In these days the country has been discovered anew. No fact of contemporary life is more significant or more hopeful than this return to nature, for breathing space, for those whose daily walk is in the tumultuous streets." Five years later, L.O. Armstrong, a CPR lecturer also known through his work with the department, wrote in the same journal, "The right thinking turn to Mother Nature, and she cures them of boredom."[10]

Others saw in nature a way of restoring what they felt was a rapidly degenerating race caused by industrialization and called for "every Canadian male to get into the woods and lakes at least once a year in order to prevent them from becoming 'helplessly soft and luxurious'." Such calls when applied to younger Canadians resulted in the growing popularity of summer camps and the success of Lieutenant-General Robert Baden-Powell's Boy Scout movement, where through activities such as camping, woodcraft, and tracking Canadian boys might prepare themselves physically and mentally to defend their empire in times of peril.[11] These ideals particularly appealed to the young assistant secretary, and despite the fact that he would have no children of his own, Harkin began a commitment to Canadian scouting that eventually saw him serve on its national executive. Closely related to those who believed in these curative and restorative values of nature were adherents of the recreation movement, which was also rapidly gaining currency in Europe and North America. It put forward the theory that man's "play spirit" had been subverted by the pressures of work and society in the modern industrial age. One American writer summed it up by stating that "in country-side and city we have cherished the ideals of work, not play; we have apologized for leisure instead of making it divine." Advocates of this movement soon became strong spokesmen for the need of playgrounds and parks in urban settings and camps and picnic grounds in the surrounding countryside. Influenced by this thinking, Harkin eventually found himself adapting its messages to support the recreational potential of more remote Canadian wilderness landscapes.

The second idea—nature as a limited storehouse—was one for which he eventually became one of Canada's foremost proponents, especially with respect to wildlife. Macdonald's national policy preached that Canada's economy was to be built up on the back of its natural resources and was based on the belief that the country possessed these in unlimited quantities. Stopping at Winnipeg on returning from a trip to the Pacific coast in August 1886 on the newly completed CPR (during which he carefully inspected the tourist potential of Banff's hot springs), the prime minister noted, "The mountains are rich in gold, and silver and all descriptions of minerals, and clothed with some of the finest timber, an inexhaustible means of supplying the treeless expanse of prairies in the Northwest."[12] This myth of superabundance was common throughout North America, as it seemed to most observers that the great forests, huge stores of minerals, and vast amounts of fish and game were present in such quantities that they would never be diminished, no matter how much they were exploited for man's wealth and pleasure. But just as some new thinking began to evoke the "back to nature" ideal in the 1890s, so too by the time the Laurier Liberals came to power did a re-evaluation of these now rapidly depleting resources result in what became known as the conservation movement. It held that the fruits of nature were not limitless and that for mankind to be able to reap and enjoy them in the future, some action needed to be taken to ensure their regeneration. Initially, at least, this early form of sustainable development did not imply that these resources should not be utilized to the fullest, only that to ensure they could be utilized some scientific principles needed to be applied.

It was in forestry where this approach came to the fore. Based on European—mainly German—thinking, the recognition that unregulated timber harvesting was threatening the industry led to articles decrying the more wasteful aspects of contemporary cutting techniques.

In Canada, the Canadian Forestry Association was formed in 1900 "to awaken public interest to the sad results attending the wholesale destruction of the forest." Largely through the columns of its official publication, *Rod and Gun*, it preached scientific harvesting of the nation's timber so that the mistakes of American foresters would be avoided. However, despite the fact that the periodical was meant to promote these specific interests, it quickly became the most influential voice of the whole conservation movement and the place where new ideas were likely to appear. The economic-inspired efforts of the lumbermen to employ new techniques were emulated by sportsmen in the idea of "harvesting" fish and game instead of following the wanton and indiscriminate fishing and hunting practices of the past. Naturalist C.W. Nash, writing in *Canadian Magazine* in 1901, warned that wildlife in Canada was being killed off so precipitously that it was likely the next generation would only know it in museum displays, and pleaded that nature should be protected for its own sake, an attitude another naturalist called "the gospel of unselfishness." *Rod and Gun* picked up on this theme, fostering more enlightened attitudes toward wildlife in its readers, publishing fish and game regulations, and spearheading formation of the League of Canadian Sportsmen, which attempted to influence government to take a more responsible approach toward wise use of natural resources.[13] Harkin was aware of the periodical, as it intersected with his department's responsibility for forestry, and although it is unlikely its messages had any deep effect on him in the early part of the decade, it would not be long before he would begin to pay increasing heed to them.

The third idea—nature as a temple–also eventually played an influential role in his outlook. With long-held religious tenets generally under attack in the final years of the nineteenth century, due to acceptance of Darwinian thought and the rapid advances of science, it was an age of religious uncertainty. In the circumstances, and with other ideas of nature gaining currency, it is not surprising that some thinkers began to see the hand of God in nature. The prospect was articulated in the work of several Canadian poets, including Bliss Carman and Archibald Lampman, who themselves were influenced by New England writers such as Ralph Waldo Emerson and Henry David Thoreau, the age's foremost proponents of transcendentalism. They held that "behind nature, throughout nature, spirit is present" and that "spirit, that is the Supreme Being, does not build up nature around us but puts it forth through us." In the Canadian case, the idea was perhaps best represented in the work of Lampman, who alternately identified the spirit in nature as "force" or "energy" and asserted, "We know with the fullest intensity of sympathy that we are of one birth with everything about us, brethren to the trees, and kin to the very grass that now... flings the dew about our feet."[14] Although these sentiments and writings would have been above the head of the ordinary man-in-the-street, Harkin's later reference to these ideals makes it apparent that he was not only familiar with them but convinced of their relevance. In fact, within a few years he came very close to equating nature with God.

Harkin was also busy learning the political ropes from Sifton. His baptism of fire came immediately after his hiring, as the minister succeeded in having one of his most bitter political opponents, R.L. Richardson, independent MP for Lisgar and owner of the rival *Winnipeg Daily Tribune*, unseated for bribing voters. A by-election was called for February 1902 and Sifton pulled out all the stops in his attacks on Richardson, including two full weeks stumping the constituency and the circulation of a mass of campaign material, preparation of which was undoubtedly one of Harkin's first assignments. The campaign was successful, a Liberal farmer who let Sifton and his political cohorts do all the campaigning taking the seat by a thousand vote majority, and it provided a quick lesson on just how serious and hard-driving Harkin's new boss could be when it came to Liberal interests. When asked how his new secretary was doing at this time, the minister responded, "He's as bright as they make them and a glutton for work. He'll do."[15] But despite Harkin's first task being to assist in the Lisgar by-election, Sifton had sought his services with a much broader goal in mind, consistent with his newspaper background. As a master political tactician, the minister was determined to keep his government's achievements constantly before his supporters between elections, to discredit opposition charges and to keep party morale high. To that end, there was a need to keep the Liberal press constantly fed with well-prepared information. In this effort, Sifton was one of Canada's first politicians to realize the importance of a well-oiled propaganda machine, known as his "Press Bureau," whose role was to keep party members informed of political opinion, to write editorials and news stories from a party perspective, and to prepare and distribute propaganda at election time.[16] Key dailies in the bureau's stable were the most powerful Liberal organs of the day, including his own *Free Press*, the *Toronto Globe* and the *Montreal Herald*, and most of Harkin's days were spent gleaning the columns of every major newspaper in the country and abroad and preparing an inexhaustible supply of material for their pages.

When an important by-election or general election was in the offing, his tasks were more directed toward creating campaign materials, and, although Sifton was always a tough taskmaster, he was particularly demanding at election time. One of his most notable quotes, made in the lead up to the 1904 Dominion election, came at the end of summing up a long list of instructions to his assistant secretary when he declared, "It should be done immediately, in fact everything should be done immediately."[17] As it turned out, Harkin did have to do everything, as on the eve of the expected election in February 1904, Collier resigned, and having been promoted to the classification of first class clerk on July 1, 1902, he was now appointed private secretary to the minister of the Interior.[18] Fortunately, the election was delayed until November, allowing him time to oversee the proper preparation, printing, and distribution of material, write appropriate newspaper articles, and generate literature aimed at particular ethnic and religious groups whom the minister had attracted as immigrants. Sifton was at the height of his powers in this election, but, nonetheless, his new secretary was undoubtedly proud of his part in what turned out to be a huge Liberal victory. The party took 138 seats to the Conservatives 75, and in the West, his particular area of responsibility, they won seven out of ten seats in both Manitoba and the North-West Territories and all the seats in British Columbia.

Apart from attention to the party's political machinery, Sifton, as one of the most influential men in government and the only minister from the West in Laurier's cabinet, had his finger in a multitude of pies. His new man therefore had to be nimble to keep abreast of many issues at once. Correspondence with Prime Minister Laurier's office reveals that Harkin was handling such diverse matters as South African war veterans' settlement, North West Mounted Police concerns and surveys on western lands. Given the emphasis on immigration in the Interior portfolio, it alone required a huge amount of departmental attention, and much of the minister's focus at the time was on improving Canada's transportation system with the addition of new transcontinental railways, capable of carrying the products of the labour of the tens of thousands of new Canadians his policies had brought to the prairies. In the North he was responsible for the Yukon during the gold rush and agent in charge of presenting the country's case to the Alaska Boundary Tribunal in 1903, tasks that were of particular interest to Harkin and undoubtedly influenced his future activity in the region. But while not the major issues of the day, Sifton also had to deal with matters arising in the park at Banff and in the park reserves at Field, Glacier, Lake Louise, and Waterton. One of the highest profile issues originated with Howard Douglas, his patronage appointment as superintendent of Rocky Mountains Park, who recommended an increase in the size of the reserve to better protect its game animals, a message consistent with the calls for improved game management from periodicals such as *Rod and Gun* and naturalists like Nash.

Douglas, who more than anyone paved the way for Harkin's Parks career, had been a coal and wood dealer in Calgary with strong Liberal connections, and in 1897 had been nominated by Calgary lawyer A.L. Sifton, after his brother Clifford had dismissed the park's first superintendent, George A. Stewart, ostensibly for some leasing irregularities at Banff. Stewart, a Dominion land surveyor, had carried out some important development work during his decade of service in the park, mainly involving improvements in infrastructure to support the growing tourist trade. These had focused on the hot springs and on roads and carriage drives, including the famous Corkscrew Drive on Tunnel Mountain, the Loop Drive on the river flats below Mount Rundle, and the King's Highway connecting Banff with the coal-mining village of

Anthracite to the east. But government purse strings had been drawn shut during the depression of the early 1890s and when Douglas took over as superintendent he needed to get the politicians' attention to loosen them. Fortunately, his appointment coincided with easing of the depression and the beginning of a real tourism boom, but he had also added momentum with his discovery that tourists were not only interested in soaking in the hot springs and admiring the scenery but also enjoyed the opportunity to view wildlife. This revelation came about almost by accident in 1898 after Toronto lawyer T.G. Blackstock had made the park a gift of three buffalo, the plains denizens that had at one time numbered in the millions but were now virtually extinct, and Douglas had convinced his superiors to build an animal paddock to house them. In 1899 Lord Strathcona had added thirteen head from his ranch at Silver Heights, Manitoba, and the paddock was soon a popular tourist destination. Seeing the possibility of repopulating some of the wildlife in the park that had been decimated during the railroad construction period, Douglas added native mountain sheep, mule deer, elk, and moose as well as a variety of introduced species to the paddock for breeding stock and a further attraction.

The idea of preservation, protecting resources for their own sake, as an extension to conservation, protecting and managing for economic purposes, was only just beginning to emerge, but Douglas was an early link between the concepts.[19] In 1899 he spoke of the value of buffalo and other wildlife from the conservation perspective in his annual report, stating that "the buffalo provide a never-failing source of attraction to all visitors to the Park, and I consider the money spent in looking after and maintaining them...will prove not only a present but a permanent valuable investment, and add to the wealth of the Dominion generally."[20] His evolving understanding of the need for preservation appeared even earlier, immediately after his appointment when, as mentioned, he pushed for enlargement of the boundaries of Rocky Mountains Park to protect game and fish from the depredations of both white and native hunters. After recommending an increase to Sifton in his 1898 report, he was joined in his call by some important voices, including A.L. Sifton and A.E. Cross, members of the Legislative

Assembly of the North-West Territories. On March 22, 1899 Douglas forwarded a letter to the minister pointing out the insignificant size of Rocky Mountains at 260 square miles as compared to Yellowstone at 3,000 square miles, and reminded him that after the expected creation of provinces from the Dominion lands in the North-West Territories it would be difficult to assemble necessary holdings. Hitting their mark, these arguments convinced Sifton to introduce an amendment to the *Rocky Mountains Park Act* in 1902 extending the park's area to an enormous 4,900 square miles. In supporting the extension in the House in one of the few speeches he made with respect to parks, he noted the increasing number of visitors and stated, "We have a thriving herd of buffalo there and a number of other animals, such as moose, elk, a couple of varieties of goat, and we are trying to get together a collection of animals that will be attractive."[21] Royal assent was given the amendment on May 15, 1902 and the newly expanded park now incorporated a reserve around Lake Louise made in 1892 as well as the watersheds of the Bow, Red Deer, Kananaskis, and Spray rivers.

It is unclear how closely associated Harkin was with these matters, but after Sifton resigned from the government in February 1905 in a dispute with Laurier over education rights in the new provinces of Alberta and Saskatchewan, his replacement as minister, Frank Oliver, took an even more proactive role in parks and wildlife affairs. Immediately upon being appointed in April 1905, after a brief interregnum where Harkin reported directly to Prime Minister Laurier as the acting minister, Oliver requested that he continue in his post. This was somewhat surprising given that there was no love lost between Sifton and Oliver. Both were realists who could bend their principles when the need arose in pursuit of their ambitions, but Sifton was more the machine politician who believed that strong party discipline was necessary to reconcile the West to the government's policies of national development, while Oliver fancied himself a populist standing up for the rights of his constituents. Oliver had been for most of his career an "Independent Liberal" and the foremost party critic of Sifton's policies at Interior, particularly those on the Yukon, immigration, natives, and party patronage. As Harkin had been involved in some of these policies, it speaks well of his performance that Oliver was willing to have him continue in the secretary's position.

The offer may well have been based on Oliver's recognition of Harkin's superior skills as a writer and publicist, as the two men shared journalistic roots. Oliver's went back to the founding and proprietorship of the *Edmonton Bulletin* in 1880, where he had made it his editorial policy to fight for the rights of the settlers, to support Edmonton's interests on the rapidly changing political scene and to damn Sir John A. Macdonald and all things connected with the Conservative Party, in particular its national policy tariff, at every opportunity. He had represented the Edmonton District in the Legislative Assembly of the North-West Territories for three terms, had successfully contested the federal seat for Alberta for the Liberals in 1896 and had been one of those convincing Laurier to agree to a platform of provincial status for Alberta and Saskatchewan in the 1904 election. His fierce support of Alberta, and particularly for Edmonton, which he was instrumental in having chosen for the provincial capital, would have a major impact on the evolution of the embryonic park system.

Another possibility is that Harkin remained in the secretary's position as part of a team with Deputy Minister of the Interior William W. Cory. Ten years his senior, Cory had been born in Strathroy, Ontario, and had accompanied his parents to Manitoba in 1870 at age five, settling northwest of Portage la Prairie at Gladstone, where his father eventually became mayor. After receiving his early education in local schools and at St. John's College, Winnipeg, he had studied law, completing his articles in the Manitoba attorney general's office in 1889 and serving as a law clerk until 1900. In 1901, undoubtedly influenced by Sifton, he had joined the Department of the Interior as clerk in charge of patenting railway lands. Within months he was transferred to the difficult position of inspector of Yukon offices, spending four years assisting as the minister's eyes and ears in the troubled northern territory, the final one as assistant commissioner of Yukon lands. By 1905 he was recognized as one of the ablest men in the department, the *Ottawa Journal*'s description "knows the West like a book" speaking to his reputation, and in one of his last acts as minister, Sifton had promoted him to the complex and influential position of deputy minister in January 1905. Cory and Harkin would have crossed paths frequently as "Sifton men" holding senior positions in his administration, and they had likely already begun to form the working relationship that bore important fruit in coming years. Cory's skill and experience were undoubtedly seen to be critical to the success of Oliver as incoming minister, perhaps even more so when combined with Secretary Harkin's.

Whatever the circumstances of Harkin's continuance in the position, it ultimately led to an important opportunity with respect to the department's responsibility for parks. Oliver's initial experience with park matters had occurred in 1903 when he was involved in establishment of Canada's first large federal game preserve near Island Lake east of Edmonton, an area that in 1913 was officially designated as Elk Island Park. The area harboured a remnant population of some seventy-five elk, one of the largest herds outside northern Canada, and concerns that hunters were about to wipe them out led to a petition from numerous Edmonton district residents to fence and protect the herd. Oliver forwarded it to Sifton with his recommendation for action, and shortly after he became minister himself, fencing of a sixteen-square-mile area around Island Lake was commenced. His interest in supporting existing parks and in creating new ones, especially when it would increase his political capital in his home province, soon became manifest when other opportunities presented themselves.[22] In southern Alberta around Waterton Lakes, Superintendent of Mines Pearce had joined with local rancher F.W. Godsal in 1893 to call for a park reserve to be made to include the beautiful lakes extending south across the International Boundary. Minister T. Mayne Daly, with foresight remarkable for the times, gave direction to his deputy, "Upon the strength of Mr. Pearce's approval of Mr. Godsal's suggestion, you have my authority for making the proposed reservation for parks purposes. Posterity will bless us."[23] Originally known as Kootenay Lakes Forest Reserve, it encompassed only fifty-four square miles, and, although much of it remained undeveloped for tourist use, some was leased for petroleum exploration purposes, leading to calls for Oliver to protect and enlarge it beginning in 1905. Although officially designated as a Forest Park until 1910, he approved restrictions on exploration and appointed area pioneer John George "Kootenai" Brown as forest ranger in charge of the reserve in April 1910.

Closer to home, he approved the creation of another forest park at Jasper along the proposed lines of two new transcontinental railways, the Canadian Northern and the Grand Trunk Pacific, providing protection to the headwaters of the Athabasca River. Oliver had hoped to establish this new park with legislation similar to that which had created Rocky Mountains Park, but potential conflict with laws of the recently created Province of Alberta required that it be carried out under provisions of the *Dominion Lands Act* by order-in-council of September 14, 1907. It not only reserved the forests and waters of 5,000 square miles of beautiful mountain country famous for its use in early fur trade days as a route to the Pacific, but also kept it in government control pending the arrival of the planned transcontinental railways when it could be transformed into a tourist park like its southern neighbour, Banff. By 1910, progress of the Grand Trunk onto park lands required the establishment of a divisional point in the area, the company favouring a site near a plateau between the Miette and Athabasca rivers at Mile 112 (as measured from the Mcleod River). Forestry Superintendent R.H. Campbell believed that the Dominion government should be responsible for the creation of a townsite, which would form the administrative headquarters for the new park, but Oliver compromised by allowing the Grand Trunk to select the location while the government controlled and developed it. The site was named after Grand Trunk Vice-President E.H. Fitzhugh but was soon changed to Jasper after pioneer fur trader Jasper Hawse, to coincide with the park. Before long, the arrival of the railway and initial development of the townsite allowed Oliver to make the case that, once developed, Jasper would be Edmonton's park, just as Rocky Mountains was Calgary's.

Although important actions, Oliver's most triumphant moment as a supporter of parks and wildlife came as a result of his involvement in the country's first major effort at species preservation. In 1906 he learned from Cory that the department's assistant immigration agent at Great Falls, Montana, had reported that there was an opportunity to purchase the largest remnant herd of plains bison in North America. Owned by Michel Pablo, a resident of the Flathead Indian Reserve, the herd, estimated at 300 head, was threatened due to the cancellation of grazing privileges on their range. Led by William T. Hornaday, the leading voice for wildlife preservation in America, the North American Bison Society had been formed in 1905 to attempt to protect the few remaining animals in the United States and had convinced Congress to establish a National Bison Range in Montana. Pablo had unsuccessfully attempted to sell his herd to the U.S. government and was suspicious that it had been trying to force his hand by opening up his grazing area for settlement, accounting for his approach to a Canadian contact. Douglas, as the man in the department most knowledgeable about the animal from his experience with the small exhibition herd at Banff, was sent to Montana to negotiate, and provided an estimate of over $95,000 to acquire, ship, and fence the herd. While this was a huge sum for the times, he argued that it was a good price, convincing Prime Minister Laurier that it was in the country's interest to acquire all the animals it could. This proved to be considerably more than anticipated, the final total standing at 716 head by the time they were all rounded up and delivered in 1912, but in the House, Oliver contended, "If we are able to corner the market by getting the whole herd that fact will appreciate the value of what we have."[24] Plans were made to ship the animals to a fenced reserve near Wainwright, Alberta, to be known as "Buffalo Park," but it would not be ready until 1909, resulting in the first arrivals being sent to the new "Elk Park" reserve, where they formed the basis of a herd that has survived to the present day. The Pablo acquisition was a high profile matter for the minister and frequently reported on in the press, partly because of its latent one-upmanship on the United States. It also required considerable attention from his secretary. Fergus Lothian, who would have spoken to him about it, wrote in his biographical sketch that "as Mr. Oliver's secretary, Mr. Harkin also

Unloading of Pablo herd at the new Buffalo Park near Wainwright, Alberta, 1909. Harkin's involvement in the Pablo buffalo purchase as Oliver's secretary provided his first experience in Canada's early efforts in game preservation. [PAA, A 4739]

was involved in the purchase of the Pablo herd of buffalo, which led to the successful experiment of saving from extinction, this magnificent game animal."[25]

In 1905, just prior to the Pablo negotiations, Harkin had been forced to take a three-month leave of absence for health reasons, probably a stress-related ailment that would plague him for his entire career, and he had recuperated on a western ranch. Perhaps learning more of the West during this sojourn and interested in it through his work on the bison file, early in 1908 he undertook some special work in the region on Oliver's behalf. The minister was concerned about the activities of a group of Russian dissenters from the Russian Orthodox Church known as Doukhobors, several thousand of whom had initially settled in Saskatchewan attracted by Sifton's promise they could farm communally and live in villages, rather than on their individual farms as was required of other homesteaders. However, by 1906, when there were many more immigrants arriving and putting pressure on available lands, Oliver took a much tougher approach than his predecessor, demanding that they swear an oath of allegiance to the British Crown in order to complete the registration of their homesteads. Having suffered religious and political persecution in their native Russia, the Doukhobors resisted this requirement, and under their leader, Peter Verigin, began to protest and cause local disturbances. As one alternative to dealing with the situation, in early 1908 Oliver directed Harkin to undertake a mission to Mexico to investigate whether the colonists could be relocated and find sanctuary there. He discovered labour conditions in the country to be abhorrent and reported that although the climate was suitable, he believed the Doukhobors would become virtual agricultural slaves if they relocated and recommended against the move. Oliver accepted the advice but meantime, taking matters into his own hands, Verigin purchased land in southeastern British Columbia and later that year led his followers to the Grand Forks district to establish their own self-contained community.[26]

It seems that Oliver wanted to keep a close eye on Verigin's activities and, in any case, needed to provide some supervision for a growing number of immigration agents along the U.S. border in the West. Accordingly, in March 1908, Harkin was sent to Vancouver, where his brother William had relocated to pursue his newspaper career. On March 20, 1908 he received a letter from Superintendent of Immigration W.D. Scott informing him that "the Minister has given instructions that you are to act as Immigration Inspector along the International Boundary in Western Canada, extending from Emerson, Man. to the Pacific Coast, with supervision over the Inspectors already appointed."[27] It was a large task, as there was some twenty such inspectors, and on April 1 Harkin received instructions concerning his duty to ensure a continuing flow of American immigrants: "It is to be borne in mind that the Department does not wish to shut out any really desirable immigrants and that therefore it is important that the Inspectors should understand that they are not to carry out the law and regulations in a very inflexible way but they are expected to exercise common sense and discretion in the performance of their duties."[28] For the first two months of his new responsibilities Harkin learned the details of immigration matters, such as enforcing rules that immigrants were required to have a minimum amount of money before being allowed to enter the country and that they had to enter Canada in a direct journey from their country of origin. By June 1908 he was out in the field carrying out inspections, early August finding him in Grand Forks, likely checking up on the Doukhobors, and at work in Regina by September. The following summer his activities caught the attention of the *Victoria Times*:

> So extensive has become the work of the Dominion immigration office in this province that throughout this summer, the work of the agencies at international points will be supervised on the ground by an officer from headquarters. The duty will be discharged this summer by J.B. Harkin, chief clerk of the department, who is now in the city in the company of his chief, W.D. Scott, superintendent of immigration....The growth of British Columbia and the increasing flow of settlers has greatly increased the importance of the stations from the Crow's Nest to the coast. Mr. Harkin will probably make his headquarters for the present at Kamloops, and will personally visit the different stations.[29]

Despite the workload of this position, by early 1910 Harkin was back at Ottawa once more acting in the secretary's role, illustrating that Oliver had again being using him as a troubleshooter. Immigration matters remained a priority, as in March he was advising Oliver on a new immigration bill, but the minister was also dealing with another pressing matter with respect to a conservation file that would soon require his almost complete attention, the work of the Canadian Commission of Conservation that had begun in 1909.[30] It had roots in the rising strength of the conservation movement in the United States, leading President Theodore Roosevelt to call a series of meetings in 1908 to consider the amount and condition of natural resources and the most effective means of conserving them. The third such meeting was scheduled for Washington in February 1909; Roosevelt had asked

President's reception for delegates of the North American Conference on Conservation of Natural Resources, Washington, February 18, 1909 [Clifford Sifton eighth from right, front row). The creation of the Canadian Commission of Conservation arising from the 1909 conference with Clifford Sifton as its chair would play an important role in focusing attention on forests and ultimately parks and wildlife conservation issues. [LAC, PA-099910]

Canada to send a representative "to consider the mutual interests of the countries in the conservation of their natural resources and to deliberate on the practicability of preparing a general plan which could be applied throughout the whole continent." The letter inviting Canadian participation was delivered by Chairman of the United States National Conservation Commission Gifford Pinchot, a key individual in the conservation movement. He was welcomed by Prime Minister Laurier, who had chaired the 1906 Canadian Forestry Convention at which Pinchot was a speaker. That meeting had focused not only on forestry matters but also had examined topics such as the effect of forest conservation on water resources and the relationship between forestry, agriculture, and irrigation. Bolstered by Laurier's personal interest, the success of this convention had led to regular meetings of the association and to establishment of schools of forestry at the University of Toronto in 1907 and the University of New Brunswick in 1908. Given this commitment, Canada was more than willing to participate in the Washington conference, and at it a "Declaration of Principles" had been adopted that included conservation initiatives in forestry, public health, water, land, minerals, and game, as well as agreement that each country should have a commission of conservation similar to that set up in the United States.[31]

The Canadian government immediately carried through with this commitment, cabinet approving establishment of the Canadian Commission of Conservation in May 1909. Laurier convinced Sifton to serve as its chair. Other members included provincial and university representatives as well as three federal cabinet ministers, one of whom was Frank Oliver. With both his former and current ministers directly involved in the commission's activities, and given its high profile through Laurier's support, its ongoing agenda became important to Harkin. Although it was meant to act as a co-ordinating agency and clearing house for conservation-related studies being done across Canada, Sifton's standing and his support of its cause soon led to it being regarded as a competitor for resources and interests that bureaucrats thought more properly belonged in their own departments. This was particularly true in the Department of the Interior, a matter that Harkin now had to deal with as secretary but which remained an issue in a new set of circumstances in the years ahead.

The growing importance of forestry and its high profile in the Commission of Conservation led Oliver to consider reorganizing the Forestry Branch's responsibilities with new legislation in 1911. In contemplating the changes in administration that would be required, it was not surprising that the name of his secretary would gravitate to the top of the list. By this time the son of the late Dr. Harkin of Vankleek Hill was well established in the Department of the Interior's complex bureaucracy and had already become a valuable commodity. His early career as a journalist and a decade of experience writing political propaganda had made him an excellent communicator. As political secretary to Sifton, one of Canada's most adept politicians, he knew the issues, players, and tactics of the game intimately, and years of dealing with the numerous and important matters that regularly confronted his ministers during a period of rapid growth in the department's responsibilities provided him with a strong political acuity. His work with Oliver as his personal troubleshooter regarding complex immigration tasks and his relationship with the Commission of Conservation contributed a background of sensitivity and administrative skill. In these circumstances, J.B. Harkin, who only a few years before had been a city editor at an Ottawa newspaper, was now on a path that would ultimately lead him to his destiny as one of Canada's greatest conservationists.

USEUM
OF
NG THE C.P.RLY

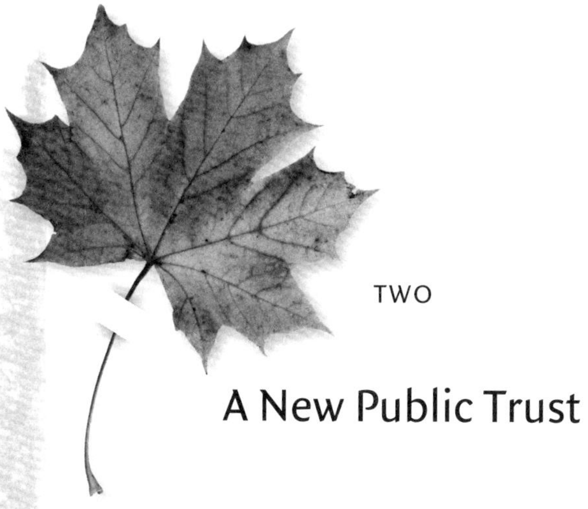

TWO

A New Public Trust

FRANK OLIVER'S RECOGNITION of the need to pay more heed to forestry matters became apparent soon after he took over the Department of the Interior portfolio, a result of its increasing profile in departmental activities. Sifton had listened to those who spoke for forest protection and had become a strong advocate for it, recognizing the potential of forestry in building up western Canada. When he became minister in 1896, some thirty-five million board feet of lumber were being produced annually from Dominion lands in the West, a quantity that had more than doubled to almost eighty million board feet by 1901. As well, acting on William Pearce's proposal to "reserve the timber as far as possible from being destroyed with the view of securing a permanent supply of water for irrigation purposes," in 1899 he had seen to it that no cutting was allowed on Crown lands on the eastern slopes and in the foothills near the Bow River. The same year he appointed Elihu Stewart, a Dominion land surveyor, as the first chief inspector of Timber and Forestry, thereby establishing the basis for a separate branch within the department.[1] Oliver followed up these important initiatives in July 1906 when the *Dominion Forest Reserves Act* was passed, placing forest reserves under the management of a superintendent of Forestry. In establishing this new, stronger basis for forestry there was to be an important by-product—the genesis of Canada's national park system and the administrative framework to guide it. Secretary Harkin soon found himself at its locus.

Succeeding Stewart in the position of superintendent of Forestry in 1907 was Robert H. Campbell, one of the most accomplished bureaucrats at Interior and a man who in this new position would exercise a powerful influence over how the country's few parks and its almost non-existent protection for wildlife evolved during a critical period. Born at Craig, Ontario, in 1867 and educated at Strathroy and the Ottawa Collegiate Institute, he had entered government service in 1887 and became chief clerk and ultimately superintendent of the Timber and Mines Branch. To this point Rocky Mountains Park and the reserves at Lake Louise, Yoho, and Glacier had drifted around the department, and in December 1907 Campbell mentioned to Cory that Oliver had informed him "he intended to place the parks in general under the charge of the Branch over which I have control."[2] The official explanation for this change was contained in the deputy minister's annual report, stating that as both irrigation and parks matters were considered to be closely connected with the preservation of the forests, the superintendent could give them the attention they deserved.[3] In undertaking the task, Campbell first reflected on the unorganized state of parks management in a memorandum to Cory—Rocky Mountains Park was administered by a departmental law clerk, T.G. Rothwell, Yoho and Glacier by the official responsible for the disposition of lands in the BC Railway Belt, R.E. Young, and no arrangements whatsoever were in place for the administration of the new Jasper Forest Park, Elk Park, or Buffalo Park. Accordingly, Campbell promised to work out "such a scheme

Picnic for J.A. Sifton (cross-legged with goatee), father of Clifford and A.L. Sifton, given by Howard Douglas (second from right), 1900. Douglas's strong Liberal connections, including those with the Sifton family, gained him appointment as superintendent of Rocky Mountains Park in 1897 and commissioner of Dominion Parks in 1908. [WMCR, V178-12]

of organization as may be necessary for the proper administration of these parks," presenting it to Cory in February 1908. This "scheme" formed the basis upon which much of future Parks administration would be structured. It involved extending his personal jurisdiction to "all matters in the Buffalo Park, Elk Park, Rocky Mountains Park of Canada and Jasper Park, which are not of a special nature and specially placed in charge of any other branch, such as mining rights," and "in Yoho Park and Glacier Park in the Railway Belt in British Columbia, the administration of the timber, the construction of roads and all matters relating to the improvement of communications for the convenience of public travel, but not the disposal of lands by sale or lease." Placed in charge would be a "commissioner" who "will have control of all officers, books and accounts and of the administration of such parks, and all matters in connection therewith shall be subject to his inspection at any time."[4] Chosen to fill this important new position was Rocky Mountains Park Superintendent Howard Douglas, likely as a result of his political connections, his good work at Banff, and his role in the

Pablo herd's acquisition. His subsequent performance merited the recognition, for over the next three years he not only helped mould the new administration into a cohesive operation but also made significant strides in forest and game protection.

Following Oliver's approval, the plan came into effect in March 1908, and despite the fact that Campbell's primary goal remained the extension of regulatory and administrative control over the ever-increasing number of forest reserves in western Canada, he did exhibit a growing consciousness for the need to protect fish and game in both the parks and the forest reserves, listening carefully to Douglas's recommendations. Most insistent was his plea for establishment of a game and fire guardian service, approved in May 1909 after a long period of false starts and arguments that to effectively protect the enlarged area of Rocky Mountains Park, he needed more and better manpower. New regulations passed in June specifically allowed for the creation of such a force, section 75 reading, "Game guardians may be appointed by the Minister of the Interior and such Guardians shall have authority to enforce the laws and regulations in force within the Parks." By then Douglas had received instructions from Cory to "appoint H.E. Sibbald Chief Game Warden, and Robert Robertson and John Hogarth of Exshaw as Assistants," and he was informing Campbell that he would "arrange with them about establishing patrols etc."[5] The choice of Howard Sibbald, an accomplished backwoodsman and former Indian agent raised among the Stoney at the McDougall Mission in Morley, proved to be a good one, as his energy and skill became critical in leading the development of the nascent warden service during the next quarter century. Initially his force consisted only of Robertson and Hogarth, but by 1912 there were twelve guardians under his authority patrolling for fires and poachers in Rocky Mountains Park as well as others in Yoho, Glacier, and Jasper parks. His appointment also provided stability to the administration at Banff, an important influence as in 1910, in an effort to ensure proper development of Jasper Park, Douglas's headquarters were moved from Banff to Oliver's home of Edmonton.

Pressures from unresolved matters respecting the forest reserves on the eastern slopes of the Rockies, questions of power and irrigation development of mountain waters, and ever-increasing tourist visitation to park lands soon convinced Oliver of the need for further changes. The forest reserves were the major catalyst, the thrust for action springing from the early activities of the Conservation Commission, where it was a major topic of concern. This was not surprising given Sifton's interest, and in his maiden speech as chairman during the commission's first annual meeting in January 1910, he specifically mentioned the reserves. Comparing the differences between the United States, where most forest lands were privately owned, and Canada, where they were largely under the control of the Crown, he stated, "The lands surrounding the head-waters of some of our greatest and most important water courses are still in the ownership of our Governments, so that extensive reserves can be made with little expense to the public treasury." Oliver sat on the commission's important Committee of Forests, which at its first meeting held on May 2, 1910 passed a resolution recommending to the government the setting aside of the eastern slopes of the Rockies for such a reserve. When this initiative was brought forward at the commission's second annual meeting in January 1911, it was duly reported that "it is gratifying to know that this area was set apart by Order in Council and, within the last few days, a Bill has been introduced for the purpose of permanently setting apart this reserve, which covers a large area of about 14,600 square miles."[6] However, the *Dominion Forest Reserves and Parks Act*, the legislation being referred to, not only solidified the direction of forest management but also determined the future of Canada's national parks by placing them in a new administrative framework, soon to be headed by a commissioner of Dominion parks having increased powers and responsibilities.

In speaking to the act after its tabling in Parliament in April, Oliver explained that "provision is made for placing all present forest and park reservations under the provisions of the Forest Reserves Act and then setting apart, within those forest reservations, park reservations with regard to which the regulations look to the enjoyment by the people of the natural advantages and beauties of those particular sections of the reserves."[7] It received royal assent on May 19, 1911, but despite the minister's assurance that the actions were carried out with an eye toward people's enjoyment of the parks as special parts of the forest reserves, in actuality it seriously weakened them. The parks were to be established by governor-in-council and when this occurred on June 8, 1911 they were substantially reduced in size. Rocky Mountains was slashed by 3,100 square miles to 1,800 square miles, Jasper by an even greater 4,000 square miles to 1,000 square miles, and the already tiny Waterton Lakes from 54 square miles to a miniscule 13.5 square miles.[8]

This action spoke to the minor importance of parks as compared with forest reserves and to Campbell's strong influence, for in his mind there was logic to these changes. Essentially, the act had set aside all lands above 4,000 feet along the eastern slope of the Rockies from the international boundary to a point 160 miles north of Jasper as a forest reserve withdrawn from sale, settlement, and disposition. As Campbell explained to the Commission of Conservation in 1912, "the two great things for which the reserve was established are protection of the timber and, as a consequence, the protection of the water supply," making particular reference to the threat of forest fires. Nonetheless, while the future of parks and wildlife were obviously not the main focus of the legislation, he did go to great pains to point out that they had not been neglected, explaining that the forest reserves were themselves important refuges for game, that some parts of them had been made game preserves and that the lands designated as Rocky Mountains and Jasper parks were also game preserves. In addition, with respect to access to the parks he stated, "The Governor in Council may from time to time, by proclamation, designate such reserves or areas within forest reserves as he sees fit, to be and be known as Dominion parks, and subject to the use of such parks and pleasure grounds for the benefit, advantage and enjoyment of the people of Canada."[9] Although the size of the parks had been reduced by the legislation, he explained that, among others, both Douglas and Sibbald had called for a reduction, particularly in the foothills country, to improve enforcement of regulations with their small staff and that the minister was merely trying to rationalize the situation.

Campbell amplified on his explanation to the Commission of Conservation in a letter of December 1911 to F.K. Vreeland, a member of the prestigious Campfire Club of America, in response to his criticism of the reductions. He stated that Oliver's policy was not well understood as his idea of a park as a place where visitors could be given as much freedom as possible only required reserves smaller than those previously created. He did, however, go to pains to point out that park reductions were not done to reduce areas where game would be protected, as that was to be provided for under forest reserve regulations.[10] As subsequent events showed, he was being somewhat disingenuous in this response, as it was primarily his idea to shrink the size of the parks, a step that allowed for as much forestry land as possible to be retained under his personal control in light of an important administrative change also incorporated into the June order. To redistribute the burdens that were obviously going to weigh down the Forestry Branch with its huge new responsibilities, Oliver had decided to create two new branches in the Department of the Interior, one responsible for water power and one for Dominion parks. According to a later report by Harkin, an examination of the Forestry superintendent's duties led to "a recognition of the potentialities in connection with National Parks and the essential differences in the administrative requirements concerning National Parks and National Forest Reserves," requiring "the detachment of the parks from the Forestry Branch and to the organization of a separate branch charged with the administration of parks alone."[11] In a fateful decision, Oliver turned to him to head the new Dominion Parks Branch; Harkin later claimed that the invitation caught him by surprise:

> It was in June, 1911, that Hon. Frank Oliver, then Minister of the Interior, called me into his office and told me that he was considering the creation of a new Branch of his department. The number of visitors, he said, who are coming to see our Canadian Rockies is increasing each year and the government feels that we should be doing more to protect this magnificent region. As you know we have one legally constituted area at Banff set aside by Act of Parliament as a "National Park," and four others set aside by Order-in-Council as "Scenic Reserves." The

> Government had decided to bring down a Bill creating them all "Dominion Parks" and establishing a separate Branch headed by an executive who will have full power to administer and protect them. "How," he said, "would you like to take on the job?"
>
> Overcome by surprise I could only say that I doubted my ability since I knew nothing about the parks or what would be expected of me.
>
> "All the better," he said, in his laconic way, "You won't be hampered by preconceived ideas and you can find out."
>
> The prospect intrigued and stirred my imagination, and, albeit with many misgivings as to my ability, I told him I would undertake the post.[12]

In another version of the event, he related that Oliver had offered him his choice of heading the new Dominion Water Power Branch or the Dominion Parks Branch, and he had chosen parks.[13]

The fact that the story was recounted in a memoir prepared from notes and reminiscences after Harkin's death makes it appear apocryphal. As pointed out, his position of private secretary would have periodically placed him in the way of issues dealing with parks and wildlife, Lothian, for example, recording that he played an important role in the Pablo buffalo matter, and his immigration service in the West required that he would often pass through Waterton and Rocky Mountains parks. Why then would he later claim that he knew nothing about parks or what would be expected of him? The answer likely lies in his propensity to never publicly discuss his work with Sifton and Oliver. His decade with them had largely been political in nature, requiring that he work in the background employing their power and influence to achieve their partisan ends, efforts that would not be seen to be of the highest calling in the public service. In contrast, his work after 1911 saw concerted progress being made on important parts of Canada's natural heritage, work for which he received an enviable reputation. While it is remarkable that he never seems to have spoken or written about his early life and work, almost making it seem like it had never happened,

J.B. Harkin, about the time of his appointment as commissioner. Two portraits taken at this sitting are the only ones known to exist of Harkin during his thirty-five years of government service. [LAC, PA-121371]

this practice had the benefit of precluding unwanted light from being shone on it. In actuality, though, that work proved to be the perfect preparation for dealing with the difficult and delicate task of moving forward Harkin's soon-to-be developed parks and wildlife messages to a not-often receptive public and skeptical politicians while keeping a low profile.[14]

The order-in-council appointing Harkin to the position was not passed until August 10, 1911, two months after the creation of the Dominion Parks Branch as a separate administrative unit, although it was retroactive to April 1st. It represented a strengthened position from that which Douglas had occupied, reporting directly to the deputy minister and headquartered in Ottawa. Douglas became chief superintendent of Dominion Parks, reporting to the commissioner, Harkin claiming that "the change in no way altered the duties performed by him, the new title being given because it was considered it more accurately described the duties of the office, viz. the supervision of the work of the individual park superintendents."[15] The appointment went almost unnoticed in Ottawa newspapers among others of the same date to more high-profile bodies, such as the International Waterways Commission, and with a major cabinet shuffle carried out by Laurier in preparation for the election he had just called. Its timing could not have been worse, for despite the fact Harkin was the perfect candidate for the new commissioner's position, the so-called "reciprocity election" would immediately throw his future in it into doubt.

The main Liberal electoral plank was support for a draft agreement to extricate Canada from high American duties imposed on agricultural products and equipment in return for extending preferred nation status to the United States with respect to tariffs on Canadian products, an idea believed to be so popular with the Canadian public that Laurier had decided to go to the hustings two years earlier than necessary. However, opposition soon arose due to latent anti-Americanism still evident from Macdonald's time and fears that such an arrangement would form a beachhead for annexation, a concept spoken of freely in the American press. A highly influential group fostering Canada's British connection came to the fore, Clifford Sifton in the vanguard. Although not running for a seat himself, he came out strongly in opposition to his own party's position, declaring, according to the *Toronto News*, "strongly and unequivocally against the trade agreement" and lending his support to the Conservatives' position. The earthshaking outcome of the vote, an unexpected Conservative victory, immediately brought into question the future of a number of appointments to senior government positions, among them that of commissioner of Dominion parks.

A well-placed observer was a noteworthy and redoubtable Philadelphia Quaker widow named Mary Schäffer, about to take up residence in the "unofficial" parks headquarters of Banff. She had just completed some amazing feats of exploration in the Canadian Rockies, including "discovery" of Jasper's beautiful Maligne Lake in 1908 and its survey for the Dominion government earlier in 1911, accomplishments that led to a reputation as one of the Rockies' most famous citizens. The guide for her early trips was a young Englishman named William "Billy" Warren (whom she married in 1915), who had initially worked for pioneer Banff outfitter Tom Wilson but who by 1911 was already gaining a reputation as one of the park's up-and-coming businessmen. Warren was a staunch Conservative and on excellent terms with MP Richard B. Bennett, the well-known Calgary corporate lawyer and entrepreneur (and a politician with whom Harkin's career would intersect more than any other), who he had just assisted in winning the Calgary West constituency that included Banff. These circumstances provided Schäffer with plenty of political gossip, and she shared some of it in letters to her Philadelphia attorney, George Vaux, who had also spent several summers exploring the mountains and knew many of the players involved. This correspondence provides an insight into the fluidity of the position of commissioner in the immediate post-election period and illustrates just how close Harkin came to losing it.

In writing to Vaux in October 1911 she noted, "Thee would be interested in all the political doings here....The Cons. won out to their own great surprise as thee knows. Absolutely *no* one dreamed of the change." She went on to state her belief that "there is bound to be a great change in the park" and speculated that the influence of the Liberal-leaning Brewster brothers' transportation interests would be broken. Furthermore, she felt that Robert Campbell, a well-known flour and grain trader in Calgary and a former competitor of the Brewsters, would be offered the Banff superintendency if he wanted it.[16] She followed up her initial thoughts in another letter to Vaux on November 21 commenting on a further change which might occur—in referring to another important figure in the Canadian Rockies who would also play a key role in Harkin's future, Arthur O. Wheeler, president of the Alpine Club of Canada, she stated, "He is trying for the Comm. Park position, but it is pretty well settled that it goes to a man by the name of Clark in Calgary, a thoro. Politician, a 'Tammany man' they call him. This is the doings of the C.P.R., and the Brewsters are jubilant." "Clark" was Simon John (Jack) Clarke, a pioneer Mounted Police member involved in the founding of Fort Calgary and later a successful hotel operator, alderman and, ultimately, city commissioner. As a prominent Conservative supporter of Bennett, he seemed to have the inside track on the park commissioner's position at this point. On November 30, Schäffer was still worrying: "I fear they are going to put in a Tammany specimen as Comm., and he (John Clark) is awful. Rob says he will not serve under him. Every one wants Rob. Nothing is settled, and will not be for some time, but Rob is the man." And again on December 3: "I saw Mrs. Campbell, but Rob is away....The Conservatives here, have asked him to take local Supt'dcy, and he has answered it depends on who is made Comm. No one seems to have a real inkling. The only thing we can depend upon is that it will be some one thoroughly incompetent."[17]

These letters make it clear that, at least in Calgary and Banff, it was expected Harkin would be removed as soon as the Conservatives could decide on his replacement. But it appears that Clarke, who was known to covet the superintendent's position at Banff as his political reward, opted not, so late in his career, to move to Ottawa away from his home and western power base. However, another interesting possibility is that support for keeping Harkin in the position came from his former boss, Clifford Sifton. Given their close association, Sifton likely played a role in his appointment in the first place, and now, with his part in the defeat of the Liberal Party and his new relationship with Prime Minister Borden, which would see him continue to chair the Conservation Commission, he may well have been asked his opinion about matters affecting his old department and stood behind the man who had served him so well as secretary. Whatever the reasons, Harkin retained the office, a quite extraordinary accomplishment given his recent appointment to the position by the outgoing minister in an age when virtually every government office was awarded on the basis of patronage. It was even more amazing in light of the new minister of the Interior being Robert Rogers, chief Conservative organizer for R.L. Richardson in the Lisgar by-election of 1901, during which Harkin had made his debut as a Sifton agent for the Liberal cause. The other pieces also fell into place, Clarke being appointed superintendent of Rocky Mountains Park in May 1913, while Campbell became the MLA for Banff in the Alberta provincial election of the same year. By the following year the man who Mary Schäffer predicted would be "thoroughly incompetent" was a guest in her home and was informing her of how he intended to open up the tourist trade in the park in the face of the opposition of livery interests by further relaxing restrictions on motorcars.

Undoubtedly aware of the speculation swirling around him in the late fall of 1911, Harkin did not let it deter him from getting on with the job. Familiar with the parks situation in a general way, he had no first-hand experience with their administrative requirements. The Parks Branch offices were initially located in the Birks Building behind Ottawa's venerable Rideau Club, and Harkin was assigned a staff of four people transferred from Forestry—engineer Frank Williamson, who was appointed deputy commissioner, naturalist Maxwell Graham, financial officer F.H. Byshe, and secretary Miss von Charles. Three more staff members were quickly added, including Mabel Williams, who apparently worked with Harkin at Interior and would handle early publicity and education responsibilities, chief clerk J.E. "Bert" Spero, and secretary Dorothy "Dora" Barber. Most remained with him for the next quarter century as they built Canada's national park system; Williams became the most important chronicler of the task. A rarity as a female university graduate, she was a native of Ottawa who had first attended Huron College in London, Ontario, studying English and Languages before completing her BA at the University of Toronto in 1900. She proved to have unique writing talents, leading to her 1936 *Guardians of the Wild*, outlining the branch's accomplishments.

In a chapter entitled "Beginnings" she asked, "Who at the time could have foreseen the changes the next decade would bring?" and described Harkin's first days on the job:

> Certainly not the young man who sat in that drab Civil Service office at Ottawa or the seven others who sat at shining new desks in adjoining rooms, though they too were at a moment of change. The young man was not looking through those rather grimy window-panes at the rather depressing back premises of the Rideau Club; he was not conscious of the beating rain. He was not thinking of the bare distempered walls, the ill-assorted furniture, the cheerless bookcase empty of books. He was studying with intense concentration two documents that lay before him—one the "Dominion Forest Reserves and Parks Act of 1911," which set aside certain areas in the Dominion of Canada for the perpetual "benefit and enjoyment of the people," under the control of an officer to be known as the Commissioner of Dominion Parks; the other, an Order-in-Council appointing him to the position.
>
> Seven thousand five hundred square miles! It was a small kingdom! And it was all henceforth to be under Government control, removed for the operation of any other Act except the Criminal Code. The Commissioner and his small staff were to initiate policies of protection and development, to discharge on behalf of the government a new public trust.[18]

Williams recalled there was little in the office to "serve for guide or inspiration," describing the files that had been transferred to the new organization as "dreary compilations of correspondence concerning transfers of land in the town sites of Banff and Field, the collection of rates and telephone charges, complaints regarding dusty roads and the absence of garbage collection." Therein, she believed, Harkin faced his first challenge: "Three thousand miles away from their inspiring reality, it was difficult to visualize these National Parks, and far more difficult to realize to what manifold uses they might be put."[19] Difficult indeed, as a dozen years later Harkin would recall, "At the outset the main impulse was to set these areas aside; to make them public possessions. What specific purposes the parks would serve, what ideals would move them, what policy should be adopted for development—these objectives were only dimly understood."[20]

Accordingly, and given his journalism background, Harkin had determined that the first order of business must be to gain an understanding of his subject matter. Cory's counsel and Douglas's annual reports provided a starting point, but the "cheerless bookcases empty of books" that Williams described began to be filled with publications and papers, largely from American sources, that could provide insight into the origins and purposes of parks and a philosophical underpinning for the decisions he would have to take. In so doing, he began a process of borrowing ideas and sharing information with Americans about parks, wildlife, tourism, and a host of other topics that lasted his entire career and became a major factor in shaping Canada's parks. Although his initial reading list is uncertain, later reminiscences provide some insights—experience of the United States with national parks had begun some fifteen years before Canada's with the creation of Yellowstone Park by an Act of Congress in 1872, and this is where he began:

> One of my first duties, I felt, must be to find out what national parks were, when they had been established, and the inspiration behind them. The word "park" seemed a very small name for so great a thing. Credit for the use of the term and honour for the vision behind it, I found, must go to Judge Cornelius Hedges, of Montana, a member of thc first authorized party to explore the Yellowstone region in 1871. After thirty-five days journey through this remarkable region, they came to their last camp on the

> Firehold [Firehole] River. As they sat about the fire, talking of the marvels they had seen, they began to speculate as to its possible future. Some wished to acquire part of it for themselves, others had rosy dreams of fortunes that might be made through commercial exploitation. But Judge Hedges—all honour to his name—said quietly: "Gentlemen, this place is too big and too beautiful to belong to any private individual. It should be set aside by the government for the use and enjoyment of the people for all time as a National Park...."
>
> It is an inspiring story, one which I have never forgotten. Here was a new "Declaration of Rights"—the right of the people to share in the use and enjoyment of the noblest regions in their own land, another expression of the great principle of Conservation—the duty of a nation to guard its treasures of art, natural beauty, or natural wonders for generations to come.[21]

Throughout his lifetime, Harkin often repeated this story, finding in it a clear example of the ability of nature to transform mankind.

The writings of John Muir, the foremost American proponent of the value of nature and the outdoors to the human spirit and founder of the conservation-oriented Sierra Club twenty years earlier, were also high on the agenda. Harkin, like Douglas before him, became an unabashed admirer of Muir's thinking and incorporated it into his own evolving philosophy of parks, quoting it freely. This first occurred in his annual report of September 1913 where he referred to Muir's words that "thousands of tired, nerve-shaken, over-civilized people are beginning to find out that going to the mountains is going home; that wilderness is a necessity and that mountain parks and reserves are useful, not only as fountains of timber and irrigating rivers, but as fountains of life."[22] Writings on park history and philosophy were supplemented by a myriad of journals and newsletters that provided technical information and discussed evolving ideas affecting the job to be done; Parks files became replete with publications as diverse as those of the United

States Biological Survey with respect to wildlife and various engineering organizations studying road-building materials.

With an understanding of the history and ideals of parks supporting him, Harkin sought a briefing on the pressing issues facing his new branch. In the past, Howard Douglas had occasionally come to Ottawa to discuss park matters, and Harkin recommended continuing the practice to Cory in November 1911, pointing out, "The conclusions regarding administrative action can be reached there but in a fraction of the time required by correspondence." And, he reported, he had a full agenda ready for discussion, including amendments to park general regulations, timber regulations, and Banff water and sewer regulations; extension of the water and sewer system south of the Bow River in order to open new lands to meet "the extraordinary demand for lots in Banff"; and several matters concerning the development of Jasper Park, such as the opening up of Fitzhugh (Jasper) and Fiddle Creek townsites, a co-operative arrangement with the Grand Trunk Pacific Railway to secure a water supply at Fitzhugh, a proposed carriage road to Fiddle Creek hot springs, and a proposed lease of surface rights to allow Jasper Collieries to open a townsite at their mines similar to Bankhead in Rocky Mountains Park.[23] As it transpired, Douglas's visit was delayed and meantime the agenda grew markedly, illustrating how quickly issues were being identified in the rapidly evolving circumstances. New inclusions were the extension of parks boundaries to "approximately their old limits"; amendments to park mining and quarrying regulations; review of plans for a new bathhouse at Banff; the application of the CPR for new guest cottage lands at Lake Louise; conditions of the CPR's occupation of the golf links at Banff; preparation of promotional materials on Banff and Jasper; and several matters concerning roads, including possible amendments to automobile regulations.[24]

The meeting was held in January 1912, and with a better grasp of the initial challenges arising from it, it now remained for him to visit the parks and get a first-hand appreciation for their physical reality and discuss issues with those on the ground. The necessity of completing his first annual report delayed Harkin's journey until July, by which time his non-appearance after almost a year in his position had begun to wear thin on those in Banff who felt that park administration was in disarray after the Conservative election victory. Norman Luxton, owner of the *Banff Crag and Canyon*, was among them; as early as the beginning of June he had directed editor Kidner to use his acerbic pen to call for the commissioner's presence: "Mr. J.B. Harkin, Commissioner of Dominion Parks, is in practical control of all the great natural parks and reservations of this country, including the Rocky Mountains Park, and it would be an excellent thing if he would take a trip to some of these reservations and see for himself what his responsibilities are.... Ottawa is a far cry from the Rocky Mountains and although distance is said to lend enchantment to the view, in this case the Commissioner would most probably discover on closer inspection that there was much hallucination about the enchantment."[25] Harkin took this criticism to heart, a week later writing Luxton to thank him for sending a copy of the issue, indicating that as an old newspaperman he could appreciate the "roast" he had received, and agreeing with its message:

> Though I have for a good many years spent a lot of time in the mountains—chiefly in the British Columbia end I'll admit—no one realizes more than I do how desirable it is that I should get on the scene at Banff at an early date to properly "get my feet in," and I am going just as soon as conditions here will permit. There cannot be satisfactory results in Parks administration unless there is a thoroughly efficient organization inside and outside. Matters are shaping up very well at this end and probably if you had an opportunity of familiarizing yourself with the details of developments taking place at Banff you would agree that there is something doing there also. But whatever my limitations may be, I naturally feel that I cannot get the best results until I have gone over the situation right on the ground.
>
> When I reach Banff I hope to meet you personally and get the benefit of your views and experience as to the best

Norman Luxton feeding his pet bear at his Sign of the Goat Curio Store, ca. 1907. George Luxton photograph. Although initially characterizing himself as a supporter, Luxton would become one of the strongest critics of Harkin's parks administrative activities in Banff. [ELHF, LUX 1/IIIB]

> line to follow in Park development, and I hope to absorb the ideas of every other Banff citizen who is willing to pass them on.[26]

Luxton's response was blunt, indicating that he and other Banff businessmen had been hoping that something would be done for the park for the past decade and while Douglas had kept up what he had built, "the last 12 months everything has gone to the devil." He complained, "Our once fine collection of wild animals and birds is a ghost of what it was. Our Roads resemble a badly patched corduroy trail some where in the wilds of northern Ontario. The Sulphur Springs are human cess pools. The inside accommodation is even worse." In these circumstances, he could support Harkin's intentions, but questioned whether he could achieve them in the face of "those fools at Ottawa," offering, "like Mr. Douglas was 10 years ago, you are starting in to do the right thing. I hope, but I cannot trust those idiots above you. They will knock your plans on the head the way they have others and make you a nice kind old horse that always does what he is told, or a rank socialist." Nevertheless, he encouraged Harkin to come as soon as possible, but warned, "Apart from any little pleasures that are in our power to give you, I promise you a line up of the warmest list of grievances you ever heard of including in Siberia, Turkey and darkest Africa."[27]

As Luxton was an influential businessman and opinion setter, Harkin's letter had undoubtedly been meant as an olive branch, and he must have been somewhat taken aback by this response. Indeed, despite the fact that it ended with a pledge that "we are heart and soul and money with you in your movement towards better conditions," it did not result in a lessening of criticism in the columns of the *Crag*. Kidner wrote in the July 13 edition that "the management of the Banff office and its district, with the exception of the Chief Game Guardian's business, is in worse condition that it ever was," and even after Harkin arrived in town on July 16, the prodding continued with the July 20 edition's challenge: "The residents of the Park will await with no little curiosity the results of his investigations into matters tending towards better administration of the People's Playground from the point of view of those who come to play." Matters were made worse when the August 3 number announced that word had been received of Douglas's release from service a few weeks earlier, commenting, "It would be difficult to convince reasonable people that Mr. Douglas's dismissal was due to any other fact than that some supporter of the present administration at Ottawa coveted his position." However, the August 10 edition was a bit more sympathetic to the circumstances he faced: "Mr. Harkin found the Banff Park office in a state of chaos and devoid of system....[he] is but a civil servant and can only use the tools the people give him. In this case the people are the Conservative Association of Banff and up to date it seems that Bennett is making a laughing stock of the Banff Conservative Association."[28]

In addition to presenting him with these administrative and political problems, the visit brought Harkin face-to-face with the conditions Luxton had alluded to. Douglas had done his best to wring the necessary appropriations out of a skeptical Parliament, using arguments about the value of tourism to the treasury to bolster his pleas, but, as Luxton had stated, results had not kept pace with needs. Banff's streets were dusty and needed attention, the electric lighting system was inadequate, the original Cave and Basin bathhouse had become decrepit and planning for its replacement had become problematic, and there was a requirement for more and better recreational facilities for those wanting to experience the West's most famous resort. Outside the village there were only a handful of narrow carriage roads, few trails, and the fire and game guardian service was inadequate to provide protection to park lands from fire and poaching. Discussions with Luxton and others led Harkin to the conclusion that while there was criticism of the new Conservative regime, opinion in town had not favoured former Minister Oliver either, as it was thought that he had not understood and supported what local residents wanted and had not provided the resources necessary for the resort to prosper. Conversation with Dr. R.G. Brett, owner of both the Sanitarium Hotel and the Brett Hospital, informed him about local agitation for improved roads and tourist amenities. Representations from the Brewsters and other transportation interests reinforced their position that the recent relaxation of regulations on automobiles was threatening their horse-drawn livery businesses. In speaking with other businessmen and park employees, Harkin heard of the statement made by Bennett during the election campaign that a company he headed, Calgary Power, intended to seek permission to build dams on park waters, including Lake Minnewanka, Bow Lake, and the Spray Lakes. He also heard complaints from local citizens about the actions of the government in cutting down the size of the park in the new act, which, it was believed, would leave wildlife vulnerable to decimation by both white and Indian hunters. But, most persistently, he was questioned about a CPR proposal that had the potential to virtually destroy the town.

When Harkin arrived in Banff, he was aware of some aspects of the CPR's idea, and it would mark the first of many occasions during his career that he would find himself dealing with railway interests, the most powerful in Canada's national parks. In May 1912 he had received a letter from Superintendent Macdonald indicating that a party of CPR engineers was running survey lines from Anthracite along the north side of the Bow River connecting with the main line about two-

and-one-half miles west of Banff. Harkin immediately wrote to C.E. Ussher, general passenger and traffic manager, bringing the matter to his attention and stating, "I know that you are quite as much interested as we are in all matters calculated to make Banff attractive and therefore equally concerned with us in regard to any matters that might arise which might possibly militate against its present attractiveness."[29] Douglas pointed out that about seven years previously a similar survey had been carried out without any effect, but that if new construction did go ahead, "it would certainly make havoc of the Townsite." In June, Macdonald followed up with further information reporting that the work was being done in conjunction with a proposal by the CPR to double track its line to the coast. He enclosed a news clipping from the *Calgary Herald* which mentioned that CPR president Sir Thomas Shaughnessy, in announcing a combined double-tracking and grade reduction, estimated the cost at some $60 million, leading the paper to speculate that the project was being carried out with an eye to increased business associated with completion of the Panama Canal.[30]

The matter was left in Williamson's hands to discuss with the Department of Justice when he departed Ottawa, and upon arrival at Banff, Harkin could judge for himself just how great an impact the new routing would have. The grade-reducing line would run along the south side of the Bow, pass through a tunnel at the foot of Mount Rundle, cross the golf links and the river, go through another tunnel in Tunnel Mountain, cross the Bow River above Bow Falls, and then run along the south bank passing between the south end of the Bow River bridge and Dr. Brett's sanitarium before heading west past the Cave and Basin. As Harkin later reported, "there was strong feeling against the proposed location of the double track," and matters were further complicated when he received a communication from Williamson in early September indicating that the Department of Justice had advised that it was possible the company had the right in its original charter to carry out the project without permission from the department.[31] This advice took the matter from concern to impending crisis, and when two members of the approving authority, the Board of Railway Commissioners, visited Banff, Harkin reported, "I made a point of driving them over the proposed location, in order that they might be familiar with the conditions as they really are."[32]

Despite facing these difficult issues, the visit deeply moved Harkin, particularly the opportunity provided by an invitation to experience some real mountain wilderness at an Alpine Club of Canada camp. The club had been holding an annual mountaineering camp since its inception in 1906, and this one was located half a mile on the BC side of the Continental Divide at Vermilion Pass, requiring an eight-mile hike from the Castle Mountain railway siding over a rough wagon road to reach. It stood at a magnificent site on islands in the headwaters of the Vermilion River, complete with ladies' and men's quarters on separate islands with the dining canopy, secretary's and director's quarters, committee tent, press tent, and tea tent in a central square in an open glade on the main island. Just outside the square was the all-important fire circle "where each evening the campers gathered in force and spent the hours between supper and bedtime in song and story and many other kinds of entertainment." Along with University of Toronto geologist Dr. A.P. Coleman and Forestry Superintendent R.H. Campbell, Harkin was invited to make a contribution, providing "a most instructive address upon Dominion parks, their boundaries, administration, and ultimate objects."[33] But the visit was intended for more than social discourse and, despite several days of inclement weather, he took part in at least some of the outings to Marble Canyon, Tokumm Creek, Boom Lake, and the striking Giant's Steps Falls in Prospector's Valley.

Overall, his attendance at the Vermilion Pass camp provided his first real opportunity to come to grips with the wilderness lands over which he had stewardship and awakened in him the realization of how the chance "to revert to more natural conditions" could produce positive effects on those participating. A few years later he recalled this experience:

> It was in 1912, shortly after I had taken charge of the administration of the parks, and while, perhaps, I was rather vague in my mind as to their possibilities and future destiny. But as I sat around the camp fire that night

Alpine Club of Canada Vermilion Pass Camp, 1912. Byron Harmon photograph. Harkin joined other participants around the campfire "luxuriating in the sense of physical well-being and spiritual peace which comes from a day spent in the clean life-giving air of the mountains." [WMCR, V263 NA-6206]

> watching the firelight play upon the faces of the climbers who were, like myself, luxuriating in the sense of physical well-being and the spiritual peace which comes from a day spent in hard exercise in the clean, life-giving air of the mountains, when I heard the gaiety of the conversation and experienced the comradeship which grows out of dangers and pleasures shared in common, culminating in the subtle fraternity of the camp fire, I realized very strongly the uses of the wilderness. I felt like saying with Walt Whitman: "Now I see the secret of making of the best persons. It is to grow in the open air, to eat and sleep with the earth."

He went on to note that the men and women with whom he shared that campfire had come largely from cities and that, tied to their desks for eleven months of the year, "every day brain and nerves were under constant strain." Now, for the few weeks they were free they were not only storing up a reserve of vitality, but were also "gathering inspiration and a new vision of life and its possibilities" and would become "better and more efficient citizens because of their visit to the mountains." Understanding this "gave me a new realization of the value of national reservations where the beauty and charm of the wilderness are conserved for all time to come and where because they are publicly administered their attractions can be opened up and developed. And I could not help wishing that the benefits they have to offer might be shared by every citizen of Canada and especially by every worker in our large cities."[34]

Mabel Williams, in the same vein, later recounted in *Guardians of the Wild* that the visit left a deep impression, as "the marvelous beauty of the mountains surpassed all the Commissioner's expectations." But she believed that it also made him realize that solving the myriad of problems that he had observed was going to require a very practical approach, which meant money, and lots of it. After all there were "hard-headed, unsentimental parliamentarians to be persuaded that National Parks were objects worthy of increased appropriations and not mere 'frills'," and Williams believed that this is where the vision for which Harkin would become famous began to be formed: "What finer issues, as yet unsuspected, could the parks be made to serve? These were problems sufficiently difficult to damp the courage of any executive. But the Commissioner was young. He had energy, enthusiasm, imagination, and an unusual capacity for disinterested service. And he cheerfully faced the task."[35]

Harkin used Banff as his headquarters for two months while making trips to other parks to gain an appreciation of their particular problems. His long sojourn was necessary for two reasons, one being organizing the construction of a replacement for the original Cave and Basin pools and bathhouses that had become such a black eye for the branch. Efforts to design a facility that would be the new Canadian park system's foremost attraction had begun immediately after he took office with the hiring of A. Van Damme, described as "the foremost bath house architect in the United States." After spending time at Banff, Van Damme had submitted his preliminary plans in September 1911, but in his first report the commissioner had speculated that "the plans before the Department may be too elaborate for present purposes" and would probably allow only one new bathhouse to be built.[36] By the time Harkin arrived in Banff, revised plans had been rejected and the search was on for a new architect. Chosen to take on this all-important task was Walter Painter, a New Yorker who had been working as chief architect for the CPR since 1905 and in 1911 had begun the design of a "new" Banff Springs Hotel with an eleven-storey centre tower and two new wings designed in a Scottish Baronial style. Painter's employment on the Cave and Basin project only increased its public profile and Harkin was present to proudly oversee the beginning of work on the excavation for its foundations on September 1.[37]

The other reason for his dalliance was to allow his attendance at a vice-regal visit by the Duke and Duchess of Connaught and their daughter Princess Patricia. The governor general's visit was much anticipated by the Banff citizenry and with the assistance of parks staff Harkin co-ordinated the greeting plans, including the erection of a large arch topped with a mountain goat at the head of Banff Avenue and the building of a speaking platform in front of the park offices at the Government Museum. On September 9, he was present to hear Dr. Brett's welcome speech and the Duke's response, which touched very much on his own thinking: "I have the most pleasant recollections of my former visit here, and my memory has often flown back to the views of the great Rocky Mountains frowning down on the beautiful valley of the Bow River. In a country where so much is constantly changing, it is pleasant to find a National Park such as this which has been set aside by the wisdom of your legislators; where Nature may be found in all her splendour; where the hand of man will never be allowed to mar the scenery."[38] The next day he lunched at the Banff Springs Hotel with the duke and duchess, Mr. and Mrs. Jim Brewster, and Luxton and his wife.

By the time the vice-regal party departed Banff on September 14, he too was headed home. Having survived his new post through a period of political uncertainty, armed with a deeper understanding of both the broad principles and the minutiae of parks from his background reading and discussions with Douglas, inspired by the opportunity to meet the wilderness face-to-face at the Alpine Club camp, and familiar with his "small kingdom," he could now contemplate how to go about creating "a new public trust" as the Atlantic Express bore him eastward. It proved to be a pivotal moment in the history of Canada's national parks.

GATEWAY
ROCKY MOUNTAINS
STOP

THREE

Dividends in Gold and Dividends in Human Units

HARKIN'S FOREMOST challenge was the branch's annual budget appropriation, which clearly was going to be inadequate to deal with all the needs arising from the rapid growth in the number and diversity of parks. His visit had given him a first-hand view of the needs in Rocky Mountains Park, where the 1911–1912 expenditure was a mere $89,915, and he had also observed that the less-developed Jasper and Waterton were going to need their own infusions of capital. Of course, these concerns were not new in park administration. They had also been faced by Douglas, and Harkin realized that, like his predecessor, he needed to educate parliamentarians about the fact that Dominion parks were not just "tulip beds and roses," as Williams put it. While organizing his Ottawa office the previous winter, he had diligently continued to read any information that might provide inspiration for ways to pique their interest, had corresponded with American parks officials to gain insights into their methods, and had begun to construct a philosophy for Canadian parks. Realizing that he had limited opportunities to make his case, he used his annual report to bring forth his considerations. They proved quite remarkable.

His first *Report of the Commissioner of Dominion Parks* was submitted to Cory on July 4, 1912, just prior to his departure for the West; in it he set out a number of ideas upon which he subsequently built to convince his superiors of the need for support. Understanding his greatest strength lay in the written word, it was cogent and evocative with a command of language that would become his hallmark. After beginning with a few administrative matters and the issue of park boundaries, Harkin launched into a section entitled "Advantages of National Parks," which clearly illustrated the influence of the recreation movement on his thinking. Noting that the act stated that the parks existed "for the benefit, advantage and enjoyment of the people of Canada," it posited that this was best achieved through the recreational opportunities they provided. And, although city parks could provide "quick aid to the people," the national parks existed for "the pure, wholesome, healthful recreation of the great outdoors" commensurate with the needs of the people of Canada.[1] Harkin constantly returned to this theme in subsequent submissions and frequently referred to mankind's "play spirit," which he identified as part of the recreation movement in the United States and Europe:

> The play spirit seems to be one of the strongest instincts in the human being....In the final analysis, people play because of the results that follow, whether the play be in the form of athletics, or entertainments, or outings, it matters not, they feel they know they have benefitted by it, the recreation has been a tonic for them....Most people take holidays in the summer in order that they may be "toned up"; and holidays after all mean play. It therefore

> seems that play is essential to the well-being of man; if he is weakened, play is one of the most important means to effect his restoration.[2]

In 1913 Harkin took this thinking near the point of transcendentalism in a section entitled "The Chief Purpose of Parks," remarking that they "are set aside because it is recognized more and more that recreation where fresh air, sunshine, beautiful natural scenery are combined, means an uplifting of spirit, a renewal of strength of body, a stimulation of the mind."[3]

At the same time as he began to put forward a philosophy of the higher purposes of parks for the health and social well-being of Canadians, Harkin also addressed the salient matter of how it could be achieved. In the posthumous compendium of his thinking about parks, *The History and Meaning of the National Parks of Canada*, he recounted where he found an answer to the conundrum of how to convince members of the House of Commons to increase appropriations. "It is an axiom that no society will pay for something it does not value," he stated, and his political experience told him any arguments put forward would need to be economically attractive:

> While I was pondering this problem my attention was called to an article in an old "Review of Reviews," stating that a considerable part of the wealth of France, Italy and Switzerland was derived from foreign tourists. I had my staff write to these countries and to California, Florida, and Maine. The replies received giving their estimates were astonishing. When questioned, the C.P.R. informed us that they estimated the amount of money attracted to Canada annually by the fame of the Rockies as about $50,000,000. This was a sum sufficient to pay the interest upon our (then) national debt, and added to estimated amounts spent in other parts of Canada, to give tourist travel fourth place among our natural resources.[4]

The large body of information his staff gathered became the focus of another section of the 1912 report headed "Commercial Side." In it Harkin argued that tourist traffic (by which he meant foreign tourism) was one of the most important sources of revenue a country could have since tourists left money but took away nothing from the country to make it poorer: "He goes away with probably improved health, certainly with a recollection of enjoyment of unequalled wonders of mountain, forest, stream and sky, of vitalizing ozone and stimulating companionship with nature but of the natural wealth of the country he takes nothing." Supporting this claim were foreign statistics—France, five hundred million dollars annually; Switzerland, one hundred and fifty million; Italy, one hundred million; and England, twenty-five million—moving him to the conclusion that "on every hand there is evidence of a powerful and prevailing desire on the part of the people to see and commune with the beauties of nature, their willingness to pay for it and the pecuniary benefit of the locality concerned." This provided the solution to how the Parks Branch could achieve its goal of developing national parks to make their benefits and beauties available and accessible to the people of Canada. Every bit of development work in the parks provided for the advantage of Canadians was of equal value to the foreign tourist business and, therefore, "the more the Branch can do in the parks to serve the recreation requirements of Canadians, the more it does at the same time to attract to Canada a share of the hundreds of millions that the public annually spend on recreation."[5]

Having linked the ability of Canadians to use their parks with the value of foreign tourism, in a section entitled "Parks Policy" Harkin turned to presenting the rationale for more investment in parks and the need for consistency in their offerings, the first such statement articulated to guide the development of Canada's national parks. In it, he contended that those who visited parks were like people everywhere and "no matter how fond they may be of nature they will not take a parks tour unless assured of some degree of comfort, convenience and safety," requiring that the policy would, first and foremost, need to relate to the quality of tourist services. He put forward a long list of these including, character of accommodation; avoidance of congestion;

protection from crime; construction of first-class roads and trails so that attractions could be safely and comfortably reached; measures to counteract "the dust nuisance and the rough road nuisance"; provision of minor attractions to fill time between longer trips; ensuring the safety of sanitary conditions and water supply; control of rates charged for services; furnishing of reliable information; and, generally, the administration of matters "so that the tourist shall be as satisfied with the treatment received while in the parks as he inevitably must be with the science wonders he has viewed." With the circumstances necessary for the parks to be successful having being laid out in this policy, Harkin concluded by stating that "the efforts of the Branch are being directed towards an organization dealing effectively with respect to details concerning all these various matters."[6]

Initial arguments made, he was concerned that their being buried in the dry and lengthy tome of a departmental report would gravitate against them reaching the attention of those whose decisions he hoped to sway. Accordingly, taking a cue from his experience as a political propagandist, he had copies of his report sent to every member of the House of Commons and the Senate as well as to leading national newspapers. Williams later recounted the results:

> As a rule government reports were dry and dusty aggregations of statistics, but Mr. Harkin deliberately used his reports to set forth his ideas and ideals. As a practical newspaperman he knew that tired editors are always on the lookout for fresh ideas which they can re-publish with a minimum of effort. At that time—1912—the very name "National Parks" was unknown to most Canadians. Mr. Harkin sent a marked copy of his report to every editor in Canada and he reaped at once a most gratifying publicity—and what pleased his hard-headed Scotch side—at almost no expense.[7]

Harkin later identified the political effect: "When our appropriations came up in the House and their increase was questioned, the Hon.

Arthur Meighen rose and defended them, quoting our figures. No man in the House was more respected than Mr. Meighen for the keenness of his intellect. The appropriations vote passed without further objection, and the economic value of the parks was thenceforth established."[8]

Having articulated compelling arguments in his first report and communicated them through the newspapers, Harkin opened his 1913 report with the disclaimer that it would be "confined largely to a statement concerning the purposes served by National Parks and the useful development work that such purposes suggest." However, it proved to be anything but "confined," as it expanded on a number of points he had made the previous year as well as adding several new ideas for consideration. Throughout, Harkin utilized the tried and true publicist's technique of the testimonial to reinforce his statements, opening with a quote (reproduced in bold type) from the governor general, who had so impressed him with his eloquence during his visit to Banff the previous fall, from an Ottawa address to a tuberculosis meeting in March 1913:

> I desire to refer shortly to the question of your Dominion Parks. I do not think that Canada realizes what an asset the nation possesses in the parks. These areas have been preserved from the vandal hand of the builder for the use and enjoyment of the public, who may take their holidays there and keep close to nature under the most comfortable conditions, accessing a store of health which will make them the better able to cope with the strenuous life to which they return after their vacation.
>
> When deciding on where to take their holidays, Canadians might well consider the claims of places within their own frontier, and spend their money in the Dominion instead of carrying it away to sell the millions annually spent in Maine, in Florida, and in California. For I do not believe that any place presents natural attractions greater than those of the Parks of Banff, Glacier and Jasper.[9]

Following this impressive introduction, Harkin left no stone unturned in his determination to quote experts, including several Americans, such as John Muir on the purposes of parks, Charles M. Robinson, author of *Modern Civic Art*, on the educational influence of parks, and even a petition of the Massachusetts State Legislature on the necessity of creating new reservations.[10] Mentioning "Are National Parks Worth While?," an address by J. Horace McFarland, president of the American Civic Federation and a leader in the efforts to establish an American parks bureau, Harkin introduced a theme that represented a further evolution in his thinking–the idea that parks performed a patriotic mission for the country. Quoting McFarland's statement "So I hold that in stimulating and safeguarding the essential virtue of patriotism, the beauty of the American park stands forth as most of all worthwhile," he suggested that by changing the word "American" to "Canadian" it "crystallizes a thought of equal application to Canada."[11] To make the point of just how worthwhile in Canada's case, he went on to cite a pantheon of pioneer alpinists concerning the Canadian Rockies, including Thomas G. Longstaff, arguably the most famous mountaineer of the day, who enthused, "In no other mountain region of the globe do peak and cliff, snowfield and glacier, alpland and forest, lake, cataract, and stream form such a perfect combination as is to be found, not in one, but in hundreds of places in these glorious ranges."[12]

A second line of thinking in Harkin's 1913 report related to less fortunate Canadians and the potential social value of parks if their role and extent were expanded. On coming to office, he recognized that with all the parks located in virtual wilderness areas in the West, the benefits of recreation and outdoor life they provided were largely unavailable to the larger populations of the east. One solution to this situation, he believed, was to have the branch become involved in the "playground movement," wherein church groups, schools, and other organizations provided facilities for poorer children to have an outing, albeit in urban areas. Seeing a potential role for parks to help provide "concerted progress" in this line of work he called for the appointment of a specially qualified officer to be associated with the parks organization to carry out a co-ordinating role. Furthermore, to address the needs of the city dweller, there was a demand to create "an area in its natural state large enough to constitute a small wilderness—an area measured in square miles—where all may roam and camp and holiday." Such areas needed to be located with comparatively easy access to cities and, Harkin warned, should be created quickly while suitable land was still available. By taking this step the poor in cities and the public in general would be guaranteed a place where they could secure the advantages of outdoor recreation, thereby having a positive effect on city children, including the reduction of juvenile delinquency. Taking a page from the success of his arguments with respect to the mountain parks, Harkin contended that these benefits should pay for themselves, as "it is surely wise to spend something on measures which will help to make better citizens and thus render penal and charitable institutions less necessary."[13]

Harkin was likely borrowing ideas from Deputy Commissioner Frank Williamson, who was particularly interested in labour matters and had a strong social conscience. In a 1914 memorandum entitled "Proposed Parks Policy," Williamson pointedly argued that "the Parks as they presently exist are for the use almost solely of the moneyed man or the middle classes who are able to save sufficient to spend several weeks' holiday in these, at present remote regions." He offered that one of the ways to prevent the "abhorrence of slumdom" was "to give the poor, especially the children every opportunity to get to the country or bring patches of country, represented by parks and playgrounds, into the city."[14] Originating in the classic liberal philosophy of John Stuart Mill, this thinking was consistent with the social reform movement of the new century's first decades and was eventually adapted by other organizations, mostly municipal parks departments and provincial parks branches. Nonetheless, it provides a measure of how progressive Harkin's and Williamson's conception of the role of the branch had become, and an early example of the commissioner's willingness to listen to and adapt the ideas of his colleagues into branch policies. In any event, the goal to have parks within the reach of the city dweller remained a powerful motivator in his future actions and, from a broader perspective, the important social role of parks continued to form a key part of his philosophy, one frequently reaffirmed over his career.[15]

A further example of Harkin's progressive thinking was evident in his 1913 comments on a subject he had mentioned briefly in 1912. In that report he had made some desultory remarks about the need to bring existing roads and trails up to standard before beginning work on new ones, and discussed at length "a road scheme in which the Canadian Pacific Railway, the Government of British Columbia and the Dominion Government are jointly interested," linking Calgary to Vancouver. He was referring to a proposed extension to the "coaching road" that had been begun by the new Alberta provincial government in 1905 with the intention of having a route from Calgary joined to an already-existing carriage road from Banff to the eastern park boundary. It was the brainchild of Scots mining engineer Randolph Bruce of Invermere, BC, who had worked for the CPR developing mines in western Canada and believed that a road joining Alberta with the Windermere district of the Columbia Valley would create both an important commercial outlet for the area as well as a spectacular tourist route. Through his railway connections, in 1910 he had convinced CPR President Thomas Shaughnessy, anxious for an alternate connection to join the CPR main line with the new Crowsnest Pass branch line, to support the concept, and together they brought Premier Sir Richard McBride on side. An agreement with the Department of the Interior was reached in 1911 that foresaw the Dominion government building the section of the road through Rocky Mountains Park to Vermilion Pass and the CPR and the provincial government completing the BC section. When Harkin attended the Alpine Club camp in 1912 he had seen the beginning of construction extending a few miles west from Banff and had hiked over the first cleared section linking Castle station with Vermilion Pass. However, in this case, the cart had got somewhat before the horse, as automobiles did not yet have free use of park roads, necessitating some timely and difficult decisions.

The issue stemmed from construction of the coach road occurring during a period of growing popularity for the recently introduced "horseless carriage," the Ford Motor Company having opened its first Canadian production facility at Walkerville, Ontario, in 1904. A few wealthy Calgarians had begun acquiring automobiles and formed a local club to organize outings and press for more and better roads. Initially conceived as a carriageway for horse-drawn vehicles, thinking about the Calgary-Banff Coach Road had begun to change as work progressed, Superintendent Douglas stating in his September 1908 report that "in another year or two it is hoped to have that part of the road in the National Park in such condition that automobiles and carriages may be able to pass between the two points." The statement was made despite Douglas himself having banned automobiles in the park in 1903 when a Calgary owner had requested permission to ship one in by rail to use for livery services and had been turned down due to the representations of the CPR, the Brewsters, and smaller livery owners. Prohibition was backed by an order-in-council of September 1905, but as time went on and the road neared completion, influential members of the Calgary club protested the restriction and in 1909 openly flaunted it, making the eight-and-a-half hour trip over the rough track to the mountain resort. By the spring of 1911 a deputation of Calgary motorists had convinced Frank Oliver to relieve the restrictions to the point of allowing them to bring their machines to Banff and park them at the police barracks during their stay. Nevertheless, to the chagrin of local residents, particularly the liverymen, on July 15, 1911 a cavalcade of club members arrived in town over the new road and drove their "buzz wagons" everywhere, including across the Spray River bridge to attend the official opening ceremonies of the Banff Springs Golf Course.

Harkin witnessed Oliver's involvement in this matter and during his last days of service as secretary in 1911 had seen the restrictions lifted to allow automobiles to be used in certain parts of Banff townsite during daylight hours. But those opposing relaxations were powerful voices and he had to be careful in pursuing further measures, determining that automobile restrictions on the roads in and around Banff should come off only slowly. Therefore, even though he continued to receive pressure from the Calgary club, which passed a resolution in July 1914 pointing out that the regulations "curtail the pleasure, recreation and enjoyment of the National Playground of Western Canada," Harkin consistently found reasons to stall. Even the powerful R.B. Bennett could not make him budge, receiving a reply to his suggestion that the Spray road should be opened with arguments that it needed improvements to make it passable and "I hesitate very much about opening it up to the general public on account of the fire danger involved."[16]

It was the Brewsters, with the solid backing of the CPR and smaller liverymen, who were most outspoken in opposition, a not surprising reaction given that they owned over 200 head of driving horses and numerous coaches, carriages, tally-hos, and sleighs to service the transportation needs of Rocky Mountain tourists. In fact, it was concern about the interaction of automobiles with horses which informed Harkin's go-slow policy, as he explained to Bennett in March 1916: "Last year the horses around Banff for the most part became remarkably well-accustomed to motors in a very short time....You are well aware that our policy has been to open up the roads to motors gradually with a view to finally having them all opened, but in the meantime getting the horses gradually accustomed to the machines."[17] On the other hand, he could see the inevitability of motor livery replacing horse-drawn livery, and when previously submitting recommendations for action by governor-in-council to open additional automobile routes in the park, he had included a draft regulation allowing it to occur. As it turned out, Jim Brewster had already modified his own thinking, and in negotiating a new livery concession with the CPR secured the rights for an automobile livery service if permitted to operate one in the park. When the draft order Harkin had prepared was adopted on June 19, 1915 it allowed the minister discretion to deal with both times and routes of travel as well as the licensing of vehicles used in motor livery. Immediately it was announced that most of the roads in and around Banff would be open to traffic. Before long Brewster was seen at the wheel of a Baby Overland, testing its possibilities for motorized livery service, and within a few years, with large Overland touring cars, Packard sedans, and White busses, the Brewster Transport Company dominated motorized transportation in the national parks just as it had with horse-and-buggy.[18]

Gateway to Rocky Mountains Park on the Calgary-Banff Coach Road near Exshaw, Alberta, ca. 1916. Byron Harmon photograph. Increasing automobile traffic to Banff after the opening of the Calgary-Banff Coach Road provided Harkin with some management challenges during his early years as commissioner. [WMCR, V263 NA-3432]

Taking up his new position on the cusp of change from the times when all visitors arrived by train and largely used these horse-drawn livery services to those when tourism was being democratized by new middle-class automobile owners arriving on roads, Harkin was not as tied to the railroads as those administering parks before him had been.[19] Nor was he slow to see the powerful influence of the internal combustion engine and adapt it to his philosophy. In his 1912 report he had enthused that in a short time "not only will it be possible to get to Calgary and other points east of Vancouver by auto but there will also be provided a round trip—Calgary to Banff, to Castle, to Vermilion, to Wardner, to Lethbridge, to Calgary—of 500 miles during which the autoist will at all times be either in the Rockies or in full sight of them."[20] This declaration indicated he made a distinction between trunk roads, with their ability to open up the beauties of the park to tourists, and local roads, which Harkin thought should be opened more slowly due to operational concerns. By 1913 he had reshaped the economic arguments put forward so forcefully the previous year by joining the value of automobile travel to the importance of international tourism, noting that "automobile traffic appears to provide a means of immensely increasing the revenue to be derived by the people of Canada from the tourist." A useful statistic he reported in this regard indicated that there were already about a million motorcars in the United States, one for every hundred of population, setting the stage for one of his most prescient quotes: "It is a well established fact that most motorists spend their holidays in their cars. Many facilities already exist which will bring the motorist to the foot-hills of the Rockies. What motorist will be able to resist the call of the Canadian Rockies when it is known that he can go through them on first-class roads. And what a revenue this country will obtain when thousands of automobiles are traversing the Parks."[21]

In marrying the economic value of tourism with the importance of the automobile, Harkin was acting in concert with the administrators of U.S. national parks. Although he had paid homage to the altruism behind the Yellowstone "creation myth," he was fully aware that economic imperatives were as much a part of American park history as the national policy was of Canada's. The setting aside of Yellowstone as a federal reserve in 1872 was supported just as completely by the Northern Pacific Railway, which intended to extend its line across southern Montana and thereby secure a monopoly on the tourist trade that would inevitably follow, as the Canadian reserves had been by the Canadian Pacific. As in Canada, tourism, fuelled by incredible scenery and a healthy climate in the as yet unvisited West, was seen to be worthy of investment and would rapidly become central to the development of U.S. national parks policy. American parks managers also became involved in the design, construction, and maintenance of roads, trails, buildings, and other facilities to serve the rapidly evolving and largely railroad-funded resort-type development in Yellowstone, in two large California parks, Sequoia and Yosemite, and in Washington's Mount

Rainier Park in the 1890s, as well as in Montana's Glacier National Park after 1910. Rivalling, if not outstripping, the CPR's first mountain hotels built in the late 1880s—the Banff Springs at Banff, Mount Stephen House at Field, and Glacier House at Rogers Pass—were the Northern Pacific's lodge built at Yellowstone's Mammoth Hot Springs in 1884, Stoneman House at Yosemite in 1886, and the Great Northern's series of tasteful lodges, led by the magnificent Glacier Park Lodge, developed in Glacier Park in the new century. In 1886 the U.S. Army had been placed in charge of Yellowstone, and had immediately turned its attention to constructing the first 152 miles of what eventually became a 400-mile road system linking the park's attractive geysers, lakes, and canyons. By 1906 a million dollars had been spent on these roads, allowing Northern Pacific to build still more hotels and lodges at ever more remote locations.[22] At Glacier Park, where Bill Brewster had gained the rights to the livery concession from the Great Northern, in 1913 he began experimenting with operating touring cars on the rough carriage roads between Glacier Park station and several outlying camps, a factor in influencing his brother Jim's decision to enter into motorized livery at Banff in 1915.[23]

Despite their longer history and greater size, American parks lacked the organizational cohesiveness that had developed in Canada's parks beginning with Campbell's efforts in 1908 and culminating with creation of the Dominion Parks Branch in 1911. In the U.S. park supervisors officially reported to the Secretary of the Interior, but in reality answered to a chief clerk who effectively ignored them, a situation that spurred the initiation of a 1910 campaign for establishment of what in 1916 became known as the National Parks Service. At least in part, this movement looked to Canada for its inspiration, a matter of some pride for Harkin. He mentioned in the opening sentences of his first annual report that those favouring the creation of a U.S. agency were using his new branch as a model, and Mabel Williams later recounted that the commissioner visited Washington to consult with American supporters of the movement. Likewise, Harkin took pride in statements such as those of Robert Sterling Yard, the campaign's promotional director, who in writing about the value of tourism to national parks in

The Nation's Business noted that Canada had entered "the scenery business" with "businessmen" in charge of its national parks.[24] However, the notoriety of Canada's achievements and the dependency of its parks on tourism also had a potential downside, setting them up as competitors for the tourists the Americans wished to attract to their own parks. A particularly powerful opponent in this regard was Louis W. Hill, president of the Great Northern, who was in the process of his initial development in Glacier Park when he spoke at a 1911 conference to discuss the establishment of a parks bureau. Hill, aware of Canada's, and particularly the CPR's, aggressive national parks promotion, stated that it was attracting traffic away from U.S. parks and argued for increased advertising to divert those headed for Canada or Europe, sentiments that were eventually picked up by America's most influential newspaper, the *New York Times*.[25]

Harkin's persistent promotion of tourism in support of Canada's national parks can only be understood when seen against the American backdrop. While he did not refer to the competitive factor in his official reports, he sometimes made veiled references that led politicians to read between the lines and did refer to it in his departmental correspondence. For example, in a memorandum to Deputy Minister Cory in May 1912, in which he informed his superior of the movement toward the creation of a U.S. parks bureau, he referred to the "See America First" initiative being directed toward the American parks "vitalized purely by the commercial side." But, after quoting American tourism revenue statistics and recommending that the U.S. tourist trade was worth competing for, he stated his belief that Canada, with its superior scenery, could get its fair share of the business if parks were properly supported:

> I think that everything the Americans do to keep the trade at home will help Canadian Parks because it is a well-known fact that the Canadian Mountains have such a reputation that the tourist trade the C.P.R. annually enjoys arises to a great extent through the round-trip business, the tourist going to the United States coast by

> an American line and returning via the C.P.R. Each satisfied tourist is an advertisement for the best kind and means increasing traffic. But no tourist is satisfied unless he is able to see the best attractions the country affords and sees them with a minimum of discomfort. Hence if Canada is to get her proper share of the money represented by tourist traffic she must have Parks containing her best attractions and of course all such attractions made readily accessible.[26]

While writing such memoranda provided Harkin with an opportunity to argue the American parks should be opposed at all costs, he did not characterize them that way. His May 1912 memorandum to Cory acknowledged that parks in both countries fostered the round-trip tourist business, and perhaps because he relied so heavily on American park ideas and models for support, he never became outwardly critical of them. For example, in responding in 1916 to a letter from F.K. Vreeland of the Campfire Club of America informing him of the creation of Mount McKinley National Park, he stated, "We feel here that everything done in regard to national parks in the United States is bound to have a beneficial reaction with respect to our own parks' work."[27] Similarly, U.S. Secretary of the Interior Lane, in advising recently appointed Parks Service Director Stephen Mather on sources of information for parks directed, "In particular you should maintain a close working relationship with the Dominion Parks Branch of the Canadian Department of the Interior, and assist in solution of park problems of an international character."[28]

Harkin's recommendation that Canadian parks be "readily accessible" meant roads, and with competition being provided by the Americans, he had to prove he could deliver the goods if he was given the necessary resources. Consequently, he often reiterated that the branch was "shaping its development work along lines calculated to make the unrivalled scenery of the Rockies accessible to automobile traffic." As indicated in his 1912 report, the first step was to improve the roads already in place and then make proper plans for additional ones. To a large extent, Harkin relied on the engineering expertise of Frank Williamson to guide this activity, and together they undertook an extensive study of the best methods of road construction. The goal for roads was "to make them all permanent, smooth, dustless, mudless, safe and altogether attractive," a tall order in a day when the most common road-surfacing technique was macadam. It used small stones rolled and tightly compacted to create a hard crust over larger gravel underneath and had been popular for a century after its invention in Scotland. Adapted for use in North America to replace earlier "corduroy" roads made of mud and wood, it had the benefit of utilizing materials that were cheap and readily available. By the time its use was being contemplated for park streets, roads and highways, it had become common to mix the stone with tar and sand to give the surface a smoother, more durable finish, but it had always been used for horses and carriages and the pneumatic tires of the new automobiles tended to create suction, destroying the surface and creating clouds of dust.

To address this problem, Harkin and Williamson contemplated several solutions. One innovation was the use of Fort McMurray tar sands, the branch arranging for a reservation of the material to be made and carrying out an experimental surfacing with it at Jasper. They also studied new commercial finishing techniques, including the "roc-mac" process, a liquid binder made largely from silica that was mixed with fine limestone screenings and water to form a matrix laid on the road and covered with broken stone and rolled until it oozed through, filling up the voids. Williamson visited Victoria Park at Niagara Falls to inspect its first Canadian use and enthused to Harkin, "I think it will be the macadam road of the future," recommending that it be tested on a section of road incorporating Banff's main street between the CPR station and the Bow River bridge at a cost of $25,000 for 20,000 yards.[29] After approval from Cory, this work was carried out in the summer of 1913, much to the delight of Banff citizens, as the *Crag and Canyon* had noted that there was strong local pressure for improved roads. Unfortunately, the branch found it impossible to follow up this experiment immediately due to the great cost of other development work in the park, and by the end of the year the outbreak of the war had intervened to put it on indefinite hold.

Outside townsites, roadwork continued to follow the less expensive method of using rock and gravel found at hand during construction. One project for which a survey was already underway when Harkin came to office was Fiddle Creek Drive in Jasper Park aimed at connecting the Fiddle Creek hot springs with the Miette railway station (Pocahontas) nine miles distant on the GTP line, but its estimated cost of $100,000 kept it low on the list of priorities. At Glacier, a road had been located linking the station with the Nakimu Caves, and during 1912–1913 five miles of grading was carried out. Williamson published an article in the March 1914 edition of *Good Roads Canada* under the title "Roads in the Parks of the Dominion," revealing how these and other park roads were selected and developed:

> First, a narrow, pedestrian trail is built, then, if this proves sufficiently popular to warrant a widening, such is done; next, if conditions justify, this pony trail will be further widened and improvements are made in the form of grading, surfacing, draining and so on, this is then a narrow roadway, which may be again widened to accommodate horse-drawn vehicles or maybe, eventually motors.
>
> It is thus seen that the location of roads in the parks is not always the best from an engineering standpoint, since the scenic route, rather than the fastest or easiest, is preferred by those having resort to the parks.[30]

Williamson concluded with a view to the day when a 200-mile highway would link Jasper with Edmonton "and this highway to eventually connect with Banff, another two hundred miles through spectacular country, undoubtedly without a peer in North America." But, with a projected cost of two to three million dollars, he believed it would probably be some time before it would be considered. Indeed, for the time being most appropriations were absorbed by pressing forward with work on the Banff-Windermere auto road toward Castle Mountain junction, with plans also being made to extend it westward to Laggan and Lake Louise. During the 1913 season the work of location surveys was picked up at Sawback, seven miles west of Banff, and carried through to Castle, where they joined with similar location work and some construction between there and the Vermilion summit.

By the eve of the First World War, both Harkin and Williamson were fully convinced that roads were the way to the future for Canada's parks and even for the nation as a whole. Williamson's vision for a road linking Edmonton with Jasper and Banff was one indication of this, but it was not the only one. After attending the American Roads Congress held at Detroit in September 1913, the deputy commissioner prepared an article that put forward other interesting premises based on what he had heard. Adapting the argument of Missouri politician J.M. Love calling for federal government support of road-building by the application of a small tobacco tax on the sale of cigars, he postulated that Canada could raise about $7 million a year by similar action and use it to construct between 500 and 700 miles of first-class highways. Such a policy would allow for roads to become a strong unifying national instrument: "Thus we could build a transcontinental highway reaching from coast to coast and with many branches aggregating a mileage almost as great in length as the main trunk line, in less than ten years by making this imperceptible sacrifice. Imagine a splendid national highway from Halifax to Toronto, and another from Toronto to Winnipeg, another from Winnipeg to Calgary, and another from Calgary to Vancouver." To assist in this task, convicts could be used as they were in the U.S. and "such work would be better for them, being of a more healthy nature and less confined than that in the prison houses and yards."[31] Harkin began using similar arguments in the fostering of roads in his annual reports, illustrating that his thinking had already begun to transcend parks concerns and focus on the greater good of Canada. Indeed, at least partly due to Parks Branch promotion, the idea of a transcontinental highway soon became a matter of public policy discussion, with the Canadian government beginning to provide funding toward realizing it in 1919.[32]

Other important supporters also saw a bright future for roads, in particular William Pearce. In the years during and immediately following completion of the CPR, Pearce had been the most influential government official in the North-West Territories, acting as the personal agent of Prime Minister Macdonald to ensure proper development and earning the unofficial title of "Czar of the West."[33] After many years with the department he had joined the railway's irrigation interests as "statistician" in 1904, but with his historic role in establishing the original park reservation in 1885, including drafting the legislation and as chairman of the hot springs discovery inquiry, he maintained a life-long interest in parks matters and commented on them frequently. While initially opposed to allowing automobiles into Rocky Mountains Park because he thought they were incompatible with horses, in 1913 he prepared a wide-ranging and influential document in which he reasoned, "It would be idle to try to prevent automobile roads being established and utilized." Instead, he recommended they be built in strategic locations and not wait until rights-of-way were prohibitive to acquire and construction costs increased. In particular he called for a road to connect the American park at Glacier Park, Montana, with parks along the CPR line, after which it could be extended north to Jasper.[34] Bennett sent a copy of the memorandum to Harkin in March 1914, noting its farsightedness and asking him to bring it to the attention of the minister. In response, the commissioner indicated that although he had heard of the report, he had not previously read it, and offered the opinion, "Perhaps we will be able to arrive at some sort of comprehensive scheme in regard to which we can prepare units from year to year."[35] Pearce's influence made his work widely read and adopted, particularly by various automobile associations anxious to see Alberta's road network expanded, and it provided a vision and common goal that both provincial interests and the branch could support.

There would be those in later years who would criticize Harkin for being in the vanguard of complete acceptance, indeed even promotion, of the commercial side of park development through linking roads with tourism. Leslie Bella, with her accusation "Harkin had entrenched autotourism as the major purpose of Canada's national parks" was

CPR Statistician William Pearce at work at his desk, 1914. Pearce, although an early supporter of Harkin's ideas concerning roads in national parks, would become one of his greatest adversaries over the control of park waters. [GA, NA-325-1]

among the most outspoken.[36] But others believed that his playing of the economic card supporting roads and automobiles had actually saved Canada's parks, long-time executive director of the National and Provincial Park Association of Canada Gavin Henderson arguing, "Harkin had no choice. Had he tried to follow a course more in line with the preservationist ideals of John Muir, for example, the whole fledgling national parks movement in Canada would almost certainly have collapsed, perhaps never to regain momentum."[37] Criticisms of his commercial proclivities tend to overlook the fact that Harkin's branch was part of the Department of the Interior, the whole *raison d'être* of which was to capitalize on the resources of western Canada for the good of the nation, an imperative that not even parks could escape.[38] However, as time went on he began to downplay the commercial factor, writing in an article on national parks in 1924 for *The Handbook of Canada*, "While those who are associated with the work have long ceased to regard the commercial side as the most important consideration, they have never disregarded the part it plays."[39] Later, in notes used for the *History and Meaning* tribute, perhaps with an eye to his conservation legacy, Harkin stated, "While we were forced in the beginning to stress the economic value of national parks we realized that there were other values far more important that would be recognized in time" and stated that he opposed any but trunk road construction in the parks.[40]

In any event, by the time Pearce's work was the focus for discussion among those interested in expanding roads in the parks and elsewhere, Harkin was tending to leave reports on the progress of road construction to Philip Barnard-Hervey, Douglas's successor as chief superintendent, while concentrating his personal efforts on parks promotion. Aware from the CPR's international tourism campaign that well-written information could sway public opinion and gain support, he had quickly reached agreement with the corporation to take on the major responsibility for tourist advertising. But from the outset he had also identified the need for brochures and pamphlets to inform the public on the value of parks in the same way as he had gained politicians' attention with his annual reports. In September 1913 he observed that there was a paucity of literature providing parks information, but noted that he had taken steps to solve the problem with a number of planned publications. Among them were a handbook on the Banff Museum, designed to provide the natural history of the Rocky Mountains in a popular way by Harlan I. Smith of the National Museum, *Glaciers of the Rockies and Selkirks* by Professor A.P. Coleman, and a handbook on the fish of Rocky Mountains Park by Fisheries Inspector Sidney Vick. Harkin was proud of these productions and even suggested that the museum handbook might be useful for teaching natural history in Alberta schools.[41]

In addition to these works, there was to be another totally unique publication, perhaps the most interesting ever issued by the Parks Branch, which Harkin both authored and designed. Work on it had begun over the summer of 1913, recorded in the report of Norman Sanson, meteorological observer and museum curator at Banff: "On July 4, 1913, acting on instruction from the Commissioner of Dominion Parks, I accompanied Mr. A. Knechtel, Chief Forester of Dominion Parks, Ottawa, on a trip to Simpson summit in order to make arrangements for collecting a quantity of some suitable flowering plants for a small pamphlet to be published in 1914....On July 17, we commenced collecting the red heather, which was then not much more than beginning to flower in any quantity, at the same time collecting some other conspicuous flowering plants in order to find which would make good dried specimens."[42] From this report it is clear that Harkin intended the brochure to be based on mountain wildflowers, and with the collection in hand he spent the winter, likely with Mabel Williams's assistance, writing and designing what was at once an informational pamphlet on the purposes of parks and "a souvenir of the Dominion Parks Branch" that visitors would want to keep and show to others. Given the predominance of heather in the gatherings, he decided that it would provide the focus, and when *Just a Sprig of Mountain Heather* appeared in 1914 each copy had a dainty piece of the plant tipped into its attractive cover. In an opening section, he explained the symbolic linkage between heather and parks: "'The top o' the world to you' is an old greeting in Ireland, but this little sprig of Mountain Heather brings to you in very reality a bit of the top o' the world. It comes from alpine meadows frequented by the wild goat and the ptarmigan, but known to few people other than those who seek solitude among the snowy summits of the National Parks of Canada." Following this rationale, he turned to emphasizing his recreational and patriotic messages: "This sprig of heather comes to call your attention [to] Canada's National Parks, which have been set aside primarily to ensure to Canadians for all time those opportunities for recreation in the out-of-doors which humanity is more and more recognizing as vital to its well-being. It is just possible that you may not know that Canada is rich in national parks and yet these parks are your parks and all the wealth of beauty and opportunity for enjoyment which they offer are yours by right of heritage because you are a Canadian."[43]

Sprig was divided into a number of sections dealing with the same messages that Harkin put forth in his annual reports. "Commercial Side of Parks" emphasized his keystone concept that the non-consumptive nature of tourism had both human and financial benefits. "Main Purposes Served" focused on an idea that had emerged from some thinking of Theodore Roosevelt which held that resource

Just a Sprig of Mountain Heather, produced by the Dominion Parks Branch in 1914. This publication was at once Harkin's first effort at publicizing Canada's national parks and a compendium of his parks philosophy. [WMCR, 04.1 C16s]

conservation was part of the bigger issue of "the problem of national efficiency, the patriotic duty of insuring the safety and continuance of the nation," and Clifford Sifton's belief that "the highest degree of conservation depends on the efficiency of the human unit." In fact, Harkin had been so influenced by this thinking that he had begun using these ideas frequently, coining some memorable phrases in the process. For example, in his 1914 report he stated that "the most important service which the parks render is in the matter of helping to make Canadian people physically fit, mentally efficient and morally elevated," and in his 1916 report he noted parks' ability to produce "dividends in gold and dividends in human units." In sections of *Sprig* entitled "Refining Influence" and "Patriotic Influence," he contended that national parks stimulated a love of nature that was "one of the purest pleasures" with "an influence akin to that of the fine arts" and "closely allied to patriotism." Finally, in "Policy and Ideals," he called attention to the necessity for new parks to be established to meet peoples' needs and went on to explain the four distinct types of parks that were required, "scenic parks, historic parks, animal parks and parks located specially to provide for congested areas of population."[44]

The publication's importance to tourism was immediately recognized by the *Toronto Globe*, which in an article in its August 14, 1914 edition entitled "Where the Heather Blooms in Canada, Novel Means of Advertising the Dominion's National Parks," reported, "Mr. J.B. Harkin, Commissioner of Dominion Parks is carrying on a campaign to make the immense playgrounds better known, and has just issued from the Department of the Interior an attractive souvenir of the mountain parks....It is a novel and very effective way to capture the tourists' interests in Canada's national parks."[45] But it was more than just a tourist pamphlet, in many respects forming a compendium of Harkin's philosophy of national parks at the time, evident in its concluding section, entitled "Meaning of National Parks Movement":

> Dominion Parks constitute a movement that means millions of dollars of revenue annually for the people of Canada; that means the preservation for their benefit, advantage and enjoyment forever, of that natural heritage of beauty whether it be in the form of majestic mountain, peaceful valley, gleaming glacier or crystalline lake, which is men's rightful heritage; that means the guarantee to

> the people of Canada to-day and all succeeding generations of Canadians those means of recreation which serve best to make better men and women, physically, morally and mentally; the protection of the country's beauty spots equally for the poor and the rich; the preservation of those places which stand for historic events that have been milestones in Canada's development—in short they represent a movement calculated to promote and maintain an efficiency and predominancy among Canadians which Canada's history and Canada's potentialities justify. [46]

This manifesto was remarkably encompassing and optimistic for having been under development for only three years, and pointed out just how broad and profound Harkin's thinking had become as well as his ability to articulate new and important ideas and instill national pride in Canadians. It also provided a clearly stated policy on national parks and their role in the country so that citizens would have identifiable goals toward which they could move. In that regard, as far as is known, it was the first separate and distinct policy document on national parks publicly issued anywhere, emphasizing Harkin's place at the forefront of pioneer international parks conservationists. Yet, in its attention to human efficiencies and patriotism, it was also preparing Canadians for the future, with a war already on the horizon when it was issued. That conflict would test many of his concepts in a crucible of world suffering where optimism and opportunities to enjoy recreation or appreciate nature would be in short supply and where the financial framework he had established to support the Canadian parks movement would come under intense pressure.

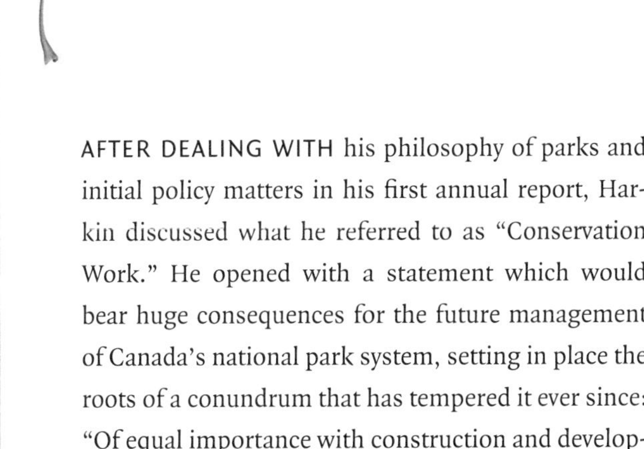

FOUR

Conservation Work

AFTER DEALING WITH his philosophy of parks and initial policy matters in his first annual report, Harkin discussed what he referred to as "Conservation Work." He opened with a statement which would bear huge consequences for the future management of Canada's national park system, setting in place the roots of a conundrum that has tempered it ever since: "Of equal importance with construction and development work in the parks is the work of conservation. This applies to the natural beauties and scenic wonders, to the forests, animal, fish and bird life."[1] The words "of equal importance" guaranteed generations of future park administrators would face the so-called "double mandate," the challenge of navigating the delicate balance between development and preservation. With conservation thinking of his day relating mainly to husbanding the country's natural resources and ideas on the related concept of preservation only just beginning to emerge, it is unlikely in 1912 that Harkin fully realized the future import of this statement. However, if his understanding of the need for protection of the parks' natural attributes and wildlife was only minimally evolved at this time, such was not to be so for long. Not beginning as a conservationist, he would quickly become one of Canada's most tireless and effective workers for wildlife and a spokesman for what he termed "inviolability," protection of parks from major development that could impair their "natural beauties and scenic wonders."

At first forest protection was the main focus of attention. Railroad operations, careless tourist parties, and even traditional native burning practices had led much of the forests in the vicinity of Rocky Mountains Park and the reserves around the Yoho Valley and Rogers Pass to being burned at the turn of the century. Early parks administrators had taken steps to mitigate these effects, and Harkin, too, called for close co-operation with the Forestry Branch to ensure forest protection through measures such as patrols, comprehensive trail systems, emergency depots, and construction of fire guards.[2] Implementation of these plans centred on the activities of the fire and game guardian (warden) service, a cadre of men shaped into his primary tool for forest and game management. In his last report as commissioner, Douglas had commented on the impact of the new service in reducing the fire menace, noting their patrols had been largely responsible for the small amount of fire damage, and other duties, such as clearing brush near the railway line, also helped "to preserve much of the natural beauty of the park."[3]

When Harkin took over he established a forestry division in the branch and supported new initiatives coming from the field to improve fire-fighting capabilities. In March 1912 Douglas reported on the establishment of a new system of fire equipment caches, the design of trails to allow emergency access, the use of old hunting cabins commandeered for park patrol purposes, and the construction of a series of cabins built by the guardians themselves.[4] Responding to a request from Chief Game Guardian Sibbald to expand the Rocky Mountains service from five to twelve men in the spring of 1913, Harkin was able to approve ten by arguing for increased appropriations. They formed the nucleus for a system Sibbald wished to establish using the cabins as a basis for seven separate patrol districts manned by guardians on horses supplied by the department (all of which, by 1915, carried the service's unique bighorn sheep's head brand at the commissioner's direction), and the practice was soon emulated in Jasper, Yoho, and Glacier.[5] Harkin also suggested the use of telephones to improve the forest fire warning plan and by 1914 had acquired the first two single-wire systems, one linking Banff with Canmore and the other the two ends of Lake Minnewanka. The same year he sought out specialized equipment and a manual on field telephones produced by Northern Electric and sent them to the parks with instructions that the guardians were to be the principal agents for extending and maintaining emergency telephone services. Particularly appealing was Sibbald's 1914 suggestion that gasoline-powered water pumps replace the hand buckets then in use, mainly along roads and the railway lines. Harkin estimated they could do the work of eighty men and saw in their use "the first practical and successful step ever taken to utilize power pumps for forest protection."[6] Ever alert for opportunities to draw attention to branch activities, he soon arranged for a demonstration on Parliament Hill.

Support for action in the field and acting on the suggestions of knowledgeable men on the front lines quickly became trademarks of Harkin's *modus operandi* for dealing with fire; he equally believed that headquarters could lead direct public education to prevent man-made fires. Influencing public opinion was second nature to him, and he had, as he explained in an appearance before the Conservation Commission in January 1916, made it a personal challenge to launch a fire-prevention campaign. Starting from the premise that fires of human origin were almost always caused by ignorance and carelessness, he had set out to convince the public through "affirmation and iteration" and "the influence of habit." To accomplish this he used as vehicles articles familiar to the public and part of their everyday experience. The most obvious cause of human-initiated fires was careless use of matches, so he "took the matter up with the match companies of Canada, and they all agreed to put a fire warning notice on their match boxes." Following the rationale that hunters were likely to be a major cause of fire, he also convinced the country's ammunition manufacturers to include warnings in their packaging. Similar success was attained with tent manufacturers, where a printed cloth notice was sewn into the tent so that "a man living in a tent would, the first thing in the morning, see a notice 'Be careful of fires'." Other participants included axe manufacturers, telephone directory companies, and the railroads, where a notice placed in each locomotive cab forcefully brought the fire prevention message home to employees:

> SAVE THE FORESTS
>
> **ENGINEMEN:** If the forest throughout the mountainous Dominion Parks through which this railway runs are destroyed by fire, passenger traffic will decrease, fewer trains will be operated and you may be out of employment. Help the Dominion Parks Branch to protect the forests by exercising the utmost possible care with the fire apparatus on this locomotive.
>
> J.B. Harkin
> Commissioner of Dominion Parks

Of particular importance was information on metal posters placed on all parks trails and roads "so that no one could even walk around without learning the gospel of fire protection."[7] So effective were these actions in reaching their intended audience that the lexicon of fire prevention became part of the thinking of generations of Canadians.

Although Harkin co-operated with and relied on the advice of the Forestry Branch in matters of fire, the relationship between the two branches was far less cordial with respect to other conservation issues. Although heading a separate branch, he recognized that the act placed parks in a subservient position to forestry and as he sought to wedge himself into the Interior Department bureaucracy, he also set out to establish his own administrative credentials distinct from the more senior Campbell. In doing so, the turf wars that erupted quickly brought

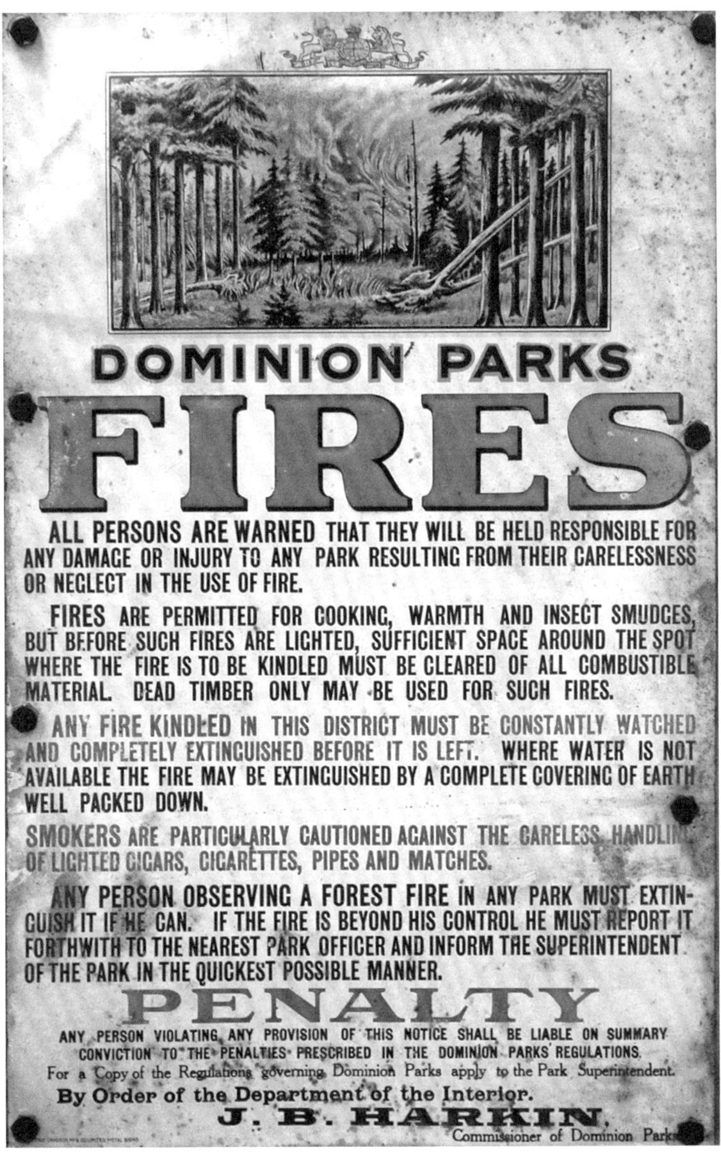

Dominion Parks fire prevention sign. These signs, placed at key locations throughout the parks, were one of Harkin's main publicity tools in his effort to bring fire protection to public attention. [WMCR, 7898]

him to the realization that in order for the parks to flourish his goal must be to change the *Dominion Forest Reserves and Parks Act* to remove park administration from under the thumb of the Forestry Branch.

Disagreement first appeared on park boundaries. Oliver's reasons for making the boundary changes of 1911 were not well understood, as witnessed by Campbell's efforts to clarify their rationale, and Harkin, too, was constantly requested to explain them. In addition to the Alpine Club, calls for reconsideration came from the new Alberta Game Protective Association, which pointed out that the past good work of game protection would be nullified, and the two new railway lines being pushed through Jasper Park, the Grand Trunk Pacific and the Canadian Northern, whose officials believed the reduction would affect their advertising campaigns. Sharing their dissatisfaction, he complained in a May 1912 memorandum to Cory that Jasper Park "is so narrow that it is only a joke so far as utility for game protection is concerned," and in referring to areas eliminated from Yoho Park stated, "Everything indicates a serious mistake was make in eliminating these townships from the park." However, it took a letter from A.O. Wheeler to Cory to bring the differing viewpoints in the department to a head, and thereafter they would become the grist for an interdepartmental battle with Campbell's branch.

Only a few months earlier a possible contender for the commissioner's post, Wheeler would soon become one of Harkin's most important allies in the work of the Parks Branch. Fifteen years his senior, he was known for his outstanding career as a Dominion land surveyor in the Department of the Interior, where, after surveying Indian reserves and railway townsites prior to 1885, he had been involved in irrigation surveys in the foothills and Front Ranges south of Calgary. In 1901–1902 he was placed in charge of work in the Selkirk Range utilizing the new technique of photogrammetry, camera-assisted surveying, leading to a life-long passion for alpine pursuits. From this experience evolved his seminal book on mountaineering, *The Selkirk Range*, in turn leading to his involvement in the formation of the Alpine Club of Canada in 1906. It quickly attracted influential Canadians from across the country to its membership, and in 1910 Wheeler retired from Interior to become its executive director, supplemented by contract work on the BC-Alberta boundary survey. With his strong character, his use of well-placed railroad and political connections, and his outspoken

Arthur O. Wheeler, executive director of the Alpine Club of Canada, 1913. Although previously a potential competitor for his job, Wheeler began to become an important ally of Harkin's in the movement over the issue of parks boundaries in 1915. [GA, NA-4376-10]

spreading of the alpine gospel he was soon a force to be reckoned with.[8] Acting on his interest in all things affecting the club's mountain playground, in his letter of April 15, 1912 to Cory he decried the boundary reductions, making specific suggestions to extend those of Rocky

Mountains, Yoho, Glacier, Waterton, and Jasper parks to their "natural limitations" rather than the artificial ones of 1911. Complaining that the revisions had eliminated spectacular alpine scenery, including some of the mountains' best advertising features, Wheeler argued that by keeping much of the territory incorporated within the old borders a more complete scenic whole would have been attained. In the case of Jasper Park, where the boundaries were set at ten miles on either side of the railways, he was particularly critical of the removal of "the beautiful Maligne Lake, which as an advertising medium might be one of the principal attractions."[9]

After examining the letter, Harkin returned it to Cory with a map showing the current boundaries as well as those suggested by Wheeler and attached his own memorandum. Noting that the order-in-council of June 8, 1911 had eliminated about 7,000 square miles of park territory, he pointed out that information from various sources indicated that areas of great value from scenic, game breeding, and other perspectives had been excluded. These included the aforementioned Alberta Fish and Game Protective Association, which asked that game breeding areas removed from Rocky Mountains Park be returned, and Chief Superintendent Douglas, who reported that the Clearwater country was the best breeding ground in the mountains for mountain sheep, goats, and deer and the Kananaskis for moose and elk. He maintained that, if reserved, these districts, together with a small area further south adjoining Waterton Lakes Park, would furnish good shooting outside the parks and keep the game inside from possible extinction.

Turning specifically to Wheeler's submission, Harkin voiced his own emerging concept of the different purposes of parks, contending that not only were the identified districts invaluable for game breeding, but also contained "natural features which should undoubtedly be preserved as recreative and scenic points of interest."[10] Like Wheeler, he was particularly disturbed by the situation at Jasper, where the "theoretical definition of boundaries, although working out fairly well on paper, on the ground prove unsatisfactory, since their precise locations were not surveyed." Accordingly, news had reached the department from guides that immense amounts of game was being slaughtered, particularly in the Brazeau and Southesk country to the south where, Douglas claimed, "the Indians hunt and kill everything in sight at all seasons of the year." Arguing that taking Wheeler's suggestion would encompass the finest mountains in that section of the Rockies, and making similar points with respect to the desire to have Waterton Lakes Park extended south to the American boundary to link up with Glacier National Park, Montana, Harkin concluded, "I think that Mr. Campbell, Superintendent of Forestry who was then in charge of Parks, as well as Forestry matters, was surprised when the Park boundaries were reduced, and that the change was hardly in line with his views on the subject." Acknowledging that the areas under discussion were part of the forest reserves and therefore under Campbell's jurisdiction, he recommended that the matter be submitted to him for his views.[11]

Harkin's opinion about Campbell likely came from reading departmental files, where there was every indication that this was the case. Being new to his position he took them at face value, although the well-seasoned Forestry superintendent actually had a far different agenda in mind. Despite Campbell's important role in the formation of the park system and apparent support for its expansion, he responded in a manner protective of his forestry mandate and his own interest in wildlife. Indeed, from the time of his appointment as Forestry superintendent he had made efforts to improve game protection, in 1909 compiling regulations prohibiting hunting or trapping in several Saskatchewan forest reserves and also taking steps to preserve antelope and wood bison. At the time he seems to have been giving the matter of a game preserve in the Waterton Lakes area active consideration, with the ability to create such preserves in forest reserves now available by virtue of the 1911 act. And, with his greater experience, Campbell may well have been annoyed at the upstart Harkin's implied suggestion that wildlife was threatened unless protected within park boundaries.

In the circumstances, it was not surprisingly that the Forestry superintendent's memorandum to Cory in reply to the commissioner's position was scornful of his ideas, pointing out that by virtue of the act "the preservation of game is a function of the forest reserve and not the park," and with respect to the game guardian service, "the organization on the Rocky Mountain reserve will this season be as complete and effective as that of the parks, and, possibly, more so as the whole reserve will be organized on a thorough basis." With respect to the suggestions for boundary changes, Campbell stated that while he had no difficulty with the proposals for Rocky Mountains, Yoho, and Glacier parks, in the case of Waterton Lakes he could see "no reason for making an extended park there or transferring the game protection power of the forest reserve to the park in that case since there is no organization already established there." He was equally critical of the suggestion for Jasper, noting, "While it may have been reduced to smaller dimensions than was necessary, the extension of it to take in the whole watershed will cut out such a large extent of the forest reserve that it will be more than a park as contemplated by the Forest Reserves and Parks Act." In closing, Campbell came to the heart of the argument: "If the parks are extended as proposed it will so seriously interfere with the administration of the timber that it will largely prevent the carrying out of the plans which are being formed for the protection and preservation of this watershed."[12]

Harkin did not take long to respond. Beginning in his typical courteous fashion, he pointed out to Cory "there appears to me that there is very little difference of opinion between Mr. Campbell and myself," but then quickly accused the superintendent of being inconsistent. In his reading of the Waterton files, he had noted that there was considerable correspondence between Campbell, local MP John Herron, and F.K. Vreeland concerning their desires to see the park extended. He quoted a passage from one of Campbell's letters of March 1911, wherein he had responded to a protest from the Campfire Club concerning reductions made to Waterton Lakes by assuring Vreeland that his own recommendations would be similar to those the club had submitted. Also pointed out was the fact that Campbell had promised Howard Douglas that once the new bill was passed by Parliament he intended to address the boundaries of Waterton Park with a view to considerably expanding them.[13] Then, in putting forth his own thoughts on the distinction between forest reserves and parks, Harkin interjected a note of cynicism: "The organization of Waterton, as you are aware, is an inheritance from Mr. Campbell. Personally I see no reason for criticizing it. Indeed I think it is quite adequate for a park containing only 13.5 square miles. The crux of the situation is that Mr. Campbell only a year ago said this Park should be enlarged....I take it this meant the area was more adapted for parks purposes than for forest reserve purposes."[14] Accordingly, he stated his belief that where these areas exhibited no remarkable features of natural beauty, they should be set aside as forest reserves, the corollary being that if they contained "features of such unique and striking natural beauty that it seems desirable to retain it with its included attractions of fauna and flora for people for all time," they should be kept aside as parks. And, he contended, while the administration of forest reserves should include game management, "I am inclined to believe, however, that where the natural attractions are the greatest there one will be most likely to find the game breeding grounds" and that making them into parks was the most effective way to protect the animals.[15]

Harkin was equally dismissive of Campbell's response on the matter of Jasper Park, pointing out that if the new branch was to concern itself with tourist promotion, as he was suggesting, some fundamental decisions had to be taken about the future of the parks:

> In this connection Mr. Campbell's main argument is not based on the question as to what is properly Park and what is properly Reserve, but is "As the organization there (Jasper) is only a new one I see no particular reason why the forest reserve powers should be transferred to any greater extent than is the case at present." I submit this argument has no real application to the case. Both the Grand Trunk Pacific and the Canadian Northern Railway will soon be pouring tourists into Jasper Park and it would appear to be the duty of the Department to provide the Parks machinery at once for opening up the beauty spots and thus helping to promote the tourist traffic which is one of the best paying businesses that any district can have.

> I can see no reason why the enlargement of Jasper Park should interfere with forestry plans in Jasper any more than the large area of Rocky Mountains Park should do so. If his argument is good then Rocky Mountains Park, and all the other Parks and Jasper Park as it is now should be abolished.[16]

Although he and Cory were close, the deputy minister was a well-seasoned senior bureaucrat and had worked with Campbell overseeing implementation of the very policies and decisions under discussion. Cory was therefore not prepared to take sides or be stampeded into a recommendation, noting on the memorandum, "Mr. Harkin, bring this up with Minister when he returns in the fall." Meantime, letters continued to arrive in the deputy minister's office from well-connected individuals with the Grand Trunk Pacific and Canadian Northern Railways supporting his commissioner's position. One from General Advertising Agent H.R. Charlton of the Grand Trunk recommended that the entire Jasper Park area should be restored "and placed under the jurisdiction of the Commissioner of Parks" and another from Assistant Land Commissioner Harvey Fitzsimmons of the Canadian Northern addressed to the minister pointed out that an extension of park lands would encourage tourism and that "the benefit to the country at large from the expenditure of these tourists would be well worth obtaining."[17]

In December, Minister W.J. Roche indicated that he wished to consider the matter more fully; however, with influential supporters such as the railways, the Campfire Club of America, the Forestry Committee of the Conservation Commission and the Alpine Club of Canada already behind him, Harkin did not rest on his laurels while waiting. As a civil servant denied the freedom to speak out publicly on contentious issues, he cleverly cultivated those with voices of authority who could do it for him, a strategy borrowed from his years as a ministerial secretary which he employed often during his career. An important supporter was William Pearce, who in April 1913 indicated he was not only sending a letter to the minister recommending that "the Rocky Mountain

Mary Schäffer, "discoverer" of Maligne Lake, at Kootenay Plains, 1907. Harkin cultivated the support of influential individuals, such as Mrs. Schäffer, to speak for policies that he could not publicly enunciate as a government bureaucrat. [WMCR, V527 NG-17]

Park of Canada be restored to its original area," but also asking that it be extended southward to join with Waterton Park.[18] Another influential voice was Mary Schäffer, who in a lecture at the Women's Canadian Club of Ottawa in 1913 called for Maligne Lake to be brought back into Jasper Park, with Roche, who was in attendance, responding, according to a report in the *Ottawa Evening Journal*, with "an intimation that the boundaries of Jasper park, which some time ago were curtailed, would be enlarged."[19] A third supporter was R.B. Bennett, who after seeing a letter on the matter by Sibbald, wrote in March 1914, "It would appear that some action should immediately be taken in connection with the extension of the park boundaries, if we are to preserve the game as it should be preserved." Harkin responded enthusiastically, "I may say that this is a matter that I have been bringing to the attention of the Department ever since I have had charge of the Parks Branch, and am very glad to know you are in sympathy with my efforts to secure an extension." Bennett followed up with a note reporting that he had written the minister and would take up the matter with him personally at an early date.[20]

Grateful for the support of others, Harkin did not leave anything to chance and took every opportunity within his bureaucratic scope to bolster his own position. Continually referring to the issue in his annual reports, he also forcefully made the point in his communications with the minister. In a brief to Roche on the state of game presented in November 1913, he stated, "So well has the public become educated as to the inviolability of these areas that infractions of the regulations are extremely rare and the increase in wild life has been so rapid during the last few years that it has been noticed by everyone familiar with the Parks," an opinion supported by observations in game warden diaries. In referring to Waterton Park, he could not resist reiterating his concern about its reduced size, maintaining, "[It] is of such absurdly small area that it cannot be considered of very great service in protecting wild life." Reminiscent of his use of counterpoint as a journalistic tool, he closed with some illustrations that drove home the point: "I am attaching photographs showing moose, elk, Rocky Mountain sheep and goat in Rocky Mountains Park and a picture of wild deer taken as they were crossing the Superintendent's lawn, Banff, also photographs showing the way in which big game is being slaughtered just outside the boundaries of Waterton Lakes Park."[21]

Cory forwarded this memorandum to the minister on November 20, 1913 with a covering letter noting that the arguments were worthy of consideration and that he was in favour of the Waterton Lakes boundary extension.[22] Strangely, though, two days earlier a memorandum prepared by Campbell had gone forward to council recommending declaration of an area extending fourteen miles north of the international boundary as "a game preserve for the propagation and perpetuation of the native birds and animals."[23] This dealt Harkin's plans a severe blow, and when made aware of it he sent Cory a long communication complaining that "authorization for this memorandum to Council was secured by the Forestry Branch without the matter being referred to this Branch" and reiterated his position that protection of game should be achieved through an enlargement to Waterton Lakes Park.

Apparently, Campbell had stolen a march in the battle of orders-in-council, and Harkin immediately put his staff to work to find a way to head him off. Maxwell Graham discovered a legal opinion to Cory on file dating from February 1913 stating that in the repealing of former parks legislation by the 1911 act all game regulations within the parks were made subject to the laws of the province in which they were situated. He pointed out that as amendments to the *Alberta Game Act* of 1910 stated that all parks within the province, either Dominion or provincial, were declared to be game preserves, "only reservations for *Park purposes* that are set aside from time to time by the Dominion or Provincial Governments, are, and will be, recognized by the Alberta Government, as game preserves," and therefore the Alberta government would neither recognize the Forestry Branch's game regulations nor protect the game itself in such a preserve.[24] An elated Harkin quickly sent a memorandum to Cory quoting the legal opinion and concluding, "Therefore, if it is important that immediate steps should be taken for the protection of game in the Waterton Lakes area—and I think both Mr. Campbell and I are agreed to this necessity—it is evident that the only effective way to establish such a reserve is to constitute it a Dominion Park."[25]

Perhaps embarrassed by his apparent slip-up, Cory did not respond immediately, but after receiving a communication from Campbell on December 30 pointing out that his approved memorandum to council had now sat inactive for a month and a half, he submitted the matter to Deputy Minister of Justice E.L. Newcombe for an opinion. It was not until April 22, 1914 that it was received, but it did reaffirm Harkin's position, with the caveat that the matter should ultimately be decided by the courts. However, it was already clear Cory had decided to opt for the park solution, having instructed Harkin in mid-March to include new boundaries for Waterton Park in a memorandum to council he had under preparation for extending the boundaries of Jasper Park.

Days after receiving the legal opinion, Cory wrote Campbell, "As you will see, there would appear to be no doubt whatever that the provincial legislation with regard to game applies to Parks and not Forest Reserves, and that it is not competent for the Governor in Council to establish game preserves as you have been attempting to do."[26] The Forestry superintendent could not agree, arguing that Justice's opinion was not unequivocal and that if such regulations could not be made "it simply means that under the legislation of last session, which placed the Dominion parks entirely under the control of the Commissioner of Dominion Parks, it is proposed to do away with the Forestry Branch altogether and turn the whole administration of the forest reserves over to the Parks Branch." He went on to remind Cory, "It was made quite clear in the discussion which Mr. Harkin and I had in your office in regard to the administration of forest reserves or parks that in his opinion as in mine, as far as administration for protection is concerned, it is unnecessary and unwise to duplicate staff of jurisdiction over the same territory."[27]

Campbell was referring to an important conference that had taken place the previous summer where he and Harkin had agreed on amendments to the *Dominion Forests Reserves and Parks Act* that would allow parks to be created from areas other than those in forest reserves and would replace the powers of the superintendent of Forestry in parks with those to be provided to the commissioner. Harkin had first brought the matter of creating parks outside forest reserves to Cory's attention in a February 1913 memorandum concerning changes in the act proposed by Senator James Lougheed, pointing out, "As the act stands, no place noted for its scenic features, no historical or monumental grounds can be set aside, unless it happens to be located in a forest reserve."[28] The original act stated in section 18 that the governor-in-council could, by proclamation, "designate such reserves or areas within forest reserves as he sees fit, to be and be known as Dominion Parks," with the suggested amendment expanding this to read "designate such reserves or areas within forest reserves *or such other areas* as he sees fit." Similarly, section 4 of the 1911 legislation declared that the director of Forestry, "or such other person as is from time to time selected for that purpose by the Governor in Council" would control and manage the reserves. This was wording from the original act of May 1911 before the strengthened commissioner's position had been created a month later. While this allowed him to be that "other person," Harkin took the opportunity to push for a change to avoid any conflict of authority and an entirely new clause was added to section 18: "The said parks shall, subject to the direction of the Minister of the Interior, be under control and management of the Commissioner of Dominion Parks, or such person as is selected for that purpose by the Governor in Council."[29]

On June 18, 1914, Harkin met with Minister Roche to discuss the new memorandum to council he had prepared for the enlargement of Jasper and Waterton Lakes parks, and these were incorporated into an order-in-council of June 24, 1914. The boundaries of Waterton Lakes Park were thereby extended to an area of 423 square miles, including the important linkage to the American Glacier National Park by incorporating the main range of the Rockies east of the Continental Divide from the international boundary north to North Kootenay Pass and the Carbondale River. At the same time, Roche kept his promise of the previous year, increasing Jasper Park to 4,400 square miles, most of its original dimensions and including the important Medicine and Maligne lakes. Meanwhile, Campbell had directed district inspector of Forest Reserves for Alberta, W.N. Millar, to prepare a report focusing on game management in the eastern slopes of the Rockies, and when it appeared in September 1914 it predictably favoured retention by Forestry. But by then the die had been cast, although Campbell, who was away on a long absence from his office, did not hear about it until returning in December. Seemingly caught by surprise, on December 9, 1914 he wrote a bitter letter to Roche claiming, "On my return to Ottawa I found that action had been taken for the enlargement of the Jasper and Waterton Lakes Parks, although I had understood from the Minister that no action would be taken on the matter until my return, owing to the objections which I have to the boundaries that were proposed for these parks." Predictably, he alleged that it interfered with his interests, in Jasper's case "taking in timber which is of considerable importance in the development of coal mines lying below in Saskatchewan valley" and in Waterton's "very important areas of timber which should be handled as part of the timber district tributary to the Crowsnest railway."[30]

Despite being outflanked, Campbell fought a vigorous rearguard action. In defence of his position, he used as cannon fodder information on the ongoing battle between foresters and conservationists over the future of American national parks and Millar's comprehensive report.[31] A few days after his letter to the minister on boundaries, he wrote to Cory to call his attention to a recent report of the United States Forester concerning game preservation in which it was asserted that "probably three-fourths of all the important wild animals of the Western States find their principal habitat within the National Forests, and the question of their proper protection and perpetuation must be reckoned with in forest management."[32] Millar's report had put forward a similar position with respect to the role of foresters in game protection, and Campbell also quoted it in making further arguments, including one in January 1915 which was strong in its opposition to Harkin's position that the Parks Branch had superior capabilities in its staff in this regard. In concluding this memorandum, Campbell also made a revealing accusation that further illustrated a reason for his intransigence:

> In conclusion I wish to say that I have no objection to Mr. Harkin enlarging the scope of his branch so long as he does not break down the forest administration, but it should be kept in mind that Mr. Harkin took strong ground, in which I agreed with him, that protection of forests and game was a problem that must be handled together. For that reason I made no objection when Mr. Harkin asked to have the Act amended so that he would be given jurisdiction over everything in the Parks, but that was apparently only a preliminary move on his part toward trying to get a legal position from which he could work to get control of a large measure of the forest administration as well as what is properly Parks administration.[33]

Further memoranda continued to flow and after the adversaries met face to face to try find some common ground their discussions resulted in a communication from Harkin to Cory, dated May 3, 1915, suggesting the general outlines of an agreement. Essentially it reiterated the position the commissioner had taken three years earlier that "any areas more suitable and more valuable for recreation purposes than forest production be parks; those areas more suitable and more valuable for forest production than for recreation and parks purposes to be reserved; any area which is essentially park area would be a park all the more because there is wildlife therein [and] game sanctuaries and bird sanctuaries which do not contain essential park features and are not suitable for forest reserves should be handled by the Parks Branch."[34] With a few quibbles, Campbell agreed, and thereafter this became the basis for a continuing shift of wildlife management away from Forestry to Parks, culminating in 1917 when, in conjunction with the passage of the new *Migratory Birds Convention Act* and an amendment to the *Northwest Game Act* concerning wildlife in the Northwest Territories, Harkin achieved his goal of receiving complete authority for game protection. Nevertheless, over the same period, his seeming victory of 1914 on boundaries was shown to be less than complete, caught up in the details of the interpretation of the agreement and the circumstances of each case.

In August 1916 he and Campbell met again to discuss the outstanding matter of the revision of the boundaries of Rocky Mountains Park, particularly the reinclusion of the Kananaskis valley which branch officers thought was necessary to protect game from the depredations of Stoney Indians, whose reserve was at nearby Morley. Arguments like this about the negative impacts of First Nations hunters on game populations were being widely made at the time, Millar, for one, identifying the Stoney as the "chief offenders" of Alberta game laws, claiming they relied almost completely on mountain sheep and that they killed two or three thousand annually in their ranges between Crowsnest Pass and the Brazeau River.[35] Despite these claims and complaints from outfitters such as Jimmy Simpson at Banff and Curly Phillips at Jasper, who made a considerable part of their income as guide for hunters active just outside park boundaries, Harkin remained remarkably restrained in his comments about native hunting amidst the outcry. This was likely in response to his experience at Indian Affairs and the fact that its officials had begun to make the case for respect of native treaty rights after a landmark legal case in Alberta where a conviction of Stoneys for hunting out of season was eventually thrown out by reference to these rights.[36] His friendship with Duncan Campbell Scott, deputy commissioner of Indian Affairs, who strongly advocated for protection of native rights, only added to this tendency.[37] However, while being careful in what he said, his actions indicate that he took the claims seriously, working toward protection of the large bighorn population of the Brazeau River district by suggesting a new park between Banff and Jasper and by attempting to regain the Kananaskis.

From his perspective, Campbell, as he had outlined in his pointed missives to Roche and Cory, remained concerned about giving up what he regarded as important forestry lands in the sole interest of parks. He therefore seemed determined to use the Rocky Mountains Park boundary issue to regain some of the authority he had lost in the extension to Waterton Lakes Park, which was now under consideration for return to the Forestry Branch, and to retain it on lands north of the CPR mainline in the Bow River Forest. The area in question, adjoining the boundary in the region of the headwaters of the Red Deer and Clearwater rivers, had been part of the park prior to being eliminated in the 1911 boundary revision and had been identified by Millar as the most important of the four Forestry Branch game preserves he had suggested. This, along with his willingness to co-operate on the Kananaskis, gave Campbell some important bargaining tools and, although he had earlier indicated to Cory that neither he nor Harkin wished "to duplicate staff or jurisdiction over the same territory," his meeting with the commissioner produced just that. Tentative agreement was reached with regard to park extensions and reductions and the creation of game preserves in connection with Rocky Mountains and Waterton Lakes parks, based on the assumption that the Parks Branch would be responsible for game protection in the areas to be created game preserves, while the Forestry Branch would be responsible for administration of such areas in all other respects.[38] The northern part of Waterton Park, which Campbell had argued so vehemently against being incorporated in the boundary extension of 1914, was one that would now feature a dual administrative model, while the Kananaskis region would be rejoined as a fully functioning part of the Rocky Mountains Park. But a small area adjacent to the South Ghost River in the foothills would be excluded and the area in the Front Ranges of the Bow River Forest extending to the Clearwater River would be under Forestry authority, except with respect to game preservation, which would fall to the Parks Branch.

In spite of their agreement to co-operate to make the model work, it became a continuing source of disagreement between the two branches, particularly regarding designation of these lands as parks or forest reserves. Campbell prepared a draft order-in-council in March 1917 which identified the areas as parts of forest reserves, resulting in Harkin's counter-argument that they be part of Rocky Mountains Park with only the parks game regulations being enforced in the northern area that Campbell desired as a forest reserve.[39] Ultimately, Cory favoured this approach and after receiving an opinion from Justice had an order-in-council, dated September 18, 1917, drawn up to set out the new boundaries of Rocky Mountains Park incorporating the clause "And whereas as regards a portion of the area above described it is deemed desirable that in so far as game protection is concerned this area should be administered as a Dominion Park but that as regards all other matters it is expedient that it should be administered as a Forest Reserve."[40] A slightly different clause made the change in Waterton Park, identifying the area north of Yarrow Creek already in the park to be placed under similar dual administration. Harkin requested his staff to co-operate with the Forestry Branch in the administration of these areas, and although he and Campbell reached an arrangement, it necessitated an unworkable requirement that the staff of each branch report infractions of regulations to the officers of the other before taking action. By 1921 the situation had become so untenable in Waterton that it had to be resolved by a departmental decision to cut the 200-square-mile area out of the park and reincorporate it into Rocky Mountain Forest Reserve. In the case of Rocky Mountains Park, joint administration continued until the mid-1920s, when the Parks Branch was awarded full jurisdiction just as Forestry had been in Waterton. Over the intervening years, though, Harkin fretted under the strictures of joint administration and they reinforced his determination to seek changes in what he believed to be the repressed status of parks under the act.

In his battles with Campbell over the size of parks, the lands to be incorporated in future reserves, and matters of joint administration, it seems that Harkin utilized the issue of game conservation as a bureaucratic weapon as much as a matter of philosophical conviction. In his early reports it was given short shrift, and there was little to indicate that he would become a spokesman for Canadian wildlife. He was not a "wilderness man" spending his free time roaming the hills and forests of Ontario in search of nature, the exigencies of life in government service dictating that the few hours he had available under the yoke of his new office be spent pursuing his passion for golf and love of reading. A slight man of medium build, Harkin soon began to put on weight due to the sedentary lifestyle necessitated by spending too many hours at his office desk and continued to be prone to illness and stress. In early park visits he often used a horse in his inspection tours, and he did occasionally get out into the backcountry, as in 1912 when attending the Alpine Club camp and in 1915 when he participated in a trip with Jim Brewster and members of the CPR Passenger Department through Simpson Pass in exploration for a scenic route to connect Banff with Lake Louise. The building of new trails was one of the branch's priorities, but apparently these ones did not measure up, presenting Harkin with some challenges that led him to complain, "The trails that I went over last summer had grades that made me swear and swear vigorously.... [and] I expressed my opinion of them in very plain language."[41] Essentially, while appreciating his few opportunities to experience wilderness firsthand, his approach at the time was more informed by its intellectual side and its effects on mankind, enunciated in the thinking of writers such as Muir and Thoreau.

Indeed, Harkin's first recorded wildlife encounter as commissioner might be seen to be less than auspicious. During his 1915 visit to Banff, where Cory and his family were vacationing, he accompanied the deputy, his son William Jr., Chief Game Guardian Sibbald, and Superintendent Clarke on an automobile trip over the partially completed coach road toward Castle Mountain in search of a bear that had been raiding camps. When the party encountered a mother black bear with two cubs, young Cory was allowed to dispatch her with a rifle under the watchful gaze of the adults, while the two cubs were captured for deposit in the Banff Zoo. In reporting the event, the *Crag and Canyon* noted that the trouble campers had been experiencing would now be considerably lessened and that "the officials sure had some day."[42] Nevertheless, this action was entirely typical of the times. Consistent with thinking going back to the establishment of Rocky Mountains Park and equally prevalent in the United States, the policy was to control canine, feline, and vulpine predators, such as coyote, wolf, cougar, and hawks, so that more desirable game animals, such as deer, moose, sheep, goats, and songbirds, could thrive, and to eliminate "nuisance" animals such as bears when they caused problems for tourists or townsfolk. The 1911 act specifically identified the powers of the governor-in-council to make regulations for "the preservation of game, birds, fish and other animals, and the destruction of noxious, dangerous and destructive animals."

These were important duties of the game guardians, and one of Harkin's first acts as commissioner was to order that they be supplied with Winchester carbines and field glasses to assist their efforts. He also wrote to the superintendents of Yellowstone, Mt. Rainier, and Glacier national parks in the United States and mentioned that "in carrying out the policy of protecting game within the boundaries of our Canadian National Parks, we find that coyote and other destructive animals become very numerous" and in the hope that they had arrived at some satisfactory solution, asked them to describe their methods of control.[43] In early 1913 this put him in touch with the head of Economic Investigations in the Bureau of the Biological Survey of the U.S. Department of Agriculture, A.E. Fisher, opening an important door for the future of wildlife management in Canada. Fisher not only sent Harkin material on the best methods for destroying wolves and coyotes, but also offered to furnish further information on the economic status

Warden Jack Warren and Chief Park Warden Howard Sibbald (right) with dead grizzlies, ca. 1920. Upon coming to office, Harkin continued to support well-established predator control policies and armed the wardens with new Winchester rifles. [WMCR, NA66-1197]

of native birds and mammals, something he believed would be valuable.[44] With respect to the control of wolves and coyotes, although all the American park superintendents indicated that they used hunting, poisoning and trapping to control these "vermin," and even supplied a recipe for wolf baits from a departmental circular, Harkin harboured some doubts about poisoning. These were reinforced in his correspondence with the suppliers of Newhouse No. 4 traps, recommended by the Americans, who argued "trapping would certainly have an advantage over poisoning, and even the gun, especially in the timberlands," and quoted their Canadian trapping expert's caution that "poison would be very dangerous to distribute around for the purpose of killing off animals as you would, to a certain extent, do away with the animals you wished to protect."[45] Heeding this advice, directions were provided to guardians that they should control predators with guns and traps alone, a rule that would bring severe criticism for years to come from the men doing the work.

Despite carrying on with traditional predator control policies and using game management to reinforce his bureaucratic arguments on boundaries and the economic value of parks, Harkin's appreciation for and understanding of the importance of wildlife soon began to be enhanced by three men. One was his fellow branch member Maxwell Graham. Son of a distinguished British military father, he had immigrated to Canada in 1897 at the age of twenty-two and after attending the Ontario Agricultural College at Guelph spent a stint farming in northwestern Ontario, becoming fascinated with the area's birds and animals and awakening a life-long interest in their study. In 1906, due to the hardship of farming in a remote area on his wife and young family, he moved to Ottawa and sought a position in the government service. He was one of the first individuals seconded to the new branch and with his superior's commitment to "conservation work," he quickly began to form a small Animal Division, recruiting among the few men in the civil service with knowledge on the subject. Soon given responsibility for the three-man unit, it fell to him to produce background on wildlife matters and to research and prepare memoranda to encourage the formation of early wildlife management policies.[46] The first such report was produced in August 1912 and opened with a blunt assessment: "The question of the proper care of the larger animals in our Parks seems to require closer supervision than has been the practice in the past." It related a sad tale of death for forty-one head of the branch's buffalo herd, of inadequate feed for the moose in the Banff enclosure and of being "unfortunate with regards to antelope." He was particularly concerned about this fleet-footed plains dweller, which some writers believed now numbered only some 4,000 in all of Alberta and Saskatchewan. Quoting a noted authority, Dr. W.T. Hornaday of the

New York Zoological Society, he stated, "This animal cannot be perpetuated by breeding in captivity and unless preserved in a wild state, will become extinct."[47] Earlier, Campbell had tried to create game preserves for their protection and had agreed to expensive attempts at live trapping for transfer to the parks, but most animals quickly died. Eager to improve the situation, and perhaps to show success where Forestry had failed, Harkin fully backed Graham's conviction that for the species to be saved the only answer was to fence them in on their prairie grassland range.

Supporting Graham in this work was another Canadian of British origin who had already gained a reputation as one of North America's foremost experts on wildlife matters. Ernest Thompson Seton had likewise immigrated to Canada as a young man and, after growing up in southern Ontario and Manitoba, had studied art at the Ontario College of Art before continuing his studies in London, Paris, and New York. Settling in Manitoba, he had begun an intensive study of its wildlife and became a prolific writer, publishing *The Birds of Manitoba* in 1891, and receiving an appointment as provincial government naturalist. Although he had moved to the United States in 1896, where he continued to write popular anthropomorphic animal stories such as *Wild Animals I Have Known* and *Lives of the Hunted*, he remained a consultant to the Manitoba government and was much celebrated as a naturalist in Canada. In seeking expertise to assist Graham in his antelope work, Seton was an obvious choice, as he had already recommended the fencing of a range near Medicine Hat, Alberta, for the purpose. As Harkin explained to Cory in justification for using his services in March 1914, "The department can hardly incur fair criticism of action taken on the advice of such an undoubted authority—in the public estimation—as Mr. Seton."[48] For Graham, working with Seton would be a dream come true, as he had been one of the writers who had inspired him while farming in Ontario, and their inspection trip to Medicine Hat resulted not only in a recommendation that "Canyon Preserve" should be set aside as a permanent antelope preserve, but also in Seton providing his blessing to Graham's skills. On returning from the trip the author complimented "his remarkable gift for accurate detail, his wide acquaintance with the subjects of animal breeding and pathology, his experience as a practical farmer, his realization of all the larger and national aspects of game propagation, bird breeding and reclamation of wild animals," all which made him "an essential member of the Commission."[49] Such encouraging words coming from someone as respected as Seton not only substantially enhanced the branch's reputation in wildlife management but also initiated a relationship that led to the author becoming a continuing source of support.

In Graham's reports, as in that on the state of park animals in August 1912, the expert he most frequently quoted was William Temple Hornaday, a leader of the wildlife conservation movement in the U.S. An avid hunter in his youth, Hornaday had graduated from Iowa State Agricultural College and had worked for Ward's Natural Science Establishment in Rochester, New York, before being appointed in 1892 chief taxidermist for the United States National Museum. Invited to join the prestigious Boone and Crockett Club, created in 1887 by Theodore Roosevelt and like-minded influential sportsmen with the objective of preserving North American big game, he became a strong supporter of the wildlife cause. Dynamic, mercurial, and often outspoken in his crusade, one writer characterized him as "one of the most interesting and complex figures in the field of conservation—a knight in shining armor rising to the defense of wildlife and swinging a mighty sword with such vigor that he often laid open his allies along with his enemies."[50] In 1896 the Boone and Crockett Club collaborated with the State of New York in creation of the New York Zoological Society and the building of the Bronx Zoo; Hornaday became its first director and set about revolutionizing zoological gardens by exhibiting native North American fauna in habitats resembling as closely as possible those in the wild. He was also an avid writer, penning the groundbreaking *The American Natural History* and *The Extermination of the American Bison* and preparing the entries on game animals for *The Encyclopedia Britannica*. In January 1913 he released *Our Vanishing Wild Life: Its Extermination and Preservation*, a book that revolutionized thinking about the future of wild birds and animals and became a virtual bible for those with wildlife conservation interests.

Hornaday's premise was that "we are exterminating our finest species of mammals, birds and fishes according to the law," because "throughout the entire United States and Canada, in every state and province, the existing legal system for the preservation of wild life is fatally defective." His dark prediction was that unless immediate steps were taken to stop the practice of legal killing, North America would become "a gameless continent." In his text Hornaday provided numerous examples of inadequate laws that were leading to the destruction of game, not sparing the large bag limits and long open seasons in many parts of Canada but also complimenting progressive actions where he saw them. While mistakenly attributing all parks and game preserves to provincial governments in a chapter entitled "Game Preserves and Game Laws in Canada," he observed, "In the creation of National parks and game preserves, some of the provinces of the Canadian nation have displayed a degree of foresight and enterprise that merits sincere admiration." He was particularly high in his praise for Alberta, noting that in creating almost ten million acres of parks (although two of those listed, Yoho and Glacier, were actually in British Columbia) it had been "splendidly progressive and liberal," the result being "fairly beyond the reach of words of ordinary praise." However, one of his clarion calls was to "let the statesmen of America be not afraid of making too many game preserves," and this situation extended to Canada where, he complained, "I have never seen a publication which set forth in one place even so much as an annotated list of the game preserves of the various provinces of Canada, and at present exact information regarding them is difficult to obtain."[51]

To spread his message as widely as possible, Hornaday provided copies of his book to those who shared his interests, one of whom was John Macoun, regarded as Canada's greatest field naturalist and recently retired from a career of thirty years as Dominion botanist for the Geological Survey of Canada. Macoun contacted Harkin in early March 1913 to advise him that the New York Zoological Society was prepared to forward him and each park superintendent a copy, an offer that the commissioner eagerly accepted. On March 4, 1913 Harkin wrote Hornaday providing addresses, thanking him, and closing with the prediction "I have no doubt that the book will be of a great deal of value not only to this office but also to the various superintendents."[52] This proved to be the case, for the book unleashed a healthy discussion on wildlife management between headquarters and the various superintendents and became the basis of a long and productive relationship between him and Hornaday in a commitment to the pursuit of game protection.[53] It was also fundamental in reinforcing Harkin's growing realization that the matter could not be limited to national parks, but must be extended to the rest of the country.

By 1915, Harkin was freely quoting Hornaday's warning about "a gameless continent" in his annual reports and, in calling for the parks to become "the natural history schools of Canada" predicted that "as civilization encroaches more and more upon the wilderness, the parks will probably be the only places where the native fauna and flora will be found in a natural state." At the same time he referred to the role of national parks as game sanctuaries and to their task of saving native wildlife from extinction: "Protective laws, while of very great importance, must be supplemented by ample sanctuaries. All Dominion Parks are wild-life sanctuaries, and everything done in connection with the extension of parks from the purely human standpoint previously referred to, will at the same time contribute in a most important and effective way towards the preservation of Canadian wildlife." He also mentioned the role of wildlife in meeting his recreational goals, describing them as an "ally" in their ability to lure mankind to activity in the out-of-doors.[54] Happily, as he noted in his 1915 report, the preservation of wildlife in Rocky Mountains Park had resulted in a situation where "thousands of tourists make special trips to see the large herds of mountain goats, sheep and other animals that are to be found roaming in a wild state," and they had become "an attraction to the tourist that is perhaps not even second to the grandeur of the mountain scenery."[55] In this case, the protection of wildlife could also be made to serve the economic and social imperatives of the branch and in *Just a Sprig of Mountain Heather*, while not mentioning the value of wildlife to Canadians, he did call for animal parks as a separate and distinct type of national park that "exists to serve the animal life of the country as other parks serve human life." And finally, in an effort to meet Hornaday's challenge, the branch had begun to involve itself in the possibility of establishing preserves outside parks, including the aforementioned antelope preserves and wood buffalo preserves, song bird sanctuaries, migratory wild fowl sanctuaries, and reserves for fur-bearing animals. Already its strongest voice for the preservation and extension of national parks, Harkin's transformation into a champion for Canada's wildlife had begun in earnest.

FIVE

Nevertheless Substantial Progress Was Made

BY 1914, THREE SHORT YEARS after receiving his appointment, Harkin could point to a substantial record of achievement in making national parks relevant to Canadians. In aligning himself with the democratizing influence of the internal combustion engine and supporting development of tourist roads, he had begun to make them more accessible to the nation's burgeoning middle classes. His use of classic publicity techniques, backed by solidly written material on various aspects of parks, was bringing his philosophy concerning their recreational, social, health, and spiritual benefits to an increasingly receptive audience. Development in new parks, such as Jasper, and older ones, such as Waterton and Rocky Mountains, meant there were improvements for both those living in and visiting parks. And his involvement in game preservation was leading to a growing reputation in the increasingly influential world of conservation. But, while not immediately apparent, the guns of August 1914 soon changed the picture dramatically; within months a much different fiscal picture was emerging, the manpower of the various parks was being drained away to battle, development work had ground to a halt, and signs were evident that the flow of tourists would soon be staunched. This meant the hand Harkin had to play for the next four years would be quite different than during his maiden period, but, in beginning a career-long propensity to adjust his actions to the situation at hand, it did not mean progress in moving his parks and wildlife agendas forward would cease.

When war broke out on August 4, 1914 the first effect on the branch was a troop to the colours by those of British extraction who were caught up in the patriotic fervor. Colonel Maynard Rogers, superintendent at Jasper, was one of the most senior, joining up within weeks to become commanding officer of a training base at Valcartier, Quebec, and leaving the decision on a replacement an immediate issue. MP Bennett quickly grasped the tenor of the times and advised that Chief Superintendent Barnard-Hervey could carry out Rogers's tasks while the assistant superintendent's position at Banff should not be filled because changes were in the offing.[1] Harkin quickly came around to this way of thinking, and with the economic and unemployment situations continuing to worsen as the war deepened and personnel left in increasing numbers, he more often than not spread out the workload among those who remained. As a result of having to deal with these new issues at a time when he was already under a great deal of stress from a myriad of irons in the fire, his health began to feel the strain. By October 1914 he was on medical leave, with his office responding to correspondents, "I may say that Mr. Harkin had to have a change, due to his health not being up to the best, hence his enforced absence at the present time." Yet, by mid-November he was back at his desk and seemed to have his feet under him as he balanced the new demands of wartime administration.

One critical issue was the branch appropriation, as the continuing economic crisis and wartime operations began to eat up available government funds. Total parks finances for 1913–1914 had been approximately $650,000, before the order had gone out for "the strictest economy with respect to the estimates for the next financial year." In December Harkin explained to Bennett that he was attempting "to keep my demand for appropriations as low as possible and have as a result provided for very little more than maintenance," submitting a reduction of about 50 per cent for the system as a whole and two-thirds for Rocky Mountains.[2] Nevertheless, although recognizing circumstances meant that only the basics could be supported, he was determined to find creative solutions to prevent his hard-won system from withering on the vine, and an opportunity that might fit the bill appeared in March 1915.

It arose from a problem Canada faced in the early war years with so-called "alien internees," men who had emigrated to Canada from the lands of the enemy Austro-Hungarian Empire. A Department of Justice report called for "detention under proper conditions and maintenance where required of said aliens as may be found necessary to intern as prisoners of war." In response, a Privy Council order of October 28, 1914 under the new *War Measures Act* put in place an enemy alien registration and internment policy. Registration officers were granted the right to confine enemy aliens if they were unable to maintain themselves or were a risk to public safety, and it also directed that "such provision as may be necessary for the maintenance of aliens of enemy nationality... shall be made by the military authorities who may require such prisoners to do and perform such work as may be by them prescribed."[3] Given this power, it was axiomatic that these men, who had been accustomed to heavy labour prior to the war, should provide work that would be beneficial to the country.

Major-General Sir William Otter, who had commanded the Second Canadian Battalion during the Boer War, was placed in charge of internment operations, and he initially concentrated on setting up forestry work camps in northern Ontario and Quebec. But this left the matter in western Canada unresolved, and while in Banff on March 12, 1915 he met briefly with Harkin at the railway station to hear a proposal on how he could help.[4] Soon after the outbreak of hostilities, the commissioner had begun to consider ways to assist the unemployed that could fulfill parks needs, and undertook several make-work projects involving regional unemployed cutting dead timber or breaking stone for roadwork. Essentially off-the-cuff solutions to deal with local problems, they did little to address reduced appropriations, and, accordingly, when the opportunity arose to make a proposal to Otter about the ability of internees to address broader park needs, Harkin made a special trip west to broach it. He later provided a description of his thinking: "At the beginning of the war large numbers of interned aliens were being maintained by the Government. It was felt that it was not good for the prisoners to live for months in a state of idleness; that it would be advantageous for them to have work to do and having to maintain them in any case it would be good business for the Government to secure with such labour the construction of roads and other public works in the parks."[5]

While Otter attempted to find the resources to implement the plan, Harkin carried out investigations to identify possible projects. To gain information on roadwork he turned to an engineer whose services he had recently obtained to replace recently enlisted park engineer A.W. Gray. At the time, James M. Wardle was a bright twenty-year-old recently graduated from Queen's University who had been working on topographic surveys, but he eventually became one of Harkin's ablest and most trusted officers. On April 17, 1915 he presented his comprehensive report, identifying such projects as the Upper Hot Springs road in Banff townsite, re-surveys of parts of the Banff-Laggan road and its possible extension to Field, and even the location of a road around Lake Louise to the foot of the Victoria Glacier. Armed with this document, Harkin returned west and was in Banff in mid-May when he received notification from Williamson that Otter had approved the transfer of 140 prisoners to a new camp in Banff, with supplies and equipment to be furnished by the branch and transportation by the Department of the Militia.[6] As the plan had still not been cleared through political channels, he wrote Bennett to inform him of the initiative and seek his views before asking Ottawa's permission. Distracted in preparing to accompany Prime Minister Borden to London to assess assistance for Britain's wartime needs and more concerned about the desperate straits of some of his park constituents, Bennett was lukewarm. He responded that if the aliens were to be utilized they "must be employed in remote portions of the park where they will not come into contact with the population of this Province" and indicated that it would be "monstrous" if they received better food and clothing than "our own people."[7] Undeterred, upon returning to Ottawa, Harkin sought out the MP and gained his grudging support to send the matter to the minister for a decision. By June 9 he could report that Roche had considered it favourably, and he quickly turned to the matter of getting the most out of the men, a task that proved far more challenging than could have been imagined.

Heeding Bennett's dictum, construction westward on the Banff-Laggan road from Castle Mountain was identified as the initial enemy alien project, and when sixty prisoners arrived from Lethbridge in mid-July they were imprisoned in a just-completed canvas camp surrounded by a ten-foot-high barbed wire fence located at the mountain's base. Within days the population had grown to 191, all employed at cutting and grubbing with hand tools, resulting in four miles of new right-of-way by the end of August. Wardle, while pronouncing himself satisfied with progress, reported that the pace of work was slower and prisoners required more supervision than he had anticipated, sounding an ominous note in his expression of hope that work would quicken once the prisoners became accustomed to it. However, the fact was that these men did not regard themselves as traitors and resisted treatment as mere government chattels paid at the starvation rate of twenty-five cents per day. They also resented the camp conditions they were forced to endure, with poor food and accommodation as well as abusive treatment at the hands of guards. Effectively, the partnership forged between the branch and internment authorities was built on a poor foundation as each pursued mutually exclusive goals, the former hoping to get the maximum work possible out of windfall manpower

Internees working on the Banff-Lake Louise Road, 1915. Harkin saw the use of alien internees as a way to accomplish important park work that would be otherwise impossible during the First World War. [GA, NA-1870-7]

while the latter was trying to keep the costs of maintenance, particularly rations, to a minimum.[8]

Nonetheless, with their inherent weaknesses not yet apparent, Harkin was intent on expanding the operations as widely as possible. Next on his list was completion of a road at a new reservation which had been created a year earlier as one of the first results of the 1913 amendment allowing establishment of parks outside forest reserves. Mount Revelstoke and its several lakes had long been a favourite hiking and climbing area for Revelstoke residents, and in 1910 a trail connecting to a rough shelter at Balsam Lake had been constructed, immediately leading to calls for a fifteen-mile road to be built to the summit to allow the remarkable views of the valleys of the Illecillewaet and Columbia rivers and the snowfield of the Clachnacudainn Range from a beautiful upland plateau. The BC government had built a rough wagon road over the first four miles, and local boosters formed a "Progress Club" in August 1912, calling on MP R.F. Green to assist in getting the area, located in the Dominion-controlled "Railway Belt," reserved as a park. Green, like Bennett one of the few elected Conservatives in western Canada, carried considerable influence, and soon Harkin had Chief

Superintendent Barnard-Hervey inspecting the area. His favourable report and renewed political pressure on Minister Roche led to the passage of an order-in-council on April 28, 1914 establishing an area of ninety-five square miles as Mount Revelstoke Park.[9]

When ordered to locate a road to the summit of Mount Revelstoke in July 1915, Wardle recommended quick completion, because "while at present the panorama of the Columbia and Illecillewaet valley that unfolds itself as the road ascends in easy swings across the mountain face is a worth while trip, the real objective of the road is the summit, where there awaits the sightseer the novel and interesting views of a mountain summit park."[10] Revelstoke merchants agreed, seeing in the road a possible solution for their ailing economy, and in addressing a public meeting organized by its Board of Trade on July 15, Green spoke of "the efforts he had made in Ottawa to secure a camp of interned Germans to work on the automobile road in Revelstoke Park." Encouraged to act quickly, he promised to wire Harkin, urging him to arrange for such a camp without delay.[11] Wardle's survey completed, Harkin was prepared to move ahead, but approval lay in the hands of the minister of Justice and Otter and it was not until a week later that they determined prisoners from a camp at Brandon could be moved to Revelstoke. Harkin had already returned west and with Cory visited the new park in late July. On July 31, 1915 an enthusiastic report appeared in the *Revelstoke Mail Herald* describing the arrangements to house 225 internees, incorporating two log sleeping cabins, a mess house, a cookhouse, and a hospital as well as the positive reaction of the two officials:

> Mr. Cory, the deputy minister, who accompanied Mr. Harkin, is spending a holiday in the mountains. Both Mr. Harkin and Mr. Cory were delighted with the view from the automobile road. "It is unique," said Mr. Harkin, "and impresses everyone who sees it and if it delights even those who are accustomed to the mountains, how must it strike visitors unused to the beautiful mountain scenery. Once the road is completed the park cannot fail to draw tourists. When the road is finished there will be

> work in the park for 35 to 50 years in building roads and bridle paths and in other development work."[12]

Although this was music to the ears of local readers, if it was not just some hyperbole for their benefit, Harkin was to be sadly mistaken.

The log barracks were built into the steep mountainside in a matter of two weeks and the first 100 prisoners were in place by September 8, with twice that number hand-clearing and grubbing the road ten days later. Accompanied by Clarke, Harkin inspected the facility on its completion, which made him think about equipping other camps to house the men and their guards over the coming winter, estimating the cost of each such establishment for 200 men at two to three thousand dollars. Returning to his Banff headquarters, he wired Williamson at Ottawa urging him to go into the financial details with Cory "fully and immediately" as "our appropriations so low fear we cannot count on any more camps unless Deputy can see means of securing additional money."[13] He had good reason to believe he would be successful in this request given his recent opportunity to have lengthy and uninterrupted access to Cory. In fact, his deputy's love of the mountains and his habit of spending his vacation at Banff at the same time as Harkin made his annual summer inspection tour proved to be of substantial benefit to Canada's national parks. Given the weight of his responsibilities, Cory had little opportunity to give his undivided attention to Parks Branch issues in Ottawa but was seemingly happy to break up the occasional monotony of the family's mountain sojourn in Harkin's company playing golf or looking over projects. In the process, he became extremely knowledgeable about park matters as the two men explored them together, and his long tenure provided at least the certainty of his understanding, if not always the guarantee of his support, in many branch initiatives.

Depending on that support regarding the camps, Harkin continued to draft plans for the additional men that Otter was now offering, including opening a new camp for 200 at the mouth of the Otterhead River near Field, finding a location for a camp of 300 near Jasper and, in an idea communicated to Otter near the end of September, moving the Castle camp to Banff for the winter and doubling the number of its

W.W. Cory, deputy minister of the Interior, 1905. W.J. Topley photograph. Cory's summer sojourns at Banff provided Harkin with unfettered access to his busy deputy, allowing them to examine and discuss various parks projects on the ground. [LAC, PA-167436]

inmates to 400. For the latter, he suggested a site near the Cave and Basin bathhouse where there were some buildings that had recently housed construction workers labouring on the new Painter facility which could be made available for the guards and provide "the great addition of running hot water from the Hot Springs and the opportunity for both soldiers and prisoners to keep clean by bathing in the hot pools."[14] This was not the first time that he had expressed concern over the welfare of the prisoners, as, unlike some associated with the alien internees, he did not consider them to be dealt with like slave labour. He had made this clear to the citizens of Revelstoke in an interview he gave during his visit: "'War prisoners are not criminals,' says Mr. Harkin, 'but are in many cases merely citizens of countries with which the empire is at war who happened to be in Canada at the time hostilities were declared. Under international law they may not be treated as ordinary prisoners but are entitled to certain consideration'."[15] Such comments likely arose from the realization were it not for the war, these men would be among those for whom he preached the health-giving value of visits to parks. Perhaps more than any other period in his career, the alien internment interregnum brought these competing sides of Harkin's psyche into sharp relief. On one hand he was the hard-driving and somewhat autocratic administrator who would go to almost any length to strengthen the parks, while on the other he was the liberal thinker who realized that it was the right of all mankind to enjoy the parks' natural benefits and recreational opportunities. For those who did not know the man personally, this dichotomy often made him difficult to understand.

Things began to unravel at Revelstoke within a month of its first arrivals when the water supply was found to be unsuitable for winter use, and arrangements were soon underway to transfer most internees to a camp at Otterhead in Yoho Park. By the end of October work at Revelstoke by the remainder had to be suspended as an early winter storm required them to spend their time shovelling snow and gathering firewood just to keep from freezing. With four feet of snow on the level and the bunkhouse roofs being propped up with timbers to keep them from collapsing, the last prisoners were removed to the new Camp Otter just prior to Christmas. With only one-and-a-half miles of new road having been constructed at Mount Revelstoke, Harkin still had great hopes for the operations at the Yoho camp, where work was focused on a new scenic road connecting the Otterhead to the Natural Bridge on the Kicking Horse, and at another camp planned for Jasper. He and Cory had visited there in August and, with the recent boundary extension once more incorporating the beautiful Maligne Lake area, had laid plans to begin construction of a road extension from the Maligne River to Medicine Lake. However, the emergency at Revelstoke and the necessity of preparing the Otterhead camp had taken priority, and by the time the fourteen-building main Jasper camp reached completion and received its first 200 inmates in February 1916, the snow was too deep for roadwork. Instead, over the next month the prisoners cut some 5,500 fence posts for Buffalo Park and hacked an excavation out of the frozen ground for the town's first water system. By the time the weather improved, the men were staging a hunger strike and then refused to work at all, only a handful being convinced to establish a new road camp at Maligne Canyon.

Similar problems were experienced at Camp Otter, where unseasonably bad weather slowed progress on the Otterhead-Natural Bridge road to a crawl, and at Banff, where progress was equally disappointing. Despite his efforts to improve conditions with the winter camp at the Cave and Basin, the cold weather, cramped living quarters, and poor clothing were exacerbated by long marches to work sites, such as a new footbridge under construction five miles up the Spray River. To address this, Otter proposed setting up two smaller camps outside Banff, but this was met by protests from residents, who were pleased with the economic boost from work in and around the townsite and wanted to see it continued. Interestingly, one of the most insistent voices was Bennett, who had come full circle in his thinking about the internees and, in reaction to local pressure, called for the men to be put to work improving the road on Tunnel Mountain and the one connecting the mining town of Bankhead with Lake Minnewanka to automobile standards. In response, Harkin indicated that he agreed with internment officials that prisoners presented a threat and should not come into contact with their own ilk: "Insofar as the Minnewanka road is concerned I am afraid we could not very well use interns. The dangerous portions of the present road are but a short distance to the north of Bankhead...too far away I think to march the aliens and moreover the internment authorities have always impressed on me that it is not desirable to have the interns near any point where there is a large foreign population."[16] There was some truth to this, as Bankhead had citizens falling under the internment regulations, and at least one of them, after boasting that he had been offered $1,500 by the Austrian consulate in Seattle to blow up the Stoney Creek bridge, was brought before Superintendent Clarke in January 1916 and "ordered interned to the end of the war."[17] Nevertheless, Bennett remained insistent, forwarding a petition signed by Banff leaseholders putting forth the opinion that the Minnewanka road could be put in shape with very little work. Harkin impatiently responded, "If it is correct that Minnewanka road could be made safe for automobile and horse traffic in two weeks time with one dozen labourers, I assure you that the necessary action will be taken." As an alternative he offered that the Upper Hot Springs road could be opened at considerably less cost and would have the benefit of increasing revenues for the bathhouse situated there, but agreed, "If it is possible to do some Tunnel Mountain road work by means of the aliens, prior to their departure, they should be put at it."[18]

In speaking of "prior to their departure," Harkin was referring to his plan to have the prisoners return to their summer work on the Banff-Laggan road. Many Banff locals argued the camp should be kept in town, but he informed Bennett he was strongly opposed to this arrangement: "The difficulty in this connection is that the internment authorities have always insisted that our summer camps should be located at points where the prisoners would not be the object of public curiosity. It is out of the question to keep an internment camp in town during the tourist season." He insisted that the work on the Laggan road was the most important in the park and "having in mind the desirability of the aliens being kept away from crowds of tourists it seems to me that it is better to concentrate our efforts on this work and endeavour to complete it this year."[19] Bennett agreed, and the prisoners carried out the promised work around town that spring before returning to Castle Mountain and recommencing work, being considerably aided by the branch's purchase of a steam shovel to assist them. Four months later another four miles stood cleared, cribbed, culverted, and gravelled as a testament to their efforts and the commissioner's strong will. But despite his insistence that the camp not become the subject of public curiosity, over the course of the summer carloads of tourists drove out on the new road to see the latest attraction, including such noteworthy visitors as the Governor General the Duke of Connaught.

Indeed, even Harkin and Cory added to the spectacle, accompanying Minister Roche to the camp in July and Surveyor General Edouard Deville in August.

Among the prisoners working on the road that summer were some 100 men shipped from the Brandon facility when it was closed down, a symptom of internment operations that henceforth had major repercussions for the park program. Essentially, by 1916 casualties in the fields of Flanders were eating up the flower of Canadian manhood and labour shortages had begun to appear on the home front. Companies which had employed immigrants in the pre-war period began approaching government officials about releasing internees to make up for the shortfall, and with the growing prevalence of strikes and escape attempts, Otter became receptive to the idea. Problems were most evident at Jasper, where some fifty men clearing the Maligne-Medicine road in June and July did so under protest and had to be forced to work, leading to Otter's decision to close down the operations and release the men, mainly to work on the GTP and CPR railways.[20] A similar situation developed in Yoho when a request for the release of men by the Crow's Nest Pass Coal Company to replace their striking workforce was quickly followed by a strike of the internees themselves. Harkin took a realistic view of the situation, reasoning that if the men could not be compelled to work, he could not afford to keep them. He relayed this opinion to Otter in a letter at the end of August and at the same time recommended to Superintendent Russell that seventy-five prisoners be released to work as loggers. Although Otter hoped to correct the situation by a change of command, matters remained unsettled and were exacerbated with the discovery in late September that over fifty prisoners had been constructing an escape tunnel from the Camp Otter compound. This sealed the matter, and after meeting with Otter in early October, Harkin wired Russell on October 7 directing that the camp be closed, with most of the prisoners being shipped to Quebec.

Fourteen men were held back to maintain the Castle complement finishing up the season's work on the road, as the releases even began to affect the most important of all the park internment projects. By July, with numbers reduced from 450 to 200 men, only the transfer from Brandon allowed progress to be made. Returned to the Cave and Basin for the winter of 1916–1917, with less crowding due to releases, the camp's conditions were somewhat better than the previous year. However, with the war going badly and casualties mounting, the Banff populace was now not so welcoming, with articles appearing in the *Crag and Canyon* referring to the internees as "foul-mouthed leering Austrians" and "slouching, bovine-faced foreigners." Work that winter did, nevertheless, result in some important local improvements, including reducing a dangerous curve on Tunnel Mountain Road, building a new rock retaining wall near Bow Falls, clearing underbrush at the Recreation Grounds and in the Buffalo Paddock, and cutting timber near Edith Pass. As well, the Banff citizenry decided to launch a carnival in February to improve winter tourism, and the prisoners were co-opted into building an elaborate ice palace and maze on Banff Avenue and a toboggan run on Caribou Street. Even so, by April 1917 large releases were underway, and with the need for industrial manpower becoming daily more acute, Harkin made no protest. Some minor work was carried out over the spring and by mid-July the few remaining men were shipped to Ontario and the camp closed, almost two years to the day after prisoners had first arrived.

It was a bitter pill for Harkin to swallow, as in their early days he had placed so much hope in the work the internment operations could accomplish. But, as pointed out, he was also aware of the darker side of the treatment of men who he himself admitted were no more than citizens of enemy countries who found themselves in Canada when war was declared. In the final analysis, it was a case of something was better than nothing, as he made clear in his annual report of March 1918. After stating that at 45 per cent appropriations allowed for "little more than ordinary maintenance," he assessed the internment program under the heading "Alien Prisoners' Camp":

> Early in the summer of 1917 the last of the internment camps in the parks was closed down. This was necessitated by the release for industrial purposes of a large portion of the alien enemies. It was not considered that

> the comparatively small number remaining would justify the continuation of the working camps and, therefore, the balance of the prisoners were transferred to camps in northern Ontario. While the operation of the alien camps in Revelstoke, Yoho and Jasper parks did not yield as great results as anticipated, nevertheless substantial progress was made on works that could not otherwise have been undertaken during the war.[21]

Significantly, the Castle and Banff operations were not mentioned in this summary, perhaps because Harkin believed they had achieved the results anticipated. In any case, this progress ensured that while his idea of using such non-traditional sources of labour was gone for the moment, it was not forgotten and was destined to reappear.

With the main source of support for development work no longer available, Harkin had to seek other creative ways for progress to be made at little cost. One area that fell under his gaze was the river flats below the Banff Springs Hotel where the CPR had built a nine-hole golf links in 1911. As an enthusiast of the game, he had taken opportunities during his annual inspection tours to play the course, designed by local professional William Thomson. This was the case in 1915 when he and Cory, who if anything was even more committed to the royal and ancient game, had formed a threesome with Superintendent Clarke, one of the Banff Springs Golf Club's leading members. Golf helped in the development of the "play spirit" that Harkin believed to be so essential to mankind's well-being, and it also met one of his policy goals by providing a diversion for tourists. Nonetheless, when the CPR approached him about increasing green fees in 1916, arguing the receipts from the course were less than the costs of operation, he flatly refused and responded that if a change were to be made it should be downward. Apparently he discussed this matter with Cory, as when the deputy minister met with a senior railway official that fall it was proposed "that the Government should take over the links, extending them to a full 18 hole course, and maintain them at its own expense, charging a nominal fee for the use of the same, which will be lower than anything than has yet been charged." Although initially opposed to the idea, CPR executives changed their minds after Shaughnessy visited and estimated the cost of the additional nine holes at $10,000. A tentative agreement was worked out in March 1917, and the following year's annual report included a section reporting on the management being taken over by the branch. In noting "there is ample room, through good country, for the extension of this nine-hole course to the full medal size of eighteen-holes," it also expressed the hope that the department would undertake the work in the coming season. This, Cory advised the CPR, would be carried out by "a number of interned aliens at Banff who could be employed in the work of clearing and preparation for the extension of the course." In fact, this was the last work carried out by the prisoners, but when they were released in early July only three holes had been partially completed.[22]

Little regular manpower was available to continue the work, partly because the branch was now involved in another project close to Bow Falls. The increasing number of automobiles reaching Banff in 1915 with the relaxation of road restrictions meant that auto camping was becoming popular. At first, there was an unofficial camping area on the station grounds, but in his 1917 report Superintendent Clarke, in noting that some 1,000 automobiles had been registered at the new park gate at Exshaw, commented on "the number of camping parties at favourable points on the main roads, parties being able, without inconvenience, to carry all camping paraphernalia in their cars and make their quarters wherever the fancy seized them."[23] One favoured location was near the confluence of the Bow and Spray rivers, and in order to bring some order to a growing management problem, it was chosen as the site for a permanent campground. Initial clearing was done by day-labourers in the summer of 1916 in conjunction with the widening of the road between the Spray bridge and the golf course, and in 1917, after further improvements, it accommodated seventy-three camping parties.

The simultaneous addressing of these two amenities reflected Harkin's goal of providing services and appropriate entertainments to park visitors. Waterton Lakes was, like Rocky Mountains, joined to a population centre by road—Pincher Creek to the north and Cardston to the

Banff Springs Hotel from the Banff Springs Golf Course, ca. 1928. Byron Harmon photograph. Harkin's and Cory's love of golf combined with the operation of their new Donald Ross-designed links at Banff in the 1920s ensured that golf courses would become important facilities in many of Canada's national parks. [WMCR, V263 NA-3760]

east—but it would be several more years before most other parks were serviced with good quality trunk roads. When they were, provision of camping grounds became a developmental priority. As for golf, the Banff course languished for its first few years under government ownership, but in 1919 Cory supported a large appropriation of $15,000 for its completion. The foremost golf architect in North America, Donald Ross of Pinehurst, North Carolina, was engaged at $1,000 to design the additional nine holes, and although there were those who thought that this was exorbitant, Harkin stood behind it, arguing, "I am advised that in the United States expert golfers will travel thousands of miles to reach a course which they know has been laid out by this man."[24] One can only imagine the pride he and Cory took in describing the attractions of their Ross-designed course in the midst of the Rockies to their fellow members at the prestigious Rivermead Club in Gatineau, Quebec, but they were to find operating a golf course was a challenging business. It took until 1924 before Ross's design was fully implemented and the course began to turn a profit, and it was soon to revert back to the CPR in conjunction with the construction of their Stanley Thompson championship course in 1927. Meanwhile, anxious to extend golfing facilities to other parks, in 1921 Harkin had sent Banff professional Thomson to Waterton to design a nine-hole course, located on a beautiful site with a view of the lakes between the Blakiston River and the townsite. That same fall, Thomson went to examine a Jasper location proposed by famous visitor and avid golfer Sir Arthur Conan Doyle near Pyramid Lake, although he found a superior site near a tent camp on Lac Beauvert. His design for a nine-hole course was under construction in 1924 when Henry Thornton, president of the newly created Canadian National Railways, determined that his recently acquired Jasper Park Lodge camp needed a more prestigious eighteen-hole links, also to be designed by Stanley Thompson.[25]

Harkin's and Cory's love of golf was to have profound consequences for the future of Canada's national parks, as golf courses would come to be regarded as a required tourist offering. Fortunately, links and the campgrounds had the benefit of costing very little as the commissioner attempted to make his wartime funding stretch as far as possible. Elsewhere, except for the work carried out by the internees, little was accomplished, and he had to find other ways to move the branch forward. One was to make important additions to the park system, as had occurred with Mount Revelstoke Park in 1914. There was no shortage of other candidates as headquarters staff had begun preparing background reports prior to the 1913 amendment, including for an area incorporating Coquitlam Lakes containing the water supply of New Westminster, BC, and the associated drainage of the Stave and Lillooet rivers; a fraction of land around Manitou Lake, Saskatchewan, the waters of which were famous for their medicinal qualities; Beausoleil Island at the east end of Georgian Bay, an area of some 2,700 acres containing ancient fortifications owned by the Chippewa Indians; and a park proposed near the Rockies' highest peak, Mt. Robson in the Yellowhead district. Of these, it was the last that was pursued the most vigorously, but, as fate would have it, Robson would be climbed in 1913 by an Alpine Club expedition and on returning to Victoria one of its conquerors, BC Deputy Minister of Public Works W.W. Foster, began to prepare legislation to create Mount Robson Provincial Park. As such, it was to be a completely unforeseen opportunity to create another mountain park in BC's Vermilion and Kootenay valleys that engaged Harkin's attention during the latter war period, and one that would also provide an opportunity for solving a thorny problem dogging the province's parks.

Despite the attention being paid to the extension of the Banff-Calgary road to the Columbia Valley in the pre-war years, after the Dominion government's completion of its thirty-mile section to Vermilion Pass in 1914, the project had languished. Although the proposed budget of 1911 was $150,000, by 1913 the BC government had invested at least $200,000 and the CPR some $75,000 in completing the extremely difficult Sinclair Creek and Vermilion Pass sections. Because of provincial financial stringency, at this point construction was halted, and in 1914 spring floods washed out most of the work on Sinclair Creek. Harkin was drawn into the situation when he was asked to query the provincial government about their future plans by the Banff Board of Trade, which, in turn, was responding to a request from the Windermere Board of Trade to support an early completion of the road. The minister of Public Works responded that, with at least $100,000 needed to complete the work, it was not likely it would occur soon. In the circumstances, and given his own belief in the importance of the road as a tourism route from the United States, Harkin was pleased to hear from Randolph Bruce, the original promoter of the Banff-Windermere Road, concerning an idea on how the impasse could be broken. Several years later in a letter to him, Bruce recalled the events:

> I got the C.P.R. interested and the provincial government, away back in 1910. The former put in $75,000 and the latter $200,000. Then came evil days in B.C. Our government had no more money. What had been built was falling into decay and I bethought myself of the Dominion Government and in conjunction with your good self, I suggested to Dr. Roche, the then Minister of the Interior,

> that he should take over the road as then constructed, as an outlet for the national park. At the time you will remember he said the Dominion Government was willing to pay for the necessary right-of-way, which we then talked about extending a mile on either side of the road. From Ottawa I went to Victoria, and asked the Government for five miles free right-of-way on either side of the road, and I got it for you.[26]

While generally correct, Bruce's recollection did not reveal the intent of the agreement or the difficult negotiations that followed. In approaching the minister, Harkin foresaw the possibility of creating a new national park in the right-of-way, incorporating one of the most historic sections of the Rockies and bringing within his administration another area with scenic and game potential. But it also offered an opportunity to address a conundrum. As part of the terms of union of BC with Canada, a strip of land extending twenty miles on each side of the CPR's projected rail line between the Kicking Horse Pass and New Westminster had been transferred from the province to the Dominion. Although it had been intended that this "Railway Belt" be used to make land grants to the CPR to support its construction, this had never occurred and the land remained under the administration of the Department of the Interior. However, it was continually a matter of contention as to whether it was Dominion or provincial law that prevailed on these lands, a problem particularly acute in the parks located within the belt. This was especially so with respect to responsibility for game administration and licensing, a constant irritation for Parks Branch employees attempting to carry out policies consistently. When discussions on the transfer of lands for a new park in return for the completion of the Banff-Windermere Road were undertaken, the opportunity for the Dominion government to address this perplexing matter was available, and, in fact, became almost as important as the transfer itself. Solicitor General Arthur Meighen drafted a bill in May 1916 incorporating an agreement on transfer of lands in return for completion of the road as well as a clause to deal with the jurisdictional matter, including wording that would provide the Dominion with "exclusive control" over legislation and regulation for "management of parks belonging to the Dominion of Canada." In forwarding it to Bruce, Harkin described it as a "necessary preliminary" that it be enacted by the province, and this was immediately followed by a telegram from Minister Roche to Premier Bowser: "Department is prepared to proceed with completion of the road if proposition endorsed by Legislature in form of the bill which Randolph Bruce will present to you Friday."[27]

On May 31, 1916 Harkin wrote Wardle, at work on roads in Jasper, that third reading of the bill had been given and that he was wiring Premier Bowser to request plans and profiles of the road be sent to Banff so that the engineer could inspect them. To his amazement, when he received a copy of the legislation ten days later, he noted a major deficiency—it extended Dominion legislative jurisdiction only to the lands to be transferred and not to all BC parks—and he fired off a memorandum to Cory pointing out that it would not do: "In the Act as passed by the British Columbia Legislature the whole question of jurisdiction over all Dominion Parks in British Columbia which was most important from the Parks' view, has been omitted. I therefore think this Department would not be justified in accepting this act, or grants thereunder, under the conditions specified."[28] Cory concurred, but unfortunately by that time the branch had egg on its face as Wardle, acting on available information, had obviously spoken with the Banff newspaper. On June 10, the same day as Harkin wrote his memorandum, the *Crag and Canyon* published a headline story "Transcontinental Motor Road," laying out the details of the supposed project, and two days later it was picked up by the *Calgary Daily Herald*. Diplomatic channels were quickly opened, Minister Roche advising Premier Bowser that the bill in its current form was unacceptable. Bowser's reply was unsatisfactory, and by early July, Harkin was cryptically responding to a request for information on the situation, "It is not the intention of the Dominion Government to establish a new park in connection with the Banff-Windermere Highway."[29]

With his star on the ascendancy in the competitive world of Ottawa's bureaucracy, having had an unexpected and career-enhancing opportunity dangled in front of him and then just as quickly snatched away was frustrating. Undoubtedly, he had cause to consider the high-handed way his department had approached the matter, providing an object lesson in the treacherous field of Dominion-provincial relations that paid important dividends later on. For the moment Harkin had to be content with the efforts of his superiors, Cory and Roche, to get negotiations back on track, something he was willing to make some significant sacrifices to achieve. At Cory's request in December 1916 he drafted a new agreement guaranteeing certain expenditures on the department's part to effect a timely completion of the road. He informed his superior that "by cutting down closely in the various parks I can extract from our regular Parks appropriations for this roadway about $20,000," but expressed doubt about whether this would be sufficient, as "probably they would expect a minimum of $40,000 to $50,000."[30] A further impediment appeared in late December while Cory was on his way to Victoria to discuss the offer when Roche announced that the parks appropriations would be cut from $348,000 to $300,000 in the forthcoming year. In informing Cory of this, he mused that it would now be very difficult "to squeeze $20,000 of the vote for the B.C. road" and expressed his doubt about the use of his deputy proceeding. Cory did decide to continue, however, and in the negotiations was successful in having the $20,000 figure, combined with a commitment to complete the road within two years of war's end, accepted. The Banff-Windermere Road Agreement was signed on this basis, but, unfortunately, there were other complications concerning the rights of logging companies and agricultural settlers along the proposed route through the Kootenay Valley. Ultimately, the BC government declared that nothing could be done until these matters were investigated the following summer.

It was October 1917 before Cory again asked Harkin's opinion about continuing negotiations. This elicited an impassioned plea of support, pointing out the "commercial potentialities of this road when it is completed," as "tourist traffic affords one of the most effective means of bringing a very large amount of foreign money into the country at a minimum expenditure." But, he indicated, the matter of jurisdiction also needed to be solved, as in his mind the two were inextricably linked, and he gave full voice to his concern about the need for overriding federal authority in national parks:

> One of the conditions laid down in the negotiations with British Columbia has been that the Province should surrender to the Dominion on the various conflicts of jurisdiction which has arisen in all Dominion Parks in B.C.....The attitude of the Dominion is that since it established national parks and invites the tourists of the world to come to them, it must assume definite responsibility with respect to them. For instance it was felt that all drivers and guides operating within Dominion Parks should be licensed by the Dominion only. The foreign tourist has a right to expect that any driver is guaranteed as to his character and efficiency by his Government. The same is true in regard to pool rooms, restaurants and other places of public resort. In addition the policy of the Dominion is to maintain all national parks as game sanctuaries, partly in order that the characteristic wild life may be preserved from extinction and partly that game may be so numerous that it may constitute one of the principal attractions to the tourist.[31]

Cory repeated these arguments in his own memorandum to newly appointed Minister of the Interior Meighen, recommending resumption of discussions. When approved in January 1918 it was expected that the commissioner would play a key role in bringing them to completion, a task that would ultimately take more than another year of painstaking effort to achieve.

While the possibility of creating a new mountain park slowly wended its way through the intergovernmental minefield, Harkin realized there were also some other opportunities for expansion of branch activities, those informed by his interest in Canadian history. Although he later modestly claimed that he had "no pretensions to any extensive knowledge of Canadian history," he had become involved with the Historic Landmarks Association of Canada (later the Canadian Historical Association) formed in 1907 as an offshoot of the Royal Society of Canada to co-ordinate interest in various regions of the country concerning heritage preservation and commemoration. Among its goals were efforts to develop the Plains of Abraham in celebration of Quebec's tercentenary in 1908 as well as plans to do an inventory of significant sites across Canada. However, nationalist rivalries within the organization all but paralyzed it, and in his 1913 report Harkin mentioned a possible opportunity for the Parks Branch to assist:

> There are many places of historic interest, poorly marked or unmarked at all. While it is somewhat out of the sphere of National Parks to deal with the marking of battlefields, it is most desirable from a national standpoint, that such should be set aside as national reserves and that the ruins, old forts, old towers and such, holding historic associations, should be preserved. Canada has much in her history to inspire the rising generations with pride of their forbears and pride of country.
>
> It would be doubly beneficial if these historic spots were not only properly restored and marked but they should be used as places of resort by Canadian children who, while gaining the benefit of outdoor recreation, would at the same time have the opportunity to absorb historical knowledge under conditions that could not fail to make them better Canadians.[32]

Accompanying these comments was a proposal to carry out "a general survey of historic sites of the Dominion with a view to preserving them as national monuments."

Well thought out, the suggestion to have the branch fill this vacuum had some real benefits in achieving Harkin's desire to expand the system, and as such it was part of the rationale for the 1913 amendment. Creation of parks in the prairie provinces and the Railway Belt was a relatively simple matter, as the land was under federal jurisdiction, but such was not the case in the east, except for a number of formerly strategic forts and battlefields in the hands of Interior's Ordnance Branch and the Militia Department. Thus association with the heritage movement offered an opportunity to help solve the perplexing problem of the lack of reserves in eastern Canada. Harkin had mentioned the necessity of establishing parks near large centres of population in his early reports and in March 1914 reiterated it in a memorandum entitled "Dominion Parks, Their Values and Ideals," where he mentioned that the tide of movement to the cities could not be stemmed and the alternative was to provide the city-dweller with an opportunity to achieve a rural and wilderness experience.[33] While a visit to a historic site did not entirely fulfill this need, it was a step in the right direction, and upon receiving support for the idea Harkin's concern about it being out of the sphere of national parks quickly disappeared. Later that year he put forward the concept of "historic parks" as one of the four distinct types of parks in *Just a Sprig of Mountain Heather.*

Steps had already been taken to put the plan into action. In September 1913 Williamson began sending letters to those who it was thought would have an interest: "The Commissioner of Dominion Parks is at present very much interested in this matter of having historical monuments, etc., in the Dominion preserved and if you could, without too much trouble to yourself send him a short resume of the facts in this connection...which will enumerate places historically worthy of preservation, I think it might result in their preservation in the future."[34] The same month Harkin began a correspondence concerning the playgrounds movement with Mabel Peters, president of the Playgrounds Association of Saint John, New Brunswick, and it was here his idea of marrying the value of outdoor recreation for Canadian children with the marking and preserving of historic sites first appeared. In a letter making this point, he concluded with the request, "It has occurred to me that you may be familiar with a number of historic places in New Brunswick which are worthy of preservation and if so, I would be very glad if you could send me any facts you possess." Peters responded enthusiastically, relating recent unsuccessful attempts to have the city's historic Fort Howe turned into a park and playground and promising to forward an historic sketch of the location. Not only did she arrange that, but she also took the matter to the local chapter of the Daughters of the Empire, the Saint John Historical Society, and the newspapers to gain support, and soon reported, "I feel sure of the heartiest support of all classes of citizens."[35] Williamson carried out the necessary background research to establish the fort's importance, finding that it had been built by the British during the American Revolutionary War to protect the harbour and then had played a significant role in the establishment of the United Empire Loyalists and the founding of Saint John in 1783.

In line with heritage movements in both England and the United States, which frequently combined heritage and land conservation but downplayed reconstruction, Harkin was not so much interested in the site for its ruins as for the opportunity it provided to create a surrounding recreational area. With the legwork done, he took the next step, drafting a letter for Cory's signature to Minister of Militia Sam Hughes on November 28 noting that "strong representations have recently been made to this Department that the site of old Fort Howe, at St. John, N.B., which I understand is owned by your Department should be created a National Park for the benefit of the people of St. John and for the sake of preserving its historic associations" and asking if there was any way that an arrangement could be made for the department to take over the location. Following this, he sent a letter to Minister Meighen's secretary, J.G. Mitchell, arguing that "from a patriotic point of view" it would be desirable to create a national park at the location for very little expenditure, and strategically presented the origin of the matter in a slightly different light, stating that "the matter was first brought to the attention of the Branch by members of the New Brunswick Historical Society," making it appear that the branch was responding to public demand rather than actually creating that demand itself.[36] Hughes was willing to hand over administration to the lands, with a proviso that they could be taken back for military purposes if necessary, and on March 30, 1914 an order-in-council directed that "the site in question be placed under control and administration of the Department of the Interior and that under the authority of Section 18 of the Dominion Forest Reserves and Parks Act, 1911, as amended by Chapter 18, 3–4 George V., the same be created and maintained as a Dominion Park to be known as *Fort Howe National Park*."[37]

With Canada's first national historic park a reality, Harkin turned his attention to its development, although the bare and rocky fifteen-acre site presented some challenges. His own preference was that "the park should be distinctly a historical park and should follow as little as possible the lines of a conventional city park" and that it "would be distinctly national in character as well as an attractive resort for the people of the town and tourists." Preliminary plans were prepared by Toronto architects Harries-Hall, but Harkin refused to approve them until he could visit, indicating, "I am anxious to go over the ground and absorb the historic atmosphere, because I think such a course will help a great deal in finally passing on the plans."[38] The necessity to travel west to discuss internment operations delayed his trip and the war soon precluded the plans being carried out in the short term. By the spring of 1916 the site was being used for military purposes, as the interdepartmental agreement allowed, and he later came to realize that it was not as important historically as he had been led to believe. Little was done to develop it, and it was eventually decommissioned and handed over to municipal authorities in 1930. Nonetheless, Fort Howe was important in establishing the precedent of national historic parks and a second initiative that quickly followed had a far better pedigree.

In 1604 in the basin around the mouth of the Annapolis River had been discovered by Samuel Champlain and the Sieur de Monts and was named Port Royal, becoming, with the appearance of Acadian farmers in 1606, one of the earliest sites of European settlement on the continent. Several forts were built in the region as it was fought over by the English and French until the conquest some century and a half later. One such settlement, named Fort Anne by the British in 1636, was renamed Annapolis Royal in 1710, and served as the capital of Nova Scotia until the founding of Halifax in 1749. As early as 1904, the Dominion government had co-operated in erection of a monument to de Monts, described as "the pioneer of civilization of North America," to mark the tercentenary of the founding of Port Royal. In February 1914, L.M. Fortier, inspector of Immigration Agencies at Annapolis Royal and one of a group of voluntary commissioners for a park around the old fortifications, contacted Harkin on hearing of the branch's activities in Saint John and suggested its involvement at Fort Anne. Fortier provided a copy of the book of Judge A.W. Savary, himself one of the commissioners, on the history of Annapolis County and Harkin promised to have a branch official look over the site in conjunction with the work at Fort Howe. As it turned out, Savary was opposed to turning over responsibility to the Parks Branch, preferring to wait for the expected extension of the authority of the Quebec (later National) Battlefields Commission to the Maritimes. Although this never occurred, it delayed matters, and it was not until 1916 that Harkin, now with a full grasp of the importance of the site, began advising in correspondence with Mitchell, "This place is of such peculiar interest from an historic standpoint that it has always been regarded as one which should eventually be constituted into a Dominion Park and made a centre for the development of the pride of country and patriotism throughout Nova Scotia."

In this instance Harkin was more interested in preservation activities, suggesting that the old fort rampart should be "put in first class condition" and the existing buildings repaired, including the establishment of a museum and library with the object of "impressing on visitors full and comprehensive significance of the great historical events that have centred on this point." This concept, the first indication of branch involvement in educational activities, would be complemented by the establishment of playground facilities for Annapolis residents.[39] Acquisition of the site once again required negotiations with the Department of Militia and while they were being carried out Williamson performed an in-depth study, providing in his December 1916 report an evocative challenge for historic sites work: "Enough was seen, however, to convince one that if a start is to be made in preserving the historic sites of the Dominion as National Historic Parks, no better commencement could be made than at Port Royal. The site, which consists of some thirty acres, possessing relics of the old fort...commands a magnificent view of the Basin, pregnant with early Canadian history and which but

Fort Anne, Annapolis Royal, Nova Scotia. Dedicated in 1917, Fort Anne Historic Park marked the real beginning of Harkin's work at creating Canada's system of national historic sites. [LAC, PA-051681]

awaits material expression in such a conservation scheme as is proposed."[40] By order-in-council of January 24, 1917, Fort Anne Historic Park was created on the lands incorporating the fortifications transferred from the Militia Department.

While the creation of the first two historic parks in the Atlantic provinces began to address Harkin's underlying concerns about all the parks being in the West, another initiative meeting this criteria was also underway when the war broke out in a group of islands in the St. Lawrence River between Lake Ontario and Brockville. These had been held in trust for many years after being surrendered in native treaty negotiations and in 1904 had been transferred to Interior "for parks purposes." Arrangement had been made by the department to pay the Mississauga band's claim for nine of the islands and to purchase additional ones, with tourist amenities such as steamboat wharves and landings and picnic grounds already being constructed before the islands came under the jurisdiction of the Forestry Branch in 1908 and then the Parks Branch in 1911. The 1913 amendment allowed them to be dedicated under the act and by order-in-council of December 10, 1914 the twelve individual island units were established as St. Lawrence

Islands Park. Soon a far more complex and time-consuming water-based eastern opportunity appeared, but in the case of Point Pelee Park its creation would arise from Harkin's increasingly important activities in the conservation field, another area where progress was being made despite the exigencies of the war.

SIX

More and Still More Sanctuaries

IN RESPONDING TO William Hornaday's warning about North America becoming "a gameless continent" and his challenge to "let the statesmen of America be not afraid of making too many game preserves," Harkin had become a strong game conservation advocate by the outbreak of the First World War. It was apparent from his statements, such as that made in relation to Kootenay Park, that preservation in the parks served a dual purpose—"partly in order that the characteristic wild life may be preserved from extinction and partly that game may be so numerous that it may constitute one of the principal attractions to the tourist." Yet, as his struggle with Campbell to gain control of game preservation activities illustrated, he recognized that work to protect some important threatened species was going to have to be undertaken outside of parks without the commercial support of tourism. Consequently, in correspondence with Hornaday in 1917 Harkin could boldly state, "So far as my wild life work is concerned, I certainly intend to strenuously work for more and still more sanctuaries." In pursuing this goal his reputation as a champion for Canadian wildlife would be fully realized.

Initially, preservation efforts were focused on plains bison inherited from Douglas's regime. The important Pablo herd, acquired while he was Oliver's secretary, had begun arriving in what was the country's first federal game preserve at Elk Park in 1907. Four hundred head arrived that year pending the completion of their final home at the new Buffalo Park near Wainwright; 325 of these were moved in September 1908 when it was completed with the erection of seventy-three miles of fencing creating a paddock of some 2,800 acres on the 160-square-mile reserve. This left a population of some forty-eight mavericks still roaming the densely-forested Elk Park, and although by 1915 this herd had increased to 106, the branch made no attempt to remove them, thereby perpetuating what would become Alberta's longest-standing fenced wildlife park. Meanwhile, by the fall of 1909, at Buffalo Park the initial Elk Park shipments had been augmented with an additional 218 animals shipped directly from the Pablo herd in Montana as well as seventy-seven head from the fast-growing exhibition herd at Banff. Because Pablo had difficulty capturing the last remnants of his herd, it was left to Harkin to recommend to the department that the contract be extended to the end of the 1912–1913 fiscal year, by which time 716 animals had been delivered. Harkin could now boast that the park contained the largest known herd of bison in the world, and in recognition of the importance of both Elk Park and Buffalo Park in their success at preservation, they were formally declared as Elk Island National Park and Buffalo National Park by order-in-council of March 27, 1913.[1]

Although his reputation as a conservationist with respect to the plains bison was largely built on the work of others, Harkin's notoriety with respect to its northern subspecies, the larger, darker wood bison, was more his own and Graham's doing. The shaggy beasts roamed a vast area in northwestern Canada between the Athabasca district and

Great Slave Lake and likely numbered several hundred thousand before beginning to fall victim to the spread of firearms in the hands of white and native hunters as well as a series of harsh winters beginning in the 1860s. After numerous reports by early sportsmen, the North West Mounted Police, and a Senate committee about their scarcity, the Canadian government passed the *Unorganized Territories Game Preservation Act* in 1894, putting in place a complete hunting ban. For the next dozen years supervision of the animals' welfare became the responsibility of the police, and periodically reports were received expressing continuing concerns about native hunting practices on their population. Amendments of continuance to the original prohibition were carried through 1907, and that year Inspector Arthur Jarvis undertook a series of expeditions, accompanied at various times by naturalists E.A. Preble and Ernest Thompson Seton, to determine the impacts of wolf predation on the herds. They found the wood buffalo confined to a small triangle between the Slave and Peace rivers and the Caribou Mountains under threat not by wolves, but by "wasteful" native hunters, who Jarvis accused of being entirely responsible for the population decline. As a solution, Jarvis suggested game guardians protect the survivors in the herd, but also mentioned that a better solution could be afforded by establishing the area as a national park.[2]

In 1911 Campbell was successful in convincing the minister that with the need for dedicated game guardians to enforce regulations, the task could best be carried out by the Forestry Branch. Immediately he directed the government agent at Fort Smith, A.J. Bell, to undertake a survey of conditions, and his report of January 1912, in noting the existence of both northern and southern herds, recommended centralizing and fencing the animals in a 220-square-mile area at the confluence of the Slave and Peace. Cory commended Campbell's efforts in this regard, and given these circumstances the matter of wood bison preservation would quickly become part of the larger debate between Campbell and Harkin over responsibility for game management outside parks.[3] It was in this vein that Maxwell Graham first exerted his influence as head of the Animal Division. In June 1912, in bringing the matter to his superior's attention, he supported Bell's recommendation but argued that the preserve should be located north of the Peace River in an unfenced area incorporating the entire wood buffalo range. As well, he stated, it should be carried out by the Parks Branch as the agency most concerned with the interests of wildlife, and cited examples of the success of the reserve principle in the game sanctuaries of East Africa and Uganda. Harkin was convinced, and in February 1913 when one of the two game guardians supervising the wood bison resigned, he contacted Cory and put forward the position that his branch should take charge, as "the Forestry Branch cannot have the same incentive for jealously guarding them."[4]

Graham was dogged, consistently reinforcing his position by criticizing Forestry's abilities and providing rationale for Parks Branch action. In July 1912 he asserted that the existing stock of plains bison, all in reserves under Parks' control, could be improved through breeding with young wood bison bulls, and by December was arguing that the game laws in the Athabasca district were ineffective and the natives were being "wantonly destructive."[5] Two years later, with the latest extension of the hunting prohibition about to expire, he prepared a memorandum to the minister, under Harkin's signature, reviewing the entire history of the matter and, predictably, ending with a recommendation that the buffalo range should be completely preserved through the creation of a national park.[6] Harkin oversaw the preparation of an order-in-council for Minister Roche that would create "Caribou Mountain National Park" near Fort Smith, and shortly afterwards, Williamson articulated the branch's position, indicating, "It is believed that adequate protection can only be afforded by centralizing the herd and driving them down into some locality where they can be confined within a restricted area, an area where proper controls can be established, where game regulations may be enforced, and where energetic steps may be taken to lessen the menace from wolves."[7]

Because of the need for interdepartmental co-operation, the issue remained unresolved for almost another two years before it came to a head with the regional Indian Affairs inspector, who opposed the formation of a park on native hunting territory, expressing doubt about the animals' use of the range and contending wolves would become a serious problem. Harkin dismissed these arguments, utilizing Graham's research about the buffaloes' long use of the area and claiming that the Indians possessed no treaty rights. His frustration was evident as he noted that the draft order-in-council of June 1914 was still awaiting submission and expressed the opinion, "The time has arrived when steps should be taken to carry out the wishes of authorities everywhere on the conservation of game." But once identified, the issue of aboriginal hunting exerted a powerful influence, and in a memorandum to Cory of July 5, 1916, in which he referred to the possibility that not all regulations need apply to the park, alluded to the possibility of natives continuing to hunt species other than wood buffalo in it. As it turned out, the park did not come up for serious discussion again for another six years, a period during which Harkin's branch was given responsibility for all northern animals.

Fortunately, the pitfalls of wood bison conservation were not duplicated with respect to the pronghorn antelope, the other large Canadian mammal believed to be on the verge of extinction. With the failure of the antelope to thrive in the Banff paddock, the remaining animals were moved to Buffalo Park in 1910, and in March 1912 its superintendent reported the presence of fourteen antelope. But they too quickly dwindled, a result, it seems, of a lack of some important ingredient in their diet. Again, it was the initiative and hard work of Graham, something that Harkin sometimes seems to have supported almost against his better judgement, which ultimately led the way to a solution. However, that support, grudging or not, was to be critical to the eventual success of antelope preserves, illustrating that even though he did not always fully understand the natural forces at work, he was willing to take some risks and support his staff in the exploration of new approaches. This was amply illustrated by the events leading to the creation of three antelope parks in Alberta and Saskatchewan, work that Williamson described to the Commission of Conservation in 1915 as "the most important new work" undertaken by the branch in wildlife conservation.

When they took their trip in May 1914 to view the proposed location for a preserve north of Medicine Hat, Graham and Seton had been directed to examine other vacant Dominion lands that might prove suitable for antelope reserves. Travelling by automobile, they inspected a number of other possible ranges near Moose Jaw and Maple Creek, Saskatchewan, keeping in touch with Harkin by telegraph as they went along. The commissioner was particularly interested in Seton's recommendation for a preserve about six miles southwest of Maple Creek, which he had found to be the most beautiful range land they had seen in "the old antelope country." Perhaps this interest was sparked by Seton's offer to personally undertake its development "at great personal sacrifice" and by his appeal to his sponsor's vanity and well-known interests: "I am convinced that there is not only a wonderful opportunity to save the antelope as you did the buffalo, but you can also secure the gratitude of posterity by establishing these parks as places of pleasure and health for the whole nation."[8] If so, the stratagem worked, as in November 1914 Williamson submitted a memorandum to the Registrar of Dominion Lands requesting that three areas—the fifty-four-square-mile Canyon Preserve, the twenty-square-mile Maple Creek preserve, and an area of nine square miles near Old Wives Lake southwest of Moose Jaw—be reserved for protection of the pronghorn antelope. The first two areas were later dedicated as Wawaskesy and Menissawok parks (Cree for "antelope" and "national property") by order-in-council of May 31, 1922.[9]

Although these were important initiatives, it was a fourth area near the village of Nemiskam southwest of Medicine Hat that ultimately played the key role in antelope preservation and best illustrates how Harkin sometimes had to make on-the-fly decisions about conservation. The saga began early in 1915 when a Mounted Police sergeant reported that about 200 starving antelope were feeding with the sheep of a rancher near the village of Foremost and recommended that the government take action to protect them. When word of their plight reached Ottawa, Harkin contacted Cory, explaining "the antelope are so tame, through hunger, that they come up to the ranches to be fed" and "the ranchers would be willing to feed them, but many have no hay, etc. to spare." He proposed feeding the animals *in situ* with a view to removing them as soon as possible to Maple Creek and recommended

Young girl feeding antelope in Buffalo National Park, ca. 1920. Lack of success with antelope at Wainwright led to Harkin's support of Graham's efforts at antelope preservation at several locations in southern Alberta and Saskatchewan. [GA, NA-5413-3]

Graham be dispatched west to take the matter in hand.[10] Cory agreed and upon reaching Medicine Hat, Graham joined forces with Saskatchewan Forest Ranger H.H. Fauquier to examine the area where the report had originated. They found the animals grazing wind-swept ridges, and Graham determined they would have to be lured to a location where they could be corralled. After baiting two sites, he wired Harkin on March 10, "Fauquier and I have located two herds here, have just succeeded enticing one herd of 32 to eat alfalfa in place suitable for corral. Recommend immediate construction corral and wings, have all lumber wire netting etc. here....Estimate cost of corral, wings, labour, under three hundred dollars." On March 11, Harkin responded, "Your wire tenth if satisfied you can control antelope until temporary corral erected proceed with the corral work." Acting quickly, Graham and a small crew constructed a corral with two wings each a quarter mile long and swing gates controlled by ropes and pulleys. But to their chagrin, even though the antelope had visited the site for five straight nights during its construction, they failed to appear on the morning of the 15th. Seven riders were sent out to try drive them in, but as Graham reported, "They no longer retained, as during the winter, the herd formation, but broke in every direction, some running back between the riders." A few days later he telegraphed word of his failure, recommending that the corral be left in place for use the following winter when, he later claimed, they could be captured "by means of perhaps two dollars worth of alfalfa hay, a little patience and the corral."[11]

In a letter of March 20, Graham referred to a second site that had been baited, a lease belonging to "a rancher, and close observer of antelope in Alberta for some twelve years" named Edgar McHugh. The rancher had been feeding a herd of some forty antelope for several months, and the failure at the first location gave Graham cause to reconsider it. By this time he was beginning to have second thoughts about the original plan of capturing and moving the antelope, noting "there is apt to be a certain dissatisfaction if antelope in Alberta are taken out of that Province and placed in Saskatchewan," and McHugh's lease offered the possibility of a more permanent solution. There were already five sections of fenced land controlled by McHugh and three other homesteaders and Graham felt with ten miles of woven wire fencing, costing under $2,000 and a month's labour, it could be made a "supply station for future stocking of reserves." Furthermore, McHugh had indicated that he would look after the fence and the antelope without charge. Graham closed by stating he could "guarantee enclosing antelope" if the department was prepared to exchange lands with the homesteaders on an acre-for-acre basis and make them a small cash payment.[12]

With Graham's request for a decision before the end of May, it can only be imagined how perplexed the cash-strapped Harkin would have been on receiving this information. Having a few days earlier approved a $300 expenditure for major corral work at one site, he was now being asked to spend at least $1,500 only eleven miles distant. In a memorandum to Cory he offered, "If I were satisfied that Mr. Graham could positively make good his guarantee I would have no hesitation in recommending that the necessary authority be given him" but admitted, "I feel a good deal of doubt as to his being able to hold the present herd until the fence is completed." Usually firm and decisive in his recommendations, this case proved an exception: "In view of the doubts which naturally arise in my mind as indicated above I can see no other course than to submit the matter to you for decision."[13] Cory declined to proceed.

Ordered back to Ottawa, Graham first took the opportunity to sow a little goodwill, touring local dignitaries around the area and providing a Lethbridge newspaper interview leaving the impression that creation of the preserve was just a matter of time. Stating he had "made a good start of preservation" and believed that all that was needed was a little more money, he said he intended to return to Ottawa to arrange for it so that future travellers on the new Lethbridge-Weyburn rail line could stop and visit "the last of the antelope."[14] He also did good work in Medicine Hat, convincing its Board of Trade to send a letter to Minister Roche advocating the fencing of the five sections until the Canyon Preserve was completed. This letter led Cory to request a further report from Harkin, and in it he noted that, since his return, Graham had expressed confidence that he could successfully enclose the herd. He then forwarded a comprehensive memorandum indicating how convincing Graham had become in his arguments: "I have now had a full explanation from Mr. Graham as to his reasons for considering his proposal perfectly feasible, and I now freely admit that his knowledge of the habits of the antelope, and the concurrence in his views by old residents in Alberta, convince me that his proposal is perfectly sound and would be good business." As a closer, he stated that the cost of fencing and labour would not exceed $1,500, while "the value of the 50 antelope is at a conservative estimate, according to recent prices, $2,500."[15] The next day the minister "approved that the department should fence an area of five sections in Chin Coulee which is now occupied by about fifty antelope" and the land agent at Medicine Hat was directed to assist Graham in arranging for transfer of the outstanding homesteader lands.[16]

Arriving back in the area in mid-April brimming with new confidence, Graham once again had to face the reality of the uncertain nature of conservation work. Upon reaching McHugh's, he found the rancher confined to bed with tonsillitis and listened while his hired man reported that some natives had been camping near the five sections intended to be reserved. Alarmed, he hired a rig and drove out to locate the fifty animals present when he left, but he could now discover only fifteen head inside and six outside the area. As he reported to Harkin, presumably the remainder had been killed or driven off and lamented, "I think you will agree with me that in view of the fact that no Indians for over ten years have been known to take the trail through McHugh's ranch, it is singularly unfortunate that they should choose a time and place such as they did in this instance." He did express confidence that the missing animals would drift back and if the eastern end of the enclosure were temporarily left unfenced, "during the winter carefully supervised drives can be made...into the Chin Coulee and through this latter into the new Antelope Reserve." Recommending fencing on the other sides proceed, he again asked if his proposals were authorized. Once more faced with a difficult decision, this time Harkin was more decisive. On April 27 he wired, "If you are thoroughly satisfied you can enclose remaining antelope and keep them there proceed with fence."[17] Two days later Graham gave an interview to the *Lethbridge Telegram*, reported under the headline "Antelope Reserve to Be Established Near Foremost," relating the decision to go ahead and giving Harkin the credit: "The Dominion Parks Branch of the Department of the Interior, we may add, is comparatively a new branch of the government service. Under its present commissioner, Mr. J.B. Harkin, much good work has been done. Mr. Harkin is a zealous official, the antelope preserve project is a case in point."[18]

A month later Graham reported that despite a delay in receiving the woven wire, he had made some real progress. Three additional sections of land where he had discovered some twenty-seven antelope were to be incorporated into the reserve, and 2,000 new cedar posts, all provided by McHugh at no cost, were to be placed. In describing the rancher, Graham stated, "his services are worth those of two ordinary men on work of this nature," and he also related that McHugh had agreed to keep a man in a house within the enclosure to carry out regular inspections. His only requirements were to be permitted to graze some cattle on the lands in the winter and, when the area ceased to be used as a temporary reserve, to be provided with a lease to the lands within the enclosure not already registered in his name. Graham felt that this was an excellent arrangement, as it secured a thoroughly competent caretaker and guardian of the antelope and the fencing at no cost.[19] In late June he reported that he had reached agreement with the affected homesteaders on relinquishing their lands, had completed fencing half the reserve, and was beginning to receive "most hearty approval from such authorities as the following: Dr. W.T. Hornaday, the eminent zoologist, and Director of the New York Zoological Society [and] Ernest Thompson Seton, famous Nature writer, and Honorary Naturalist to the Province of Manitoba." He also provided his view of the importance of the work in the face of wartime conditions: "The question of preserving from extinction the few remaining Prong horned Antelope, may not in itself appear of much importance during times such as these. Nevertheless, it is felt that such action on the part of Canada redounds to her prestige as showing how she can still pursue the even tenor of her way, and carry out a construction project of practical conservation, in spite of 'furor teutonicus'."[20]

Once his work was completed, Graham's enthusiasm, in this case framing conservation work as akin to a patriotic duty, was shared by others. Undoubtedly relieved at how the once rather tenuous situation had turned out, Harkin observed to Cory, "The wisdom of Mr. Graham's proposal to enclose wild antelope in their natural habitat, which proposal was favourably recommended in my memorandum to you of March 31 last, appears to be fully vindicated."[21] Both Cory and Minister Roche agreed and five days later, on December 18, 1915, the minister approved the formal reservation of some seven square miles as Nemiskam National Antelope Park. Accolades from another important voice soon followed. Hornaday sent his personal compliments to Graham and officially recognized Canada as the first country to create a fenced preserve for antelope in the annual *Bulletin* of the American Permanent Wild Life Protection Fund in 1917. In his tribute, he observed that, so skilful was Graham in not scaring off the animals in his fence work, he must have been using "padded hammers and velvet-headed nails." Harkin, too, later referred to his success in difficult circumstances, writing in an article for the American Game Protective and

Propagation Association, "It seemed a wild goose proposition to us at Ottawa, and we refused him permission, but he was so insistent that he was finally authorized to go ahead," producing a result that was by then evident to all.[22] By 1920 this success led to reassessment of the temporary nature of the preserve. With Old Wives Lake reserve having been dropped, likely due to financial stringencies, and the other two reserves not fenced, Harkin wrote to McHugh informing him, "It is doubtful if a more suitable area can be selected and it is considered that steps should be taken to have this area established as a park and made into a permanent reserve."[23] A protracted series of negotiations with McHugh and another ranching interest ensued, but, in the meantime, the rancher was appointed as temporary caretaker at a small salary. After the reserve had been re-designated as Nemiskam National Park by the 1922 order-in-council creating Menissawok and Wawaskesy parks, he became a full-time warden responsible for over 100 animals in 1925.

By the time Harkin's standing as a game conservationist had been enhanced by these efforts, he could also bask in the glow of his work with migratory birds and bird sanctuaries. In fact, that work would propel his reputation into the rarified world of international conservation and establish the Parks Branch as the foremost agency for preservation in the country. However, he did not accomplish this alone, but rather as a part of the efforts of the most influential group of Canadian naturalists and scientists yet assembled in the interests of wildlife. It grew from attention to the issue of migratory birds in North America, beginning with a communication from Graham on March 18, 1913 in which he proposed "the time would appear propitious for the enactment of suitable legislation by which these birds could be efficiently protected," and, in referring to a recently passed American migratory bird bill, suggested the branch draft similar laws for presentation to the Canadian government. The initiative came at a key moment in the story of bird preservation in North America, as after generations of slaughter by suppliers to the milliner's trade, market hunters and hunters killing migrating birds in spring shooting, populations had been decimated and some species, such as the passenger pigeon, had been driven to extinction. The United States government had responded by passing the Weekes-McLean Bill, aimed at providing some consistency in migratory bird game protection from state to state, including a reduction in open seasons and the elimination of spring shooting. Although bird protection was not as pressing a matter in Canada with its smaller hunting population and fewer excesses, there were some voices calling for action, including an influential international game organization, the North American Fish and Game Protective Association. It included prominent members from both sides of the border, and at its first annual meeting in 1902 it had passed a resolution calling for the banning of spring shooting in New York State and the Province of Ontario, a sentiment later picked up by leading American sportsman John Burnham in his 1911 creation of the powerful American Game Protective and Propagation Association.

In January 1913 the matter of what level of government, federal or provincial, should be responsible for migratory birds was placed before a meeting of the Commission of Conservation by J.W. Jones in a report on fur farming. Although wildlife was the responsibility of the provinces, he vociferously argued that only federal government jurisdiction in both Canada and the United States could ensure the passage of laws strong and consistent enough to ensure migratory bird preservation. As he put it to the commission, "Of what use would provincial authority be when one hundred and fifty-four species of insect-eating birds are being legally slaughtered, and when most of them nest in Canadian territory, and winter in the United States, Mexico and other parts of America?"[24] Harkin was aware of these matters, and they coalesced at the same moment as he received his copy of Hornaday's book with its damning indictment of hunting practices and game regulations in North America. Accordingly, he was receptive to Graham's idea, particularly its initiative in providing strength to the recently passed American legislation. He therefore brought the matter of bird sanctuaries and protective legislation to the minister's attention in his 1913 report, borrowing some of Jones's points:

> For the preservation of bird life it is felt that small sanctuaries at suitable places should be established throughout the country to ensure the birds protection during the breeding season....
>
> It should be pointed out that at the last session of the recent United States Congress a Bill was passed for the federal protection of migratory birds. It was shown that the United States producers sustained an annual loss of $800,000,000 through the disturbance of nature's balance consequent upon the destruction on insectivorous birds. Officers of the Geological Survey, who are authorities on bird life, calculate that the annual loss sustained in Canada from this cause is probably $80,000,000.
>
> In view of these facts the question arises whether Canada should not follow the example of the United States and deal with these matters from a Dominion standpoint.[25]

Fully realizing he was opening a can of worms with the sensitivities of Dominion-provincial relations, Harkin was equally aware that a Canadian act could form the basis of an international treaty with the United States on migratory birds. This would ensure that the American legislation itself would not be breached, as the Weekes-McLean Bill was of doubtful constitutionality in its assertion of federal over states rights. Supporters in the U.S. Senate suggested that if a treaty were concluded with Canada (through the agency of Great Britain, which still retained treaty powers on its behalf), it would supersede federal law and ensure that the issue of federal jurisdiction was unassailable. Consequently, when word arrived at Ottawa from the British ambassador in Washington that the American government was interested in discussing an international migratory bird convention, Harkin suggested to Cory that the communication be circulated to provincial authorities and then be followed by a federal-provincial conference to discuss the matter. This proposal was supported by a motion of the Fish and Game Protective Association, meeting at Ottawa in December 1913, and the following month the Commission of Conservation carried a resolution recommending it to the prime minister.

A draft treaty drawn up by the United States Biological Survey arrived at Ottawa in February 1914 and was given to both Interior and Agriculture for study. After Graham examined it to ensure it incorporated all the major requirements and National Museum of Canada ornithologist Percy Taverner was consulted, Harkin provided Parks Branch approval for submission to the provinces for their input. New Brunswick and British Columbia expressed opposition, mainly concerning their right to establish open seasons on certain species and traditional spring shooting, but these objections were serious, as any international treaty would need to have full provincial compliance. However, as it was believed these problems could be overcome, Harkin and Graham, as leading voices in the matter, looked forward to participating in the international negotiations. The outbreak of war immediately thrust them into the background, and it was not until the spring of 1915 that an order-in-council was passed approving in principle the idea of an international convention and not until June that the information was conveyed to the British ambassador at Washington. Meantime, and apparently without the branch's knowledge, Dr. Gordon Hewitt, Dominion entomologist in the Department of Agriculture, had become the primary Canadian contact for the proposed treaty. Having received a PhD in zoology at the University of Manchester, Hewitt had been recruited to fill the vacant entomology position in 1909, possessing a concern about both the economic value of insectivorous birds and an appreciation of birds' importance to the human psyche. Initially pursuing the matter of protection as a personal interest, he had established contact with the head of the U.S. Biological Survey and had visited Washington in the spring of 1914 to discuss international protection of migratory birds. A trained scientist, an attribute possessed by neither Harkin nor Graham, a man with important connections in Washington and with the added benefit of being married to a niece of Borden, he was an obvious choice to conduct the negotiations on Canada's behalf and was directed to do so by the minister of Agriculture in January 1916.

C. Gordon Hewitt, Dominion entomologist. Hewitt was to lead Canada's efforts in the Migratory Birds Convention negotiations with Washington and would become one of Harkin's most important peers in Canadian wildlife conservation. [LAC, PA-143057]

The activities of Hewitt's and Harkin's organizations in efforts toward bird preservation only became known to each other as a result of a meeting of the Commission of Conservation's Committee on Fisheries, Game and Fur-Bearing Animals held in Ottawa on November 1–2, 1915. Game had been somewhat neglected by the commission and the assembly was meant to address this lack of attention. It included a number of papers dealing with game laws and conservation, including those of Millar and Williamson previously mentioned, and Hewitt, too, spoke on "Conservation of Birds and Mammals in Canada." But he was particularly interested in what Williamson had to say about Parks Branch efforts in sanctuary creation, making welcome remarks concerning his belief that the Forestry Branch should defer to the Parks Branch and "delegate the duties of game preservation to a Branch which has an efficient staff engaged for that purpose." He also went on to express amazement at his lack of knowledge of branch bird activity: "I was very pleased to hear from Mr. Williamson of the formation of bird sanctuaries and I have, therefore, to correct the mistaken views which I derived from other sources. But there is some ground for my making such a mistake, as the Park authorities keep their activities so dark. Those of us who are working hard to obtain bird sanctuaries should certainly be the first people to hear that such refuges have been set apart."[26] Nonetheless, once aware of each other's efforts, the matter became an important point of contact for future Canadian wildlife preservation efforts.

Unfortunately, Graham felt slighted by the choice of Hewitt to carry out the important international negotiations, pointing out in communications with his superior the work he and others in the branch had done since 1913. Distracted by wartime considerations, Harkin did not record his own thoughts, but appears to have been satisfied with the decision. In correspondence with Hewitt he became somewhat of an honest broker in attempting to soothe the ruffled feathers of his staff while paving the way for a positive outcome. On returning from his first negotiating session in Washington in late January, Hewitt wrote the commissioner expressing his regret at Graham's reaction and conveyed the hope he would continue his good work, as he felt the efforts of the branch on bird protection were fundamental to its future success. He also put forward a new idea, perhaps the most important outcome of the disagreement, stating he would like to see migratory bird administration handled by an advisory group made up of representatives of the major departments and agencies involved.[27] As it transpired, the negotiations, in their challenging attempt to balance the local concerns of Canadian provinces with the national interests of the American government, proved difficult and protracted, and Hewitt would have to rely heavily on the continuing advice and support of the branch and other wildlife protection interests.

On August 16, 1916 the Treaty for the International Protection of Migratory Birds was signed at Washington by the British ambassador and the United States secretary of state, and was followed by the passage in Parliament of the *Migratory Birds Convention Act* in August 1917 giving legislative force to the treaty's provisions. Despite the fact that Harkin and his branch had only played the role of supporting cast to this point, the new *Convention Act* and associated changes in wildlife protection quickly placed them front and centre in nationwide species preservation. The act was the first important achievement of the Interdepartmental Advisory Board on Wild Life Protection, which became a key element in formulating Canada's conservation mandate and moving it forward. Hewitt, as originator of the idea, had prepared the order-in-council creating the board, which was enacted on December 28, 1916 after completion of the treaty. It was decided that all those appointed should be senior officials who could use their influence in key areas to play a role in effecting meaningful wildlife protection. Taken for granted were membership appointments for Hewitt, as Dominion entomologist, Harkin, as commissioner of Dominion Parks, and James White, as assistant chairman of the Commission of Conservation, but choices for the remaining two positions were not so obvious. Ultimately, with game conservation in the North being so critical, they went to men who had knowledge and influence in the region—Dr. Rudolph Anderson, a zoologist with the Geological Survey and a member of the Canadian Arctic Expedition of 1913–1918, and Duncan Campbell Scott, deputy superintendent general of Indian Affairs. In referring to the board's creation, Cory called it "an important step...with regard to game protection" and stated that under its direction "the Dominion Parks Branch will have charge of all those matters which come under Federal authority."[28]

Cory's words confirmed that Harkin had been provided with important powers in creation of the new interdepartmental board, recognizing that his was the ablest government body in the country to take responsibility for national as well as international wildlife protection matters. This was reiterated in the language of the *Convention Act* proposed by Hewitt, directing that while the governor-in-council would be empowered to make regulations to protect migratory game, non-game, and insectivorous birds inhabiting Canada, the Department of the Interior would be tasked with their enforcement through the Parks Branch. This move recognized that Harkin, with his extensive connections across the country and the influence of his position, would be well placed to convince provincial governments to co-operate on intergovernmental bird and game protection issues. To provide the necessary tools, the Advisory Board drafted the first migratory bird game regulations, establishing hunting seasons in the various provinces, and these were approved by order-in-council of April 23, 1918. In May 1920 they were amended and strengthened with the addition of bag limits.

As the *Convention Act*'s mandate was to be supported by a separate parliamentary appropriation, a new migratory birds section was created within the branch, allowing for the hiring of an ornithologist to administer the *Convention Act* and assist with the *Northwest Game Act*. Capturing the first public competition for a senior position in the branch by virtue of new public service regulations was Hoyes Lloyd of Toronto. Born in 1888, Lloyd had been fascinated by birds since his youth and had begun field collecting in 1903, sometimes in the company of Stuart Thompson, a nephew of Ernest Thompson Seton. Although attracted to studying biology, it was part of the Faculty of Medicine at the University of Toronto so instead he chose chemistry, receiving his MA in 1911. During his student years he worked as seasonal forest ranger and game warden in Ontario's Temagami Forest Reserve, continuing his ornithological work and receiving a gold medal for a collection of bird skins at the Canadian National Exhibition in 1909. Upon graduation, he received a position with the Health Laboratories of the City of Toronto testing milk, but after becoming an associate member of the American Ornithological Union (AOU) in 1916, he had been supported by several of its members in his application for the new parks position. He began his service on December 11, 1918, marking an important milestone for the branch in addressing its strengthened wildlife mandate.[29]

The cornerstone of his responsibilities was Harkin's vision for bird sanctuaries, work that would often only be successful after difficult negotiations with provincial authorities and discussions with other federal interests as efforts were made to establish them across the country. One of the section's first successes came as a result of an initiative by National Museums ornithologist Percy Taverner, who in 1915 had sent Harkin a proposal entitled "Recommendation for the Creation of Three New National Parks in Canada," calling for Percé Rock and Bonaventure Island in the Gulf of St. Lawrence as well as Point Pelee in Ontario to be included in the national park system as localities "of special scientific interest and which exhibit natural phenomena under conditions particularly well adapted for study to the advance of the world's knowledge and the increase of the nation's intellectual development and prestige."[30] By order-in-council in March 1919, Percé Rock, Great Bird Rocks, and part of Bonaventure Island were created as bird sanctuaries, and Lloyd was beginning to take action on the world's largest "duck factory," the potholes and lakes of the prairies, resulting in the establishment of seven sanctuaries in Alberta in June 1920.

His superior's dedication to the power of the written word and the branch's educational role also came strongly into play, as Lloyd was tasked with both creating and supervising the production of a number of publications and other media relating to the protection of Canada's birds. Harkin described these in his 1919 annual report: "A comprehensive publicity campaign has been organized; pamphlets have been prepared and distributed to the press, schools and generally throughout Canada; lectures with motion pictures and coloured lantern slides have been prepared for outsiders, or given by members of the staff. A very successful series of lectures was delivered at the Central Canada Exhibition during the fall of 1918."[31] Over the ensuing years, these pamphlets would become some of the most successful Canadian government publications ever issued, including *Canada's Feathered Friends*, *No Spring Shooting Means More Migratory Game*, and *Protection of Bird Neighbours* all produced by Lloyd himself, as well as contributions from others, including *Vanished and Vanishing Birds* and the tremendously popular *Bird Houses and Their Occupants* by Taverner and *Lessons in Bird*

Protection by migratory bird officers Tufts, Lewis, and Munro. In 1921 the branch purchased and distributed to its field officers and honorary officers a substantial number of the first comprehensive book on Canadian conservation, *The Conservation of the Wild Life of Canada*, written by Hewitt and published posthumously.[32]

Even before Lloyd was brought on board to head the convention and sanctuary program, the Interdepartmental Advisory Board was well on its way to orchestrating the creation of Canada's first national park based solely on bird protection. As mentioned, the idea of creating a park on Point Pelee in Essex County, Ontario, on a spit of land extending into Lake Erie, the most southerly extension of the mainland of Canada, had initially been presented to Harkin by Taverner. Pelee, a triangular piece of land about six miles across at its base and extending some nine miles south into the lake, was largely composed of sandbars and swamps but held representative samples of vegetation and fauna normally found further south. As Taverner pointed out, it formed "one of the most important migration highways in America and is a station from which such phenomena can be studied with extra-ordinary advantage, as almost incredible numbers of birds follow along its length on both their spring and autumn journeys."[33] A former naval reserve administered as ordnance and admiralty lands by Interior, in 1884 large portions of it had been leased to a group of area sportsmen, known as the South Essex Gun Club, and hunting had quickly become a popular activity in the area. By the time of Taverner's memorandum, two Essex County conservation organizations were calling for steps to be taken to make the area a bird sanctuary and game preserve.

In responding to Taverner's appeal and representations of the conservation organizations, Harkin had discussed the matter with the minister and obtained approval to undertake negotiations with the Province of Ontario, as part of Pelee was comprised of privately held lands. However, this initiative had been abandoned when the superintendent of Ordnance and Admiralty Lands expressed his opposition. But with formation of the Advisory Board, the conservation organizations had renewed their call for action and, after direction from an Advisory Board meeting in May 1917, Hewitt had drafted a resolution that set out the background and suggested "the Board recommend that such portion of Point Pelee as still remains the property of the Dominion Government be created a Dominion Park in order that the migratory and other birds and the unusual southern vegetation...may be adequately protected, and that the Government of the Province of Ontario be asked to co-operate by prohibiting shooting at any time on the privately owned land." He also included a clause recommending that duck hunting, under certain restrictions, be allowed in the park after October 15 each year to encourage public acceptance.[34]

While recognizing this recommendation as problematic, Harkin could see its importance in assuaging local opinion and recommended only that private landowners be allowed the same privilege, noting in his memorandum to Cory, "It seems to me that what we really want to ask the Ontario Government to do is to make provision by which regulations applying to privately owned lands shall be identical to those applying to the Dominion owned lands."[35] Hewitt compromised by working out an agreement in February 1918 whereby shooting on the marshes would be open by permit to any bona fide applicant, and he then turned the matter back to the commissioner "for the definite establishment of Point Pelee as a game reserve or National Park" with a plea that "no further time be lost in taking the necessary steps."[36] Given the private land holdings and the fact that Pelee's beaches were popular with day tourists, Harkin decided on the national park model, and within a month had drafted the necessary order-in-council and obtained the consent of the previously hesitant superintendent of Ordnance and Admiralty Lands. On May 29, 1918 the area know as the Point Pelee Admiralty and Naval Reserve was established as a "Dominion Park and Bird Sanctuary" known as Point Pelee Park, with the order including notice that Ontario would enact regulations to harmonize with the Dominion regulations.[37]

While the creation of Point Pelee and the setting aside of other bird sanctuaries were important initiatives, the Advisory Board's interests went beyond birds into all manner of wildlife conservation issues. A further area where it proved to be useful to Harkin was in providing advice on another emerging preservation initiative. Elk in the mountain parks, although never abundant, had been almost completely extirpated by the turn of the century, leaving only a few animals wandering over the British Columbia divide into Rocky Mountains, small herds in Jasper and Waterton, and several dozen head in the Banff animal paddock as representative of the species. Howard Sibbald, as the branch's most experienced wildlife manager, was constantly looking for ways to improve populations of native animals, and a 1916 conversation with Dr. Charles Walcott, secretary of the Smithsonian Institution in Washington, provided such an opportunity. Walcott visited the Canadian Rockies frequently in carrying out paleontology studies, and Sibbald learned from him that the Smithsonian's zoological park had recently acquired some elk from Yellowstone Park and that, in fact, the U.S. Department of the Interior was distributing elk widely in an effort to decrease pressure on its overgrazed Yellowstone range. After expressing interest in "securing a couple of cars" of the animals, in October 1916 Walcott wrote him and suggested, "If your Department of Parks cares to obtain a number of elk, will you not request Mr. Harkin, or whoever may be the proper official, to write me to that effect. I will at once take the matter up with our Park department, so that arrangements can be made for securing them." In return, he requested some sheep and goat be donated to the Smithsonian collection, a not uncommon request from zoos and scientific organizations. Sibbald turned the letter over to Superintendent Clarke with a recommendation that if some animals could be obtained before the next spring, they could be maintained in the paddock over the winter and then, while keeping some for "new blood" for the paddock herd and placing a few east and west of Banff, "part of them [could be] turned north where they would work over on the Red Deer."[38]

Harkin was excited by this prospect and enthused in a memorandum to Cory: "This I think would be a splendid idea as there are comparatively few elk at large in Rocky Mountains Park, and it is possible that some of those which have been raised in confinement, turned loose in the vicinity of Banff, might become as tame as the mule-deer about the town and would certainly be an added attraction. Further, as there is a very small loss among elk when they can secure food, Rocky Mountains

Park would soon become stocked." Supporting Walcott's proposal he offered, "I would be glad to have your authority to write to Dr. Walcott, as he suggests in his letter, advising him that we would be pleased to secure a number of elk, say (2) carloads, and ascertain what arrangements can be made for securing them; and also that we will be glad to furnish Dr. Walcott with the mountain goat and sheep which the Zoological Park desires." On the letter, Cory scribbled "I heartily concur" and Minister Roche, with reference to Harkin's information that the cost of capture and feeding should be $5 per head, added "OK if can be secured at above cost."[39]

Harkin immediately contacted Walcott and the scientist's reply at the end of November indicated he had received permission from the superintendent of the National Parks Service "to grant authority to the Commissioner of Dominion Parks to secure two carloads of elk from the Yellowstone National Park" and advising "to get in communication with acting Supervisor Chester A. Lindsley, Yellowstone National Park, Yellowstone Park, Wyoming, and secure from him all detailed information necessary in connection with the capture and shipment of these elk."[40] As it turned out, with Yellowstone's elk population numbering somewhat in excess of 3,000 head and a target of disposing of 500 head during the fiscal year, it was providing good business for local shippers in nearby Gardiner, Montana. At Lindsley's suggestion, contact was made with C.B. Scott, who had already sent seventy-five head to Wisconsin and could meet the minister's requirement of $5 per head, and the acting supervisor also co-operated by volunteering the services of his men to identify the best specimens. Sibbald and Clarke proceeded to Gardiner by train, arriving on February 17, 1917, and after supervising the loading of sixty-three animals and making a quick inspection of Yellowstone Park, departed the next day. They arrived at the Banff paddock a day and a half later, losing only four head in shipping and two more shortly afterwards.

Harkin had provided strict instructions that the new elk be kept in the paddock with the existing herd until further notice, and discussions as to their ultimate disposition soon engaged branch wildlife staff. His thought was that some older and tamer elk could be released immediately to become an attraction for tourists around Banff, but there was concern about safety if such a step were taken. As the branch did not possess expertise in the matter, in July 1917 Graham prepared a letter to Hornaday requesting his point of view, and while awaiting a reply he carried out some research into the zoologist's writings on the deer family. Here he discovered a mention that male elk were dangerous at mating time: "I have seen stags that were wild and gentle during 8 or 9 months of the year suddenly transformed into murderous demons, ready and anxious to stab to death any unarmed man who ventured near." Graham consequently concluded that as it would be a mistake to keep the "liberated" elk around Banff, Sibbald's suggestion for their release should be followed. Harkin believed this unnecessary, responding that "all the elk would be far away at that season," but allowed, "as there are thousands of elk at Yellowstone," directed Graham to prepare letters to Lindsley and E.W. Nelson, chief of the U.S. Biological Survey, seeking their opinions.

Illustrating the variety of views current with respect to wildlife management at the time, the responses were mixed. Hornaday believed that releasing the original paddock elk would entail a certain amount of danger, but stated "the object to be attained is so praiseworthy, I would not hesitate to take the risk;" Nelson observed that while the elk would unquestionably interest tourists, "I regret to say however that the bull elk during the rutting season is an extremely dangerous animal to man, particularly if he is a tame animal whose natural fear of man has been overcome"; and Lindsley offered, "Like bears, I consider that elk are not a dangerous class of animals so long as they are wild, but when tamed and fearless of men they are not entirely safe to have running loose."[41] Harkin was now consulting members of the Advisory Board on the matter and in October 1917 decided to go along with the recommendations of his own people, informing Superintendent Clarke that he would accept Sibbald's plan, but not until the following spring as it was now too late in the season to implement. Eighteen of the animals jumped the gun, escaping over the course of the winter, another twenty-one head were released in June, and in August they were joined by ten of the old paddock herd.

Yellowstone elk released near Jasper, 1920. Harkin's arrangement to ship surplus elk from Yellowstone National Park in the United States beginning in 1917 gradually reintroduced the species into the mountain national parks. [JYHS, 84.32.280]

By the fall of 1918 all the released animals were still near the paddock, and Harkin was sounding a completely different tone in a letter to the superintendent: "Mr. Sibbald should use all means at his disposal to ensure these Elk [are] not remaining at large during the rutting season in and around the Banff townsite."[42] Apart from this concern, the animals appeared to fare so well that when he read an article in the *Ottawa Journal* the following December concerning a campaign being conducted by the National Parks Association to preserve the Yellowstone herd in the face of terrible winter conditions, Harkin took further action. Querying Superintendent Wardle at Banff, he was informed that the park could accommodate 1,100 animals if they were unloaded at different points, and he then approached Cory with a recommendation that the branch be authorized to accept shipments provided that they be obtained at no cost other than transportation, care, and feeding. Approval in hand, on December 27, 1919 he again contacted Walcott and asked him to act as go-between, presenting a plan that illustrated some lessons had already been learned about elk management. It proposed "to release them at certain points along the railroad traversing the park, where by means of trails broken through the snow and hay scattered along the same it is expected that the elk can be lured to the selected winter range areas."[43] Walcott contacted Secretary Lane of the Department of the Interior, and within days received approval from Superintendent Horace Albright at Yellowstone to allot 200 head to the branch for shipment within ten days. On January 21, 1920 Sibbald again found himself aboard a train hauling 206 animals out of Gardiner, and a few days later the 194 survivors were deposited in two groups at Duthill east of Banff and Massive to the west, where wardens had laid out some hay and beaten down trails to suitable grazing. All but a few "made for the hills," and despite concerns about their survival in the cold winter conditions, they appeared to immediately adapt to their new surroundings.

One of the benefits of this "trial" shipment was the bridgehead it established with the new administration of the U.S. National Parks Service. At the time of the first transfer, the service had only existed for a few months and its first director, Stephen Mather, had not yet been appointed. But Mather took a personal interest in the second shipment, writing Harkin on the day it left Gardiner, "I am very glad that this bureau could co-operate with the Dominion Parks Branch in the capture and shipment of these elk, and I trust that the animals may thrive in their new refuges." The commissioner responded in kind, assuring him that the animals would do well in their new location and would be fully protected by the park regulations enforced by wardens and thanking him for the courtesy and co-operation extended to Sibbald by his people at Yellowstone.[44] These good sentiments resulted in a further offer by Mather to secure additional animals before spring, leading Harkin to immediately request that Sibbald provide his opinion concerning placing some animals in Jasper Park. It was agreed that it could accept 100 animals and before the end of February the Chief Game Guardian had delivered them to the Henry House flats.

With establishment of elk at Banff and Jasper, Harkin could once again take pride in the branch's conservation efforts in favour of a major game species in the parks. Nevertheless, even by then there were some dark clouds beginning to gather on the wildlife conservation horizon. At Buffalo Park, Graham had spoken out as early as 1914 about the practice of allowing cattle being used in cross-breeding experiments to graze with the bison because of the possibility of spread of disease, and by 1917, when the first buffalo in the park died of tuberculosis, it was spreading rapidly through the herd. At the same time, the animals were proving incredibly fertile, by 1920 numbering almost 5,000 head, the theoretical carrying capacity of the Wainwright range. Similarly, the Yellowstone elk soon illustrated why they had become such a problem, Sibbald reporting in 1921 that they had spread from Castle Mountain to Kananaskis and worrying, "We may have trouble, in future years, of supplying them with sufficient feed, and thus be in the position the Yellowstone Park has been placed." These matters were just the thin edge of the wedge in the increasingly complex world of game management that Harkin's focus on sanctuaries had engendered, and they would lead him into increasingly difficult ground in the years ahead.

SEVEN

One-Man Rule

WHEN HARKIN BECAME commissioner in 1911, the Canadian civil service was lacklustre. In 1917 an MP speaking in the House remarked, "From my experience, my advice to my friends and acquaintances has been to keep clear of the Civil Service above everything else. If you have any ambition; if you ever expect to make any headway in the world; if you place any value on your initiative, your freedom, then, for Heaven's sake steer clear of the Civil Service."[1] It was a revealing statement, for the civil service was regarded then, and remained for nearly two more decades, as a place where red tape prevailed and full of men with little ability. A later history of the bureaucracy of the time identified some exceptions in what were referred to as the "technical branches of government"—surveyors, agronomists, entomologists, and foresters among others—who "made substantial and valuable contributions to their country."[2] The Parks Branch should be counted among these, for throughout his career Harkin exhibited determination in the direction he wanted it to go, and he succeeded in making it an effective and high-functioning agency. But he did not do it alone.

In launching the branch, he had benefited from the support of the headquarters staff he had recruited within the department as well as some good men in the field inherited from Forestry. Despite their long service, during the period of rapid growth in branch responsibilities through to the end of the First World War, his relationship with those working with him became increasingly more complex. With the growth in his staff complement, it might have been expected he would begin to relinquish his strong grip on personnel matters, but this did not fit with his view of the proper administration of so far-flung a responsibility, believing only a strong central authority could make the system workable. As mentioned, an assessment by Alan MacEachern has portrayed him as being almost redundant to the parks story, merely a "conduit for the philosophy germinating in the Branch," but this presents an incomplete picture. While he did incorporate the views of subordinates and the knowledge they brought to the task, he also exhibited a keen ability to seek out opinions and information from his many peers and a variety of other sources and synthesize it into a coherent policy before selling it to his superiors and politicians. Without this skill, Canada's national park system would not have become what it is today.

For the Ottawa-based "inside staff," hired according to the principles of merit under the provisions of the Civil Service Commission created in 1908, it was necessary to share their superior's philosophy and support his direction to achieve it. As noted, the fact that some remained with him through his entire parks career speaks to the loyalty Harkin commanded. Men like Frank Williamson and James Wardle benefited from this constancy, later going on to more senior posts. For his part, the commissioner was proud of the work of his staff and often publicly supported their accomplishments and extolled their virtues. For example, in a letter to Norman Luxton in June 1912, he stated, "The staff is so enthusiastic that my chief difficulty is to prevent them overworking altogether too much. Nearly every day, long after regulation closing hours are past I have to practically order them out of the office. They are after results and I am convinced there will be gratifying results."[3] Likewise, he stood up for their professionalism, particularly in the struggles with Forestry. As mentioned, both he and Campbell used the work of their experts to buttress their positions, and in so doing Harkin favourably compared his people with the older and well-established United States Biological Survey. In response, Campbell declared such a comparison "rather far-fetched," eliciting a rebuttal containing a long list of supporters for the Animal Division's work, including the prime minister and the chairman of the Society for the Preservation of Fauna in the British Empire.[4]

Harkin's support extended to headquarters staff actions affecting those living in the parks when they led to conflict. Such disagreements were inevitable, particularly given his constant effort to uphold Ottawa's overriding authority on matters affecting administration and governance of park towns. One such instance occurred in July 1914 when Bennett, with respect to matters at Banff, accused, "While you are endeavouring to administer your office fairly and honourably...I cannot say the same for some of the officials in your head office." In response, Harkin thanked Bennett for his "personal reference," but indicated he would not have his people bear the brunt of the criticism:

> I am responsible for all parks administration and do not desire blame put on anyone else. In the first place I do not believe any Head Office clerk attached to my staff is animated by any other motive in his work in relation to Banff, or any other park, except to see what is done is done right. The "Square deal" is the motto that has been held up to them and the one that I believe they implicitly follow. I do not pretend that we do not make mistakes, but I feel absolutely assured that no action ever taken here can be pointed out in regard to which it cannot be shown there were reasons convincing...that the action taken was the right action....My own conscience has no misgivings

> whatever in connection with the subject of your letter and that to me is the supreme test.[5]

In these circumstances, those taking a position at head office tended to be both inspired and somewhat awestruck by the commissioner. Secretary May Lafranchise, hired in 1918, recalled a rather surprising introduction to "The Chief." Upon reporting for duty she was being interviewed when he suddenly leapt from his chair and landed on his knees in the middle of a large polar bear rug on his office floor in an effort to catch a wayward moth! A few years later when Migratory Bird Officer Harrison Lewis was undergoing a similar introduction, Harkin carefully went through the expectations for the position, but when Lewis rose to leave, he gave one last admonishment, "Now, remember! You are on duty twenty-four hours a day—and twenty-five if I need you." The young officer regarded this as an inspiring remark and a good omen with which to begin his service.[6]

If headquarters was small and closely-knit, field administration was completely the opposite, growing rapidly, widely dispersed, and far from cohesive, inevitable results of the isolation of one park from another and the influence of patronage. As the 1907 Royal Commission on the civil service had pointed out, "Politics enters every appointment and politicians on the spot interest themselves not only in appointments but in subsequent promotions of officers."[7] Harkin now found himself on the other side of the table from his days as a ministerial secretary, as in all the parks under his purview he had to contend with influential government supporters who expected to have a say in choosing "outside staff," those working directly in the parks. In Bennett's case, as the only elected Conservative in Alberta, all regular staff appointments in Rocky Mountains Park had to be presented to him for approval, and he often suggested constituents for positions, while requiring junior appointments to be cleared with the Banff Conservative Association. In 1912 when appointing temporary fire wardens Harkin contacted the MP and asked him to submit the names of "four or five persons who would be suitable for the work and the order of priority," promising "your suggestions will of course be carried out in that respect."[8] Patronage also extended to suppliers of goods and services, and later that year Harkin again contacted Bennett and asked for a list of "reputable hay dealers who would be able to supply hay of good quality for horses and buffalo at the park this winter."[9] This practice did not ensure the branch was getting the best people or goods available and meant that some parks suffered from poor organization and a deficit of skills in key positions.

Harkin's experience in running the branch was to be considerably affected when some senior members exhibited the system's pitfalls. Douglas, the epitome of a political appointee, had proven an exception during his brief period of service as chief superintendent, but his partisan loyalties had quickly caught up to him. As his position was charged with supervision of all the superintendents, it required considerable skill and tact, and his Conservative-appointed successor, Philip C. Barnard-Hervey, lacked a measure of these. Little is known of him except that he had emigrated from England in 1890 and was engaged in surveying, an important skill in a period of rapid growth and development. However, Harkin often questioned his decision-making capabilities, particularly with respect to Waterton Lakes Park, where he seemed powerless to solve a series of problems. Likely this contributed to the elimination of his position at the end of the 1917–1918 fiscal year; on the other hand, perhaps the necessity of "making do" as the war dragged on and appropriations continued to shrink made him a victim of the numbers game.[10] Those lower in the ranks had always answered to the commissioner anyway and the elimination of the position just made it official while at the same time considerably flattening the organizational structure.

The most important branch relationships were those between Harkin and individual park superintendents. In normal circumstances, the superintendent's job involved supervision of office staff and the chief game guardian, as well as responsibility for all financial matters to ensure the park was fairly and efficiently administered. In some instances he could also be called upon to oversee development work, as for example in March 1913 when Harkin instructed the Rocky Mountains superintendent, "Your foremost duty shall be to see that the best possible results are obtained at a minimum of expenditure with respect to roads, the trails, buildings and all other outside work. This will naturally involve you personally supervising the work of the Engineers, the general foremen and all other employees."[11] In the carrying out of these duties, there was extensive correspondence with head office on a variety of topics, often involving several communications a day, as branch procedure required dealing with each matter in a separate letter. As well, the superintendent had to provide official weekly, monthly, and annual reports, the latter being included in the comprehensive summary published in the annual Department of the Interior report. Superintendents were not particularly well compensated (the salary at Rocky Mountains Park was $2400/annum in 1913) and they lived in a variety of circumstances depending on the location and prominence of their park. Whatever their situation, though, their ability to be decisive, effective, and able to articulate their park's needs to Harkin were important factors in the developmental history of each park.

Unquestionably, the key superintendency was at Banff, responsible for the flagship Rocky Mountains Park, and it was also here where political interference was most conspicuous. As mentioned, the Conservative election victory had been followed by a period of turmoil at the Banff office, largely due to Bennett's influence; he seemed to take almost as much interest in the Banff situation as Harkin himself. The MP was in constant contact with him about local conditions, and in February 1913 began taking steps to address some outstanding issues. He cultivated a mole in the Banff office, accountant R. Alford, who described Superintendent A.B. Macdonald as "a very conscientious man...but a figure head who has no ideas of discipline or office organization...I foresaw this difficulty from the first, and pressed Mr. Harkin very strongly on the subject, but he could only promise to take the matter into consideration when the reorganization took place."[12] Bennett's solution was to replace Macdonald with Clarke and to increase the staff complement, writing Harkin on February 14, 1913 to inform him of Clarke's appointment and stating, "I will now direct my attention to getting you an assistant Accountant and an engineer and I have written regarding the position of Storekeeper, and I hope to let you have complete information at an early moment."[13] Alford had also complained about the influence of the Banff Conservative Association in the making of local appointments, while on the other hand some of the Banff party faithful began levelling accusations that Calgarians were receiving preference for new positions. Bennett dismissed these out of hand, grumbling, "It is the old story...[they] seem to think that a Government position is one where you need not work." But, as time would prove, it would not be quite so easy for Harkin to disavow such claims of favouritism. When Chief Clerk Spero and Branch Auditor Courtice were brought to Banff "to improve the chaotic conditions prevailing," Bennett began to hear accusations that "Liberals are being preferred over others in connection with the Park," and the commissioner had to remind him that, with the exception of those approved by the minister, "I think every person on the list was nominated by you."[14]

Interestingly, in a reorganization memo, Harkin left the position of superintendent vacant, likely a reflection on the recently appointed incumbent Jack Clarke. As a one-time contender for his job, he distrusted Clarke and perhaps feared his strong political connections, but most of all believed he was not up to the task of administering the complex Rocky Mountains Park. Although Bennett had made it clear that the commissioner was to be in control and could count on his support, in reality Clarke's circumstances protected him from virtually every misstep. Harkin therefore rarely missed an opportunity to bring his shortcomings to the MP's attention; sometimes these were petty, as in January 1914 when he complained the superintendent had requested coal be supplied to his home, a policy discontinued during Macdonald's service, and sometimes they were more serious, as in March 1914 when Clarke was absent without leave on his return from a trip to Ottawa and Harkin reported on his success in "making him feel he must submit to the discipline of the Department."[15] Shortly afterwards, he made some notes about Clarke for discussion with Bennett, including, "lacks ideals; no sense of responsibility; anything he did he was told to do; Clarke vs. Child; Slams Ottawa; Finances; Dodges responsibility." He wrote Bennett on "Clarke vs. Child," an ongoing battle between the superintendent and Resident Engineer J.T. Child:

Superintendent S.J. Clarke (second from right) and Jim Brewster (right) visiting Castle Mountain Internment Camp, ca. 1915. Clarke, as a politically well-connected friend of R.B. Bennett and rumoured to have been a rival for the commissioner's post, was both feared and disdained by Harkin. [GA, PA-3571-13]

"From my viewpoint it is desirable that drastic steps should be taken to put a stop to this interminable warring but as both these men were your appointees and both are friends as well, I do not want to take any action that might make trouble for you."[16] In a crossing letter, Bennett declared, "So long as Mr. Clarke remains there he is Superintendent and I suppose it will be well for all parties to take notice and govern themselves accordingly."[17]After this thinly veiled warning, and in the face of Clarke's local popularity and the increasing exigencies of wartime administration, Harkin largely left his criticisms in abeyance, perhaps intending to take them up later.

If so, fate intervened as in June 1918 Clarke died unexpectedly after an operation for "internal troubles." An editorial in the *Crag and Canyon*, in commenting on his career, left no doubt as to who was responsible for his not having achieved more success: "His executive ability was always held in check by the authority at Ottawa and if Mr. Clarke did not make the best of Superintendents he could not be altogether blamed, for larger and better men would have fallen down just as hard on this one-man rule which has set itself up at Ottawa as Mr. Clarke did."[18] The *Crag*'s assessment makes it clear Harkin had not failed to take a firm hand or to provide specific direction to Clarke despite his personal association with Bennett, and this became typical of his relationship with all superintendents in line with his belief in strong central authority and consistent procedure. Often they toed the line and performed well under such discipline, but there were other cases where the results perplexed or at times even infuriated him, requiring decisive action. An examination of his relationship with two men who filled the superintendent positions at particularly critical times in the history of Jasper and Waterton parks provides examples of the range of these experiences.

At Jasper, responsibility for the park was initially placed under a non-resident superintendent, but soon Harkin sought the services of a resident superintendent, turning to an accomplished and strong-willed citizen of Ottawa who was well connected to the sporting fraternity. Lieutentant-Colonel Samuel Maynard Rogers, born at Plymouth, England, in 1862, had served in the Guards Sharpshooter Company during the North-West Rebellion of 1885 and had received his commission as commander of "D" Company, 2nd Special Service Battalion, Royal Canadian Regiment during the Boer War in 1899. After serving as chief staff officer of the Rockcliffe Training Camp near Ottawa from 1905 to 1907, he left the army to work in the insurance industry, first at Edmonton and later in eastern Ontario and Quebec. But exhibiting the strong discipline and attention to detail that was going to be needed in the rapidly changing Jasper circumstances, in March 1913 Rogers was an obvious choice for appointment to the Jasper position. In late 1914 he volunteered for service with the 9th Battalion, 101st Edmonton Fusiliers and again served as a training camp commanding officer before returning to Jasper in 1918. Henceforth, he would serve as superintendent until 1927 and from late 1931 to 1934, becoming one of Harkin's most trusted field officers.

Rogers was remembered by one early Jasper resident as "something of a martinet, a military disciplinarian," and was noted for being disdainful of resident's sensibilities. One of his annoying habits was to pick mushrooms on the village's boulevards at three or four in the morning, letting it be known that all competitors should desist from similar activities. If he spotted a garbage can lid askew during these nocturnal ramblings, he had no hesitation in knocking on the offending householder's door and demanding that it be corrected at once. He also came down hard on neighbourhood cats, shooting any that deigned to come near the chicken coop he proudly kept near his office.[19] Despite the occasional complaint he might receive, Harkin easily overlooked them in light of the devotion to duty with which the colonel carried out the branch's emerging policy direction as well as his enthusiasm for the protection of wildlife and the support for the sanctity of park lands that he shared with his superior. Even in the short span between his appointment and departure for war, Rogers made an impact on opening the region to tourist traffic, overseeing the building of a four-mile road to Pyramid Lake to make it accessible for a party led by author B.W. Mitchell and convincing the surveyor general to lay out 150 lots for summer residences there. The same year he initiated construction of a new trail from the railway line to the Fiddle Creek springs, including a side trail to the interesting Punch Bowl Falls, and after exploring several possible routes to Maligne Lake decided on the Maligne River valley "as possessing the easiest gradients, and opening up the most interesting country, especially three wonderful canyons." This trail was designed so that it could be converted to road width in future, and the following year it was linked with a temporary pile bridge over the Athabasca River.

Rogers was also quick to see the necessity for the branch to impose its administrative authority over what was essentially a railroad townsite, convincing Ottawa to support the erection of a combined park office and superintendent's residence at a prominent location at the junction of Pyramid and Miette streets. Designed by Edmonton architect A.M. Calderon, its use of local stone and log in what the superintendent referred to as a "boulder bungalow," resulted in "a credit to the department in design and construction." Soon he was requesting that all major edifices be of "rustic style of architecture," either log or stone, already recognizing the benefit of such uniformity in that it "will result, in after years, in our having a harmonious appearance in the class of

"The Ruling Spirits," Superintendent Lieutenant-Colonel S.M. Rogers and his wife at Jasper. W.J. Topley photograph. Rogers's military discipline and strong interest in wildlife made him the perfect superintendent for the challenging Jasper Park in Harkin's estimation. [JYHS, 991.113.65]

buildings."[20] So pleased was Harkin that at the end of Rogers's first year on the job he was already publicly recognizing his efforts in the branch's annual report: "During 1913–1914 the first real development work in Jasper park took place. Lieutenant-Colonel S.M. Rogers, the Superintendent, proved equal to the great task of transforming a wilderness—a wilderness of extraordinary scenic beauty—into a park; and even in one year he accomplished striking results."[21]

Harkin's implicit trust in Rogers was made evident by his placing in the colonel's hands the government's first effort at publicizing the new park, the aforementioned visit of one of the era's most popular authors, Sir Arthur Conan Doyle. Harkin's involvement in organizing the 1914 visit is not known, but he undoubtedly understood that much

Sir Arthur Conan Doyle (standing at edge of gorge) and party on the Maligne River, 1914. W.J. Topley photograph. Rogers's successful handling of the Conan Doyle visit resulted in important publicity for the new Jasper Park. [LAC, PA-011196]

of Jasper's tourism potential hinged on it, providing the superintendent with detailed instructions on the arrangements. The *Edmonton Journal* reported, "Sir Arthur Conan Doyle, the famous English author, and Lady Doyle are in Edmonton en route to Jasper National Park, where they will be the guests of Col. Maynard Rogers," and, indeed, they did stay in his home.[22] During the visit the party, accompanied by a government-appointed photographer from Ottawa's W.J. Topley studio, were escorted to the spectacular Maligne Canyon and taken on a pack trip to Yellowhead Pass, resulting in the author's penning of the oft-quoted poem "The Athabaska Trail." These efforts bore fruit, Conan Doyle publishing a serialized account in *Cornhill Magazine* in which he described Jasper Park as "one of the great national playgrounds and health resorts which the Canadian Government with great wisdom has laid out for the benefit of its citizens." In his 1924 widely-read *Memories and Adventures*, he commented further, "When Canada has filled up and carries a large population, she will bless the foresight of the administrators who took possession of broad tracts of the most picturesque land and put them forever out of the power of the speculative dealer," and complimented Rogers personally for the building of trails to open up the park to adventure.[23]

Although his efforts were interrupted by the war, when Rogers returned in 1918 he immediately used his few available funds to upgrade roads on the east side of the Athabasca River (later the basis for the Jasper-Edmonton Highway), utilizing the abandoned Canadian Northern Railway grade. Beyond quickly and efficiently carrying out important development work, he also gained his superior's approbation because of his philosophy of parks and the role of their wildlife. In fact, in his own first annual report of April 1, 1914, under the heading of "Humanitarian Ideals," he made a statement focusing on the benefits of parks that might well have come from Harkin: "The Canadian parks, I believe, possess vast potentialities for the betterment of the Canadian people in body, mind, and resultant energy and activity, and each year, as their attractions become better known, they will undoubtedly draw increasingly larger numbers to share in the benefits of the out-of-door life....Jasper park has many such attractive points where a reasonable altitude, perfect water, pine clad hills, and a delightful climate would restore to health and activity many who would otherwise pass quickly over the Divide, and every life thus saved and restored to health means an added asset to Canada."[24] Similarly, as an avid sportsman, Rogers was an enthusiastic supporter of the branch's emerging wildlife policy, reporting frequently on the increase in big game and bird life in Jasper and being particularly proud of the reappearance of bighorn sheep and moose, which had virtually disappeared during railway construction. He also exhibited a progressive approach to patrol activities. The first airplane to arrive in Jasper Park landed on the flats near Henry House in 1920, and, familiar with its wartime use, in 1922 he took part in air photography trials in remote sections of the mountains and recommended that with availability of abundant water resources it was suitable for "future operations in connection with fire protection and aerial photo-topography."[25]

If the hard-driving Rogers was the epitome of a progressive parks officer in Harkin's view, just the opposite was the case with respect to Superintendent Robert Cooper at Waterton Park. Beginning in 1910, area pioneer J.G. "Kootenai" Brown had begun serving as game guardian and unofficial superintendent, but in November 1913 Bennett had referred to him as "an old man of 73 years of age and much addicted to the use of intoxicants...absolutely unfit for his position." After the 1914 boundary extension, Chief Superintendent Barnard-Hervey recommended he be replaced due to his inability to supervise the enlarged area, and although he continued to serve as a warden until his death in 1916, on September 1, 1914 his one-time assistant, Cooper, became the park's first official superintendent. His qualifications for the job are unclear, but as a Pincher Creek harness maker who had served on the town's first municipal council in 1906 and familiar with the area through assisting Brown, he was possibly the best person available with the proper political credentials to take Waterton through an expected period of development. However, he would quickly run into difficulties.

Initially, Cooper's problems stemmed from his inexperience with proper procedures, inadequate working conditions, and ongoing disagreements with his chief warden, George Allinson. Harkin had accountant Donald Matheson from the Banff office go to Waterton in the fall of 1915 to help establish administrative procedures, and he reported that the staff did not understand how to enter accounts and the superintendent did not even keep a correspondence ledger. This, he stated, was partially due to poor working conditions, as Cooper had only "a decrepit table and has absolutely no facilities for keeping his papers in order," an old wooden box acting as the filing cabinet. The administrative facility itself was equally inadequate, containing a storeroom and a combined office and living room with a lean-to kitchen attached at the rear, forcing his family to live in a tent in the summer and to move to Pincher Creek in winter.[26] There was little the commissioner could do given wartime financial restrictions, and shortly after receiving Matheson's report he began to hear reports of other administrative concerns and rumours of disagreements with the chief warden. Dispatching Barnard-Hervey to investigate, in December 1915

John George "Kootenai" Brown at his cabin in Waterton, Alberta, 1914. Brown, a pioneer of the Waterton area, became its first "unofficial" superintendent until replaced by Robert Cooper in September 1914. [GA, NA-1253-3]

he was informed that Cooper had spent money without authority, had failed to properly record income, and had, on occasion, not collected payments for cattle grazing on park lands. The chief superintendent recommended that Commissioner of Police Silas Carpenter be sent to Waterton to investigate, and his February 1916 report, the third now received in five months, found that Cooper and Allinson had "not been working in harmony for some months past, owing to their being too

Hazzard's Hotel, Waterton Lakes Park. F.H. Riggall photograph. John Hazzard presented a conundrum for Superintendent Robert Cooper—running afoul of liquor regulations while operating the only tourist accommodation in Waterton Park—typical of problems faced by superintendents in small parks communities but met with a call for strict adherence to regulations by Harkin. [WMCR, V26]

familiar with each other at first, and, in part, to both being ignorant of their duties and responsibilities in the park." Carpenter recommended that they be given six months to better familiarize themselves with their responsibilities, and to work out their personal differences, or be replaced.

When he received Carpenter's report, Harkin immediately wrote Barnard-Hervey and admonished him, reiterating his responsibility for the proper administration of the park, pointing out that any negligence was a reflection on his administrative abilities and reprimanding him for not properly instructing the two officials and not reporting unsatisfactory conditions.[27] Cooper and Allinson thereafter seemingly tried to work more co-operatively, but other problems with the superintendent were coming to light. In his 1916 report Carpenter had mentioned concerns with the operation of a steam launch on Waterton Lakes, owned by hotelier John Hazzard but run by Carl Danielson, who was "said to be of a drinking character and very often under the influence of liquor while running this boat, which is a pleasure craft, said to be often taxed beyond its capacity." Carpenter recommended the boat's operator be required to pass an examination and that the number of passengers be limited to its capacity.[28] With his attempts to develop tourism amenities, Harkin was already working through the Marine Department to arrange for a set of rules that would adequately protect the public yet still allow tour boat owners to make a profit. In the Waterton case, he arranged for a steamboat inspector to visit Waterton and assess the situation, and in his subsequent report it stated that both Hazzard and Danielson had overloaded the boat and the general opinion of the public of the latter was that while not operating the boat while intoxicated, "at other times he may take a little drink." He also indicated that Cooper had promised to "give the matter his personal attention, [and] if Mr. Hazzard does not properly conduct his business he will have the license he now has permitting him to do business in the park cancelled."[29]

As Hazzard was the proprietor of the only tourist hotel in the park, Harkin undoubtedly hoped problems would now subside, but within days he received a letter from Cooper enclosing a recommendation to approve an application from one H.H. Hanson to operate a passenger boat for the coming summer. An attached note revealed, "This is the H.H. Hanson who has been living on the Park and he has asked me to mention the fact that he has removed himself and family from the Park area." The reference related to Hanson's having been ordered to leave the park due to the breaking of regulations in operating a sawmill for his brother's company and being under suspicion of smuggling in liquor. Harkin was not amused, indicating that while new regulations were in preparation "in the meantime however the department will not countenance a man who has recently been turned out of the park for defying the law operating a boat for passengers within the park boundaries" and admonished that "it is very surprising that you, who represent the department's interests in the park, should recommend such permission being given to Mr. Hanson." In trying to explain his actions, Cooper noted that Hanson had been misled by his brother, had severed his connection with him and "is trying to make a living as best he can for his family, as well as educate his children at the Parkview School." The response makes it clear the superintendent was struggling to operate within confined local conditions against a background of knowing on a personal basis those he was responsible for overseeing, a situation faced by many superintendents in remote parks. But it did not cut any ice with Harkin—he noted Carpenter had recommended Hanson be barred from the park and warned, "I would be glad for you to bear this in mind and in future to exercise more care in making recommendations." In closing, he stated his core belief in the proper role for a superintendent: "It is imperative for departmental interests that the Superintendent of the Park who is on the ground as the department's representative should protect the park and public therein in every way. If this is not done then the Superintendent's position becomes a sinecure."[30]

By this time Cooper's days were numbered, as new problems had arisen between him and Allinson, leading Lethbridge Police Commissioner B.W. Collison to launch an investigation in February 1917 into alleged irregularities in park administration. His conclusion was that the superintendent was negligent in the matter of the erection of a new warden's cabin, including missing receipts, a shortage of supplies and equipment, and poor siting due to exposure to high winds, resulting from a disagreement with the chief warden about the best location. Tellingly, he also pointed out that Cooper was "evidently under the impression that he is bound by the rules of Party patronage, or the rules of his department...to get any supplies in the town in the riding in which Waterton Lakes Park forms a part." Expressing some sympathy, Collison concluded that Cooper was doing his best but was led astray "listening to friends who perhaps had something to do with getting him the position he now holds" and, as the problems were not entirely his fault, with "proper office assistance, the work would be gotten along with alright."[31]

Although no action was forthcoming, in March 1918 Howard Sibbald was directed by Barnard-Hervey to investigate further from a warden service perspective, and he expressed the opinion that the strained relationship between the two officers had not improved. On March 18, 1918, in one of his last acts as chief superintendent, Barnard-Hervey recommended that a change in superintendent take place as soon as possible. In an effort to be absolutely fair, Harkin launched his own investigation and meanwhile seconded Superintendent Maunder of

Revelstoke Park to proceed to Waterton and organize it "on an efficient basis" by acting as "Superintendent of the Superintendent." Maunder also found the differences irreconcilable and the commissioner thereafter recommended to Cory that both men, being "hopelessly incompetent in their work," should be dismissed. Despite Cooper having overseen a visitation increase from 2,000 to 9,000 annually over the difficult war period, in June 1919 George A. Bevan became Waterton's new superintendent.[32]

While it is apparent that Cooper was, to a degree, a victim of circumstances, it is equally clear that Harkin would not long tolerate anything that negatively affected the branch's reputation or operations. Cooper was not the only superintendent to feel his wrath when matters went off the rails, as all had to the bear the brunt of his pointed criticisms from time to time. Usually they simply quietly accepted the direction, most of it bearing their superior's signature but often prepared by other headquarters staff, and responded with an explanation and a report on the action taken. But sometimes his desire to be on top of every aspect of every park verged on the picayune, driving them to distraction and occasionally even backfiring. A case in point occurred in June 1914 when an article appeared in the *Crag and Canyon* under the byline "A Mighty Hunter," recounting the attempt of one Dave Murray to adorn his hat with porcupine quills. According to the story, Murray was driving his carriage near Lake Minnewanka when he spied "a big porky" and decided to fulfill his wish, throwing his hat on the beast in the expectation it would release its quills. But, to his amazement, it lumbered away through the bush with the hat on its back and he had to give chase, eventually knocking the quill-filled hat off its back with a club.[33] On reading the account when the paper reached Ottawa, a perplexed Harkin immediately fired off a letter to Superintendent Clarke:

> Under the caption of "A Mighty Hunter" the Crag and Canyon of the 27th ultimo gives an account of the recent attempt of some person, named Dave Murray, to secure the quills of a porcupine at large in your park. The occurrence in itself may appear to be of trifling moment, especially as

> the animal would not appear to have been either killed or injured; but, it should be apparent to you that the Parks Branch cannot afford to even risk the appearance of evil in any matters that concern the Park regulation for the protection of animal and bird life in your Park....
>
> You will kindly, therefore, investigate the truth, or otherwise, of the statement in this connection which appeared in the issue of the newspaper referred to, and if the facts are as stated, you will take the necessary steps in order to prevent further repetitions of such violations of the Park regulations.

A smile likely crossed the superintendent's face as he replied, "I made enquiry into this case at the time and found that the paragraph was in the nature of a joke on a person who is evidently closely acquainted with the manager of this newspaper. So far as I can discover there was no serious attempt to capture or interfere with the porcupine."[34]

Harkin usually did not directly concern himself with the field staff below superintendent, but sometimes made an exception with members of the warden service as the park officers most in touch with what was occurring outside park towns. Although the chief warden reported to the superintendent, the commissioner occasionally truncated this relationship by contacting them directly, particularly Chief Warden Howard Sibbald at Banff, whose knowledge and opinion he especially valued. He also regularly read the chief wardens' reports, and set up a system to have headquarters staff review individual warden diaries and accompanying summaries, which formed the cornerstone for detailed information-gathering in the parks. The diaries were carried on patrol so that notes could be recorded promptly, including patrol routes followed, time spent in such activities as trail clearing, fire prevention or telephone line maintenance, observations of game, enforcement of regulations, and logging of hours worked. The arrival of the reviews on Harkin's desk prompted a flurry of memos and requests for additional information. Typical of issues falling under his gaze were those mentioned in a letter to Superintendent Maunder at Waterton Lakes in

July 1918 where Warden McDonald, while not mentioning the number of hours on duty, had reported the planting of a garden as "maintenance," an activity he directed be charged against annual leave as it did not relate to fire and game protection. The letter closed with the warning, "If the Wardens' diaries and summaries are not filled in, in the proper manner, it will be necessary to withhold their salary cheques, until they have done so."[35]

The procedure also had the benefit of making headquarters aware of problems in the parks and served as a check that policy and directives were being properly carried out. One such area concerned Harkin's directive that no poison should be used in predator control activities. Entries in Banff warden diaries in early 1913 relating to the use of poison in exterminating coyotes elicited a reminder to Chief Warden Sibbald: "Game warden W. Noble mentions in his diary of January last, that he was using poison to rid the park of coyotes. In previous letters to you, I referred to the use of poison by wardens Peyto and Brown, and both these men promised to desist from the practice. Would you please broach the matter with Mr. Noble and point out the danger in this method of combating the coyote nuisance? The use of the gun and the trap should be quite sufficient for the purposes at the present time."[36]

The fact that the diary system made him acutely aware of wardens' activities and the conditions they operated under resulted in a strong interest in their role and welfare. This was especially true with respect to longer serving men, such as Warden Bill Peyto, who had been a trapper, prospector, and mountain guide after his arrival in the Rockies in 1887. Peyto was one of the first wardens appointed in 1911, and, with his strong outdoors background and determined character, came to be regarded as the quintessential role model for what a warden should be. This standing led to Harkin's personal involvement over the matter of compensation for two of his horses killed on the railway tracks while on patrol in November 1912, illustrating the lengths he would go to support his men. In August 1913 Peyto requested the superintendent take up the matter of compensation on his behalf with headquarters. Out of pocket some $170, he also pressed the matter with Bennett, who wrote Harkin in April 1914, offering, "When a valuable man loses his horses while on duty, it seems to me that it is the duty of the Government to purchase other horses in their place" and querying, "Do you not think it would be possible to purchase horses of equal value for him and justify the expenditure in that way?" In response, Harkin reported he had made "a very persistent effort to secure compensation," with the CPR and the government, but had been refused at every turn. As an alternative, he had secured an additional $5.00 per month in salary and "would have recommended a larger increase had it not been that an increase of even $10.00 per month would have given him a larger salary than that received by Mr. Sibbald, the Chief Game Warden." This was not satisfactory to either Peyto or Bennett and the matter dragged on, with the commissioner reporting in May that Treasury Board was considering another similar case that, if approved, would be a good precedent for the claim. Unfortunately, this did not occur and in September he was forced to admit defeat, writing Bennett, "This matter was again submitted to the Deputy Minister and it was considered not advisable to reopen the question."[37]

Despite these efforts, Peyto was undoubtedly upset by the decision and, like many of his confreres moved by world events transpiring that autumn, left the service and joined the 12th Canadian Mounted Rifles in May 1915. Wounded by shrapnel in fighting with the Canadian Expeditionary Force at Hooge, Belgium, in July 1916 he returned to Banff and had to undergo a long convalescence before rejoining the warden service on a temporary basis in 1919. He returned to permanent staff in 1921, assigned to the Healy Creek district where he became notorious for his success at hunting predators and enforcing regulations on unwary offenders, but his actions continued to illustrate the test of wills that sometimes went on between men in the field set in their ways and their equally stubborn superior. One such instance occurred in May 1923 after Harkin decreed that pelts of all mountain lions killed by wardens be turned in, rather than kept for their own use as in the past. That month a package arrived at head office containing a fresh lion skin and a note from Peyto reading, "Enclosed Mt Lion skin treed by my dog near Banff & shot. If you care to accpt same for your office alright."[38] This was undoubtedly Peyto's way of commenting on what he believed to be the ridiculousness of the situation. However, while their relationship underwent ups and downs, Harkin's respect for the warden would remain high, and in the period before the retirement of both men in 1936, he supported Peyto's continuing employment despite disabilities limiting his effectiveness.

As indicated, in all "outside staff" matters in the mountain parks, Harkin's ability to find good men up to the end of the war was constrained by his relationship with Bennett. As an important western voice in government and a strong supporter of parks, he was something of a double-edged sword, requiring constant assurances that administration was being carried out to his exacting political standards but, on the other hand, providing critical support where objectives might otherwise have been unachievable. His advocacy on the boundary disputes was indicative of this, but far from unique. One of the most persistent criticisms at Banff related to the fact that most of the justices of the peace were senior park staff members, resulting in the superintendent frequently having to sit on the bench when offenders breaking park regulations were arraigned for trial. In August 1913 Harkin brought this matter to the MP's attention, stating that the local Mounted Police officer had told him that "last year there were in the Park about six hundred cases for trial and that in many cases the most difficulty was to find a J.P. to try them," and suggesting that a resident police magistrate be hired to deal with the problem. Bennett consulted fellow Conservative and law partner Senator James Lougheed, a Banff summer resident and confidant on park matters, and responded that as the season was almost over, there was no hurry to act. Undaunted, Harkin contacted him every time a new case came up and within a month Bennett had relented and promised to secure the services of a qualified magistrate.[39]

There were numerous other instances where Bennett's influence was valuable. Prior to the war, his advocacy was important in the rebuilding of the Cave and Basin, the building of a new bridge across the Bow at Banff, the construction of a pavilion on the Banff Recreation Grounds, and building of the bridge and road linking the Banff-Castle road with Vermilion Pass. In return, Harkin kept his ear to the ground and advised him of potential pitfalls. For example, in July 1914 when he received a patronage list for Calgary containing the name of Bennett's legal firm, he wrote, "I presume local people at Calgary had the name put on it when a general list was being prepared, not knowing anything about the independence of Parliament Act. I thought it well to bring this matter to your attention." Bennett was astounded that this could have happened and warmly thanked Harkin for helping to avoid a serious misstep.[40] As time went on, his respect for the MP went beyond the immediate matter of parks, sharing his concerns about the Canadian nation as a whole, and by 1915 he was using him as a sounding board for ideas about how Canada could play a larger role in the postwar world. This was a topic of particular interest to Bennett, who thought the country should have more influence in the British Empire. An interesting exchange of correspondence occurred in February 1915 when, moved by reading an H.G. Wells article in *The World Wide Review*, Harkin wrote, "This article inspired the thought that why might Canada not have a thinking department for collecting, testing and developing new ideas? Not as regards the war but looking principally to the advancement of the country in its multiphase developments. I pass the suggestion on to you as I know if there is any national value in it its development will be assured." Bennett responded in a remarkable missive, agreeing "all departments will require a branch for collecting, testing and developing new thoughts and ideas," but decrying Canadians' lack of responsibility in wartime compared to "the supreme stimulus of a lofty patriotism" evident in Germany. He called for "a sound patriotism, without which there can be no commercial or industrial expansion, to say nothing of that sense of moral responsibility which is absolutely necessary if our civilization is to be better than that which we are now doing our best to destroy." Responding enthusiastically, Harkin forwarded several memorandums prepared by Frank Williamson containing suggestions for actions on behalf of Canadian soldiers when they returned from the war.[41]

Bennett likewise respected Harkin's potential and regarded him as a civil servant trying to do his best in difficult circumstances. In a letter to Norman Luxton in May 1915, he confided, "I regard Harkin as a reasonably good efficient public servant and a man who is trying to do

Prime Minister Robert L. Borden, R.B. Bennett and Police Inspector Deane. Harkin's relationship with Calgary West member of Parliament Bennett proved to be a double-edged sword in his efforts to administer Rocky Mountains Park during the war years. [GA, NB-16-173]

something for the Parks and for Canada generally. He is a young man of ideals and many of his suggestions are of great value and can be worked out to secure very desirable results."[42] Regrettably, as time went on this cordial relationship began to be strained, largely because the politician was increasingly called upon to take the side of his constituents against unpopular head office decisions. In most cases Bennett tried to work these out, suggesting a course of governmental action that would solve the problem and get the branch off the hook. During the war such solutions became more difficult as Harkin was constantly being called upon to relax regulations with respect to leasing and building requirements in Banff, a result of tight financial conditions and many residents serving overseas. His point of view concerning such decisions had been consistent, set out in his own letter to Luxton of June 1912: "I know that in the course of administration I often have to take stands that the other party to the transaction may not approve but we all have to follow the course which we believe is the right one and abide by the results."[43] While trying to be co-operative where he could, when he felt that the branch was being taken advantage of he would draw the line, even at the risk of incurring the MP's ire.

In March 1916 in making representations in favour of a Mr. Stokes, who in 1913 had purchased a lot to build a house but, due to financial hardship, was unable to do so within the allotted time, Bennett put forward the opinion, "I think each man should be written to and asked if he desires to keep his lot, and if he does, it should not be taken away from him." As Stokes's and a few other leases had been cancelled, he followed this up with a pointed letter to the minister: "I cannot but think that a very great injustice has been done by Mr. Harkin in connection with the cancellation of contracts for the leases of lots in Banff. Under the conditions that exist in that locality, having regard to the enormous enlistments that have taken place there, and to the financial situation generally, I cannot understand how any Government official can do what Mr. Harkin has been doing. It is creating a little less than a revolt in the minds of the people, and I desire to protest most strongly against his action." The same day he sent a copy to the commissioner with a blunt note berating him for his "entire and utter disregard of conditions in Western Canada" and warning "I do not propose to let the matter drop until one or the other of us understands the situation much more clearly than it is apparently now understood." Harkin responded with an explanation emphasizing that the matter was essentially one of fairness: "It was not considered that it was a justice to the parties who felt that they were forced to build on the understanding that no extensions were to be granted and who established their good faith in the face of the financial depression, afterwards to find that the Department was carrying on a few parties indefinitely when they had not done anything at all to establish their bona fides." Bennett, known for supporting the rights of the individual, was unconvinced, and he sent a further letter to Minister Roche throwing another barb in the commissioner's direction: "I venture to think that Mr. Harkin has permitted his zeal to outrun his discretion in dealing with this and other matters at Banff this year."[44] Roche did not become involved and, meanwhile, regular and cordial correspondence between Bennett and Harkin resumed, perhaps leading to the conclusion that such letters were sometimes written mainly to illustrate to a prominent constituent that the politician was taking action on his behalf.

If so, such subterfuge was only temporary, as other problems soon arose, an inevitable result of the two men's diverging philosophies on central authority. One was a result of a letter sent to Bennett in January 1917 by Banff resident Hugh Dyer, who claimed his rifle and the skin of a lynx "which was after my chickens, not four yards from my door" had been confiscated. Claiming that the chief warden had previously allowed him to keep the gun to protect his poultry, he said Sibbald was now denying this and refusing to return either it or the lynx skin. Bennett passed the letter on, commenting, "On the facts stated, I certainly think Dyer's request should be granted, although you may know some good reason why it should not." Harkin's reaction was tough, arguing the skin could not be returned as "all the animals in the Park belong to the Government in trust for the general public of Canada and the fact that any individual should kill one, even for a good reason, cannot give such individual any right to ownership in the animal." This would mean "the doors would be thrown open in a way that would mean endless difficulties for the game service and a great temptation to people to destroy game on the chance of getting possession of a valuable pelt." With respect to the gun, Harkin stated he would have the superintendent investigate Dyer's assertion of having received permission to keep the weapon and "to let me have his own views in light of local conditions," pending which he would then make a final decision as to its disposition. An incredulous Bennett, who was noted for his short fuse, responded with an attack that showed this seemingly minor incident had provided a spark for him to vent his displeasure with the difficulties Banff was presenting, his disagreement with the commissioner's methods, and, perhaps, even suspicions of Liberal Party sympathies:

> I am at a great loss to understand why there has been such increased friction at Banff since you became Commissioner of Parks in 1911.
>
> Is this to be attributed to your political zeal or to your inefficiency? I am asking a perfectly plain question and

> without any personal feelings. I am in the habit of getting down to the bottom of things, and as the representative of Banff in the House of Commons, I have been wholly unable to understand why the present situation exists....
>
> I think that you might revise your whole ideas with relation to Park administration. I would like you to think it over at any rate from that standpoint as I am now doing. I propose to discuss the question with the Minister at an early date and, if I can see no possible chance of improvement in the administration, I will have to of course bring the matter to the attention of Parliament when the vote to pay the salaries of Park officials at Ottawa is being considered.[45]

Given these increasing stresses, it was not surprising Harkin's relationship with Bennett, which sometimes entailed more than one piece of correspondence a day, should cease. Bennett, discouraged at not being taken into cabinet and expecting to be appointed to the Senate, decided not to run in the 1917 general election for Prime Minister Borden's new Unionist government. Appointed minister of Justice in Arthur Meighen's brief successor administration of 1920–1921, he carried out only a desultory correspondence with the branch on statistical matters. He was unsuccessful in a reelection bid in December 1921, and for the next few years, before reentering politics in 1925, concentrated on his business interests. One was Calgary Power, and its ambition to develop waters on park lands for power purposes inevitably brought him into direct conflict with his former Parks ally. When he became leader of the Opposition at the head of a rejuvenated Conservative Party in 1927, the two men's relationship had been irretrievably damaged by their disagreements over wartime administration of Banff and subsequent power development wrangles.

Meantime, the huge social upheaval caused by the First World War quickly eroded the excesses of the patronage system and replaced them, first with returned men's preference and gradually with the merit principle. In November 1917 the press reported that "the Dominion government has abolished the patronage system—a system of taxation to give political bosses an undue advantage over their fellows. Canadians should never have to bend the knee to political parasites for jobs or favors."[46] As the end of the war approached, notices went out to the parks to do away with patronage lists for purchases, and Harkin no longer had to submit suggested appointments to MPs, that requirement now being taken on by the Civil Service Commission. This change proved beneficial in choosing a replacement for Clarke at Banff, allowing Harkin to hand pick a man he knew would be motivated by branch, rather than political, concerns. His choice was James Wardle, who had proven invaluable in carrying out park surveys and construction projects under difficult wartime conditions and who, with his superior's distrust of Clarke, had become his main Rocky Mountains Park confidant. The *Crag and Canyon*, expressing surprise to see "the familiar chair of the boss-in-chief occupied by a clean shaven, dark young man, and not as one expected, a bewhiskered and staid-looking old chap," protested that it could "hand out no bunch of roses to J.B. Harkin for his appointment, because we believe at this time the Commission should have considered the men who have returned from the land of death, the men who have risked their ALL for Canada and the Empire." This opinion, the newspaper stated, was shared by recently elected Calgary West Unionist MP Thomas Tweedie, but "as patronage is a thing of the past at Ottawa, he says he had nothing to do with this appointment."[47]

The change also provided Harkin with the advantage of being able to send the applicants for lower level positions directly to the commission. These were numerous, as by 1918 the branch had grown significantly, with thirty-five employees at head office organized into six sections (chief, accounts, engineering, wildlife, forest, and clerical), ninety-six in Alberta parks (including five superintendents and twenty-seven wardens), and ten in BC parks. While the new policy did not entirely root out all vestiges of patronage and certainly did not mean that staffing issues would not arise from time to time, the administration of the parks and the quality of employees coming up through the civil service system took a decided turn for the better. This only strengthened Harkin's hand in maintaining the firm grip he had placed on the rapidly growing organization.

OE REPAIRS
C. A. VANZANT
HARMONY
DRUG
STORE
Ladies + Men's Wear
EDWARD HOTEL
DRUG STORE
FILMS

EIGHT

The Business of Selling Scenery

THE IMMEDIATE POSTWAR reconstruction period was to prove a difficult time for Harkin and his branch, just as it was for Canada as a whole. Not only was the country faced with reintegrating thousands of returned men, but it also had to wrestle with an enormous national debt as a result of the conflict and an unfavourable balance of payments with the United States. In these circumstances, as was evident from his discussions with Bennett about Canada's post-war role, Harkin believed that his task was not just to head an important branch within a government department but through that position to contribute to broader national considerations. As early as 1915 Bennett had noted in his letter to Luxton that he was "trying to do something for the Parks and for Canada generally," and this two-pronged approach would become a hallmark of Harkin's career. His philosophy on tourism in his early years had been that it would help to sustain and expand the park system in its infancy when its very survival was still somewhat tenuous. But now tourism, increasingly fuelled by the huge new auto-tourism market, was to become an end in itself for the good of Canada, leading to his 1921 declaration, "The Canadian National Parks may be said to be in the business of selling scenery."[1]

Harkin had first given voice to this idea in his 1919 report, stating, "the possibilities of Canada's mountains and in addition of Canada's recreational areas elsewhere have forced the Parks Service to the conclusion that all its work must be developed primarily with the view to promoting the tourist traffic because it appears to offer a very effective means of helping meet the country's financial conditions." To illustrate the potential he developed a concept of "exporting the scenery," estimating that $16 million of income had been generated by the 65,000 visitors to Rocky Mountains Park in 1915 spending an average of $250 each. This, he contended, could be valued the same as Canadian exports, and in a clever manipulation used the figures to calculate a return per acre of scenery. If the park's total acreage were divided into the total tourism income, it would yield $13.88 per acre; if the $74 million of wheat exports for the same year were divided into the wheat acreage under cultivation, it would yield $4.91 per acre. And, he argued, not only was the value of the scenery almost three times greater on a per acre basis, it was entirely non-consumptive, a point illustrated with reference to some fairy tales:

> As I have pointed out before, the sale of scenery never diminishes the capital stock. When we sell a bushel of wheat we sell so much of the constituents of the soil, so many nitrates, so many phosphates etc., which leaves the soil poorer, but when we dispense scenery we are like the two old people in the Greek fairy tale who entertained Jove and his son. No matter how much we give our guests there is still as much wine left in the pitcher. The dispensers of all other natural commodities are bound in the end,

> unless they partially replace what they sell, to find themselves in the unfortunate position of Mother Hubbard.[2]

The success of such arguments was attested to by Minister Meighen's 1920 speech supporting increased appropriations for the branch: "The returns per acre...[are] figured by the officers of the department as being more for the rocks and waste lands of our parks than even for our wheat fields...[and] speaking from the whole national standpoint, it is good public business to maintain these parks."[3]

Harkin believed that if the annual expenditures of American visitors reached $60 million, the unfavourable balance of payments could be wiped out. For him, the key was a large increase in motor traffic, and it is not surprising then that much of his attention in the immediate post-war period was focused on the completion of the Banff-Windermere Road. When the possibility of resuming negotiations was being considered early in 1918, he forcefully pointed out in a memorandum to the minister drafted for Cory's signature that "when it is considered that the completion of the Banff-Windermere road will make the Canadian Rockies accessible to over four million automobilists from the States, and that thousands of these will be annually attracted to Canada, the possibilities of tourist revenue is evident." Of course, Harkin also mentioned other benefits, including "a grant to the Dominion of some 384,000 acres of land which at a valuation of only $1.00 an acre would be worth $384,000" and "the satisfactory adjustment of the numerous difficulties arising from the present conflicting jurisdiction of the Dominion Parks in British Columbia."[4]

It took some time to get the stalled negotiations restarted, but in April 1918, BC Attorney General Farris had the aborted 1916 Banff-Windermere Road Agreement amended to provide the lieutenant-governor-in-council with authority to give the Dominion "any rights, power or control which otherwise might be had or exercised by the Legislature of the Province within the area of such public lands or parks."[5] That fall Harkin and Cory visited Victoria and met with Farris, resulting in a consensus that Deputy Attorney General Johnson would draft a new agreement and make arrangements for legislation to incorporate its provisions. Unfortunately, the matter languished through early 1919, and it was only when the province was faced with finding employment for the flood of returning men did it realize how important timely action had become. This created a frenzy of activity in the three months before the estimates were due to be tabled, virtually monopolizing Harkin's time. However, despite the pressures being brought to bear, he proved his mettle as a canny and unflappable negotiator ensuring the Dominion's interests were being fully met.

As foreseen, in Johnson's draft agreement the federal government undertook to complete construction of the road within four years of war's end while, in return, BC agreed to grant a strip of land approximately five miles wide on either side of the right-of-way (but generally following the crests of the mountains) between the provincial boundary at Vermilion Pass and the road's intersection with the Golden-Windermere Highway at Sinclair Creek. All minerals, coal, petroleum, and water would remain under the control of the province, but with a requirement that it would release no more mineral claims without Dominion concurrence and all timber and other leases were to revert to the federal Crown upon their expiry or cancellation. As well, the province agreed to extend authority to the minister of Lands to relinquish any private rights over lands needed for the road or the park and vest them in the ownership of Canada, and in return it agreed to compensate any person whose rights were so removed. And, most importantly from Harkin's perspective, the Dominion would exercise exclusive authority, except in the matters of schools, liquor, and shared revenue from automobile licensing where allowance would be made for the Province's legislation to prevail, along with its ordinary powers of taxation.[6]

Even before receiving a draft of the agreement, the department was being pressed by Minister of Works J.H. King to complete the road in two years, but despite the fact that he was absent from the office much of February with bouts of illness and with the time to have the estimates completed fast approaching, Harkin refused to be stampeded. His primary concern focused on the status of lands within the ten-mile belt and he therefore demanded both maps and information on the standing of all applications, leases, and licences. When King protested that this would require a topographic survey, Harkin requested at least a list of alienations and reminded the minister that in seeking an appropriation for the road he had to be prepared to answer Parliament concerning the amount of lands to be deducted to settle any rights-holders' claims. At the same time he informed a fellow bureaucrat that the provincial government's draft of the enabling act didn't meet requirements, and therefore "a proposed Act covering the understanding of the Dominion in the matter is now being prepared by this Branch for submission to the British Columbia Government." Although not extensive, the required changes were important as they largely related to ensuring that any provincial legislation would be "conformable to and correspond with the legislation of the Dominion governing Dominion Parks generally...so that there will be at all times uniformity." As mentioned, the department had attempted to dictate legislation with somewhat disastrous results in May 1916, but in this case Harkin felt it had an ace-in-the-hole: "Upon the action of the Government of British Columbia in passing legislation at the present session covering the terms of the draft Act will depend whether an appropriation towards constructing part of this road will be provided for in the estimates for this year."[7]

Likely due to this tenuous situation, Randolph Bruce soon resumed his role in the discussions, meeting with Harkin to go over matters on March 11 before departing for Victoria to "camp on the ground" until the new agreement was approved. On the same date, the commissioner wired Johnson the approved text and Cory likewise wired King explaining that the new draft had been considered necessary by the Justice Department and that if the BC legislature approved it, work would commence immediately. It was signed by the respective governments the same day. Interestingly, departmental law officer Newcombe, who assisted in the drafting, indicated to Cory that it was the best that could be done given the timelines available and that "in the last analysis it is very much a gentleman's agreement." Gentleman's agreement or not, Harkin had no intention of signing off until he was convinced that every step to protect his government had been taken. In the telegram to

Johnson laying out the required changes, he mentioned, "Please note grant of land will have to be made to Dominion before any expenditure can be incurred by Dominion & kindly have your legislation drafted to permit of this."[8] Ultimately, there was insufficient time to have the legislature take all the necessary steps and the department had to take the province's word that it would introduce a bill in the next session to repeal any conflicting legislation.

The agreement and subsequent land transfer in July 1919 represented a significant victory for the branch after three years of painstaking negotiations, but Harkin had little time to savor it due to his involvement in organizing the relinquishment of rights. Settling with the rights-holders proved no easy task, as some regarded it as an opportunity to make money on properties that had previously been relatively worthless. Harkin's approach was to inform holdouts that they were under no obligation to surrender their interests, but if they chose not to, they would have to conform to park regulations. To those seeking compensation for prospective future property value, he responded that this was impossible and somewhat speciously argued that it was questionable whether their holdings would increase in value because of the building of the road and the park. Not surprisingly, some complained to their MPs and the commissioner received letters seeking his assistance in providing an explanation for the refusal. One such communication in April 1921 from MP Bonnell, familiar with his reputation in handling such matters, requested, "As Chisolm is a particular friend of mine, and I realize that nothing can be done for this claim, I would appreciate if in your usual diplomatic way you would furnish me with as nice an answer as possible. I would like this question dealt with considerable diplomacy and I am sure you can tone down your refusal very nicely."[9]

Disgruntled rights-holders in the Kootenay Valley were not the only park residents upset with Harkin in the spring of 1921. Building of the Banff-Windermere Road was only one aspect of his tourism program, and other parts affected those living in Banff, the system's oldest and most influential community. As it had shifted away from its early spa period dominated by railroad and horse to its resort era when visitors increasingly arrived in automobiles, Banff's service, amenity, and accommodation needs had begun to change and its business community had emerged to find a voice. The Banff Board of Trade was created in 1912 in reaction to the same issue that he had addressed during his first visit—possible construction of a new CPR line with its attendant threats to the fledgling village. Upon returning to Ottawa from his western sojourn that year, Harkin had continued to press the company for a solution, and fortunately it soon thought better of the double-tracking project and dropped its application. However, when the threat disappeared local leaders such as Jim Brewster, Norman Luxton, and Dr. Harry Brett decided to change the Board of Trade's focus to matters concerning the relationship between the community and the Dominion government. Effectively, the branch's administration of park townsites placed it in the position of a municipal authority, with those it governed having no say in local decisions. Particularly controversial at Banff were actions on regulations and financial matters, with complaints against the raising of water rates being heard as early as 1909. But things really began to heat up a few years later in the face of deepening controversy over increasing departmental regulation of citizens' lives and livelihoods.

When Harkin appeared in Banff for his second annual inspection tour in June 1913, everything was sweetness and light so far as the *Crag and Canyon* was concerned: "J.B. is a friend of the National Park. He almost gets tiresome the way he talks about the park....Stay with it—'Oh you J.B.' Crag and Canyon is with you now and always."[10] But its faith was apparently misplaced, as when the Board of Trade requested the opportunity to review and advise on proposed actions in January 1914, Harkin told Bennett, "Although any suggestions from the Board of Trade in connection with matters of this nature might be helpful in framing any regulations concerning Banff, my idea is that since the Department is responsible for all the regulations, it might be a dangerous precedent to offer the citizens of Banff the opportunity of advising the Department in a matter of this kind."[11] Bennett, with his "red" Tory proclivities, did not entirely agree, believing the board might be allowed to at least make "suggestions." But Harkin's reasoning was consistent with his view of efficient, headquarters-directed administration, as it would preclude any local lobbying for improvements that, while perhaps needed, were not branch priorities. Already rates being charged for utilities such as the telephone system, sewer, and water did not cover their costs, and he was equally concerned that, if it was given a voice, any financial changes suggested by the board might create a precedent for other park towns. This point of view was reiterated in response to another Bennett letter in May 1914 suggesting that the Canmore school be supported for a much-needed expansion: "The moment even a small grant was made a precedent would be created and I am afraid that very soon Banff and all other towns would agitate that the Department should bear practically all the educational expenses....It is impossible to get away from the outstanding fact that the parks are a federal institution maintained and developed at a cost much in excess of the revenue derived and that they exist for a specific purpose, viz. for providing recreation for the people of Canada and tourists generally."[12]

Nevertheless, in May 1915, likely at Bennett's insistence, Harkin met with the Board of Trade to discuss matters, clarifying his policy with respect to park towns. In discussion about the province's initiative to license moving picture houses, he refused to discontinue the Dominion fee, arguing that it was intended only as a regulatory tool. Similarly, he declined to budge on the matter of a local health board, and to the suggestion that the telephone service be twenty-four hours, he noted that it was already running at a deficit. As the *Crag and Canyon* reported, "The Commissioner also pointed out that the park belonged to the whole dominion; that the total revenue of the park was trifling in comparison to the total expenditure and that they had to consider very seriously any suggestion calculated to increase that expenditure."[13] The meeting's failure marked an end to the Board of Trade's lobbying activities; however, it became the starting point for an increasingly more adversarial relationship with the community.

The torch for local rights was carried mainly by the newspaper under the direction of its publisher, Norman Luxton. Harkin and Luxton knew each other relatively well by this point, having corresponded on and

Banff Avenue, ca. 1925. Byron Harmon photograph. The transformation of Banff into a resort community with the introduction of the automobile created a tenuous relationship between Harkin and town leaders seeking a greater voice in the community's governance. [WMCR, V263 NA-3412]

discussed numerous issues concerning the businessman's many interests and the operations of the park. Initially, they had hit it off well, but after Luxton's King Edward Hotel burned to the ground in a February 1914 fire and the department refused to provide compensation despite that fact that the town's fire hydrants had been frozen, the relationship became less cordial. As a strong Liberal, Luxton was unhappy with the state of government activities in the park after Bennett had secured a Conservative grip on its administration, being particularly displeased with Superintendent Clarke, who he regarded as an out-and-out drunkard and a disgrace to the service. In attempting to rebuild his hotel, he met with difficulty getting Clarke's approval of his plans, for which he blamed Harkin, complaining, "It was very unfair of you to put me at the mercy of one Jack Clark[e]."[14] Matters were not helped by Ottawa's insistence that the new building be two storeys, rather than the less expensive one-storey structure Luxton was hoping to be allowed until business improved.

Against this backdrop, the *Crag and Canyon* became more querulous, and its earlier news items welcoming Harkin to Banff for his annual inspection were replaced by cryptic one-liners such as "J.B. Harkin is in residence at the Banff Springs Hotel—who the Hell cares?" The paper complained about the CPR's monopoly on electrical power supply, departmental favouritism toward the company in deteriorating tourism conditions, the poor state of roads, and the general "tortoise-like manner in which the department moves in all matters relating to Banff." In 1916 Luxton promoted a petition aimed at local unhappiness over regulations, ones the newspaper claimed were designed and enforced "by men who live in Ottawa, by fly-by-night men who visit Banff in the summer only, by men who have no knowledge of local conditions the year round." The source of the condition, it claimed, was a basic flaw in the park's formation: "With the few inhabitants at that time it did not work such a hardship, but with increased population and more irksome regulations it now does not afford the citizens of Banff as much protection and right to exist privileges as accorded to the conquered Red Man." Accordingly, "as British subjects, as business men, as property owners [and] as thinking men and women," each person was invited to sign and have the petition sent to Minister Roche, MP Bennett, and Senator Lougheed with a request that "a body of citizens composed of men and women, be appointed to confer with one or more appointees of the government on all subjects beneficial or inimical to the prosperity and well-being of the people of Banff."[15] Luxton contacted Bennett in February 1917 explaining how the petition had been gathered and expressing frustration that despite all his powers even he seemed incapable of getting Harkin and the branch to budge, pleading, "The good God knows you have done all we can expect and then some more. But the good feeling of the people that should be going to you is being killed by this stranglehold Ottawa has on every businessman's throat in Banff, and this little thing, such a little thing, we ask for, an advisory board, get the word 'advisory,' simply to discuss with Ottawa these appointments."

Bennett was distracted by Meighen's idea of an alliance between the Conservatives and the Liberals in a union government for the balance of the war and was motivated by the advisability of not making waves in difficult times. Despite a further Luxton letter making it clear that townspeople were looking to him as "the only man who has the power to effect a change," he expressed annoyance in his reply "that you should have taken this moment of all others in which to complain with respect to the administration of the Park," and while stating that he opposed Harkin's efforts to centralize work at Ottawa, had decided to take "no political action since the war broke out." He also took issue with Luxton's contention that things were better when Howard Douglas was in control of Banff, perhaps providing a further clue for the Conservative's support of Harkin in the commissioner's position: "Have you studied the reports from the Department; do you realize the price the country paid for having him [Douglas] in Banff? If you did, I am sure that you would see that it was because of what happened during his regime that Mr. Harkin believes that centralization is the proper method to pursue."[16]

In any event, no action was forthcoming, and Luxton and the *Crag* became less outspoken in worsening wartime conditions. That is until the editor's chair was taken over by P.W. Stone in early 1918, whereupon the newspaper began a vicious campaign of attacks on Harkin's character and "imperialist" policies. In announcing the campaign, Stone indicated that it would be kept up "until such time as proper recognition is given by the little boss at Ottawa of the rights of the citizens of the Park." Even the most basic decision, he alleged, required approval from the commissioner, chiding, "If the teeth of the monkey in the zoo need manicuring, or the nails of the polar bear need cleaning, 'you may consult me by wire,' is the little man's imperialistic command; if a bear or a lynx come along and rob your pig pen or hen roost—or perhaps your children's lives are imperiled—'you can't shoot is the imperialistic "ha ha," your gun will be sealed and both your property and your lives are in my hands. I AM THE BOSS'." With respect to the superintendent's position, the editor contended that it required a yes-man: "It would make no difference who sat in the superintendent's chair here—that man must be wholly subservient to the little chief, the little autocrat, the little king enthroned at Ottawa, or he could not hold his job. It apparently is one of the stipulations of the position that the superintendent be a nonentity, that he must have no power whatever apart from the wishes of Mr. Harkin."[17]

These scurrilous outpourings continued with great regularity, containing observations such as "Mr. Harkin is prejudiced against the Banff populace because at one time it asked him to take their opinions into consideration," and, "We have always held the opinion that Mr. Harkin was the commissioner, the minister of the interior and in fact the whole cheese in regard to the fate of Banff, and until some further proof is forthcoming to show that its power is curtailed, we must maintain the very same opinion."[18] Such slanders could not remain unaddressed, but when Harkin and Cory met with Banff representatives in October 1918, the results were frustrating for the local delegates who found the deputy minister intentionally insulting in his answer to questions and felt that the two officials were "evading" and "camouflaging" in their responses.[19] The *Crag and Canyon*'s outbursts abated somewhat after Stone's departure in early 1919, but relations with the Banff populace and the newspaper remained frosty, and Harkin would be unflinching during seven years of dispute over a greater voice for townspeople.

Yet, while not wanting Banff residents directly involved in discussing difficult issues, it did not deter Harkin from trying to find solutions to those he agreed with, such as the contentious dual licensing matter discussed with the Board of Trade in 1915. By 1916 Alberta was levying fees in accordance with its legal right to do so, leading to further calls for fair treatment and the opening of federal-provincial discussions to find a solution. A tentative agreement was reached between Cory and Premier Sifton in May 1917, in some respects similar to the approach being taken in the BC negotiations where the Dominion would leave the province with complete jurisdiction in educational matters, the administration of justice, and licensing of liquor. However, there would be shared revenue on automobile licensing, and the province would agree to federal responsibility for licensing motion picture houses, poolrooms, and other public gathering places in the parks as well as management and control of guides, camping parties, and all other activities connected with the parks as pleasure grounds. Regrettably, the agreement was not ratified by Alberta and when the matter was raised again a year later, Harkin advised Cory that it now appeared it might be necessary to take court action, believing that the Dominion's case for exclusive jurisdiction was a strong one. As usual, he quoted the corresponding situation in the United States where a state had to pass an act ceding exclusive jurisdiction to the federal government before a new park could be created within its precincts. Ultimately, Cory's cooler head prevailed, opting to resurrect the original agreement with the province in 1918 and providing at least one positive note in the relationship with Banff residents. Nevertheless, Harkin continued to believe it was a serious mistake.

The status quo with respect to community representation remained in place until 1920 when circumstances caused erosion in Harkin's long-held position. That summer, Senator James Lougheed became minister of the Interior, and as a seasonal resident of Banff since 1911 and a solicitor for many of its prominent residents, he had promised Luxton to try to obtain an advisory board for its citizens. Upon his appointment, the minister called a meeting attended by some thirty Banff residents, and agreed to meet with a smaller delegation to discuss the specifics of their demands. Reported to be "greater authority vested in the local superintendent to settle local conditions, and the establishment of a committee of citizens to confer with the superintendent upon matters which demanded immediate attention instead of referring the affairs to Ottawa," Lougheed declared himself in sympathy with reestablishing the Board of Trade, which in turn would appoint the committee to deal with the superintendent.[20] By February 1921, local leaders had gone well beyond this idea, holding an organizational meeting for the "Banff Citizens' Association" and calling an election for March 21. Nine councillors emerged from this first effort at democratic local representation and immediately they began to hold monthly meetings to communicate issues, not only to the superintendent but directly to Harkin himself. While not commenting on this turn-of-events, he could not have been pleased he now had to answer, at least in a cursory fashion, to others than his departmental and political superiors.

Nonetheless, Harkin soon came to recognize that the situation having changed over the years, there could be some real benefits to more open communication. Long-standing grievances that began to be addressed with the Banff Advisory Council, as it became known, included the establishment of a board of health, the organization of an annual "clean-up day," and discussion of the establishment of an ambulance service for the park. These topics were on the agenda when he held the first of what was to become regular annual meetings with the council on September 21, 1921, a step that would ease, although by no means eliminate, conflict between Ottawa and Banff. At it, while reiterating federal powers with respect to licensing and pointing out the inability of the community to levy taxes to set up a fireman's fund, Harkin was more amenable on tourism matters, speaking of the desirability of Banff developing a "community spirit" and identifying the need for the manufacture of handcrafts as a local cottage industry to compete with the "cheap souvenirs" coming from Europe and the U.S. He was particularly pleased with a suggestion that the branch build a tourist information bureau, even supporting the idea of paying for the printing of a guidebook if council arranged to prepare one. By the time they met again the following July, his approach had completely changed from the contentious period leading up to 1921, agreeing that it should have the right to input on amendments to business licensing regulations and supporting an assessment being made for additional manpower at the fire hall through an increase to water and sewer rates. Remarkably, after ending the meeting with an announcement that the Banff-Windermere Road would be opened the next summer, "a vote of thanks was tendered Mr. Harkin by the council."[21]

Despite being able to move ahead on many local issues with the Advisory Council, there was one area of disagreement on which Harkin was not prepared to bend—planning and development approval. From the earliest days of parks, responsibility for leasing and approval of building design and construction activities had rested with the superintendent, with difficult issues often being referred to Ottawa for direction. This *laissez-faire* approach resulted in a hodge-podge of building designs being evident in Banff, essentially reflecting interpretations of rustic design popular in both American and Canadian parks. But with the village on the cusp of a major boom in the early 1920s, better planning and stricter regulations aimed at improving buildings and tourism infrastructure needed to be developed and explained to residents. Harkin and his departmental superiors had recognized the need for better town planning immediately before the war, taking advantage of English civic planner Thomas Mawson being at work on a plan for Calgary to engage him in 1913. Mawson was an adherent of the City Beautiful movement promoting urban aesthetics, focusing on variations in street patterns featuring curving boulevards leading to parks and squares and, most importantly, a grand civic centre. In Banff he thought this could be accomplished if Banff Avenue formed a central axis with Dr. Brett's hotel on the south end and on the north a new "Banff Avenue Radial," a circular focal point where Parks administration and other public buildings would be located, with important streets radiating outwards. All new buildings would be constructed of local stone and building materials.[22] Unfortunately, wartime budgetary restrictions intervened to make most of Mawson's plan unachievable, although a few elements, such as a recreation grounds and a new Bow River bridge, were eventually built. By the early 1920s, the City Beautiful movement was being rapidly supplanted in urban planning circles by the Garden City or New Town movement, one tenet of which was that planners would have a great deal of control in changing existing urban structure and in planning new towns. And circumstances dictated that Harkin soon had one of its foremost proponents at his disposal.[23]

In 1921, with the disbandment of the Commission of Conservation, the Parks Branch inherited its town planning responsibilities, developed in recognition that proper urban planning was part of better public health standards. Thomas Adams, a noted British planner of the Garden City school, had been engaged by the commission in 1914 as an advisor and he made his influence felt in calling for more government regulation of town planning, as occurred in Britain, and by promoting planning education.[24] Why the commission's town planning activities, and with them Adams's contract, were transferred to the branch are unknown, but with current thinking being that conservation and urban planning were related in using nature to ameliorate the effects of

Gateway, Kootenay National Park, ca. 1925. Byron Harmon photograph. The creation of a Town Planning Division in 1921 under the direction of Thomas Adams allowed Harkin to plan and design major parks projects in-house. [WMCR, V263 NA-5554]

urban living, it made some sense. In any event, creation of the Town Planning Division (later the Architectural and Town Planning Division) provided Harkin with the tool he needed to impose the central authority he sought for the difficult situation arising in park towns. Adams was ably assisted by William Cromarty, a fellow Englishman who taught architecture at the University of Alberta and had worked with Alfred Calderon, the designer of the "boulder bungalow" administration building at Jasper, providing him with experience in a vernacular of rustic design. After Adams's contract expired in 1923, Cromarty became head of the division, remaining as its driving force until 1937. In this position he heavily influenced the design of both public and private buildings in the parks in his favoured Tudor Revival and English Arts and Crafts styles, modified by the use of local materials and rustic elements. Despite this expertise, Harkin remained directly involved in the design of key buildings, both in his efforts to extend operational control over all branch matters and through personal interest in architecture and design.[25]

As early as 1922 he was reporting that the division's services were "available for the planning of community life within the limits of the national parks and for the better provision of the needs of tourists" and a year later that the requirement for developers to submit plan drawings would result in "establishing more suitable and effective architecture" and would "greatly improve the appearances of villages and towns from a modern town planning view."[26] Hitting full stride in 1923, the division carried out a diverse and impressive body of work: "Plans were made for a new subdivision at Radium Hot Springs and for the layout of the station grounds at Jasper; for automobile camping grounds and a new subdivision at Waterton Lakes park; a subdivision for summer cottages at Lake Edith, Jasper Park; the proposed layout of the grounds at Fort Howe, St. John, N.B.; Banff ave. boulevard and automobile parking place at Banff; preliminary drawings of the proposed police quarters and entrance gateway at Waterton Lakes; fort Chambly layout of cemetery grounds and central memorial."[27] From the outset, the Banff Advisory Council dealt with issues that fell into the town-planning sphere, including the location of the new business category of public garages and granting permission for house tents in village backyards to service lower-cost tourist accommodation needs. As well, it frequently acted as a lobbyist for residents or businessmen in their attempts to have a design or a building approved, matters that created tension and conflict as the authority of the new agency gradually increased.

While these influences took hold, Harkin was distracted by completion of the Banff-Windermere Highway, as it was now being referred to, that he had so proudly announced to council in July 1922. Their pleasure was occasioned by the fact that its completion was scheduled to be almost a full year early, a result of an important change in road construction practices. When planning for postwar construction, the branch had decided to carry it out by contract rather than day-labour, a result of its previous experience of tendering being more cost-effective. Bids were called for the road in May, along with those for three other tourist road projects—completion of the Banff-Laggan Highway to Lake Louise as well as the Mount Revelstoke Highway to the summit of Mount Revelstoke and further work on a road south from Jasper to the recently named Mount Edith Cavell. The letting of these large contracts proved to be tricky, placing Harkin in a position of being lobbied by those with influence at Ottawa, a situation he had to deal with often during his career as one controlling substantial government development funds. In this instance, Captain J.A. Stephen, an acquaintance connected with the Militia Department, had written a personal note concerning the tenders and posed the leading question, "I suppose 'Bun' there is no advantage to getting one's tender in early?" As in all such instances, Harkin's reply had been courteous but firm, consistent with his trademark integrity: "Dear Stephen....You are quite right in your idea that there would be no advantage in getting a tender in early. As long as the tenders are received within the time limit set all are given equal consideration."[28] Indeed, the use of contracts on these projects would prove disappointing, only seven-and-one-half miles of the over twenty-one miles contracted for that year being completed.

The 1919 work had been placed under the direction of Chief Highway Engineer Captain A.W. Gray, but after he resigned due to an injury sustained in a fall from his horse, Rocky Mountains Superintendent J.M. Wardle was appointed to take over Banff-Windermere supervision. The promotion of Wardle to acting chief highway engineer proved to be a godsend, and was just the first of his many steps up the departmental ladder. An energetic and highly organized individual, he instigated two changes that proved vital to the road's timely completion—winter

James M. Wardle, 1926. Byron Harmon photograph. The promotion of Wardle to highway engineer on the Banff-Windermere Road in 1919 was the key to success in Harkin's efforts to have a timely completion of his most important postwar tourism project. [WMCR, V263 NA-3995]

clearing of the right-of-way and utilization of day labour under his direct supervision. Although the commissioner preferred contract work, results spoke for themselves as the costs were relatively equal and the practice allowed for more time to be spent on finishing, resulting in a better road. In comparing the two methods, Wardle firmly stated, "I might say that the quantity and quality of the work done is vastly better than that of the latter contracts."[29] By 1921 he had 180 men and forty-five teams of horses at work on construction with four trucks hauling supplies to the various work camps, and he was estimating the final project costs at $500,000. In his desire to adopt improved methods and techniques, he soon came to be regarded as an innovator and one of the ablest highway engineers in western Canada.

With the Banff-Windermere work well in hand under Wardle's capable direction in late 1919, Harkin turned his attention to other important matters looking toward the day of its completion. One concern was a lack of an organized national approach to tourism promotion, something he had identified as early as 1913 in mentioning that some countries were creating a "department for tourists" and in 1915 when he had suggested Canada needed "a federal Tourist Bureau." These earlier suggestions had been focused on supporting the role that tourism played in the parks, but his emerging desire to help solve Canada's greater economic ills now led him to shift attention to tourism development in the country as a whole. For example, in his 1921 annual report he described Canada's, not just national parks', attributes: "In her climate, her virgin forests, her big game and fishing, her picturesque Indian and French Canadian traditions, her great hinterland of wilderness, [Canada] possesses a wealth of natural attractions capable of practically unlimited development."[30] But despite his visionary proposal for a national approach, no action was forthcoming, and Harkin therefore concentrated on a number of the "good roads" associations that had sprung up to promote regional travel systems.

In particular, he co-operated closely with the Calgary Good Roads Association and its influential president James W. Davidson, a booster for upgrading of the Calgary-Banff road and the improvement of connections between American and Canadian parks. So successful was Davidson that in 1919 he managed to get private American subscriptions and financial support from the U.S. Parks Service to have his organization make improvements to "the trail between Waterton Lakes, Alberta and the Glacier Park Highway System." Upon doing so, he appealed to Harkin to contact National Parks Service Director Stephen Mather and help the cause by bringing the work to his attention and inviting him to visit Banff so that he could inspect it en route.[31] While the commissioner did not comply, it did not mean he was not interested in the role of roads in bringing the two countries' parks closer together. Remaining positive about the relationship between American and Canadian parks, in his 1921 report he postulated that new roads could help create a pan-park movement:

> As soon as the Vermilion-Sinclair road is completed the Canadian parks will automatically become part of the United States park-to-park system of highways forming a link in what will be an international park-to-park route unequalled in the world. There is I believe no room for jealousy between the two park systems. The aims of both are identical and they cannot help rendering an international service to each other. Everything that is done by the United States service to make its parks more attractive will help to swell the tide of travel which will eventually touch the Canadian parks and vice versa every improvement in the Canadian parks will have a similar effect where the United States parks are concerned.[32]

In time, his association with the good roads movement led to an invitation for Harkin to speak at the June 1922 national convention of the Canadian Good Roads Association held in Victoria. By the early 1920s his reputation in the tourism and conservation worlds had led to several such engagements, and that year he also spoke at the meeting of the International Association of Game and Fish Commissioners at Madison, Wisconsin. The Victoria speech was typical of Harkin's approach, preferring to speak extemporaneously rather than from a prepared text, a habit he made light of in his opening remarks: "Mr. Chairman and gentlemen: As I watched the proceedings I realized that before I left Ottawa I made a serious error. I have a very strong objection to reading papers, although I often have to write them. I always think we can reach an audience much more effectively if we talk about our ideas directly, even though we stumble more or less. However, as the time has come to speak, I feel I could have done better if I had put my thoughts on paper, particularly on a subject as big as 'National Parks'." In using this off-the-cuff approach, he had to be careful about keeping his audience's attention, and often interjected notes of humour. For example, early in this speech he made the point that Canada's national parks were entirely democratic, "administered on the basis of no monopoly, no special privilege for anyone" where "a poor man shall have just as many rights as a rich man," providing a small illustration for emphasis: "We are something like a clerk in a departmental store when dealing with a fussy old woman who claimed some particular privilege and was told it was against the rules. She said: 'I would have you know that I am one of the directors' wives.' He said: 'It would make no difference, madam, if you were his only wife'."[33]

In this speech, Harkin pointed out the value of the Banff-Windermere project in completing the International Grand Circle Route: "A motorist can start at Calgary for instance and proceed to Banff with a side trip to Lake Louise, then proceed through the very heart of the main Rockies to the Columbia Valley, south to Cranbrook, proceeding to Spokane and then on to Vancouver and Victoria; turning southward one can then proceed along down the Pacific Coast, taking in the United States National parks at Crater Lake and Mount Rainier and the various coast cities, Yosemite National Park and the Sequoia Giant Trees; then crossing the Rockies again proceed to the Grand Canyon of the Colorado, Yellowstone National Park, United States Glacier National Park, Canada's Waterton Lakes Park and thence back to Calgary." Quoting a travel expert, he expected that in its first year the highway would bring into Canada something over $5 million. Apart from its emphasis on the importance of tourist roads, the speech also called for more and better publicity if the potential of this huge market was to be unlocked. As he admitted, the branch had been somewhat deficient in this regard: "We have never done very much propaganda...we have a working agreement with the railways that they shall do the publicity work regarding Parks and we devote our energies and appropriations to making the Parks accessible to the public." But there was a price to pay, as "when our estimate comes up in the House and we are asking for large sums... we find people even in the House of Commons who have no idea what parks are."[34]

As a former newspaperman, concern about this situation was not new—it had bothered Harkin since 1914 when the last significant funds had been available to publish *Sprig* and the two or three other pamphlets in circulation at the time. Some steps had been taken to attempt to keep the park message in the public's consciousness, including the creation of several productions in co-operation with the Exhibits and Publicity Branch of the Department of Trade and Commerce featuring the new medium of motion pictures. In 1919 he reported that "a number of very fine films of the parks were secured by them and sent out through exchanges practically all over the country," and was already looking forward to their distribution in the U.S. and abroad. As well, the branch had put together a large collection of hand-coloured lantern slides and these were loaned to church and other organization for projection, and some of the same images were available to magazine writers and others needing illustrations for publication.[35] In his 1922 speech, Harkin could report that a small appropriation had been made available for publicity purposes, and material was being prepared for a number of "fresh publications" and some souvenir items. One, "a new descriptive booklet on the parks through the central Rockies along the mainline of the Canadian Pacific Railway," was to pave the way for many more branch guidebooks to follow. Its prototype was a 1917 co-operative publishing effort between the Parks Branch and the Topographic Surveys Branch, the ninety-seven-page *Description of & Guide to Jasper*, co-written by DLS surveyor M.P. Bridgland and Geographic Board of Canada secretary Robert Douglas. The new guidebook, entitled *Through the Heart of the Rockies and Selkirks*, was written by Mabel Williams, who had assisted with *Sprig*. Over 100 pages in length, it contained chapters describing the mountains and the various parks; trails, drives, and climbs around Banff; vegetation and wildlife in the parks; advice on trail trips and information on place names and altitudes, all copiously adorned with photographs and accompanied by a fold-out map. Harkin wrote the foreword, similar in tone to the closing of *Sprig*, informing Canadians of their birthright to national parks and promoting their healing powers.[36]

While these initiatives were a first step, by the time he mentioned the need for more and better publicity in his Victoria address further changes were afoot that were to assist in meeting this goal. In 1920, he had begun drafting new legislation to replace the *Dominion Forest Reserves and Parks Act*, incorporating a proposed change of name for the parks from Dominion Parks to Canadian National Parks. As he explained, "It is considered that the word 'Canadian' is preferable to the word 'Dominion' because it identifies the parks at once with Canada. The word 'National' alone might have been used but the United States use it for their National Parks and it might be confusing to the public."[37] With the expectation that the new parks act would soon be in place, the department decided to go forward with the new name in the 1921–1922 fiscal year, creating a somewhat confusing situation when the legislation failed to proceed; the parks were still legally described as "Dominion Parks" but their administrative body was the "Canadian National Parks Branch" (later shortened to National Parks Branch), an anomaly that would continue for almost a decade. At the same time, the branch began to go through a major reorganization, reflecting Harkin's success at expanding its mandate, including an enlargement to the Historic Sites Division, the aforementioned addition of the Town Planning Division, and the creation of a formal Publicity Division. The reorganization was extremely important for the future of promotional work, as through the efforts of J.C. Campbell, who was appointed director, the new Publicity Division immediately began to make the newly named organization's presence felt.

Harkin was most interested in using his new resources to celebrate the major accomplishment represented by the completion of the Banff-Windermere Highway. The 587-square-mile Kootenay National Park had been created with little fanfare by order-in-council of April 21, 1920, and he intended that it be celebrated in conjunction with the official opening of the road, scheduled for June 30, 1923. Its name had been adopted to recognize the Kootenay Indians, who had frequented the area in earlier times, and the similarly named river flowing through it, although Randolph Bruce, who always expressed a certain pride of ownership as the source of the idea for the road and the park, argued strenuously in 1922 that the park name should be changed to "Columbia." Harkin understood his argument that being located in the Columbia River watershed and as a name "venerated" by Americans, it had a great power to attract tourists. Accordingly, he sought to include the name change in yet another draft of a new parks act being prepared for the 1923 session, but when it again failed to proceed he apparently abandoned the idea. He did not, however, ignore another of Bruce's admonishments, his call that promotional efforts could "by no means cease when the last load of gravel goes on this new road" and that as partners in its creation, "it will be up to us to prove that our judgment is right by going out and getting the tourist business, so the C.P.R. and the Provincial Government, as well as the Dominion, get some return for their money."[38]

Indeed, much was at stake for Harkin's reputation in the road's fate, and consequently he pulled out all the stops in its promotion. As part of its new publicity activities, the branch issued monthly news releases in both French and English in the form of the *Canadian National Parks News-Bulletin*, containing information on the pending completion of the highway. Similarly, with numerous small Canadian radio stations hungry for material, scripts under the titles "Completion of the Banff-Windermere Highway" and "Parks Along the Banff-Windermere Highway" were made available. However, these measures were overshadowed by the two main thrusts of the campaign–production of a high quality guidebook focusing on the road and a major lecture tour undertaken by Campbell. By late 1922 Harkin was being inundated with requests from writers wishing to provide promotional material, but he was replying "my publicity division is loaded down with work and has about all it can take care of for the winter," noting that the branch itself already had a guidebook in preparation.[39] *The Banff-Windermere Highway* was once again composed by Williams, concentrating mainly on the history of the park, the great engineering achievement the road represented, and descriptions of the links it forged with Canadian and

American highway systems. Proving to be an immensely popular souvenir of the new roadway, within months its first run of 25,000 copies was depleted, requiring a reprint of 15,000 copies, and it would soon reappear in a revised edition under the title *Kootenay National Park and the Banff-Windermere Highway*.

Campbell's efforts were equally fruitful, beginning with a tour of Ontario and Quebec in the autumn of 1922 and proceeding to western Canadian cities early in 1923. A letter Harkin received in April from A.B. MacKay, president of the Calgary Automobile Club, spoke to its reception:

> Since arriving in this City, Mr. J.C. Campbell has been hard at work in our midst and has attracted the very keenest interest in our citizens to the work which you are so strongly developing in your Department. Mr. Campbell lunched with the Directors of this Club on Wednesday and afterwards addressed them, and a once created the impression upon his hearers, that, in quite a unique way, your Department is carrying out a great work in the National Parks. He has addressed several meetings of a public nature in the City during the last few days, and has obviously established a very excellent impression in the minds of the public, and we look for the very greatest success to follow from his tour in the States.[40]

Harkin shared this hope and was not disappointed—the Publicity Division, manned by Campbell, an "official lecturer," and a "motion picture operator," visited fourteen western and Pacific coast states during 1923–1924, delivering 277 lectures and 753 film screenings, reportedly reaching 74,375 persons.

As the date for the Banff-Windermere opening approached, Harkin became distracted with ensuring that the guests in attendance would reflect the importance of the event to Dominion-provincial relations and the reputation of the department. No effort was spared in his attempts to cajole, beg, or otherwise convince prominent representatives to attend, and in this he proved highly effective. The guest list was gold-plated, including Minister of Public Works Dr. J.H. King, representing the Dominion government; Premiers J. Oliver and H. Greenfield and Lieutenant Governors W. Nichol and R.G. Brett representing the provinces of British Columbia and Alberta; Vice-President D.C. Coleman, representing the CPR; R. Ross Eakins, representing the U.S. Department of the Interior; Harvey M. Toy, representing the Governor of California; and a host of Harkin's friends and supporters, including A.O. Wheeler, James Davidson, and Randolph Bruce. His annual report for 1923–1924 indicated just how successful his efforts had been:

> The formal ceremonies took place at Kootenay Crossing, B.C., in the presence of distinguished representatives of the Dominion, Provincial and United States Governments, the Canadian Pacific Railway and other organizations.... Hon. Dr. J.H. King, Federal Minister of Public Works, representing the Dominion Government, presided at the simple but impressive ceremony and at its conclusion Dr. R.G. Brett, Lieutenant-Governor of Alberta, and the Hon. Walter Nichol, Lieutenant-Governor of British Columbia, severed the ribbons barring the highway and the first motor way across the Central Rockies was declared open to the motorists of the world....Most of the chief Canadian cities had newspaper men in attendance while special representatives secured an account of the proceedings for Boston, Pittsburgh, New York, Chicago, Portland, Tacoma, Seattle, Minneapolis, Los Angeles and San Francisco journals. In addition, syndicates and magazines obtained particulars of the occasion through special correspondents.[41]

In its coverage, the *Banff Crag and Canyon* focused on the importance of the event to the country, noting that the opening was "a large feather in Canada's national plume," bringing home to the nearly 1200 in attendance "the fullness and richness of the glorious scenery to be

Lieutenant-Governors R.G. Brett of Alberta and Walter Nichol of British Columbia officially open the Banff-Windermere Highway, June 30, 1923. As he typically did, Harkin (third from left with cap in hand) remained in the background during the official ceremony for what was one of the major infrastructure accomplishments of his career. [GA, NA-3705-20]

beheld in the Canadian Rockies."[42] The commissioner was not among the speakers, playing his usual background role, but he was pleased with the results, writing his old friend Tom Wilson two days later, "The opening took place Saturday, and was most successful from every point of view."[43] However, tangible recognition for his efforts was not long in coming. Surveyor M.P. Bridgland, who had been mapping the new park and was acquainted with him from his earlier work in Jasper, secured agreement from Surveyor General Deville the same year to name a prominent peak visible from the highway in the Mitchell Range south and east of Vermilion Crossing as Mount Harkin.

Harkin's dream for the new highway was quickly realized; although 1923 proved to be a particularly wet season and some of the connecting roads were in bad condition, the Banff-Windermere saw 8,000 vehicles pass over it, contributing, he believed, to the "combined advance of 15,000 visitors" recorded at Banff and Lake Louise that summer.

The following year, 1924, saw traffic on the road essentially double to 15,500 vehicles, leading to a record attendance at Banff of over 104,000, fully half arriving in their automobiles. With his 1912 vision being fulfilled, the results sparked renewed work on other important roadways, the major one being the "Kicking Horse Trail," leading from Laggan to Field utilizing in part the old CPR railroad grade through the Kicking Horse Pass made available by construction of the Spiral Tunnels. The extension of this road on to Golden from Field linking up with the route up the Columbia Valley from Golden to Invermere, while not officially opened until July 1927, would provide another popular motor tour known as the "Scenic Lariat."

The Banff-Windermere Highway completed and work on other roads progressing rapidly, the branch began to pay increasing attention to the amenities available for tourists. Good accommodation was a necessity, but its supply was beyond the purview of the department, and Harkin could readily agree with Davidson's comment in a July 1920 letter, "You have doubtless heard about the camp at Windermere established by the CPR. This will be of great help to us after the Windermere road is completed."[44] This camp turned out to be only the forerunner of a whole series the railway built in the twenties to address the needs of the new middle-class motoring public in the mountains, in the case of the Banff-Windermere beginning with establishment of the Radium Hot Springs Bungalow Camp in 1923, followed by later developments at Storm Mountain and Vermilion Crossing. The same year Harkin could also happily note the completion of the first unit of the Jasper Park Lodge by Canadian National Railways, contributing to a record season at Jasper.

With private enterprise taking on structural accommodation, his own attention could be focused on the services to be provided by his new Town Planning Division, including the laying out of townsites at Marble Canyon (which was never built) and at Radium Hot Springs, both of which were designed by Thomas Adams, and the more rudimentary requirements of the growing number of budget-conscious tourists arriving in cars. He had first spoken to these in March 1920 in response to a request from the Good Roads League of BC soliciting his support

Douglas family motoring on the Sinclair Creek section of the Banff-Windermere Highway, ca. 1923. As Harkin had hoped, the new road and its amenities attracted auto tourists to Canada's mountain national parks. [WMCR, V178-90]

for a resolution it had passed with respect to "Parks along Highways," stating, "For some years I have advocated the development of small areas at intervals along automobile roads for the use of the motoring public for picnic and camping purposes. It seems to me that this is a natural and obvious development in connection with motor roads."[45] Addressing this issue with Cory, Harkin repeated his belief that with more people travelling by automobile each year, "I do not think there is any other feature that would contribute more to tourist motoring than reservations of this kind."[46] As mentioned, he had already grasped the importance of such tourist amenities in the pre-war period, and in 1923 a major expansion to the Rundle campgrounds at Banff was undertaken incorporating 277 campsites serviced by nineteen shelters, two service buildings, and a caretaker's residence, all designed "with a view to establishing more suitable and effective architecture in the various social settlements."[47] At the same time, smaller camping facilities and picnic grounds were under development along the new Banff-Windermere route, again under Adams's creative direction.

These accomplishments were heartening in Harkin's efforts to have tourism play an important role in Canada achieving financial stability, and by 1925 he could already report that success was at hand. He also noted some other important benefits: "While the increasing volume of travel is important from the economic point of view, the most gratifying feature is the more democratic use that is being made of the parks themselves. Time was when visitors consisted almost wholly of wealthy tourists who made the parks a stopping place for a few days on a transcontinental tour. The coming of the motor and the establishment of motor camp sites and small bungalow hotels in practically every one of the parks has brought the national playgrounds within the reach of thousands."[48] Having set out in 1919 to accomplish economic goals for Canada, by 1925 Harkin found himself in the happy position of also achieving unforeseen humanitarian and social benefits in the national parks in line with his long-held aspirations.

NINE

Hands Off Our National Parks

HARKIN'S CHALLENGES IN HIS efforts to have the Parks Branch play a significant role in Canada's postwar recovery were not the only ones he faced in the reconstruction period. The same recession and drought that affected the country's economy brought with them direct threats to park lands and waters. Industrial activities such as logging, mining, petroleum exploration, and limestone quarrying had been a fact of life in the reservations he inherited in 1911, a manifestation of the *raison d'être* of the Department of the Interior in developing western Canadian resources. But now the nascent conservation movement looked askance at these activities and perceived grave danger in proposals to improve agriculture and spark development through utilization of water for irrigation and power purposes. The Dominion Water Power

Branch, the body regulating these matters, was a sister agency within the department, and, having learned from his struggles with Forestry, Harkin would have to walk a fine line and find creative solutions in his emerging goal to protect parks in the face of its opposing position.

Upon Harkin's coming to office, resource extraction activities in parks were an accepted fact. Commercial logging and coal mining had been actively carried out in Rocky Mountains Park for a quarter of a century, the Eau Claire and Bow River Lumber Company acquiring a number of timber berths in the Kananaskis and near Castle Mountain as early as 1883 and the Canadian Anthracite Coal Company beginning operations in the thirty-six-square-mile Cascade Coal Basin near the confluence of the Cascade and Bow rivers in 1886. The thriving mining village of Anthracite had rivalled pioneer Banff in size, and mining activity had also been commenced at nearby Canmore in 1888 and Bankhead by 1904. These resource towns and their attendant coal mines resided within the park after the boundary extension of 1902, as did some early limestone quarry operations further east near Gap Lake. On the lands incorporated into Waterton Lakes Forest Park in 1895, staking of petroleum claims had begun in 1889–1890 along Oil (Cameron) Creek, and in 1901 John Lineham formed the Rocky Mountain Development Company to begin drilling near the planned townsite of Oil City. Given the permissive tenor of the new *Forest Reserves and Parks Act* and the influence of the Canadian Commission of Conservation as background, Harkin well understood the role these industries played. Most importantly, they provided significant revenues to the treasury, as they were all on government leases and, in addition, paid royalties on the coal, timber, or rock extracted; in 1911–1912 alone the revenue of the Mining Lands Branch in the parks was some $58,500, more than double the $27,700 of the Parks Branch.

Accordingly, the years immediately after his appointment were a very active period in the expansion of industrial activities. At Canmore, which had superseded Anthracite by 1900 with better steam coal, various leases were consolidated under the Pennsylvania-headquartered Canmore Coal Company in 1911. A year earlier a new English interest, Georgetown Collieries, began supplying the steamship trade from a

No. 1 mine at Canmore, Alberta, ca. 1915. Natural resource development, in particular mining on park lands, was part of the situation Harkin inherited on taking office. [GA, NA-4074-5]

mine to the west and had established the forty-residence Georgetown townsite by 1913. Also, by 1910 the cement works at Exshaw, which had experienced operating difficulties and were shut down, had been reinvigorated by the Canada Cement Company, a conglomerate headed by entrepreneur Max Aitken (the future Lord Beaverbrook) and his frequent business partner R.B. Bennett. But it was to be Jasper Park, where there was demand for coal by the two new transcontinental railways penetrating its lands, which received Harkin's particular attention. Its resource development coincided with his appointment and, as mentioned, his initial agenda for discussion with Douglas in late 1911 had included the matters of amendments to mining and quarrying regulations and the proposed lease of surface rights to allow Jasper Collieries to create a townsite in association with the mines. By the following April the new town, named after the Virginia mining community of Pocahontas, had thirty residences already completed and ten more under construction in response to the company's initiation of operations utilizing 150 miners. At the same time a small limestone quarry was put into operation by the Fitzhugh Lime and Stone Company near Disaster Point on the Athabasca River, its first production being used in the construction of Edmonton's Macdonald Hotel. Another mine, the Blue Diamond at Brûlé Lake just inside the eastern park boundary, appeared in 1916; both Pocahontas and Brûlé were larger than early Jasper.

Despite the importance of these resource extraction industries, with the exception of the surface operations that were his responsibility, Harkin initially took only a passing interest in their operations. Direct supervision was to be carried out by the Mining Lands Branch, while the needs of the associated communities were the responsibility of the companies themselves. In these circumstances, Harkin's point of view was that park appropriations should not be spent on development relating to their activities. In April 1914 he wrote to Bennett after being advised by the park engineer of the need for a road to connect the new village of Georgetown with Canmore: "You will note he states that such would be of no particular use insofar as Parks work is concerned there, other than to access one place to another. I do not therefore think we would be justified in spending such a large amount of money necessary to build this road."[1] Similarly, in June he responded to Bennett's concern about the public health risk associated with the lack of a proper water system in Canmore with the information that he had been unsuccessful in getting a supplementary appropriation to allow for its installation. He did, however, express the hope that a projected surplus in the Banff waterworks could help address the matter.[2] Unfortunately, no surplus materialized and little or no work was done, leading to an outbreak of dysentery in October 1916 that killed at least three Canmore children.[3] But its fate was certainly not the norm, as some towns, particularly Bankhead and Pocahontas, had, in their owners' attempts to make them model communities, much better municipal amenities than either Banff or Jasper. During the First World War they would thrive under the demands of wartime production.

Nonetheless, with growing conservation concerns, Harkin gradually paid more attention to resource development on park lands. A first step at increasing control was achieved on August 15, 1916 when an order-in-council was passed withdrawing all parks from quartz and placer mining regulations. Although existing mines were allowed to continue, the action was particularly effective in managing mining in the BC parks, where the provincial government continued to own the mineral rights. On the more intensively mined Alberta coal lands, a critical adjunct to park creation was a provision which allowed the minister the right to refuse the entry of any mineral claim if he felt that it unduly interfered with the park's primary purposes. However, this move still allowed for bona fide interests to operate under proper conditions. It was at Jasper, with its more recent resource development, where this most frequently occurred, Superintendent Rogers reporting in 1918 that applications for coal leases had been made on some of the lands added to the park and commenting, "You are no doubt aware that a coal mine does not improve the scenic beauties of any area where located...a coal camp is one of the hardest districts there is to protect game in the vicinity of...[as] the coal miner poaches if he gets the chance." Rogers thereafter continually and forcefully recommended against granting these leases, arguing that since the existing mines were experiencing labour shortages, there was no need to open more, and that the proposed holdings were in the best moose-breeding habitat in the park. But his pleas fell on deaf ears. From Ottawa's perspective, Harkin pointed out, the reasons for withholding approval did not meet the test of sufficiently satisfying the public interest and the leases would therefore be granted.

Even when a similar question came up in 1923 concerning applications for leases around Brûlé Lake, this time, according to the superintendent, with the agreement of the director of the Mines Branch that he "would back our Department in refusing any further grants of mining leases within the Park area," Harkin demurred. In this case, though, his explanation shed some light on his approach: "I think your argument...is a very sound one, but so long as our parks are open to applications for coal mining purposes under the regulations we cannot justly refuse any such applicants unless it can be clearly shown that the granting of such application would seriously interfere with the park."[4] These responses were effectively a case of bureaucratic demands subverting his own particular conservation beliefs, a product of the requirement of his job to respect laws and regulations in force when dealing with the specifics of a particular case.

Scope for taking a more progressive stance had first been provided in 1919 when a fundamental policy shift had been initiated by Interior Minister Arthur Meighen with respect to renewal of oil exploration activity near the original Lineham works at Waterton Lakes. Existing policy discouraged "promiscuous prospecting" by speculators who might cause fires and destroy game but did allow work to take place if it could be proven that park land was "of sufficient commercial value to justify developing." Harkin recommended to Cory in December 1919 that permits be issued for development of specific areas not to exceed forty acres, known to be of commercial value. Surprisingly, Meighen indicated that further mining or oil exploration in the mountain national parks should be prohibited, at least insofar as they were speculative ventures.[5] This change in emphasis provided Harkin with an opportunity to voice a new perspective. When Minister of Public Works King broached the idea of opening up the parks to further commercial development in October 1922, his response suggested that park lands should be maintained in their natural state for the recreational and aesthetic benefit of the public, arguing that tourism would soon be much more important in producing revenue than the utilization of forest and mineral resources.[6] This viewpoint was reiterated in a letter to Norman Luxton in 1927 in response to a request for assistance in gaining mining rights in Rocky Mountains Park for a friend, providing a picture of his thinking on the relationship between resource exploitation, tourism, and mankind's well-being:

> I think you are well aware that all of us who are concerned in the perpetuation of National Parks deem it imperative that we oppose all efforts at commercial development of natural resources lying within any park....We feel that the comparatively small areas constituting National Parks must be kept in their natural state for all time to come. We believe that these Parks kept in their natural state of beauty, unspoiled by mining camps, lumbering operations and such, will continue for all time to bring in more money to the Dominion of Canada than any utilization

> of any of the natural resources as such. From a commercial standpoint therefore, we believe that the preservation of the Parks will work out with the greatest advantage to the Dominion but at the same time the perpetuation of the Parks, with all their wonderful beauty, will continue to administer to the recreational, aesthetic and spiritual needs of our people.[7]

Harkin's changing attitude about resource development was at least partly informed by a growing concern about water. The subject was almost completely tied up in the person of William Pearce who, as pointed out, had initially been a useful ally, in particular in matters of boundaries and roads. But water was different. Pearce's main concern was irrigation, which he believed could provide a solution to making the large semi-arid areas of southern Alberta productive. After launching a successful, albeit short-lived, demonstration project near Calgary in 1893, he had recognized that huge capital investment and land holdings would be necessary to make it possible on a commercial basis. Accordingly, he had turned his attention to the Canadian Pacific Railway as the most likely candidate able to carry it out. Through persistent arguments, he convinced the company to become involved in the Bow River Irrigation Scheme, whereby they would increase their existing landholdings along their southern Alberta mainline by completing their outstanding construction land grants and, through a diversion of the Bow River near Calgary, build works that could irrigate up to two million acres of semi-arid lands. In 1903 these irrigation lands were transferred to the CPR *en bloc*, and at the same time the railway convinced Pearce to leave government service and join its employ to supervise this and other projects, hoping that his wide connections would assist in greasing the skids.[8]

In 1916 Pearce was asked to sit on the Royal Commission on Economics and Development investigating the control and exploitation of Canada's natural resources under the chairmanship of Senator Lougheed, his particular task being to report on the condition of western lands and to recommend how to control their future disposition.

His studies had shown that the West's agriculturally based economy was close to total collapse due to the onset of the prolonged drought and a high rate of farm abandonment. Pearce believed the solution lay in irrigation, although his research concluded that under their present management there was only sufficient water in all mountain watercourses to successfully irrigate six million acres. He recalled a 1910 visit to India where he had witnessed the massive irrigation canals being used to take Himalayan waters to far distant plains, and believed that a similar scheme using the water of the Rockies could expand the potential to nine million acres. Suggesting the construction of a number of upstream dams and storage reservoirs to trap spring runoff and make it available for irrigation purposes, he also stated his belief that the works could provide a means for flood control and a basis for future hydroelectric power development.[9] One initiative that formed part of his CPR responsibilities was the Lethbridge Southeast Irrigation Project, aimed at establishing irrigation districts in the Lethbridge area to supply water to farmers through private canal systems. The department's irrigation services had carried out extensive hydrometric surveys of east-slope rivers, and in 1920 after a study of Waterton Lakes, Irrigation Superintendent F.H. Peters recommended them as an ideal location for a reservoir in connection with the Lethbridge project.

As mentioned, despite the problems associated with Robert Cooper's superintendency, between 1917 and 1920 visitation to Waterton had doubled, mainly due to road and bridge improvements, and in the latter year Harkin confidently predicted that, "All indications point to this becoming one of the most popular of the Dominion parks in the future." His success in gaining the 1914 boundary extension to join the park with the American Glacier National Park set the stage for an eventual cross-border connection with an automobile road, and also the possibility, first vetted the same year by Great Northern Railway president Louis Hill, of railway lodge development at Waterton similar to that occurring in the American park. Therefore his reaction was cautious when first contacted in November 1919 by E.F. Drake, director of the Reclamation Service, asking if raising the water would impair the park's scenic beauties. Harkin stated his main concern as potential impacts on the recently surveyed Waterton townsite, since its recreational potential could be affected, but he delayed a full response until he had an opportunity to weigh the benefits to agriculture against those of the development of the park. Once he heard the study's preliminary results, though, his position hardened. The project would see the creation of some 100,000 acre feet of storage with the erection of a forty-foot dam at the narrows between Upper and Lower Waterton lakes, completely inundating the townsite and requiring its removal to a new location near Linnet Lake. In indicating that the lakes would still be useful for boating and fishing, Peters did admit that some scenery would be engulfed, although he claimed the public would prefer the irrigation scheme to a recreational park. Fortunately the project needed ministerial approval, which offered Harkin an opportunity to make a case for preservation, something he rapidly became convinced was required.

Although Harkin initially left it to recently appointed Superintendent Bevan to attempt to influence local opinion and gain support for opposition, it was not long before his growing alarm led him to use his own position and act behind the scenes to attempt to gain the upper hand in the widening debate. He first staked out his position on the Waterton scheme in his annual report of March 1921 when the project was still being held in abeyance due to lack of funding to undertake it. Unequivocal in his remarks, Harkin made what was perhaps the most visionary statement of his entire career about the need to protect park lands in their natural condition:

> The stand taken by the Parks Branch with regard to such applications is that the parks are the property of all the people of Canada and that consequently they should not be developed for the benefit of any one section of the country or of private interests; second, that such development constitutes an invasion of the fundamental principles upon which parks have been established, namely, the conservation of certain areas of primitive landscape with all their original conditions of plant and

Upper Waterton Lake with emerging townsite in the middle ground, ca. 1910. F.H. Riggall photograph. The proposal that Waterton Lakes be dammed for irrigation purposes in 1919 thereby flooding the new townsite sparked Harkin's career-long battle for the sanctity of park lands and waters. [WMCR, V26]

> animal life and other natural features intact. National parks are in reality natural museums of undisturbed nature. As time goes on they will probably be the only places which will present a perfect picture of natural conditions such as existed when the white man first came to this continent. The national parks from this aspect are valuable now but they will be many times more so 100 years hence when probably every part of the country will have been settled.[10]

Few were interested in these remarks, and as information on the benefits of providing water to 75,000 acres of unproductive lands began to be discussed after the release of Peters's report, Harkin found himself facing some powerful interests. It took time for the debate to heat up, but by early 1922 Alberta newspapers strongly favoured irrigation, and at the same time the minister was being lobbied with resolutions from the councils of Fort Macleod, Lethbridge, and several irrigation districts as well as petitions signed by virtually every community in southern Alberta, all supporting the scheme. The United Farmers of Alberta (UFA), which had recently won the Alberta provincial election, predictably favoured it and organized their southern Alberta locals to work for its approval. A welcome exception was Pincher Creek near Waterton, where both the town council and the UFA local sent resolutions opposing the idea, and Bevan, through his hard work, organized a few individual voices of opposition. One of the strongest was area resident L.E. Dimsdale, who in a letter to the editor of the *Lethbridge Herald* in November 1921 stated that "this is the first move of private interests to get a hold of our National parks, and if it is granted, the government can scarcely refuse similar requests."[11] This mirrored Harkin's own concern, which he shared in a letter to a supporter at the University of Alberta written seven months later: "The creation of a precedent in the commercialization of our parks seems to me to be a most serious matter. If the Waterton Irrigation Scheme goes through, how can the power interests be turned down; if the power interests are recognized, how can the lumbermen be refused permission to destroy the forest which is such an essential beauty to the parks...the next step would be a demand on the part of sportsmen for an open season with respect to wildlife."[12]

Although the forces arrayed against him were strong, Harkin did have a few arrows in his quiver. The decision on the project was to be made by Minister of the Interior James Lougheed in the spring of 1922, but in the federal election of December 1921 the Liberals under the leadership of William Lyon Mackenzie King squeaked out a narrow minority government. After the farmer-based Progressive Party, which had taken all the seats in Alberta, refused to have one of its members take a cabinet seat, Prime Minister King invited Alberta Liberal Charles Stewart to accept the position of minister of the Interior. A central

Minister of the Interior Charles Stewart, 1926. Stewart was to be a key decision-maker in Harkin's efforts to regulate park waters and to gain passage of a new national parks act. [GA, NC-6-11900]

Alberta farmer, he had held several ministerial portfolios until replacing A.L. Sifton as premier in late 1917, but then he had been swept aside in the rising tide of the UFA political movement in the 1921 election. Appearing to understand what was at stake, Stewart held the key Interior portfolio for most of the next decade, an extremely important one for the future of resource control in his home province as well as the park system that incorporated a good deal of its mountain lands.

At the same time as these new, perhaps more sympathetic ears appeared on the federal scene, another government with an interest in the issue also began to weigh in. As international waters, Waterton

Lakes were subject to the control of the International Joint Commission, a Canadian-American intergovernmental body established by the Boundary Waters Treaty of 1909 to deal with the conservation and development of waters extending across the international border. If the minister approved the project, specific plans would have to be drawn up and referred to the commission for approval before construction on the dam could begin. To the surprise of the Reclamation Service when its survey party sought access to the American side in March 1922, permission was denied. The same month the *Bulletin* of the country's National Parks Association argued against the dam, stating that it would do "irreparable damage to broad shores and magnificent valleys covering the floor of the Kootenay Valley at our end of the lake at a point which is the key to the entire future development northward of Glacier National Park."[13] In addition, in February 1922 Harkin began receiving strong support from some influential Americans, including A.O. Weese of the Ecological Society of America and George Bird Grinnell, one of the United States' foremost conservationists as head of the University of California's Museum of Vertebrate Zoology and founder of the powerful Audubon Society, who called the project "to the last degree shortsighted."

With no organized voice of opposition in his own country, Harkin's correspondence with these American interests indicated an attempt to find support among the myriad of game preservation and conservation organizations flourishing in their country. He was aware that the earliest conservation movement in the U.S., the influential Sierra Club formed in 1892, had opposed an American dam project, the 1913 Hetch Hetchy works, which had seen a portion of Yosemite Park removed for reservoir purposes in the provision of water to San Francisco. He also knew of the success of his American counterpart, Stephen T. Mather, appointed the first director of the National Park Service after its creation by Congress in August 1916, in organizing an effective public voice specifically in support of parks. Mather was his complete antithesis, a successful Chicago businessman with strong political connections who had made a fortune from western borax mines and had no qualms about using some of it to support the drive for a parks bureau and then, once created, to help fund it. In 1919 he personally sponsored the formation of the National Parks Association, under the direction of publicist Robert Sterling Yard, who he had employed in the struggle to create the Parks Service. The principal objectives of the organization were to protect the parks, to enlarge the park system (with a view to making it "an American trademark in competition for the world's travel"), and to promote public enjoyment of parks without impairing them.[14] Harkin's initial opposition to the Waterton scheme had likely been informed by his knowledge of this body, and it provided a model that he would dearly have loved to copy. This wish was conveyed in a letter to Weese in June 1922 when he again expressed concern about the important precedent of the Waterton issue, identifying "the greatest need in Canada for an organization something along the lines of the American National Parks Association which, being independent of the Government is free to actively carry on work in defence of National Parks."[15] Little could Harkin realize that comments he had made in recent correspondence with A.O. Wheeler were about to lead to that desire being fulfilled.

Ironically, that correspondence concerned a matter upon which he and the Alpine Club's director had been disagreeing for some time. Harkin was a strong supporter of the club, seeing in it an opportunity for those of limited means to experience nature and partake of health-giving recreational activities in mountain surroundings and believing its members to be effective spokespeople for the parks' alpine attractions. As mentioned, Wheeler had left Interior in 1910 to work as the club's director, and although continuing to occasionally work as a contract surveyor, he was always seeking ways to increase his own and the club's income. In 1914 he had developed a concept for affordable walking tours, which would overcome the expensive costs of travel and accommodation for those using the railway, and by 1920 had been able to acquire a substantial property adjacent to the club's Sulphur Mountain clubhouse and had set up the Banff to Mount Assiniboine Walking and Riding Tour. Utilizing cabins and camps leased from the CPR and the Eau Claire Lumber Company at strategic points on the way into the fabled peak, Wheeler offered conducted trips on a circle route as well as the option of a horseback side trip through the aegis of his outfitting associate, the Alpine Pack Train. However, local outfitters objected to the side trip service and, although he strongly supported the walking tour concept, Harkin found himself trying to play the role of honest broker in settlement of the dispute.

Wheeler mounted a letter writing campaign from club members to the minister characterizing the outfitters' objections as a threat to the future of the walking tours. In fact, in a gross overstatement, in his New Year 1922 club greetings he even indicated it was a threat to the Alpine Club itself, stating, "There is a cloud upon our horizon that not only threatens the freedom, but the very existence of the Club and its life work of opening up the mountain areas of the Canadian Rockies."[16] Harkin was outraged, and in a pointed missive to Wheeler complained that the members' letters "seem to have the impression that the opposition is largely against the Walking Tour Scheme and not confined to the one phase of the matter as is actually the case," and, with respect to the threat to the club, "I do not see how this statement can be justified." In addition, he noted that the department's support came at some risk: "The financial support afforded by the Department to the Walking Tour has been so large as compared with the number of patrons to date, that it has possibly laid itself open to criticism in this respect." In summary, he put forward his belief that "the circular greeting in question does not make clear the point at present in dispute and conveys...an erroneous idea of the Department's attitude to the Walking Tour and Alpine Club organizations."[17] When Wheeler claimed to the assistant deputy minister that agreement to a ban on side trips would result in the cancellation of a proposed Alpine Club camp at Palliser Pass, it was the last straw. In a memorandum to Cory, Harkin recommended "Mr. Wheeler be advised that the Department cannot agree to the condition he imposes with regard to side trip service on the Walking Tour routes, and that if such service is supplied by the Alpine Club pack train the Department must withdraw its financial support."[18] The recommendation was approved and forwarded to Wheeler on March 31, 1922.

While this tempest in a teapot wended its way through the departmental bureaucracy, Harkin was distracted by the Waterton matter.

During March he was preparing what proved to be an eighty-six-page memorandum to Cory refuting the Reclamation Service's claims in favour of the dam, and presenting maps and statistical data to support the Parks Branch position. On March 6, in a letter to Wheeler on the walking tour issue, he made a passing reference to the departmental debate and public controversy. In his March 20 response, which opened with the conciliatory observation that "we have not seen quite eye to eye, but I know that we both have the same object in view," the director referred to his lack of awareness of the matter: "What you say about the clash between Parks and Irrigation interests at Waterton Lakes Park is quite new to me. I have heard nothing of it. If you will be so good as to put me wise, and let me know if the Alpine Club can help, I shall be glad to move in the matter. I think you know that our interests and sympathies lie with the parks."[19] Wheeler's alternately aggressive and friendly approach in support of his position was consistent with his *modus operandi* in dealing with important interests such as the CPR and the Parks Branch, but he realized, at the end of the day, that he needed good relations with Harkin. In one of his earlier letters he had assured him, "In expressing myself as I have I intend nothing personal. I am speaking in the best interests of the mountains as I and many others see them."[20] Harkin likewise understood Wheeler's value as an ally, and on April 6, after returning from an illness likely related to the matter, responded with a letter that spoke to that understanding. It opened with his concern about the precedent the Waterton project would create and then, in stating his philosophical position that it was necessary to retain certain areas inviolate, identified the struggle going on in the department:

> There naturally is a difference of opinion between the Park Service and the Irrigation Service with respect to the scheme....We in the Park Service are quite convinced that the lake cannot serve two purposes and also feel that the lake with its wonderful beauty is of more value to Canada, even financially, than the irrigation of 75,000 acres of land. Of course the precedent that the erection of this reservoir would create in the matter

> of commercializing National Parks is a matter of momentous concern to anyone who believes that a limited amount of virginal mountain scenery should be maintained absolutely in its natural state for the benefit of present and future generations.

He went on to express his surprise that, given the club's concern about the preservation of mountain scenery, "there was no action as far as I could see on the part of the Alpinists to present the other side publicly." Having thrown down the gauntlet, he ended with an admission: "I have some diffidence in writing to anyone upon a subject of this kind. Personally I believe in matters being settled on their own merits and not as a result of propaganda."[21]

This statement was quite remarkable, for it is one of the few times that Harkin shed light on his approach to carrying out his sensitive role as a senior bureaucrat. But despite this stricture and a stated dislike for "propaganda," desperate times called for desperate measures, and the thinly veiled suggestion that the Alpine Club "present the other side publicly" made it clear that, at least in this case, he was prepared to accept the director's offer "to move on the matter" and bend the rules. In the circumstances, it is interesting to speculate whether or not Harkin's initial mentioning of the Waterton matter was calculated to elicit a particular response or was merely a simple expression of frustration. Given Wheeler's success as a lobbyist on park boundaries and his obvious ability to mobilize support from the most significant recreational group in the parks in the walking tour debate, it is not out of the question that the commissioner had cleverly maneuvered his adversary to become his supporter. Intended or not, he had unleashed a powerful force in the cause of parks preservation, as Wheeler moved decisively to make good on his offer.

In advance of the annual meeting at the club's Palliser Pass camp, Wheeler circulated a memorandum to its executive and section heads citing Harkin's letter and enclosing a circular received from the U.S. National Parks Association on the same topic, asking that they "ascertain whether it is desired that action should be taken by the Club as a body." At the camp, W.W. Foster made a point in his presidential address of stressing that "the future of the Club was one of illimitable possibilities, not only from a mountaineering point of view, but that of preserving the great mountain playgrounds for the people, free from improper encroachment," before Wheeler reported on the results of his survey. The responses had been inconclusive, some considering that the raising of the water was an economic necessity and others that the matter was outside the club's jurisdiction. Nevertheless, the executive found there was sufficient support to draft a resolution for discussion: "With regard to the Waterton Lakes Irrigation Scheme, the Alpine Club of Canada, while it recognizes the undoubted economic value of the project, deplores the necessity of the action to be taken if it involves the destruction of the natural beauties of a park which the Government has already decided shall be set aside for the benefit of the public. In this resolution it realizes that its voice of protest is weak, but it considers it is a necessity to affirm its stand on a principle which involves a precedent, and desires that it may be kept fully informed by the Government of the details of the development of the scheme." In the ensuing debate, rancher F.W. Godsal spoke of "the absolute necessity of the dam to keep the southern Alberta farmer from total ruin due to drought," but the chairman disagreed and responded, "The desire is to prevent the establishment of a precedent which will enable any corporation to go in and take away any part of the parks," and was joined by the head of the Calgary section who proclaimed, "The government must not trespass on the people's rights." Aroused by these words, some of those present stated that they were not comfortable with the rather meek tenor of the resolution and an amendment was carried dropping the phrase "in this resolution it realizes that its voice is weak."[22] This was a significant change, for by passing a stronger resolution the club was indicating it was not a humble mouthpiece for protest but rather a committed body intent on having its position taken seriously.

As it transpired, even before this proposition was adopted there were signs that the Waterton project was in trouble. In response to the American decision to bar access to the Reclamation Service's survey party, Drake had complained, "It would be a practical impossibility now, or at any time in the near future, to secure the consent of the United States authorities to making any use whatever of that portion of Waterton Lake within Glacier National Park for reservoir purposes in connection with irrigation in Canada."[23] The intervention of the U.S. National Parks Association, Harkin's comprehensive memorandum prepared for the expected submission to the International Joint Commission, and the need for the Alberta government to be consulted also had influenced the minister. By the end of 1923, against the backdrop of a retreat of drought conditions as well as continuing hostility from the U.S. Parks Service, a decision was taken not to present the matter to the commission for adjudication. However, despite the initial impetus for a public voice for conservation in Canada beginning to fade with the Waterton irrigation project receding, there was already a greater threat lurking in the background that would require support of Harkin's position. By 1923 a controversy over the potential for water power development in Rocky Mountains Park had superseded the Waterton matter on both the branch's and the Alpine Club's agendas.

Along with exploitation of natural resources, use of park waters for power purposes was something Harkin had to deal with in coming to office. In previous legislation power development had not been addressed, but section 17 of the *Forest Reserves and Parks Act* stated that "the establishment and use of reservoirs, water power sites [and] power transmission lines" could be permitted by order-in-council. In 1910 a new and aggressive power company with a problem had anxiously awaited the passage of the new act. Calgary Power Company was the brainchild of thirty-year-old Montreal industrialist Max Aitken, who during a rail trip through the upper Bow Valley recognized its suitability for providing the electrical services that were going to be required by rapid development of the Calgary district. His interest first emerged in 1908, but at the time he could not get his Calgary associate R.B. Bennett to participate, and it was not until 1909, after the two became involved in the organization of the large Canada Cement venture at Exshaw, that the company was formed. Bennett was appointed a director and solicitor and remained part of its ownership structure until 1919 when it was sold to Isaak Walton Killam. Even after that he continued to act as solicitor, a factor that was to colour his relationship with Harkin while he was both inside and outside of political office.

Studies of upstream water sources had recently been carried out by the Department of the Interior, and in 1908 two engineers, C.B. Smith and W.G. Chase, had gained the rights to develop Horseshoe Falls, just downstream from Kananaskis Falls, as the best site for hydroelectric generation on the Bow River. Once formed, Calgary Power had quickly acquired their interests and by mid-1910 had the Horseshoe plant under construction, while Bennett went to work negotiating a lucrative long-term power contract with the City of Calgary. Incredibly, all this had been done without accurate stream flow information, and the company's promoters soon found that the depth of winter flow in the river slowed to a trickle. With contracts and demands for power they could clearly not meet, the ownership group had begun to madly search for alternatives. A second site was identified just upstream at Kananaskis Falls, but as the reservoir for this location would back up into a small piece of Rocky Mountains Park, the department hired the best hydro engineer in Canada, C.H. Mitchell, to examine the proposals of both Calgary Power and a competing interest. Mitchell submitted his report on September 8, 1911, noting that February stream flow was a paltry 600 cubic feet per second, but also advising that these flows could be doubled or tripled if the proper water storage facilities to impound spring runoff were built upstream on the tributaries of the Bow in the park, which was by then possible with the passage of the new act. He also recommended one company control the two facilities, a matter sealed by the election of September 21. Only a month previously Bennett had taken over presidency of Calgary Power and now he was the MP for the constituency in which these projects were located. In the spring of 1912 he wrote Aitken, "I have succeeded in getting the Dept. to agree to give us Kananaskis Falls & we will have the leases in due course."[24] This provided Calgary Power with the monopoly it sought; meantime, the company had not been slow to see the direction of Mitchell's work and as early as February 1911 Smith and Chase were busy on a preliminary survey of Lake Minnewanka, as Chief Hydrographer P.M Sauder reported, "with a view to making an application to the Department to create a storage reservoir for the Calgary Power and Transmission Company."[25]

These water power matters ultimately bore huge consequences for the future of Canada's national parks and the man at their helm. When Harkin took office several months after the passage of the new *Forest Reserves and Parks Act*, he was aware of ongoing discussions between the department and Calgary Power, but as a neophyte he could only stand by and watch as other, more seasoned government officials decided the fate of an important part of the park. With an agreement of March 1, 1912 between the minister and Calgary Power allowing for the construction of a control dam on Minnewanka's outlet raising its level by twelve feet, he was faced with a *fait accompli*. He attempted to put as good a face as possible on the decision in first annual report, noting, "Elaborate provisions were incorporated in the agreement adequately to protect park interests," and also pointed out that, from a practical perspective, the agreement's main advantage was that Calgary Power made provisions in the dam's construction to allow for the future development of a generator able to produce up to 1,000 horsepower, allowing the production of "an abundance of electric lighting for Banff, especially during the tourist season."[26] By 1913 both the Minnewanka dam and the Kananaskis plant were completed as foreseen, and further development lay dormant through the difficult war period until beginning to re-emerge in the 1920s. Now more experienced, Harkin was well prepared to take on the challenges it presented.

Beginning in 1918 the Water Power Branch made frequent reference to the growing population and industrialization of the prairies and to the fact that harnessing the Bow River's potential could take care of the electrical needs of up to 300,000 people. At the same time, Calgary was growing, leading city officials to express concern about the costs of operating a municipal steam-generating plant which supplemented power purchased from Calgary Power, as well as the availability of additional purchased power. Against this background, Calgary Power first made application to develop the Spray Lakes southeast of Banff as a hydroelectric reservoir in 1920, but this expensive initiative was dropped the next year in favour of a proposal to enlarge the existing

Lake Minnewanka works. In January 1921 its secretary, V.M. Drury, applied to Director Challies of the Water Power Branch "for permission to use the additional storage...it being understood that this permission would be subject to cancellation in the event of the Dominion Government proceeding with its development on the Cascade River."[27] Challies undertook to have the renewed application studied by engineer J.T. Johnston, and after meeting with him, Deputy Commissioner Williamson prepared a memorandum to his superior warning, "I would also say that the granting of the additional storage to the Company would no doubt lead to further application from the Company... and any affirmative action in the present case would possibly weaken the Department's stand in the case of further applications."[28]

As he typically did, Harkin took this advice under consideration and in a handwritten memo dated March 21, 1921, laid out the pros and cons. On one side of the ledger was "price we pay," which included "mud flats, fish, irrigation, steamboat," while on the other was "price public get," which, according to Drury would be a $10,000 addition to the company's revenue and a savings of $40,000 per annum for Calgary on its steam plant operation. This simple doodle turned out to be an important document in the history of Canadian park conservation for it is apparent that it convinced Harkin that the benefit to the public of further water storage at Lake Minnewanka, and in this case mostly shareholders of a private company, was too great a price to pay. His conclusion was reached at an important moment, as on August 30, 1921, obviously frustrated by delays and growing demands, the Montreal Engineering Company, Calgary Power's parent company, applied for permission to construct generating facilities in conjunction with their Minnewanka operations. This would involve raising the water level by some forty-seven feet and include a right of way for a pipeline paralleling the Cascade River from Minnewanka dam to the vicinity of Anthracite and a power house site on the Cascade capable of supplying up to 7,000 horsepower to the City of Calgary through the Calgary Power system.[29] Likely distracted by the Waterton Lakes irrigation matter, Harkin did not hear about the proposal until November when he received a Calgary newspaper clipping from Superintendent

Stronach at Banff and confirmed with him that company surveyors had recently been on the ground. Asked for a report, Wardle, who had recently been appointed chief engineer, did the math and concluded, "It appears from the figures on hand that the estimated development of 7000 h.p. from Cascade Creek would just about meet the average deficiencies of the Kananaskis plants during the winter months."[30]

In corresponding with Stronach, Harkin noted that in addition to the penstock and power house, the project would require the building of a transmission line from Anthracite eastward to the park boundary, which "would constitute a very great eyesore along the automobile road and the C.P.R." He stated unequivocally "this is a proposition which the Parks Branch should strongly oppose," and wrote a memorandum to Challies on February 13, 1922 advising of his decision: "It is considered that the construction of the necessary pipe line, transmission lines and power house in the heart of our most popular and developed park cannot fail to detract from its scenic value and that the power development work in view is consequently opposed to the best interests of the park. It is also felt that in view of the comparatively small magnitude of the project it would be inadvisable to sacrifice those interests which represent the purpose for which the National Parks were created."[31] Communication of this rejection to the company predictably threw the matter into the political arena, bringing the minister into play.

Charles Stewart visited Banff in July and was escorted around by Harkin and Wardle, providing a perfect opportunity for the commissioner to put forward his concerns face-to-face. On July 27 a conference between himself, Stewart, A.L. Ford of the Water Power Branch and R.A. Brown, superintendent of the Calgary Street Railway (and the leading voice for city power needs), was held to discuss the situation, the results of which, Brown reported, were agreement by the minister "to take the matter up on his return to Ottawa" and by Harkin "to give the matter his unbiased consideration."[32] However, two days later in meeting with a delegation of Banff citizens, Stewart assured them, "Under no circumstances would Lake Minnewanka be injured, and that consideration would only be given to a request that the water level be raised for storage purposes in the event that the public welfare was vitally concerned."[33] This elicited a strong letter from Montreal Engineering to the minister, arguing, "It is evident that the only immediately practicable water power sites in Alberta are those of the high head type, that all accessible high head sites are situated in the National Parks, and that of these the only one which is commercially feasible today is the proposed Cascade development."[34]

The forcefulness of this letter, with its spectre of major power development in the park, and Stewart's promise to fully consider the application resulted in his calling a meeting in September with Cory, Challies, and Harkin to reach a common position. In advance, he was lobbied strongly by those in opposition, including the influential Calgary Automobile Club and the Banff Citizens' Association which, with a weather eye to the potential effect on the tourist trade, carried a motion by Councillor Jim Brewster to communicate with Harkin and Stewart protesting any interference with water levels in the lake and speaking against "any attempt on part of irrigation or power interests to invade our National Parks."[35] Later reports make it clear that the two branch heads were asked their opinions (Cory had previously requested that Harkin and Challies "get on common ground and present a joint report") after which Stewart and Cory huddled privately to consider the arguments. The result, later confirmed in a letter from Harkin to his deputy, was that "both you and the Minister definitely turned down the Company's Minnewanka project," a decision not publicly announced until the following January. In a parliamentary debate the following June, Stewart stated that he was "keen on scenic beauty" and believed that Minnewanka was "an attraction close to Banff that should not be damaged by changing water levels."[36]

Undeterred, Calgary Power shifted gears, stating that it now intended to give closer examination to its earlier Spray Lakes proposal and requesting Stewart "not give a final reply to our demand regarding the Cascade site, should it be found that the Spray development cannot be financed," and "allow both of our demands (Spray and Minnewanka) to remain in status quo until this investigation has been completed by us." Harkin believed that this was just a ploy "to mix up the Spray and the Minnewanka scheme and have them considered together, not independently," with an aim "to get the Department more or less committed to the idea that the Company is entitled to further consideration in its Minnewanka application." In October 1922 he completed an extensive missive to Cory which laid out seven reasons why the Spray project should not be allowed, including its effect on fish-spawning beds and wildlife habitat, on scenic views of the confluence of the Bow and Spray rivers from the Banff Springs Hotel, and, in a clever turning of the tables, on water levels in southern Alberta's western irrigation bloc. He then turned to a recitation of the public's rights in the matter and brought forward an argument about the fate of parks similar to that used to good effect in the earlier boundary disputes: "99 3/4 percent of the public domain is available for commercial exploitation. If the principle is admitted that even the 1/4 percent must also be open to exploitation then the issue should be faced squarely and the parks abolished altogether. For piecemeal invasion will just as surely accomplish that purpose and straight abolition would be honest with the public, and prevent the waste of development money in the interval."[37]

By this time, the Alpine Club was committed to acting as a voice for conservation, and Wheeler had moved decisively to oppose each of the Waterton, Minnewanka, and Spray projects. As Harkin had undoubtedly hoped, public debate began to revolve around the forthright director as he spoke out in newspapers and club publications, replacing himself and the branch as the focal point of opposition for those who supported the various power schemes. In the same way, William Pearce became the lightning rod for upholding their position, as he took it upon himself to lobby all who would listen about Parks' mistaken ideas concerning the effects on mountain scenery of creating reservoirs and the economic necessity of developing park waters. Pearce and Wheeler, old acquaintances from their days at Interior, corresponded frequently on the topic, and Pearce noted in a letter to Bennett that "next to Mr. J.B. Harkin, Parks Commissioner, in fact, I think [Wheeler] almost exceeds him in the strenuous opposition to utilizing any portion of our Park reservations for storage of water," and, while admitting the value of the Alpine Club, complained, "Through his influence with that Club he is continually having resolutions passed—many of them going outside the scope of said Club—and this opposition is one of them."[38] That this letter was expected to bear fruit was suggested by Pearce in a subsequent communication to irrigationist Charles Magrath: "Mr. Bennett is solicitor for the Calgary Water Power Company which have applied for commission to create storage at Lake Minnewanka and Spray Lakes. I am led to infer that if Mr. Bennett sees fit to pull the wires to the fullest extent, he can probably make Mr. Harkin sit up regarding his views of the sanctity of our Parks, and that no storage should be allowed therein."[39] In his response of May 18 to Pearce's earlier letter, Wheeler gave his own view of the club's actions: "It is not so much this particular scheme, although I think it is objectionable for many reasons, as the fact that there is one thing here, another there and something somewhere else and so on, ad infinitum. Once a precedent is established there is no chance of stopping it no matter how it may affect the interest of the parks or what injury may be done."[40] Harkin could not have said it better himself, and this response unleashed a torrent of letters to the editor of the *Calgary Herald*, turning the debate into one of the most topical issues of the day.

In closing a letter to Harkin, Wheeler referred to the "pressure from commercial purposes that has been fought for so long in the United States and which has in many cases been so disastrous," and contended that only through "very much labour and hard fighting" had the Save the Redwoods League recently been successful in preserving the last redwoods of California. This letter indicated that he, like Harkin, was in touch with American conservation interests, and it seems certain the two discussed this subject whenever the opportunity arose. In any event, in the June 1923 edition of the Alpine Club of Canada *Gazette*, an article by Wheeler entitled "National Parks Association" related the attempts of commercial interests "to encroach upon our park reserves, and utilize their scenic beauties to pay dividends to power companies." Happily, he could report, recent attempts at encroachment had been largely defeated "through the careful watchfulness of the National Park authorities," then went on to argue that the club must look to the future to protect against similar attempts. This required those sharing the benefits of the parks to work together, and he called attention to the "combination such as had taken place in the United States, where a National Parks Association, numbering millions, now watches over the interests of the people in the enjoyment of their national heritage." In concluding, he reported that at the club's forthcoming annual meeting it was intended to bring forward the matter of the formation of a national parks association for Canada, and that "the slogan 'Hands Off Our National Parks' is a good one to adopt and to employ measures to maintain."[41]

"Hands Off Our National Parks," borrowed from the American association, became a rallying cry for the movement, and that Harkin was behind, or at least in support of it was evident from Wheeler's report that he would attend the club's annual camp two months hence. Accordingly, he made a brief appearance at the Larch Valley camp and was present for the annual meeting held on August 2, 1923. When the discussion came up on the agenda, Wheeler explained that the policy of the club did not deal with such matters but it "was vitally interested in defending the entire system of national parks from commercial encroachment and despoliation of their beautiful scenery," and suggested that a national organization in their interest should be formed. He then asked Harkin to speak to parks policy:

> Mr. Harkin said the policy of the parks was the policy of the Alpine Club of Canada, the preservation of the natural beauties of Canada for the people of Canada, free from all monopolies and special privileges. The general opinion was that the parks were a sort of frill, of no especial value. From a commercial standpoint, however, they were a great asset to the nation, bringing enormous amounts of money into the country and paying a huge dividend on the outlay....There were also the human dividends to be considered—the greater mental, physical and spiritual efficiency acquired through time spent in the National Parks.[42]

Alpine Club of Canada members and guests at the Larch Valley Camp, August 2, 1923. Harkin (fourth from right, back row) is joined by Wheeler (second from right, back row) in a group photograph of those involved in the creation of the Canadian National Parks Association, Canada's first public conservation organization. [GA, ND-24-94]

Representatives of each club section then spoke against the spoliation of the parks and in favour of the creation of an association, and the motion carried that "this meeting of the Alpine Club of Canada hereby declares itself in favour of the immediate formation of a National Parks Association of Canada whose objects shall be the conservation of the Canadian National Parks for scientific, recreational and scenic purposes, and their protection from exploitation for commercial purposes."

With the rest of those in attendance, Harkin retired to the formative meeting of the Canadian National Parks Association. At it, a constitution was passed that laid out three objectives—"the preservation of the National Parks of Canada in their entirety for the use of the people of Canada and the world, and the prevention of detriment to them through the invasion of commercial interests; the spreading abroad of propaganda with the object of attracting people to them; and the preservation of their natural beauties for the benefit of mankind, and of the fauna and flora intact, for educational, scientific, artistic and recreational purposes [and] to maintain them inviolate as symbols of the great heritage we possess in this wide-spreading Dominion of Canada."[43] The national voice that Harkin had longed for was now a reality, its objectives encapsulating his own philosophy on park conservation and the principle of inviolability. But while undoubtedly satisfied with its creation, he did not assume that there would not be difficult days ahead. His state of mind at the time was perhaps best revealed in a letter he had written exactly one month earlier to pioneer Banff outfitter Tom Wilson in response to his admonishment about working hard to keep the power companies out of the park: "Whether the parks' view, or the power view prevails, there is one thing certain and that is the power side will know they have been through a fight."[44] Little could he realize how important the support of the new parks association he had fostered was going to become in that struggle.

TEN

An Embarrassment of Riches

CONCERN WITH MAJOR conservation issues relating to park waters in the early 1920s dovetailed with Harkin's growing dedication to wildlife protection. His search for American support of inviolability combined with work on the *Migratory Birds Convention Act* to keep him in touch with developing North American conservation interests. In this regard he was at the height of his influence by mid-decade, but the only dimly understood natural forces that were at work soon tried him mightily. Sanctuaries, which stood at the very heart of his game conservation philosophy, exhibited some stresses as rising populations stretched their capacities and efforts to make adjustments brought Harkin into unaccustomed controversy. At the same time, his gradually emerging understanding of the interaction between game populations and the branch's predator control activities, with an attendant need for more study and a role for science, soon led to calls for a fundamental shift in the direction of its wildlife policies.

After being given responsibility for the new *Migratory Birds Convention Act* in 1917, one of his first acts was to work with the Advisory Board on Wild Life Protection to ensure its successful implementation. As mentioned, Hoyes Lloyd had been hired as ornithologist to spearhead this task in December 1918, and within a year had been promoted to the new position of Supervisor of Wild Life Protection. At the outset, attention was paid to bringing the provinces into conformity with the new act. The Maritimes, British Columbia, and the Yukon had all spoken against certain aspects of it, and the east coast provinces in particular continued to resist its implementation. Lloyd's first task was, therefore, to overcome some of this opposition, and he immediately began to work with provincial authorities to address it. However, Harkin also realized that education needed to be backed with strong enforcement, and his appointments of temporary federal migratory bird officers had within a year become permanent civil services positions. R.W. Tufts of Wolfville, Nova Scotia, was the first, appointed chief migratory bird officer for the Atlantic region, but he was quickly joined by Harrison F. Lewis of Quebec City responsible for Ontario and Quebec and J.A. Munro of Okanagan Landing, BC, for the western provinces. Over the next few years these men were assisted by Lloyd's recruitment of a large number of honorary game officers throughout the country, numbering some 190 by 1921, effectively assisting in upholding the act's provisions.[1]

An opportunity to explain the act and bring the provinces into the fold was provided in 1919. The goodwill engendered by the 1915 fish and wildlife conference had again largely been squandered due to lack of follow-up, and, in response, the Commission of Conservation scheduled a "National Conference on Conservation of Game, Fur-Bearing Animals and Other Wildlife" for February 18–19, 1919 at Ottawa. Harkin agreed to deliver an address, and, as he had missed the earlier conference, greatly anticipated an opportunity to discuss the recently passed *Convention Act* regulations with provincial delegates as well as some high-profile Americans, such as Hornaday and Burnham.

Unfortunately, he fell ill on its eve and in his absence it was Hewitt who shone, stating in his presentation that Canadians had slowly awakened to the fact that "they bore a responsibility to future generations for the nation's wildlife" and stressing three important points setting the convention's tone—the need for foresight in wildlife preservation, the need for a national effort to achieve it and, most importantly, the need for Dominion-provincial co-operation.[2]

It fell to Williamson to deliver Harkin's address, entitled "Wild Life Sanctuaries," an affirmation of his belief that they were the answer to effective wildlife conservation. The paper opened by citing the case of the western parks, all of which were game sanctuaries, where "if an exceedingly great increase in wild life is the test of their success, then there can be no doubt that sanctuaries, properly and fearlessly administered, will inevitably result, not only in the preservation, but in the very great increase of all forms of wild life." It went on to describe conditions in Rocky Mountains Park where the situation of ten years previously, when virtually no deer, sheep, or goats were seen near Banff, had been totally reversed. Visitors sitting on the piazzas of the Banff Springs Hotel could now pick out goats on the slopes of Mount Rundle, black bear were becoming so plentiful that they sometimes had to be shot when they became too fond of "the larders of the citizens," and a person on the road west of town commonly saw up to 200 sheep. These observations were supported by warden diaries reporting an abundance of game in all parts of the park, at least partly due to "the fact that animals very quickly learn that they need have no fear of molestation by man." In closing, Harkin suggested that the experience of the parks as sanctuaries should provide inspiration for other wildlife agencies so that "there may be an absolute assurance that, for all time, there shall be no danger of the disappearance of the characteristic wild life of the Dominion."[3] His call to action hit the mark, a number of delegates relating their own experiences with sanctuaries and Benjamin Lawton of Alberta paying tribute to other Dominion efforts, such as Buffalo Park, Elk Island Park, and the antelope preserves.

The success of the conference strengthened Harkin's resolve to improve provincial relations, which he believed to be one of the

Advisory Board's main responsibilities. However, two factors made it difficult to heed the meeting's call for regular wildlife conferences. One was Hewitt's premature death in March 1920, removing the man who had been largely responsible for the *Convention Act*, revisions to the *Northwest Game Act*, and creation of the Advisory Board as well as one of Harkin's few peers in the wildlife conservation movement. The other was the dismantling of the Commission of Conservation in 1921, an action led by Prime Minister Arthur Meighen, who felt that it was competing with regular government departments. Its meeting in February 1920, at which Hewitt had presented a paper on the economic importance of fur-bearing animals less than a month before his death, proved to be its last.[4] With the wind taken out of the sails of Canadian wildlife conservation for the moment, Harkin persevered virtually alone, keeping up pressure for further Dominion-provincial meetings, which he saw as an opportunity to hold open and friendly round-table discussions with delegates rather than a traditional reading of papers. Not until December 1922 was he able to convince Cory and his minister to support another gathering, with the department paying travel expenses and a small stipend to each participant to encourage attendance.

Unlike the 1919 conference, there were no big-name American conservationists or representatives of local game organizations invited, consistent with Harkin's belief that provincial delegates should roll up their sleeves and get down to serious business on solving some important problems. Indeed, this is what occurred, as the *Migratory Birds Convention Act* and Regulations were again gone over in detail, and discussions took place on matters such as uniform bag limits across the country, predator control policies, and the need for more and better educational material. The delegates appreciated this approach, passing a resolution that "assures him of the continued hearty co-operation in this great work of all the provinces and territories here represented, and regards the calling of this conference a very valuable step toward still closer co-operation and productive of a much better understanding between Dominion and Provincial officials entrusted with this work."[5] Few accolades would have pleased Harkin more, and the organization of biennial Dominion-provincial wildlife conferences and attendance at interprovincial conferences of game conservation officials henceforth became regular parts of his agenda.

Apart from improvement in Dominion-provincial co-operation, the Advisory Board also paid increasing attention to the North, which held the last large free-ranging herds of mammals on the continent. This led to one of the most interesting sidelights of Harkin's career as well as his most controversial conservation involvement. As pointed out, the region had been of particular interest to him in the branch's early efforts to be made responsible for wood bison conservation, although, with the utilitarian approach to conservation of the times, he was equally concerned about the economic value of its resources and the fate of its peoples in the face of decades of exploitation by non-native trappers and traders.[6] His earliest involvement had been concerned with schemes to introduce domesticated Norwegian reindeer, meant to address a number of issues, including depleting caribou herds, the provision of a local and, potentially, national food supply, as well as an effort to have indigenous peoples become herders. The success of reindeer herding in Alaska had resulted in a similar attempt being proposed by the Yukon Territorial Council in 1914, and in supporting the idea Meighen had recommended to Prime Minister Borden that "the first step would appear to be an investigation under the Interior Department conducted by the head of the branch which takes care of our Canadian buffalo preserves."[7]

Harkin had supplied the prime minister with a report by Graham addressing the difficulties of an earlier unsuccessful attempt by Dr. Wilfred Grenfell, a medical missionary on the coast of Newfoundland, to move fifty animals from Newfoundland to Fort Smith, NWT. He recommended that, instead of reindeer, attention should be focused on the barren grounds caribou, quoting Graham's observations of their large numbers, the great value of their meat and hides, and Seton's work on the use of their hair in the development of flotation devices. This was followed up in Harkin's 1915 annual report where he quoted Hornaday's prediction that despite their large population, without steps being taken the caribou would "be swept away in a hundred years or less." He also stated he shared the belief of others that the caribou offered a source for a future meat supply, as "their flesh is as palatable and nutritious as venison and their numbers are still estimated in the millions," so that "under proper protection and with an adequate system of transportation, there seems no reason why they could not be utilized for food in the not distant future."[8]

Similarly, after creation of the Advisory Board in December 1916 Harkin's reports reflected its shared anxiety about all northern wildlife. In particular, the muskox appeared to be under extreme pressure, Hudson's Bay Company reports showing that it had almost entirely disappeared throughout the Mackenzie district. The Advisory Board's proposed amendments to the *Northwest Game Act* could help prevent destruction of both muskox and caribou, and when they were adopted by Parliament in 1917 and supported by new regulations in 1918, Harkin felt there was then in place "a modern system of protection for the valuable fur and game resources." A graded licence system controlled hunting and trapping, excluding foreigners and incorporating a nominal fee for bona fide residents while remaining free for Indians, Inuit, and resident mixed-bloods, with enforcement being left in the capable hands of the Mounted Police.[9] Despite these initiatives, the question of domestic reindeer lingered, and one who declared an interest in the matter was controversial Arctic explorer Vilhjalmur Stefansson.

Canadian-born, American-raised and Harvard-educated, Stefansson believed that the Arctic was not the vast wasteland many made it out to be but rather a "polar Mediterranean," habitable, developable, and capable of making Canada a world power. In 1913 he had convinced Borden to support an expedition to explore the Beaufort Sea, with the intention of finding new Canadian territories as well as proving it was possible for Arctic explorers to live off the land. Dr. Rudolph Anderson, one of Harkin's fellow Advisory Board members, had been second-in-command of the Canadian Arctic Expedition, but he and Stefansson had violently disagreed after the venture had come to near-disaster in 1914 when its ship *Karluk* was wrecked near Wrangel Island, 110 miles north of Siberia, and some of its crew marooned. However, Stefansson did find some hitherto undiscovered islands and proved his theory about self-sufficiency. When he returned south in 1918 he pursued his idea of "the friendly arctic," and in 1919 gained the attention of Meighen with a proposal to utilize the North's grazing potential for breeding reindeer and muskox as a government enterprise. The "Royal Commission on Possibilities of Reindeer and Musk Ox Industries in the Arctic and Sub-arctic Regions (Canada)" was struck on May 20, 1919 to investigate the matter, and Harkin, with his background in reindeer matters and as the departmental official responsible for northern wildlife, was appointed one of its four commissioners.[10] Consisting of himself, Stefansson, J.S. Maclean of the Canadian meatpacking concern Harris Abattoir, and Dominion Railway Commissioner J.G. Rutherford, it began public hearings in January 1920, although soon without Stefansson, who resigned in March to pursue a private reindeer venture on Baffin Island. Its April 1921 report was lukewarm to commercialization, but its hearings did confirm a wider Canadian problem, one that was to engage Harkin well beyond his normal duties.

Sovereignty in the Arctic had been under active discussion in the latter nineteenth century, with occasional interest from Norway, Denmark, and the United States in what Canada contended were its possessions in the Arctic Archipelago. In 1907 the so-called "sector theory" had been enunciated, claiming Canadian ownership of all lands in an area bounded on the west side by a line from the North Pole along the 141st meridian and on the east side by a line from the pole along a zigzag route through Baffin Island and Davis Strait. However, the case for Ellesmere Island, the most northerly island in the archipelago, had been regarded as somewhat circumspect due to its location near Danish-controlled Greenland. The Advisory Board succeeded in having a closed season declared on muskox throughout the region, but in 1919, as the official responsible for administering the prohibition, Harkin had received a report through Stefansson that Greenland Inuit were ignoring it and hunting on Ellesmere. He sent a communication to the Danish government and in May 1920 received a reply from Knud Rasmussen, head of Thule Station on Greenland, that he would attempt to wean his people off muskox by importing reindeer hides, but declaring the territory fell within a "No Man's Land" and there was no authority in the district except that which he exercised.[11] The Danish government supported this position, thereby immediately propelling Harkin into the wider world of international diplomacy.[12]

By this time Stefansson was pushing for a two-pronged approach on Canadian Arctic sovereignty—forcefully and by concerted action reinforcing its claims in the eastern Arctic and more quietly strengthening its case in the western Arctic by encouraging settlement of Wrangel Island through the means of a "development company" led by himself.[13] While Harkin had initially been drawn into the matter because of his responsibility for muskox, with its increasing national importance his advice was regularly sought by Cory and the minister and he was given special responsibilities by Prime Minister Borden for orchestrating a government response in the challenge to its authority. Along with other civil servants concerned with northern affairs, he was appointed to the new Advisory Technical Board on Canadian Sovereignty and appears to have been the source of much of its thinking. Relative to the Ellesmere situation, he proposed a secret plan with several courses of action; he recommended that an expedition be sent to locate permanent RCMP posts on the Island, that Canadian Inuit be established on it, that the HBC or another northern fur company be encouraged to establish there, and that detailed explorations of Ellesmere and neighbouring islands be sponsored by the government.[14] Stefansson, who was close to Borden and intimately involved in these matters, later reported, "The men at Ottawa who were most actively concerned were Desbarats and Harkin—also Christie," and in his autobiography recalled, "I never knew why Harkin was brought in, but I do know that he came to be the best informed man in Ottawa, or anywhere, on both overt and secret matters connected with our plans. I was told that the only files our project ever had were in either Harkin's private apartment in Ottawa or in his office."[15] Although fully supported by Borden, the need to mount a major expedition to achieve the plan was anything but straightforward, and, accordingly, Harkin became involved in some delicate maneuverings with respect to Stefansson and Canada's position after Meighen became prime minister in July 1920.

Stefansson was not a believer that the sector theory could protect Canadian claims and, as mentioned, was more interested in securing occupation and control of key northern locations. Consequently, in the fall of 1920 he lobbied to lead an expedition to Wrangel Island, having received reports from survivors of his shipwrecked crew that it was filled with resources and believing that it was of great strategic importance. Early in 1921 he wrote to Harkin to gain support for his vision, putting forward his belief the island should be British territory and that in the forthcoming decades "there will be traffic across the polar basin from Europe to Japan, by way of the polar ocean, certainly with dirigibles and submarines and probably aeroplanes....As naval bases for our submarines and as way stations for aircraft we need a chain of islands across the polar basin."[16] He had begun discussing this possibility with Borden as early as 1916, and as the prime minister had become an enthusiastic supporter of this strategic vision for Canada, when he made a similar request to Prime Minister Meighen, occupation of Wrangel had initially been approved. But within a few weeks Meighen had reversed himself, apparently after External Affairs convinced him that the island was of no strategic or military importance, that Stefansson's assessment of its resources was only speculative, and that other powers, including the USSR, Britain, and the United States, had far better claims.

Having once referred to the explorer as "an extremely difficult man to handle," Harkin was nonetheless sympathetic to some of his thinking while being aware of his publicity-seeking proclivities, unpredictability, and penchant to play one country off against another. For his part, Stefansson believed the commissioner to be a strong supporter of his cause, later referring to him as such in a book he wrote about Wrangel Island. In the circumstances, and aware that the explorer could exert either a positive or negative influence on Canada's claims, Harkin recommended humouring him and engaging in a bit of subterfuge. In early 1921 the matter of who should lead the expedition to the archipelago, either Stefansson or British south polar explorer Sir Ernest Shackleton, was under consideration by the government, and in a March 2 memorandum to Cory, Harkin expressed fear that there could be trouble if it were the latter: "There is a grave possibility that if any aid or recognition is given the Shackleton expedition either (or both) the United States and Denmark may receive advance information from

Stefansson....Stefansson is a Canadian in the sense that he was born in Canada but that is all. It would therefore be unwise to bank on his Canadian loyalty too much. The Canadian expedition has been developed in the line of keeping him with us through self-interest." Accordingly, he suggested Stefansson be informed he was the prime candidate to lead the expedition, diverting him from the Wrangel scheme and keeping him in sympathy with the Canadian position until it was underway. He could then be sent north "where he would not be able to do damage to the Canadian cause."[17]

As it transpired, Shackleton's demands for funding were found to be unacceptable and, in the end, the whole expedition was cancelled. Stefansson never figured out the machinations involved and recalled that after Borden's death in 1937, he asked Harkin to explain, only to be met by reticence: "At first I felt sure he would eventually release his information, but the last time I saw him his position was that Borden had trusted him to keep certain matters secret. He had not been released from that pledge during Borden's lifetime. With the Prime Minister's death, Harkin felt, the secret became inviolate."[18] However, the commissioner had assisted him in recruitment of Allan Crawford of the University of Toronto as a leader for his own expedition mounted when Meighen refused to extend government approval. In September 1921 a group of four men and an Inuit woman, led by Crawford, occupied the island—an uncomfortable situation for the Canadian government that would drag on for almost two years. By then Harkin's role in sovereignty matters had lapsed, although the Wrangel matter continued to bedevil Mackenzie King's government and in 1926 its jurisdiction was turned over to the Soviet Union. Meanwhile, a more limited expedition was sent to Ellesmere Island in 1922 under the command of Captain J.E. Bernier and a Mounted Police post established, as Harkin had suggested, securing the Canadian claim. As far as can be determined, he kept his covenant with Borden and never publicly discussed the circumstances of the episode.[19]

Harkin's removal from the sovereignty file was occasioned by the creation of a new Northwest Territories (and later Yukon) Branch of the Department of the Interior on April 21, 1921. The complex nature of Canada's policy in the Arctic had already long illustrated the need for an administrative body devoted to the North, but the immediate cause for the new branch's creation was an expected exploration stampede after the discovery of oil near Fort Norman and valuable minerals near Great Slave Lake in the summer of 1920. O.S. Finnie, former chief mining inspector, was appointed director and on January 1, 1922 responsibility for the *Northwest Game Act* and other conservation matters in the North was transferred to the new branch. However, despite the removal of his authority over wildlife in the North, Harkin did not lose interest in the region. The Wild Life Advisory Board, on which his influence had only amplified after Hewitt's death, increased its membership in 1922 to include representation from seven government departments, including Finnie, the Mounted Police commissioner and the commissioner of Fisheries. Henceforth, fully two-thirds of its agenda would be concerned with northern wildlife, and one important matter that came up concerned revival of the movement to establish a sanctuary for wood bison. As related, this had long been of interest to both Harkin and Maxwell Graham, who had been the most directly involved in this campaign and had a special interest in northern wildlife, in particular caribou. Given his work in the North and his knowledge of its game, it was not surprising that Graham accepted the position of chief of thc Wildlife Division in the new Northwest Territories Branch, a loss for Harkin of a long-serving and trusted colleague in his own branch and one that had important repercussions. After the branch's creation, Finnie immediately revived interest in establishing a wood bison preserve, and in May 1922 Graham took part in a survey of the separate northern and southern wood bison herds, estimating the northern one at 500 animals and the southern at 1,000. Harkin, who had come to believe that animal sanctuaries should not be classified as full national parks, therein found himself in a difficult position. As it stood, the *Forest Reserves and Parks Act* was the only legislation available to create a large sanctuary on Dominion lands and while he expressed concern about its being formed as a national park, he knew there was no alternative.

Wood Buffalo National Park was established by order-in-council of December 22, 1922 in an area of 10,500 square miles astride the Northwest Territories-Alberta boundary, encompassing both herds.

Although Harkin was now in the position where the largest national park in the country was not under his authority, he accepted it with apparent equanimity, writing to CPR Tourist Agent A.O. Seymour, "As it is being set aside purely for sanctuary purposes and not for any of the other purposes for which a park is naturally established, there were no reasons why, though nominally a park, this area should be administered by this Branch."[20] In any case, he soon came to see an unforeseen benefit to Wood Buffalo in helping to solve a problem in a buffalo park that was his responsibility. Buffalo National Park at Wainwright had been developed after its formal establishment in March 1913 as a showplace for the government's famous Pablo herd. Extensive grain growing and haying operations had been undertaken to provide feed for the animals during the winter and fencing was put in place to divide the range into winter and summer grazing areas, with the herd multiplying rapidly. Nevertheless, Harkin had quickly realized that public support for buffalo conservation would wane if steps were not taken to increase its importance, leading in 1912 to considerations toward breeding experiments with cattle to produce a hardier beef animal.[21] By 1916 he had reached agreement with the director of the Dominion Experimental Farm Service to locate a hybridization experiment at the park, cross-breeding male bison with female cattle. These activities occurred separately from the buffalo enclosures and although the branch provided stock, they were under the control and management of the Department of Agriculture and therefore not regarded as impinging on buffalo preservation efforts.[22] Harkin was proud of branch activities at Wainwright, particularly its role in increasing the original herd, and spoke about it frequently at wildlife conferences. One was the September 1922 meeting of the International Association of Game and Fish Commissioners at Madison, Wisconsin, where, in speaking to the importance of bison in his organization's conservation program, he referred to a developing problem with them.

His talk, "Federal Game Activities in Canada," began by assuring the largely American audience of his country's dedication to wildlife preservation, calling Canada "the last stamping ground for big game... [and] the great game bird breeding grounds of the continent." This situation, he indicated, placed a responsibility on the country, one that it recognized and resulted in both Dominion and provincial authorities "working whole-heartedly with the idea of preventing the fulfillment of Dr. Hornaday's prediction that America might become a gameless continent." In these efforts, the branch's success with sanctuaries stood out as a shining example and Harkin repeated some of the phrases used in his 1919 presentation to put the idea across. But he also interjected another thought that illustrated he was beginning to understand there was more to be learned about wildlife protection. Identifying "the need of more intensive study of the field habits of animals," he noted that even though the U.S. Biological Survey and his own organization had been working with wildlife for years, "we have not even scratched the surface of knowledge with respect to wildlife—either bird or animal life." He provided examples in the difficulty of setting open seasons for animals with cyclical populations, such as the Arctic fox, and in understanding the interaction between birds and the insects on which they preyed, concluding by urging that "study and more study is necessary if we are intelligently to administer the law and preserve our wild life."[23]

Following these opening remarks, the remainder of Harkin's talk was devoted to bison. He related that the Canadian government had originally saved the buffalo as a matter of sentiment as "the great characteristic animal of the plain," and informed his audience that if they visited the park, they could relive the experience of the early pioneers: "Last fall I drove for hours through Buffalo Park, which is a large, rolling area, and so far as the eye could see there were little black groups of buffalo, extending away off to the horizon. As I looked at it I said: 'this is undoubtedly the same view that the first man who came through the west saw—buffalo everywhere'." To further illustrate the success of the efforts, he explained that the government was on the verge of recouping all the expenditures made in acquiring the bison and keeping them at the park. He estimated the cost of the herd at one-half million dollars and in noting "our range is exhausted" and could no longer carry the approximately 8,000 animals utilizing it, explained that plans were in place to slaughter 1,000 head annually, something which would prove a very valuable source of income when the mounted buffalo heads were sold at the Montreal fur auction for between $325 and $1,035 each. While admitting that such prices would be difficult to sustain, he pointed out that the robes could also be sold for $100 apiece and that the meat too could be marketed. Taken together, these steps would, over the course of a few years, "absolutely recoup us and from that time on we shall be on velvet." In completing the speech with a summary of the strides made in wildlife conservation, Harkin put forth his personal thoughts on their deeper meaning:

> There is just one thing more that I want to say. We have from time to time heard here, and we hear everywhere, this cry of nature being our mother. A clever English writer said recently that we no sooner discovered that nature is our mother than we resorted to matricide. I am afraid that is true. However, in recent years organizations of this kind and, perhaps a gradual change in public sentiment, have been bringing about a new condition of affairs. After all, we are more interested to-day in the life of the wild thing than we are in its death....We are gradually changing our outlook; we are realizing that wild life was created not for us to destroy but for us to preserve and conserve and utilize intelligently. Personally, I am quite convinced that if we persist in this policy the result will be an enrichment not only in a material sense, but in a spiritual sense as well.[24]

Remarkable for its insights into Canada's role in North American wildlife preservation, the success of sanctuaries, the need for species research, and the spiritual dimensions of conservation, the address was equally noteworthy in its mentioning of the slaughter and for what

Bison at Buffalo National Park, Wainwright, Alberta, 1921. Harkin described scenes of bison "as far as the eye could see" to his audience at the International Association of Game and Fish Commissioners in Madison, Wisconsin, in September 1922, hinting that their very abundance was becoming a management problem at Wainwright. [GA, NB-16-309]

it did not admit—his idea of wildlife conservation developed solely around the idea of sanctuaries was beginning to develop some serious problems. With optimum range conditions, winter-feeding, and few predators, the Pablo herd was growing exponentially—731 animals had been delivered when the last shipment was received from Montana in 1912, by March 1916 the population stood at 1,640, and then it grew rapidly, by March 1921 standing at 5,152 head, increasing at about 1,000 annually. These circumstances had led to the decision Harkin conveyed to his American audience; an experimental slaughter of buffalo bulls was to take place in the winter of 1923 with their heads, hides, and meat to be test-marketed to the Canadian public. Preparations had begun in 1922 with the construction of a small abattoir in the northern part of the winter range, and that fall the commissioner had reached agreement with California's Ince Studios to have a silent movie, *The Last Frontier*, filmed at Wainwright using some of the animals with a view to earning revenue and bringing them to public attention in preparation for marketing. Unfortunately, the October 1923 filming had resulted in some negative press, including reports about natives "shooting feathered barbs into vital spots from bows," 4,000 buffalo being stampeded

Publicity photograph for Thomas Ince's *The Last Frontier*, filmed at Buffalo National Park in October 1923. William Oliver photograph. This effort at drawing public attention to the Wainwright herd backfired when negative reaction arose from natives shooting arrows into the animals and thirty-four animals, including cows and calves, were killed. [GA, NA-3164-345]

instead of the 100 agreed upon, and thirty-four being killed, including cows and calves, rather than the ten bulls anticipated.[25]

Despite some positives, including significant visitor increases to Buffalo National Park and outtakes from the Ince film being used in the branch's own production, *The Return of the Buffalo*, released in 1933, adverse publicity brought the plans to reduce the herd by means of slaughter widespread negative reaction. Regardless, the experimental slaughter of 264 animals took place under the supervision of a trio of veterinarians. Their examinations showed that 75 per cent exhibited some form of tubercular lesion. One, pathologist, Dr. Seymour Hadwen, recommended complete destruction of the herd, but when the department refused he suggested changes to feed and concentration on the slaughter of older animals. The experiment being deemed successful, later in the winter of 1923–1924 an additional 1,847 animals were shot and processed in the park abattoir, their heads and hides being marketed as Harkin had foreseen. Issues with tuberculosis were not revealed to the public, but all the meat was inspected to the same standards as domestic cattle before being approved for sale through various Canadian meatpackers.[26]

Meanwhile, in December 1922 Harkin had begun receiving letters from those who supported releasing surplus animals to the wild or moving them to new park areas. In one response he indicated that although "the buffalo represents an embarrassment of riches to us who are charged with the administration of the herd," those released to the wild would inevitably migrate to settled areas while creating new parks would involve large expenditures for fencing and maintenance.[27] Shortly afterwards he received a variation on these suggestions from Howard Sibbald, now occupying the new position of Inspector of Dominion Parks, akin to a chief warden for all the parks. Sibbald, in noting the recent creation of Wood Buffalo, had examined its boundaries on a map and, observing that the Peace River formed its southern perimeter, offered a possible solution: "It has occurred to me that should the country be suitable, this would be a probable outlet for the surplus stock at Wainwright. I have made enquiries from one of the dog drivers now at Banff with the Trimble-Murfin Production Company, who is familiar with that country, and he informs me that the Peace River is navigable from where the Railway crosses the river to within a few miles of the Park, where there is a rapids about a mile long, and that scows are let through the rapids by ropes; if this is the case buffalo might be taken by rail to Peace River Crossing and then down the river in scows. If the scheme is feasible it would relieve the situation."[28] In response, Harkin had observed that such a solution would be expensive and queried, "What particular object is to be served?" He contended that his solution would solve the problem while dealing with an issue that constantly distracted him: "It is likely that by annually slaughtering one thousand animals or thereabouts, at Wainwright, the Department will be able to secure a substantial revenue. In the present condition of this country financially it seems to me that this would be better policy than spending more money to transport these animals to the north."[29] This may have been true, but before long public opinion and financial considerations led to a change of heart.

Documentation is scarce, but it is clear that, with continuing public outcry making the slaughter likely to prove unsustainable, the idea of shipping some bison north was under active discussion within a few months of Sibbald's letter. Following a series of departmental conferences, during which the tuberculosis problem was discussed but effectively ignored, Harkin provided his thoughts to Cory in November 1923. While agreeing "it is desirable that an experiment should be made in the matter of transfer of young buffalo from Buffalo Park to the habitat of Wood Buffalo," he believed that there were so many unknowns it should be strictly limited in its first year. Particularly important was ongoing concern about the spread of TB, but it was only one of many issues that Harkin believed should be addressed before a final decision was reached.[30] However, in replying to critics of the slaughter, Minister Stewart indicated that the feasibility of moving excess animals to the Northwest Territories the following year was being studied and stated his opinion that, "When we have completed our inquiries the scheme will be found to be feasible and we will be in a position to announce something definite along this line."[31] This implied promise was published in the newspapers, and thereafter the transfer became a somewhat self-fulfilling prophecy. Finnie soon reported that Graham had researched and satisfactorily addressed all concerns, including discussions with transportation companies which showed that between 2,000 and 2,500 animals could be shipped over the summer season and agreement to carry out tuberculin testing, if required. He asked for a conference with Cory to finalize the matter, and after Harkin gained the somewhat grudging agreement of C.E. Nagle, Graham's replacement, to approve sending an experimental shipment of not more than 500 animals, it took place on April 9, 1924. In writing the next day to Superintendent Smith directing him to prepare 500 yearlings for shipment, Harkin informed him, "My present understanding of the proposal is that the yearlings are not to be subjected to the tuberculin test."[32]

It appears that Harkin's concerns about TB were tempered by the results of the 1923 slaughter, where postmortems had shown that many tubercular scars were no longer active. Accordingly, he had reported to

Cory, "I am pleased to report [tuberculosis] is not as serious as first thought."[33] But Hoyes Lloyd, with his background in milk inspection in Ontario, could not agree, stating in a memorandum of April 22, 1924, "It is thought to be very bad epidemiology to ship buffalo from a herd known to be diseased and place them in contact with buffalo in the Wood Buffalo Park, which are not known to be diseased, so far as I am aware." He also identified another difficulty: "The wood buffalo has been described as a separate sub-species, and whether this is so or not has not been finally established by naturalists. The possibility of solving this natural history problem is removed once the two sub-species, plains buffalo and wood buffalo, are crossed by introducing plains buffalo into the wood buffalo area." In support of this position, he quoted a letter from Professor M.Y. Williams of the University of British Columbia who, having heard a rumour about the proposed transfer, appealed for the plains herd to be kept separate from the wood bison so that "they will not interbreed and spoil that fine geographic race which is one of the most attractive faunal assets of Canada." Lloyd completed his argument by stating, "No doubt other similar views will be expressed as soon as the proposal to make this transfer of buffalo is known to naturalists."[34]

It was now too late in the year to arrange for the transfer and it was not until September 24, after further discussions with Finnie, that Harkin contacted Smith, informing him that up to 2,000 animals would be shipped in 1925, 1,300 from the 1924 increase and the balance from the 1923 increase, in a ratio of five cows to one bull. As well, he stated "as it had been decided the tuberculin test could be dispensed with," no squeeze pens needed to be constructed. Both Lloyd and Nagle initialled this letter, presumably providing their agreement, but Lloyd remained concerned about the subspecies matter and requested his former colleague, Graham, address it in writing for possible publication in *The Canadian Field Naturalist*, the periodical of the Ottawa Field Naturalist Club of which he had recently become president. Graham produced a three-page report entitled "Further Utilization of the Wood Buffalo Park near Fort Smith, N.W.T. for the Conservation of Canada's Buffalo," in which he repeated a statement made in an earlier report: "Our wood buffalo has been classified as a sub-species of the American bison and is referred to as Bos (Bison) Bison Athabascae, but whatever differences there are between it and the buffalo of the plains are largely owing to environment." To those who continued to believe it was a distinct subspecies, based on analysis of a specimen in the Victoria Memorial Museum killed by natives north of Fort Resolution in 1892, Graham mentioned that the reports of Dr. Charles Camsell of the Geological Survey, active in the area in 1916, indicated that there was no contact between the northern and southern herds. As the Buffalo Park animals were only to be released in the south, the northern herd, he argued, "will remain inviolate so far as admixture with the introduced bison is concerned."[35]

In sending the report to Lloyd, Graham indicated it was up to him to determine whether or not it should be published. Lloyd elected to publish an edited version, likely believing it would spur some debate on such a fundamental issue, and it appeared under the title "Finding Range for Canada's Buffalo" in the December 1924 issue of *Field Naturalist*. If controversy was Lloyd's intention, he was successful, as a response from Francis Harper, an Ithaca, New York, zoologist who had inspected the wood buffalo range in 1914 as a member of the Geological Survey, in predicting inbreeding and the spread of TB, asked, "Would it not be wiser to send them to the slaughter house at once, rather than to undertake the enormously expensive and difficult job of transporting them to northern Alberta, and leaving them there to work slow but sure havoc through inbreeding with the superb Wood Buffalo?"[36] Having earlier argued this point himself, Harkin might well have asserted himself and possibly nipped the movement in the bud; instead, he knuckled under to decisions being made over his head. As a result, he had to respond to the numerous letters from those with whom he had worked on wildlife conservation and had read Harper's letter when it appeared in the February 1925 issue. Replying to one such missive from Edward Seymour of the American Bison Society, Harkin took refuge in the postmortem evidence of healed lesions and the difficulty being experienced in dealing with such a complex wildlife issue:

> It is true that a number of very old animals, many of them original ones brought from Montana, did show tubercular infection, but even in the case of some of these, old lesions had healed. When the Department began to slaughter younger animals, the health record was remarkably good, especially when the congested condition of the Park is considered. As none but young animals will be sent north, I think the chance of transferring infection is slight, in view of the very great area of range in which they will be placed. The Department is doing its utmost to meet the many complicated problems that arise in administering a wildlife question of this magnitude and, of course, is pleased to receive your views and those of Dr. Hornaday on the points at issue.[37]

Harper ended his letter by calling for the matter to be submitted to the annual meeting of the 700-member American Society of Mammalogists in April, and its response proved even more damming, pointing out that "serious results would occur from carrying out the...plan." The society passed a resolution expressing "the earnest hope that some other means may be found of disposing of the surplus Plains Buffalo" and requested Harkin "take such energetic action in the matter as seems appropriate." Instead, the department having closed ranks, he sent a standard response to those writing to protest: "I beg to say that the officers of the Canadian Government concerned in this matter have given careful consideration to all aspects of this subject...and that it is dealing with the matter on the lines which it considers to be in the best interests of the Dominion."[38] When it released its official position to the press on May 5, 1925, it was reported the department "while admitting that they have received protests from zoologists and mammalogical societies of the United States and Canada...are going ahead with their plans, claiming their own experts are better qualified to judge the policy, because of experience and practice, than are zoologists at a distance."[39]

Its reputation tarnished by this contretemps, there were repercussions for those in the branch directly involved. Lloyd, as the instigator of the *Field Naturalist* article, and Migratory Bird Officer Harrison Lewis, its editor, were forced to resign their positions with the Ottawa club under threat of dismissal after the organization passed a resolution, moved by Lloyd, that a letter be sent to the minister opposing the transfer on the basis that "the government would be negating their own action of setting aside a national park for the northern wood buffalo." This threat was not formally conveyed but, as Lewis later recalled, "It just came down from the Deputy Minister's office by the grapevine."[40] The first shipment of buffalo left Wainwright on June 15, 1925 and the second seven days later under the watchful eye of Governor General Byng, and before the season ended, 1,634 animals had been moved to the new range. The following year 2,011 head were sent in lots at two-week intervals and in 1927, 1,940 were shipped, this time including animals varying in age from one to three years. When the last shipment arrived at the Wood Buffalo range in June 1928 a total of 6,673 buffalo had been transferred. Even at that the measures failed to staunch the natural increase and during the winter of 1926–1927 it was found necessary to recommence the slaughter, with a 2,000-head reduction that year and an average of 1,000 each year thereafter. At Wood Buffalo, the increased herds had immediately begun to move south across the Peace River and by order-in-council of April 30, 1926 this area was added to the park, bringing it to a total of 17,000 square miles, and the combined herd had increased to 10,000 within three years.[41]

Harkin's involvement in the movement of bison to Wood Buffalo was a low point in his wildlife conservation career. Of course, we cannot know if he had stuck to his earlier arguments of an annual slaughter as a better solution whether things would have turned out differently. Regardless, he seems to have fairly quickly and willingly bought into the shipments, and as pointed out, became the foremost apologist for them. Environmental historians have heaped criticism on all those involved and, while appropriate, I also believe some have failed to understand the influences Harkin was working under that tempered his actions. Jennifer Brower harshly concludes "the decision to move the

Barge carrying plains bison arriving at Fort Smith, NWT, 1927. Between 1925 and 1928 a total of 6,673 plains bison were shipped to Wood Buffalo National Park using this method, leading to harsh criticism of the department and Harkin from wildlife experts. [LAC, PA-020182]

buffalo north with the knowledge of their condition was inexcusable and raises the question of the Parks Branch having any preservation ethic at all."[42] John Sandlos, although critical, sees it more in light of the accepted practice of the day: "The principles behind the transfer proposal were entirely consistent with the contradictory amalgamation of preservationist sentiment and quasi-agricultural approaches to wildlife management that dominated Canada's conservation bureaucracy during the 1920s."[43] In a comment on the bison shipments to American writer Lewis Freeman in 1927, Harkin pointed out the animals' value as a guaranteed food and fur supply for both natives and white explorers in the North and closed by noting, "Thus, quite apart from the sentimental side of the preservation of the native people, there will be a distinct commercial necessity which will be met by this planting of buffalo in the North."[44] The words "commercial necessity" speak to his view that this work was primarily being carried out to address economic concerns. Just as he described his branch as being in "the business of tourism" after the war, he might equally have described his wildlife work in the North as being in "the business of wildlife conservation," both aimed at improving the general economic condition of Canada in the difficult postwar reconstruction period. Too often those examining Harkin have seen his tourism and conservation activities in the 1920s to be at odds, while in reality they were largely carried out toward what he saw as the same end—the well-being of the nation.

If the bison shipments to Wood Buffalo were indicative of the problems faced by Buffalo National Park as a game sanctuary, there were also issues arising with populations of game animals in other parks that provided further troubling auguries. In 1923 deer were becoming a menace in Banff townsite with incidents being cited where the public were accosted by aggressive animals, something that Sibbald attributed to the feeding of "tame" animals. At Waterton Park bighorn sheep became the issue, Harkin informing Cory in April 1924 that there were too few and within six years the superintendent complaining that there were too many and, as high populations would inevitably lead to disease, further efforts to protect them should be discontinued.[45] But, as Sibbald had forewarned, it was to be elk that would present the greatest management quandary. In shipping 194 head from Yellowstone to Rocky Mountains in February 1920, Mather had mentioned in a letter to Harkin, "I trust that these animals may thrive under the care of your officers." This they did, and by the spring of 1923 Rocky Mountains Superintendent Stronach was reporting 337 elk in the park in ten separate herds. At Jasper, they were even more prolific, Supervising Warden Langford likewise reporting in 1923 that the original 100 animals planted in the park had already tripled in number. Stronach had noted in his report that twenty animals frequented the Loop and Golf Links area, and it was here that Harkin's tourism development and wildlife conservation efforts began to come into conflict.

By April 1924 Assistant Superintendent Wood was complaining, "This herd is increasing in numbers very rapidly and they are doing a tremendous amount of damage to the greens and fairways." He noted that they had barked all the aspens in the vicinity of the course, left deep holes in the turf and greens, and during the rutting season acted extremely aggressively toward players. Wood suggested that there were two ways to deal with the problem—transplant the herd to an outlying district, which would be costly but effective, or destroy it, which he did not recommend until all other avenues were exhausted. The only other possibility he could see was erection of a fence around the part of the course not bounded by the Bow River to keep the animals out. Harkin demurred, indicating that a fence would be too costly and suggested that a shotgun be used to scare them off the links until they moved to higher altitudes for the summer. But the elk had become habituated to the lush fairways and difficulties with these animals remained an irritant between local golfers and the government until September 1926 when, after a further spate of destruction by rutting bulls, Harkin relented and informed the superintendent, "You should take some steps to destroy some of the animals if other means fail."[46] Within a few years, the six-mile-long, nine-foot-high "elk fence" Stronach had suggested was in place.

By 1924 Harkin was being constantly informed by Lloyd that the strict predator control policies active in the parks were at the root of many of these troubles. Although he had unequivocally sided with Graham on the bison matter, it did not mean he failed to respect Lloyd's opinions on other wildlife issues. Indeed, Lloyd had acquitted himself admirably in organizing the convention work and in setting up bird sanctuaries, and he had also developed strong ties in U.S. conservation circles. His attendance at the AOU annual meetings put him in direct contact with those in the United States with similar responsibilities, but even more importantly, in 1919 he became a charter member of the aforementioned American Society of Mammalogists, composed of men such as Joseph Grinnell, Joseph Dixon, and some of the foremost American scientists in the new field of animal ecology. This placed him at some of the most fateful meetings in North American wildlife conservation history, including the spring 1924 meeting of the society where a group of scientists largely connected with universities attacked the U.S. Biological Survey's use of poison in their national predator control campaign, charging that the survey was not merely controlling predators, but actually exterminating them.[47] Both sides in the debate presented papers on predator control and one by Dr. Charles C. Adams, author of one the first works in the field, *Guide to the Study of Animal Ecology* published in 1913, was of particular interest in its identification of national parks as virtually the only areas in North America where the survival of predators could be assured.[48] Adams was already known to the branch because of a written critique he had provided, apparently in response to Hewitt's call in his book for strict predator control, putting forward some new thinking with respect to those working with wildlife, and particularly predators, in Canada's parks: "The intelligent formulation of satisfactory rules for the protection of wildlife and their enforcement is a subject that should receive the most careful attention of Canadian naturalists, until the Canadian Parks are properly staffed with scientific men, clothed with authority as well as responsibility. Naturalists are only beginning to awaken to the seriousness of this matter. There is an urgent, acute need for careful scientific study of the predatory animals in these parks (and everywhere for that matter), because of a prevalence of a strong prejudice against the predatory animal."[49]

Lloyd obviously thought he was the "scientific man" being referred to and was able to convince Harkin of the relevance of the scientist's position, resulting in the commissioner later distributing a copy of Adams's paper "The Conservation of Predatory Animals," published in the *Journal of Mammalogy* in February 1925, to each of his superintendents.[50] The upshot of his interest in, if not yet his outright support for the position espoused by Adams and embraced by Lloyd, proved to be the starting point for a fundamental shift in branch wildlife policy.[51] In May 1924, shortly after the mammalogists' conference, Harkin directed that the Wildlife Division poll the superintendents for information on which birds and mammals were being shot in the Canadian parks in the belief that they were injurious. In forwarding the results of this work, Nagle provided the first indication of the new thinking that was emerging in the division:

> Attached herewith is a table showing in detail the birds and mammals reported as being killed by the Wardens. According to this list the Wardens are killing many interesting birds and mammals to no apparent purpose.
>
> Animals are by nature dependent upon one another. When you kill off the hawk[,] the coyote etc., the weaker

> birds and mammals survive and increase, and in their abundance do more harm in various ways than the combination when evenly divided by the laws of nature. If man offsets nature he must readjust the balance....
>
> Something good on behalf of any alleged predatory animal could be said. Sufficient to say, however, I understand that as well as providing Parks for recreation, our aim is always the protection of wild life within these preserves, and in furthering our efforts in this regard, feel that we would be well advised to enroll the services of nature instead of to combat its influence to too great an extent.[52]

A letter immediately went out to the superintendents under Harkin's signature looking for arguments to support the birds and animals being eliminated in each park and asking if they thought it advisable to discontinue killing any species previously destroyed. In summarizing the arguments received, Nagle indicated that the strongest case had been made for killing wolves, wolverines, coyotes, lynx, goshawks, Cooper's hawks, horned owls, crows, and magpies. Harkin agreed to allow some restrictions on predator destruction and on September 29, 1924 he sent out a circular letter to the superintendents, heralding the beginning of the shift in official branch policy:

> In view of the fact that so many people are interested in seeing the various kinds of wild life within the Canadian National Parks, even though in some instances some of these species may be more or less injurious, it is felt that there should be a strict tightening up in the matter of killing birds and mammals because they are alleged to be predatory.
>
> It has been decided, and all Superintendents are being advised, that no fur bearers, except wolves, wolverines and coyotes, are to be trapped. All skins of fur bearers

> taken by wardens and properly prepared by them may be turned in to the Superintendent who will credit the particular warden with the skins turned in, if these skins are of the species allowed to be trapped. All such skins are to be disposed of by the Department and the warden will be paid the amounts received for these pelts.

When queried by Stronach about why some of the most noteworthy predators had been left off the list, he provided further details: "Before issuing these instructions, the whole matter received careful study and consideration. It is not felt that cougars are so numerous in any of the parks as to be considered of very great danger to game. As parks are set aside for the preservation of fur bearers, as well as other wild life, it was decided not to allow lynx or weasel to be taken."[53]

In sending the September 1924 policy letter, Harkin promised to "furnish a general discussion of the question of predatory animals in the National Parks," and work began on another circular letter in early January. Lloyd prepared several drafts before the commissioner agreed to a final version, which went out under his signature on January 31, 1925. It went right to the heart of the matter: "The question of predatory animals in the National Parks arises frequently. It is held that the policy should be to have the wild life conditions in the National Parks remain as natural as possible. Whenever stringent steps are taken by man to curtail the natural numbers of any wild creature because he considers it to be doing damage, there is almost sure to follow a reaction because some of the prey of this predatory animal are causing other damage." Numerous sources and examples were quoted to back up this position, such as exploding populations of varying hares when lynx were eliminated and the troubles with Wyoming elk and deer in the Kaibab National Forest near Grand Canyon. In summing up, the four-page statement justified the action in light of the larger role of national parks: "In the large national parks there is a special need for a policy of preserving the balance of nature, exercising only the control necessary to maintain the balance against such human interference as

Don Harmon feeding deer in the Harmon family yard, Banff, ca. 1920. Byron Harmon photograph. Problems with overabundance of ungulates, such as elk and deer, led Harkin to accept the advice of his Wildlife Division to re-examine the role of predators in achieving a "balance of nature." [WMCR, V263 NA-2931]

may unavoidably occur. One of the greatest accomplishments of these parks is the preservation of large areas of Canadian nature, or the great out-doors, as nearly in its original condition as possible, while the rest of the continent undergoes inevitable change."[54]

While the changing perspective on predators was beginning to be implemented within the branch by early 1925, there was already a challenge looming with respect to the idea being accepted by the general public. In February 1925 influential Calgary businessman and rancher A.W. Cross began a correspondence with Cory protesting the policy of not killing cougars, claiming they were destructive to his livestock, and Harkin, with advice from Lloyd and Nagle, had to respond to support the new policy. In doing so, he used papers just published in the *Journal of Mammalogy*, which, in addition to Adams's, included topics such as "The Scientific Value of Predatory Animals" and "The Predatory

Mammal Problem and the Balance of Nature," to supply scientific support for the Canadian position. In a May 20 memorandum to Cory, Harkin provided an explanation that could be communicated to Cross:

> The largest of the Canadian National Parks are ideally situated as sanctuaries for the preservation of predatory animals in as large numbers as the conditions will permit. Scientists of note state that it is worth years of effort to secure just such areas where all control measures are absolutely prohibited....Other scientists are pointing out that much of the antipathy towards the predatory mammal is not backed by evidence obtained from a study of food habits, that it is becoming apparent that predatory animals have a real place in nature and because they feed upon animals in which we are interested is not a valid excuse for organizing campaigns of killing.[55]

Cross was unmoved, but for Harkin dependence on his Wildlife Division and the work of other scientists in the field henceforth formed the backbone of his position, and he thereafter fostered less aggressive predator measures in larger parks where greater populations of game animals could withstand it while approving more active measures in smaller parks where the superintendent was concerned about vulnerable wildlife populations or nearby livestock.[56]

ELEVEN

The Fine Italian Hand

THROUGHOUT THE CHALLENGES presented by wildlife and water development matters, Harkin did not lose sight of his objective of removing restrictions on parks under the *Dominion Forest Reserves and Parks Act*. Although several amendments had increased his powers and the scope of his branch, he remained restive under the strictures of working with Forestry and regarded the act as an impediment to preserving and protecting park lands as well as to effectively administering new responsibilities, such as sanctuaries and historic sites. The formulation of a dedicated parks act could have been a fairly straightforward task of detaching park matters from Forestry and encompassing them in new legislation that Cory could take forward to the minister and Parliament. But Harkin's efforts increasingly intersected with the rapidly shifting ground of irrigation and water power development on park lands and soon with the equally contentious issue of the transfer of natural resources to the prairie provinces. In these circumstances, he proved tenacious in the face of what became a protracted struggle, masterfully manipulating the bureaucracy and public opinion in moving forward his message of inviolability and the need for new legislation to protect Canada's parks.

Apart from the enforced partnership with the Forestry Branch, at the end of the First World War Harkin was bothered by Parks Branch weakness in controlling park lands. This became manifest when, in connection with a proposal to acquire lands from the St. Regis Indian Band for an extension to St. Lawrence Islands Park, the Department of Justice indicated that an amendment to the act would be necessary to allow for an expropriation of native land. In fact, it pointed out that there was no authority in the *Expropriations Act* to acquire any lands for park purposes. Requesting that Cory take forward an amendment to rectify this, Harkin indicated that it "should not be confined to the acquisition of Indian Reserves but should provide the necessary authority for expropriating any property required for parks purposes."[1] Although he worked with departmental law officers drafting wording, the matter failed to proceed, and by the time the opportunity again came forward in the spring of 1920 the situation had changed dramatically. The Waterton Lakes project was rearing its head, and Harkin began to weigh his options on the need for additional legislation to protect park interests in light of its perceived threat.

Initially, he took comfort from a precedent—the Bear Trail Springs case—which had provided for the primacy of the *Forest Reserves and Parks Act* over the *Irrigation Act* on the control of park waters in 1911. It had arisen as a result of a Grand Trunk Pacific Railway request for water from the springs for the Chateau Miette hotel they intended building at Fiddle Creek in Jasper Park. Harkin had countered that the water was needed for the Miette townsite, planned for a nearby location. The Irrigation Branch had insisted on the primacy of the *Irrigation Act*, even arguing that the railway's application would take precedence over an application submitted by the Parks Branch. This could not go unchallenged, and a few years later in reminding his deputy of the outcome, Harkin recalled, "This stand seemed so unreasonable that this Branch in self-protection was forced to raise the question as to the application of the Irrigation Act to Parks and Justice Department subsequently decided that the Act did not apply."[2] But despite this case providing support for the branch's opposition to irrigation development at Waterton, he was under no illusions the case would be sufficient to fully protect its interests. Accordingly, he began drafting a new parks bill in early 1920, incorporating the expropriation clause and updating many other aspects of the existing legislation, but most importantly addressing the issue of water.

Subsection 3 of section 19 of the draft indicated that any waters "which are not required for the purposes of such parks" could be made available for other purposes under the direction of the director of reclamation or the director of water power and according to regulations set down by governor-in-council. Cleverly conceived, this did not deny the use of water for irrigation or power purposes but implied the decision as to what water would be made available rested entirely with the Parks Branch. Reclamation Director Drake was not easily fooled, and his response to the draft suggested alternative wording providing that the *Irrigation Act* and the *Dominion Water Power Act* hold primacy.[3] Given these opposing perspectives, the battle lines were clearly drawn and a long and acrimonious inter-branch war for control of water resources on parks lands ensued. Importantly, many of the arguments Harkin would put forward to support his position eventually found their way into the *National Parks Act*.

Foremost was his contention in a memorandum to Cory of May 14, 1920 that "the whole spirit of national parks legislation both in Canada and the United States has been to provide that parks set aside for the people, present and future, shall be maintained inviolate." Based on this assumption, he felt Parliament intended that parks waters primarily serve parks purposes, making the Canadian circumstances consistent with the United States. In response to bills before Congress in 1917–1918 to permit water development in parks, a clause had been inserted in the legislation which required that power permits only be issued after a determination by the secretary-in-charge that such development would not be at odds with the purposes of such reservations. If similar thinking was not accepted, Harkin argued, "the outlook for parks would indeed be hopeless," as "the Mining Lands Branch might come along and claim the right to unconditionally deal with minerals in Parks; that the Dominion Lands Branch might claim it should administer Parks lands...that Public Works Dept. might claim it should do all the construction work in the Parks; that the Fisheries Dept. might claim the right to handle Parks fisheries." Instead, minerals were to be administered "under conditions and limitations approved by the Parks Branch," while "fisheries are administered by the Parks in harmony with the principles suggested by the fisheries authorities." Only the Irrigation Branch, he charged, demanded "a free hand independent of the Parks Branch or Parks interests." Recalling the Bear Trail Springs case, he asserted that in these circumstances the public interest would be sacrificed, including subordinating the Crown's interest in favour of private corporations in opposition to parks interests and a necessity for the Parks Branch to apply to the Irrigation Branch to use its own water. He drew an analogy to illustrate the point:

> The Crown represented by the Branch has a supply of water which may be likened to a bank account. It requires most of this for its own purposes. It admits that it may be able to spare some of it to the Irrigation Branch. It proposes that whenever the Irrigation Branch needs any of it, the Parks Branch will offer no objection to a withdrawal if such withdrawal will not embarrass the Parks account. On the other hand the Irrigation Branch wishes for a free hand to issue cheques on this account to all comers. It even goes further and contends that the Parks Branch should use none of these funds itself without getting the consent of the Irrigation Branch, and moreover doing without if the Irrigation Branch on its own responsibility should choose to cash out all the available funds.[4]

Drake was unmoved, and Harkin was forced to reconsider his section 19, agreeing to change the wording to have the decision-making authority moved to the minister from governor-in-council, although he now did make specific reference to the responsibility of his own office. The suggested change held that water not being used for parks purposes be made available for irrigation or water power purposes, but not until "the Commissioner has concurred in writing to such action being taken," or "in the event of his non-concurrence, until the Commissioner and the Director of Reclamation or of Water Power as the case may be, have made full and detailed reports thereon to the Minister, and the Minister has prescribed in writing the conditions under which action may be taken." Drake was willing to agree to the role of the minister, but only on the basis of the *Irrigation Act* and the *Water Power Act* taking precedence and the right of concurrence resting with their directors.[5] With disagreement rampant, the draft bill did not make it past the minister's desk, nor did it appear on the parliamentary order paper the following year.

Meantime, the Waterton irrigation case and the emerging Spray and Minnewanka power projects had moved from mere concepts in 1920 to real possibilities by 1922. With Liberal Charles Stewart now occupying the Interior portfolio and the water issue the subject of heated public debate, a departmental decision to try to amend the existing *Dominion Forest Reserves and Parks Act* rather than table a new one was taken, perhaps an attempt to get some important principles in place before the projects progressed further. Harkin drafted an amendment incorporating some significant improvements on his 1920 efforts, working at the same time on his eighty-six-page memorandum to Cory providing the background to the Waterton matter in preparation for the expected International Joint Commission submission. Therefore, it was not surprising it was tough, adding a requirement that the decision-making authority over the use of parks waters now be placed directly in the hands of Parliament, accomplished through insertion of a clause reading, "Notwithstanding anything in this Act, no permit, license, lease or authorization for dams, conduits, reservoirs, power houses, transmission lines or other works for storage, transmission or utilization of power within the limits of any Canadian National Park, shall be granted or made unless such permit, license, or authorization is authorized by specific Act of the Parliament of Canada."[6] Along with the concept of inviolability, this proposal to strengthen the mechanics of approval for major development or change in parks through the involvement of Parliament became one of Harkin's most important conservation contributions.

But its acceptance was still some time off, as the draft was not tabled in 1922, likely due to its controversial nature making it too contentious given the current state of disagreement and public debate. Harkin persisted, complaining to Cory in February 1923, "For three years now this Branch has been endeavouring to have a new Parks Bill passed. Last year we had a draft ready but owing to the desire of the Minister to curtail the legislation it was left over until this session. We are at present revising this draft and will have same ready in a few days. It is imperative that this bill be passed this session and I beg to recommend that the necessary provision be made for same."[7] Abandoning the amendment route, in early March Harkin tabled a proposal "to have a separate Act dealing solely with Parks, Historic Sites and other Reservations administered by this Branch." Officially titled "An Act Respecting National Parks and Reservations," or, in short form "The National Parks Act," it provided the framework on which much subsequent park legislation was crafted.

In section 2, "Interpretation," key terms, such as "Park," "Boundary of a Park," "Minister," and "Lands of the Dominion" were defined, with the latter being identified as lands "title to which is vested in His Majesty and includes the natural resources of the land and the waters thereon." Section 3, "Establishment of Parks," began by stating that all reserves or areas previously set apart as parks "are hereby dedicated to the people of Canada and set apart as Canadian National Parks for the purposes and subject to the terms of this Act," an early form of what became the famous "dedication clause" of the 1930 act. The concept of "dedication" was borrowed from recent American legislation establishing Grand Canyon and Mount McKinley national parks, and it was later defined as "to devote, as land or other property, to the use of the public" or "to set aside in trust for the public." In an accompanying memorandum explaining the bill, Harkin identified what he had in mind by including this phrase and made a farsighted prediction: "The idea of parks has been that of a *permanent* reservation for the benefit of the people. I think the term 'dedicated' strengthens the idea of a national heritage for future generations as well as emphasizes the sanctity of the parks. The term will have a distinct bearing on all decisions in regard to park matters."[8]

Section 4, "General Purposes," set out Harkin's idea of the reasons for which parks needed to be established, a modification of his thinking first expressed in *Sprig*, including: "as national recreation areas and pleasure grounds and as natural museums; as animal sanctuaries for the preservation of wild animals as near as possible in their natural state; as historic sites and monuments to commemorate historic events and to preserve historic landmarks, prehistoric structures and other objects of historic, prehistoric or scientific interest." To these specific uses were added several more general conditions:

> All parks shall be maintained and made use of for the enjoyment, education and benefit of the people of Canada and for the purposes of attracting tourists to Canada. The natural scenery, the animal life and vegetation and the historic and other objects of interest within a park shall be conserved. Any development work within a park shall be carried out so as to interfere as little as possible with the maintenance of such park in an unimpaired condition in order that future generations may know and enjoy the beauties and wonders of nature in their original form. The national interest shall dictate all decisions affecting parks.

Particularly important in this section was the reference to development work and leaving parks in an unimpaired condition, as it spoke to how, in Harkin's mind, the mandates of both development and preservation could be reconciled. There was no question that development work should occur; however, in doing so the precautionary principle "to interfere as little as possible with the maintenance of such park in an unimpaired condition" should be followed. Two years later, in 1925, when writing about parks policy, he described this thinking slightly differently: "Broadly speaking the purpose of National Parks is to serve the people of Canada. While the preservation of the original wilderness has been the fundamental idea it has been recognized that the parks cannot serve the public unless they are made readily accessible and unless they can be visited in safety and comfort. This has forced the construction of roads and trails throughout the parks. However, in all construction work of this kind everything has been carried on with a view to it making as little change as possible in the original appearance and character of the parks."[9] Not addressed was how this development fit with the concept of inviolability, although the context in which that word was used makes it clear it was to be reserved for major actions that outside interests might take with respect to natural resources or waters on park lands, not those that the branch itself would take or sanction in connection with infrastructure and tourism development.[10]

Section 5, "Park Lands," dealt with circumstances in which parks could be used by outside interests. Restrictions on private holding of lands or park resources were primary, setting out the principle of leasehold over freehold and the requirement of approval of occupation for use of lands, with the exception of railways where lands could be sold or leased for right-of-way or station uses, but with a reversionary clause if such uses were discontinued. The defining clause read, "Notwithstanding the provisions of any other act, no right or interest shall be granted to or acquired by any person in any such lands, nor shall any person enter upon, use or occupy any such lands except under the authority of this Act; and no lands shall be deemed to be withdrawn from any park or shall any rights be deemed to be granted therein by any Act, unless it is clearly specified in such Act that Canadian National Park lands are so withdrawn or affected." In his memorandum, Harkin explained, "The main principle behind parks is their preservation in their natural state for the public in perpetuity. The clause under consideration reasserts this principle and makes it impossible for any invasion of parks lands without it being perfectly clear to Parliament that such invasion is to take place." This section also incorporated two "sunset" clauses, one that indicated that any rights on freehold land granted prior to the establishment of a park would be maintained and the other that any special exemptions previously granted would be retained under the provisions of the new act. Finally, it addressed the matter of acquisition of lands, stating that the governor-in-council could authorize the minister to purchase, expropriate, or otherwise acquire lands for parks purposes, including Indian lands, and, in cases where it was required, the *Expropriations Act* would apply and compensation be awarded.

Section 6, "Park Administration," set out the administrative framework, powers, and duties of the Parks Branch, including Harkin's own position: "There shall be a Commissioner of Canadian National Parks who, subject to the direction of the Minister, shall control, manage, administer and supervise the parks and all matters arising under this Act." Next came superintendents, wardens and other employees "necessary for carrying out the provisions of this Act," each of whom was to swear an oath of office. To be able to enforce regulations under the act, each officer would have all the powers of a justice of the peace, and all wardens would have the powers of a police constable. This section also gave the governor-in-council authority to appoint stipendiary magistrates to try cases within the parks and, in instances where there was believed to be "irregularity" or "misconduct," to appoint a person with the powers of a commissioner under the *Inquiries Act*.

Section 7, "Regulations," specified the rules that these officers were to carry out in "the proper control and administration of the park." First were those that supported the conservation system that the branch had put in place, including "the protection and control of wild mammals and birds within the boundaries of a park; the destruction of noxious predatory and superabundant mammals or birds and the taking of specimens of wild mammals and birds for scientific purposes; the protection of all fish, including the prevention of obstruction or pollution of streams and the remedying of any obstruction or pollution of streams and the management and regulation of all fishing...[and] the prevention and extinguishment of fires upon or threatening park lands." Next were regulations guiding the use of resources, such as "lands for the accommodation and entertainment of persons resorting to the park," the grazing of cattle and horses, the removal of sand, stone, and gravel for construction purposes in the park and the cutting and removal of dead or green timber for forest protection. This section was particularly important to Harkin, as the restrictions on disposal of lands included natural resources and water, providing a further layer of protection for inviolability, as well as strictly controlling those who occupied park lands in that "it means that these lands shall only be leased or licensed in so far as is necessary or advisable for development of the parks and their use and enjoyment by the people." These were followed by regulations controlling different aspects of occupation of these lands, including the establishment and maintenance of utilities, such as sewers, domestic water supply, street lighting and fire protection; the establishment and maintenance of roads, sidewalks, bridges, and "other ways within the park," and the regulating of buildings that might be erected, including their accompanying signage. In support of these regulations was section 8, "Penalties and Procedure," which levied fines of up to $500 for a summary conviction for a first offence, and, at the discretion of the convicting magistrate, "to imprisonment with or without hard labour for any term not exceeding six months" for a second conviction.

The final parts of the proposed act concerned two of the more specialized types of parks—animal sanctuaries and recreation areas—identified in section 4. In the case of animal parks, the exclusion of the Northwest Territories from the lands to be reserved was outlined, as was the inclusion of game sanctuaries and public shooting grounds (such as Point Pelee). The governor-in-council was empowered to make regulations governing the control and management of game preserves and for the "breeding, care, protection and disposal of game on lands of the Dominion." It could also authorize the minister to co-operate and enter into agreements with provincial authorities in the pursuit of game conservation goals. With respect to recreation areas, they were to be "administered as recreational and summer resort areas and...made available for the use of the public for building sites and recreational grounds for the benefit and enjoyment of the people of Canada."[11]

The all-encompassing nature of the 1923 draft reflected Harkin's progression in thinking about parks and wildlife in the nine-year-period since he had written *Sprig*. It was a fully developed position, touching on all aspects of conservation, development, and administration, and as such, it was probably more than Stewart had bargained for. Or so it seemed, for ten days after its submission Assistant Deputy Minister Roy Gibson wrote, "The Minister has read the proposed Parks Bill.... Mr. Stewart has asked that, if possible, we carry on under the existing legislation and avoid the necessity of introducing any Bill at the present Session as his programme is somewhat extensive and he does not like to undertake anything additional that can be postponed."[12] Reacting quickly, Harkin penned a note on the letter to Spero, "see if short bill will do," and made an impassioned plea to Gibson for reconsideration in light of the great threat the parks were under:

> In view of the urgent necessity for adequate provision to insure the sanctity of the parks and their maintenance in their original form, it is considered that provision should be made at once whereby Parliament alone shall have the power to say whether or not there would be any interference in the parks. If this provision is made, it will first of all free the Minister from the necessity of continually fighting private interests and will fully protect the parks as no intrusion can be made without full discussion on the floor of the House....
>
> I appreciate the Minister's position, but I am confident that Parliament as a whole is in sympathy with the parks idea and that there will be very little criticism of our Bill. The only contentious point so far as we are aware would be the question of water power. I think in this connection that all recognize today that the parks are one of the greatest revenue producing resources of the Dominion and

> will, therefore, gladly accept the provision that none of the resources should be disposed of without open discussion in the House.[13]

In arguing to free the minister from having to fight private interests, he seems to have struck a chord given Stewart's experience with water matters the previous summer. By mid-April the minister was suggesting that the bill would be put forward, and an amended draft was printed and delivered to Stewart for introduction as Bill No. 185. It was given first reading in the House on May 28, 1923.

Amazingly, until first reading the proposed act did not catch the attention of those most likely to oppose it. On June 1, Dominion Water Power Commissioner J.B. Challies received a memorandum from branch employee M.F. Cochrane which, in analyzing the legislation, noted that "it is clearly apparent that the general effect of this proposed bill would be to prevent, indeed to prohibit, the storage of water or the development of power within a park for any purpose whatsoever outside a park," and warned that once parks were established "only further legislative action can provide a remedy."[14] Challies forwarded the memorandum to Cory, asking that it be considered with respect to water power and promising to provide a further opinion from irrigation. J.A. Symes of the Reclamation Service condemned it in even stronger terms, pointing out that over one million acres of lands were being irrigated by water flowing from the parks that would be affected and "there is no recognition of any of the rights administered under the Irrigation Act or even of riparian rights." He insisted these rights must be protected as millions of dollars had been spent on irrigation development, thousands of people in semi-arid tracts were dependent on irrigation for their living, thousands of vacant acres would remain undeveloped without it, and "under the proposed Act this protection would be removed and disaster would inevitably ensue."[15]

Harkin was dismissive of these positions. With respect to the Water Power submission, he stated, "I cannot see that the memorandum from the Water Powers Branch is a serious argument against the Bill beyond the fact that it appears to hold up as a crime the idea of

Parliament alone having authority in the matter of commercialization of the Parks natural resources." And equally, in response to the Reclamation Service's position, he asserted, "It is not flattering to Parliament that the Reclamation Service considers that 'disaster would inevitably ensue' if these matters are to rest in the hands of Parliament."[16] Despite this, it is unquestionable that in conjunction with powerful opposing departmental interests, the issues raised were sufficient to have the minister withdraw the legislation. As it transpired, this proved to be extremely damaging for Harkin's cause, as the 1923 session, during which Stewart went on record as opposing water power development at Lake Minnewanka, represented the best chance for timely passage of a national parks act. Following the minister's decision on Minnewanka, Calgary Power changed tactics and began to publicly pursue development of the less-well-known Spray Lakes, while at the same moment another important element entered the picture.

The farmer-led Alberta provincial government had made it clear it had some interest in controlling provincial electrical power, leading to concerns about granting power rights at Spray Lakes. Immediately on the heels of the 1923 session a letter arrived on Stewart's desk from Alberta Attorney General J.E. Brownlee drawing attention to sections 2 and 5 of the proposed act and making a pointed request: "The Province is bound to be interested in the future in the possible development of the Spray Lakes water power resources and this Government is therefore interested in knowing just what legislation is proposed with respect to the granting of such resources, and if you propose proceeding with this Act at the present Session we would be glad if you would let us know just what is intended."[17] Although Cory was able to respond that the legislation had not been dealt with, the Alberta letter would prove to be just another shot-across-the-bow in the growing debate over control of natural resources, one that would prove an impediment to a new act again being seriously considered for some time.

Led by William Pearce, there were also strong opposition voices in Calgary from those associated with civic power matters who were successful in swaying public opinion. Pearce consistently criticized Harkin and the Parks Branch for opposition to what he thought was a clear case of common sense, as, for example, in a letter to the editor of the *Calgary Herald* concerning the Spray project: "Many of our guardians of public interest make a vital mistake of opposing in toto any movement when the best policy would be to guide it....Would it not therefore be good policy to provide for this contingency by guiding this matter on lines that would do the least damage to the scenic effects of the mountains—in fact, I contend that it could be guided so that it will not injure at all said scenic effects."[18] Harkin understood that Pearce's reputation, long experience, and tenacity made him a formidable opponent and behind the scenes used his own considerable influence to negate this position.

In early June 1923, Pearce began receiving letters from senior CPR officials questioning, as a representative of the company, his broad public profile in the matter. He protested that he was not making such statements as a CPR representative but rather as a private individual with a long history in water interests, and he expressed his suspicions about the source of the complaint. On June 16 he wrote Stewart concerning a recent letter to the minister regarding the necessity for water storage in the mountains after which he had begun to be criticized by his CPR superiors and queried, "It would be of very much interest to ascertain which particular official or officials of your department made such an assertion, and on what grounds he based it."[19] A week later he received a message from T.L. Naismith of the CPR's Natural Resources Department in Calgary concerning a coded telegram he had received from Vice-President D.C. Coleman which, while acknowledging that Pearce was expressing his personal views, nonetheless requested, "I wish you would tell him that his engagement in the controversy is causing us some embarrassment in Ottawa...[and] would regard it as a personal favor if he would desist from further controversy." Pearce responded with a promise "to follow the wishes of the Corporation," but in the next breath complained, "There are occasions when it may be the duty of an individual to continue action, even though it may cause 'some embarrassment in Ottawa.' I submit the parties at Ottawa who are making complaints against my actions have a good deal to learn about their duties as public officials, and if they truly appreciated their responsibilities they would welcome criticism and not try to choke it off. They are treating it as a personal matter when they should recollect that they are merely public servants." In a later comment to Coleman he added, "Mr. Harkin told me in March last he was going to 'fix' those who were advocating storage. If this Bill had been carried as drafted by him, he certainly would have succeeded so long as the Bill stood and he and his partisans had been permitted to enforce it."[20]

In his struggles with the Alberta government and Calgary civic power interests, the newly minted Canadian National Parks Association (CNPA) proved useful to Harkin. Within days of its formation in August 1923, Secretary A.S. Sibbald of Saskatoon informed the minister of its creation, offering "to co-operate and be of any possible service" in connection with the Parks Branch. An official letter also went to Harkin, noting that, "We would like to be kept closely in touch by the parks branch with any applications for concessions made in the Parks...and with proposals for legislation...which may affect conservation matters in Parks," and requested "a statement of the methods by which in your opinion the new association may be of assistance to the Parks Branch."[21] Careful about responding officially, it is unclear how Harkin dealt with this invitation, but it appears that at the very least he worked behind the scenes to assist the association in its campaigns. Pearce alluded to this assistance in a letter referring to his difficulty in getting across the message about the necessity of reservoirs in parks and claiming "owing to the attitude of the Canadian Park Authorities—an active propaganda started by them, through letters to newspapers, has resulted in a great many people, who know nothing at all about the subject, to write to the papers under the heading of 'Hands Off Our National Parks'."[22]

Although Wheeler had been appointed the CNPA's chair, on its executive was a prominent Calgary insurance broker and real estate developer, W.J. Selby Walker, son of Fort Calgary founder Colonel James Walker, who directed most of this "active propaganda" and eventually replaced Wheeler as the association's head. Walker was a real gadfly, poking, prodding, and rocking the boat as the Spray Lakes controversy took hold. Within a few weeks of creation of the association, he was asking Banff Superintendent Stronach, "Would it be possible to stir up something in Banff regarding the possible breaking of the dam and havoc in the Spray Valley extending to Banff?"[23] Harkin responded that he would be happy to receive any "information and suggestion which you can give us in this connection," but Walker was already off on a new tack, writing letters to the editor of the *Calgary Herald* on his position and supporting the commissioner's call for parliamentary involvement: "The National Parks Association views this application with great apprehension on account of the precedent involved, which, if granted would jeopardize all our parks. We trust that before any encouragement is given to this application, that the case be considered not solely on its merits as a storage basin, but that full consideration be given to all the probable consequences of this power dam at Spray Lakes....No effort should be made to pass this by order-in-council, but full opportunity should be given to the people of Canada through their representatives in parliament to express their desires."[24] A few months later the association began a successful letter-writing campaign to Stewart indicating that the correspondent endorsed the CNPA's objects, and stating, "I also wish to place myself on record as being opposed to all such concessions or franchises in the Canadian National Parks as are illustrated by the present application of The Montreal Engineering Company for reservoir and power rights in the Spray Lakes Basin."[25]

In reply to one of Pearce's earlier letters in May 1923, Stewart had noted, "I expect that before a decision is reached upon the conflicting representations which have been made I will take an opportunity of looking into matters on the ground."[26] This spoke to the possibility that he never intended to see the act through in 1923, instead putting it forward as a "straw man" to see what reaction it would bring. The Liberals were in a minority, requiring the support of the western farmer-led Progressives to keep them in office, which accounted for the minister's tendency not to be too definitive. In any event, by July he was in the West carrying out his inspection and talking to many of those with opinions on the matter. According to Pearce, upon visiting Spray Lakes he described it as "a marshy, mosquito-breeding area" and "expressed astonishment that the Parks authorities had objected to said storage." That fall, Stewart addressed the Lethbridge Board of Trade and stated

W.J. Selby Walker (second from left) on a Skyline Trail Hikers of the Canadian Rockies hike to Sentinel Pass, August 1933. As an avid outdoorsman, Walker became the chief spokesman for the Canadian National Parks Association and a strong supporter of Harkin in his battles with Calgary Power. [GA, NA-5566-4]

that in the matter of water storage projects, each one would have to be dealt with on its own merits. Despite this, as G.R. Marnoch of the Lethbridge Irrigation Council reported to Pearce in November, the Parks Branch was going ahead with surveying an expansion to the Waterton townsite, indicating "that if the Minister will not do what they tell him, they will take care of what they consider to be the Parks' interest behind his back."[27] However, CPR Chief Commissioner of Colonization and Development Colonel J.S. Dennis, also a former civil servant familiar with irrigation matters, provided Pearce with a more intuitive view: "I have no expectation that Mr. Harkin will make any further effort at the approaching session to obtain the passage of the Bill which he prepared and submitted at the last session. Both his Minister and other members of the Government are now better informed as to the situation and are not likely to be stampeded as they apparently were in the first instance."[28]

Dennis was wrong about attempts to get the bill passed, but right about Stewart digging in. In November 1923 Harkin informed Cory he would like to reintroduce the parks act for the spring session with few, if any, changes, but as the session drew near he reported on a recent discussion with Stewart and an important strategic decision emerging from it:

> A few days ago, I mentioned the Parks Act to the Minister and gathered from our conversation that it was improbable that the opposition which last session, manifested itself with respect to the Act would not likely be so aggressive this year. I therefore take it that there is a reasonable possibility of the Bill getting through.
>
> In this connection, however, Mr. Stewart seemed to think that it was not good policy to tie up to Parliament such large areas as are now included in National Parks. He seemed to think that absolute sanctity might be alright with respect to areas extending approximately twenty-five (25) miles from a centre like Banff but that any areas beyond that should be open to commercial exploitation. I told him I was not tied up to exceedingly large areas and that if reducing the areas would expedite the passage of the Bill I would be glad to go carefully into the matter and see what boundaries could be devised to meet his views....
>
> To me, getting the principle of absolute sanctity established appears to be the most important subject in connection with the National Parks. While I feel that our present parks are not a bit too large to take care of Canada's future recreational and educational needs, I would rather make some sacrifice in areas than sacrifice the principle of sanctity.[29]

In informing Cory of this epiphany, he was baring his soul in a way he rarely did. Having made this difficult decision, though, he was better prepared to tread the still treacherous path ahead, and it heavily influenced subsequent negotiations.

Nevertheless, Harkin would not again mention his willingness to bend until it became absolutely necessary and that this was still some time off was already becoming clear as a result of a debate in the House of Commons on April 10, 1924. In it, Stewart, while noting that there was no doubt that Calgary Power would require more electricity, indicated there was strong opposition on the part of authorities and therefore he was keeping an open mind. Conservative H.H. Stevens, known to be a supporter of parks, offered, "I gather from the minister's remarks that the power company still has some units that they can develop on the Bow River site, so that there is no need for great haste at this time." Stewart interjected, "And plenty of coal." This remark spoke volumes about the Parks Branch's stance at this point, as Harkin and the CNPA were arguing the coal resources of Alberta that could be used in steam-generated power production were massive, cheap, and would spare development of park waters. Stevens responded, "Exactly," and continued, "Having these things in mind I would think it would be a very fine thing if the government would declare that for a period of a year nothing will be done, and then in the interim let the public opinion adjust itself and familiarize itself with the circumstances." To this Stewart replied, "I think I can give my hon. Friend at once that assurance. I am not in any hurry to deal with this particular question because I think it is of much importance."[30]

Meanwhile, in January 1923 Stewart had made public his decision not to allow Calgary Power's generating project at Lake Minnewanka. In response, company President Drury had sent him a long epistle indicating that studies on the feasibility of the Spray project were underway but that power contract negotiations with Calgary had taken place based on the assumption of the Cascade plant and "we may not be able to get the City to agree to the higher price represented by the Spray project." The letter closed with an implied threat, "While we are naturally anxious to meet your views, we would in this event be forced to abandon the Spray project and to press for the Cascade site instead."[31] However, its main purpose was to protest against the department's own actions at Minnewanka. In an ironic turn-of-events, exactly six days before the announcement refusing Calgary Power's development, Harkin had informed the company in a cryptic communication, "I beg to advise you that this Branch is proceeding immediately with the construction of a Hydro Electric Power Plant for the town of Banff, utilizing the thimble in the Dam at Lake Minnewanka. The using of this thimble in connection with the proposed project and the taking of water through it for departmental power purposes is provided by the Agreement with regard to the storage of water in Lake Minnewanka and which was executed by the Department of the Interior and your Company on March 1, 1912."[32]

This action was occasioned by the CPR's decision to close down its steam plant at Bankhead, which provided Banff's power supply, as a follow-up to closing the mines themselves a few years earlier. It was just such a situation that the 1912 agreement had foreseen, but Drury protested it would reduce the water supply available for his company's proposed works, arguing that as the water needed to be conserved for high head usage during the winter season and the parks' development would operate year-round under less than a fifth of the head, its plan was wasteful. He further stressed that his proposal would improve the scenery by virtue of the lake being fed through the diversion of the Ghost River and complained, "Over two years ago we expressed verbally to the Park Commissioner our willingness to supply the Park with its power requirements and since then the point has been raised a number of times." And, in stating the plant was inevitable whether the Spray Lakes development went ahead or not, he declared that the parks plan was "not in the public interest" and expressed frustration "in view of the Calgary Power Company having offered to supply the power at a lower cost and in less time than the Parks could generate it themselves."[33]

In analyzing this letter for Cory, Harkin observed, "It appears, without doubt, from this letter that the Lake Minnewanka or Cascade development is the development the Company have in mind" and "their application policy stands revealed as one of expediency and of apparently trying to confuse the Department as to the ultimate object of their applications." He reminded his deputy that the parks project had been designed to only use the amount of water that the company, by the

Calgary Power's Cascade dam at Lake Minnewanka with penstock (lower right) for Banff power development, 1931. The Department of the Interior's 1923 decision to build a power-generating plant in Calgary Power's control dam at Lake Minnewanka, as allowed in the original 1912 agreement, enabled Harkin to steal a march on his corporate foe. [WMCR, V488-161-1]

terms of its agreement, must allow to pass over or through the existing dam and, therefore, the lake level would not be further affected. As to the claim that the proposed reservoir would be a visual improvement over existing conditions, Harkin contended there were already aesthetic problems for tourists visiting the lake early in the year due to mud flats and noted that as the company admitted that there would be an additional thirty- to thirty-five-foot annual rise and fall in the reservoir, it would delay its filling to as late as the first of August. With respect to the company's offer of power to supply Banff's needs, he claimed, "This Branch has not received any definite offer from the Calgary Power Company to supply Banff with power at a certain rate nor have they even stated that they could guarantee a continuous supply of power to Banff."[34] Convincing in his arguments, no halt was made in construction and the project was completed within a year, including installation of two generating units and taking over of the CPR's power distribution system in Banff townsite.

It seems Calgary Power was pressing this matter hard because of concerns about the provincial government's interest in developing its own power sources. Indeed, according to a press report, Superintendent Brown of the Calgary Street Railway and other electrical engineers were "of the opinion that the provincial government would make a paying investment by establishing a power plant in or near the mountains which would supply all the leading towns of Alberta with power."[35] As mentioned, Attorney General Brownlee wrote Stewart in June 1923 concerning the effect of the proposed parks act on provincial interests in water, but it was not his government's first communication on the matter. On March 29, Premier Herbert Greenfield had wired Prime Minister Mackenzie King concerning Calgary Power's attempts to secure rights at Spray Lakes, stating that it was "an exceptionally valuable power site" and that "in public interest these power rights should not be alienated without careful consideration."[36] This position was part of the larger question of control of natural resources, which had remained in Dominion hands upon the creation of Alberta and Saskatchewan in 1905, an issue that had been actively discussed in regular conferences since 1921 but had foundered on the matter of compensation to the provinces for already alienated lands and resources. As it transpired, Stewart's agreement to a one-year hiatus in the decision on power development would result in the ongoing debate co-opting both Harkin's agenda for passage of a new parks act and Calgary Power's plans for park waters.

The principals in the discussion were Brownlee, Mackenzie King, and Harkin's minister, Charles Stewart, with the task not being made easier given that Stewart had been routed as Alberta premier in 1921 by Brownlee's UFA government and that the two men disliked and mistrusted each other. In 1924, as a result of several deficit budgets and the falling price of agricultural commodities, the province attempted to impose a tax on holders of mineral lands, leading to a protest from the two most affected interests, the CPR and the HBC, and federal disallowance of the provincial statute. This served to sharpen Alberta's focus on the main objective, the transfer of minerals and other resources. Lawyer and Chief Electoral Officer O.M. Biggar was tasked to work with Brownlee, also a lawyer, in drafting an agreement, and in May the work was reviewed by a ministerial committee representing both governments. Their discussion resulted in the redrafting of several clauses but King then indicated his cabinet wished to study the draft further over the summer. During the attempts to reach agreement, Harkin had periodically been asked his opinion, but this effort marked the first time that he was given a full voice. Cory requested on January 8, 1925 that he provide "a statement setting forth what special matters should be taken into consideration in order to safeguard the interests of the Dominion in the Canadian National Parks, game reserves, bird sanctuaries, etc."[37]

As a first step, Harkin consulted Wardle, who pointed out that of primary importance was that the national parks in Alberta should remain under Dominion control, both with respect to their lands and their natural resources, and that the province should have no right, other than that granted by the Dominion, to carry out any river control, water storage, or power projects in park areas. Wardle also offered that in the absence of any park or Dominion regulations to carry out administration on park lands, such as liquor control, health, and education, Canada should be able to request that provincial laws and regulations in these areas be applied. Harkin held extensive discussions with Biggar on this matter of dual control, with the lawyer noting that despite the agreements of 1918 there would be several areas of friction, particularly with respect to taxes and water rates. Accordingly, he suggested that it would be worthwhile to examine the possibility of excluding the parks from the province, such as was done in the United States and Harkin, never a supporter of sharing administration, eagerly concurred. Not surprisingly, then, when he wrote to Cory concerning this matter on February 12, Harkin came down firmly on the side of removal:

> I understand the Province does not wish to take over the National Park areas and therefore the only question at issue is whether these areas shall be withdrawn from the Province and made Federal areas or whether they shall continue to constitute part of the Province. There are many difficulties on both sides of this question but the more I study it the more I am convinced that the better

> course to follow is to create the Parks Federal areas as is the case in the United States....
>
> The Parks now are part of the Province. This means that on many matters there is dual jurisdiction and that on some important matters there is only provincial jurisdiction....To permit of the continuation of dual jurisdiction is to imperil the whole future of national parks. In matters of local taxation there is only provincial jurisdiction. The Federal Government has to spend large sums of money annually on purely municipal activities but is without any authority to impose taxation within the Parks to help meet such expenditures.[38]

Stating that this was unfair to the rest of Canada, the matter formed a significant section in a twenty-five-page memorandum submitted to Cory on February 21, 1925.

At this point, when it was not apparent exactly what difficulties would arise with respect to the resources agreement, this document was meant to stake out a position and prop it up against any potential provincial attack. That it was warranted became apparent when Premier Greenfield wrote Stewart and asked if it was intended to change the existing legislation affecting the resources in the Alberta forest reserves and national parks. This was a clear indication that, while not interested in national park lands, there was provincial interest in park resources, an issue that became even more apparent after a Commons debate on the transfer in June. On June 23, while the session was still in progress, Harkin wrote in a note to Spero, "Kindly see that before next Session a suitable Bill is drafted which will place the Natural Resources of the National Parks entirely under the control of Parliament. This should be on the lines of the recent discussion in the House."[39] Spero drafted an amendment to the *Forest Reserves and Parks Act* and in the preamble of the section dealing with the occupation and use of parks lands it included wording stating "there shall be no alienation of any of the natural resources in the said park except such as is necessary for

John E. Brownlee, n.d. Brownlee began negotiations for the transfer of Alberta's natural resources in 1923 and in 1926, shortly after becoming premier, he completed a preliminary agreement staking out a provincial position in the control of park waters and resources. [GA, NA-1451-11]

railway right of way and as hereinafter provided, unless such alienation is provided by an act of Parliament."[40]

On November 23, 1925, Brownlee succeeded Greenfield as premier of Alberta and, facing the necessity of an election, visited Ottawa in early January and played his ace, assuring King of continuing support for his minority government by the Progressives if the speech from the throne announced the transfer agreement. The tactic worked perfectly and on January 9, 1926 he and Minister of Railways Vernor Smith signed an agreement with King and his ministers Lapointe and Stewart.[41] Early versions of this agreement had been in departmental circulation since the previous summer, and Harkin had been asked by Cory to supply "the benefit of any observations that you would care to make" as part of the departmental opinion that would be set before the minister. The draft contained some fourteen sections, dealing with such important matters as "subsidy in lieu of lands terminated," "transfer of public lands generally," "school lands fund," "waters and fisheries," "Indian reserves," "other forest reserves and parks," and "historic sites, bird sanctuaries etc.," but Harkin confined his remarks only to those impacting directly on branch interests.

Under section 6, "waters and fisheries," the commissioner requested that the wording be strengthened to make it crystal clear that "the Dominion shall be absolutely free to do as it pleases and that the Province shall have no right, implied or otherwise, to demand water within a park." Most alarming was section 12 under "other forest reserves and parks" which read, "The Crown lands, including the rights of fishery, but not the mines or minerals or the royalties incident thereto, included...in the parks specified in Schedule A hereto attached shall continue to be vested in the Crown and administered by the Government of Canada for the purposes of Canada." This Harkin found "absolutely objectionable," arguing that the future welfare of the parks could only be guaranteed if minerals remained exclusively under Dominion control. Even though the province's right to grant or lease mineral rights was to be subject to the consent of and conditions imposed by the minister, he pointed out, "The essential point is that the Province has a definite right to demand the development of minerals...[and] mineral development is certain in practically all cases to be detrimental to the parks and the agreement as it stands means that there will always be friction between the Province and the Dominion on this subject." Believing the province to be mainly interested in the revenue from natural resources, Harkin suggested, "The minerals remain in the

Dominion but that at any time should the Dominion authorize the development of any mine in the park such mine shall immediately become subject to provincial law as well as to any provisions that may be stipulated by the Dominion for the protection of park interests." Other concerns included a need for assurances that wording indicating the application of the existing parks act to the agreement would be carried on if a new parks act was passed; a need for interpretation of the wording giving the Dominion exclusive jurisdiction to legislate for the parks; assurances that any laws of the province that would be applied that were "not repugnant to the provisions of the Forest Reserves and Parks Act" would include future laws as well as those presently on the statute books; stronger wording concerning the province's responsibility for bird sanctuaries; wording requiring that the province not only refrain from disposing of identified historic sites but actually transfer them to the Dominion; and "a clause clearly applying everything in the agreement to all new parks that may later be created in Alberta and to all changes that may be made to the boundaries of existing parks."[42]

In forwarding these suggestions to Cory on July 29, 1925, Harkin requested assurances that should there be any doubt about incorporating them in the resources agreement, he be given the opportunity to make further representations. However, when a new draft was forwarded to him on January 5, 1926, he responded with a blistering critique expressing with astonishing frankness his unhappiness with the fact that the minerals in the parks were still to be vested with the province and maintaining that, "Everyone with administrative experience knows that such safeguards against damaging the park as are provided will in the first place open the way for constant conflict, constant pressure and almost certainly will in the end mean commercial exploitation of mines within the Parks." He then went on to make the old argument, "If these parks are to be not in reality any different to the contiguous areas then there is no justification for expending Dominion money on their care and development as parks...[and] the only fair course to the rest of the people of Canada is to be honest about the matter and either preserve the parks in reality as parks or hand them over in their entirety to the province and relieve the rest of Canada of the burden of maintenance." He completed this diatribe by attacking the dual authority still evident, stating that it could never work out satisfactorily and that "either parks are worth while or they are not. If they are worth while then I submit the authority charged with their conservation and development should have its hands free and not be embarrassed by questions of dual authority."[43]

By the time Cory received this pointed missive the signing of the agreement was only two days off, and, although Harkin had not alluded to it, some of his arguments had actually been heard. The final version contained an additional clause, number 18, which more specifically indicated that Canada would not dispose of its interests in any parks lands unless there were compelling reasons for doing so, to the extent that it would actually transfer the lands to the province in that eventuality.[44] This was highly reminiscent of his position in his earlier battle with Irrigation over the use of park waters, implying that park lands could be used by other interests, but only if they were not required for parks purposes. Inviolability would be maintained because decisions on administration of resources and control of lands would remain firmly in Dominion hands, subject only to the powers of Parliament. Accordingly, the agreement immediately came under attack from Mayor George Webster of Calgary in a letter of February 13 to Brownlee, noting, "The first part of the clause is worded in such a way that, if the Dominion Government Department of the Interior were so disposed, they could refuse a permit to either the Provincial Government or a private company for the leasing of any of the lands for storage reservoirs" and suggested "now is the time for changing the wording of this clause," understanding that once in place it would be highly doubtful that Parliament would do so. In closing the letter, the mayor identified the source of the offending clause: "I might say that, in my opinion, the wording of this clause was dictated by Mr. Harkin, the Parks Commissioner, as part of his propaganda against any development in the park area."[45] Similarly, in a letter to Pearce a few days later, he made the bemused observation, "It is evident to me that Mr. Harkin got his fine

Italian hand in clause 18 in the agreement between the Dominion and the Province regarding the transfer of natural resources."[46]

Webster's assessment was correct, but this apparent victory was not enough for the hard-driving commissioner. A few weeks earlier Harkin had again written to Cory complaining, "In view of the representations made in this memorandum and made in my previous memorandum I cannot help feeling that the Agreement as executed is unsatisfactory in many particulars on the Parks' standpoint and that if it is not changed it will result in many difficulties and complications in connection with Parks' administration."[47] While important, from his perspective the inclusion of clause 18 was only one more step along the way to his ultimate goal of complete inviolability.

TWELVE

A Park in Every Province

AS HE SLOWLY MOVED forward his concept of inviolability and the need for new parks legislation at the beginning of the postwar reconstruction period, steps toward the furthering of the branch's tourism and recreation mandates and ministerial direction to rationalize the organization of historic sites led to an expansion of Harkin's responsibilities. Along with his questioning of the status of wildlife sanctuaries as national parks, these activities would soon come to be viewed through the lens of a growing North American acceptance for a "national park standard." This was not a straightforward process of moving toward a well-defined goal, but rather an uneven and sometimes difficult change in emphasis and direction. At the same time, Harkin's accomplishments in making parks important to Canadians led to increasing demand for national parks across the country, and the public and their political representatives did not necessarily see them in the same light as did he and others in the branch. Ultimately, these concerns merged with his ongoing efforts toward creating a new act, providing important influences in defining the future role of Canada's parks.

In terms of helping Canadians appreciate their nation's rich heritage, the branch's efforts in the field of historic sites grew significantly, but not always smoothly, in the 1920s. During the war years there had been no funds available to follow up the first tentative steps taken with Fort Howe and Fort Anne, but Minister Roche had begun to be pressured by the Ontario Historical Society as early as 1914 to preserve the site of the 1813 Battle of Beaver Dams near Thorold, Ontario, as a national battlefield park. Similarly, in 1919 Meighen became concerned about the fate of some of the old western fur posts in Saskatchewan. These concerns led Meighen to turn to the Parks Branch as the only agency with experience in historic sites, and he asked Harkin to prepare a policy dealing with heritage matters, a request it appears the commissioner was none too happy to receive. Given his manifold postwar challenges and the scarcity of available resources, he complained to the prime minister's secretary that he "very reluctantly took on this additional work." But, having done so, he was determined not to make any missteps. With insufficient expertise within his own staff and with the model of the Wild Life Advisory Board to guide him, in March 1919 he proposed the formation of a new expert board: "It was considered that the best results could be obtained, both from an historic preservation standpoint and also from the economy, if the Department had access to the advice of a Board composed of men who would give their services gratis, and whose advice would be authoritative and at the same time utilize the existing machinery of a Branch of the Government service for carrying into effect the recommendations of this advisory board."[1]

Meighen accepted the proposal, and in his annual report for 1919–1920, Harkin recorded creation of the Historic Sites and Monuments Board, henceforth a key element in Canada's heritage administration:

> The work with respect to the preservation of historic and pre-historic sites, which had been laid aside on account of the war, was resumed during the year and an important step taken in this connection. This was the formation of what is known as the Historic Sites and Monuments Board. In carrying on this work it had been found the development of a policy concerning so wide a field demanded expert knowledge with regard to practically all the historic sites in Canada and their relative value. The Government, therefore, thought it advisable to endeavour to secure the assistance of experts intimately acquainted with these matters and a number of prominent Canadian historians kindly consented to serve as members of an advisory board.[2]

In addition to himself, the board membership included Chairman Brigadier General E.A. Cruikshank, Benjamin Sulte of Ottawa, James Coyne of St. Thomas, Ontario, W.C. Milner of Halifax, and W.O. Raymond of Saint John, New Brunswick. Its first meeting, held in October 1919, determined that it should carry out a survey of Canadian historic sites so as to be in a position to recommend which should receive government attention.

Unfortunately, while all members were knowledgeable historians, they quickly began to promote their own particular interest or region, leading to competition and rancour, and the West was not represented at all. Another source of disappointment was a lack of resources, as the finances the branch was able to obtain were earmarked for higher priorities, leaving little for the historic sites initiative. Accordingly, the stratagem of creating national parks from historic sites was largely dropped as expensive and ineffective, while the sites that were identified had differing needs—some important for a particular historic event that could be marked with an inexpensive plaque and others featuring historic buildings or remains requiring costly preservation actions and more formal interpretation. Commemoration efforts tended to be favoured by the Ontario and Quebec members, while Maritimes member Milner wished to see more preservation activities so that historic sites would help form a distinctive regional landscape. The board also agreed that only sites of "national significance" should be commemorated, again begging differing interpretations.[3]

Within a year of its first meeting these differences had led to a crisis atmosphere and Milner, an employee of the Public Archives of Canada collecting in the Maritimes who never believed the board should be created, began attempts to have it abolished. He appealed to now retired Prime Minister Borden to use his influence in the matter, describing the board as "a hopeless body" and while criticizing all its members, saved his most pointed barbs for Cruikshank and Harkin: "This leaves Harkin and Cruikshank; these are clerks in the Public Service who show indications from either travel or reading of no fitness for the service. I would think it somewhat presumptuous in such men accepting a position that demands an intimate knowledge of the country and its history, had I not learned that Mr. Harkin in particular had been for some time working up this 'job.'...I think the Board ought to be relieved of all further duty and a new Board struck; if that cannot be accomplished then an Eastern Forts and Monuments Board ought to be organized."[4] Borden forwarded this letter to Dominion Archivist Arthur Doughty for his opinion and he concurred, offering, "I still think the plan I recommended to you at the time this commission was formed would have been better. I suggested the powers of the Battlefield Commission should be enlarged and should be termed the National Memorial Commission."[5] Borden passed the letters on to Meighen with the note, "Mr. Doughty's observations are undoubtedly well-founded."

In response, the prime minister strongly supported the board, particularly the commissioner, whom he had come to know and respect during his recent term as minister of the Interior: "I think that Mr. Doughty is not quite right with regard to the Historic Sites and Monuments Board, nor is Mr. Milner right. Mr. Harkin is one of the most competent officers in the Government Service and certainly was not desirous of taking on unnecessary responsibilities."[6] Harkin gave his side of the story in a memorandum to Meighen's private secretary, recounting the circumstances surrounding the board's creation and explaining, "It is quite true that I am a member of the Board and equally true that I have no pretensions to any extensive knowledge of Canadian history. The reason that I am on the Board is that as I have charge of the executive work in connection with historic matters it was considered advisable that I should sit with the other members of the Board when they were formulating their recommendations." With respect to the membership he offered that all the names had been carefully considered and approved by Meighen and "that apparently the only mistake made was in the nomination of W.C. Milner as a member." Expanding on this, he outlined his objection: "With the exception of the first meeting of the Board his presence has been productive of nothing but delay and trouble. In fact conditions had become such that some weeks ago it became clear to me that it would be utterly impossible to retain any other members on the Board if Mr. Milner was to continue as a member and I am recommending to the Minister that Mr. Milner be removed."[7]

Action on this front was not immediately forthcoming, leading to the first few years of the board's efforts getting off to a rather shaky start. Funds were made available in 1920 to hire Arthur A. Pinard, a former army officer and one of the few francophones in the branch, to head up the program under the direct supervision of Deputy Commissioner Williamson, but the legislative backing to give it teeth proved elusive. Without a coherent approved policy and with a penurious budget limited to $10,000 annually, Pinard was forced to deal with his many responsibilities on an ad hoc basis. Accordingly, even though the initial survey identified 547 prospective sites, in its first four years the accomplishments under the new program were minimal. In 1920, the board commissioned a design for a commemorative plaque from Major Ernest Fosbery, RCA, and the first one was placed in 1922 at Port Dover, a site nominated by Coyne to mark the claiming of the Lake Erie basin in 1670 for New France. It was followed by the erection of twenty-four plaques in 1923, fifteen in Ontario, mostly at sites chosen by Cruikshank commemorating his particular interest, the United Empire Loyalist defence of Canada. Although several other sites were identified for possible preservation—Louisbourg in Nova Scotia, Fort

Beauséjour in New Brunswick, Forts Chambly and Lennox in Quebec, Fort Prince of Wales (Churchill) and Fort Garry in Manitoba, Fort Pelly in Saskatchewan, and Fort Langley in British Columbia—there was little interest among board members and even less money available to take any real action, other than identification of remains and a few surveys.[8]

Matters improved somewhat after the major Parks Branch reorganization begun in 1921–1922 when a new Historic Sites Division was added. Pinard was provided with an assistant, the engineering and town planning divisions were seconded to provide expertise and by the 1923–1924 fiscal year the historic sites appropriation had doubled. In March 1923 Harkin got his wish, as a reinvigorated Historic Sites Board was appointed, dropping Milner and adding J.P. Edwards of Halifax, J.C. Webster of Shediac, New Brunswick, and F. Howay of New Westminster, BC, considerably strengthening its Maritimes and western Canadian influences. At its insistence, Harkin made a further effort to gain legislative backing for the program, drafting a new *National Historic Sites Act* in the spring of 1924. But once again this proposal and an accompanying new draft of the parks act failed to move forward and thereafter historic sites were amalgamated with proposals for the larger act. However, the new program carried on with the commemoration of historic sites being rationed to a maximum of five each year in each of four regions—the Maritimes, Quebec, Ontario, and the West—and attention being given to gaining control of important ruins for later development, including the aforementioned forts and the citadels at Halifax and Quebec City.

While the resources to carry out extensive restoration work were unavailable, some efforts were made on a few existing preserved sites, such as Fort Chambly, where repair work was performed on the fortifications and the cemetery and a museum was created, and at Fort Lennox, where a custodian was appointed, an interpretive brochure issued, and attempts made to improve the museum collection. Other sites were obtained and some modest work carried out to make them attractive for tourists. At Prescott, Ontario, the blockhouse and caretaker's residence at old Fort Wellington were acquired in 1924 and,

Members of the Historic Sites and Monuments Board of Canada, 1924. The appointment of a new Historic Sites and Monuments Board in 1923 strengthened the branch's historic sites program in the Maritimes and the West. [LAC, PA-066730]

after minor repairs, became a functioning historic park, while in 1925 the branch acquired Fort Langley on BC's lower mainland and created a museum similar to that at Fort Lennox.[9]

As indicated, some historic sites had advantages in helping to achieve the branch's tourism goals. For example, Fort Lennox, located on Ile-aux-Noix in the Richelieu River, a strategic location near the U.S. border dating from 1609 alternately occupied by the French, Americans, and British, was already a functioning heritage attraction and a stopover point for river cruises when its operation was conveyed to the branch in 1921. Development of the 210-acre, five-island complex was therefore akin to creating a recreation area similar to the St. Lawrence River Islands Park, an idea that was gaining popularity in the post-war period. Harkin had, of course, long been a proponent of having parks or recreation areas close to large cities, and he first mentioned the idea for a more extensive system of recreational reserves outside the parks proper in his 1922 report: "These are reservations of Crown lands which are adapted for public use and enjoyment for summer resort and recreational purposes but which do not possess scenery of sufficient importance to justify their creation as national parks. They are usually lands about a lake, which are unfit for agriculture and so have remained unpatented, but which are adapted for summer cottage sites and recreational purposes."[10] As was the case with the soon-to-be-created animal park at Wood Buffalo, the only legislation available to accomplish these reservations was the *Forest Reserves and Parks Act*. Accordingly, when the first of these areas, a seventeen-acre promontory known as Vidal's Point on Lake Katepwa north of Indian Head, Saskatchewan, was transferred from the control of the Forestry Branch in 1921 in order that its amenities could be better developed, Harkin referred to it as a "national park recreation area," but it had to be set aside by order-in-council of October 31, 1921 as "a Dominion Park...to be known as Vidal's Point Park."[11] Another area around Brereton Lake in the Whiteshell district of eastern Manitoba joined it in 1922, and a third site at Lesser Slave Lake, Alberta, was reserved but not given full recreation park status.

Apart from the new directions represented by historic parks and recreation areas, by the early 1920s Harkin's perspective on the traditional parks had also been enhanced by a new emphasis on their spiritual dimensions. From the outset interested in the social, recreational, and health-giving benefits of national parks to mankind, he had now become a full believer in the transformational value of their wilderness landscapes. The concept, clearly an outgrowth of his admiration for transcendentalists such as Whitman, Emerson, and Thoreau, was first stated in an article he wrote for the 1918 Alpine Club of Canada journal

Bathing beach at Vidal's Point, Katepwa Lake, Saskatchewan, 1923. Vidal's Point was the first park created specifically for recreation purposes in response to regional demands for national parks. [LAC, PA-019357]

under the title of "Our Need for National Parks." In it, while recognizing the social value of recreation in the wilderness for Canadians occasioned by his attendance at the club's 1912 Vermilion Pass camp, he also noted its higher meaning:

> If life in the wilderness revitalizes the body of a man and frees and clears his mind, the contemplation of beauty liberates that deepest part of him which we call the soul. It takes us, as the common phrase puts it, "out of ourselves," that is, it lets us out of the prison of the ego and brings us into contact with the Universal....
>
> Almost everyone who goes to the wilderness experiences, however dimly, a consciousness of recreation which is the result of something more than mere exercise and the effects of sunshine and fresh air, a finer ether in which his soul is enlarged and purified, a perceived sense "of something far more deeply infused," which answers a greater need than that of mind or body."[12]

Although not often referred to, it is clear that this belief had begun to significantly influence Harkin's thinking, and it likely helped to sustain him during his frequent bouts of stress-related illness, probably accompanied by depression, while also reinforcing his belief in the need for the inviolability of park lands.

In his postwar efforts to expand the branch's activities and influence, Harkin's actions had borne important fruit by the mid-1920s. His success at carving out a niche for the branch in the Department of the Interior was attested to by the statistics—in 1912–1913 the branch budget was $223,588, or 4 per cent of the departmental appropriation; by 1923–1924 it was $1,269,827, slightly over 18 per cent. Over the same period the staff complement had quadrupled to some two dozen officers in its five divisions.[13] At the same time, Harkin had reached full maturity as commissioner and entered a period where his missionary zeal of earlier years was replaced by efforts to solidify the gains. This consolidation was also evident in his personal life as the frenetic and often unhealthy pace of earlier times gave way to a more normal lifestyle. His unrelenting schedule had provided little time for social activities and he had lived in an apartment close to his new headquarters in the Bryson Building on Queen Street in order to be as efficient as possible. He had continued his work with the Boy Scout movement and his passion for golf remained, mainly carried out through his membership in the prestigious Rivermead Club in nearby Gatineau. Introduced in 1922 to Rotary, a service organization linked to one's profession, he had quickly become an active member of Ottawa's club, his particular contribution being the organization of stage shows it regularly put on for charity purposes. But, most important, having reached the half-century mark as a bachelor, was Harkin's decision to marry. His bride was the former Jean McCuaig of Ottawa and after their wedding in 1925 the couple settled down to domestic life at 222 Clemow Avenue in Ottawa's Glebe, a district popular with senior bureaucrats.

An opportunity to reflect on his accomplishments was provided in the department's 1926–1927 annual report, marking the fifteenth anniversary of the Parks Branch's creation. Recalling that in 1911 national parks consisted of a combined area of 4,020 square miles represented by five scenic reserves in the Rockies, two animal reserves on the prairies, and the Thousand Islands of the St. Lawrence River, Harkin noted that currently there were ten scenic parks, three animal reserves, and two historic parks encompassing 10,300 square miles. Even more satisfying was how the idea of national parks had been embraced, not only in Canada, but also on a global basis:

> There is, indeed, nothing more surprising that the way in which the national park idea has spread and taken hold of public imagination. Fifteen years ago the sound philosophical and economic principles back of this form of conservation had scarcely been recognized. Canadians, as a whole, were indifferent to their great possessions.... In recent years, however, there has been a remarkable change in the public attitude. The widespread growth of travel, which is one of the marked features of this century, has given places of outstanding scenery a new interest and value. Alarm at the changes in the face of the country due to the rapid extension of our present industrial civilization, has emphasized the necessity of conserving a few untouched areas. In consequence, in the past few years, we have seen the national parks movement spread over the entire civilized world.[14]

This evolution in thinking with respect to parks and conservation, at least in part a result of Harkin's own efforts, was also referred to by Cory, who, in addressing the importance of Canada's parks as a model for other nations, mentioned the creation of a separate service for parks in 1911 was "well ahead of public opinion in most countries," including the United States, and that foreign representatives were now investigating Canada's parks organization.[15]

In closing his remarks on progress, Harkin noted that national parks were a "magnet" for tourist travel, which led to a "demand for the creation of new parks in sections of the country where they do not exist and in consequence a new responsibility arises, that in the creation of any new areas there be no lowering of the national standard already established." This statement encapsulated two threads that were to become fundamental to Harkin's actions over the remaining decade of his career—a growing desire for new parks in parts of the country where they did not exist and conformity to a standard in their selection. He had begun referring to the concept of a standard in 1922 when envisioning the creation of recreation areas, which, he stated, "do not possess scenery of sufficient importance to justify their creation as national parks." Scenic qualities were, therefore, regarded as critical in the application of a standard, but recreational attributes and wilderness character were also important. For example, in a memorandum to Cory in 1925 concerning the establishment of new parks, he argued, "According to the standards which we have adopted with respect to National parks, park areas must be outstanding in their scenic and recreational values. In addition our inclination has been towards large areas preferably in wilderness condition because one of the purposes of a National park is to preserve bits of original Canada for all time."[16]

Consideration for using a standard appears to have come from the United States where, after nearly a decade of discussion, the idea would be drawn up by the Camp Fire Club of America into a treatise entitled "National Park Standards" and published in the August 1929 edition of the periodical *Parks and Recreation*. Among its tenets were that park areas "must be of national interest to warrant their commitment to national care," and that they be "justified and insured by the educational and spiritual benefits to be derived from contact with pristine wilderness." For the first time, the idea of integrity of ecological systems was referred to in the requirement that they form "a logical unit, embracing all territory required for effective administration and for rounding out the life zones of its flora and fauna," and be "a sanctuary for the scientific care, study and preservation of all wild plant and animal life within limits, to the extent that no species shall become extinct." The treatise also incorporated Harkin's thinking about inviolability: "Parks must be kept free of all industrial uses, and that sanctuary, scientific and primitive values must always take precedence over recreational or other values." In addition, it was necessary for the standard to be rigorously enforced, eliminating those parks failing to meet it; adding those that met its scenic, scientific and educational goals; and withdrawing legislation that, in certain circumstances, allowed for utilization of park resources. Finally, it addressed some issues concerning the expansion of park systems, indicating that parks should differ in their physical aspects and should represent as wide a range of land forms "of supreme quality" as possible.[17]

These emerging ideas had informed Harkin's view in 1923 when his attention turned eastward to the need for parks in Ontario and the eastern provinces where "there are still wilderness areas that are specially adapted for recreational purposes and that could be acquired now and set aside at slight expense." One region suggested was the Laurentians, within reach of the large eastern Canadian population centres. He also favoured a Maritime park "including some part of the beautiful sea coast and the original forest if any area where this remains can be secured."[18] Therein lay the rub, as "can be secured" meant money, either paid to purchase private holdings or compensate for Indian lands or satisfy a provincial government averse to freely turning over Crown lands to a senior government. This was initially the case with respect to the best opportunity to create a new eastern park on a group of islands in Lake Ontario's Georgian Bay. As related, the islands were one location that the branch had considered after the 1913 amendment as, like Thousand Islands, they consisted of lands formerly occupied by natives, in this case Chippewas, that could be acquired for very little. Part of an archipelago along the lake's north and northeastern shores, they were a boating, fishing, and camping paradise. Formal steps to acquire the largest island, Beausoleil, were initiated after Historic Sites Board Chair Cruikshank recommended it for national park purposes in 1921, but the matter was delayed while Harkin examined twenty-eight smaller neighbouring islands. In January 1923 he sought a $25,000 appropriation to extinguish native claims on Beausoleil and, although funds were approved by the minister for this and several succeeding years, they were consistently cut in favour of higher priorities. Only after private offers were made to Indian Affairs did the department finally relent, and the islands were purchased for Interior and established as Georgian Bay Islands National Park on December 28, 1929.[19] It became one of only two eastern parks created in the 1920s, the other being Fort Beauséjour National Park, a French fort dating from the mid-seventeenth century located near Amherst, New Brunswick. Fifty-nine acres were transferred to the branch in 1923 and, through provincial political influence, including that of Historic Sites Board member J.C. Webster, they were designated as an historic park in 1926.[20]

While these small parks were important beachheads, the lack of appropriate eastern lands in federal hands meant that it was more likely that larger new parks would continue to appear in the West. Neither Saskatchewan nor Manitoba yet had parks, and so it was not surprising that it would be on the prairies where Harkin worked out the competing aspects of making what were essentially recreational areas into national parks while still paying heed to the standard. In both provinces, it was interest in wildlife that kick-started national park movements. Early activity in Manitoba focused on the Riding Mountain Forest Reserve, established in 1906 north of Brandon and south of Dauphin, featuring a thousand-foot escarpment rising above the surrounding plains and a number of beautiful lakes. One, Clear Lake, featured a subdivision for resort cottages established by the Forestry Branch in 1914, but the reserve also contained one of the largest herds of elk in Canada, and it was the potential for their preservation that initially caught Harkin's attention. He and Hewitt first discussed the matter in 1917, the latter strongly in favour of turning the reserve into a park to protect the animals, and suggesting it be discussed by the Wild Life Board.[21] But before that could occur, a petition was received from area residents pointing out "the Game Reserve is one of the beauty spots of Canada having beautiful lakes and forests and would be an ideal spot for an Animal Park." Asked by Cory to provide his view on the matter, Harkin responded that the reserve would not only be useful for protection of elk and other wildlife but "this area being high, well wooded and well watered, if properly developed on park lines would provide a recreational resort of special service to the people of Manitoba." However, given his ongoing discussions with Forestry, he equivocated, admitting, "On principle I have not felt like recommending the establishment of Dominion Parks within forest reserves in the prairies proper and I have on several occasions made it clear to Mr. Campbell, Director of Forestry, that this is the policy which I favour." Seeking Campbell's view, the deputy minister was informed that, at his request, he and Harkin had worked out an agreement "that where the forest interests predominated the protection of game should be handled by the Forest service," and in Riding Mountain he believed this was the case.[22] Not surprisingly, the initial attempt to establish a park at Riding Mountain ended with this letter.

The issue lay dormant until January 1923 when, in one of the many initiatives for buffalo parks in connection with the proposed slaughter at Wainwright, the Archbishop of Rupert's Land suggested that part of the Riding Mountain reserve would make a fine location for such a purpose. In conveying the idea to Harkin, Cory enthused, "It would certainly be a great thing for Manitobans if we could establish the Riding Mountain Forest Reserve as a Dominion Park and set aside a part of it at the southern end as a Buffalo Park." But there were also other areas in Manitoba being touted, with several old timers' associations supporting a "Manitoba Buffalo Park" at Gladstone, northwest of Portage la Prairie, MP Robert Forke favouring a Brandon Board of Trade resolution to use the Spruce Woods Forest Reserve east of that city, and Mayor Webb of Winnipeg suggesting the possibility of such a reserve in eastern Manitoba. These initiatives were not the first time Harkin had heard a proposal for establishment of a new buffalo park on the prairies, a similar request from Saskatchewan having been made in June 1921 when the Wainwright herd was reported to be increasing rapidly. The Prince Albert Board of Trade asked that such a park be created in a portion of the Pines Forest Reserve southeast of the city, but after consulting departmental officers, Harkin indicated that the area was largely fenced by ranching interests and suggested efforts be combined with a provincial government initiative to have an antelope park established in southern Saskatchewan. The movement was revived in 1926 as part of a tourism plan promoted by the Saskatoon Board of Trade, although once again heeding Harkin's argument not to create any new buffalo parks, it suffered the same fate as the Manitoba requests when the department pleaded lack of funds. But, as with Manitoba, talk of the possibility of a national park in the province had wider repercussions and became entangled in a web of politics—in this case prime ministerial politics—taking the matter of park-making to a whole new level and requiring modification in Harkin's thinking about a national park standard.

North of Prince Albert lay the Sturgeon Forest Reserve and surrounding territory comprising a beautiful area of rocks, rivers, lakes, and forests entirely distinct from the open prairies to the south and containing good potential for recreational development. A traditional hunting and trapping area for the Woodland Cree of Montreal Lake to the east, in the early part of the century it had also been commercially fished and heavily logged before being burned over in 1919. With its forest regenerating, in 1924 the Forestry Branch had surveyed a summer cottage subdivision similar to that at Manitoba's Clear Lake on the reserve's major lake, Waskesiu (Red Deer), and in 1925, when the Prince Albert Board of Trade again brought up the issue of a national park for Saskatchewan, it was this area, where several members held rights to lots, that was suggested. Prince Albert citizens, led by T.C. Davis, a minister in the provincial government and former mayor, asked Minister James Gardiner to investigate the possibility, and he had Commissioner of Labour and Industries Thomas Molloy write the Parks Branch to find out what would be involved. Harkin identified the required qualifications: "You will realize that National Parks so far adopted have set standards, whether of scenery, as animal sanctuaries or in special recreational usefulness and any proposed National Park should reach these standards of quality....Any new park scheme would therefore have to be considered very carefully and be of exceptional character to receive endorsement at present." Although the commissioner did invite a proposal, in his reply Molloy expressed doubt that the area being considered would qualify and was concerned that the exclusion of hunting and trapping necessary in a park would be unacceptable.[23] Not so the Board of Trade, which created a national park committee to put together a proposal for the area around Waskesiu and also agreed to further investigate the buffalo park idea. It soon had what appeared to be very influential support for, as luck would have it, Prime Minister Mackenzie King had lost his North York seat in the

Dominion election of October 1925 and in January 1926 was invited by Gardiner, now premier of Saskatchewan, to run in a by-election for the safe Liberal seat of Prince Albert.

King's decision to accept led to a constituency visit on January 31, 1926 for his nomination meeting and during discussions with supporters, Davis presented him with a list of local demands, including a request that a national park be established north of Prince Albert.[24] It is unclear if King actually agreed to this demand, as he did not speak directly about it, but it was widely assumed that he had. After his victory in the by-election, Davis attended a dinner at the prime minister's home in the company of Charles Stewart to discuss it further. Stewart subsequently met with Cory and Harkin to inform them of the proposal, leaving the latter in a difficult position. In a May 1, 1926 memorandum to Cory, he agreed, "If a scenic and recreational area of National Park standards can be found in Saskatchewan a National Park should be established there." He also suggested that "there should be at least one large National park in each Province, if at all possible," an important deviation from strict application of the standard but one consistent with its call for park systems with as many different landscapes of "supreme quality" as possible and a recognition of political realities.[25] However, the standard as applied in the United States called for the choice of lands to be made not by individuals, committees, or commissions, but rather by the park service, "which alone possesses the requisite knowledge, tradition, and experience, united with responsibility to the people."[26] Harkin firmly believed this process should be applied in Canada, and mentioned to Cory that while he favoured a Saskatchewan park, "whether the area suggested would be suitable is another question," and recommended that a parks officer be sent to the region to carry out an evaluation and that Forestry be consulted. But King had already pre-empted this proposal by announcing in a cabinet meeting of May 12, 1926 that he desired to create a park in Saskatchewan, and when the decision was communicated to Davis it was met with jubilation by the Prince Albert Board of Trade.[27]

Precluded from the decision as to whether there was an area in the province meeting the standard for a park, Harkin nevertheless remained convinced that the decision on its locality should be in departmental hands. But events moved too quickly for him to arrange for the in-depth examination he thought was necessary, and in mid-June he was directed by Gibson to investigate the suitability of the Sturgeon Forest Reserve and an area extending east to Melfort by consulting with departmental officers and reporting back within ten days. Given the timelines, the examination was cursory and, relying mostly on reports of the surveyor general and the Department of Mines and Dominion Lands, he reported, "According to Topographical records the land in parts of the said area covered by their surveys is comparatively flat, largely covered with muskeg and scrub growth of timber; the soil chiefly light loam and sand....The general impression seems to be that this is comparatively flat country, with very little outstanding scenic attractiveness." He believed that there was little justifying the establishment of a national park and instead suggested it could be "developed into a recreational area along the lines followed in connection with our recreational areas at Brereton Lake," thereby protecting the timber and a good game breeding area while making the waters available for recreational purposes. As in all reports on the issue, he closed by recommending, "Before anything of this nature is done, I think the first step is to have a Head Office official who is familiar with the development of parks and recreational areas visit the area and as far as possible look over conditions on the ground."[28] In another memorandum, he even more succinctly laid out his position: "A national park in the true sense of the term is something created by nature; it cannot be artificially created by simply establishing boundaries. Careful examination is therefore imperative before action is taken."[29]

At this point, the famous King-Byng constitutional affair and the appearance of a short-lived Conservative government derailed the matter, and it was not until the Liberals had gained a majority in the September 1926 election that it received further consideration. Meanwhile, the department had prepared a memorandum that favoured the country further north around Lac la Ronge and the Churchill River as a park, but when this idea was communicated to Davis he protested vehemently to Stewart. In a letter of November 10, 1926 he reminded the minister that "the Right Honourable W.L. Mackenzie King has already publicly announced to the people of Prince Albert the intention of the Government to create a national park North of Prince Albert," and, while admitting that Lac la Ronge was more scenic, indicated that it would be absolutely useless as a park as there were no roads and it would take years until it was accessible. Davis stated the matter was one of fairness, as while there were several parks in Alberta and British Columbia, there was none in Saskatchewan, and he argued that tentative boundaries should be promulgated immediately by order-in-council and then be looked over by a branch representative.[30] The Board of Trade's national park committee seconded this position in their own submission to the minister, strongly supporting the area around Waskesiu, Big Trout (Crean), and Little Trout (Kingsmere) lakes and stating their view that the matter was simply one of common sense: "We have summed up our park argument something like this: Some really highly developed park expert had been told to get together the exact materials to make up a perfect park, he had accumulated the right proportions of everything and left them at our back door step and told us to help ourselves. Well, we are shy on business acumen if we don't do it."[31]

Harkin reluctantly followed orders, examining information on four possible configurations in areas favoured by the board and others and determining that, from a practical perspective, all were too large or interfered unduly with forestry reserve operations. In reporting back to Gibson, he reiterated the need to have an inspection made and, as it was now too late in the season, suggested that it be postponed until spring and be limited to "Area D," the smallest identified. But Chief Engineer Wardle had taken the opportunity to closely examine the situation and supported the selection, offering that at 600 square miles it was economically feasible to administer and acknowledged that while it lacked the rugged grandeur of the Rockies it had "many features which would make it highly desirable as a National Park," and, as it included lands recommended by "the parties in P.A.," it could at least temporarily meet the demands of all those pressing for the park.[32] It was Wardle's implied recommendation in recognition of the political realities that Cory heeded, and by the end of January 1927 Harkin had been directed to draft an order-in-council defining the park's proposed boundaries. On the eve of its proclamation, he made one final request—that the park not be named Prince Albert because the impression would be that it was being set aside for that city and not the whole province, suggesting "The Saskatchewan National Park" or the name of some important topographic feature instead.[33] As with virtually all of Harkin's advice in the matter of this park, it was ignored.

Prince Albert National Park was established by order-in- council of March 24, 1927, encompassing, at 1,377 square miles, an area much larger than either Harkin or Wardle had contemplated. It included all of the Sturgeon River Forest Reserve, eight townships to the north containing Crean and Kingsmere lakes, and various lands around Bittern and Montreal lakes. Having seen first-hand the power of politics in setting the agenda, Harkin had moved quickly to establish branch authority over administration before there could be more interference, recommending for superintendent his assistant superintendent at Banff, James Wood, even before the park was officially created. Ultimately, Stewart thought that the appointment needed the prime minister's blessing, and after Wood passed muster upon visiting King in June at his Gatineau summer home (Kingsmere), Stewart informed the Prince Albert constituents that Wood would lead the new park. In the company of Wood, J.C. Campbell, and Davis, Harkin made his first visit to the park in mid-August and, according to an interview in the *Prince Albert Daily Herald*, was quite taken with the surroundings. Later, he predicted to Cory that Waskesiu and its associated lakes would provide adequate cottage sites for the whole province of Saskatchewan, and dispatched Wardle and Cromarty to investigate future development possibilities.

By the time Prime Minister King arrived on August 10, 1928 to officially open the park and receive the gift of a cottage from his grateful constituents, the Waskesiu townsite had been designated, an all-weather thirty-four-mile highway accessing it from the park boundary was under construction, and the location for future cottage development and a campground determined.[34] A year later, during a second visit, Harkin attended a meeting to form the Saskatchewan National Park Committee and in his remarks reported in the *Prince*

Camping at Prince Albert National Park, ca. 1928. Despite his initial skepticism, by the end of the 1920s Harkin had to admit there was more regional enthusiasm for Prince Albert Park than he had seen anywhere else in Canada. [GA, NA-3887-1]

Albert Herald, while indicating that the government could not provide the organization formal recognition, stated that "he was glad to find such enthusiasm as had been shown regarding the new national park," and that he had never anticipated that attendance figures would be as strong as they were.[35] Upon his return to Ottawa he sent such a glowing memorandum to Cory that Stewart forwarded a copy of it to the prime minister with the note "I think that you will be interested in the attached report which I have received from the Commissioner of National Parks telling of the popularity of Prince Albert Park."[36] It revealed that despite his initial skepticism, Harkin had now been fully converted to the Prince Albert cause, closing with the observation, "From what I heard...it is quite clear that Saskatchewan, as a whole, is thoroughly behind Prince Albert Park. There is a tremendous provincial pride in it and an enthusiasm which I have never found elsewhere in relation to national parks."[37]

From one perspective the Prince Albert affair could be interpreted as a failure of Harkin to achieve the standard. But taking a more positive view, it illustrated that in his efforts to make national parks relevant to Canadians, he had been so successful that they had now become instruments of public policy and even political expediency. However, this tended to erode Harkin's influence, and in the circumstances, as he had learned to do through long bureaucratic experience, he had to adapt his views to the situation as it existed rather than to what he wished it might be. His thinking on the standard and new parks creation was revealed in October 1927 correspondence with James McKenna, president of the *Saint John Telegraph-Journal* and an old acquaintance from his newspaper days. Reminding him that "we were 'kids' together in the Press Gallery," McKenna complimented the fine work carried out in Banff and Jasper parks, which he had recently visited, and queried, "Have you ever thought anything of a National Park for New Brunswick?" Indeed, by this time there was considerable departmental discussion around the possibility of a Maritimes park and Harkin responded with unusual frankness, reserved only for those with whom he was on the closest terms: "For years we have discussed here the question of a National Park in your Province. As a matter of fact, one of my ambitions, unrealized as yet, has been the creation of one National Park in each of our Provinces. Of course, in the Rockies of Alberta and British Columbia, we have more than one for each province and anybody will admit that there are exceptional conditions there which justify this." He then enumerated some attributes required of parks by virtue of the standard and the roadblocks that stood in the way of their achievement in McKenna's region:

> Our difficulties with respect to the Maritime provinces are numerous. In the first place, it is important that a National Park be of a very considerable area. I would say a minimum of a couple of hundred square miles. It is imperative that the area have a standard of scenic beauty equal to the best within the province. It is important that the area be such that there will be every opportunity for conserving in it every form of life typical of the province,

> including vegetable life, mammal life and bird life. It is important that the area should also be exceptionally suitable for recreation. As you know, fundamentally a National Park is created for the purpose of preserving in perpetuity a little bit of the original Canada as far as possible in its original state in order that Canadians for all time, by right of citizenship, may have access to such areas and there get the subtle values the wilderness has to give for one's physical, mental and spiritual advantage. Insofar as the eastern provinces are concerned, it probably would not be very difficult to find suitable areas but the main difficulty is to acquire them.[38]

Given these impediments, it was not surprising that establishment of a new Maritime park was still several years away, but Harkin's Prince Albert epiphany concerning a park in every province certainly made matters easier for him when the next opportunity in the West came along.

In his letter to McKenna, Harkin had mentioned, "There has been a very strong movement for a park in Manitoba. As a matter of fact, for the past six months there has been a violent conflict between the East and West sections of that province as to where he park should be." He was referring to the issue that had been brought to the fore by Mayor Webb of Winnipeg in 1925 in his promotion of a national park in eastern Manitoba, in particular an area drained by the Whiteshell River contiguous with the Ontario border. This idea had been around since 1919 and in addressing it with Cory in July 1925, Harkin had reminded him that it faced difficulty in that "Eastern Manitoba is intimately connected with water power developments and...such developments do not harmonize with the ideals associated with National parks." The Brereton recreation park had already been created in the area, but local MP Dr. E.D. Bissett had gained the support of Manitoba premier John Bracken for a full national park, and after receiving departmental compliance on the condition park policy on resource conservation be respected and the province take responsibility for all road construction, he sought endorsement from Manitoba's other members. All nineteen agreed, and in April 1928 an order-in-council reserved the Brereton lands from public disposal as a "provisional reservation for Park purposes."

Meanwhile, those with park interests in central and western Manitoba, who still favoured the old idea of developing a park in Riding Mountain Forest Reserve, had been awakened by the events taking place at Prince Albert and news of a possible eastern Manitoba park. In May 1927 Cory directed Harkin "to have one of your officers obtain from the Forestry Branch and plot on a map, full information regarding the Riding Mountain Forest Reserve, which I feel should be made a park." Cory had always been an enthusiastic proponent of Riding Mountain, and in a June 1, 1927 letter to J. Allison Glen, MP of the Russell constituency, admitted, "I must confess that it touches a responsive chord as the writer spent his boyhood days at Gladstone and has a keen appreciation of the scenic beauties of Riding Mountains."[39] Given his influential position, it seems likely the deputy minister played a behind-the-scenes role in the promotion of Riding Mountain in opposition to eastern Manitoba. It was well orchestrated and effective, based around the efforts of Glen, other area MPs, and influential Dauphin lawyer J.A. McFadden in organizing regional municipal councils to flood the minister with resolutions supporting Riding Mountain and, not unlike their Prince Albert counterparts, to create a powerful lobby, the Riding Mountain National Park Committee. In November 1927, Cory, noting the volume of correspondence arriving on the minister's desk favouring the western location, happily commented to his commissioner, "I am inclined to think that the weight of public opinion in Manitoba supports the creation of a park in the Riding Mountain Forest Reserve rather than in Eastern Manitoba."[40] This was confirmed by a vote in the legislative assembly in February 1928 where, by a margin of twenty-eight to ten, MLAs supported the Riding Mountain location, although they also called for the creation of a second park in eastern Manitoba.

Nevertheless, Stewart had made it clear that there was to be only one park in Manitoba and Cory, conscious of Harkin's strong feelings on inspections, called for an expert examination. In July 1928 the commissioner was able to arrange for the department to send surveyor

Prime Minister W.L. Mackenzie King pets a famous rescue dog at the official dedication of Prince Albert National Park, August 10, 1928 (T.C. Davis, leader of the park movement is at the left, Harkin's hand-picked superintendent James Wood is third from the left (crouching) and Minister of the Interior Charles Stewart is second from the right). On their way to this event, King and Stewart stopped at Brandon and were inundated with requests for a park at Riding Mountain. [LAC, C-051825]

R.W. Cautley, who had been working on boundary surveys in the mountain parks, to report on both areas. He initially examined the region between Ontario's Lake of the Woods and the Whiteshell River and recommended against establishment of a park confined to its Manitoba section. In August he followed up with a study of Riding Mountain but found it, too, lacking in the qualities necessary for a national park and more valuable for its timber resources, suggesting instead only a small recreational area around Clear Lake. Even before he could present his reports, Stewart had taken matters into his own hands, as in early August, he and King had stopped at Brandon on their way to officially open the new Prince Albert Park and had been assailed by residents demanding that Riding Mountain be allowed to achieve the same status. Possibly already aware of Cautley's forthcoming opinion, Stewart attended a large picnic at Clear Lake on August 16 put on by the supporters of the Park Committee with the expectation that he would announce his intentions with respect to a Manitoba national park. In a clever speech he indicated that with the forest reserve likely to soon fall under provincial jurisdiction as a result of the resources transfer, he was prepared to recommend that all or a part of it be set aside "for the purpose of creating a Federal National Playground here." While stating "I am not going to say that we will call this a National Park," he did promise "all the facilities of a National Park," including a golf course, cottage sites, a playground and a campground, and "a road which will provide facilities for people coming here every day."[41]

Essentially, Stewart was proposing a recreational park much like that already present at Brereton Lake and similar to what Harkin had suggested for Riding Mountain as early as 1917. Harkin had by then ceased offering his own opinions on the situation, although he likely supported this approach, particularly after Cautley presented his negative reports. But the members of the National Parks Committee soon became resentful of the idea of a "second-class" park and once again organized nearby towns and municipalities to forward resolutions promoting the idea that the whole reserve area should be administered completely either by the federal or the provincial government. Chairman McFadden, when provided with Cautley's report, informed Stewart "that the people of this part of Manitoba will consider the formation of a national recreational area of the size and extent outlined in the report given to me is a very poor substitute for a national park" and also opposed division of responsibility along federal-provincial lines.[42] By March 1929 Gibson was directing Harkin to assist in drafting a memorandum on disposition of the matter for discussion between Stewart and Bracken in conjunction with the transfer of Manitoba's natural resources, and in a July press report Stewart was quoted as stating that both areas of the province were still under consideration for a park. But, as foreseen, the matter quickly became enmeshed in resource transfer negotiations, and only when Bracken returned from Ottawa with the final agreement in hand in December was the announcement made that the matter had been decided in favour of Riding Mountain. Harkin recommended to Cory on December 17, 1929 that, the decision having been made, it would be best to have the park established by governor-in-council so that it would not have to be part of the pending new parks legislation. Accordingly, by order-in-council of December 28, 1929, the same date as the Georgian Bay Park declaration, the 1,148-square-mile Riding Mountain National Park was created from the lands of the former Riding Mountain Forest Reserve.

Stewart had neatly sidestepped the controversy over the site of a national park in Manitoba by ostensibly leaving the decision in Premier Bracken's hands, and was naturally somewhat gun-shy about becoming embroiled in similar debates in other provinces. But continuing demands for a park in the Maritimes precluded that possibility, and Harkin's joining of the call for a full representation of national landforms of supreme quality across the country with his idea of a park in every province soon required the matter to be resolved. In discussions concerning the possibility of a park in New Brunswick, he wrote Cory in February 1929, trying to bring the matter to a head: "I think your general attitude always has been that if suitable territory could be secured it was desirable to extend the National Parks to the Eastern Provinces. In view of this, I beg to suggest that Mr. R.W. Cautley be asked to inspect the two areas...with a view to a decision as to whether they are suitable for National Parks purposes."[43] With no answer forthcoming, he reiterated his request on February 28: "As you know, I have long felt that it would be good policy to make a wider geographical distribution of our Parks activities, but in any case I should like to have your views on the general point of whether you desire to establish a National Park in New Brunswick."[44] Part of the problem was the acquisition of suitable lands and finally, in late September, Cory acknowledged that Stewart was considering the matter, but pointed out, "the Minister takes the view that it should not be necessary for the Dominion Government to purchase land for National Parks but that if through the Province or otherwise areas suitable for National Parks can be provided free of charge then this Department, after verifying suitability, should be in a position to recommend formal dedication as a National Park and the undertaking of expenditure for development and maintenance at National Park standard."[45]

This position was consistent with Harkin's own thinking and affirmed in recent communications with respect to practices in the United States. In late February, in carrying out background research on new park formation, he had contacted U.S. Parks Service Director Horace Albright for information on the amount his organization had spent on purchase of private lands for parks over the past decade and what the costs were of acquiring land for its proposed Great Smokey Mountain National Park. Albright had responded that Congress never appropriated lands for national parks, that nearly all parks in the country had been set aside from public lands and that exceptions occurred only in cases such as Acadia National Park in Maine, where lands were donated by private individuals or organizations or, as in the case of Great Smokey in North Carolina and Tennessee, where legislation establishing the park only became operative after sufficient lands were provided.[46]

Albright's information, when combined with his commissioner's insistent calls for an expanded park system, eventually had a salutary effect on Stewart. As early as January 1930 he began making comments in small group situations concerning his desire to have a park in every province, and in March, in the departmental notification of the official proclamation of Riding Mountain Park, it was stated, "The establishment of this Park is in accordance with the policy of the Department to, as far as possible, extend the National Park System throughout Canada setting aside in each Province the most outstanding area from a scenic and recreational point of view."[47] Finally, in a speech in the House of May 26, 1930, Stewart went public: "It is the policy of this government to develop a national park in each province provided the province makes available for this purpose, free of charge and free of encumbrance, a compact area of national park standard."[48] With his own conversion to the idea some four years earlier and his attempts to have it recognized in this way, Stewart's words were music to Harkin's ears. But when the speech was given, they inevitably took second place to the major subject being addressed in it—the *National Parks Act*—which was even more important to his parks philosophy.

14

THIRTEEN

A Great Achievement for Us

CHARLES STEWART'S POLICY of a park in every province had been announced in the debate on the legislation for the new parks act that Harkin had worked on for a decade. In his view, the possibility that either water power or mineral exploitation might take place in the parks under the aegis of a province envisaged in the resource transfer negotiations presented a serious impediment to inviolability, and he had attempted to remove that potential by enshrining the concept under the control of Parliament. Meanwhile, Calgary Power and its supporters continued to demand both levels of government allow more storage capacity and hydro development at Spray Lakes and Lake Minnewanka to meet the growing need for electrification in Alberta. As it transpired, both sides were to be offered new opportunities to achieve their objectives during the final act of the resource transfer drama, one that would have major repercussions for the future of Canada's national parks.

In 1926 the Alberta resource transfer agreement became caught up in a reignition of the age-old Dominion-provincial debate over Roman Catholic school rights, in this case focusing on the control of school lands, resulting in long delays fraught with court challenges and two changes of government. As matters dragged on, Harkin continued to speak out on his concerns about the transfer's proposals for mineral development, noting that while no mining would occur in the parks without the consent of the minister, "I feel that this proviso in the first place puts too much responsibility upon the Minister and at the same time leaves the Minister open to tremendous pressure on the part of interested people." He feared that while most ministers would respect their trusteeship of the public's interest, there could also be those "whose ideals will not be nearly so high" and might agree to exploitation of resources where serious damage to park lands might occur.[1] He specifically attacked clause B in the proposed Dominion ratification bill, allowing the Dominion government to dispose of any park or forest reserve lands for any purpose other than those specified in the agreement. Recommending the elimination of this clause, he also requested the opportunity for his branch to make its own representations should provincial arguments for change continue.[2] Accordingly, at a meeting between Stewart, Gibson, and himself on March 9, 1926 it was determined to request a rewording allowing for disposal of park lands only in accordance with concurrent statutes of the Dominion and the province. Although Brownlee refused to accede to this request, his observation—"We feel it is entirely unnecessary that [the] Dominion and provincial parliament be consulted before [a] site can be granted for power or any similar purpose"—identified exactly was at stake.[3] The natural resources legislation was subsequently introduced into the House unchanged, but by mid-May, Harkin was answering queries with the response that the matter was not acute because of King's decision to take his time in its consideration.

Meantime, he continued his quest to have a new parks act put before Parliament, and his arguments about the necessity of it taking park resources into account began to have some effect. Accordingly, in January 1927 the focus shifted to introducing an amendment to the *Dominion Forest Reserves and Parks Act*, the purpose of which, as Harkin described it, was "to establish the principle of absolute sanctity for the national parks, that hereafter none of the natural resources shall be disposed of without a special act of Parliament." The amendment (Bill 54) also suggested that a section be added "to overrule the provisions in the existing Water Power Act which provides that it shall be applicable, under certain restrictions, to the Dominion Parks."[4] In accompanying explanations, Harkin trundled out the usual arguments that "the development of natural resources within this area certainly is not in keeping with the fundamental principles of the parks" and "the question is whether the parks or the resources are of greater value to the country." With specific respect to minerals, he made the observation that as coal mines had been closing down for several years "now, while there is no demand for further coal mines, is a good time to withdraw the park areas."[5]

Concentrating on efforts getting legislation to protect park resources, Harkin was nevertheless distracted fending off proponents of the Spray Lakes project. With the Dominion government otherwise occupied, Brownlee had time to give further consideration to possible power projects, and in November 1926 he agreed to seek a meeting with Stewart and representatives of the City of Calgary and Calgary Power in an effort to work out an agreement whereby a development licence could be issued. Stewart had wired that he was too busy to come west but indicated that "the Spray Lakes matter can easily be adjusted" as "[the] Dominion Government now own and will continue to own [the] territory upon which [the] proposed reservoir is to be constructed and naturally will not care to do business with any except parties intending to develop on their own behalf."[6] Brownlee persisted, agreeing to come east with Alberta representatives, and upon hearing of this, Harkin suggested to Cory that as all their arguments were general in nature, the proponents should be required to provide specifics before the minister agreed to a conference. He even enclosed a draft letter to the premier for the minister's signature to this effect, but Stewart chose not to communicate it. On January 11 the meeting, attended by Stewart, Brownlee, Cory, Calgary MLA George Webster, and Isaak W. Killam, president of Calgary Power, took place in Ottawa. As reported by Webster, while upholding his position that the provincial application for Spray Lakes should have primacy, Brownlee did not commit to going ahead, while Killam indicated that he would start development immediately if issued the permit. Stewart explained he had promised to consult Parliament "to determine the policy as to whether or not water storage reservoirs were to be permitted within the limits of the Banff National Park," but "expressed as his own opinion that he could see no objections to water reservoirs being located within the Parks area, particularly a reservoir at Spray Lake" and "if the House decided on a policy of allowing reservoirs in the Parks area, he would give immediate consideration to the two applications before him and dispose of them forthwith."[7]

Aware that Stewart was soft on the Spray issue, Harkin had by then taken further steps to shore up his position. One important initiative was convincing Cory to support an investigation into the economics of steam plants fuelled by gas or coal. Arrangements had been made in January 1927 to send Wardle to Toronto to meet with two expert engineers from the Ontario Hydro-Electric Power Commission and in the chief engineer's subsequent report he stated that one of them believed that a natural gas plant at Calgary "was one of the most attractive power propositions from all angles that he had known."[8] Then, in early February, informed that a Calgary MP had tabled a notice of motion in the House aimed at gaining approval for the Spray project, Harkin took the extraordinary step of writing Walker recommending that, with the fate of the Spray Lakes so tenuous, the Canadian National Parks Association should call its members to action. After assuring themselves that the suggested thinking was in line with their own position, the association's executive issued a pamphlet on February 15 under the headline "*Attention! Most Important!!* The Spray Lakes in the Banff National Park," with Harkin's requested call-to-arms front-and-centre: "All Canadian members and Club members of the Association should lose no time in advising their representatives in Parliament that they are strongly opposed to granting any such application, and in requesting their representatives to carefully watch the proceedings."[9] This action unleashed a new flood of letters to the minister opposing the project.

As Stewart had promised, Bill 54 received first reading on February 10, 1927 and as it affected negotiations on the transfer of resources, it was immediately sent off to Edmonton for comment. Brownlee cut to the chase in his response to King on March 2, pointing out that with most Canadian parks in Alberta incorporating the only substantial opportunity for provincial water power development as well as rich coal deposits, a solution needed to be found that could break the log-jam on both the issues of resources on park lands and Spray Lakes. In his view there were such vast areas of the Rocky Mountains suitable for pleasure and recreation already in national parks, "the interests of the people of Canada will not be prejudiced if the small area necessary for the Spray Lakes development is used for this purpose and if a resurvey is made which will eliminate some of the areas containing coal or other mineral deposits, and other areas of the Rocky Mountains substituted therefor."[10] The idea of redrawing park boundaries had likely already been broached in negotiations between Dominion and provincial representatives and clearly, with Stewart anxious to find a way to see the project go ahead, it could be seen as a way for it and the equally contentious issue of resources to be successfully dealt with.

In the circumstances, Harkin's moment of truth had arrived. Principle demanded he protest, and in his memorandum to Cory of March 23, 1927 he certainly did. But the situation he had foreseen in May 1924 when he had decided that he would sacrifice some park areas for the certainty of inviolability was at hand. Brownlee had implied in closing his letter that he would accept sanctity on the remaining park lands, stating, "The Government of this Province would be willing to co-operate with your Government wholeheartedly in such a resurvey and endeavouring to safeguard, as far as possible, the scenic beauty of such areas as are finally defined, as we realize these National Parks form one of the great Provincial assets in the number of tourists that are attracted annually."[11] Harkin therefore made a conciliatory suggestion to Cory, while explaining in the clearest terms yet why park lands must remain inviolate:

> The Government has taken the stand that the parks are areas primarily set aside for the development of two specific resources, viz., natural scenery and wild life. As it so happens these resources are more intangible, more difficult of conservation than any other of our natural resources. Unless special safeguards are erected these resources may easily be impaired or destroyed and it is practically impossible to conserve scenery and wild life side by side with the development of other resources such as coal, minerals or water powers that the areas may possess....
>
> With regard to Mr. Brownlee's suggestion for a resurvey of park areas to ascertain whether these areas as now set aside include valuable deposits of coal and minerals which should properly be released and other areas substituted therefore, Mr. Brownlee might be advised that the Government is willing to introduce an amendment to Bill No. 54 authorizing the Governor in Council to exclude from the park any areas which appear to be more valuable for industrial than parks purposes.[12]

Nonetheless, in making this concession and thereafter co-operating in departmental decisions regarding Brownlee's proposal, he was not yet ready to entirely give up on the boundary issue. For example, in May 1927 Harkin was responding to a query from Gibson indicating that Cory, who was absent, was "emphatic in the view that the Spray Lakes should be retained within the park."[13] But the same day, May 13, Gibson provided him with a copy of a May 4 letter from Brownlee to Stewart in which the premier stated, "I assume that you have agreed to the suggestion of a resurvey of the parks areas," and suggested that it be done prior to discussion of resource transfer again being taken up in the House.[14] Stewart responded that he wished to delay his decision until he visited the parks in July, and in the meantime Harkin was directed to brief him on the issue. The minister headed west in late June to engage in face-to-face discussions with the prairie premiers, leading to agreement with Brownlee on his proposal, and representatives of the two governments were immediately appointed to carry out investigations and report on "the selection of permanent boundaries for Rocky Mountain and Jasper Parks." They were Dominion Land Surveyor R.W. Cautley, an experienced mountain surveyor who later did the Manitoba park analysis, and L.C. Charlesworth, chairman of the Irrigation Council of Alberta.

According to Cautley's later report the principle followed was "that the areas investigated shall be classified on the basis of their being used for such purposes as shall yield the greatest return to the nation. Many areas are so outstanding in their scenic, recreational, and educational characteristics that there can be no doubt their natural and proper place is in the National Parks. Other areas may be more suitable for forest reserves than parks. Again there may be areas where certain natural resources indicate that such areas will serve Canada best by their being open to industrial development." Cautley's rationale in making the redetermination included two critical factors—that it was intended to change the government's title to lands within the parks by making them inviolable, and that in order to ensure the "extent and tenure" of the parks they would only be able to be changed by an act of Parliament.[15]

This and the fact that Stewart had withdrawn Bill 54 offered Harkin an opportunity to bring the new parks bill back for reconsideration, and, as Cautley carried out his survey work on a 750-mile horseback trip examining locations for the eastern boundaries of the two parks, he began to search for an opportunity to do so. In early December one appeared when Stewart invited him to attend a meeting with Cory and Cautley to discuss the new boundaries. At it the minister agreed to extend the agenda to deal with "the proposed Parks Bill," and by April 1928 Harkin was providing departmental solicitor K.R. Daly with background information to assist in preparing a new draft.[16] But it was apparent that with boundary changes now tied to both a new act and the passage of natural resource transfer legislation, the matter could not be expected to move quickly. Cautley was unable to complete his surveys in 1927, requiring him to spend part of the summer of 1928 examining the northern boundary of Jasper Park, and as King had successfully referred the school lands matter to the Supreme Court, the Judicial Committee of the Privy Council was now awaiting additional submissions. Brownlee, upset with King's gambit, refused to participate, and the matter of final agreement on this key issue remained in limbo.[17]

Although disheartened by the incessant delays, Harkin kept the faith, his determination evident in a letter to Norman Luxton in October 1927: "No stand which I have taken in regard to National Park matters has given me more trouble than this one in favour of absolute sanctity for our Parks. It would be very much easier and more pleasant for me to relax but I feel that if I did I would be signing the death warrant of the Parks."[18] Accordingly, in January 1928 he forwarded a new version of the draft act to Cory noting, "Aside from making the necessary changes in the boundaries of the Alberta Parks to meet the recommendations made by Mr. Cautley and approved by Alberta, the Bill is designed to adequately provide for the inviolability of the National Parks." In format and content it bore a close resemblance to 1923's Bill 185. Harkin called particular attention to the definition of "land" in the interpretation clauses, where, with words similar to those in the earlier version, it stated, "'Land' means any land the title to which is vested in His Majesty, and any interest therein, and includes the waters thereof and the natural resources of the land." When read in conjunction with clause 6 under "Park Lands," which directed that lands within parks would not be disposed of except under authority of the act, and clause 7 under "Regulations," which allowed for licensing or leasing of lands only for specified purposes, he believed inviolability was protected. Furthermore, he stated, "The force of these provisions is clarified and emphasized by Clause 4." In its "General Purposes" section it read, "The Parks are hereby dedicated to the people of Canada for their benefit, education and enjoyment and such Parks shall be maintained and made use of so as to leave them unimpaired for the enjoyment of future generations."[19]

This wording was a decided improvement over that in the 1923 version where the concepts of dedication to the people of Canada and leaving the lands unimpaired for future generations had appeared in separate sections. In this new form, Harkin was confident that the phraseology would better withstand legal challenge, perceptively commenting, "This clause will always be of great weight in any Appeal Court which is interpreting the Act and Regulations."[20] But it was still inadequate to provide the department with the flexibility it needed to secure inviolability, also requiring a strong "Regulations" section, the reason for which he described in a memo to Cory: "When Mr. Stewart has from time to time discussed the question of a new Parks Act he has always stressed the desirability of a general clause which would give the Governor-in-Council adequate power to make necessary regulations and give the Department a fair degree of freedom. We have consulted with the Justice Department and other Law Officers on many occasions on this subject and there has been unanimity that it is not possible to devise a general clause which will be adequate to meet our necessities. I offer this to explain the number of particular powers which are taken under the Regulation Clause."[21] This solution, using the "General Purposes" part of the *National Parks Act* to set out its philosophy and supporting it with a strong "Regulations" section capable of being adjusted to meet the circumstances of the day, was to prove fundamental in protecting Canada's parks during times of peril. The "dedication clause" as it became known, became Harkin's most important contribution to Canadian parks conservation and he gained much fame for it.

Another change was related to "Part II" of the act, which combined concepts concerning recreation areas and game resources in Bill 185 with a new schedule identifying historic sites. Clause 1 of the new Part II stated: "The Governor in Council may set apart any land, the title to which is vested in His Majesty, as (a) a National Historic Site to commemorate an historic event of national importance, or preserve any historic landmark or any object of historic, prehistoric or scientific interest of national importance; (b) a Game Sanctuary for the conservation of wild animals in their natural state; (c) a Recreational and Resort

Area for the use of the public." These inclusions in a separate part of the act illustrated the fundamental shift in thinking in the branch since Harkin had identified the four types of national parks in *Sprig* some fifteen years earlier, all relating to the increasing importance of the standard. In background notes to Daly he mentioned that game sanctuaries no longer passed the test of being regarded as national parks: "You will remember that the Wood Buffalo Game Sanctuary had to be created a National Park because the Forest Reserves and Parks Act was the only Dominion legislation which gave the Governor in Council the necessary authority. Drawing the line as sharply as we propose to draw it with respect to National Parks in the new Act makes it desirable that there should be legislation under which areas like Wood Buffalo Park and other sanctuaries could be created without imposing on the land concerned the many restrictions that have been applied to parks."[22] In the circumstances, he believed it was better to establish a new category of park incorporating large animal reserves such as Wood Buffalo and Nemiskam as well as the bird sanctuaries created under the Migratory Birds Convention. These changing circumstances also extended to historic sites where, despite the increasing importance of the historic sites and monuments program, Harkin now believed they did not meet the criteria of national parks either: "Such areas, while important from an historic standpoint, are absolutely different from the modern conception of National Parks and therefore it would seem desirable to have legislative provisions by which they can be controlled without their being given the status of National Parks."[23]

The final part of the proposed act was the "Schedules" section, which identified and laid out the boundaries of each park. Apart from some small adjustments to Yoho and Glacier parks associated with the dismantling of the BC Railway Belt, the main changes from the 1923 draft were in the new boundaries for Rocky Mountains and Jasper parks. In his work Cautley had sought to substitute "natural" boundaries, those based on heights of land or watercourses, for "straight line" boundaries laid out by survey, which lent themselves to efficient administration by park authorities and reduced the necessity of surveying over difficult terrain. This approach resulted in the addition of a small amount of territory when the new western boundaries were located at the height of land, but much larger changes were recommended for administrative purposes or in line with eliminating potential industrial lands. As a first step, by order-in-council of February 6, 1929 an area of 976 square miles south of Sunwapta Pass, more easily accessible from Banff than Jasper, was transferred to Rocky Mountains Park, and an area of 103 square miles around Mount Malloch was added, presumably to replace some of the lands that were to be eliminated in the forthcoming act. Subsequently, in the new act's schedule, 630 square miles were excluded in the Kananaskis and Spray watersheds, including the proposed Spray Lakes power site, coal mining lands in the Bow Valley, and the Canmore and Exshaw townsites; seventy-five square miles of the Ghost River watershed, cut off from the rest of the park by a high mountain range; 291 square miles of the Red Deer River watershed containing valuable grazing lands and good timber reserves; and 377 square miles of the lands recently transferred from Jasper to Rocky Mountains between the Cline and Siffleur rivers. This left an area of 2,585 square miles to be incorporated in the new Rocky Mountains Park. In Jasper, Cautley recommended that "the territory now contained therein is of such a character as to be of greater value as a National Park than it could possibly be if put to any other use." Two small areas containing coalbeds were, however, recommended for exclusion—329 square miles around Brûlé Lake and 106 square miles around Rock Lake—leaving a park area of 4,200 square miles.[24]

Although Harkin continued his call for the Spray Lakes to remain in the park, on January 30, 1929 the matter was unequivocally laid to rest when he received a short communication from Gibson indicating that "it is the Minister's wish that Spray Lakes should be left outside Rocky Mountains Park."[25] It was now expected that the bill would be tabled in the spring session, so he was surprised when King did not mention it in a late April speech concerning proposed legislation. He complained to Cory, "I think the time is very opportune for introducing such a Bill.... The debates on the resources question to date definitely commit the Opposition to control by Parliament."[26] Unfortunately, while a resolution on the language of the school lands issue had finally been reached between the Dominion and Alberta, a new roadblock in the resource transfer had appeared in the details of financial payments in lieu of lost revenues. With the passage of a new parks bill now inextricably linked to the transfer of the natural resources, Cory informed Harkin on May 21, "It will not be possible to introduce a Parks Bill at this session of Parliament." Once again Harkin had come to the brink of getting his principles sanctioned in legislation only to see final resolution delayed, and once again that delay resulted in attacks on the vision of inviolability he had fought so hard to achieve.

Killam, perceiving in the results of the Ottawa conference of February 1927 that the development of Spray Lakes would not take place in the immediate future, had turned his attention to possible further power development outside the park at the confluence of the Ghost and Bow rivers near Calgary Power's Horseshoe and Kananaskis plants. Stewart had quickly agreed to transfer the necessary lands in 1928, and while this took care of its immediate power needs, the company was still casting covetous eyes on Lake Minnewanka. When it became apparent that a new parks act would preclude development there, Calgary Power ramped up calls for a reservoir to be built immediately. In making their case, its officials had two things in their favour—deteriorating economic conditions marking the onset of the Depression in the fall of 1929, which made large projects capable of utilizing unemployed workers attractive, and the fact that the leader of the Opposition in Parliament calling for such projects was none other than Calgary Power champion, and Harkin nemesis, R.B. Bennett.

After losing the election of 1921 by a whisker, Bennett had concentrated on his law practice and business interests, and by the time he returned to politics as the candidate for Calgary West in October 1925, he was a millionaire. Running on a protectionist platform, he had won the seat handily and served as minister of Justice in Meighen's brief government before being elected leader of the Conservative Party at its October 1927 convention. In his acceptance speech, he had mentioned that he had gained his wealth by his own untiring efforts, but now being called upon to serve his country as the leader of a great party, "no longer can the claims of my business or my profession be upon me."[27]

Nonetheless, as Calgary West embraced the disputed Spray Lakes, he could support the development as purely a matter of constituency business. Even so as economic conditions deteriorated, Bennett's Calgary supporters began calling for even greater access to park waters at the same time as he determined that duty and democratic tradition required him to take up the cause of his park constituents' rights in any forthcoming legislation.

These issues came to a head after the final clearing of roadblocks on the natural resources transfer. In November 1929 a first ministers' conference reached general agreement on the subsidy to all the prairie provinces in lieu of lost resource revenue being continued in perpetuity. This set the stage for a visit by Brownlee to Ottawa in early December to complete the Alberta negotiations, and although they proved difficult because of his demands for an additional cash payment at least as generous as that negotiated with Manitoba, the impasse was broken by referring the issue to a commission. Similarly, the premier was uncomfortable that there was nothing in the agreement to prevent development of resources in national parks if they were left entirely in Dominion hands, something that it was believed Stewart quietly supported, and the two parties also settled on a process of handling this by a side agreement. In advance of the signing ceremony a letter from Stewart was delivered to Brownlee at the Chateau Laurier stating, "I am authorized by our Government to assure you that should Federal Parliament decide at any time to permit the development of the mineral resources of any of the National Parks in Alberta, and should such commercial exploitation result in revenue exceeding the expenditure by the Federal Government on the Parks in Alberta, then the Government of Canada will discuss with the Province of Alberta the equitable division of such excess revenue."[28] This contentious issue out of the way, the revised transfer agreement was signed under King's watchful eye by Stewart on behalf of Canada and Brownlee and George Hoadley on behalf of Alberta.[29]

Brownlee returned home to a hero's welcome, as the new agreement was infinitely better than that signed three years earlier. But Harkin, too, must have been elated, since it also represented a significant

Prime Minister King and Premier Brownlee signing the natural resources transfer agreement for Alberta, December 1929. The natural resources agreement between Alberta and Canada affirmed Harkin's position that resources should remain under federal control in national parks and that Parliament would have exclusive jurisdiction. [PAA, A 10924]

improvement in his position, containing key clauses ensuring the lands and minerals in the scheduled areas "shall continue to be vested in and administered by the Government of Canada as national parks," and "the Parliament of Canada shall have exclusive legislative jurisdiction within the whole area included."[30] As well, the agreement's promise to introduce legislation on boundaries clearly referred to the likelihood of a new parks act, and the path to achieving his long-sought goal now seemed clear. Once again, though, any optimism he might have had was short-lived, as five days later in far-away Calgary a meeting was held that challenged the very sanctity he believed was secured. Called by Mayor F.W. Osborne to deal with possible solutions to the city's increasing employment problems, it requested R. Bruce Baxter, managing director of Calgary Power, to indicate if his company was contemplating any development plans. In his response, Baxter stated, "If permission is secured from the Dominion Government to heighten the present dam on Lake Minnewanka by about 30 feet, 400 men will be placed at work on the project within three weeks," and claimed that work at Minnewanka could begin as soon as a licence was granted, while at Spray Lakes almost a year of preparatory work would be required.[31] Two days later Osborne contacted Stewart and forwarded a resolution of a meeting of "employers of labor and representative citizens of Calgary" urging him "to immediately grant the necessary license to the Calgary Power Company in order that the work may be proceeded with and thereby give immediate employment to at least four hundred men as well as those employed in tributary industries."[32]

When provided with this information, Harkin wasted no time in venting his spleen, ripping to shreds in a December 23rd memorandum the whole idea that the proposed project could be got on with immediately and use 400 of Calgary's unemployed, astutely perceiving the game Calgary Power was up to. Noting there was no application in front of the department for the project, he charged, "There is no doubt that both the Calgary Power Co. and Mayor Osborne know perfectly well that licenses of this kind, even if the claim was meritorious, cannot be put through on a moment's notice and that, therefore, the only effect of the telegram is to put the Dominion in an unfair position in regard to the unemployment situation." Furthermore, he suggested, the claim that 400 men could be immediately employed on such a project was one "to be taken with a great deal of salt" and that even if it were, there was no guarantee that Calgary men would have a claim on the jobs. He also found it strange there was no mention of Spray Lakes: "These people at Calgary are undoubtedly familiar with the fact that the Alberta Resources Agreement had been executed and that this involves the exclusion of the Spray Lakes from the Park....Having in mind the tremendous propaganda and agitation carried on in connection with the Spray during the past seven years, it does seem extraordinary that when the Spray is practically available the Calgary Power Co. is now turning its eyes on Lake Minnewanka and ignoring the Spray." The reason seemed obvious: "One cannot help feeling that the real purpose is to challenge the inviolability of National Parks. An agreement has just been concluded with Alberta under which the Province definitely withdraws from its former position as against the principle of inviolability. In this connection the Parks boundaries are being revised. This contract is no sooner made than the principle is being challenged under the guise of unemployment necessities." Harkin summed up by stating that after seven or eight years of refusals at Lake Minnewanka, it appeared that the company was trying to put the minister in an unfair position by bringing forward the matter again in association with the unemployment problem. It was distinctly aware of the effect of inviolability on the future of such projects and, therefore, the scheme "at this time would be carried on with motives which are very obvious."[33]

Meanwhile, Stewart sent a telegram to Mayor Osborne pointing out that since 1922 the government had been consistent in not allowing development at Minnewanka, that the Spray Lakes had been offered instead, and that "all the Calgary Power Company need to do is to make that application and secure the consent of the Provincial Government and they can start work at once."[34] Inevitably, though, the matter became a *cause célèbre* in Calgary, with both its newspapers and city council calling on Stewart to reconsider, and despite the fact that the minister continued to support the principle of inviolability, the pressure steadily mounted. The Calgary Board of Trade launched a campaign to convince other boards of trade around the province to support its position, charging, "An agitation has been raised and fostered by officials of the National Parks department at Ottawa to prevent the use of any waters in the Banff National Park for hydro electric power development. The excuse for their unwarranted action in this matter is that the National Parks belong to all the people of Canada and should not be used for the benefit of the citizens of Alberta even though such use will in no way despoil the scenic beauty of the park or lessen its attractiveness in any manner, shape or form."[35] In the face of this growing maelstrom, on January 8, 1930 Stewart made the announcement that Harkin had so long waited to hear: "In order to protect the parks from private exploitation in the future, I will introduce a measure in the next session of Parliament to make it necessary for a private bill to be enacted before any leases or other rights for commercial development could be granted. This legislation will take the protection of the parks out of the hands of the Minister and place it in this respect directly with the people's representatives in Parliament."[36] Not surprisingly, given what was at stake, with this announcement both the proposed legislation and the Minnewanka matter again quickly found their way into the political arena.

The Calgary Board of Trade's call to action resulted in eighteen other Alberta boards passing resolutions urging the Dominion government to support the city's request, and each MP was circularized to gain their backing. The *Manitoba Free Press*, consistently a backer of the branch's position on inviolability, reported in its March 28 edition, "In the case of Lake Minnewanka, Hon. R.B. Bennett, Conservative leader, is on record as favoring the building of a storage dam within the park."[37] Bennett did make his feelings known, but at the same time seemed more concerned with the effects that the parks clauses of the resource transfer acts would have on the provinces and park residents in the West. Always a stickler on constitutional issues and the effect of government on citizens' rights, he saw the implementation of a system where federal regulations approved by governor-in-council could supersede provincial laws on park lands as unfair, in fact similar to Harkin's earlier efforts to suppress Banff's efforts to gain a voice in local affairs and akin to the battle which Canada itself had fought to get its own law-making capability from Westminster. His position was most clearly stated during a March 21 debate with Stewart on the resources transfer, during which the Parks Branch, and by extension Harkin, came under direct attack:

> [The western provinces] are to be told that hereafter because the Dominion reserves parks in their provinces, a few officials in a departmental office here in Ottawa are to draw up regulations to be approved by governor in council, for the government of these areas, and that the legislatures in the respective province are to [be] subordinated to those regulation in respect to taxes, if ever there is a conflict....
>
> How would the minister feel about it if he were one of the inhabitants? We might as well face the matter frankly. I regard it as unfair, and I am very much surprised that

> the minister would permit the permanent officials of the country to create what Lord Howard has described as the new despotism.[38]

To correct this situation, Bennett suggested that any Dominion regulations should be subject to approval through provincial order-in-council.

In a memorandum prepared to respond to this assault, Harkin began by referring to his long-held principle that national parks must be for the good of the whole country:

> The Dominion is the owner of these Parks in trust not for the Provinces of British Columbia or Alberta alone but for all the provinces of Canada. That fact emphasizes at once that these areas must be administered from a national and not a local standpoint. The resident of Prince Edward Island is just as much the owner of these Parks as the residents of British Columbia or Alberta and pays just as much for their preservation and development.
>
> The moment one admits the principle that any area should be a National Park, that moment he admits that therein the interests of all the people of Canada are paramount over the interests of the people wherein the area lies.

He then went on to advise that the "dual authority" which had been agreed to in Alberta in 1918 would remain, modified by Dominion insistence on regulating matters dealing directly with tourists as first recognized in the Banff-Windermere Road Agreement with British Columbia would remain. As well, provincial legislation not repugnant to Dominion laws would continue to be applied, so that "permanent residents of the Parks will continue to live under provincial laws," except where Dominion and provincial laws conflicted. Furthermore, with respect to Bennett's charge that park regulations were "oppressive," he

R.B. Bennett's return to Calgary after winning the leadership of the Conservative Party, July 1928. Bennett's gaining of the position of leader of the Opposition in October 1927 raised the stakes for Harkin in the battle over park waters and the passage of a new parks act. [GA, NB-16-180]

recalled, "The law under which regulations are made—the Dominion Parks Act—was amended in 1913 when Hon. R.B. Bennett was in the Commons representing the constituency in which Banff lies and the most extensive powers of regulation were provided by these amendments." He also attacked the leader of the Opposition for his stand on having regulations subject to provincial approval: "Mr. Bennett is too good a lawyer to fail to recognize the utter hopelessness of satisfactory results from such an arrangement....To agree to his Provincial approval scheme would be equivalent to surrender of the legislative authority the Dominion now possesses. The scheme is both impracticable and unjustifiable."[39]

Bennett was not the only one criticizing the forthcoming legislation, as the Calgary press constantly wrote about it and the Minnewanka proposal. Like Bennett's thinly veiled criticisms, its broadsides, although debunking the branch and the department in general, were sometimes personal, as, for example, in the *Calgary Albertan*'s reference to the proposed parks bill in its January 11 edition:

> Theoretically, it places the responsibility upon the Canadian people's elected representatives. Whatever they do with it the Minister is free from responsibility. But in practice the fact is that the Minister proposes to hand the duty of administering the national parks over to a bureaucracy in the person of the superintendent of the parks branch, including the power sites which, as such are not part of that official's responsibilities at all.
>
> That the Minister is simply shirking responsibility in this instance is only too obvious and he will be well advised to proceed no further with his projected bill whose effect will be to place the people of Alberta at the mercy of an unsympathetic civil servant.[40]

To defend himself and buttress his superiors' resolve, Harkin wrote numerous other memoranda, providing the information they needed in the debate. Never one to use a sentence when he felt a point could be more emphatically made in a paragraph, these were often long and repetitive, as for example his missive of April 23 dealing with the Minnewanka issue which went on for an amazing thirty-seven pages!

While stressful and tedious, there was some benefit in these matters being debated early in the year when Minnewanka was the topic of the day and the resource transfers were under discussion in both the Dominion and provincial houses; when Stewart tabled the *National Parks Act* (Bill 135) for first reading on May 7, most arguments related to it had already been made. After second reading on May 9, he and Bennett did rehash their earlier wrangle during discussion in committee, with the leader of the Opposition primarily focusing on the lack of power available to the Banff Advisory Council and charging that the town was controlled by a Liberal Party machine under the Brewsters' direction. He also threw another barb in Harkin's direction in his remarks concerning the branch's control of townsite affairs, charging, "You cannot have a game of baseball unless Mr. Harkin says so, and he is in Ottawa three thousand miles away." In closing his comments, Bennett referred to the unsuccessful efforts of the Advisory Council in establishing municipal institutions and stated ominously, "I am really powerless in the matter, but I cannot help thinking that it is my duty to direct attention to the matter, and I believe a remedy can be found. If I had the power, I would do it."[41] As there was a desire to clear the order paper quickly with the session winding down, the committee stage was short, and before the day was out the act had received third reading. It was forwarded directly to the Senate for consideration and, along with the resource transfer acts, was given royal assent on May 30, 1930.

The *National Parks Act* approved that day closely followed the template of 1923 as modified by the draft of 1929, but there were a few important differences. Most concerned section 3, "Establishment of Parks" and the related Part II dealing with special types of parks. An earlier version had proposed changing the name of Rocky Mountains Park to the more commonly used "Banff," but it had been subsequently dropped and Bill 135 had been drafted keeping the older terminology. On March 1, J.O. Apps, general executive assistant to the CPR president, complained to Cory, "The name 'Rocky Mountains Park' is not sufficiently distinctive or easily understood as to its location....Kindly reconsider the matter and advise me that the name Banff National Park will be used." Harkin immediately agreed with this recommendation, noting that the general public had almost "universally adopted" the term and that "Rocky Mountains" was confusing because there were other parks in the same range and there was a similarly named park in the United States. The change was made on the very eve of the bill going forward for printing.[42] Of even greater moment, though, were changes in the same section dealing with game sanctuaries, recreation areas, and historic sites, reflecting obvious compromises and an inability to rationalize disparate parts of the branch's mandate.

As mentioned, Harkin had recommended Section II parks be regulated by governor-in-council with direction that Wood Buffalo, Wawaskesy, Nemiskam, and Menissawok would be changed to game sanctuaries, Vidal's Point to a recreation area and Fort Howe to an historic site. But in the 1930 version only National Historic Sites remained in Part II. In a briefing document and accompanying explanatory notes, Harkin emphasized the importance of applying the park standard, recommending that the criteria in the recent *Parks and Recreation* article should be adopted. While supporting the movement of provincial or local authorities to create recreational areas or resorts to stimulate tourist traffic, he felt that such areas should not be national parks unless they met the standard. On the other hand, "The idea of regional parks may be successfully defended to the possible extent of having a national park in each Province, this park to represent the best from a parks point of view in each Province." In the final analysis, "Parliament should decide on a matter of such importance," as they would be viewed from a national perspective, although even in this case an official investigation should take place before deciding to establish any new parks.[43] This thinking had affected the recreational park classification, as Harkin went on to note that since the Manitoba and Great Slave Lake reservations were not active and Vidal's Point was not of a standard to justify its continuance as a national park, a decision had been made to transfer responsibility for it to Saskatchewan in the resource transfer agreement, altogether eliminating the necessity for a category of recreational parks in the act.

Such decisive action did not prove possible in the case of animal sanctuaries. Although he specifically mentioned the elimination of Menissawok Park and its return to Saskatchewan because "two small animal parks in this district is considered ample," Harkin did not address the broader question of animal sanctuaries as national parks. The decision to keep larger sanctuaries as full parks likely related to provincial authority for game management outside the parks and the fact that there had been a myriad of sanctuaries created under the *Migratory Birds Convention Act*. The smallest were returned to the prairie provinces under the resources transfer agreements while the largest, such as Buffalo, Elk Island, Point Pelee, and Nemiskam, and including Wood Buffalo now returning to the branch's fold, remained under federal control all as full national parks. Only national historic parks remained in the Part II category, the explanatory notes stating, "This is to provide for the preservation and marking of sites and the commemoration of events of national importance," but without the necessity of extending all the provision of the act to these areas. This allowed the governor-in-council "to apply to such areas those provisions of the Parks Act and Regulations as are considered necessary," which, while consistent with application of the standard, did not provide the formal recognition of the program that Harkin had so long sought.[44]

Despite its weaknesses and compromises, on balance the act's main goals of protection for inviolability and change only by Parliament had been well met. Supportive elements in the Canadian press celebrated the achievement and the bright future it heralded for the country's national parks, even before it received final assent. The May 12 edition of the *Manitoba Free Press* called it "an important achievement in the movement for the protection of the parks and will be cause for satisfaction to the growing number of Canadians who recognize the necessity for that movement." The *Prince Albert Herald* offered, "Passage of the act is a great victory for the parks department and those park-minded citizens of the Dominion deeply concerned about protecting the parks from the inroads of commercial interests." The *Saskatoon Star-Phoenix* of May 15 seconded this sentiment with particular reference to the agitation for the proposed Lake Minnewanka development, noting, "A bill just passed by the House of Commons will put such questions outside the scope of executive action at Ottawa."[45] While undoubtedly gratified, Harkin was too busy to pay these plaudits much attention, preparing his superintendents and others in administration for changes about to occur. However, on June 17 he received a communication from Horace Albright, and in response to his question as to whether the pending legislation had been passed, he finally let a bit of his pride in the accomplishment show through: "We consider that this Bill pretty well meets the situation in regard to inviolability because its effect is that there can be no commercialization of National Parks except by Act of Parliament....Prior to the enactment of this Bill mining, water power, irrigation and similar rights could have been disposed of by order-in-council without Parliament being consulted. The new Bill, therefore, is a great achievement for us."[46]

While certainly true, hailing it as a *fait accompli* for inviolability proved to be somewhat premature. Within a month any hope that the controversy surrounding it with respect to power development would subside was thrown into limbo with the calling of a general election for July 28, with some of Bennett's strongest backers being power interests from Calgary and region. The election produced a majority for Bennett and his Conservatives, immediately changing the equation; the politician Harkin had disaffected during the First World War, the corporate foe who had lurked in the background during his protracted battles with Calgary Power, and the leader of the Opposition he had so severely criticized on the resources transfer and parks acts now held the nation's reins of power. He would have immediately realized that his circumstances were about to change, and others too recognized the ground had shifted. Within a day, Mayor Davison and the Calgary Board of Trade announced that they would formally petition the prime minister-elect to grant Calgary Power a licence to develop Minnewanka. Returning in late August to his constituency for the first time since the vote, Bennett was already deeply immersed in plans for an emergency session of Parliament to deal with the unemployment situation, and was fully aware that, apart from his long support for the project, the Minnewanka development could alleviate that situation in the Calgary area. The meeting took place on August 27 and, according to reports in the Calgary dailies, he agreed to consider the matter, but stated, "Transfer of the natural resources to the provincial government had somewhat complicated matters....and the legal points to be cleared up in this regard might take some time."[47] Two days later the *Free Press* more fully identified these legal considerations: "There certainly are difficulties. Thanks to the late Government the National Parks Act became law last spring....All matters affecting the parks must be given 30 days' notice in the Canada Gazette and the proposed changes must then be incorporated in a bill and passed by Parliament, and Parliament will most decidedly have something to say about these repeated proposals emanating from Calgary for the spoliation of park areas."[48]

Leaping into the fray, both the Alpine Club of Canada and the Canadian National Parks Association immediately opposed any action to remove or develop Lake Minnewanka, and the new minister of the Interior, Thomas Murphy, was soon inundated with letters of protest. In a communication to Murphy, Cory warned, "I anticipate that we will be asked for a lot of information," and provided Harkin's memorandum of the previous May, suggesting, "The Prime Minister may be interested in the Parks Branch statement."[49] If he read it, Bennett would certainly have been galled to see the lengthy and critical opinion of the position of Calgary Power and its supporters from the man he so disdained. Regardless, with his legal and political acumen, he would have been aware that the advice it contained on the need for parliamentary action and the likelihood of involvement on the part of the Alberta government was accurate. Accordingly, while continuing to indicate his sympathy for the Calgary position, he turned the file over to Murphy and threw himself into round-the-clock preparations for the special parliamentary session scheduled for early September.

Fuel was added to the fire by the Banff Advisory Council's decision to hold a plebiscite on Minnewanka, wherein a majority of residents strongly supported not the thirty-foot increase in the height of the dam Calgary Power was now proposing but rather an earlier suggestion for a full fifty- to sixty-foot augmentation. By mid-September, Harkin was once more doing his utmost to keep the project at bay, responding to a letter from the private secretary to the minister of Trade and Commerce that any act of Parliament necessary for the project to proceed would bring section 14 of the *Natural Resources Transfer Act* into play. If this occurred, "My interpretation of Section 14 is that the dominion has the right to operate these park areas only as National Parks and that authorization by Parliament for power development would be equivalent to declaring that the areas concerned were no longer required for parks purposes and that they would forthwith revert to the Province."[50] Meanwhile, Calgary Power, despite having pulled out all the stops in its efforts to lobby for approval, had come to the realization that parliamentary involvement could not be avoided if the project were to proceed. On September 6, 1930, Secretary E.J. Chambers submitted an application to Murphy, indicating the company would spend $3.4 million and employ 500 men over a one-year period and pointing out the support of a large percentage of boards of trade and municipal councils in Alberta, including the people of Banff. Addressing the matter of approval, he stated, "I am aware of the fact that the Parks Act passed at the regular 1930 session of Parliament may necessitate the matter being dealt with by Parliament....Notwithstanding the provisions of the Parks Act, such work might and could be carried out in the name and under the direction of one of your departments at the risk and expense of the Company."[51]

Unwittingly, this put the matter even more fully into Harkin's hands. In an analysis of the application for the deputy minister, Water Power Director J.T. Johnston confirmed that the project would need parliamentary approval and that in order to carry out preliminary investigation, "It would appear to be required under the Act that any such investigations as the Department may feel inclined to permit, should be carried out under the direction of the Commissioner of Dominion Parks."[52] In the circumstances, Bennett would have understood there would be no way to avoid a fight should the government attempt to grant approval for the proposal, one that undoubtedly would spill over onto the floor of the House where there were far weightier issues he wished to have debated. And, immediately after the House prorogued two weeks after being called, he departed for the Imperial Conference in London to argue the case for a reciprocal preference in trade with Great Britain and the countries of the Empire, which he thought would help solve Canada's difficult economic situation. The conference kept him in London until mid-November, and during his absence the *Free Press* reported that in reply to a query from the Banff Advisory Council he had indicated that, due to the legal difficulties, there would be no immediate development of a storage reservoir at Lake Minnewanka.[53] Nevertheless, the *Calgary Daily Herald*, in speculating what he might eventually do, was certain he would put Harkin and his minions in their place: "But those who know the present prime minister are sure of one thing, that the continued propaganda of officials of the department of the interior, their newspaper friends and organizations will not have the slightest effect on his decision. We fancy Mr. Bennett is well aware of the source of the propaganda and on more than one occasion has publicly expressed his views regarding bureaucratic methods of government officials."[54]

Although Murphy stated in an interview before departing for a visit to the West that the matter would ultimately be decided by cabinet, after visiting Lake Minnewanka with Wardle, he advised that a more complete survey by Calgary Power would be necessary before any action could be taken. Following this, Harkin communicated directly with Bennett in a letter of January 23, 1931 reviewing the situation: "Our Departmental Solicitor tells me that it is in my power to authorize an investigation." While frequently disagreeing with Bennett, he could not decide this matter without reference to the chief decision-maker and reviewed the points to be considered, including whether an investigation should be held and, if so, should it be carried out by the Parks Branch alone or with the involvement of the company and perhaps the province. In closing, he indicated, "I will hold these papers on my desk pending word from you."[55] No response to this letter appears in the file, almost certainly a result of matters becoming even more complicated on March 5, 1931 when the members of the Alberta legislature voted unanimously in favour of a Labour party motion stating, "This assembly believes that the best interests of this province will be served by the Dominion authorities transferring to the Provincial authorities all water power sites in the National Parks, providing, however, that no development of such sites shall take place without the mutual consent of both governments." In advising the department on the effect of this resolution, Johnston pointed out that it would require that Parliament declare the *Dominion Water Power Act* applicable to park waters and have the work carried out without removing Minnewanka from the park.[56] Understandably, this requirement provided the final knockout blow to the project's further consideration.

The commissioner and the National Parks Branch had won, or at least sidestepped, the first challenge to the *National Parks Act*, but the question remained whether the outcome would have differed had other priorities not conspired to distract Bennett. In any event, by a strange twist of fate, circumstances were bringing the two men closer together, and the immediate future saw their relationship become ever more tortuous, markedly affecting Harkin's remaining career.

FOURTEEN

The Prime Minister Telephoned

WITH THE ONSET of the Depression in 1929, Harkin entered a period much like that he had experienced during the First World War when creative approaches were needed to keep national parks relevant and supported during a difficult economic and social period. But despite the challenges this situation presented, the years from 1930 to 1936 proved to be an incredibly productive period for parks infrastructure, as the branch became one of only two national agencies tasked with carrying out extensive depression relief projects. In these circumstances, Harkin had to by turns be patient and forceful to keep matters on an even keel, a challenge made all the more difficult given that he was operating under a hostile prime minister and in an environment where his control of the parks agenda was gradually slipping.

As the issue of power development in Banff National Park began to subside following the election, Harkin's relationship with Bennett continued to influence parks, a result of the country's declining circumstances. Earlier the branch had benefitted from limited relief funding for the Banff-Windermere Highway, and with that precedent and conditions deteriorating toward the end of the 1920s, it became involved in discussions with Minister Stewart about the possibility of again playing a role in providing work for relief purposes. A list of projects had first been assembled in November 1929 and updated in July 1930, and within days of the election Harkin wired his superintendents inquiring, "In case opportunity offers to get extra work done in parks through unemployment situation what work might be undertaken in your Park."[1] Some responses identified town improvements and upgrading of trails and campgrounds, but most involved work on improving or building new roads, all expensive undertakings difficult to fund with regular appropriations. Information in hand from ten parks, he and Wardle combined it into three different schedules, details of which were communicated to departmental officials while the special parliamentary session was underway. Harkin could not fail to recognize that such work lent itself to being addressed similarly to that carried out by alien internees during the war years and that it might fill some gaps in the looming financial circumstances. Undoubtedly he hoped that Bennett, too, would see the similarities, but at least for the moment this was not to be as the *Unemployment Relief Act* that emerged from the session supported the government's position that relief was a local responsibility. While limited funds were to be provided to the provinces to help alleviate the situation, federal departments were barred from receiving them. Nonetheless, as conditions continued to deteriorate, opportunities emerged for a role that made the branch's assistance invaluable in helping the prime minister solve his problem.

The sole benefit to national parks under the *Relief Act* lay in providing individual provinces with an opportunity to use a portion of their grant for improvements in park areas. Both Manitoba and Saskatchewan opted to do so in recognition that development work in Riding Mountain and Prince Albert would be labour-intensive, would remove some of the unemployed from urban centres, and would provide much-needed new tourist facilities. That fall unemployed men arriving in the parks were provided with up to two months' relief work to a maximum income of $100, contributing to the cutting of seventy-five miles of Prince Albert's boundary, the enlargement of Waskesiu campground, and the building of roads at Riding Mountain to connect Clear Lake with surrounding towns.[2] Conversely, in Alberta the provincial government refused to spend any of its $900,000 allocation on national parks projects, resulting in Banff, Jasper, and Waterton beginning to keenly feel the effects of a worsening situation, particularly as residents living on federal lands were declared ineligible to receive provincial relief. The advisory councils in Banff and Jasper were not slow to let their MPs know the impacts, especially the former as part of the prime minister's own constituency. By mid-October the Banff council had passed a resolution to write the ministers of Interior and Public Works "re-outlining the programme of much needed works in this vicinity that have already been suggested by this Council" and "re-opening the question of obtaining a grant for the construction of a public building in Banff, particularly for a post office." Impatient at the lack of response, three weeks later the council passed a further motion to contact Bennett as their MP "expressing disappointment that was felt over the delay in the building of the new Bath House at the Upper Hot Springs [and] the curtailment of funds that it was understood had been allocated for definite purposes in the Banff National Park, but which had been withdrawn or transferred."[3]

Bennett could not long ignore Banff's complaints, and ultimately took a fateful step. On Saturday, January 10, 1931 he telephoned Harkin at home and, as later reported to Cory, made "enquiries as to unemployment conditions in the parks and asked for information as to how much it would cost to take care of the unemployed in Banff, Jasper and Waterton Lakes Parks."[4] Subsequent events make it seem likely the conversation included the commissioner conveying information on former Minister Stewart's recommendation in January 1930 that a special sum of $33,000 be included in the supplementary estimates for relief work at Banff, including $10,000 specifically earmarked for the Upper Hot Springs, which had inadvertently been overlooked. The prime minister apparently found this sufficient to immediately approve relief funds for the Alberta parks without stepping outside the intent of the *Relief Act*, except for one significant difference. The new money was to be administered directly by the Department of the Interior, a change Harkin had perhaps also recommended in light of the need for expediency. That same day Minister of Labour Robertson forwarded a report to Privy Council laying out the background and advising, "In order, therefore, to enable certain improvements to be carried on to relieve present unemployment in these Park areas, the Minister recommends that the sum of $33,000 be allocated from the monies authorized by the Unemployment Relief Act, 1930; the said amount to be administered through the Department of the Interior." Privy Council concurred on January 14, and it was immediately sanctioned by governor-in-council.[5] Informed of the action, Harkin wrote Bennett on January 29 to advise him of the funds' allocation between the three parks and to inform him that superintendents had been directed to provide part-time work only, alternating gangs on a weekly basis.[6]

Although these resources paled in comparison to the more than $400,000 Harkin had initially requested for work in the three parks, it was still a victory to gain Bennett's approval, and it provided the key for future relief monies to go directly to a government department. And, although limited, the funding accomplished its goal. For example, in Jasper there were seven rotations in the first eleven weeks, each comprised of between eighty and ninety men, and according to the foreman, "A strong evidence of willingness and thankfulness to work was shown throughout the job by 98% of the men and the amount of work exceeded estimates and anticipations."[7] Similar reports quickly came from other parks, but, unfortunately, the *Unemployment Relief Act* expired at the end of March and the workers had to be laid off. Nonetheless, in the subsequent budget debate both Labour Party MP J.S. Woodsworth and Leader of the Opposition King acknowledged the opportunity that relief operations in the national parks provided to do something meaningful for the country while they provided much-needed work.[8] Accordingly, the new *Unemployment and Farm Relief Act* passed in August 1931 gave the government a free hand in determining the amount to be expended on relief, allowing the entire Parks Branch program to be reconsidered. After Murphy's approval in early September, Harkin confirmed and organized numerous new projects.

To this point, the commissioner had played a key role in gaining approval for and administering the initial branch efforts, but the very nature of the work demanded specialized skills to accomplish the more intensive work ahead. An obvious choice to carry out these tasks was Chief Engineer James Wardle. By nature meticulous and efficient, he had much experience through supervision of the alien internee projects, more than a decade serving as chief engineer, and successful completion of the Banff-Windermere and other branch road-building endeavours. The job of supervising park relief activities in Jasper Park was assigned to him in mid-September, Harkin wiring the superintendent, "All relief your Park is under direct supervision of Chief Engineer Wardle. All matters this connection should be taken up through him and not direct with head office."[9] Effectively, this directive soon became the rule in all western parks, but while making perfect sense, it was just one further step in what was becoming a devolution of control from the commissioner's office.

This tendency was also evident in his relationship with Bennett. Although the prime minister had forged a relationship of convenience to further relief efforts, he had not forgotten or forgiven past transgressions. Indeed, Bennett was famous for holding grudges, and Fergus Lothian recalled that during this period the prime minister regularly telephoned Harkin and requested his resignation.[10] This situation likely influenced decisions when Deputy Minister Cory reached retirement in 1931, a state of affairs from which Harkin might otherwise have benefitted. Practice dictated that Assistant Deputy Minister Roy Gibson, a Manitoba native brought into Interior by Cory in 1908, would succeed to the deputy's position and Harkin might have expected, with his long service and wide reputation, to be considered for assistant deputy. But the timing was wrong. Gibson was not promoted, like Harkin probably being seen as a Liberal placeman with connections going back to Oliver's time, and instead Hugh Rowatt, a veteran of the Mining Lands and

Yukon Branch, was awarded the position. At the same time, the Parks Branch faced huge attrition within its ranks, occasioned by the natural resources transfer to the western provinces. The handing over of files took place during the summer of 1931, affecting the careers of 1,295 employees in the Department of the Interior, including the loss of thirty-two positions within the Parks Branch alone, while it retained all its responsibilities.[11]

On the other hand, Wardle's increase in responsibilities marked another step up the departmental ladder for him. In the days ahead, while communicating with his superior on a daily basis concerning the various relief projects, he took direction from higher authorities, mainly from Minister of Labour Senator G.D. Robertson, the man with overall responsibility for the program, but sometimes from Bennett himself. When relief camps were being set up in the fall of 1931 shortly after his appointment, Robertson informed Murphy that the prime minister had agreed that while the Dominion Unemployment Service would provide for the urban unemployed, the chief engineer would have sole authority to "select the local labour...necessary to be drawn from within the Park areas."[12] Soon Wardle was in direct communication with Bennett's secretary concerning Banff relief projects and was also invited to conferences of senior government officials to discuss relief matters, with Rowatt and Harkin being conspicuous by their absences. Typical was a meeting held in April 1932 in response to a request from Premier Brownlee to keep relief work on park road construction going to alleviate the provincial unemployment situation, which Wardle attended in company with Bennett, Murphy, and Alberta minister George Hoadley. In reporting on it to Harkin, he noted he had expressed some operational concerns, but Bennett had dismissed them and, in speaking to the grave emergency the country faced, assured him that funding would be found as soon as it was necessary.[13] This commitment not only indicated that the prime minister was relying heavily on the Engineering Division to achieve his agenda, but also had found an effective way to get around the roadblock he perceived Harkin to be.

This situation did not affect Harkin's and Wardle's relationship or their success in teaming up over the next five years to accomplish an unprecedented record of infrastructure improvement in and beyond Canada's national parks. In fact, when Wardle was given responsibility for relief activities, they had already been at work for two years carrying out the "Big Bend" project, which itself would be placed on a relief basis in November 1931, providing the last link in the western Canadian section of a transcontinental highway connecting five national parks. As mentioned, the idea for this road had been promoted by Harkin and Williamson as early as 1913, and the completion of the Kicking Horse Trail to Golden in 1927 and subsequent linking of Revelstoke with a road through the Fraser Canyon to the coast left only a section between Golden and Revelstoke for a highway from Winnipeg to Vancouver to become a reality. Eventually an understanding between BC and the Dominion had been reached whereby Canada would contribute some $800,000 towards construction of fifty-six miles of the ninety-six-mile route passing through Glacier Park over Rogers Pass. However, another possibility would see a 190-mile road following the Columbia in its northern arc circumventing the Selkirks, thought to be easier to build and maintain and potentially providing another scenic national park route to the coast via a connecting highway from Canoe River to Jasper. Harkin had been involved with Cory in the intergovernmental discussion of the options and ultimately recommended, based on information received from Wardle, that the Parks Branch undertake construction of the "east leg" of the Big Bend from Golden to Canoe River rather than have the government make a cash contribution. Approved on September 30, 1929, Wardle had successfully commenced work with an appropriation of only $15,000 in hand more quickly than anyone had thought possible.[14]

Given this background, it did not take the pair long to clarify their thinking around the huge volume of new projects facing them in the fall of 1931. The program's goal was to accomplish "the maximum amount of essential work at a minimum cost in materials, in order to give effect to the policy of the Government to employ as many men as possible."[15] So that this work would only be that of permanent benefit to the parks it was necessary "to canvas the situation thoroughly," but despite there being needs in all eighteen parks in the system, Harkin

Chief Engineer J.M. Wardle (second from left) discussing construction on the Big Bend Highway, 1932. Byron Harmon photograph. Wardle's skills as an organizer and a highway engineer resulted in an increase in his power and authority at the expense of Harkin as the Parks Branch focused its attention on relief projects during the Depression years. [WMCR, V263 NA-1736]

and Wardle understood that politics would play a significant role in the choices ultimately made. Having recently won a number of western seats, the Conservatives knew that relief measures in their ridings could help to solidify support. Indeed, Bennett's favouring of funding for Banff, Jasper, and Waterton had already been emulated a few months later when similar largesse was extended to Riding Mountain, bordering on Minister of the Interior Thomas Murphy's home town of Neepawa, Manitoba. It was therefore not surprising the new monies provided by the *Unemployment Relief and Farm Act* continued to be allocated in the same fashion; with roughly equivalent needs, Riding Mountain received four times the funding of Prince Albert in King's riding. In fact, the Manitoba park had its operations up and running by November 1931, soon having nearly 1,000 men under canvas in ten separate camps constructing roads from Wasagaming to the eastern park boundary and Dauphin, working on municipal improvements in the townsite, and enlarging the golf course. In the process is wracked up a bill of $209,000, four times greater than any other park. Records make it clear Murphy favoured his park, as when relief funds ran short in December 1931, Harkin wrote Rowatt noting that the minister had intervened when it appeared operations might close down: "The Minister's notation on our memorandum in this connection is 'stand for the moment.' Our understanding, therefore is that you will furnish us with instructions in a few days to be sent to Mr. Wardle in regard to Riding Mountain Park work."[16]

Nor were other parks represented by Conservatives forgotten. At Waterton, General J.S. Stewart, a Lethbridge dentist and First World War veteran, was determined to build on the fivefold increase in visitation registered in the three years after the 1927 opening of the Prince of Wales Hotel at Waterton Lakes. As American visitors still had to use the long roundabout route through Cardston to access the park from the Great Northern's lodges in Glacier Park, Montana, better road connection was a priority. This would involve further work on the Akamina Road begun in the 1920s. Road construction was also the priority in Minister of Trade and Commerce H.H. Stevens's East Kootenay riding, with work being carried out by local unemployed in the fall of 1931 on widening the road between Field and Golden, building a new bridge at Leanchoil in Yoho Park, and improving the Banff-Windermere Highway. When Wardle warned Harkin that winter weather threatened to shut down this work prematurely, the commissioner acquired a truck and snowplough to allow it to continue. Likewise, roadwork in MP Bury's riding would see Jasper townsite connected to tourist destinations at Maligne Canyon, Mount Edith Cavell, Pyramid Lake, and Miette Hot Springs.[17] However, while these individual park projects were important in allowing local politicians to look good in benefitting mostly local unemployed, there were bigger concerns and a requirement for larger projects to take care of the growing ranks of the unemployed in the major Alberta centres. This resulted in a commitment for a unique inter-park project that had long been promoted by Harkin and the branch.

As mentioned, Williamson and Pearce had touted the possibility of a road connecting Banff with Jasper in the pre-war years, and with the circumstances now making it appear feasible as a relief project, building of the 147-mile Banff-Jasper Highway through some of the grandest scenery on the continent was seen as a high priority. The first thirty workers were marshalled at the Lake Louise and Jasper ends in late September 1931, with their numbers expected to grow rapidly. Regrettably, many of those appearing over the coming months were ill-prepared for work at clearing in mountain country in winter conditions, providing the first taste of the difficulties Harkin and Wardle often faced in coming years. It was the branch's understanding that relief workers would be supplied with clothing, but when it was found not to be the case with those appearing at Jasper, Harkin obtained permission from Rowatt to provide the essentials charged against future wages. Wardle had established commissaries in the camps for this purpose, but at the rate of twenty-five cents per hour many men found other uses for the little money earned. Also, they were housed in canvas tents, and although this did not cause problems at first, when a blizzard brought with it frigid conditions in the third week of November, men were confined to their tents trying desperately to keep from freezing. As they only got paid when they worked, their purchase of warmer clothing was precluded, and eventually stories began to appear in the Edmonton press concerning their plight. Bury wired Murphy about the problem and probing questions and finger pointing began to appear in Jasper relief files. Wardle believed conditions were no worse than in Alberta's provincial camps, and accused the Jasper minister who had brought the matter to the newspaper's attention of bad judgement. In a November 23 memorandum he claimed that "this whole matter was given unnecessary publicity" and that if the cleric had discussed the matter with the resident engineer, "he would have thoroughly understood the circumstances, and the Department would not have been wrongly blamed."[18]

Concerned about the controversy, Harkin advised Wardle to prepare a full report laying out the facts "for your own protection and the protection of the Department." In apologizing for the request, he stated his concern that the accusations would become grist for the political mill and wanted to be prepared: "I fully appreciate how tremendously rushed you are. At first sight it might appear to you unnecessary to ask for such details as I have indicated. The way I feel is that some of these allegations may be brought up in the House and that we therefore should have our information so complete that no question could be asked that we could not answer."[19] Matters were complicated by a negative report from J.B. Harstone, assistant director of Alberta Relief, moving Wardle to complain that the branch was the only organization doing effective relief work for Alberta's transients and that Harstone "could help us rather than hinder us by securing better prices on clothing products purchased through him." Noting that frame and log buildings were already under construction for winter quarters, he let his frustration show in signing off his telegram, "Doing best possible under winter conditions with equipment available and if further unreasonable complaints feel we should close down transient camps concerned."[20] In discussing the situation with Rowatt, Harkin laid out the choice that the department would have to make with respect to the camps: "There will be no objection on the part of Mr. Wardle or by this Branch to very greatly raise the standard of these camps but it must be kept in mind that to do so will involve large expenditures for materials and supplies and will, to that extent, defeat the purpose of the camps which is to supply any minimum of work for transients with reasonable accommodation."[21] Within days Wardle received a letter from Harstone indicating an inspection bore out the chief engineer's claims that the reports had been exaggerated, and in writing to Harkin, Wardle acknowledged the men had now received a considerable amount of free clothing and observed, "In any winter canvas camp there is a certain amount of hardship, particularly to men not used to this kind of life."[22]

After the waning of this contretemps, winter conditions continued to affect all relief projects, as deep snows brought progress to a virtual standstill. As well, relief funding was due to expire at the end of December, and only after the Bennett government granted an eleventh-hour extension to the end of February were operations allowed to continue. But work on the Big Bend and highways in Kootenay and Yoho parks had to be discontinued in January in any event because of the extreme snowfall and, with the exception of a few priority projects such as the

Upper Hot Springs in Banff, others wound down as spring approached. Nevertheless, despite the few rough spots with getting the Banff-Jasper project underway, most parks had good results with the work undertaken. In his annual report, Rowatt referred particularly to the Banff-Jasper project as "the most important work inaugurated" and noted, "this highway opens up some of the most spectacular mountain scenery of the Rockies." Likewise, Harkin stated that the year was one of "sound progress," and mentioned that, most importantly, "through the appropriation of unemployment relief funds numerous important works were proceeded with during the winter season which would otherwise have had to be held over for better times." He produced a table showing the work accomplished in each park; it illustrated the impressive impact of the relief projects—4,354 men had been employed in over 265,000 man-days of labour with a total expenditure on wages of $642,500.[23]

However, it was not long before Harkin's fear that relief conditions would come under public scrutiny in Parliament was realized. During 1932 attention focused on the growing number of transient single homeless men in western Canadian cities and the danger they were perceived to represent as potential Communist sympathizers, something Bennett greatly feared. After he consulted with Wardle in mid-September, the Parks Branch received $200,000 of funding specifically targeted at these men, who under Bennett's new directive were to be provided only with food, shelter, and a clothing allotment in addition to a penurious allowance amounting to $5.00 per month. In Banff and Jasper, some work was carried out on the Banff-Jasper Highway until it shut down in November, after which the men were used on local roads, clearing brush and doing maintenance projects. However, the largest use of the new labour force occurred in Prince Albert and Riding Mountain, where by the end of the year more than a thousand workers carried out similar works in each park.

It was at Riding Mountain where the men were congregated in large camps of several hundred at Wasagaming and Clear Lake that problems with housing them in hastily-erected shacks appeared. On November 22, Woodsworth rose in the House and read a letter from a man

Hillsdale Relief Camp, 1933. Living conditions in relief camps caused Harkin and Wardle difficulties when they came under the scrutiny of Parliament. [WMCR, V488-255-2]

representing a group of the camp occupants claiming that they were forced to "double bunk" in beds that were so close together they had to be crawled into from the end. The letter went on to make a particularly damming observation: "The terrible thing about it is that many of the men who are congregated in the camp are teenaged Canadian boys forced into close association with mature men, who have tramped the country, with the result is that the outlook for these boys stands a good chance of being completely warped and their characters so degraded and demoralized that their future is unquestionably seriously menaced."[24] This created an uproar and Murphy vigorously denounced the accusations the next day by reading into the record laudatory comments on the camps from Manitoba newspapers and attacking Woodsworth's motives. Fortunately, at this point the House prorogued for Christmas, but Harkin, concerned about the future of parks relief camps, went to great lengths to get to the bottom of the matter. The author was eventually found to be a suspected Communist sympathizer who had been expelled from a Riding Mountain camp as a rabble-rouser, comforting information except that Harkin already had a report from Superintendent James Smart that indicated the allegations were essentially true. Smart had already taken steps to correct the situation and proudly boasted of the activities the men in the camps were enjoying, but at the same moment Harkin received communications from Wardle warning that perhaps too much was being done to keep the men entertained in their spare time.[25]

Such issues only added to the pressure-filled aspect of Harkin's daily routine. Juggling the demands of overseeing the myriad of projects while keeping senior officials informed of the details was taxing, and he sometimes became impatient in his correspondence with Wardle, particularly when timely information was not forthcoming. But it was communications flowing the other way concerning uncertainties around the conditions and timelines of the government's rather haphazard approach to relief projects that was most frustrating. As each program neared its end, a flurry of correspondence from Wardle asked about rules regarding expenditure of surplus funds, whether or not it was the government's intention to continue successful programs, if he should allocate monies and begin demobilization in advance of expiry dates, and even about the fate of the unemployed should new funds not be forthcoming. These were queries that Harkin could not answer and there was increasing urgency in his contacts with Rowatt as he sought information. Each new episode took its toll and his already troubled health seems to have suffered; yet he never lost his sense of purpose or composure in the myriads of letters and memoranda flowing through his office. Like all others in the civil service, he had been forced to accept a 10 per cent decrease in pay by the *Salary Reduction Act* of 1932, but clearly recognized that he and his confreres in government service were infinitely better off than the thousands on the bread line.

Over the winter of 1932–1933, Canada tumbled to the depths of the Depression and was gripped with hopelessness, the unemployment rate standing at 30 per cent by the spring of 1933. Everywhere hapless men rode the rails back and forth across the country in an endless search for work, and Harkin was therefore pleased in April 1933 when the government approved funding for summer relief camps, hitherto only a small part of the overall program. He advised Wardle that $250,000 had been approved "for the undertaking of works in National Parks, National Historic Sites and on the Golden-Revelstoke Highway to provide for unemployment relief purposes," adding that "our Minister says this sum of $250,000 will be used especially for the relief of homeless men." Projects included road construction in Riding Mountain, Elk Island, Jasper, and Banff parks and the building of a second nine holes at the Riding Mountain golf course, using an authorized strength of 1,675 homeless men.[26] But the branch did not have the relief field entirely to itself, as General Andrew McNaughton, chief of the general staff at the Department of National Defence (DND) and a Bennett confidant, had convinced the prime minister in 1932 that he could deal with the single unemployed threat by setting up a system of work camps under his department. Engaged in building airfields over the winter of 1932–1933 using some 2,000 men, his success led to a proposal in the spring of 1933 that he become responsible for the rapidly growing numbers of single homeless. The BC government had abandoned its work on the western leg of the Big Bend in late 1932, and it was decided to give McNaughton this project as one of his first tasks.

Initially, Harkin was not concerned that there was another agency assisting in addressing relief, perhaps even welcoming it given the numbers of those needing assistance. But this began to change when the requirement to co-operate with the dogmatic McNaughton led to disagreement, competition, and the need to be protective of park relief operating procedures. From the outset Harkin had expressed his belief that his branch was the superior organization for road construction, given its road-building experience in mountainous terrain requiring numerous camps and long supply lines compared to DND's work on airfields on flat ground supplied from a central camp. Furthermore, he thought that there was a distinct difference between the goals of the two bodies, identifying the work of Defence's camps as "the care of the maximum number possible of single homeless transients with the funds available" while the branch aimed "to employ as many men as we could handle and obtain reasonable results." However, it was the general's demeanour that was most frustrating, particularly his aggressive demand that branch projects be made consistent with his own. McNaughton wrote him in early May 1933 suggesting a meeting, as "it appears there is need for co-ordination in respect to rates and conditions," and in advising Rowatt of the outcome Harkin noted there were a number of policies operational in national park camps on which agreement had been reached but other matters on which it was impossible.[27] He confirmed, "Our opinion was that where in view of our past experience, certain practices were working out well, there would seem no reason for us to change to practices proposed by the National Defence Department and which to a certain extent were still untried as regards highway construction with single homeless men."[28] Disagreements were related to the relative economy of the differing operations and the best way of administering and operating the camps, resulting in the two organizations engaging in a war of attrition that continued well into 1934.

McNaughton continued to criticize clothing and food policies in the branch compared with his own organization throughout the winter of 1933–1934, and in a memorandum to Rowatt of February 16, 1934 Harkin finally indicated he'd had enough: "I think it may be stated quite fairly that the relief camps operated by the Department have been operated with a minimum of labour troubles and taking into consideration the nature and location of the work, at a cost which compares favourably with those operated by the Department of National Defence. I also wish to remark that the constant recurring criticism of our policy in attempt to cause the lowering of our operating standards is entirely out of place."[29] The branch's record was enviable, to the extent that there were only two brief work stoppages in park camps that winter compared with fifty-seven incidents in DND camps.[30] Harkin undoubtedly felt vindicated, then, when Murphy announced in early March 1934 that he intended to make a statement in the House on the work of the national park relief camps as part of the debate on new relief funding. A briefing prepared by Wardle reported that as many as 3,360 single homeless men had been simultaneously accommodated in the camps; there were twenty-four different types of projects or activities being undertaken; wholesome and substantial meals were being provided, with the single homeless receiving exactly the same fare as the supervisory staff; in camps where the men were concentrated in one location, such as Riding Mountain, there were extensive recreational facilities

Steamshovel loading truck on Big Bend Highway construction, 1932. Byron Harmon photograph. Competition to build the Big Bend was only one area of disagreement between the Parks Branch and the Department of National Defence beginning in 1933. [WMCR, V263 NA-1724]

being provided, including skating rinks, so that "many of the men are living a fuller life than ever before"; and that as a consequence of all these factors and the competence of engineers and foremen, there had been no serious labour trouble.[31] The information provided the grist for Murphy's speech during which he presented the record of his department's relief efforts. This defence assured continued funding and parks relief operations were again underway by the end of May 1934, but now concentrating on road construction and using fewer men, in light of Wardle's belief that the availability of single homeless workers was on the wane.

There was also an expectation that a major public works program would soon be announced, as Bennett had promised as much in a November 1933 radio broadcast and President Roosevelt had provided a compelling American model with his "New Deal," making the huge sum of $3 billion available to fund major public works pump-priming projects. Bennett ultimately reacted with a pale imitation, the

Public Works Construction Act (PWCA) announced in the summer of 1934, financed by printing $40 million of new money on the basis of an increase in the value of Canadian bullion reserves due to escalating gold prices.[32] The new act dictated that McNaughton would finally get his wish and become responsible for all single homeless unemployed, while major projects such as the Big Bend and the Banff-Jasper were to go on a PWCA footing aimed specifically at giving a real working wage to the married unemployed with dependents. In effect, this move allowed the Parks Branch to dodge a bullet. After the single homeless were gradually transferred to DND camps discontent festered in increasingly rough conditions with penurious compensation, and in the spring of 1935 a mass walkout in the BC camps culminated in the On-to-Ottawa Trek and the disastrous Regina Riot when Bennett decided they must be stopped.[33] On the other hand, the PWCA proved a huge boon to the Parks Branch, as it was to receive $2 million earmarked for its projects, which could now be extended to construction of public buildings and other public works projects that Harkin and Wardle had kept on the shelf for some time. However, in no-holds-barred pork-barrelling Bennett made sure the lion's share of Alberta's funding was directed to his Banff constituents, the effect being to increase park infrastructure spending but further isolate Harkin from decision-making.

Bennett's powerful grip on his constituency resulted in a new *modus operandi* for Harkin vis-à-vis the town's residents. After initiating annual meetings with the Banff Advisory Council in 1921, he had patched up some of his earlier disagreements during the 1920s. One particularly beneficial action occurred in 1927 when he reached agreement with the CPR to provide them with the Rundle campgrounds, allowing the building of a new Stanley Thompson-designed golf course and resulting in the company reciprocating by funding a new campground on Tunnel Mountain. However, the prime minister had characterized Harkin as an enemy of national parks residents in the natural resources transfer and parks act debates, and although not being expressly forbidden from visiting Bennett's constituency, he was apparently not particularly comfortable doing so. Accordingly, his annual inspection tours to the park effectively ended, his only further recorded contact with the Banff

Council coming in August 1933 during a visit to the western parks with Murphy, when they met with a committee to discuss lack of progress on local roads and a proposed airfield. Much more frequently, with the ear of Bennett available, he was effectively by-passed, council's contact being made directly with the prime minister or the minister.

The corollary to this situation was that, after the initiation of the PWCA, Wardle began to fill the gap in the branch's western administrative role. His influence at Interior had reached lofty heights, with Bennett, Murphy, and Minister of Labour Gordon becoming ever more dependent on him as relief projects progressively co-opted regular government activities. When a minister or the prime minister visited western parks to review relief activities or announce new ones, Wardle was at their side. This development was further amplified after Rowatt's retirement in April 1934 and the decision taken to leave the deputy minister's position vacant, requiring Gibson to juggle all departmental responsibilities, also relying heavily on the chief engineer. Even Harkin succumbed to the tendency, constantly seeking Wardle's opinion when action was required and often quoting it verbatim in his reports to senior officials. Banff residents had long called for the chief parks position to be headquartered in the West closer to the scene of its major responsibilities, and with Wardle in place, ably seconded by engineer and new superintendent Major P.J. Jennings, he was now effectively acting as a western commissioner. Having moved seasonally between the district office in Banff and the Ottawa headquarters early in the Depression, by 1934, with the need for his constant supervision of the many complex relief projects underway in the West, he lived year-round in Banff.

However, Harkin was still nominally in control and the partnership forged with Wardle and other branch employees working toward the completion of relief projects resulted in important accomplishments during the PWCA period. Proposals for public works went back to Banff Council's 1930 identification of a new post office and upgrades to the Cave and Basin, and while theoretically still to be built using relief labour, the combined administration building and post office, proudly announced by Bennett during a visit July 1934 visit to Banff, was to be

Banff Administration Building from Cascades of Time gardens. Byron Harmon photograph. The construction of Banff's new public building designed by Harold Beckett was one of the foremost achievements of PWCA funding. [WMCR, V263 NA-3583]

built on a contract basis. Virtually all PWCA buildings in other parks were designed by the branch's Architectural and Town Planning Division; however, an exception was made for the special status of the administration/post office building and a new Banff east gate entrance structure. These were the work of well-connected Windsor, Ontario, architect Harold Beckett, who adopted a Tudor revival design using Rundle limestone for what were seen to be landmark structures. Beckett, an avid amateur geologist, also created the design for one of the most interesting PWCA projects, the "Cascades of Time" gardens surrounding the new administration building, an attempt, in his words, to "depict in rock, plants and models evolution of life from its first known forms of microscopic size of millions of years ago."[34] As it turned out, the architect became one more burden for Harkin as lack of funding prevented him from fully realizing his dream, an outcome he could not understand and laid responsibility for at the commissioner's door.

Although the PWCA incorporated public works, parks road construction also fell under its auspices, providing a shot in the arm for the Banff-Jasper and the Big Bend projects. It also provided impetus for another road that had been languishing for some time, the so-called "Belly River Highway," aimed at linking Canada's Waterton and the U.S. Glacier parks when the Akamina Road proved impossible to complete because of BC's opposition. The Belly River route had initially received support at a July 1931 gathering of one hundred Rotary members from Alberta, Saskatchewan, and Montana at the Prince of Wales Hotel in Waterton, which had passed a joint resolution to petition their respective national governments to declare Glacier and Waterton an international peace park. Rotary membership had always been a useful tool for Harkin in forging important relationships by virtue of its requirement for members to attend a weekly meeting no matter where they were. His presence at the regular Ottawa meetings had brought him into contact with other senior bureaucrats and a good sprinkling of politicians, while being a visiting Rotarian had allowed him to meet influential local decision-makers informally. When in Banff, Harkin always attended Rotary and was often asked to update members on recent branch activities and plans, information that reached the entire populace when reported in the next week's newspaper.[35] The Waterton-Glacier resolution, while fitting perfectly with the international focus of Rotary, at the same time provided him with an opportunity to achieve one of his longest-standing goals—improving relations and tourism opportunities with the American parks system.

The Alberta sponsor of the peace park was Canon S.H. Middleton, principal of St. Paul's Anglican School on the Peigan Reservation and noted for his attempts at integrating native peoples into western society. Middleton was president of the Cardston Rotary Club and Harkin likely would have met him on early trips to the park, perhaps even attending a few of his club's meetings. The energetic minister later wrote that the idea of an international park had first come to him as a result of discussions with Waterton chief warden Kootenai Brown, who as early as 1910 had suggested that something be done between the two countries to preserve the game crossing the border, a factor that had eventually become important in the park boundary arguments Harkin himself had mounted in 1912.[36] Middleton's concept of holding reciprocal goodwill meetings between clubs on both sides of the border and extending Brown's conservation thinking to cultural ties had been embraced by fellow sponsor Harry Mitchell of the Great Falls Rotary Club, with the "peace" aspect celebrating the long record of harmonious relations between the United States and Canada.[37] Understanding the achievement of their plan would require support at the highest levels of both governments, the sponsors had recruited local MP General J.S. Stewart and Montana congressman Scott Leavitt to their cause. Both had legislation passed in their respective countries, after which an impressive dedication ceremony was held at Glacier on June 18, 1932, a crowd of 2,000 Rotarians and guests hearing messages from President Herbert Hoover speaking of the initiative as "an appropriate symbol of permanent peace and friendship" and Prime Minister Bennett as "a permanent memorial of all that neighborly relations should be between adjoining nations."[38]

Tied to his desk by relief concerns or perhaps prevented from attending by Bennett's strictures, Harkin was nonetheless pleased with the attention the dedication focused on his branch as a partner in the first such transborder park in the world. The occasion was extensively reported in Canadian newspapers and Harkin, too, waxed eloquent in his 1932–1933 report:

> Glacier National Park in Montana and Waterton Lakes National Park in Alberta are peculiarly adapted for the purpose of an international park. Situated side by side and complementary to each other, the parks encompass a region of the Rocky Mountain range of surpassing beauty

> and charm, and, together, constitute a playground of exceptional attraction from the tourist standpoint. Without impairing the autonomous rights of either country in respect to administrative matters, the union in spirit of the two parks should prove a powerful force for continued good will and sound understanding between the peoples of the North American continent who, although separate and distinct, have many aspirations in common.[39]

Given his belief in co-operation between Canadian and American parks, Harkin undoubtedly hoped to take a more active part in a reciprocal dedication planned for the Prince of Wales Hotel the next summer. But the Depression had begun to weigh heavily on its house count and Great Northern decided to keep it closed until conditions improved. Rotarians thought that as it was the location where the peace park idea had originally been adopted, they should await reopening before holding the ceremony. Meantime, influenced by the prospect, the Parks Branch announced that preliminary work was to begin work on the Belly River road as a relief project, while funding for the Kennedy Creek cutoff providing more direct access to Glacier National Park had been secured on the American side.

A connection between the parks had been under discussion for many years, dating back to its promotion by James Davidson of the Alberta Good Roads Association, and it had proven an important point of contact between the Canadian and American parks administrations. Harkin had first been approached in 1919 by Horace Albright, then acting director of the U.S. National Park Service, his letter noting "the tremendous enthusiasm of motorists of this country for national parks" and stating that this brought forward the possibility of a project "linking the national park system of the Dominion of Canada with the national park system of the United States by the construction of a motor highway to connect Banff, Rocky Mountains Park (Canadian) via Waterton Lakes Park (Canadian) with Glacier National Park and the entire park system of the United States."[40] However, the two men disagreed on the route to be followed, Harkin believing it should proceed to Glacier directly from the south end of Waterton Lake while Albright thought it should circle the mountains and join the St. Mary's River road near Kennedy Creek, and, by following up the St. Mary's River a short distance, connect with Glacier's east side road system. This difference if opinion had effectively put the matter on the back burner and during the 1920s both countries were distracted by other roadwork, the Parks Branch engaging in its Banff-Windermere and Kicking Horse Trail projects, which were seen to have benefits in improving road communication with the United States, and the Montana Highway Commission upgrading the road between Babb and the Canadian border, reducing the distance by twelve miles. But after the opening of the Prince of Wales Hotel attention had periodically continued to be focused on improving the connection between the two parks, and, although Harkin now supported Albright's Belly River route as the most feasible, financial strictures dictated that the branch continued to pursue the Akamina Pass path instead, expending money and effort on what by mid-Depression would merely be an extremely well-built tourist road to Cameron Lake.

On December 30, 1931, over twelve years after he had originally broached the subject, Albright, now director of the National Park Service, once more wrote Harkin attempting to revive the idea, stating that "this project appears to have considerable merit" and "upon receipt of assurance as to construction of that part of the road in Canada, I shall concern myself relative to arrangements with all other interested officials as to the construction of the balance of the project."[41] Again, the commissioner had pleaded poverty given recent restrictions on appropriations but, "as the project, in my opinion, has many points of value," agreed to keep it in mind for reconsideration. It would not be until June 1933, against the background of the peace park creation, that he could report that full construction of the road had been approved as an unemployment relief activity, and, fortuitously, Acting U.S. Parks Service Director A.E. Demaray replied that funding for Montana's section was also proceeding.[42] A few weeks later at the official opening of the Going-to-the-Sun Highway, a major Glacier Park road project, Senator Buchanan and Congressman Leavitt again spoke of the peace

Overlooking Waterton townsite, 1934. Obtaining a road connection with Glacier National Park in the United States proved to be a fifteen-year-long effort on Harkin's part. [GA, NA-4868-140]

park initiative and plans for a ceremony at Waterton while Middleton was busy convincing Governor Cooney and Senator Wheeler of Montana to attend.[43] But work on the Belly River proceeded at a snail's pace, and when Montana began construction in the summer of 1934 on its ten-mile section between the Blackfeet Highway north of Babb and the corner of Glacier Park, where the federal government would take over with a four-and-a-half-mile section connecting with the international boundary, only six miles in Canada had been graded and half of that gravelled. Fortunately, after Harkin informed Gibson that the U.S.

section would be completed that fall, the first major infusion of funding, $120,000, was approved through the PWCA.

The project proceeded throughout 1935, but was further retarded, first by Murphy's directive that available money was to be spread over the entire season and then by total depletion of funds in mid-September. Although an additional $20,000 was found, it was apparent to Canon Middleton that the highway would not be completed until 1936, and in planning for his long-awaited Waterton peace park dedication, he proposed that "a certain amount of prestige would be added" if the road's opening were combined with his ceremony on July 4, 1936.[44] Superintendent Knight recommended to Harkin that this "most appropriate" opportunity be embraced: "This Highway is in some respects unique in the Department's many undertakings in that it was built for the express purpose of connecting an American and a Canadian National Park and with a view to fostering international traffic, thus we feel that in this instance it might be a happy gesture to do all in our power to keep any ceremonies attendant upon its opening on an international basis."[45] Sadly, Harkin had to reply that no official opening was foreseen.

Canada ultimately beat its partner in completing its part of the road, work on oiling the Canadian section being finished only days before the peace park dedication while the American section through Glacier Park remained without gravel. American authorities had suggested "Chief Mountain Highway" as a name, in recognition of the route's most prominent feature seen from both sides of the border, but J.C. Campbell rejected it because it was not a "selling name." But by November 1936 the new minister, Thomas Crerar, had agreed to Knight's suggestion of "Chief Mountain International Highway," and some months later in a letter to Harkin, Director Cammerer concurred. In preparing for the peace park dedication in May 1936, Middleton informed Knight that the minister would be present "provided his Parliamentary duties will allow such absence" and that he would be "accompanied by Commissioner Harkin of the Parks Branch."[46] Once more, though, Harkin would be denied the opportunity to celebrate his combined Rotary and national park convictions, this time being tied to his office by a pressing file concerning parks in the Maritimes. However, he was present vicariously, writing the speech for Senator Buchanan, the minister's representative, which read in part, "I can think of no finer memorial in international goodwill than a park where the beauties of Nature are so vividly revealed, and it is my fervent hope that the ideals which inspired its creation will ever remain, intensifying the friendship and the mutual confidence which have served to make the American-Canadian boundary line unique in the annals of history."[47] After a fashion, the memorial represented the success of Harkin's career-long efforts toward harmonious relations between American and Canadian parks.

Completion of the Chief Mountain International Highway put an exclamation point on the Parks Branch's achievements during the Depression. By then relief programs were ending, with the winding up of the last of the winter single homeless camps in Prince Albert Park and smaller camps for permanent park residents in Banff, Jasper, Yoho, and Waterton on March 31, 1936. Apart from the satisfaction of knowing he had played a part in providing meaningful work to thousands of men through these difficult times, Harkin could total up what the various relief projects had meant for Canada's national parks in his annual report that year. The figures were impressive—Relief Acts, $3,358,735; PWCA 1934, $1,931,600; Supplementary PWCA 1935, $1,013,882, a total of some $6,300,000. Branch expenditure for the 1935–1936 fiscal year alone, including the regular appropriation of $1,130,000 and relief funding of $2,220,000, was $3,350,000.[48] To some degree, this funding had only replaced that which had disappeared from regular parks appropriations through Bennett's budget-cutting exercises, but as Harkin had predicted early on, it had provided a way that projects that would not otherwise have been carried out could be achieved in difficult times. Happily, attendance figures were also on the upswing, standing at 771,794 visitors for 1935–1936, and he could take considerable pride that his branch, having successfully educated Canadians about the importance of national parks and having convinced them to visit over the previous decades, had now provided them with the means of access and facilities to make their experience enjoyable for generations to come.

FIFTEEN

A Tremendous Magnet

SOME TEN MONTHS before the Waterton Peace Park ceremony an important event occurred that would provide Harkin with a new lease on life after five years of repressed status under the Bennett regime. The prime minister had planned to leave the deputy minister's position at Interior vacant given the likelihood of an election, but by August 1935 this plan was causing difficulties with respect to major departmental construction activities. Accordingly, and against the usual practice of making a political appointment, he decided to go inside the service to solve the problem. Bennett had mentioned in correspondence that "the leading official of the Parks Branch was the engineer, Mr. Wardle," and on August 19 made it official, telegraphing him offering "heartiest congratulations on your well deserved appointment."[1] The news was reported a few days later in the *Crag and Canyon*: "Announcement was made by Premier Bennett on Saturday last of the appointment of Chief Engineer James M. Wardle to the office of Deputy Minister of the Interior. Mr. Wardle will leave Banff as soon as possible to take over his new duties at Ottawa."[2] Harkin therein found himself in an unusual position—Wardle had been his protégé in his early career and later, apart from Deputy Commissioner Williamson, his most trusted and valuable confidant, but now would be his superior. However, no outcome could have had a greater impact on the National Parks Branch's aspirations and needs. If the appointment had been intended to be temporary, it did not turn out that way, and, combined with a brief revitalized role for the Department of the Interior, allowed Harkin to take care of some important unfinished business.

As indicated, in advance of the passage of the *National Parks Act*, he had become a strong advocate for a park in every province and was particularly concerned about the lack of Maritimes representation. Attention to national parks for the region already had a long history of debate, discussion, and negotiation by the time serious action was taken. The first proposal for a national park on the eastern seaboard had come in 1914, when H.F. McDougall of Christmas Island, Nova Scotia, had recommended an area in the Bras d'Or Lakes of Cape Breton Island southwest of Sydney be acquired for this purpose. This had been supported by officials of the Intercolonial Railway and Premier George Murray, but investigation found the lands in question were almost all privately held and accordingly "considerable expense would consequently be involved in the acquiring of such lands," something that became a familiar refrain throughout the 1920s when Harkin was approached about park creation in the region.[3] In October 1922, in response to a request for information concerning the possibility of establishing a park at Boat Harbour, Pictou County, he had declared that "the Dominion in the past has created national parks only where it directly owned the land or where a Province was willing to transfer the necessary land to the Federal Authorities" and that "the Dominion has not adopted any policy involving the purchase of lands for national parks purposes."[4] Similarly, in reaction to the request from MP D.A.

Mackinnon for a requisition of $10,000 toward establishment of a park at Port Lajoie, PEI, Harkin had suggested to Gibson that it was unlikely that the minister of Finance would approve such a supplementary estimate in light of the branch approaching him for funding for the slaughter of 2,000 buffalo.[5] Equally important was the availability of lands suitable for parks, since in the pre-Prince Albert and Riding Mountain parks era the idea that reservations should measure up to the sublime landscapes of the mountain parks was well-entrenched and the national park standard was in its early stages of formulation. Harkin had made this point in his October 1927 letter to James McKenna of the *Saint John Telegraph-Journal*, marrying it with his concern about availability: "I have some doubts as to whether any of the eastern provinces have Crown lands that would be suitable. Prince Edward Island has not. I think it is almost equally true with respect to Nova Scotia. Even if New Brunswickers may have some suitable areas, there is always the probability that the province would not be willing to cede such lands to the Dominion."[6]

Mackinnon had been the most persistent of those seeking approval, first querying Harkin in a delightful letter of April 2, 1923, "Will you give consideration to the matter of establishing a Canadian Park Branch in PEI? The modest natural beauty of the spot should not be a cause for its being overlooked. The larger freaks of nature are in the public eye today, but I think you can help the Province into the limelight. As to the sunlight, it's the first Province every day to enjoy that without government aid!"[7] In support of his position the MP asked the opinion of Provincial Secretary Arthur Newbury, a city parks planner by profession, and received a reply that could have been written by Harkin: "We have a most pleasing land scape (which is conducive to rest and quietness) but with a few variations from one end of the island to another, the whole Province being really one immense cultivated garden rather than a Park, no one spot seeming better than another. We lack grand mountain scenery, bold cliffs, dense forests, extensive valleys, great water falls, cascades and rapids, etc., some or most of which are essential in the formation of a National Park." However, he took pains to point out that the island's attractions were different from those of any other province or place in the United States, including its wonderful summer climate, red seashores, and blue ocean waters, and, on its north side, "natural sand dunes which bar the sea from the land for many miles along the coast, and beyond the dunes beaches of white and firm sand affording the best sea surf bathing in America."[8] Hearing that Harkin planned a trip to the east coast that summer, Mackinnon frequently visited his office, and in May wrote to indicate that the island did, indeed, possess a few "freaks of nature," including a series of very ancient mounds around a lake near Avondale and off Hog Island in Richmond Bay "a mass of lava thrown there ages ago by volcanic disturbances." Significantly, in his response Harkin did not mention these, but perhaps with a view toward the recreational parks recently established in the West, noted, "It seems to me that the sand dunes and the beautiful bathing beaches of the North Shore offer perhaps the finest recreational opportunities on the Island and possibly some plan might be devised for the reservation of areas where the land is not too valuable from the viewpoint of agriculture."[9]

Influential voices from the Maritimes had kept up the pressure, and, seemingly against his better judgement, by 1925 Harkin was forced to react to a strong representation from the Amherst, Nova Scotia, Board of Trade to Minister Stewart to make Fort Beauséjour, recognized as an important historic site by the Historic Sites and Monuments Board, into a full national park. In January 1925 the Board of Trade had carried a resolution quoting his 1923 report stating that "tentative plans were made showing possible locations for National Parks in the Maritime Provinces and the Gatineau district of Quebec," and pointing out that "the Department of the Interior has already made appropriations for National Parks in other sections of the Dominion in large sums."[10] Stewart had previously discussed this matter with Harkin as a result of representations made by area MP and Minister of State A.B. Copp, and, undoubtedly seeing it as an easy way to take the pressure off for new parks creation, had expressed himself open to the idea. In reporting to Cory, Harkin stated, "Some time ago Mr. Stewart approved of a letter to the Honourable Mr. Copp in which it was intimated that if Mr. Copp desired that Fort Beauséjour should be constituted a National

Fort Beauséjour National Historic Park showing museum and restored wall. Fort Beauséjour was the only Maritime province national park created in the 1920s. [LAC, PA-051686]

park the Department would take the necessary action."[11] However, he did his best to throw cold water on the idea. In response to letters from the Amherst Board of Trade, he referred to the change of emphasis that had occurred within the branch around the practice of creating national parks at historic sites: "With the exception of Fort Anne at Annapolis, this Branch has not dealt with historic areas on the basis of National parks. Even at Fort Anne there is not a great deal to plan for in connection with development. Our duty there was primarily one of preservation."[12] At the same time he renewed contact with Secretary of Industries and Immigration W.B. MacCoy, with whom he had discussed the possibility of finding Crown land suitable for a park in Nova Scotia in May 1923. MacCoy responded negatively to his March 1925 enquiry as to whether he had made any progress with respect to land they had been discussing in the Stillwater-St. Margaret's Bay area, effectively eliminating it as an option. With no available alternative, an order-in-council of June 10, 1926 established Fort Beauséjour National Park.[13]

Although the seventy-five-acre Fort Beauséjour did not measure up to national park standards, its dedication took immediate pressure off for Maritime parks creation. But agitation recurred in 1926 from a new direction; as a result of representations to the government by the New Brunswick Fish and Game Association, a campaign including boards of trade and influential individuals called for a national park in the province. By this time, though, Harkin's tune had begun to change. In a communication with Minister of Mines and Lands C.D. Richards, he mentioned his decision to support modification of the standard toward a selection of the best quality of typical national landforms and indicated that he fully supported Maritime national parks, making points similar to those he would put forward to McKenna a few months later. "I have dreamed for many years that sooner or later we might be able to find areas in the Maritimes which would include ample seashore and which would be incorporated in National Parks," he stated, and suggested they should be "typical of the early conditions of a province rather than for the protection of some particular outstanding physical feature."[14] As pointed out, with this change of emphasis finding its ultimate expression in the 1930 policy of a park in every province, it was not surprising that renewed pressure appeared in the three Maritime provinces in the early 1930s.

At the same time, regional government officials had come to appreciate the importance of tourism to their somewhat underdeveloped provincial economies, and increasingly challenging conditions were heightening that awareness. One of the impediments to park creation in the 1920s had been the large number and somewhat competitive requests coming from a variety of interests and the lack of knowledge in the branch concerning the geography and attributes of the areas being suggested. Harkin's own beliefs about the necessity for professional evaluation had led to a suggestion to Stewart for such action concerning a New Brunswick park in 1929. However, with the minister's indecision about creating new parks at the time, it was only after he, Cory, and Harkin met with a provincial delegation headed by Richards in January 1930 that an agreement was reached that would see a departmental officer investigate possible sites. Cautley had done excellent work in Manitoba and on mountain park boundaries, and the two men shared views about the importance of the standard and tourism to new parks establishment. At the end of May, Harkin contacted his deputy, advising, "The officer who I think should do this work is Mr. R.W. Cautley who did such excellent work in connection with the investigation of the boundaries of the western parks. I know that Mr. Cautley is very busy in his new position in the Topographical Surveys Branch but I think this matter of the selection of a Park area in New Brunswick is so important that the Department would be justified in asking Topographical Surveys to make a sacrifice in this matter for the general good."[15]

Although approval was delayed, Cautley eventually arrived in Fredericton on September 8 with directions to "investigate the physical characteristics of the various sites and in the light of this investigation and his own knowledge of Parks requirements to make a report for the consideration of the Government."[16] The surveyor examined six possible park locations with the province's chief game warden, favouring a site near Lepreau on the Bay of Fundy featuring a beautiful sandy beach. In his subsequent report he observed, "It may be said that it is unfair to compare the mountains and lakes of New Brunswick with scenic features of a similar kind in other Provinces, but it must be remembered that the object of my report is to select a National Park of Canada—not a Provincial Park—and that the two main objects of a National Park are:—(a) To set apart an area which shall truly represent the best of each distinctive type of Canadian scenery, (b) To attract tourists from other Provinces of Canada and all over the world."[17] The report also pointed out that with a requirement that the province hand over all land free of encumbrance, there would be a cost to it of approximately half a million dollars to acquire the lands at Lepreau.

In a December 1930 memorandum to Cory, Harkin discussed the issue of transfer of unencumbered lands, which thereafter became a critical consideration in timely Maritime park creation. It would be a reasonable expectation for the province to spread out its acquisitions, say over a period of five years, but "naturally there would be some difficulty in such arrangement since if a National Park were created with a great amount of alienated land within its boundaries complications in administration would ensue." Indicating that the branch's experience showed that enforcing regulations in such circumstances was difficult, he noted "where such areas have existed we have always endeavoured to purchase them as soon as possible." Another consideration was whether any allowance would be made for the province having expended money on improvements, Cautley estimating the value of the roads at the Lepreau site at some $190,000. If this were done "the Dominion will be saved spending that amount of money in the future on roads but on the other hand the Province will have no expense in connection with the maintenance of these roads." For the moment at least, Harkin favoured this approach, recommending that the province be credited with up to $50,000 per year if the funds were used to purchase alienated lands.[18]

Unfortunately, these considerations occurred at the same time as the 1930 election and a prolonged bout of illness causing Harkin's absence from the office. The New Brunswick government did move ahead, passing legislation in March 1931 allowing lands to be expropriated for national parks purposes and then be transferred to the Dominion. However, depression conditions were making further progress on any parks files difficult, and in October 1931 Harkin mentioned to Rowatt that, in the wake of Bennett's recent unsuccessful involvement in a possible transfer of the provincial park at Mount Robson to federal control, "the Government has decided on a policy of not extending the Parks System at present."[19] In April 1933, Richards, now New Brunswick's premier, made a formal offer to have his government make lands available in the Lepreau area provided the Dominion would develop it with roads and buildings and provide compensation for structures already in place. By then Harkin had determined that nothing could be done anywhere in the Maritimes in the circumstances, and in a communication to Nova Scotia Premier Harrington in September 1933 pointed out that all proposals for new parks were "temporarily suspended" while more pressing national demands were addressed.[20]

This restriction originated in the failing state of the Canadian economy, and one issue connected with it was the repressed state of Canadian tourism. As mentioned, from his earliest days as commissioner, Harkin had called for a national approach to the matter, but failing this the work of his Publicity Division had been virtually the only government-based tourism promotion carried out during the 1920s. Meanwhile, another body within the department, the Natural Resources Intelligence Service, had become responsible for investigating and promoting all aspects of Canada's industrial and natural resource development, and finally, in 1929, with a name change to the National Development Bureau, it took on responsibility as a clearinghouse supporting tourist travel in Canada. The work was mainly carried out through contacts with chambers of commerce, boards of trade, hotels and service stations, having them distribute maps and tourist reports on the country's attractions, but it also included preparing newspaper and magazine articles and making contacts at conventions and meetings. Eventually it became obvious that much of the work of the two agencies overlapped, and early in 1933 it was announced that the bureau's tourism work would henceforth be carried out under the aegis of the National Parks Branch. As Rowatt's annual report indicated, this placed a large responsibility on Harkin's shoulders: "The development of Canada's recreational resources is not only a source of national income but serves as a stimulus to further development of her other great natural resources....Commercially as well as geographically it benefits a very wide field, the income therefrom flows among all classes and helps to build up the prosperity of town and country. An extension of Canada's tourist business is therefore a line of constructive action that enters largely into the work of national development."[21]

These sentiments fit perfectly with Harkin's view of the role of Canadian tourism formulated in the postwar reconstruction period, and were, in essence, the recreational philosophy of his early parks tourism program writ large on the national scene. He explained that the "tourist division" would be distinct from the "publicity division," the latter acting "wholly as a media agency promoting interest in and travel to the National Parks" while the former "coordinates within certain limits the activities of the provincial tourist bureaux and traffic organizations interested in the development of tourist travel throughout the length and breadth of the Dominion."[22] Of further benefit was reassignment to the branch of a number of the bureau's employees engaged in tourist work, including its director, H.A. McCallum. Finally having an opportunity to see his vision fulfilled, Harkin made sure the work was carried out with purpose. During his first year of responsibility, he reported, "New avenues to increase Canada's tourist business were explored, new publications were issued and a number of other ones revised and updated." One "new avenue" was a systematic follow-up with those previously requesting recreational information, while regular work included distribution in the United States of 150,000 copies of five separate road map sheets featuring the various geographic regions of Canada and their American road links, placement of seasonal articles in Canadian and American periodicals and newspapers, and distribution of large numbers of lantern slides, photographs, cuts, and transparencies "depicting the recreational resources of the Dominion." During the year more than a quarter million were distributed, again mainly in the United States, and the following year the division fielded 12,750 individual requests for information "principally with motor routes, hunting and fishing districts, canoe routes, camping areas, lakes and seaside resorts, and to a lesser extent, golf courses, hotel and campsite accommodation, hiking trips and health resorts."[23]

Although satisfied, Harkin had actually been handed somewhat of a "hot potato" in his new responsibilities. Dominion Bureau of Statistics information indicated that in 1929, its peak year, the Canadian tourist trade had a value of some $309 million, but by 1933 this had slipped by almost two-thirds to $117 million. He had precious few resources at his disposal to address this massive problem—the Publicity Division had an appropriation of $40,000 per annum, $18,000 for publicity and $22,000 for salaries, and the Tourist Division an equivalent amount, a total of only $80,000.[24] The crisis created by the loss of almost $200 million a year in national revenue was eventually recognized in April

1934 with the appointment of a Senate committee "to consider the immense possibilities of the tourist traffic, to enquire as to the means adopted by the Government looking to its encouragement and expansion, and to report to this House." Eight senators were appointed to the Special Committee on Tourist Traffic under the chairmanship of Senator W.H. Dennis of Halifax, including Senator R.F. Green, former MP for the West Kootenays, who had played a role in the creation of Mount Revelstoke Park, and Senator W.A. Buchanan of Lethbridge, a moving force behind the development of Waterton Lakes Park.[25] This was the first in-depth examination of Canadian tourism, and as a recognized authority as well as the individual with the most responsibility for it in the country, Harkin was the first witness at hearings beginning on May 2, 1934.

His testimony would prove revealing, providing a picture of what he had accomplished in a long career in national parks and tourism work and his vision for the future of Canadian travel promotion. In opening his remarks, he gave a brief summary of the branch's role in the development of tourism in national parks:

> The main purpose of the National Parks organization is the preservation and development of what I might call the raw material for tourists, that is, the ultimate in scenery. As a matter of fact when I took charge of national parks in 1911 I found conditions very unsatisfactory, very little attention having been given to this end. From that time on I got very active financial and other support, and we have accomplished a great deal in developing and approving and preserving and extending our parks area.
>
> In the development of our parks we attach great importance to the foreign tourist trade, and while we always have in mind that the parks are primarily for our own people, we feel that whatever we do to make them more accessible and encourage their use by the home tourist, incidentally attracts the foreign tourist. At the outset, I approached the railway people and had a definite

> understanding with them from the start that they would take care of advertising. But that does not mean we have done no publicity of any kind. We have done a great deal and have had very satisfactory developments.[26]

In turning to a discussion of the extent of the parks system and, in particular, the lack of parks east of Ontario, Harkin noted that "we have two areas in the Maritimes that we call parks, though they are really historic sites," and in describing Fort Anne and Fort Beauséjour said, "We have authority to set aside historic sites as such, and while these, like the parks, are being developed primarily for the benefit of our own people, they are also being developed from the standpoint of attractions for tourists." In this vein, he mentioned the work being carried out at Louisbourg on Cape Breton Island: "When we complete our development there will be a tremendous magnet, particularly for New England tourists, the ancestors of many of whom took part in the capture of Louisbourg." He also informed the committee of recently taking over responsibility for the National Development Bureau, and in response to a question, described his activities: "Yes, I am the nominal head. I simply received the organization as it stood. It has been carrying out a great deal of work of a somewhat specialized character, but quite effective....Primarily it is an information bureau. It also gets out a considerable volume of newspaper material." He then recounted its work in co-operation with the Canadian Radio Commission, activities at the previous year's Chicago World's Fair, and the use of travelling lecturers in the United States.[27]

In summarizing, Harkin identified the need for better planning going forward: "What I have been trying to do since I took over the work last summer is this. My problem has been to ponder on a general plan. While there is a great deal of very good work being carried on now, it is rather haphazard....Co-ordination is what I think is most required." Pressed for an opinion on current federal activities with respect to tourist promotion and associated expenditure, he was more evasive; however, he provided recommendations concerning advocacy and support, ones that heavily relied on models developed in the branch. First, he suggested calling together representatives—from the provinces, the railways and other transportation companies, the hotels, the Canadian Chamber of Commerce, and the Press Association—who through general conference or the appointment of committees could tackle aspects of the problem. This gathering would appoint a general committee that would meet once a year: "It should be purely an advisory organization, pretty much along the lines of our Historic Sites and Monuments Board. We can only get the benefit of the best advice through such a conference." Second, behind the advisory board there should be an interdepartmental committee of government, composed of representatives of Customs, Immigration, Trade and Commerce, Justice, the Bureau of Statistics, and the Radio Commission. Unlike the advisory organization, this committee would meet frequently to deal with specific problems arising within the various departments, emulating the structure of the Interdepartmental Wild Life Advisory Board. A third proposal involved undertaking research and appropriate product development: "As a preliminary step it is of utmost importance that we divide the United States into four or five zones and put to work there surveyors or investigators to study local conditions with a view to ascertaining the peculiar likes and dislikes of the people in regard to tourist attractions, and then try to sell them the attractions that appeal. We must develop our tourist business more intelligently than we have been doing in the past." Finally, he referred to something that he had been thinking about for some time, the growing prevalence of "remittance men," 105,000 Canadians who had gone to live in California but had left their investments in Canada and were drawing out of the economy an estimated $100 million a year. In a brief accompanying his testimony, entitled "Tourist Industry—A Five Year Plan," Harkin described how to address this group, including encouraging retired Canadians to take up residence in British Columbia, promoting wintering outside Canada in countries who traded fairly with it, and, most thought-provokingly, "that some suitable island in the West Indies be secured by the Dominion and be administered as a National Park of Canada."[28]

Twenty-nine witnesses followed Harkin, including branch employees J.C. Campbell and H.A. McCallum, major railway executives, such as J.O. Apps and John Murray Gibbon of the CPR and C.K. Howard and J. Van Wyck of the CNR, as well as executives associated with local, regional, and national tourist bureaus and associations. The fact that Harkin had appeared first, was recognized as a leader in the tourism field, and had set out a comprehensive proposal for action meant that many of them found it necessary to react to his ideas. Most were positive, an exception being railway interests who argued against the idea of government becoming directly involved in paid advertising. Foremost was Gibbon, general publicity agent of the CPR and a man gaining a reputation as an authority on Canada's cultural and ethnic make-up, who in reporting on the CPR's co-operation with other agencies, specifically singled out the Parks Branch and some recreational activities Harkin was known to strongly support:

> As indication of co-operation with the Parks Branch of the Department of the Interior, we may mention that the Canadian Pacific organized in 1926 the Trail Riders of the Canadian Rockies to encourage greater use of the trails in the National Parks in that territory. This Order has 1,500 members, and among its various activities conducts an annual four-day cross-country riding and camping trip. Last summer there was organized, under the company's auspices, the Sky Line Trail Hikers of the Canadian Rockies, which will encourage Trail Hiking within Banff and Yoho National Parks....The Chalet-Bungalow Camps of the Canadian Pacific provide moderate-priced accommodation for hikers in Banff and Yoho National Parks and the Assiniboine Lodge, at Mount Assiniboine. We suggest that the Parks Branch might do well to study the Youth Hostel organization, with a view to encouraging hiking in Canada and in other National Parks, where there is at present inadequate accommodation.

Gibbon also recognized the national role parks played, recommending in a proposal for the organization of a week to celebrate Canada's beautiful fall foliage that "the Parks Branch of the Department of the Interior be authorized to contribute $5,000 toward this Canadian Maple Leaf Publicity Campaign so as to make it a truly National Movement." He also said, "We welcome the suggestion of Mr. J.B. Harkin to establish a Committee of Federal Department officers at Ottawa... to smooth out any troubles arising in connection with the tourist business." But he objected to pooling advertising funds in a central office, and when asked directly whether he recommended government expenditure to encourage tourism from the U.S. to Canada, he replied, "I do not, candidly, recommend the Government advertising in its own name, Mr. Chairman."[29]

Gibbon's comments touched on the question of what role the Dominion government should play in tourism from a financial and structural point of view, something Harkin had avoided directly commenting on as a matter of government policy. However, it seems certain he agreed with most of the witnesses, who thought that the Dominion should lead the tourism movement with a dedicated agency directed by a strong head, although whether or not he saw himself as continuing in that position is unclear. In any event, when the Senate report was released on May 22, 1934 an important recommendation was for "a central organization at Ottawa to co-ordinate the activities of the multitude of tourist agencies, public and private, throughout the Provinces, as well as the work of those Federal Departments and Services interested in the promotion of tourist travel within and to Canada." With a proposed name of "The Canadian Travel Bureau," it would be a branch of an appropriate department of government with a director, and, with a nod in Harkin's direction, to be assisted by an advisory council consisting of provincial directors of information, representatives of federal departments interested in promotion of the tourist trade, and executive members of the Canadian Association of Tourist and Publicity Bureaus. Its expenditures would supplement and not supplant what was already being done; a figure of $500 million annually was proposed as "the objective of a progressive permanent program of Canadian tourist trade promotion."[30] Bennett reacted quickly to this advice, creating the new Canadian Travel Bureau within a few months and placing it under the mantle of the Department of Railways and Canals in an obvious attempt to pair up the interests of the government and railroads in tourism promotion. Leo Dolan, director of the New Brunswick Bureau of Information and Tourist Travel, one of the most outspoken witnesses calling for a strong central organization, was appointed director. At the very least, Harkin would have been pleased to see his twenty-year-long call for a dedicated national tourism agency finally realized even if it was no longer under his authority.

Nevertheless, another recommendation in the report fully engaged his attention, one that related to his ongoing interest in Maritime park creation and his long practice of linking parks with tourism. An important focus of the Senate committee had been the need for greater tourism development of the Maritimes, with three of its members hailing from the region, including chair W.H. Dennis, publisher of the *Halifax Herald*.[31] Dolan had effectively portrayed the potential of Maritime tourism in his testimony, arguing, "We have there, mountain, lake and sea-shore resorts; trout and salmon streams; beaches, where warm water bathing is the rule rather than the exception; and surely a portion of Canada that is rich in historic lore. In other words, we have every natural asset for tourist development and we have them in abundance."[32] Another influential witness, F.W. "Casey" Baldwin, a Baddeck, Nova Scotia, MLA and an associate of Alexander Graham Bell, took this idea a step further with the suggestion that Maritime tourism be combined with national park creation.

Baldwin was highly complimentary of the National Parks Branch in his remarks, stating that the most effective federal activity in the tourist trade had been creation of national parks and "the success of our National Parks venture has been due in no small measure to the able administration of the National Parks Commission." He reviewed the situation of land availability in the West leading to the early parks, and although he placed no blame for the lack of parks east of Ontario, argued that it was time for things to change: "It is not my intention to complain in any way that Nova Scotia has been neglected, so far as National Parks are concerned, because the natural development came logically from the West, but since National Parks are now such a tremendous factor in directing the course of modern tourist traffic it becomes desirable that Nova Scotia should now have one or more National Parks within its boundaries." If this were done, he contended, it would help form an irresistible attraction, as "a National Park is an objective, and a string of National Parks forms a chain of points of interest which the modern motor tourist follows as instinctively as he does a trunk highway." He foresaw the day when airplanes would figure in this equation and closed his presentation by looking forward to a triumvirate of irresistible attractions: "Trans-Canada highways, Trans-Canada airways and Trans-Canada Parks should be joined together in one great national effort to stimulate, promote and develop the Tourist Industry of Canada."[33]

The testimony of witnesses with Maritime interests was seconded by written briefs from both the premiers of Prince Edward Island and Nova Scotia which, combined with the senators' focus, ensured that the region would not be forgotten in the final report. The committee specifically stated their thoughts about what they had heard concerning national parks. Pointing out that evidence submitted showed that over $22 million had been spent on the establishment and maintenance of national parks in Canada, and while indicating that such expenditures were desirable and to be commended, they observed that parks had been concentrated in one part of the Dominion, Quebec and the Maritimes having none. Therefore, "Your Committee agrees with the strong representations of witnesses that the establishment of National Parks by the Dominion authority should now be extended, as a truly national policy, to embrace all the provinces; and that these ideal settings for the scenic and historic attractions of Canada justify greater and more effective efforts to induce visitors to see and enjoy them."[34] This recommendation ensured that Harkin, who had begun his career by fostering tourism to prop up national parks, would end it by setting up parks to support tourism.

Although no immediate steps were taken to adopt the Senate committee's recommendations, it eliminated the federal government's restrictions on examining new parks creation and provided new impetus within Interior to consider ongoing arguments emanating from the Maritimes. Attention focused on Cape Breton Island, where both Baldwin and McLennan favoured a 540-square-mile northern area for a national park, reflecting a movement that had been afoot since 1928 backed by several boards of trade and tourist and game associations. Harkin had believed from the outset that this area was not ideal for park purposes and favoured an area forty miles further south around the Bras d'Or Lakes, first suggested in 1914. He had recorded his thinking in a June 1931 memorandum, stating, "From what information we have available, it would not seem that the area suggested by the above organizations would measure up to our standards for National Parks; the Bras d'Or Lakes region on the other hand, has always been considered as the outstanding Park area in the Province and it would accordingly appear to be desirable that the possibility of establishing a National Park in this area should be the subject of complete survey and report."[35] Cautley shared this perspective, but to both men's disappointment when Murphy finally agreed in August 1934 to inspect three possible sites in Nova Scotia, Bras d'Or was not among them.

Now regarded as the departmental specialist, Cautley was appointed to inspect potential park areas and that fall examined sites at Cape Blomidon and in Yarmouth County before spending several weeks in Cape Breton. Using the recently built Cabot Trail highway to access the relatively remote area, he was amazed at what he saw. The park movement in Cape Breton had been largely focused on the interior of the island, excluding farms and villages along the coast, but Cautley recorded in his December 1934 report that "the interior of northern Cape Breton is singularly devoid of scenic attraction" and only valuable as a park asset from a game preservation perspective. On the other hand, "the great scenic value of the site is the rugged coast itself with its mountain background," and "the merits of the Cape Breton Park site rest on the coast line scenery and the Cabot Trail as a means of accessing it." While admitting that upgrading and rebuilding of the Cabot Trail would be necessary, the need to provide a park that could attract tourists was foremost in his mind, and he observed, "As a scenic route for

H.F. Lawrence, J. Barrington, and R.W. Cautley on the Cabot Trail, 1934. R.W. Cautley photograph. Cautley drove the newly-built Cabot Trail to inspect possible national park locations in Nova Scotia in 1934. [LAC, PA-121468]

motoring tourists, its attractions and drawing power is inter-related to all the other scenic attractions of Cape Breton Island."[36]

Harkin was not so sure, expressing doubts in correspondence with the surveyor that the interior, being devoid of interesting scenery, might become "a Parks liability rather than a Parks asset." After Cautley's complete report was received, he expanded on his concerns in a memorandum to Gibson: "I have grave fears that if we name the northern portion of Cape Breton Island a National Park and then find ourselves with nothing more to sell than a highway, even though a considerable portion of it has real scenic value, we may do more harm than good from a tourist standpoint. We cannot afford to have any visitors go away feeling that what we called a National Park was not of a quality which they had reason to expect." However, in another memorandum two months later, he observed that the only serious problem with Cape Breton was shortage of recreational facilities required to stimulate the tourist trade.

Consequently, while gradually coming to accept that there would be a park in Cape Breton, Harkin did not give up the idea that it be complemented by a smaller recreational-oriented area at Bras d'Or, which he believed fundamental to the successful encouragement of Maritime tourism. He made this point strongly in his communications to Gibson, pointing out that Cautley believed that a reasonably sized parcel at Bras d'Or would make a better park than the Cape Breton site and that, in his own opinion, it possessed "the most beautiful and internationally remarkable features of Nova Scotia scenery" with "extraordinary facilities for recreational development."[37] Apparently he made his point, as when Murphy corresponded with Premier A.L. Macdonald in February 1935 the desirability of having the two sites made available for park purposes was specifically mentioned. In his telegraphed response, Macdonald promised, "Province will provide clear title such lands as are selected by mutual agreement as are suitable site for national park and will also supplement national park site with grant of land in Bras d'Or Lakes district for national park recreational facilities and will introduce necessary legislation."[38]

At this juncture matters slowed while the provincial government prepared legislation to allow Macdonald's agreement to be met, the branch attempted to identify the areas to be transferred to the Dominion, and the Department of the Interior attempted to find park development money in its still constrained financial circumstances. Furthermore, as the park area in Cape Breton was now to include the picturesque coastal areas, the province had to undertake the tricky political task of expropriating lands and their improvements in several small fishing settlements dotting the coastline. Meantime, while Harkin consulted with the Department of Justice for advice on drafting the federal act necessary to accept the lands and create the park, everyone waited to see what would result from the federal election campaign being waged in the fall of 1935 between Bennett's Conservatives and King's Liberals. Fortunately for Harkin, the Liberals, running under their slogan of "King or Chaos," swept the Conservatives from office, ending his five years in the bureaucratic wilderness but immediately providing a new set of circumstances.

King, with the obvious intention of creating a smaller and more efficient government, coalesced the Department of the Interior and Indian Affairs with two other departments, Mines and Immigration and Colonization, placing them under the authority of one minister,

Thomas Crerar. Wardle remained as one of four deputies reporting to him. It might have been expected that with his full plate Crerar would pay little attention to new parks creation, but, surprisingly, he took a personal interest in extending the park system across Canada. But as the new minister got his feet under him, the Maritime Board of Trade was growing impatient about the lack of action, and in December 1935 sent a communication indicating that a motion had been adopted calling on the Dominion government to get busy in Nova Scotia. Crerar was initially willing to have Harkin take care of such matters, but with his hands-on proclivities, he had Wardle gather the information necessary to be better informed. This resulted in a series of requests. One was to identify the costs of the proposed park in Cape Breton, to which Harkin replied that Cautley had estimated it at $500,000 for capital, mostly to be spent on upgrades to the Cabot Trail to make it more suitable for tourist purposes, and $75,000 for annual operating costs. He appended a further estimate of $200,000 for capital and $5,000 for annual maintenance "if, as has been strongly pressed, an additional area in the Bras d'Or Lakes district should be included in the Park."[39]

Early in 1936 Harkin went on an extended medical leave, and by the time he returned in March, Maritime park issues had become a priority due to a recent federal-provincial conference decision to accept the Senate committee's recommendation to extend the system, with a particular focus on the Atlantic region. Accordingly, Crerar had agreed to go ahead with the Nova Scotia park, and after Harkin discussed this with Wardle it was determined that he would draft a letter for Crerar's signature to Premier Macdonald advising that the Dominion was prepared to proceed and asking that the province turn over the necessary lands. He was also tasked with preparing "a draft of an agreement between the Dominion and the Province of Nova Scotia relative to matters of jurisdiction, and which might be incorporated into any legislation regarding the National Park put through by the Province."[40]

In carrying out this direction, Harkin could rely to some extent on his experience with Kootenay National Park twenty years earlier, although by virtue of the *National Parks Act* it now required endorsement by Parliament. He had the draft of the letter to Macdonald available the day after his conversation with Wardle, as he had been at work on the details for some time, and it included a number of vital points. First, it outlined a recent decision that the Bras d'Or Lakes could not be part of the Dominion legislation, but would be added by order-in-council later. Second, since it was imperative that the Dominion have exclusive legislative authority it would be necessary for the province to provide by statute "that its legislation and regulations applicable to the said area shall at all times hereafter be conformable to and correspond with the legislation and regulations of the Dominion governing National Parks generally so that there will, at all times, be uniformity in the legislation applicable to the area." As in Kootenay, this legislation was being drafted by the department and would be forwarded for inclusion in the suggested provincial legislation. Harkin also pointed out that while work was underway on the Dominion legislation it would not be likely Nova Scotia could formally transfer ownership of the land before prorogation of the current session of Parliament and the bill would have to contain provisions for the legislation to become effective by order of the governor-in-council upon receipt of title to the lands.[41]

At this point provincial politicians, undoubtedly becoming concerned about the looming costs of expropriation, made suggestions about the lands to be included in the new park, particularly with respect to leaving several small fishing settlements outside its boundaries. Harkin and Cautley agreed on what would henceforth be a key point in Maritime park creation: "An important detail in connection with this whole matter is that the coast line is the best feature of the whole park and these small settlements are undoubtedly placed in the choicest section of the coast line. It will, therefore, be recognized that if the coast line is to be featured successfully the Department must have control over whatever is within the park boundaries."[42] Harkin sent this memorandum to Wardle on March 27, and the same day received one in return informing him that Crerar had sent the letter he had drafted to Premier Macdonald, but containing no mention of the Bras d'Or. Apologetically, Wardle stated that while he had brought the desirability of including a mention of the area to Crerar's attention and had reminded him that Nova Scotia had expressed its willingness to turn over a small piece of land, "It was the Minister's wish, however, that for the present no mention of the Bras d'Or Lakes area be made."[43]

On few occasions did Harkin express absolute outrage about a decision to his deputy, but in this case he responded that he hoped this omission was only temporary and that "when the Northern area is eventually transferred to the Dominion the Bras d'Or Lakes area will be transferred at the same time...because I want to stress in the strongest possible way the belief of this Branch that an area in the Bras d'Or Lakes is absolutely indispensable if the Department expects this Branch to make a success of the Nova Scotia National Park from a tourist standpoint." He then described the area's attributes, particularly the seashore access that he firmly believed necessary for any successful Maritime park: "The Bras d'Or Lakes are outstanding in their scenic beauty and already have a reputation well established in North America. They afford, I understand, salt water bathing in water of reasonable temperature,—a very rare condition on the Atlantic coast. They also offer first class sailing, boating, fishing. Therefore, a site on these lakes would make a first class central point for holding the touring public and gradually distributing them to the various attractive points in the island." Turning to Cape Breton, Harkin stated his belief that the area did not incorporate sufficient attractions for tourism to flourish and reminded Wardle, "It must be kept in mind that while the name 'National Park' has a very great selling value, particularly in the United States, even a National Park must deliver the goods."[44]

Given their long experience of working together, Wardle obviously understood how important the Bras d'Or matter was to his mentor, and apparently continued to make strong representations to Crerar. Harkin meanwhile continued work on the agreement with Nova Scotia and when it was ready to be sent in mid-April, he was asked to draft a new letter to Macdonald to forward with it. On the eve of its transmittal, Wardle made some final changes and forwarded them with the notation, "Provision has been made for the matters which we discussed verbally." The letter sent the next day under Crerar's signature, while focusing primarily on the agreement, closed, "It is also our understanding that a suitable area in the Bras d'Or Lakes is to be included in the park area as soon as the Province and the Dominion authorities have agreed on the area and the title to the land has been secured."[45] Vindicated, Harkin quickly completed work on the Dominion bill, although there were further complications with respect to Prince Edward Island. Although no investigation had been carried out and no particular area identified for a park in the province, provincial lobbying for a future park had been kept up over the years. In May 1930, Stewart had received a letter from MP A.E. MacLean on this score, and, in line with his recently announced policy of a park in every province, he wrote that he could see no reason why PEI should not be so favoured. However, it was not until agreement on the Nova Scotia park was imminent, in February 1936, that Premier Thane Campbell forwarded a letter to Minister of Transportation C.D. Howe indicating that the province was considering a national park and requesting that the Dominion government allow in its annual appropriations a sum sufficient to establish and develop one.[46] In March, Wardle directed Harkin to include an amount of $25,000 for parks development in PEI in addition to the $100,000 earmarked for Nova Scotia in a new public works funding request, indicating that the minister was prepared to move on the matter.

In his correspondence with Crerar, Campbell stated, "I hope to convince your Department of the position which I stressed before Mr. Harkin, that in the case of our small Province, the Park should be taken to include not only the actual appropriated area, but the surrounding characteristic districts, and that therefore the highway traversing such surrounding districts and leading to the nucleus of the Park should logically be considered as being within the Park."[47] It was significant that he had initially addressed the minister of Transportation on the matter, indicating that unlike his counterpart in Nova Scotia, who saw creation of a national park as purely a tourism enterprise, Campbell believed that it could result in some much-needed provincial infrastructure.[48] But Harkin, having toyed earlier with the idea of compensation for any improvements carried out by provinces previous to parks creation, had now, after corresponding with Horace Albright to ascertain American practices, rejected that notion and any other associated with related outside expenditures. Crerar contacted Campbell to inform him that his government could not promise to carry out roadwork to any park location, but did agree to include an amount for park establishment in the departmental estimates, to have an inspection carried out that summer, focusing on a Victorian mansion and related grounds at "Dalvay-by-the-Sea" at Grand Tracadie in Queen's County on the island's north shore, and to provide an amount for its acquisition from private hands.

These decisions required PEI to be taken into account in agreements and legislation, and in being directed by Wardle to prepare documents similar to those for Nova Scotia, Harkin was asked to consider whether there should be separate legislation for the two provinces given that no site had been chosen in the former. He agreed that two bills were preferable, but pointed out that Crerar's offer of $25,000 toward the purchase of Dalvay was inconsistent with policy and would open a can of worms with other provinces requesting similar assistance.[49] Furthermore, when he presented the two draft bills on April 16, he indicated that it was his understanding that they could not be addressed by Parliament, "pending the preliminary steps to be carried out by the provincial authorities which include the securing of the land and the transfer of title to the Dominion."[50] Crerar did not agree and directed that both parks be included in separate sections of one bill, and ultimately the new draft Harkin forwarded included identification of the lands in Nova Scotia to be transferred, with allowance for further small areas to be added later, and in PEI powers for the governor-in-council to proclaim a park once a suitable area had been transferred. This still left the matter of the transfer of the Nova Scotia lands outstanding before Parliament could act, and this too had to be addressed by the same means as in PEI. "The Nova Scotia and Prince Edward Island National Parks Act, 1936" was approved for presentation to Parliament on May 4, 1936.[51]

Awaiting its consideration, Harkin turned his attention to the proposed survey of PEI sites, conferring with Premier Campbell in early May concerning details. He recommended to Wardle that the inspection team be made up of Deputy Commissioner Williamson and Architectural and Town Planning Division head Cromarty, a result of the differing nature of a park in the province: "A decision will, in part, result upon a visualization of the development treatment that will be necessary or desirable in any site. On that account I am specially anxious that Mr. Cromarty, who is our specialist in landscaping should apprise the various sites from that standpoint. Ordinarily, National Parks are established in what are virtually wilderness areas and development and treatment are therefore quite different to what will be the case in Prince Edward Island where this is nothing of a wilderness character."[52] Williamson had provided a similar assessment to his superior some two months previously: "It will be impossible to apply the same National Park standards to the proposed park in PEI since its characteristics are almost totally different from any of the National Parks so far established in Canada....It is my opinion that we should not plan its development in terms of attracting only hundreds of tourists but many thousands a year."[53]

It was understandable, then, that in their inspection Williamson and Cromarty identified a twenty-five-mile-long strip of coastline west of Dalvay extending from Stanhope to New London and containing the striking Cavendish Beach with its impressive sand dunes and the famous Green Gables cottage nearby as being particularly suited for parks purposes. Nor was it surprising that this area was exactly the one Harkin had referred to as being possible of reservation in his remarks to MP Mackinnon thirteen years previously. In supporting the selection in the report to Harkin, Williamson and Cromarty gave full voice to the evolution that had occurred in park policy with respect to the creation of parks over the course of his career: "When the idea of National Parks was first conceived over fifty years ago the intention was to preserve spectacular mountain scenery and the lakes streams, flora and fauna of the region. Subsequently however this policy has been expanded in Canada, in order not only to conserve some of the outstanding scenery of the country, but to create in each province at least one National Park whose setting is representative of the best natural features of such province. Prince Edward Island is typically a seaside province and therefore your inspecting officers felt its contribution would be of greatest value to the system of National Parks decided upon in that Province."[54]

Inspection of New London Bay, PEI, 1936. Harkin sent Williamson and Cromarty to inspect possible sites for a park in Prince Edward Island, resulting in their recommendation of a strip of beach extending from Stanhope to New London. [LAC, PA-203583)

By the time this report was in hand in late July, the Cape Breton lands had been transferred to the Dominion and had become Cape Breton Highlands National Park by virtue of the new act, which received royal assent on June 23, 1936, and steps were under way for similar action in PEI. Harkin would have been pleased, but as usual with new parks he was already distracted with getting the administration established. He recommended to Wardle that James Smart, who he had entrusted with the initial development of Riding Mountain and who he had identified as "the ideal man to get things started in Nova Scotia," be appointed to carry out the duties.[55] He then turned back to the matter of a park in New Brunswick, and over the course of the summer of 1936 successfully arranged for Cautley to re-examine the province's potential sites in Smart's company. However, he could not know that passage of the new act and establishment of Cape Breton, the first real national park in the Maritimes and the largest in eastern Canada, marked his last accomplishments in creating Canada's national park system.

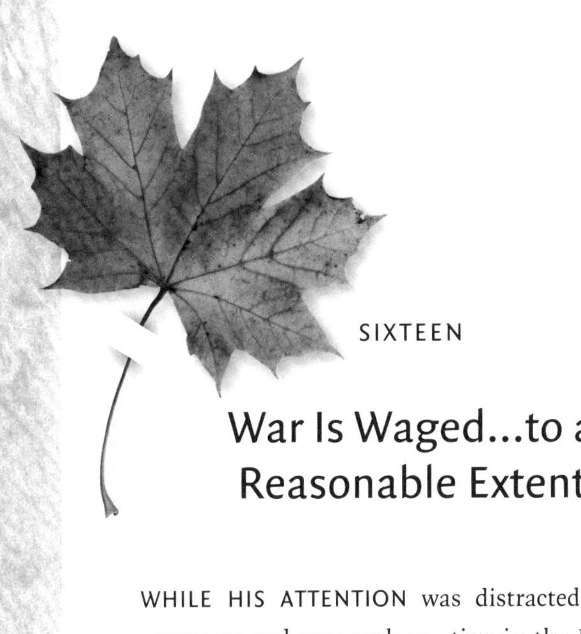

SIXTEEN

War Is Waged...to a Reasonable Extent

WHILE HIS ATTENTION was distracted by relief programs and new park creation in the Maritimes during the Depression years, Harkin did not ignore the branch's other responsibilities. Balancing these proved equally challenging, given the gutting of his staff in the natural resources transfer and constantly reduced appropriations. Some fields, such as historic sites and migratory bird work, languished as he struggled to keep them relevant during times of constraint, but one of his greatest challenges was the Wildlife Division, particularly with respect to the task of educating the public on wildlife matters and walking the tightrope of predator control. In these efforts the branch would employ some new educational techniques and Harkin would be called upon to muster all his experience and broad reputation to assist in moving wildlife policy forward. But faced by an uncomprehending public, an often openly hostile field service, and the opposition of influential game associations, he found himself constantly under attack and frequently in a compromised position.

Apart from the Engineering Division, it was the Architectural and Town Planning Division on which he had to rely most directly to support the branch's Depression-era activities. Between 1923 and 1926 William Cromarty had been the sole staff architect tasked with the duty of preparing drawings for Parks' own buildings, drafting site plans for campgrounds, bungalow camps and townsite subdivisions, and reviewing and approving buildings for private interests in the parks. In 1926 he was joined by K.D. Harris as assistant staff architect, but there is no evidence, apart from an assistant to administer the branch-supported Town Planning Institute founded by Adams, that they had any additional resources despite their increasingly heavy workload.[1] This was remarkable in light of the large number of relief-funded projects the division supported in the years after 1930, particularly in the PWCA period when public works were added to the mix. The spate of public building construction that resulted fully expressed Cromarty's favoured Tudor Revival style, featuring mock half-timbering combined with elements of Arts and Crafts design and strong rustic elements, all of which were fully supported by Harkin in his efforts to oversee virtually every plan approved.[2] Perhaps the finest expression of Cromarty's work was his plan for the Banff Upper Hot Springs Bathhouse, one of the first major public buildings constructed with relief funds, heavily utilizing native Rundle limestone, henceforth a standard for local building construction. Another design featuring its use, this time built as a PWCA project in 1935, was Banff's main public works garage (currently the Banff Firehall), located immediately adjacent to downtown on Beaver Street.[3]

Cromarty's services were also employed in eastern Canada designing PWCA buildings for several historic sites. Of all branch responsibilities it was the Historic Sites Division that suffered most acutely the consequences of post-1930 retrenchment. As part of the contribution to departmental downsizing, the division was eliminated in 1931 and

Arthur Pinard took early retirement, leaving only his assistant, G.W. Bryan, to carry on a modicum of historic sites work. The failure of the *National Parks Act* to provide the legislative standing that the Historic Sites Board had so long sought made this almost inevitable, and, dependent on other overstretched divisions to carry out its programs, the board's activities and effectiveness were likewise constrained. Harkin had little time to devote to the program and its day-to-day activities were mainly carried out by Williamson, who served as board secretary. Limited to placing one or two commemorative plaques each year, several of its members believed that the situation dictated that no new initiatives should be undertaken and some retired. The only way forward was to access relief funding for previously identified, labour-intensive projects, designed by the Architectural and Town Planning Division and carried out by the Engineering Division. In accomplishing designs for these locations, Cromarty took inspiration from the historic architecture on their sites or implied by their setting, and made them attractive locations for Harkin's Maritime tourism initiatives. Entirely new stone buildings were constructed at Fortress Louisbourg and Fort Beauséjour, appearing as though they had been present for generations, at Fort Chambly a museum addition was made to an extant historic structure, and at Fort Anne the officer's quarters were rehabilitated for a museum.[4]

The Migratory Birds Section faced equally difficult challenges, affected by changes brought about by the natural resources transfers and by extreme drought conditions gripping the prairies. The transfer agreements had dictated that most federal bird game sanctuaries and public shooting grounds would revert to provincial hands, seriously weakening direct federal involvement. Then by order-in-council of October 14, 1932, complete responsibility for enforcement of the *Migratory Birds Convention Act* passed to the RCMP, leaving in the branch's hands only inspections for reservation of bird sanctuaries, scientific research on bird problems, publicity and education work, and performance of liaison duties with the police and conservation organizations. Assistant migratory bird wardens and associated appropriations also went to the RCMP, effectively handcuffing chief federal migratory bird officers in their ability to carry out important tasks. Ironically, the change created even more work as many of the police were uninterested and officers had to act as information resources, suppliers of technical advice, and providers of expert testimony in court cases.[5] These changes occurred simultaneously with the huge impact of the drought exacerbating depression conditions, particularly with respect to waterfowl populations on prairie marsh breeding grounds, and at the same time the state of the economy meant that more poaching and illegal activity was happening. Each year in his annual report Harkin referred to the inroads being made into waterfowl numbers by these conditions and called for increased enforcement, something the branch could no longer deliver.

Another program impacted by the 1931 changes and depression conditions was the Publicity Division, but despite being affected by the largest staff reductions and having an extremely tight budget, it kept up the high public profile for national parks that Campbell had achieved in the 1920s. In addition to undertaking his new responsibilities for Canada-wide publicity under the auspices of the National Development Bureau, Harkin understood that continuing to attract visitors to the parks was fundamental to keeping the branch relevant during the Depression, providing at least some Canadians with an escape from daily drudgery. One particularly successful method was using the still relatively new medium of motion pictures as both an entertainment and educational device. In 1929–1930 the branch offered lectures illustrated by moving pictures and coloured lantern slides at 140 locations in Canada and the United States, and in addition to those used in its lecture series, employees screened 1,788 films in the parks, 718 outside the parks, and made 355 loans to others.[6] These were largely drawn from the extensive film library Campbell had established, using footage of parks, wildlife, and scenery purchased from professional photographers and assembled in Ottawa. Initially silent films, many were later complemented with sound tracks through co-operation with the Canadian Government Motion Picture Bureau and Associated Screen News in Montreal.[7]

One of the most prolific suppliers was former *Calgary Herald* photographer W.J. "Bill" Oliver, who eventually became synonymous with national parks publicity through his extensive work in both still and motion picture photography. He had cut his teeth photographing the annual winter buffalo roundups at Wainwright in the early 1920s, mainly working with Fox News and other commercial film companies but also for the Ince Studio on their 1923 extravaganza. Later he had accompanied a buffalo shipment north to Wood Buffalo, and by 1930 made films directly for the branch, work that appeared as part of *The Return of the Buffalo* in 1933.[8] However, it was a film about a native writer and conservationist working with young beaver in Riding Mountain National Park in 1931 that would solidify his reputation. Significantly, working with the same enigmatic naturalist Grey Owl involved Harkin in one of his own most interesting educational and promotional efforts for conservation.

Despite the branch's efforts at publicizing Canada's parks and wildlife through the print media and illustrated lectures, what most Canadians knew about wildlife came from the anthropomorphic stories of Seton and other writers of the genre. Many, in fact, still regarded predators as the villains of children's fairy tales. This situation, and an ever present desire to publicize the conservation work the branch was carrying out, came into focus in 1930 when Campbell presented Harkin with an interesting idea. The publicity director had just visited a mixed-blood Apache in Quebec who was working with two trained beaver and had recently parlayed writing articles on conservation for magazines such as *Country Life* into a contract with an English publisher. Campbell didn't realize that he was being drawn into one of Canada's greatest hoaxes, as his supposed Indian conservationist was in reality Archie Belaney, an Englishman who had immigrated to Canada in 1906 and in 1928 had adopted a native persona as Grey Owl. Instead, the publicity director, recognizing the role he could play in national parks publicity, contacted Harkin suggesting having him continue his activities in one of the national parks. The commissioner was well-disposed to the proposal, as Grey Owl would not only provide an attraction for tourists

Photographer W.J. "Bill" Oliver visiting Grey Owl at his cabin at Lake Ajawaan, Prince Albert National Park, ca. 1932. W.J. Oliver photograph. Oliver's photographs and films of Grey Owl helped popularize both the conservationist and the work of the National Parks Branch in the 1930s. [GA, NA-4868-201]

but could also illustrate branch efforts concerning wildlife preservation. While not predators, beaver were fur-bearers, a class of animals long of concern to the department, were recognized by the public as Canada's national animal and now, within reason, were to be protected by new conservation policies in the parks.[9] Riding Mountain Park was selected as the site to reconstruct the beaver colony as an area that possessed several important attributes, including being in need of tourism promotion as the newest park and, perhaps most importantly, being in Minister Murphy's riding. In a memorandum to Rowatt of April 7, 1931 requesting approval for Grey Owl's appointment to the Riding Mountain staff, Harkin noted that "this work might be developed to become one of the most interesting and valuable features of the park" and "the man has a unique personality and his success with beaver has aroused the interest of scientists all over the continent and in England."[10]

Efforts to feature Grey Owl's work immediately proceeded, Oliver visiting him to begin filming for a movie entitled *The Beaver Family*, which appeared the following year. Unfortunately, though, within months of his arrival, Grey Owl complained that the water levels in the ponds and dams at Riding Mountain were too low to achieve his goal of increasing the progeny of his one pair to up to 200 animals. In August, he wrote Harkin a long, plaintive letter laying out his feelings about his work and appealing for the understanding of a kindred spirit:

> Only a man who thoroughly understands the needs of beaver could appreciate the difficulty, or see how utterly futile it is for me to attempt anything here....By means of the beaver I had hoped to teach an object lesson, to preach a parable that would have resounded across the length and breadth of the continent to elevate them in the public mind to the position that rightly belongs to them, to the end that preservation of animal and other forms of wild life would be supported by widespread public opinion so that our national animal would become more than just a name; conservation would follow as a matter of course....I feel a little queer at times putting the beaver through their paces before a crowd, but never lose sight of the ultimate object; seed may be sown in a number of instances where little suspected."[11]

This plea seems to have struck a chord and if the commissioner had any doubts they were quickly dispelled, as he became one of Grey Owl's strongest supporters. He wrote to Gibson, "Grey Owl is an Indian with exceptional talents and education. His principal characteristic is the faculty he possesses for gaining the confidence of wild life for which he has an almost fanatic devotion."[12]

Impressed by Grey Owl's concern about the inadequacy of his location and not wanting to lose his services, Harkin requested that Rowatt approve transferring the operations to Prince Albert or a mountain park. Within weeks the conservationist had visited Prince Albert and identified a suitable location at Ajawaan, a small isolated lake north of Kingsmere Lake, although Harkin wanted to make sure the situation at Prince Albert was better than at Riding Mountain and that Grey Owl would not find the circumstances more inviting in one of the mountain parks. There were also the matters of finances and concerns about the minister's reaction. Murphy was responding positively to the work going on at Riding Mountain, writing to a cabinet colleague in May that efforts were underway to ascertain "to what extent Grey Owl, with his ability for the training of wild life, would serve as a means of attracting people to the Park," and that if the experiment were successful "we will then be able to take up the question of having others trained for this work in other National Parks."[13] Ultimately, Rowatt informed Harkin that the minister was relying on his advice and agreed "If conditions for the beaver were unsatisfactory at Riding Mountain and the transfer of Grey Owl and his charges to Prince Albert was recommended by you, it should be proceeded with."[14] By the end of October, Grey Owl and his wife Anahareo were ensconced in their new cabin, christened Beaver Lodge, on the shores of Ajawaan Lake.

Only after the transfer was Prince Albert Superintendent Wood made aware by Riding Mountain Superintendent Smart that his new tourist attraction could be difficult to handle, often being moody and imperious and overly fond of the bottle. Grey Owl's location close to Wasagaming had led to him being too accessible to both the townsite and tourists and Campbell in a letter to Smart admitted "the further he is from civilization the better for all concerned." He did, however, reassure Wood, "There is no doubt he [has] the greatest publicity value of anything we have ever done." This proved to be the case, as the beaver constructed part of their lodge on the cabin floor next to their plunge

Grey Owl working beside beaver lodge in his cabin at Lake Ajawaan, Prince Albert National Park, ca. 1932. W.J. Oliver photograph. Enthusiasts' desire to see Grey Owl's unique living arrangements with his beaver and see him put them through their paces helped to increase Depression-era visitor statistics at Prince Albert. [GA, NA-4868-206]

hole and when readers learned of their antics in one of Grey Owl's articles, many wanted to make the pilgrimage to Beaver Lodge. This helped to increase Riding Mountain's visitation as Harkin had hoped, but the real value of the exercise lay in the media coverage provided to parks conservation work in newspapers and popular journals. Despite this, his reputation required a short leash be kept on his activities and while "Archie" could usually be trusted to behave when tourists were visiting, parks officials were not wont to let him stray too far. When replying to Rowatt about a request for him to speak at the Medicine Hat Fish and Game Association banquet in February 1932, Harkin indicated that it would not be wise for him to leave the beaver and noted, "Grey Owl has not been trained in Departmental policy and this is an additional reason why I feel his speaking in public while employed by this Department might not be advisable at this time."[15] This may well have been code for a desire to avoid one of his famous benders. Even the warden service, while supporting his work, became disenchanted with his indiscretions and haughty attitude in his demands for help with the beaver. Consequently, within a year of his arriving at Prince Albert, Grey Owl presented somewhat of a double-edged sword.

Nevertheless, by 1934 the release of a Bill Oliver movie entitled *Grey Owl's Strange Guests*, a sound version of an earlier silent film, captured the attention of an increasing number of Canadians, and this was supported by the appearance of his autobiographical *Pilgrims of the Wild* the same year. The book proved so popular that its British publisher, Lovat Dickson, arranged a speaking tour for Grey Owl in England in the fall of 1935, incredibly without first checking with the branch about a leave of absence to allow him to do so. Herbert Eayrs, the representative for Macmillan, its Canadian publisher, appealed to Harkin to overlook this slight and extend permission, noting that the book had already sold over 10,000 copies in England and pointing out that he would "lecture alike to the learned societies and to more popular constituencies describing his activities with the beaver, and their conservation, and in general the work of the National Parks."[16] Despite responding that there were "grave difficulties" with this proposal, after Campbell corresponded with Dickson, Harkin recommended the leave, arguing, "It would not be in the best interests of the Department to refuse this leave as we are anxious to retain his services and control his activities as far as possible."[17]

The four-month British tour was a huge success, Grey Owl regularly speaking to audiences of up to 3,000 people. On each occasion, he repeated his central theme, "The difference between civilized man and the savage is just this—civilized people try to impose themselves on their surroundings, to dominate everything. The Indian's part of the background. He lets himself—not just drift—but go with Nature."[18] Audiences loved this self-deprecating approach, and from the Parks Branch perspective it also got its message out, particularly through the Oliver films projected at each lecture. On his return to Canada, Grey Owl stopped off in Ottawa to provide details of his tour, and later sent a copy of one of his books, inscribed, "To J.B. Harkin. In remembrance of the happy occasion of my first meeting with him."[19] However, whatever good feeling was engendered by this meeting was short-lived. Grey

Owl remained in the east for almost a month, lobbying the influential to support publication of a new book, including the governor general and Prime Minister King. He was also a frequent visitor at Interior, but upset with his inability to gain firm commitments, he went on several well-reported drinking sprees before returning to Prince Albert in April 1936. Gibson, hearing of the escapades, contacted Harkin by telephone and demanded an explanation, resulting in a letter of April 25, 1936 in which, complete with some native stereotyping typical of the times, the commissioner supported the conservationist's work but agreed that a decision about his future needed to be made:

> I am sorry to hear that Grey Owl has been indulging too freely in liquor. As a matter of fact, with so much Indian blood in his veins I suppose it is inevitable that from time to time he will break out in this connection. We ourselves are quite annoyed. Sometimes we feel that it would be just as well if we did wash our hands of him, though I do feel there still is quite a field for additional publicity for us in connection with him. With the great success he had on his recent winter lecture tour in England, he has obviously become more difficult to handle and I fear it will only be a matter of time until we definitely have to decide on a break with him.[20]

Harkin advised sending Grey Owl an "emphatic letter" pointing out the tenuousness of his position, and when he forwarded it in June 1936 it was firm, stating, "you will realize that if you conduct yourself in a manner which arouses criticism it reflects not only on yourself but also on the Department" and "the work in which you are now engaged, together with the high position you now hold in the field of conservation, demand that your conduct be absolutely beyond reproach."[21] When provided with a copy, Superintendent Wood reported that his own conversations with Grey Owl on this matter were "not all that could be desired," but allowed, "I am of the opinion that your letter will have a very salutary effect and in all probability things will be different from now on."[22] Sadly, this proved not to be the case, as he continued to be difficult. Not until two years later, after his untimely death, would the reasons become apparent in the revelation of his true identity, creating a controversy that resulted in undoing much of his worthwhile parks and wildlife conservation efforts.

Despite this outcome, the branch's use of Grey Owl had done much to alert the Canadian public to the importance of Canadian wildlife conservation, particularly in national parks. At the same time, Harkin's own conservation reputation was increasingly recognized, as he received many letters from those sharing his interests and complimenting him on the branch's activities. For example, in April 1926 Norman Biddle, entomologist for Manitoba, wrote, "I am heartily in agreement with your stand in attempting to preserve all kinds of wild life in the National Parks. I have no doubt that adjustments will need to be made from time to time which will necessitate reducing the numbers of certain animals but apart from that all animals should be permitted to make the parks a permanent home."[23] In response to such comments and in support of the efforts of those who shared his commitment, Harkin consistently tried to be supportive and optimistic. A case in point was a June 1929 letter to Judge W.A. Dowler of Kenora, Ontario, who had sent him a copy of his article entitled "Earth's Unclaimed Wilderness": "It is indeed a delight to find people like yourself taking such an interest in Nature and the wild things. As you know, I am intimately mixed up in the administrative details of these matters and regret to have to admit that I frequently get rather pessimistic, especially in regard to our wild life. However, there are some hopeful signs and perhaps the best is that a constantly increasing number of people like yourself are taking a real interest in the wilderness and the wild things."[24]

Many other individuals wrote in a similar vein and several organizations sought his support, in response to which he attempted to co-operate despite the little time he had available. In 1929 he was associated with an effort to organize a Dominion fish and game association, responding to a letter from J.R. Dymond, Secretary, Royal Ontario Museum, Zoology, with the view, "I am most thoroughly convinced that a strong federal organization for the protection of our wildlife is essential." Reacting to Dymond's call for a significant role for research into problems affecting wildlife, Harkin provided a picture of the importance he believed the matter had taken on: "Without adequate scientific investigation game conservationists are largely groping in their search for ways and means of perpetuating wild life. No conservation organization will ever achieve real success unless it links up its activities with scientific investigation."[25] Another important body seeking Canada's assistance in large game conservation at the time was the Society for the Preservation of the Fauna of the Empire, and its secretary, C.W. Hobley of the Zoological Society of London, wrote seeking his help, perhaps better than anyone summing up the reputation Harkin had gained: "By your position and reputation in this sphere you would appear to be marked out as the man who could lead this movement in Canada and I earnestly beg that you will see your way to initiate this closer union." Typically, Harkin did not acknowledge the compliment, instead agreeing to bring the matter to the attention of the new association.[26]

Unfortunately, the goodwill and positive views expressed by his peers for his wildlife activities were not shared by those working for the branch in the field. The new wildlife policy of the 1920s had dictated that superintendents and wardens pay closer attention to fur-bearers, particularly the predatory variety, but the message had not been widely embraced by those whose old habits and attitudes remained well engrained. This situation was only exacerbated after further changes emerged from a January 1928 conference of superintendents held in Ottawa. As described by Lloyd, "It was the opinion of the conference that wardens should not be allowed to keep the furs of any animals trapped or killed in the Parks."[27] Harkin followed up with a letter in October 1928 to each superintendent directing that park wardens should not be allowed to keep the fur of any animal, predatory or otherwise, trapped or killed in the park, skins of those animals accidentally killed should be turned over to the superintendent, and that when any animal other than wolves, wolverines, coyotes, and cougars were killed by order of the superintendent because they were damaging property, full particulars needed to be submitted to headquarters.[28] Although this policy had apparently been agreed to by all the superintendents at the Ottawa meeting, it seems likely that Harkin only prevailed on them after providing a compelling rationale, one later conveyed in a memorandum to Cory. In it, Harkin made clear that the decision was, at least to a certain extent, based on operational concerns. Reminding his deputy that the wardens had not only been encouraged to trap but had also been allowed to keep the skins, he offered, "Gradually we came to the conclusion that...the system encouraged the Wardens to spend far too much time in trapping and too little on the more important part of the duties of their position; and also that some of them at least were trapping numerous fur-bearers not on the predatory list." The result was "we were in the winter time virtually paying them a salary to carry on a general trapping business" and "having in mind the frailties of human nature, we are convinced that the old policy was not a good one."[29]

While likely having grudgingly accepted this decision, the superintendents were shocked, if not outraged, at a further directive received from Harkin a few weeks later, one on which they had not been consulted: "In future the use or possession of traps by park wardens is prohibited. Please notify all wardens accordingly, allowing them a limited period in which to dispose of any which are now in their possession."[30] Predictably, protests immediately began to cross Harkin's desk, one of the most forceful coming from Howard Sibbald, now superintendent of Kootenay National Park but still recognized as the most knowledgeable field officer in the branch with respect to game: "The trap is the only known means by which these animals may be kept down, for in a timbered district such as we have here, the chances of killing any of the animals listed with a rifle are very small and it will not be long before a howl will go up that we are protecting such animals to the detriment of which might overflow into the outlying territory and thus reduce the chances of the hunter getting sufficient sport."[31] The reasoning behind the order is not entirely clear, although the Wildlife Division frequently mentioned that traps were indiscriminate with respect to the animals taken and the likelihood of wardens being less inclined to keep their income up by trapping animals on the side was also hinted at. Harkin's only reaction to the protest was to write to each

Buffalo National Park warden Bud Cotton with coyote pelts, n.d. Harkin's "no pelts" and "no traps" policy at the end the end of the 1920s with respect to predators was akin to a declaration of war for wardens in the field. [PAA, A 4737]

superintendent in February 1929 reminding them of the ban and impressing upon them the necessity of having the wardens "use their best efforts in the shooting of coyotes," and ordering them to "submit here quarterly with your usual report a statement of the kill by each warden of wolves and coyotes."[32]

In September 1929, Harkin described the branch's wildlife policy to a correspondent in terms of an even-handed approach: "Wildlife is given absolute protection with the further exception that war is waged on predatory animals to a reasonable extent in order that the safety of the remainder may be made more secure."[33] But it was inevitable that introduction of these changes to predator control would not be seen as at all balanced by many of his staff, marking the beginning of a difficult period in his wildlife conservation efforts during which he was often caught between competing voices. On one side were Lloyd and Nagle of his Wildlife Division, which had become one of the branch's most influential agencies by the eve of the Depression. From their memorandums, it is apparent that Lloyd's strong connection with American naturalists, in particular the ecologist "dissenters" in the Society of Mammalogy who continued their fight against the U.S. Biological Survey, provided them with ample ammunition to keep up their side of the debate. On the other side was the majority of the field staff involved in wildlife work, including most, if not all, the wardens. They had largely been chosen for their jobs because of their experience as hunters and trappers, and permission to keep the skins of the animals taken had provided an important supplement to their income.[34] Now they were not only to be denied this perk but were also to be hampered in their jobs by being denied use of the trap, the most useful tool at their disposal.

After a brief hiatus, this struggle heated up again in the early 1930s, a result of increasing numbers of predators, tough depression conditions, and the influence of voices from beyond the branch supporting the wardens' cause. At the time, the war against wolves and coyotes was raging outside park boundaries, with bounties being paid on 100,000 pelts annually in Canada during the 1920s, the Biological Service's poisoning activities carrying on unabated in the United States, and agricultural interests in both countries pushing hard for more stringent controls as conditions worsened.[35] Harkin considered reintroducing trapping, but the Wildlife Division took every opportunity to dissuade its consideration. In response to an October 1930 memorandum making observations about the poor results being achieved by the wardens under the new rules, Lloyd responded to his superior by stating, "Of the two evils, trapping and coyotes, I prefer the latter.... I would recommend that the ban on trapping be continued as otherwise we will be removing one interesting form of native life because it follows its life habit of preying on another form, which is, after all, the way of Nature."[36] Even he and Nagle did not call for a complete ban on predator control, nor were wildlife managers anywhere, Lloyd believing that populations were much more affected by natural conditions than by the few killed with rifles. But before long Harkin was receiving renewed pressure to have both of the "no pelts" and "no traps" restrictions lifted, several superintendents being critical, albeit respectful, in their remarks. Surprisingly, one who overstepped these bounds and became outspoken to near outright insubordination was Superintendent Rogers at Jasper.

Rogers had returned to Jasper after a four-year hiatus in November 1931, and likely his long relationship with Harkin, his knowledge of wildlife, and the fact that he had been absent when the new restrictions were implemented helped account for the tone of his comments. In January 1932 he wrote Harkin a letter headed "Re Coyote Jasper Park" which began by describing a recent event that spoke volumes about field reaction to predator issues. Indicating "we had a bad scare Thursday," he related that a railway employee had come in on a westbound freight and reported seeing eight large timber wolves near the Snaring River. Believing the man well qualified to identify the animals, he "instructed the Supervising Warden to detail every available Warden that could be spared to have a round up from different directions, commencing early Friday morning." This had been carried out and resulted in one large coyote being killed and another wounded, Rogers speculating that they had probably come in as part of a band from the north and been mistaken for wolves because of their unusual size. But this report only provided an opening for what was really on his mind:

> In this connection I am more impressed every day that Ecologists and other "gists" to the contrary, the policy of preventing Wardens from trapping coyotes is causing a most serious, and in my opinion, shameful waste of our wildlife. I appreciate the difficulty of keeping down predatory animals by rifle fire. Very few of the Wardens are what I call good shots, and most good shots in the ordinary sense can do very little good with a rifle at running animals, and I would recommend most strongly that you reconsider the late instructions preventing the warden service trapping predatory animals, such as are permitted to be destroyed.

Harkin sent a brief note acknowledging receipt of the letter and stating, "It is not considered advisable to change the regulations in this regard at present." Within days an incensed Rogers responded that he would abide by the decision, but not without expressing his disgust: "We shall of course carry on as per your ruling contained in this letter, but I am compelled to place myself on record as completely disagreeing with your finding. You seemingly do not appreciate that my request is governed by not only a very large number of coyote this Winter but the absolute fact that next Winter and for many more following the almost undisturbed breeding of these animals is going to result in a tremendous decimation of our game animals." Harkin was unmoved, and, in going right to the point in his response, illustrated he had learned much about wildlife population dynamics: "As I explained in my letter to you of the 27th of January 1932, it is considered inadvisable to change the regulations in this regard at present. What disposal would you propose to make of the surplus deer population if it were not controlled by natural means? According to your annual report for 1931, it would appear that all game in the Park is in a normal healthy condition, and increasing in numbers." The final communication in the exchange came from Rogers a week later simply noting the letter's contents; he was undoubtedly aware that he could go no further without causing himself grievous harm.[37]

Although he continued to support the procedure in this and other exchanges with his superintendents, the pressure was obviously building and Harkin regularly called upon the Wildlife Division to prepare memoranda to support the status quo. In one of January 1933, Lloyd went on for eleven pages and, while forced to admit that the trap was more effective than the gun, noted that neither the superintendents nor supervising wardens could provide figures on the number of game animals taken by predators. He concluded by calling for the employment of "resident naturalists" to keep in touch with conditions on the ground: "This is specialized work on which the word of a warden or a Superintendent is not sufficient."[38] This observation on the abilities of field staff when juxtaposed against Rogers's concerning ecologists indicates the depth of the gulf that existed between the two groups.

Given the necessity of choosing between them, Harkin was consistent in his support of the Wildlife Division; his comments on the critical importance of science made to Dymond in 1929 make it clear that he fully embraced the need for its application and accepted the growing North American voice of ecologists in the 1930s, including those within his own branch. He infrequently publicly defended his position, but an exception occurred in April 1933 in correspondence with Dr. D.M. Kennedy, MP for Jasper Park: "The whole situation respecting predatory animals in the National Parks is under the observation of competent officials. No other parties or organizations could possibly have a greater interest in the conservation of all the wild life in the parks than have the officials responsible for the administration of the parks."[39] For his part, Lloyd attempted to leverage this support to convince his superior to further relax predator control. A case in point concerned his observation in a memorandum of March 1933 that "there is no justification for the killing of Hawks and Owls in wilderness areas such as national parks." To support this position, he used an argument that he knew would be telling: "It would be most disconcerting if the Parks Administration was attacked on the ground that it permitted the killing of Hawks and Owls at a time when this is a live question in conservation, especially since these birds have been subjected to such severe attack, particularly in the United States." He proposed instead that only crows be kept on the predator list, and magpies if they became a nuisance in the opinion of the superintendent, providing a draft of codified regulations, entitled "Policy Governing Predatory Animal Control in National Parks of Canada," with the change incorporated. Considering the argument, Harkin forwarded a copy of the document to all superintendents asking for their views and suggestions.[40]

With debate simmering within his organization, he kept a lid on it through his usual disciplined approach, but he had no such control over public discussion. Sibbald's prediction that a "howl" would go up from sportsmen over the new predator policy had proven correct, particularly harsh criticism coming from two sources. At their annual meeting held on December 3, 1932, the Athabasca Guides and Trailmen's Association resolved "that this Association recommend that the Wardens of Jasper National Park be allowed to trap and shoot all Predatory animals and retain their skins." In an accompanying letter, the organization's secretary noted that predatory animals had been on the increase in recent times, that in past years the remains of deer and other animal kills had been found in large numbers along the banks of the Athabasca River, providing "a mute testimony to the necessity of drastic dealing with this great menace," and that the previous procedure of allowing wardens to trap and keep the skins had kept coyotes and lynx to a minimum.[41] Similarly, on December 7 the Banff Advisory Council carried a motion resolving "that this Council ask the Park Superintendent to recommend that the Game Wardens be empowered to kill off Mountain Lions, Coyotes and other predatory animals, and that they be supplied with ammunition, and be paid a bonus, or, at least, be given the pelts as a reward."[42] The December 23 edition of the *Crag and Canyon*, in an editorial concerning the resolution, put forward arguments that virtually mirrored the Guides Association's, adding for good measure comments on the disappearance of bird life due to weasels and marten, described as "bloodthirsty killers," and crows and magpies, which "no one, not even wardens, dare raise their hand to destroy." It, too, recalled the results of the old procedure: "When wardens were allowed to use traps, coyotes were kept down to a minimum, as the wardens had an incentive to make it their business to catch every coyote possible....Quite true, the wardens made good money but they were doing their work and predatory animals were held in check."[43]

Not surprisingly, this two-pronged attack generated a flurry of memoranda from the Wildlife Division. To a great degree these focused on what Lloyd described as "the motive behind the concerted effort to rid the Parks of predatory animals by means of traps—and bonus," in which he suspected collusion. Admitting that while it was possible those responsible were acting in good faith, he concluded, "There is however such a meager element of fact to support their allegations that one is forced to the view that they have been cajoled into a movement the success of which would be beneficial only to the wardens." As proof, he critiqued the phrase "the wardens made good money" in the *Crag and Canyon* editorial, postulating that if this was the case it must have come from trapping valuable fur bearers and not the two-and-a-half coyotes a year the wardens averaged. In summary, he said, "The whole mass boils down to additional compensation for the wardens."[44]

Harkin agreed, and, in writing MP Kennedy, reiterated the reasons for the predator policy as first that national parks were sanctuaries for all types of wildlife and not solely for big game animals; second that it was fact, not theory, that a reasonable number of predators in an area would destroy weaklings and thereby eliminate disease; and finally "that virtually every recommendation that we have recently received with regard to this predatory animal question has been accompanied with the suggestion not only that our wardens should be allowed to trap in the parks but that they should be allowed to retain the skins for their own use." Having made this observation, Harkin spoke to what was really galling him—his sense of disappointment and anger at what he felt was the wardens' unfairness in pressing for this consideration in the difficult times:

> Our wardens are well paid. They have free cabins and, beginning at a minimum of $1320, their pay is increased to $1740. In addition they are entitled to holidays, sick leave, compensation for injuries received when on duty and superannuation. I do not believe that there are many men in private employment carrying on similar duties who are any better, or perhaps as well, looked after and still the agitation goes on that these men should be privileged to trap predators and keep the skins for their own use.[45]

Be that as it may, the "agitation" continued, reaching higher levels. The Guides' Association continued to press Kennedy for action, but to his credit he met with Lloyd in April to hear his arguments, and, after a further letter of explanation from Harkin, wrote, "It seems to me the contention of the trail rangers is well answered."[46] But influential Alberta fish and game associations had now entered the fray in support of the Guides' resolution, and Harkin received letters from both President L.E. Wize of the Northern Alberta Game and Fish Protective League and Secretary George Spargo of the Alberta Fish and Game Association, withering in their criticisms of the branch. Spargo contacted Minister Murphy calling for the wardens to be permitted to trap in the parks and after speaking with Harkin on the telephone, Rowatt sent a memorandum indicating that Murphy understood the reasons for the policy but wanted further information as to whether the superintendents were investigating if the claims of disappearing game animals were accurate. Lloyd replied with comments on the codified policy that had been received from the superintendents, which indicated that most recommended some level of trapping be reinstated, but reported that Chief Engineer Wardle had stated, "I certainly think it would be inadvisable to revert to the old arrangement whereby the wardens obtained the revenue from the sale of skins of predatory animals they killed."[47] Apparently, Lloyd also prepared an accompanying memorandum and when Harkin did not forward either it or the letter, he was queried by Gibson about a response to the minister, eliciting an explanation on July 11, 1933 illustrating his uncertainties concerning the matter:

> Quite frankly, I have delayed reports and action on this subject because of the difficulties I find in definitely making up my mind as to the action that should be taken. I cannot say that I fully concur in the memorandum prepared by Mr. Lloyd for my signature, though it is very largely correct. I do not concur fully in it because I am inclined to believe that it will probably be found necessary for us to take some further steps than we have yet taken in this matter of predator control....
>
> There is no doubt in my mind that predators were rather numerous last winter. Whether there were too many or not I am not at all certain....There is not the slightest doubt that for the well-being of the game itself, it is necessary that there be a reasonable proportion of predators. There will always be uncertainty as to whether the proper state of equilibrium in this connection exists....
>
> I may add that I am inclined to the belief that if we make it very clear to the wardens that better results than

> they have been having in the past by the use of rifles are expected of them and will be considered an important factor in appraising their efficiency, we may get some more satisfactory reports in that connection.[48]

This letter illustrates that despite being pressed hard and harbouring doubts, Harkin still supported the Wildlife Division's stance and placed the blame squarely on the wardens for their failure to adequately control predators. Rowatt accepted the argument, writing to Murphy the next day, "We are inclined to believe that the agitation is instigated by our own wardens. The remedy lies in insisting that our wardens perform the duties for which they are remunerated." The letter bears a hand-written notation, "Approved T.G.M."[49]

Harkin had won the battle for the day, but soon it became apparent that he had not won the war. As mentioned, both he and Murphy toured the mountain parks in August 1933 after the dedication of Riding Mountain, and before the trip the minister had written to Bert Wilkins, president of the Athabasca Guides' Association, agreeing to meet with him. In forwarding a copy to Harkin, Rowatt had directed that he "give special attention to this matter when you are in the Parks this year."[50] That Wilkins made his point in the meeting was evident in a letter from Rowatt to Harkin at the end of August: "The Minister does not see why it should not be possible to direct our Wardens to take whatever steps are necessary to preserve the balance as between predatory and other animals, even to the extent of setting traps for predators. We explained that whenever we give Wardens an opportunity to trap, it always happens that valuable furbearers are caught in the traps. The Minister asks why it is not possible to require the Wardens to turn in all the pelts."[51] Knowing of the minister's meeting, Harkin had foreseen such an outcome and had taken steps to head off the inevitable political repercussions. Therefore, in his response to Rowatt he related that during his own visits to the individual parks, he had met with the superintendents and chief wardens and insisted that "a genuine, whole-hearted, well planned and organized campaign on the part of the wardens against the predator could be made absolutely effective without traps." To ensure this outcome, he had required that the chief warden and superintendent meet and set a monthly quota for each warden which was fair and reasonable, taking into account factors such as the location and elevation of their district and seasonal occurrences of predators. And, to make it plain that the requirement was serious, he had insisted, "The Warden is to be given very clearly that he must get his quota and that if he fails to get it, it will be evidence of his own incompetence." He ended the letter with a promise, "If the Department insists as I did when I was in the West that the wardens must deliver a monthly quota of predators, there will be no more trouble in connection with this subject." Impressed by this tough new stance, Rowatt again supported him, advising Murphy on a copy sent to brief him, "Evidently the Wardens have been a little slack and I hope the visit of yourself and Mr. Harkin and the instructions which he has given the Chief Wardens will have the desired effect." Murphy simply scrawled a note, "Please keep me advised as to the success of the plan monthly."[52]

The hope that "there would be no more trouble" was quickly dashed, as the new quota requirement simply added fuel to the fire of field staff discontent and caused more grief on the political front. On September 27, Rogers once again pleaded with Harkin to reconsider the whole trapping matter, noting that "the small abuses that crept in would not be very serious" and indicated that the wardens could "be absolutely trusted in this respect." A response came on October 17, reminding him of the previous summer's conversation and ordering him to "forthwith proceed with the organization and development of plans for effecting this purpose." Rogers expressed his grudging compliance, but again querulously: "I feel that you must, like myself appreciate the very great difficulties of establishing what would be a fair quota for the different areas within Jasper Park, as they naturally present so many totally different conditions affecting the destruction of predatory animals. I cannot agree with your statement that when a quota for each warden is fixed that such warden will have no excuse whatever at the end of the month if he fails to get his quota." Forwarding his figure of seventy coyotes for the coming winter, he was greeted with the response, "In view of the large number of predators reported in Jasper Park it seems to me that a greater number should be taken by the Wardens than that suggested and it is hoped that such better showing will be made." Two months later the superintendent was forced to report that only one coyote had been killed in December due to fifty degree below zero weather and snowstorms, pleading that it would be impossible to set a quota for January, and suggesting "you consider 50% or under as the very outside we could expect under these abnormal conditions."[53] These circumstances were common to all the parks, and when Harkin's February report went forward to Rowatt summarizing the predator kills in each park in January, the numbers were far below what had been set. Again, Murphy made a telling notation on the copy of the report sent to him: "Apparently our wardens are not very active in this work."[54]

Murphy's remarks on the ineffectiveness of the wardens in February 1934 were both accurate and deeply felt, as Harkin complained in a letter to Wardle noting the minister's dissatisfaction and observing that the take of coyotes was only about one per man per month.[55] Nevertheless, within a short time the situation improved at Jasper, with ten coyotes reported killed in February and Rogers reporting in March that the tracks of very few predators had been observed. By November 1934 Supervising Warden Phillips reported normal increases in game populations and that headquarters instructions had been carried out with respect to destruction of coyotes. However, this report also noted that increasing numbers of cougars were appearing in the park and requested that dogs be brought in to track them, as this was the only known method to effectively hunt the animal. As this was also becoming a concern at Banff, in April 1935 Harkin approved the idea. Although Superintendent A.C. Wright, Rogers's replacement at Jasper, reported that trained dogs were available from a breeder in Tennessee, Phillips recommended acquiring young dogs that could be trained in about three years to leave other game unmolested when hunting cougars. This matter was discussed by Harkin and Lloyd, and on May 31, 1935 the latter reluctantly sent a memorandum acknowledging that on the basis that hunting of cougars by wardens using dogs was already permitted and "you expressed the opinion that dogs should be brought into Jasper Park for this purpose, it seems necessary that in order to carry out this policy...that two young coonhounds be purchased at an estimated cost of $160.00." By June, Harkin was recommending this course of action to Gibson, indicating that there was a Jasper warden capable of training the dogs and increasing their proposed number to four so that, once trained, there would be two available for Jasper and two for Banff. This was approved by both Rowatt and Murphy, and by November, Phillips proudly reported, "The four cougar hounds, in charge of Warden Wells, were successful in getting a cougar on their initial tryout."[56]

While the program seemed to be proceeding smoothly at Jasper, such was not so in Banff. Immediately upon receiving instructions on the new procedure in early November 1935, two Banff wardens wrote an official letter to Superintendent Jennings challenging headquarters' ideas on effective predator control activities and stating their opinion that control with firearms alone was impossible, an opinion Jennings shared.[57] As in Jasper, the first results were disappointing, the quota for November being set at forty animals and only seven reported being taken, and the March 1934 year-end statement showing only fifteen coyotes taken in comparison to thirty-one at Jasper. Even these figures were hard to confirm, given that the stubborn Bill Peyto was the foremost predator hunter on staff and he failed to submit evidence of his kills.[58] By the beginning of 1935 Jennings was complaining of growing predator population in the park and suggesting a round-table discussion with the wardens and others with knowledge of the matter, while Harkin was pointing out that the Banff wardens had killed only forty animals, or three per month, over the past thirteen months. To encourage better results, he enclosed a survey prepared by the Wildlife Division, "in order that the Department may be advised as to the exact nature of the activities of the wardens in their pursuit of predators."[59] When the completed questionnaires were received in Ottawa, the comments they contained were the last straw, and in a May 29, 1935 letter to Jennings Harkin charged that the Banff wardens' work was unsatisfactory, noting "only thirty-five coyotes and one cougar were taken by the Banff Wardens and of these thirty-five predators, twenty were taken by the Peytos" and that "the Banff Wardens are either inefficient or indifferent in actively carrying out this branch of their work."[60]

Issues around the cougar problem were also on the Banff agenda and even before the four coonhounds had been purchased, a local movement led by Norman Luxton called for employment of an outside cougar hunter to take the matter in hand. Further pressure for action was brought to bear in the wake of a July 1935 incident where Dr. J.H. Allan, a professor at the University of Alberta, witnessed the killing of a goat by a mountain lion on the road west of Banff in broad daylight, an event widely reported in the newspapers. Initially, Harkin planned to resist calls for paid bounty hunters, observing in a draft of a letter to Jennings, "The bringing in of outside hunters for the purpose of hunting Cougars would constitute a reflection on the warden service." But the same day he noted on a memorandum prepared by Lloyd opposing the hiring of outside hunters, "Mr. Lloyd, I am not sure that it wd not be well to hire an experienced Cougar hunter for a while." On July 23, he forwarded a new draft of his letter to Jennings directing him to make enquiries concerning the terms on which a capable hunter could be employed.[61] E.R. "Cougar" Lee of Rock Bay, Vancouver Island, one of BC's most prominent mountain lion hunters with a record of thirty-three kills in 1933 and a man strongly recommended by Luxton, was ultimately contracted in October 1935 for six months at $50 per month and a bonus of $10 per animal. He commenced work in November and the *Crag and Canyon* regularly recorded his success, but not without ongoing criticisms of headquarters staff:

> Mr. Lee was induced to consider the proposal to come to Banff through representations made to him by Mr. N.K. Luxton. After getting Mr. Lee's consent to bring his dogs here Mr. Luxton then took the matter up direct with Parks Commissioner Harkin, and it took many months of correspondence to gain that official's permission to use dogs in the hunting of lions. Mr. Harkin, evidently also a believer in letting Nature look after itself—another arm-chair administrator who refused to take advice of men who have the experience to give wise counsel, until he was finally convinced that something would have to be done.[62]

Banff warden Harold Fuller with dead cougar, ca. 1925. An increase in cougars in Banff National Park led to the hiring of a professional hunter in 1935, but Harkin felt it was only one more example of warden ineptitude. [WMCR, NA66-1881]

The newspaper's opinion about the infestation of cougars was not shared by Lee himself, who noted in a telling letter of December 19, 1935 to Jennings requesting an increase in his base rate to $100 per month, "I feel satisfied in saying that there are not nearly the number of lion in this Park that have been reported."[63] Harkin consulted Wardle on the matter and as the chief engineer stated that in the circumstances increasing the stipend would not produce any better results, Lee returned to the coast at the end of January 1936 after killing nine cougars. For Harkin, the whole episode was one more indicator of how the branch's wildlife policy was misunderstood as well as a testament to the ineptitude of the warden service. This perspective, and his unwavering support for the policy, was perhaps best described in reaction to the newspaper campaign in a December letter to Selby Walker of the National Parks Association, who had become one of his few confidants on the subject:

> I was rather amused at seeing in the newspapers a statement that we had changed our policy in regard to predators because we happen to have engaged a cougar hunter to reduce the cougars in Banff Park. The fact of the matter is our wardens have always been free to kill

> cougars, but, between you and me, these wardens have not met our expectations in the matter of either cougar or coyote killing.
>
> While I recognize that it is undesirable that predators become too numerous, the fact remains that, so far as Parks are concerned, our policy must be to preserve all types of indigenous wild life. We are not running the Parks purely to preserve the deer, sheep and other game animals and, as a matter of fact, I know you understand that the worst thing that could be done insofar as the game animals are concerned would be to entirely eliminate the predators.[64]

Unquestionably, though, the test of wills with his field staff over predator control combined with the faltering Grey Owl program cast a long shadow over Harkin's final years of service. Particularly tragic was the relationship with the warden service, which earlier in his career had been based on mutual respect and a common purpose but now was one of scorn and disillusionment on both sides. But as sad as the whole predator control period was on a personal level, it was important for the future of Canadian wildlife conservation. As pointed out, the issue turned on the role of his wildlife experts and science in the Wildlife Division, and although Harkin questioned the approach at times and had to adjust to pressures coming from all sides, he never hesitated in his fundamental support. At the same time, he was overseeing important, but largely unseen, activities carried out by the branch that also fostered a new ecological approach. The issue of fisheries in the national parks had always been of concern, particularly because of its attraction to tourists, and in 1928 Dr. Donald S. Rawson of the University of Saskatchewan carried out consulting research on fish habitat and distribution. As well, after establishment of the Migratory Birds Section, its officers had improved their credentials and done important research in ornithology, particularly Harrison Lewis, who received his PhD from Cornell University in 1929 after completing a groundbreaking project studying Double-crested Cormorants. In 1934 the need for a chief migratory bird officer for the prairies, duties that had largely been carried out by Lloyd, saw the hiring of J. Dewey Soper, a graduate of the University of Alberta already noted for his Arctic research with the National Museum, in particular his discovery of Snow Goose nesting grounds on Baffin Island. As well, research began to be carried out intermittently in the parks by scientists working for the National Museum through agreement with the Parks Branch, most notably Dr. Ian McTaggart Cowan of British Columbia, who did his first collecting for the Museum in Jasper in 1930.[65]

If Harkin had wavered in support of the role of science and research under Parks administration, the whole subsequent story of Canadian wildlife conservation might well have been different. While in many respects it would have been easier for him to give in to the many voices assailing him and back down on the predator issue, this was not the measure of the man. Giving into public pressure, which for many years would remain averse to the acceptance of the predatory role, would likely have set back the work of the Wildlife Division, and it may well have affected the new role for wildlife management that emerged with creation of the Canadian Wildlife Service in 1947.[66] However, holding his ground in this hard-fought battle just served to add more stress in the difficult circumstances the branch was experiencing at all levels during the Depression. It soon caught up to him.

JAMES BERNARD HARKIN
COMMISSIONER OF NATIONAL PARKS, 1911 – 1936
EDITOR, PUBLIC SERVANT, CONSERVATIONIST AND HUMANITARIAN, HE REORGANIZED THE ADMINISTRATION OF OUR NATIONAL PARKS AND GUIDED THEIR DEVELOPMENT THROUGH THE CRITICAL FORMATIVE YEARS. THROUGH HIS VISION, INTEGRITY, AND DEVOTED SERVICE THESE SPLENDID AREAS NOW SPAN CANADA – DEDICATED TO HER PEOPLE FOR THEIR BENEFIT, EDUCATION AND ENJOYMENT.
BORN IN VANKLEEK HILL, ONTARIO, 30TH JANUARY, 1875
DIED IN OTTAWA, ONTARIO, 27TH JANUARY, 1955

SEVENTEEN

Passing the Torch

IN A TWIST OF FATE, the same session of Parliament that passed the new *Nova Scotia and Prince Edward Island National Parks Act* in June 1936 also dealt with legislation eliminating the Department of the Interior as a separate agency, rolling its remaining responsibilities into the new Department of Mines and Resources. The consolidation had been foreseen by Bennett as early as 1935, the inevitable outcome of the natural resources transfer, and had been partially achieved in the reorganization carried out by the Liberals under the direction of Thomas Crerar. In speaking to the 1936 legislation, King pointed out the governmental efficiencies that joining Interior, Indian Affairs, Mines, and Immigration and Colonization would create; it would consolidate a number of services that were being duplicated or triplicated, merge twenty-three existing branches into not more than eight, and eliminate the positions of three deputy ministers. In these circumstances, the bulk of Parks Branch responsibilities would become part of the mandate of the new Land, Parks and Forest Branch under a director, while the engineering services provided by Wardle's former division would become part of the new Surveys and Engineering Branch aimed at providing support to the entire department. Over the years, Harkin had always regarded himself as an employee of the department as a whole, not just one of its branches, and undoubtedly would have been aware that change was coming. As the position of commissioner of National Parks was now slated to become controller of the National Parks Bureau reporting to a director, the question for him as the December 1, 1936 implementation date drew near would likely have been where he fit in the new structure.

The only comment on the situation from one in a position to know was provided by Fergus Lothian in *A History of Canada's National Parks*, written from the perspective of more than forty years in the service. He stated, "Faced with demotion from the status of a director to that of a division head in the new Lands, Parks and Forest Branch, Commissioner Harkin chose retirement. He had given thirty-five years of outstanding service public service to Canada, of which twenty-five years had been devoted to the development and administration of Canada's national park system. The new post of Controller of the National Parks Bureau was filled by F.H.H. Williamson, for many years the Deputy Commissioner of Parks." Lothian also noted that long-serving Assistant Deputy Minister Roy Gibson was awarded the position of director of the new branch, while Wardle became director of the Surveys and Engineering Branch.[1] Every writer who has dealt with Harkin's career has repeated this explanation, no evidence to the contrary seemingly being available to dispute it. Indeed, it may have been as simple and straightforward as that, as his health continued to suffer and his energy appeared to have flagged under the weight of a myriad of Depression projects, reduced appropriations, and problems with field staff. But despite this indication that his retirement was a matter of personal choice, there are also hints from the waning months of his service and a statement made after his retirement that, perhaps, point to a more complex explanation.

First and foremost is that there was no sign of impending retirement in his correspondence with departmental officers or others, even after passage of the legislation creating the Department of Mines and Resources. It was business as usual as he went about getting the new Cape Breton Park up and running and preparing for those to follow in Prince Edward Island and New Brunswick. He likewise continued to provide direction, including to Deputy Commissioner Williamson who succeeded him, with his usual forthright manner and typical progressive outlook. Even after he went on medical leave in September 1936, correspondence continued in his name but signed by other headquarters officials, mainly Williamson, who, as late as mid-September responded to a query "in the absence of Mr. Harkin, who unfortunately had to undergo a slight operation but who is improving very rapidly and is expected back in the office shortly."[2] Similarly, those reporting to him gave no indication in their memoranda that any change was contemplated. Of equal interest is a letter to the Banff Advisory Council of March 1937 after his retirement thanking them for the good wishes they had extended, but in which he admitted, "I have one outstanding regret and that is that so much I planned for and had visions of, remains unstarted. True, substantial progress has been made; perhaps the foundations have been laid but no one can yet visualize to the full what National Parks can do for Canada. Every day it seemed to me new possibilities were looming up."[3] There appears to be a touch of regret and a sense of unfinished business in this statement, and it may be that, approaching sixty-one years of age, Harkin still hoped to see some of these possibilities fulfilled.[4]

Why he did not, apart from not wanting to face an organizational "demotion," is unclear. However, a strong possibility is that it had something to do with his health, a debilitating factor throughout his career and one that apparently was worsening in 1936, requiring an extensive medical leave early that year and the unspecified operation referred to. A clue appears in a letter he wrote to an acquaintance exactly two years later, in December 1938, from Lakeland, Florida, where he spent the winter: "I am feeling very much better since I came here and expect by spring I shall have taken at least 25 years off. If the change of the past few weeks can be taken as a criterion, that certainly will be the result."[5] This sounds like a man who is completely exhausted from the "25 years" referred to. However, another possibility may be that his financial circumstances allowed him to take early retirement, although if so these resources must have come from his wife, as there was no apparent Harkin family fortune. Yet money does not seem to have become an issue as the Harkins continued to live in their Clemow Avenue home and took winter vacations to Florida and he also remained active in his clubs and engaged in social activities equating to comfortable middle class living. Harkin's salary when he left is not known, but it likely would have been equivalent to that of his peer in the Water Power Branch, E.H. Finlayson, who received $6,000 per annum in 1935. This was a good wage in the 1930s, particularly so in light of Harkin's lack of formal education, equivalent to one being paid a university professor. That lack of education may too have been a factor. The education and ability of those entering the civil service by the early 1930s was on the upswing, and by 1935 it was coming to be dominated by a group of bright young men, revolving around O.D. Skelton at External Affairs, who were educated at Queen's or the University of Toronto and who, as historian J.L. Granatstein has pointed out, formed "a meritocratic elite."[6] In comparison to this new wave of "mandarins," Harkin would have been seen as part of the "old guard," and there were younger, ambitious men such as James Smart associated with him who would be seen to have lots of potential. Perhaps it made more sense for the government, given his medical problems and its efforts to decrease costs in the consolidation exercise as well as to rejuvenate the civil service, to extend his eligibility under the *Superannuation Act* to the equivalent of full term.[7]

Whatever the circumstances of his leaving, it appears that Harkin's retirement, at least during its early years, was a time of personal fulfillment and pleasant relaxation after an unrelenting and pressure-filled career. He filled his former working hours by lending his administrative and public relations talents to the Boy Scout movement. Three or four days a week he volunteered at the national headquarters in Ottawa and he served many years on the national executive as chairman of its publications committee. Upon retirement from this work in 1946, he was presented with the Silver Wolf Award, the highest decoration of the Boy Scouts Association. At the same time he continued active involvement with the Ottawa Rotary Club, continuing to look after its publicity functions and serving a term as club director. He also continued to enjoy golf, and in recognition of his service to the Rivermead Club was made one of only two life members.[8] Little is known of the details of his married life, although in later years Mrs. Harkin was an invalid and it may well have been that much of his time was devoted to caring for her.

At the same time he did not lose interest in national parks matters, and in his quite remarkable letter to the Banff Advisory Council provided a clear picture of his hopes for the system's future:

> I am passing the torch on and my earnest prayer is that the work will continue to be based on idealism. If that is ever lost, Parks will lose their soul, will become like the tens of thousands of ordinary resorts throughout the world.
>
> When God made the Rockies he never intended them to be ordinary resorts. Every action I ever took in regard to our beloved Parks was based on that belief....
>
> While henceforth I shall be an on-looker from the sidelines watching the evolution of the Parks, their welfare will be first as much a matter of supreme concern to me as they always have been in the past. And in this connection my most earnest hope is that the people of Banff will champion the inviolability of the Parks and will ever demand the most rigid adherence to idealism in their development.[9]

He would have watched with interest, then, as Williamson, Gibson, Wardle, and Wood began development of Cape Breton Highlands and

Hon. T.A. Crerar, minister of Mines and Resources, speaking at official opening of Cape Breton Highlands National Park, Nova Scotia, July 1, 1941. Although it took five years after its creation to be officially dedicated, Harkin would have rejoiced in the event in his retirement. [LAC, PA-058361]

later of Prince Edward Island National Park, formally established by proclamation on April 24, 1937 in a 7.65-square-mile area focused on Cavendish Beach and Green Gables cottage. Undoubtedly, he would have been happy to avoid some of the difficulties surrounding appropriation of private lands that were faced in both instances. As well, with the outbreak of the Second World War in 1939, he would have been grateful to escape another period of retrenchment like those he had endured during the First World War and the Depression. But the war and postwar periods brought other events and changes that would have been troubling. Most disappointing would have been development of Calgary Power's Lake Minnewanka project, including a dam, penstock, powerhouse, and transmission lines, carried out under the auspices of the *War Measures Act* in 1942 to provide emergency backup power for wartime purposes. Like other knowledgeable observers, he likely would have seen this as pure opportunism on the company's part, taking advantage of the circumstances to achieve what they been unable to gain over a fifteen-year period on his watch and seeing it as a direct attack on his treasured inviolability. Perhaps of concern would have been the 1947 abolition of both Buffalo and Nemiskam parks and the decision to create the independent Canadian Wildlife Service out of the Wildlife Division, even though his own support of science had paved the way for this evolution. In any event, by the 1950s these and other changes in administration had led him to the conclusion that the "idealism" he had called for had been lost, and he became, at least privately, a critic of the direction national parks were taking.

Because of lack of material, it is difficult to determine just how much Harkin kept up the associations of his park days. However, it is clear that some of his Ottawa friendships continued and he corresponded, at least at Christmas, with some old acquaintances in the West. One was Norman Luxton, his oft-times critic and adversary on parks issues. In the late 1920s, Luxton's criticisms in the *Crag and Canyon* had abated as the opinionated and hardbitten businessman undoubtedly began to recognize that they were hurting both his own and Banff's interests, but they had continued in his private correspondence. For example, in a September 1928 letter to recently appointed Prince Albert superintendent James Wood, a close friend from his days serving at Banff, Luxton had observed, "J.B. is here and I have had my annual round with him. He is a dandy little fellow if he could only get it out of his head that God appointed him to the job. So long as he thinks that he also thinks he can't make a mistake." Even more succinct were his thoughts in a note to another acquaintance about the same time: "King Henry 8, J.B. Harkin, God and the Pope will have a great time some day when they all meet."[10] Given these opinions, a seasonal letter written to his old nemesis on the first day of 1952 was quite amazing. Luxton began by relating the current circumstances of some of Harkin's former co-workers, including engineers and wardens and not sparing, in his typical acerbic fashion, recent superintendents. These he described as "some terrible specimens of humanity," with the exception of the current incumbent, J.R.B. Coleman, who he described as "a rather high class chap." He thought that Coleman would soon succeed to the position of director as "Jim Smart is shelved next summer," an allusion to the retirement of Harkin's hand-picked officer entrusted with the direction of new national parks who had succeeded Williamson as controller of the National Parks Bureau in 1941 and became chief of the National and Historic Sites Division in 1950. But after these comments and relating his own rather restricted activities due to advancing age, Luxton closed with a tribute that indicated time had made him reconsider earlier opinions of Harkin and that he now understood the importance of his legacy:

> We never did have a Parks Commissioner like you. I can realize it now after what has been going on ever since you left. I am glad you were strong enough to take all the worry you had, less has killed a lot off. I suppose you feel like me, traveling does not appeal, but it would be nice to see you come West once more. I would take a month off and show you all the dreams that never came true, but still at that, when one thinks at what you started and each park clean across Canada will always be a monument to your great ideas, you would realize it more if you could see the thousands of people who come here each year; an education that no school or university could have ever given them.[11]

Another correspondent and confidante in these years was Mabel Williams, his long-time assistant and the only one who made an effort to record his work in *Guardians of the Wild*, written in 1936 when she was living in England.[12] In an August 1954 letter to her, after reading a copy of the American periodical *The Living Wilderness* which she had sent him, Harkin referred to their shared disappointment at the way parks and parks policy in Canada had recently evolved: "It is good to see that many in the U.S. are seeing the light and are willing to work in accordance with it. But I fear there is no hope for success in Canada. All who were schooled in the proper principles are out and the newcomers seemingly can see nothing but tourist biz. I suppose you knew that several amendments have been made to our Parks Act which are contrary to all the old policies."[13] In the circumstances, he felt compelled to put down some of his own thoughts in reflecting on his experiences, and this too he discussed with "M.B.," as he called Williams. Believing that the Canadian parks system had gone off track, he stated the purpose of his writing as being to "jolt the public into seeing things as we see them." Throughout his career he had kept a file of index cards and notebooks in which he jotted down ideas when they occurred to him or quotes when he read them, using headings such as "Beauty," "Inviolability," "Recreation," "Tourist Traffic," and "Roads," and it appears he had continued to add to these after his retirement with this project in mind. In an outline, he came back to points he had made as early as his first series of annual reports, including: the inspiration provided by Yellowstone; the necessity of demonstrating parks' economic value; and, while they should be preserved in their natural state as far as possible, that there must be trails and roads for the public to enjoy them.[14] Unfortunately, he had difficulty in bringing this work to a conclusion, as he complained in the same August 1954 letter to Williams:

> I never seem to get anywhere....Sometimes I almost get superstitious about it. During the years I have made five or six starts. No. 1 was crude and was cast out. A number of others looked better to me. One which had developed 9 or 10 chapters disappeared; presumably it got mixed up with old papers or fell off [the] desk and got into [the] wastepaper basket. Several minor starts got underway but finally I had what pretty well satisfied my own criticism. It was an introduction which covered a lot of ground and was, I think, well-worth [while] material. But almost a year ago it too disappeared and has never shown up since. During the past year conditions have not been favourable to my making any real progress though I have accumulated an amplitude of ideas.[15]

By the time he wrote this letter Harkin was seventy-nine years old, he mentioned that "conditions had not been favourable" during the past year, and his handwriting was shaky. He recognized his own failing, closing the letter with the sad admission, "Incidentally I fully recognize that my writing is indicative of my slipping, slipping."

During this period he was still working on his notes and in one of them recorded what, perhaps, he hoped would become his epitaph: "In a few years we shall 'pass and be forgotten like the rest,' but the parks we earnestly hope will remain, and the feeling that at least something was attempted, something done for our beloved Canada, seems reward enough before we, too, go to the long nights' repose."[16] Nevertheless, despite some signs of failing, he was seemingly still in good health, and five months later his wife was planning his 80th birthday party for friends and former colleagues at their home on January 30. Several days before the event, the invitees were shocked to hear that their friend Bunny had been confined to hospital for a few days and had died on January 27, 1955. The man who in recent years had come to be referred to as "the father of Canada's national parks" was gone. Instead of a birthday party, the January 30 gathering at his home was for a funeral service, officiated by Reverend Dr. Charles Donald, with burial following at Ottawa's Beechwood Cemetery.

Despite the fact that that he had been retired for almost twenty years, both the Ottawa dailies and other major Canadian newspapers carried extensive obituaries and articles highlighting Harkin's career. The *Ottawa Journal*, his own former paper, provided the most comprehensive coverage in its January 28 edition, including a front-page portrait taken in 1947 by famed Ottawa photographer Yousuf Karsh. Under the headline "J.B. Harkin Dies in Ottawa at Age 79," it provided a detailed account of his many accomplishments:

> J.B. Harkin brought organization out of the former laissez-faire chaos in establishing the parks and preserving the wild animals. Taking the park lands in hand, he drafted modern regulations under the headings of game protection, fire protection, construction of essential buildings and park facilities. He established the Warden Service and planned to throw the areas open to the Canadian public.

> Envious eyes of promoters were turned on the newly-created National Parks. They wanted not only part of the Crown-held lands, but also wanted to develop potential water powers for private profit. Mr. Harkin fiercely resisted these attempts at encroachment on the park reserves and succeeded in attracting important support. Sometimes he lost out, but in the main had his way with the lands by a determined doctrine of "What we have, we hold."...
>
> Well over 40 years ago, J.B. Harkin realized that the vast system of National Parks from Cape Breton to British Columbia was not only a chain of marvelous playgrounds for Canadians but would pay important dividends through visitors from other countries. He was one of the first Canadians of his time to realize the values and wealth of the then new industry of catering to tourists. His parks were instrumental in bringing many thousands of visitors from the United States and other countries to visit Canada for the first time.[17]

Such tributes indicated that Harkin's efforts had not been forgotten, and soon other steps were taken to provide memorials to his life and work. At some point a Canadian Geographic Board sign had been erected at the Mount Harkin pull-out on the Banff-Windermere Highway, describing the background of the man for whom the peak had been named in 1923. Apart from this, as might have been expected, the first move to recognize his accomplishments after his death came from his own creation, the Historic Sites and Monuments Board. His work in the board's establishment had been recognized as recently as the previous year when, during his presidential speech at the 1954 annual meeting of the Canadian Historical Association, M.H. Long referred to him as "the physician attendant upon the birth of the Board."[18] Three days after reading of his death in the *Toronto Globe and Mail*, Professor Fred Landon of Queen's University, chair of the board, wrote Secretary A.J.H. Richardson recommending, "He was a big figure in the establishment of the National Parks and it might be that we would want to add his name to our list of distinguished Canadians." This list was kept as a source from which future historic markers could be chosen, and in a further note to Richardson a few days later asking him to put the matter on an upcoming agenda, Landon noted, "I do not think we need draft an inscription for a secondary tablet at once as no action would be taken this year....Perhaps in a couple of years we might think of erecting a tablet."[19] On approval of a motion by Landon at the board's meeting in early June 1955, Harkin's name was added to the list for future consideration.

Meanwhile, the irrepressible Norman Luxton had, as president of the Southern Alberta Old Timers' Association, approached National Parks and Historic Sites Chief Coleman during his 1954 summer inspection tour to Banff suggesting the erection of a plaque during his friend's lifetime recognizing his contributions to national parks "as a particularly appropriate gesture." Luxton had actually come up with this idea as early as 1937 and had even convinced Wardle to have some designs completed, but the costs of having the work done on his own proved a deterrent to carrying it out. Coleman did not act on the renewed proposal at this time, but with Harkin's death he recommended to Director J.A. Hutchison in February 1955 that a plaque be erected on the grounds of the Banff Administration Grounds at the department's expense. Hutchison foresaw some difficulty in that other individuals, particularly Howard Douglas, had also "contributed rather extensively to the National Park system" and thought that what was being proposed should be reviewed by the Historic Sites and Monuments Board.[20] From this discussion emerged what might be referred to as the "unofficial" Harkin memorial. Hutchison's direction and the subsequent recommendation to the Historic Sites Board resulted in no immediate action, and Banff Advisory Council Secretary R.E. Edwards wrote now Director Coleman two years later again recommending erection of a memorial cairn: "During the many years which he occupied the position Mr. Harkin did more towards bringing the National Parks, and especially Banff National Park, to their present high repute throughout the world...and the Council feels that it is fitting that future generations, both of visitors and residents, should be continually reminded of the man to whom, to a very great extent, they are indebted for the opportunity of enjoying the beauties of the world's most scenic areas spread before their eyes."[21] Perhaps embarrassed, Coleman responded positively and directed Chief B.I.M. Strong to have Fergus Lothian draft the wording for a tablet that could be "affixed to a nicely shaped boulder and erected in a suitable location on the Administration Grounds" similar to a plaque and boulder recently placed at the Banff School of Fine Arts in memory of John Murray Gibbon.[22] By the end of April 1958, Lothian had completed the wording and it had been approved by Strong and Coleman:

JAMES BERNARD HARKIN
COMMISSIONER OF DOMINION PARKS, 1911–1936

Editor, Public Servant, Conservationist and Humanitarian.
He reorganized the administration of our National Parks
and guided their development through the critical formative years. Through his vision, integrity, and devoted service,
these splendid areas now span Canada—dedicated to her
people for their benefit, education and enjoyment.

Born in Vankleek Hill, Ontario, 30th January, 1875.
Died in Ottawa, Ontario, 27th January, 1955.

Erected by the National Parks Service
Department of Northern Affairs and National Resources

1958

A suitable boulder and location near the Cascades of Time gardens had been chosen and plans for the memorial's completion to be accomplished in time for the beginning of the 1958 summer season were in place when the Banff Advisory Council again wrote Coleman on June 6. This time Edwards indicated that it had received no word of the proposed completion date and urged, "The Council would also like to suggest that, when completed, the unveiling of the memorial might be performed by yourself, failing which, it might, perhaps, be undertaken by either Prime Minister Mr. Diefenbaker, or Minister of Resources Mr. Hamilton on the occasion of their tour of the National Parks this summer." On receiving a copy of this missive, Strong wrote to Banff superintendent Harry Dempster and pointed out that the Advisory Council's suggestion was going to cause problems: "I do not know whether you are aware that authorization for erection of this plaque was made without reference to the Historic Sites and Monuments Board or senior Head Office officials. It was the thinking that the plaque could be erected without any ceremony and that would be the end of it. If the Council carry on agitation for a special ceremony it is certainly going to complicate matters."[23] Somewhat reluctantly, Council agreed, so it was that a most fitting and handsome memorial to Harkin just appeared in the Administration Grounds one day in July 1958. Ironically, it had been the Council, who Harkin had tangled with so frequently in the 1920s, that had virtually shamed the parks service into erecting the memorial. It would also recognize its importance to informing Canadians of Harkin's national parks accomplishments in a letter of thanks to Coleman: "The Council feels that this memorial will be of great interest to innumerable visitors and also be a public recognition of the wonderful work done by Mr. Harkin in earlier days in laying the groundwork for the magnificent system of National Parks which has since developed."[24] This plaque was joined by two official Historic Sites and Monuments Board versions unveiled on August 28, 1987, one attached to the Administration Building and one attached to the back of the building's sign overlooking the famous view down Banff Avenue to Cascade Mountain beyond.[25]

If the National Parks' memorial was somewhat surreptitious, such was not the case with another effort at recognition occurring at the same time. In the letter to Mabel Williams in 1954 concerning his difficulty in finishing his manuscript, Harkin had chided, "Do you recall some years ago I warned you that it might be to you would fall the task of completing the job."[26] Williams took this charge seriously, and after his death began work on carrying through with what he no longer could. She had returned from England in 1938 and was making her living as a writer,

J.B. Harkin memorial in Banff National Park administration grounds, July 1958. This was the first, "unofficial" memorial erected to Harkin in Banff's Administration Building grounds. [WMCR, V488-384-21]

her most noteworthy project being a commercial guidebook entitled *The Banff-Jasper Highway* published in 1948. An outline under the title of "Divisions of Work" indicates that she intended this work to be an expansion of that presented in *Guardians of the Wild*, including chapters on "Fire & Game Protection," "Roads, Trails and Telephones," "Publicity," "Recreation and Education," "Wildlife," "Historic Sites," and several other topics. She made at least one attempt to write a manuscript based on this plan, but it sounded much like her earlier work and it appears she did not have sufficient material available to develop the various subjects to the depth that Harkin had been seeking. It is likely that at this point she was in contact with Dorothy Barber of Ottawa, another surviving member of the early headquarters staff, and received from her many of the notes previously referred to. Five years later, in correspondence with Dr. Robin Winks of Yale University, Williams described the circumstances: "Mr. Harkin's notes and papers when they reached me were a great disappointment. They were nothing but a mass of jumbled ideas, often one line or a few words, just as they occurred to him. If I had not known his mind so well, I could have made nothing of them."[27]

She did make something of them, although the result was probably less satisfactory than she might have hoped. Using the haphazard jottings and copies of the annual Department of the Interior reports, she constructed an essay by stringing together the topics he had used to head his notes. In 1957 the work was taken on by her publisher H.R. Larson of Saskatoon in a sixteen-page pamphlet entitled *The History and Meaning of the National Parks of Canada*, "extracts from the papers of the late Jas. B. Harkin, first Commissioner of the National Parks of Canada." Its frontispiece featured the Karsh portrait and the title-page was followed by an "Acknowledgement" which paid tribute to the work Williams had accomplished: "The publisher and lovers of national and provincial parks are deeply indebted to Miss MABEL B. WILLIAMS, an authority on Canadian National Parks, for the completion of 'The History and Meaning of the National Parks of Canada' from the original notes of the late Jas. B. Harkin, first Commissioner of National Parks....Miss Williams willingly volunteered to complete this volume and in doing so derived much pleasure and satisfaction because of her profound admiration and deep appreciation for and of Mr. Harkin's contribution to the weal of Canada."[28] This appreciation was followed by a "Foreword" written by Larson, which began by highlighting the commissioner's role as a public servant and conservationist: "The late Jas. B. Harkin, first Commissioner of the National Parks of Canada, was an eminent member of that long list of distinguished public servants who have added so much to Canada's prestige abroad and prosperity at home. His work carried him to many fields of conservation, in each of which he had to break new ground."[29]

The following dozen pages of *History and Meaning*, the result of Williams's efforts, formed a very readable but rather incomplete summary of Harkin's thinking, probably intentionally weighted toward his point of view later in life. They began with the story of his appointment in June 1911 by Frank Oliver—the unexpected offering of the new post to someone who "doubted my ability since I knew nothing about the parks or what would be expected of me," but found "the prospect intrigued and stirred my imagination and, albeit, with many misgivings as to my ability, I told him I would undertake the post." This account, perhaps the most apocryphal of those quoted by writers dealing with Harkin's background, is not part of the notes or reports that most of the recollection is based upon, nor have I been able to trace a source prior to Williams's use of it. In the circumstances, it seems likely that she received it orally—Harkin's own telling of the story of how he came to create the Canadian park system by a chance set of circumstances—perhaps a Canadian version of the famous "creation myth" of the founding of the American park system at Yellowstone in which he put so much stock. This seems all the more likely since after recounting Harkin's gaining of the position the narrative immediately turned to the inspiration he took from the Yellowstone discovery story and Hedges' "noble and public-spirited idea" which resulted in an Act of Congress establishing the first North American national park.

History and Meaning then described the establishment of Canadian parks and the gaining of political support, identifying the economic impetus of tourism, the influence of automobiles, and the final achievement of success when Meighen rose in the House to support the parks appropriation "and the economic value of the parks was thenceforth established." With the system created and secure, the remainder of the treatise focused on Harkin's thinking about the value of parks to mankind in the future and their higher purposes. The future was foretold with phrases such as "the day will come when the population of Canada will be ten times as great as now," and "Even the face of Canada has seen many changes in the last fifty years. What will it be like a hundred years from now?" The inference was, of course, that national parks would have a significant role to play in that future: "Our national parks will be the recognized schools for the study of natural history and geology"; "Canada has now a fine series of national and provincial parks of which we may well be proud, but we need more parks"; and "as Canada expands northward we shall need more northern parks too, particularly sanctuaries for wild fowl and other migratory birds which breed there."

Williams also made sure that the issues bothering Harkin concerning the direction of Canadian parks were identified. During his career he gave a few hints that he recognized that tourism and recreational development could impair parks in ways similar to larger-scale irrigation and power projects, an awareness alluded to in the statement that "There are increased demands for more and more roads, cheaper forms of amusement, commercial exploitation, and the danger is that if these demands are acceded to, the parks may lose the very thing that distinguished them from the outside world." Williams followed up with his later, seemingly revisionist statement about the role of park roads: "I have always believed that the building of motor roads should be restricted as much as possible. Though trunk roads, of course, there must be, and they should be made as good and as safe as possible. But road building in the mountains is extremely expensive and—what is more important—it is only from the trails that one can get into real intimacy with the parks." Everyday matters concerning infrastructure were counterbalanced with his thoughts on what today we would call intact ecosystems, and, with the same broad brushstrokes used in his annual reports, they were combined with those on beauty and spirituality:

> Man can maim, disfigure, and weaken Nature, but once he has destroyed original conditions, he can never replace them. Each citizen of Canada is the owner of one share of stock in the National Parks. Our part is to see that the value of their holdings is kept up. I feel that everything our engineers construct in the Parks should be dominated by the spirit of beauty. People sometimes accuse me of being a mystic about the influence of the mountains. Perhaps I am. I devoutly believe that there are emanations from them, intangible but very real, which elevate the mind and purify the spirit.

Finally, Williams turned to Harkin's most important message to Canadians, the one concerning the necessity of keeping parks inviolate: "The battle for the establishment of National Parks is long since over but the battle to keep them inviolate is never won....Future generations may wonder at our blindness if we neglect to set them aside before civilization invades them. What is needed in Canada today is an informed public opinion which will voice an indignant protest against any vulgarization of the beauty of our National Parks or any invasion of their sanctity....Every principle of enlightened patriotism should inspire us to keep them inviolate." Although not its publisher, *History and Meaning* was initially distributed through the National and Historic Parks Branch, and in 1961 it took on the publication of a second edition under the title *The Origin and Meaning of the National Parks of Canada*. In the half century since its appearance, and despite its rather limited content, it has become the most widely quoted source for Harkin's ideas, in view of the paucity of other readily accessible material.

It would be another fifteen years before a final memorial, probably the one Harkin would have appreciated most, was created bearing his name and witnessing his pioneering conservation efforts. In his writing, Harkin had called for "an informed public opinion which will voice an indignant protest against any vulgarization of the beauty of our National Parks or any invasion of their sanctity," and after the Canadian National Parks Association waned in the war years, an organization fostering this role had disappeared. The National and Provincial Parks Association of Canada (now the Canadian Parks and Wilderness Society) was created in 1963 as the successor to the CNPA; its goals included "the use and management of National and Provincial parks in a manner that will contribute to the education, inspiration and well being of the general public; to cooperate...in protecting the integrity of National and Provincial Parks, historic sites and nature reserves...and to encourage the expansion of both the National and Provincial Park systems and the preservation of places having outstanding natural or historical significance."[30] These were positions consistent with those Harkin had espoused in calling for a public voice for conservation in the early 1920s, and it was therefore not surprising that the NPPAC would choose to name a new conservation order it intended to award in his honour. At a Vancouver press conference in October 1972 announcing creation of the J.B. Harkin Medal and its first recipient, President Gordon Nelson explained, "The idea of the Harkin Medal is to keep alive the memory of this exceptional Canadian and what he believed in and accomplished and to honour others who serve the cause of parks with equal distinction. It is not an annual award and will be given only to those who, in the opinion of the Association, merit the recognition."

The Honourable Jean Chrétien, minister of Indian Affairs and Northern Development, was to receive the first award, and Nelson, in providing the reasons for his choice, compared the work of the two men in parks creation: "In the space of four short years, he has established eleven new National Parks, including the first three major parks in the north other than Wood Buffalo Park—Kluane, Nahanni, and Baffin Island Parks—as well as twenty new National Historic Parks and Sites. This is all the more remarkable when set beside the fact that in the thirty-two years between Commissioner Harkin's retirement and Mr. Chrétien taking over the parks portfolio, only four new parks were created." Although the bronze medal, then being designed by prominent Canadian medal artist Dora de Pedery Hunt, was not officially presented until several months later, Chrétien, in acknowledging the letter informing him of his selection, expressed his pleasure at being the first recipient and, in identifying the work yet to be done in Canada's national parks, stated, "Because of the growing commitment of all Canadians to the ideal which the J.B. Harkin Medal commemorates, I have confidence that the immense task we still face will be tackled with vigour and success in the years ahead."[31] This comment is as relevant today as it was when it was made. Harkin's precautionary principle and the need to find a balance between development and preservation, identified almost a century ago, is still being worked out.

It is difficult to know where to turn for the final word on the importance of J.B. Harkin to Canada and its national park system, since there have been so many superlatives written over the years. Perhaps it is best left to the man himself. In the last paragraph of *History and Meaning*, Williams used one of his statements, originally included in his 1916 annual report, that she obviously believed best summed up his work and what it meant to Canadians, and I can do no better:

> National Parks are maintained for all the people—for the ill, that they may be restored, for the well that they may be fortified and inspired by the sunshine, the fresh air, the

beauty, and all the other healing, ennobling, and inspiring agencies of Nature. They exist in order that every citizen of Canada may satisfy his craving for Nature and Nature's beauty; that he may absorb the poise and restfulness of the forests; that he may steep his soul in the brilliance of the wild flowers and the sublimity of mountain peaks; that he may develop in himself the buoyancy, the joy, and the activity he sees in wild animals; that he may stock his mind with the material of intelligent optimism, great thoughts, noble ideals; that he may be made better, happier and healthier.[32]

Notes

INTRODUCTION

1. Whyte Museum of the Canadian Rockies, Library and Archives (WMCR), Winks fonds, handwritten manuscript [Mabel Williams], "James Bernard Harkin."
2. Roderick Nash, "Wilderness Man in North America," in *Proceedings of a conference organized by the Canadian Parks and Wilderness Society and the University of Calgary, October 1968* (Calgary: The Canadian Parks and Wilderness Society and The University of Calgary, 1968), 66–93.
3. Ibid., R. Craig Brown, "The Doctrine of Usefulness: Natural Resource and National Park Policy in Canada, 1887–1914," 94–110. See also J.G. Nelson, ed., *Canadian Parks in Perspective* (Montreal: Harvest House, 1970), 46–63.
4. Janet Foster, *Working for Wildlife: The Beginning of Preservation in Canada* (Toronto & Buffalo: University of Toronto Press, 1978), jacket notes. It has been suggested that part of the reason for Foster's work was to refute Nash's contention that Canada seriously lagged the United States in conservation action.
5. Ibid., 13.
6. Ibid., 219.
7. A good source for understanding the focus of environmental history is *Consuming Canada: Readings in Environmental History* edited by Chad and Pam Gaffield. It brings together a number of articles concerning the theory and

method of the discipline and addresses numerous aspects of the topics of interest to its practitioners. In "Doing Environmental History," Donald Worster, a pioneer of environmental history in the United States, explained its principal goal as "deepening our understanding of how humans have been affected by their natural environment through time and, conversely, how they have affected that environment and with what results," or, in the vernacular, "the role and place of nature in human life." See Donald Worster, "Doing Environmental History," in Gaffield and Gaffield, ed. *Consuming Canada: Readings in Environmental History* (Toronto: Copp Clark Ltd., 1995), 18–19.

8. Leslie Bella, *Parks for Profit* (Montreal: Harvest House, 1987), 39–81.
9. Alan MacEachern, "Rationality and Rationalization in Canadian National Park Predator Policy," Gaffield and Gaffield, ibid., 197–212.
10. Alan MacEachern, *Natural Selections, National Parks in Atlantic Canada, 1935–1970* (Montreal and Kingston: McGill-Queen's University Press, 2001), 27–28.
11. Karl Jacoby, *Crimes Against Nature: Squatters, Poachers, Thieves, and the Hidden History of American Conservation* (Berkeley: University of California Press, 2001), 1–3.
12. Theodore Binnema, "'Let the Line be Drawn Now': Wilderness, Conservation, and the Exclusion of Aboriginal People from Banff National Park," *Environmental History*, October 2006; Tina Loo, *States of Nature: Conserving Canada's Wildlife in the Twentieth Century* (Vancouver: UBC Press, 2006).
13. John Sandlos, *Hunters at the Margin: Native People and Wildlife Conservation in the Northwest Territories* (Vancouver: UBC Press, 2007), 7–11.
14. Recently a respected Canadian institution has joined in this assessment of Harkin's contribution to Canada. The National Museum of Canada has unveiled a new exhibition entitled *Face to Face: The Canadian Personalities Hall*. Presenting background on twenty-seven "men and women whose ideas and contributions have transformed this country," Harkin appears with four others, including Samuel de Champlain and David Thompson, in the "We built" section: "We shaped Canada's landscapes: waterways, mountains, cities and countryside." Visit *www.civilization.ca/hist/biography/biographi200e.html*.

ONE

1. Although religion appears to have played no major part in Harkin's daily life, in official records he listed himself as Roman Catholic.
2. Library and Archives Canada (LAC), MG 26 A (Macdonald papers), Vol. 222, John Hamilton to The Right Honorable Sir John A. Macdonald, January 24, 1876 & May 31, 1877.
3. Ibid., Vol. 39, Wm. Harkin MD to Macdonald, April 12, 1878.
4. The terms "order-in-council" and "governor-in-council," used frequently in this work, refer to the process whereby administrative action is taken by the Privy Council (the prime minister and/or his cabinet) by advising the governor general to make an order to carry out the details of an act of Parliament.
5. Canada. House of Commons. *Debates*, May 3, 1887.

6. Harkin provided support to his mother and sister for the rest of their lives, and, according to his assistant, Mabel Williams, was entirely devoted to them.
7. *Ottawa Evening Journal*, June 24, 1896.
8. LAC, RG 10, Vol. 3052, To His Excellency the Governor General in Council from Superintendent General of Indian Affairs, December 5, 1901.
9. George Altmeyer, "Three Ideas of Nature in Canada, 1893–1914," *Journal of Canadian Studies*, 11, 3 (1976), 22.
10. Ibid., 22–24.
11. Ibid., 26.
12. Cited in Brown, "The Doctrine of Usefulness," 48.
13. Altmeyer, "Three Ideas of Nature in Canada," 28–30.
14. Ibid., 33.
15. Williams, "James Bernard Harkin."
16. David Hall, *Clifford Sifton, Vol. 2* (Vancouver: UBC Press, 1985), 146.
17. Ibid., 156.
18. Vol. 3052, Extract of a Report of a Committee of the Honourable the Privy Council approved by His Excellency on June 30, 1902. Through an administrative oversight, Harkin was not transferred from Indian Affairs to Interior until April 26, 1907 at a salary of $1,650 per annum.
19. The changing terminology with respect to preservation and conservation is difficult to follow. Originally used in conjunction with reference to the management of reservoirs and grazing in the western U.S., "conservation" had by the early twentieth century come to identify a movement for wise use of all natural resources. Later it was divided into two concepts—"utilitarian conservation" and "aesthetic conservation," with the latter incorporating the preservation idea—and the word "conservation" thereafter embodied both concepts. See Richard W. Sellars, *Preserving Nature in the National Parks* (New Haven: Yale University Press, 1997), 43.
20. Canada. Department of the Interior. *Annual Report for the Year Ending March 31, 1899*, Part V, Rocky Mountains Park, November 22, 1899, 4.
21. *Debates*, April 23, 1902, 3305.
22. Banff pioneer Pat Brewster in his book of reminiscences, *They Came West*, wrote: "I recall my uncle Jim remarking on several occasions that Frank Oliver, not socialistically inclined, suggested from time to time that large portions of our beautiful country be set aside for public use while the country was still young, and spaces were still available." F.O. Pat Brewster, *They Came West* (Banff: The Author, 1979), 23.
23. Cited in W. F. Lothian, *A History of Canada's National Parks*, 1 (Ottawa: Parks Canada, 1976), 32.
24. *Debates*, March 20, 1908, 5795.
25. WMCR, Lothian fonds, Fergus Lothian, "James Bernard Harkin, a brief biographical sketch," 3. Jennifer Brower, in her thesis "Buffalo National Park and the Second Demise of the Plains Bison in Canada, 1909–1940," argues that while acquisition of the Pablo herd was touted as the greatest preservation

effort of its day, it had much more to do with Canadian cultural considerations of the time centred around nationalistic fervour and the mythical status of the buffalo. See Jennifer Lynn Brower, "Buffalo National Park and the Second Demise of the Plains Bison in Canada, 1909–1940," Master's thesis, University of Alberta, 2004, 41–64.

26. George Woodcock and Ivan Avakumovic, *The Doukhobors* (Toronto: McClelland and Stewart, 1977), 208–28. While Mabel Williams recalled that this mission was to Mexico, a request from Cory to the Secretary of State for a letter of introduction for Harkin to the governor of British Honduras indicates his investigation may actually have been there rather than Mexico. See LAC, RG 6, Vol. 135, File 2084.
27. LAC, RG 76, Vol. 509, File 784040, W.D. Scott to J.B. Harkin, March 20, 1908. Harkin's brother William, whom he much admired, was then working for the *Vancouver Daily Province*. In 1912 he participated in a series of interviews with Sir Charles Tupper concerning his career and, after publishing them in his newspaper, was involved in helping turn them into a book when he died suddenly in September 1913. Two of his friends completed the task. The book appeared as *Political Reminiscences of The Right Honourable Sir Charles Tupper* (London: Constable & Co., 1914).
28. Ibid., April 1, 1908.
29. *Victoria Times*, "J.B. Harkin Will Supervise," August 10, 1909.
30. Vol. 509, Harkin to Mr. Oliver, March 3, 1910.
31. F.J. Thorpe, "Historical Perspective on the 'Resources for Tomorrow Conference'" (Ottawa: Department of Northern Affairs and National Resources, [1961]), 2–5.

TWO

1. David Hall, *Clifford Sifton, Vol. 2* (Vancouver: UBC Press, 1985), 54.
2. LAC, RG 84, Vol. 1960, U2, Memorandum to Deputy Minister from R.H. Campbell, December 4, 1907.
3. Canada. Department of the Interior. *Annual Report for the Fiscal Year ending March 31, 1908*, "Report of the Deputy Minister," x.
4. Vol. 1960, R.H. Campbell to W.W. Cory, February 20, 1908.
5. Ibid., H. Douglas to Campbell, May 10, 1909.
6. Canada. Canadian Commission of Conservation, *First Annual Report*, 1910, 7; *Second Annual Report*, 1911, 6.
7. *Debates*, April 28, 1911, 8085.
8. P.C. 1338, June 8, 1911.
9. Canada. Commission of Conservation, *Third Annual Report*, 1912, 67–69.
10. LAC, RG 84, Vol. 2166, W2–1, Campbell Memorandum, December 18, 1911. See Brown "The Doctrine of Usefulness" for a discussion of parks as developed tourist sites contributing to the goals of the national policy in this period.
11. Canada. Department of the Interior. *Annual Report for the Fiscal Year Ending March 31, 1912*, "Report of the Commissioner of Dominion Parks," 1.

12. J.B. Harkin. *The History and Meaning of the National Parks of Canada* (Saskatoon: H.R. Larson, 1957), 5.
13. Lothian, "James Bernard Harkin, a brief biographical sketch," 4. Although Douglas had been identified as Commissioner of Dominion Parks, the new Act formalized the position as head of a separate branch known as the Dominion Parks Branch.
14. See page 495 for a discussion of the possibility that this story was used to establish a "creation myth" for the Canadian park system.
15. "Report of the Commissioner of Dominion Parks," 1912, 4. The reason why Douglas was not himself appointed to the strengthened position is not clear but appears to have been related to his loss of influence in Ottawa because of his earlier resistance to the transfer of his position to Edmonton and to suspicion of his activities concerning land dealings in the parks. See LAC, MG 26 G, Vol. 55 (Laurier papers), 175094, Frank Oliver to Laurier, September 24, 1910 and Foster, 243, footnote 75. Despite this outcome, his important work on behalf of parks and wildlife over a career of fifteen years had been groundbreaking in Canada, and it provided a solid base upon which his successor would build.
16. WMCR, Vaux family fonds, Mary Schäffer to George Vaux, October 10, 1911.
17. Ibid., November 21, 30 and December 3, 1911.
18. Mabel Williams, *Guardians of the Wild* (London: Thomas Nelson, 1939), 2–3.
19. Ibid., 7.
20. J.B. Harkin, "Canada's National Parks," *Handbook of Canada* (Toronto: University of Toronto Press, 1924), 95.
21. Harkin, *History and Meaning*, 6–7. Mabel Williams later related "how much store he laid upon that moment in the Yellowstone Park when Hedges and his party sat around the campfire and discussed the future of the reserved region....Mr. Harkin thought there was something almost mystical in that vision that came to Hedges." Winks fonds, M. Williams to R. Winks, January 9, 1960.
22. Canada. Department of the Interior, *Annual Report for the Fiscal Year Ending March 31, 1913*, "Report of the Commissioner of Dominion Parks," 5.
23. Vol. 1960, J.B. Harkin to Cory, November 23, 1911.
24. Ibid., Byshe for Commissioner to H. Douglas, December 18, 1911.
25. Eleanor Luxton Historical Foundation (maintained at the Whyte Museum of the Canadian Rockies, Library and Archives), Luxton family fonds, Harkin to N. Luxton, June 8, 1912.
26. Ibid., Harkin to Luxton, n.d.
27. Ibid., Luxton to Harkin, n.d.
28. *Banff Crag and Canyon*, July 13, July 20 & August 10, 1912.
29. LAC, RG 84, Vol. 718, B17CP-5, Harkin to C.E.E. Ussher, May 6, 1912.
30. Ibid., A.B. Macdonald to Harkin and enclosure, June 12, 1912.
31. Ibid., F.H.H. Williamson to Harkin, September 4, 1912.
32. Ibid., Harkin to Cory, November 19, 1912.
33. *Canadian Alpine Journal*, 1912, 132.

34. J.B. Harkin, "Our Need for National Parks," *Canadian Alpine Journal*, 1918, 102–3. This article, written at the request of the club, underscores Harkin's understanding of the social reform movement at the beginning of the twentieth century. The ideas expressed in it mirrored many of those in his annual reports and became the foundation for much of his justification for the work of the Parks Branch.
35. Williams, *Guardians of the Wild*, 19.
36. "Report of the Commissioner of Dominion Parks," 1912, 9.
37. Work on the new Cave and Basin would soon prove to be expensive because of the need to support the whole building on 300 piles, causing Harkin to appeal for larger sums to complete the work. Not finished until December 1914, with its beautiful arches and belvederes and 150-foot concrete pool, the largest in Canada, it was hailed as an architectural masterpiece and immediately became popular with the public and indicative of the new branch's success.
38. *Banff Crag and Canyon*, September 14, 1917.

THREE

1. "Report of the Commissioner of Dominion Parks," 1912, 4.
2. Canada. Department of the Interior. *Annual Report for the Fiscal Year Ending March 31, 1914*, "Report of the Commissioner of Dominion Parks," 3. Within a few years, Harkin had developed his recreation philosophy of parks to the point that they not only served as locations for recreation, but also provided an example capable of instilling the need for recreation generally in the minds of Canadians. See Canada. Department of the Interior. *Annual Report for the Fiscal Year Ending March 31, 1918*, "Report of the Commissioner of Dominion Parks," 15–16.
3. "Report of the Commissioner of Dominion Parks," 1913, 5.
4. Harkin, *History and Meaning*, 8.
5. "Report of the Commissioner of Dominion Parks," 1912, 4.
6. Ibid., 6. The need for services and operations of a high quality became the basis for Harkin's belief that the Dominion government had to be responsible for all major activities in national parks and could not allow other levels of government to exercise significant powers.
7. Winks fonds, Williams to Winks, January 9, 1960.
8. Harkin, *History and Meaning*, 8–9. Although Harkin implied that Meighen had done this in the earliest days of the branch's efforts, it actually occurred in 1920 (see *Debates*, June 8, 1920, 3283). It is more likely that his strategy of sending a printed extract of his report to politicians and newspapermen led to the initial support for his increased budget appropriations and that these were later sustained by Meighen's support.
9. "Report of the Commissioner of Dominion Parks," 1913, 6.
10. Environmental historian Alan MacEachern thinks that Harkin's quoting of recognizable names associated with conservation in the United States such as Muir was done in the belief that his readers would recognize the American

"and because to quote him was to become identified with him." Alan MacEachern, *Natural Selections*, 30.

11. "Report of the Commissioner of Dominion Parks," 1914, 8.
12. Ibid., 9.
13. Ibid., 11. The interest expressed in underprivileged youth in this quote helps to explain Harkin's interest in the Boy Scout movement, meant to help address similar concerns.
14. LAC, RG 84, Vol. 103, U36, Memorandum to Mr. Harkin Re proposed Parks' policy by F.H.H.W.
15. Parks historian C.J. Taylor states that Deputy Commissioner Williamson was tasked with collecting sociological studies "showing scientific evidence of parks' importance as antidotes to some of the evils of modern life," that this research led to the discovery of the "playground movement" and that Harkin refined the arguments for urban playgrounds to apply to national parks. See WMCR, C.J. Taylor, "A History of National Parks Administration, Part One: The Harkin Era," unpublished manuscript, June 1989, [16]. Taylor also believes that Harkin was willing to use any and all arguments to support parks, a practice that sometimes led to ideas that did not jibe and created some difficulties in him squaring his position. C.J. Taylor, personal communication, August 2006.
16. LAC, RG 84, Vol. 45, BENNETT, R.B. Bennett to J.B. Harkin, July 17, 1914; Harkin to Bennett, July 22, 1914.
17. Ibid., Harkin to Bennett, March 20, 1916.
18. E.J. Hart, *The Brewster Story: From Packtrain to Tour Bus* (Banff: Brewster Transport, 1981), 53.
19. Unlike previous parks administrators who had worked closely with the CPR, Harkin sometimes expressed concern about being too cozy with the company. For example, in 1914 when Bennett conveyed the substance of some discussions with it about building a trail or road to the base of the Victoria Glacier at Lake Louise to improve tourist access, Harkin stated, "I hesitate about making any large expenditures in the vicinity of Lake Louise in case we might leave ourselves open to the charge of spending Parks' money for the exclusive benefit of the CPR company." Vol. 45, Harkin to Bennett, July 22, 1914.
20. "Report of the Commissioner of Dominion Parks," 1913, 8.
21. Ibid., 1914, 5.
22. Sellars, *Preserving Nature in the National Parks*, 10.
23. Hart, *The Brewster Story*, 52.
24. Sellars, *Preserving Nature in the National Parks*, 28.
25. Ibid., 33 and footnote 13, 300.
26. Vol. 1960, Harkin to Cory, May 7, 1912.
27. LAC, RG 84, Vol. 535, Harkin to F.K. Vreeland, June 5, 1916.
28. Cited in Lary M. Dilsaver, *America's National Park System: The Critical Documents* (Baltimore: Rowman and Littlefield Publishers, 1993), 51.
29. LAC, RG 84, Vol. 104, U60, F.H. Williamson to Harkin, December 19, 1912.

30. F.H.H. Williamson, "Roads in the Parks of the Dominion," *Good Roads Canada*, Vol. II, No. 1, 1.
31. F.H.H. Williamson, "Good Roads for Canada," *Good Roads Canada*, Vol. 1, No. 10, December 1913, 1 & 6.
32. The idea of a transcontinental highway had been first conceived by the Canadian Highway Association of Alberni, BC in 1911. For a history of early highway building in Canada and the role the Parks Branch played, see Daniel Francis, *A Road for Canada: The Illustrated Story of the Trans-Canada Highway* (North Vancouver, BC: Stanton, Arthur & Dos, 2006).
33. E. Alyn Michener, "The Development of Western Waters, 1885–1930" (Edmonton: Department of History, University of Alberta, 1973), 26.
34. Vol. 104, Memorandum of William Pearce, April 8, 1913.
35. Vol. 45, Bennett to Harkin, March 19, 1914; Harkin to Bennett, April 2, 1914.
36. Bella, *Parks for Profit*, 81.
37. Gavin Henderson, "The Father of Canadian National Parks," *Borealis*, Fall 1994, 30–31.
38. An examination of any one of the voluminous annual reports of the Department of the Interior will bear out the importance of revenue generation. For example, Deputy Minister Cory's noted in the opening sentences of his annual report of August 25, 1913, "Attention is called to the financial statements submitted, showing that the total cash revenue from all sources has increased during the year from $6,714,734 to $9,533, 945, an advance of almost $3,000,000. This revenue has increased about seven-fold in the last ten years." See "Report of the Deputy Minister," 1913, pp. xi-xiii.
39. Harkin, "Canada's National Parks," 98.
40. Harkin, *History and Meaning*, 9.
41. Vol. 45, Harkin to Bennett, October 8, 1914.
42. "Report of the Curator of Banff," 1914, 27.
43. [J.B. Harkin], *Just a Sprig of Mountain Heather* (Ottawa: Dominion Parks Branch, 1914), 8.
44. Ibid., 8–13.
45. *Toronto Globe*, August 14, 1914.
46. [Harkin], *Just a Sprig of Mountain Heather*, 16.

FOUR

1. "Report of the Commissioner of Dominion Parks," 1912, 6.
2. Ibid.
3. "Report of the Commissioner of Dominion Parks," 1911, 1–4.
4. Robert J. Burns, *Guardians of the Wild: A History of the Warden Service in Canada's National Parks* (Ottawa: Parks Canada, 1999), 33–34.
5. Ibid., 59.
6. Canada. Department of the Interior. *Annual Report for the Year Ending March 31, 1916*, "Report of the Commissioner of Dominion Parks," 7–8.
7. Canada. *Sixth Annual Report of the Commission of Conservation*, 1916, 102.

8. See Esther Fraser, *Wheeler* (Banff: Summerthought Ltd., 1978) for a biography of this important figure in the history of the Canadian Rockies.
9. Vol. 1960, A.O. Wheeler to W.W. Cory, April 15, 1912.
10. Ibid., Harkin to Cory, April 17, 1912.
11. Ibid.
12. Ibid., R.H. Campbell to Cory, April 24, 1912.
13. LAC, RG 84, Vol. 2167, W2–1A, "Waterton Lakes National Park—Park Property—Encroaching on a Game Preserve," 1912–1914.
14. Vol. 1960, Harkin to Cory, May 7, 1912.
15. Ibid.
16. Ibid.
17. Vol. 2167, H.R. Charlton to Cory, April 30, 1912; Harvey Fitzsimmonds to Hon. Robert Rogers, September 21, 1912. Fitzsimmonds's remarks referred to a proposed enlargement in the region of CN's Brazeau branch line in lieu of an enlargement to Jasper itself. This would become part of a new park being proposed by Harkin between the boundaries of Jasper and Rocky Mountains Park, tentatively to be known as "Bighorn." See Vol. 2167, Harkin to Cory, October 24, 1912.
18. University of Alberta Archives, William Pearce papers, W. Pearce to J.B. Harkin, April 1, 1913.
19. Vol. 1960, clipping, "Expand the National Park."
20. Vol. 45, Bennett to Harkin, March 16 & April 2, 1914; Harkin to Bennett, March 21, 1914.
21. LAC, RG 84, Vol. 35, U300, "Memorandum to Hon. W.J. Roche," November 18, 1913.
22. Vol. 2167, Cory to Roche, November 20, 1913.
23. Ibid., draft of P.C. 2863.
24. Ibid., Maxwell Graham to Harkin, December 5, 1913.
25. Ibid., Harkin to Cory, December 5, 1913.
26. Ibid., Cory to Campbell, April 29, 1914. In this letter Cory goes on to say, "Under the circumstances, I think that steps should be taken to rescind the Order in Council of the 18th November last establishing a game preserve within the Rocky Mountains Forest Reserve." Apparently he was referring to the draft order-in-council Campbell had presented, as there is no record of it having been adopted by governor-in-council. In any event, Cory's decision to come down on the side of parks expansion under the Parks Branch instead of game preserve creation under Forestry would be the key to both the enlargement of the existing parks and his later decision to give all Canadian wildlife management responsibilities to Harkin's branch.
27. Ibid., Campbell to Cory, May 2, 1914.
28. LAC, RG 84, Vol. 1955, U1, Harkin to Cory, February 22, 1913.
29. Canada. Dominion Forest Reserves and Parks Act, 1–2 Geo. V, c. 10 and amendment 3–4 Geo. V, c. 18.
30. Vol. 1955, Campbell to Roche, December 9, 1914.

31. W.N. Millar, *Game Preservation in the Rocky Mountains Forest Reserve* (Ottawa: Department of the Interior, 1915), Forestry Branch Bulletin No. 51. Millar's report was the most comprehensive of its time on game populations and conditions in the front ranges of the Rockies.
32. Vol. 35, Campbell to Cory, December 18, 1914 enclosing "Extract from the Report of The Forester, United States Department of Agriculture, Washington, September 23, 1914 on Game Preservation."
33. Ibid.
34. LAC, RG 84, Vol. 7, R300, Harkin to Cory, May 3, 1915.
35. Millar, *Game Preservation*, 18–19.
36. See George Colpitts, *Game in the Garden* (Vancouver: UBC Press, 2002), 98–100.
37. In a presentation at the National Conference on Game and Wild Life Conservation in 1919, Duncan Campbell Scott, in speaking to complaints from provincial delegates about native hunting practices, stated, "On the whole, it may be said that the Indian obeys the hunting and fishing regulations as well as the white man. The Indian, who has to maintain himself on the hunting grounds by killing animals for food, is entitled to a measure of sympathy...." Duncan Campbell Scott, "Relation of Indians to Wild Life Conservation," *Proceedings of National Conference on Conservation of Game, Fur-Bearing Animals and Other Wildlife* (Ottawa: Commission of Conservation, 1919), 21.
38. LAC, RG 84, Vol. 654, B2–1, "Report on Proposed Extensions and Reductions in the Rocky Mountains Park, for Game Preservation and Park Purposes, Respectively," December 1, 1916.
39. Ibid., Harkin to T. Rothwell, April 19, 1917.
40. P.C. 2594, September 18, 1917.
41. Vol. 45, Harkin to Bennett, March 14, 1916.
42. *Banff Crag and Canyon*, July 24, 1915.
43. Vol. 35, Harkin to H. Douglas, January 30, 1912; Harkin to Superintendent, Yellowstone National Park, March 8, 1912.
44. Ibid., Harkin to A.E. Fisher, February 7, 1913.
45. Ibid., S.A. Griffith, Oneida Community, Ltd. to Harkin, March 27, 1913.
46. The evolving nature of the Parks Branch structure at this early date is attested to by Graham sometimes signing himself as head of the Animal and Zoological Division and sometimes simply as head of the Animal Division, with the latter becoming the accepted terminology until changed to the Wildlife Division in the early 1920s.
47. Vol. 35, Memorandum to Mr. Harkin, August 3, 1912.
48. Cited in Foster, *Working for Wildlife*, 98.
49. Vol. 7, Knechtel to Harkin, February 1, 1915.
50. James B. Trefethen, *An American Crusade for Wildlife* (New York: Winchester Press and the Boone and Crockett Club, 1975), 177.
51. William T. Hornaday, *Our Vanishing Wild Life* (New York: Charles Scribner's Sons, 1913), ix, 351–52. Hornaday's experience with Canada and its game laws was limited, mainly coming from a 1905 trip to southeastern British Columbia

to hunt mountain goat with John Phillips, Pennsylvania state game commissioner. In his 1906 book on the trip, he stated, "The perpetual preservation of the grand game of the grand mountain land just beyond our northern boundary is of interest to every American sportsman...." See William T. Hornaday, *Camp-Fires in the Canadian Rockies* (New York: Charles Scribner's Sons, 1906), 9.

52. Vol. 7, Harkin to W.T. Hornaday, March 4, 1913.
53. Superintendent J.G. "Kootenai" Brown at Waterton, after reading *Our Vanishing Wild Life*, wrote Harkin and indicated that he had been most impressed by Hornaday's words "the wild things of Earth are not ours, to do with as we please. They have been given to us in trust, and we must account for them to the generations which will come after us and audit our accounts." See Vol. 2167, John George Brown to Harkin, June 1, 1913.
54. "Report of the Commissioner of Dominion Parks," 1912, 6.
55. Canada. Department of the Interior. *Annual Report for the Fiscal Year Ending March 31, 1915*, "Report of the Commissioner of Dominion Parks," 7.

FIVE

1. Vol. 45, Bennett to Harkin, September 11 & 22, 1914.
2. Ibid., Harkin to Bennett, December 1, 1914.
3. *Canada Gazette*, October 31, 1914.
4. W.A. Waiser, *Park Prisoners: The Untold Story of Western Canada's National Parks, 1915–46* (Saskatoon: Fifth House, 1995), 8.
5. "Report of the Commissioner of Dominion Parks," 1916, 11.
6. Vol. 45, Williamson to Harkin, May 19 & 20, 1915.
7. Ibid., Bennett to Harkin, May 24, 1915.
8. Waiser, *Park Prisoners*, 15.
9. Lothian, *A History of Canada's National Parks*, 1, 55–56.
10. Vol. 104, Wardle to Harkin, August 5, 1915.
11. *Revelstoke Mail Herald*, July 17, 1915.
12. Ibid., July 31, 1915.
13. LAC, RG 84, Vol. 190, MR176, Harkin to Williamson, September 17, 1915.
14. Ibid., Harkin to Otter, September 28, 1915.
15. *Revelstoke Mail Herald*, July 31, 1915.
16. Vol. 45, Harkin to Bennett, March 20, 1916.
17. *Banff Crag and Canyon*, January 15, 1916.
18. Vol. 45, Harkin to Bennett, March 20, 1916.
19. Ibid., Harkin to Bennett, May 2, 1916.
20. Waiser, *Park Prisoners*, 34–35. The parks camps accounted for about 10 per cent of the internees in the country.
21. "Report of the Commissioner of Dominion Parks, J.B. Harkin," 1918, 6.
22. E.J. Hart, *Golf on the Roof of the World* (Banff: EJH Literary Enterprises, 1999), 20–22.
23. "Report of Superintendent of Rocky Mountains Park," 1917, 16.
24. Hart, *Golf on the Roof*, 24.

25. Ibid., 38–40.
26. LAC, RG 84, Vol. 631, K2, R. Bruce to Harkin, June 22, 1922.
27. Ibid., Harkin to Bruce, May 23, 1916; Roche to Bruce & Roche to Bowser, May 23, 1916.
28. Ibid., Harkin to Cory, June 10, 1916.
29. Ibid., Harkin to J. Black, July 4, 1916.
30. Ibid., Harkin to Cory, December 27, 1916.
31. Ibid., Harkin to Cory, October 18, 1917.
32. "Report of the Commissioner of Dominion Parks," 1913, 11.
33. William Russell, "James Bernard Harkin (1875–1955)," National and Historic Parks Branch, Manuscript Report Number 216, Miscellaneous Research Reports, 112.
34. Cited in C.J. Taylor, *Negotiating the Past: The Making of Canada's National Historic Parks and Sites* (Montreal and Kingston: McGill-Queen's University Press, 1990), 29–30.
35. LAC, RG 84, Vol. 1965, U2-13-1, M. Peters to Harkin, September 22, 1913.
36. Ibid., Cory to S. Hughes, November 28, 1913; Harkin to J. Mitchell, December 6, 1913.
37. Ibid., Certified copy of the Report of the Committee of the Privy Council approved by His Royal Highness the Governor General on 30 March 1914.
38. Ibid., Harkin to Harries, (n.d.).
39. LAC, RG 84, Vol. 1041, FA2, Harkin to Mitchell, February 2, 1916.
40. Ibid., Williamson to Harkin, December 12, 1916.

SIX

1. P.C. 646, March 27, 1913.
2. Sandlos, *Hunters at the Margin*, 26–31.
3. Foster, *Working for Wildlife*, 110–11.
4. Cited in Foster, *Working for Wildlife*, 116.
5. Ibid., 112.
6. In *Hunters at the Margin*, John Sandlos identifies Graham's great influence in the establishment of a federal wood bison preserve: "Graham's compelling and forceful personality dominates the early history of Wood Buffalo Park: no other individual shaped the early policies and local ecology of the park region to the same degree." On the other hand, he abhors his lack of respect for local and native rights: "The most conspicuous theme in Graham's writings on the wood bison preserve was a profound antilocal sentiment that denied any parochial claim of an inherent right to access local resources." Sandlos, 34, 37.
7. F.H.H. Williamson, "Game Preservation in Dominion Parks," *Proceedings at a Meeting of the Committee on Fisheries, Game and Fur-Bearing Animals, November 1 and 2, 1915* (Ottawa: Commission of Conservation, 1916), 132.
8. LAC, RG 84, Vol. 74, Seton/Graham report, May 10 & June 10, 1914.
9. W.F. Lothian, *A History of Canada's National Parks*, 4 (Ottawa: Parks Canada, 1981), 22, 24.

10. LAC, RG 84, Vol. 1699, N2, Harkin to Cory, February 26, 1915.
11. Ibid., Graham to Harkin, March 20, 1915.
12. Ibid., Graham to Harkin, March 20, 1915 (second letter).
13. Ibid., Graham to Harkin, March 20, 1915 .
14. *Lethbridge Herald*, March 26, 1915.
15. Vol. 1699, Harkin to Cory, March 30 & March 31, 1915.
16. Ibid., Nelson to Dominion Land Agent, April 1, 1915; Harkin to Mitchell, April 7, 1915. This provides a concrete example of how Harkin took the work and expertise of his staff and "sold" it to more senior government officials, resulting in an important conservation achievement.
17. Ibid., Graham to Harkin, April 19, 1915; Harkin to Graham, April 27, 1915.
18. *Lethbridge Telegram*, April 29, 1915.
19. Vol. 1699, Graham to Harkin, May 27, 1915.
20. Ibid., Graham to Dominion Land Agent Cuttle, June 24, 1915.
21. Ibid., Harkin to Cory, December 13, 1915.
22. Cited in Foster, *Working for Wildlife*, 103.
23. Vol. 1699, Harkin to McHugh, October 26, 1920.
24. J.W. Jones, "Fur Farming in Canada," *Annual Report of the Commission of Conservation for 1913* (Ottawa: Commission of Conservation, 1913), 42–48. For a full description of the branch's involvement in the migratory bird field see Foster, Chapter 6, "Protecting an International Resource."
25. "Report of the Commissioner of Dominion Parks," 1913, 13.
26. *Proceedings at a Meeting of the Committee of Fisheries, Game and Fur Bearing Animals, November 1 and 2, 1915*, 138.
27. Cited in Foster, *Working for Wildlife*, 141.
28. Canada. Department of the Interior. *Annual Report for the Year Ending March 31, 1918*, "Report of the Deputy Minister," 28–29. Elizabeth Hewitt, in the foreword to her late husband's book *The Conservation of the Wild Life of Canada* published in 1921, commented on the co-operation of those involved with him in his work: "Indeed, the relation that existed between my husband and his associates was like that which animates a group of friends, where each one gives the best that is in him and looks to the best in others—a bright record in Civil Service history of loyalty and disinterestedness." C. Gordon Hewitt, *The Conservation of the Wildlife of Canada* (New York: Charles Scribner's Sons, 1921), v.
29. C.H.D. Clarke, "In Memoriam, Hoyes Lloyd," *Auk*, Vol. 96, No. 2, 1978, 204–06.
30. LAC, RG 84, Vol. 1700, P2, "Recommendation for the Creation of Three New National Parks in Canada," [1915], 1.
31. Canada. Department of the Interior. *Annual Report of the Department of the Interior for the Year Ending March 31, 1920*, "Report of the Commissioner of Dominion Parks, J.B. Harkin," 8.
32. Lothian, *A History of Canada's National Parks*, 4, 55.
33. Vol. 1700, "Recommendation for the Creation of Three New National Parks in Canada," 3.

34. Ibid., Hewitt to Harkin, May 22, 1917.
35. Ibid., Harkin to Hewitt, May 25, 1917.
36. Ibid., Hewitt to Harkin, February 15, 1918.
37. P.C. 1264, May 29, 1918.
38. LAC, RG 84, Vol. 68, R234, C.D. Walcott to H. Sibbald, October 9, 1916; ibid., Sibbald to Clarke, October 16, 1916. Walcott was the discoverer of the Burgess Shale in Yoho National Park, now a World Heritage Site.
39. Ibid., Memorandum to Cory, October 26, 1916 and notations.
40. Ibid., Walcott to Harkin, November 28, 1916.
41. Ibid., Harkin to Hornaday, July 9, 1917; Memorandum to Mr. Harkin from [Maxwell Graham] and notation, August 7, 1917; Hornaday to Harkin, August 9, 1917; E.W. Nelson to Harkin, August 23, 1917; C.A. Lindsley to Harkin, August 24, 1917.
42. Ibid., Harkin to Superintendent, September 6, 1918.
43. Ibid., Harkin to Walcott, December 27, 1919.
44. Ibid., S.T. Mather to Harkin, January 22, 1920; Harkin to Walcott, February 5, 1920.

SEVEN

1. Cited in R.M. Dawson, *The Civil Service of Canada* (London, 1929), 233.
2. Cited in J.L. Granatstein, *The Ottawa Men: The Civil Service Mandarins, 1935–1957* (Toronto: Oxford University Press, 1982), 23.
3. Luxton family fonds, Harkin to Luxton, June 8, 1912.
4. Vol. 7, Harkin to Cory, December 30, 1914 & January 13, 1915.
5. Vol. 45, Harkin to Bennett, July 15, 1914.
6. Harrison Lewis, "Lively: A History of the Canadian Wildlife Service," unpublished manuscript, 1976. While Harkin seems to have been friendly and approachable with those at headquarters, he apparently did not socialize with them outside its confines. Mabel Williams, one of his closest associates, many years later recalled, "I never knew much about his private life. Outside the office we never met. He had different friends and different tastes and our paths never crossed." Winks fonds, Williams to Winks, May 16, 1960.
7. Cited in Granatstein, *The Ottawa Men*, 22–23.
8. Vol. 45, Harkin to Bennett, June 13, 1912.
9. Ibid., Harkin to Bennett, September 26, 1912.
10. The booklet *50 Switzerlands in One, Banff the Beautiful: Canada's National Park* issued by the Banff Board of Trade at this time clearly indicated the real situation with respect to park's administration. In the section "Parks of Western Canada," while noting that Barnard-Hervey was the chief superintendent of Dominion Parks with headquarters at Edmonton, it stated, "J.B. Harkin is Commissioner of Dominion Parks with headquarters at Ottawa. All park business goes through his office." C.J. Taylor believes that the growing number of professionals in the headquarters staff provided it with a greater central planning capability so that the chief superintendent's position

became redundant. See Taylor, "A History of National Parks Administration, Part One: The Harkin Era," [16].

11. LAC, RG 84, Vol. 219, R 174–1, Harkin to Cory, March 23, 1913.
12. Vol. 45, R. Alford to Bennett, February 7 1913.
13. Ibid., Bennett to Harkin, February 14, 1913.
14. Ibid., Bennett to Harkin, September 24, 1913; Harkin to Bennett, July 20, 1914.
15. Ibid., Harkin to Bennett, January 27 & March 26, 1914.
16. Ibid., Harkin to Bennett, July 24, 1914.
17. Ibid., Bennett to Harkin, July 23, 1914.
18. *Banff Crag and Canyon*, June 8, 1918.
19. Great Plains Research Consultants, *Jasper National Park, 1792–1965: A History* (Ottawa: Parks Canada, 1984), 219.
20. "Report of the Superintendent of Jasper Park," April 1, 1914, 63–65.
21. "Report of the Commissioner of Dominion Parks," April 1, 1914, 9.
22. *Edmonton Journal*, June 10, 1914.
23. Sir Arthur Conan Doyle, *Memories and Adventures* (Boston: Little Brown, 1924), 298. In their *Description of & Guide to Jasper Park*, published by the Department of the Interior in 1917, surveyor Bridgland and fellow author Robert Douglas of the Canadian Geographic Board reproduced "The Athabaska Trail."
24. "Report of the Superintendent of Jasper Park," April 1, 1914, 68.
25. "Report of the Superintendent of Jasper Park," 1922, 127.
26. Ian L. Getty, "The History of Waterton Lakes National Park, 1800–1937," a research paper prepared for the National Historic Parks Branch, 1971, 73–74.
27. Ibid., 76.
28. Vol. 103, S. Carpenter to Harkin, April 10, 1916 (extract).
29. Ibid., J.T. Mathews, Steamboat Inspector, to T.R. Ferguson, Chairman of the Board of Steamship Inspections, May 7, 1916.
30. Ibid., Harkin to R. Cooper, May 22 & June 20, 1916.
31. Cited in Getty, "History of Waterton Lakes National Park," 77.
32. Ibid., 77–80.
33. *Banff Crag and Canyon*, June 27, 1914.
34. Vol. 7, Harkin to Clarke, July 8, 1914; Clarke to Harkin, July 15, 1914.
35. Cited in Getty, "History of Waterton Lakes National Park," 69.
36. Ibid., 70.
37. Vol. 45, Bennett to Harkin, April 8, 1914; Harkin to Bennett, April 18 & September 16, 1914.
38. Federal Records Centre (Edmonton), RG 84, E 1985, S1–52, Peyto Personnel File, Ref. # 166.
39. Vol. 45, Harkin to Bennett, August 27 & September 19, 1913; Bennett to Harkin, September 24, 1913.
40. Ibid., Harkin to Bennett, July 14, 1914; Bennett to Harkin, July 24, 1914.
41. Ibid., Harkin to Bennett, February 24 & March 6, 1915; Bennett to Harkin February 26, 1915.
42. Luxton family fonds, Bennett to Luxton, May 25, 1915.

43. Ibid., Harkin to Luxton, June 8, 1912.
44. Vol. 45, Bennett to Harkin, March 31 & April 3, 1916; Harkin to Bennett, April 7 & April 17, 1916; Bennett to Roche, April 3 & May 8, 1916.
45. Ibid., Dyer to Bennett, January 22, 1917; Bennett to Harkin, January 27 & February 13, 1917; Harkin to Bennett, February 5, 1917.
46. *Banff Crag and Canyon*, November 10, 1917.
47. Ibid., June 29, 1918.

EIGHT

1. J.B. Harkin, "Canadian National Parks and Playgrounds," *Annual Report of the Historic Landmarks Association of Canada*, 1921, 37.
2. Canada. Department of the Interior. *Annual Report for the Fiscal Year Ended March 31, 1919*, "Report of the Commissioner, J.B. Harkin," 4.
3. Cited in Taylor, *Negotiating the Past*, 36.
4. Vol. 1631, Memo: Deputy Minister, February 4, 1918.
5. Ibid., "An Act to amend the 'Banff-Windermere Road Act' passed Third Reading on April 22, 1918."
6. Ibid., "Memorandum of Agreement," [January 25, 1919].
7. Ibid., Harkin to Johnson, March 15, 1919.
8. Ibid., Harkin to Johnson, March 12, 1919.
9. Ibid., S. Bonnell to Harkin, April 7, 1921.
10. *Banff Crag and Canyon*, June 21, 1913.
11. Vol. 45, Harkin to Bennett, January 28, 1914.
12. Ibid., Harkin to Bennett, May 22, 1914. *Banff Crag and Canyon*, May 29, 1915.
13. *Banff Crag and Canyon*, May 29, 1915.
14. Luxton family fonds, Luxton to Harkin, April 9, 1914.
15. Ibid., December 23, 1916.
16. Ibid., Luxton to Bennett, February 4, 1917; Bennett to Luxton, February 13, 1917.
17. *Banff Crag and Canyon*, February 2, 1918.
18. Ibid., September 17, 1918.
19. Ibid., October 28, 1918.
20. Ibid., September 4, 1920.
21. Ibid., July 8, 1922.
22. Canada. Department of the Interior. *Annual Report for the Fiscal Year Ended March 31, 1914*, "Report of Proposed Artistic Lay-Out of Banff," by Thos. H. Mawson, 73–79.
23. See A.F.J. Artibise and G.A. Stelter, "Conservation Planning and Urban Planning: The Canadian Commission of Conservation in Historical Perspective," *Consuming Canada: Readings in Environmental History*, edited by Chad and Pam Gaffield (Toronto: Copp Clark Ltd., 1995), 154–55 for a discussion of early twentieth-century Canadian urban planning.
24. Ibid., 158–59.
25. Edward Mills, *Rustic Building Programs in Canada's National Parks, 1887–1950* (Ottawa: Parks Canada, 1994), 47–48.

26. Canada. Department of the Interior, *Annual Report for the Fiscal Year Ended March 31, 1922*, "Report of the Commissioner, J.B. Harkin," 103; "Report of the Commissioner, J.B. Harkin," 1923, 73.
27. Canada. Department of the Interior, *Annual Report for the Fiscal Year Ended March 31, 1924*, "Report of the Commissioner, J.B. Harkin," 69.
28. Vol. 104, J.A. Stephen to Harkin, May 10, 1919; Harkin to Stephen, May 14, 1919.
29. Ibid., J.M. Wardle to Cory, March 30, 1922.
30. Canada. Department of the Interior. *Annual Report for the Fiscal Year Ended March 31, 1921*, "Report of the Commissioner, J.B. Harkin," 2.
31. Vol. 104, J.W. Davidson to Harkin, September 8, 1919 & July 24, 1920.
32. "Report of the Commissioner, J.B. Harkin," 1921, p. 5.
33. Vol. 104, "National Parks Address: J.B. Harkin, Commissioner, Canadian National Parks, Department of the Interior, Ottawa, Ontario," [June 10, 1922].
34. Ibid.
35. "Report of the Commissioner of Dominion Parks," 1919, 7.
36. M.B. Williams, *Through the Heart of the Rockies & Selkirks*, "Foreword" by J.B. Harkin (Ottawa: Minister of the Interior, 1921).
37. Vol. 1955, Parks Act citation. For a fuller description of Harkin's efforts to get a new park bill approved, see Chapters 11 and 13.
38. Vol. 631, Bruce to Harkin, June 22, 1922.
39. LAC, RG 84, Vol. 169, U109–25, Harkin to D. McCowan, December 15, 1922.
40. Ibid., A.B. MacKay to Harkin, April 6, 1923.
41. "Report of the Commissioner, J.B. Harkin," 1924, 65–66.
42. *Banff Crag and Canyon*, July 5, 1923.
43. LAC, RG 84, Vol. 217, R60–6, Harkin to T. Wilson, July 2, 1923.
44. Ibid., J. Davidson to Harkin, July 20, 1920.
45. Ibid., Harkin to H.F. Bird, March 19, 1920.
46. Ibid., Harkin to Cory, March 20, 1920.
47. Canada. Department of the Interior. *Annual Report for the Fiscal Year Ended March 31, 1923*, "Report of the Commissioner, J.B. Harkin," 73. It is important to note that while Harkin supported campgrounds in major park tourist centres and along parks highways, he was opposed to campgrounds being placed beside park lakes. In 1926, in a letter to the Yoho and Glacier superintendent, while acknowledging that "most motor tourists would no doubt like to camp at Emerald Lake," he stated, "It is felt that scenic points such as Emerald Lake, Lake Louise, Moraine Lake, Cavell Lake etc., should be kept as far as possible in their natural state of beauty and that motor tourist camps on the shores of such lakes would be most objectionable." This policy would have profound implications for the preservation of riparian habitats in the mountain national parks. See Vol. 103, Harkin to The Superintendent, Yoho and Glacier Parks, January 5, 1926.
48. Canada. Department of the Interior. *Annual Report for the Fiscal Year Ended March 31, 1925*, "Report of the Commissioner, J.B. Harkin," 90.

NINE

1. Vol. 45, Harkin to Bennett, April 11, 1914.
2. Ibid., June 26, 1914.
3. *Banff Crag and Canyon*, October 7, 1916.
4. Nora Findlay, *Jasper: A Backward Glance at People, Places and Progress* (Jasper: Parks and People, 1992), 141–42.
5. Getty, *A History of Waterton Lakes National Park*, 51–52.
6. Ibid., 51–53.
7. Luxton family fonds, Harkin to Luxton, October 5, 1927.
8. Michener, "Western Waters," 271.
9. Ibid., 325–26.
10. "Report of the Commissioner of Dominion Parks, J.B. Harkin," 1921, 14.
11. Cited in Getty, "History of Waterton Lakes National Park," 119.
12. Ibid., 123.
13. Ibid., 118.
14. Sellars, *Preserving Nature in the National Parks*, 59.
15. Cited in PearlAnn Reichwein, "Beyond the Visionary Mountains," PhD thesis, Carleton University, 1995, 230.
16. LAC, RG 84, Vol. 102, U136–1, Wheeler to ACC members, January 1, 1922.
17. Ibid., Harkin to Wheeler, February 16, 1922.
18. Ibid., Harkin to Cory, March 23, 1922.
19. Ibid., Wheeler to Harkin, March 20, 1922. For a detailed description of Wheeler's and the Alpine Club's involvement in support of the Parks Branch in the struggle over parks waters, see PearlAnn Reichwein, "'Hands Off Our National Parks': The Alpine Club of Canada and Hydro-development Controversies in the Canadian Rockies, 1922–1930," *Journal of the Canadian Historical Association*, Vol. 6, New series, 1995, 129–55.
20. Vol. 102, Wheeler to Harkin, January 23, 1922.
21. Ibid., Harkin to Wheeler, April 6, 1922.
22. Alpine Club of Canada *Gazette*, December 1922, 13, 17–18.
23. Cited in Getty, "History of Waterton Lakes National Park," 121.
24. Cited in Christopher Armstrong and H.V. Nelles, "Competition vs. Convenience: Federal Administration of Bow River Waterpowers, 1906–1913," *The Canadian West*, Henry Klassen, ed. (Calgary: University of Calgary Press, 1976), 176. This paper provides the full background of Aitken's and Bennett's early involvement with Calgary Power.
25. LAC, RG 84, Vol. 491, R39–5, P.M. Sauder to Campbell, February 6, 1911.
26. "Report of the Commissioner of Dominion Parks," 1912, 8–9.
27. Vol. 491, Drury to Director, Water Powers Branch, January 28, 1921.
28. Ibid., Williamson to Harkin, February 4, 1921.
29. Ibid., G.A. Gaherty to Minister of the Interior, August 21, 1921.
30. Ibid., Wardle to Harkin, January 10, 1922.
31. Ibid., Harkin to Challies, February 13, 1922.
32. *Calgary Daily Herald*, July 28, 1922.

33. Ibid., July 29, 1922.
34. Vol. 491, Montreal Engineering to Minister of the Interior, July 31, 1922.
35. WMCR, Banff Citizens' Association Minutes, September 17, 1922.
36. Vol. 491, Harkin to Cory, October 7, 1922; Reichwein, "Beyond the Visionary Mountains," 239.
37. Cited in Great Plains Research, *Jasper National Park, 1792–1965: A History*, 175.
38. University of Alberta Archives, William Pearce papers, W. Pearce to Bennett, May 12, 1923.
39. Ibid., Pearce to C. Magrath, May 14, 1923.
40. Ibid., Wheeler to Pearce, May 18, 1923.
41. Alpine Club of Canada *Gazette*, June 1923, 4–5.
42. Ibid., December 1923, 22.
43. Vol. 45, Harkin to Bennett, April 11, 1914.
44. Vol. 217, Harkin to T. Wilson, July 2, 1923.

TEN

1. J. Alexander Burnett, *A Passion for Wildlife: The History of the Canadian Wildlife Service* (Vancouver: UBC Press, 2005), 14.
2. Foster, *Working for Wildlife*, 201.
3. Canada. Commission of Conservation. *National Conference on Conservation of Game, Fur-Bearing Animals and Other Wildlife*, February 18 & 19, 1919, 50. In an article published in *Rod and Gun* in October 1919, Harkin reiterated the points in this address and summed up his position on sanctuaries by stating, "Sanctuaries do result in a very great increase in wild life and these results are obtained primarily through the following courses:—that the animals themselves recognize and take advantage of sanctuaries; that the public, including Indians, can be very readily educated as to the sanctity of sanctuaries; and that energetic, fearless and unrelenting pursuit of offenders, together with intelligent patrol work and the insistence of sealing firearms practically eliminates any destruction of wild life within sanctuary areas." J.B. Harkin, "Wild Life Sanctuaries," *Rod and Gun*, Vol. XXI, No. 5, October 1919, 570.
4. Thorpe, "Historical Perspective," 6; Foster, *Working for Wildlife*, 209–14.
5. Cited in Foster, *Working for Wildlife*, 219.
6. See John Sandlos's *Hunters at the Margin* for a description of how Canadian conservationists were motivated by a belief that northern wildlife could be managed and developed like an agricultural resource to spur economic development so that the North could realize its potential in Canada and how, in the process, native peoples were dispossessed of their hunting rights.
7. LAC, MG 26 H, Vol. 187 (Borden papers), A. Meighen to R. Borden, August 23, 1914.
8. "Report of the Commissioner of Dominion Parks," 1915, 7.
9. "Report of the Commissioner of Dominion Parks, J.B. Harkin," 1919, 8.
10. John Sandlos believes that Harkin's service on this commission is part of the evidence that shows he and his peers were "pragmatic bureaucrats rather than

visionaries," and "demonstrate that wildlife policy in the North was based on the rational production orthodoxy of the American progressives." See Sandlos, *Hunters at the Margin*, 233–34.

11. Cited in Morris Zaslow, *The Northern Expansion of Canada* (Toronto: McClelland and Stewart, 1988), 13.
12. See Sandlos, *Hunters at the Margin*, 122–25 for a view of Harkin's involvement in sovereignty matters that focuses more on its conservation aspects.
13. R. Diubaldo, "Wrangling over Wrangel Island," *Canadian Historical Review*, Vol. 48, No. 3, September 1967, 204.
14. LAC, MG 30, E169 (R2033-0-7-E), Harkin Papers, Vol. 2.
15. Ibid., Stefansson to H.L. Keenleyside, November 3, 1949 ; Vilhjalmur Stefansson, *Discovery: The Autobiography of Vilhjalmur Stefansson* (New York: McGraw-Hill, 1964), 232. Loring Christie was officially legal advisor to the Department of External Affairs but was also one of Borden's most trusted advisors; G.J. Desbarats was deputy director of the Naval Services Department to whom Stefansson reported when carrying out government work. Both men were fellow members with Harkin on the Advisory Technical Board, and the files to which Stefansson referred were compiled by Harkin for it.
16. Cited in Diubaldo, "Wrangling Over Wrangel Island," 204.
17. Cited in Russell, "James Bernard Harkin," 208.
18. Stefansson, *Discovery*, 239.
19. All of the files in the Meighen papers concerning this matter were marked "secret," and Harkin, as one who strictly followed bureaucratic rules, obviously felt that this restriction did not end after the fact.
20. LAC, RG 84, Vol. 2226, WB2, Harkin to A.O. Seymour, May 23, 1923.
21. In writing Cory in January 1912 about possible cross-breeding, Harkin stated the "Department sooner or later [would] be subject to criticism if it takes no steps on these lines but simply maintains the buffalo for show purposes." LAC, RG 84, Vol. 52, BU233, Harkin to Cory, January 27, 1912.
22. Brower indicates that while there was no controversy surrounding having the cross-breeding experiments carried out at Wainwright, there was realization that there was risk of disease and contends that it played a role in the spread of TB. She states that the experiments were carried out only to prove that the buffalo herd could be made useful and that they showed "the blatant disregard officials displayed for the protection of the species." Brower, "Buffalo National Park," 162–63, 186.
23. Vol. 35, "Federal Game Activity in Canada" [1922].
24. Ibid.
25. Lothian, *A History of Canada's National Parks*, 4, 32–33.
26. Ibid.
27. Vol. 52, Harkin to C.C. Moncrieff, December 15, 1922.
28. Ibid., Sibbald to Harkin, January 17, 1923.
29. Ibid., Harkin to Sibbald, January 23, 1923.
30. Ibid., Memorandum to Cory, November 22, 1923.

31. Ibid., C. Stewart to F.E. Leushner, November 24, 1923.
32. Ibid., Harkin to Smith, April 10, 1924. By the time Nagle joined the branch, he was part of what was being referred to as the Wildlife Division, a combination of the old Animal Division, Wild Life Protection and the Migratory Birds Section, headed by Lloyd. Although he became an important figure as assistant to Lloyd, I have been unable to discover any biographical data on him.
33. LAC, RG 84, Vol. 58, BU299–2, Harkin to Cory, May 23, 1923.
34. Vol. 52, Lloyd to Harkin, April 22, 1924.
35. Ibid., "Further Utilization of the Wood Buffalo Park near Fort Smith, N.W.T. for the Conservation of Canada's Buffalo," October 2, 1924. Harkin clearly supported this position, as he had been privy to Camsell's 1916 reports through Hewitt, who was vitally interested in this matter for inclusion in his book. See Hewitt, *The Conservation of the Wild Life of Canada*, 129.
36. Lewis, "Lively,“ 112.
37. Vol. 52, Harkin to E. Seymour, American Bison Society, April 2, 1925. Hornaday had already expressed his objections to the move in a letter to Harper a month earlier when he learned the herd was diseased, but, likely with an eye to his important conservation relationships with Harkin and other Canadian officials, stated that he felt that there was nothing that could be done without seeming to be interfering. Vol. 58, W.T. Hornaday to Francis Harper, March 17, 1925.
38. Ibid., A.B. Howell, American Society of Mammalogists to Harkin, April 13, 1925; Harkin to Howell, April 17, 1925.
39. *Edmonton Journal*, May 5, 1925.
40. Lewis, "Lively," 113; Lothian, *A History of Canada's National Parks*, 4, 34.
41. Lothian, IV, 35. The advisability and effects of sending plains bison from Wainwright to Wood Buffalo have remained contentious among zoologists and naturalists. By 1932 biologist J. Dewey Soper was actively studying the Wood Buffalo herd and found it to be largely hybridized, and in 1947 Canadian Wildlife Service mammalogist W.A. Fuller discovered some older slaughtered animals were tubercular. After an outbreak of anthrax in the early 1960s, a program of testing and inoculation was undertaken in an attempt to control both it and tuberculosis. In 1960 a previously isolated herd of 200 "purebred" wood bison was discovered and in 1965, twenty-four head were transferred to Elk Island Park and kept separate from the plains bison to reestablish the subspecies. Disease control measures at Wood Buffalo proved unsuccessful and in 1991 a proposal to eradicate the whole herd and begin anew with the Elk Island stock almost came to fruition before being cancelled by the government. As this book was being written a new proposal by scientists and park managers foresees eradication of the infected herd over a ten-year period and a restocking that would take another ten years.
42. Brower, "Buffalo National Park," 163.
43. Sandlos, *Hunters at the Margin*, 59.
44. Vol. 52, Harkin to L. Freeman, November 14, 1927.

45. Vol. 36, Harkin to Cory, April 3, 1924; Thomas R. Dunlap, "Ecology, Nature and Canadian National Park Policy: Wolves, Elk and Bison as a Case Study," *To See Ourselves/To Save Ourselves: Ecology and Culture in Canada* (Montreal: Association of Canadian Studies, 1991), 143.
46. LAC, RG 84, Vol. 69, B234, J. Wood to Harkin, April 30, 1924; Harkin to Superintendent, May 26, 1924; Harkin to Superintendent, September 30, 1924.
47. See Thomas R. Dunlap, *Saving America's Wildlife* (Princeton: Princeton University Press, 1988), 48–61 for a description of this important wildlife debate.
48. Charles C. Adams, "The Conservation of Predatory Animals," *Journal of Mammalogy*, Vol. 6, No. 2, February 1925, 90.
49. Vol. 35, undated quote from Charles C. Adams. This quote appears in Wildlife Division files in 1924 under a heading identifying Hewitt's book and was apparently written to challenge its predator position.
50. Ibid., Harkin to Superintendent, Buffalo National Park, November 15, 1925.
51. The influence of Adams and the American ecologists on Harkin and branch policy is detailed in Dunlap, "Ecology, Nature, and Canadian National Parks Policy," 140–42.
52. Vol. 7, Nagle to Lloyd, May 2, 1924.
53. Vol. 36, Harkin to Superintendents, September 30, 1924; Harkin to Superintendent, RMP, November 25, 1924.
54. Ibid., Harkin to Superintendents, January 31, 1925.
55. Ibid., Harkin to Cory, May 20, 1925.
56. It is interesting to speculate whether or not Harkin would have become so firm in his support of the new wildlife policy if the Wood Buffalo transfer and his face-off with U.S. scientists had occurred prior to its implementation rather than after. Suffice it to say that throughout his career he continually exhibited a balanced approach to each issue he dealt with, indeed often with several of them overlapping, and that he was adept at judging each on its own merits.

ELEVEN

1. Vol. 1955, Harkin to Deputy Minister, November 22, 1918.
2. Ibid., Memo to Cory, May 11, 1920.
3. Ibid.
4. Ibid., Harkin to Cory, May 11, 1920.
5. Ibid., Harkin to Cory, May 14, 1920.
6. Ibid., "Draft of an Act to Amend the Dominion Forests and Parks Act, 12–13 George V," 1922.
7. Ibid., Harkin to Cory, February 21, 1923.
8. Ibid., Harkin to Cory, March 7, 1923.
9. LAC, RG 84, Vol. 2071, U127–1, Memorandum dealing with the proposed transfer of resources from the Dominion to the Province of Alberta, February 21, 1925.
10. Harkin was clearly oblivious to what today might seem to be an incongruity, as in his mind (and his contemporaries') it simply did not exist.

11. Vol. 1955, Printed draft of "An Act Respecting National Parks and Reservations," 13–14 George V, 1923; Harkin to Cory, March 7, 1923. Vol. 1955, Printed draft of "An Act Respecting National Parks and Reservations," 13–14 George V, 1923; Harkin to Cory, March 7, 1923.
12. Ibid., Gibson to Harkin, March 17, 1923.
13. Ibid., Harkin to Cory, March 20, 1923.
14. Ibid., M.F. Cochrane to J.B. Challies, June 1, 1923.
15. Ibid., Memorandum of J.A. Symes, reclamation service, June 5, 1923.
16. Ibid., Harkin to Cory, June 7 & June 13, 1923.
17. Ibid., J.E. Brownlee to Charles Stewart, June 29, 1923.
18. Pearce papers. Pearce to Wheeler, May 19, 1923.
19. Ibid., Pearce to Stewart, June 16, 1923.
20. Ibid., Pearce to Coleman, June 25 and November 2, 1923.
21. LAC, RG 84, Vol. 107, U 125, Sibbald to Stewart, August 14, 1923; Sibbald to Harkin, Aug. 9, 1923.
22. Pearce papers, Pearce to unidentified, December 17, 1923.
23. Vol. 1955, W.J. Selby Walker to Stronach, August 23, 1923.
24. *Calgary Herald*, September 1923.
25. Vol. 107, Christina Henry to the Minister of the Interior, November 21, 1923.
26. Pearce papers, Stewart to Pearce, May 23, 1923.
27. Ibid., Pearce to P. Robson Black, Canadian Forestry Association, December 22, 1923.
28. Ibid., Dennis to Pearce, November 10, 1923. Parks historian C J. Taylor maintains that Stewart probably did not initially understand the implications of the bill and that it was not until 1924 that he raised concerns about the extensive new powers it would provide to the Parks Branch. C J. Taylor, "Legislating Nature," 131.
29. Vol. 1955, Harkin to Cory, May 7, 1924.
30. *Debates* April 10, 1924.
31. Vol. 1955, Drury to Stewart, April 12, 1923.
32. Ibid., Harkin to Calgary Power, January 23, 1923.
33. Ibid., Drury to Stewart, April 12, 1923.
34. Ibid., Harkin to Cory, April 18, 1923.
35. *Calgary Morning Albertan*, July 29, 1923.
36. LAC, RG 84, Vol. 214, R39–8, H. Greenfield to Mackenzie King, March 29, 1923.
37. Vol. 2071, Cory to Harkin, January 8, 1925.
38. Ibid., Memorandum of O.M. Biggar, February 3, 1925.
39. Vol. 214, Harkin to Spero, June 23, 1925.
40. Ibid., draft of amendment to Subsection 3, Section 18 of the Dominion Forest Reserves and Parks Act.
41. Franklin L. Foster, *John E. Brownlee: A Biography* (Lloydminster: Foster's Learning Inc., 1996), 119–20.
42. Vol. 2071, Memorandum "Alberta Natural Resources Agreement," n.d.
43. Ibid., Harkin to Cory, January 7, 1926.

44. Ibid., Agreement Made on the Ninth Day of January, 1926 between the Dominion of Canada and the Province of Alberta on the Subject of the Transfer to the Province of Its Natural Resources, 5.
45. Ibid., Webster to Brownlee, February 13, 1926.
46. Ibid., Webster to Pearce, February 15, 1926.
47. Ibid., Harkin to Cory, January 28, 1926.

TWELVE

1. LAC, MG 26 I, Vol. 29 (Meighen papers), Harkin to Cory, October 13, 1920.
2. "Report of the Commissioner of Dominion Parks, J.B. Harkin," 1920, p. 8.
3. Taylor, *Negotiating the Past*, 33–34.
4. Vol. 29, (Meighen papers), W.C. Milner to R. Borden, October 29, 1920.
5. Ibid., A. Doughty to Borden, November 4, 1920.
6. Ibid., A. Meighen to Borden, November 25, 1920.
7. Ibid., Harkin to G. Buskard, December 8, 1920.
8. Harkin provided his thinking on restoration in a letter to Meighen's secretary on May 31, 1920: "It has not been considered advisable that restoration should be part of this historic work. If there is nothing but a pile of stones, it is not considered to be good policy to erect a fort on the lines of the original one. On the other hand, it is considered of the utmost importance that where any forts or any other works are still in existence, they should be jealously preserved." LAC, MG 26 H, Vol. 163 (Borden papers), Memorandum to Mr. Mitchell by [J.B. Harkin], May 31, 1920.
9. Taylor, *Negotiating the Past*, 69–71.
10. "Report of the Commissioner of Canadian National Parks, J.B. Harkin," 1922, 101. It seems likely that the influence of Thomas Adams, head of the town planning division, came into play with respect to regional parks, as he was a strong believer in the importance of parks for urban areas.
11. LAC, RG 84, Vol. 2165, V2, Cory to Thomas Mulvey, Undersecretary of State, November 11, 1921.
12. Harkin, "Our Need for National Parks," 104–05.
13. Taylor, "A History of National Park Administration," 16.
14. "Report of the Commissioner of Canadian National Parks, J.B. Harkin," 1927, 16.
15. "Report of the Deputy Minister," 1927, 6.
16. LAC, RG 84, Vol. 983, CBH2, Harkin to Cory, February 11, 1925.
17. "National Park Standards," *Parks and Recreation*, August 1929.
18. "Report of the Commissioner of Canadian National Parks, J.B. Harkin," 1923, 111.
19. Lothian, *A History of Canada's National Parks*, 1, 87–88.
20. See Chapter 15 for information on how this historic site became, at least for a time, a national park.
21. LAC, RG 84, Vol. 1841, RM2, Hewitt to Harkin, June 16, 1917.

22. Ibid., Harkin to Cory, June 21, 1917; Campbell to Cory, June 28, 1917.
23. LAC, RG 84, Vol. 1726, PA2, Harkin to Thomas Malloy, September 4, 1925; Molloy to Harkin, September 10, 1925.
24. W.A. Waiser, *Saskatchewan's Playground* (Saskatoon: Fifth House, 1989), 25–26.
25. Vol. 1726, Harkin to Cory, May 1, 1926.
26. "National Park Standards."
27. Vol. 1726, Davis to Harkin May 15, 1926; Harkin to Davis, May 26, 1926.
28. Ibid., Harkin to Gibson, June 16, 1926.
29. Ibid., undated memorandum.
30. Ibid., T.C. Davis to Stewart, November 10, 1926.
31. Ibid., Cory to Harkin, November 30, 1926.
32. Ibid., Wardle to Cory, December 21, 1926.
33. Ibid., Harkin to Cory, February 7 & March 18, 1927.
34. Waiser, *Saskatchewan's Playground*, 30–38.
35. *Prince Albert Herald*, September 3, 1929.
36. LAC, MG 26 J1, Vol. 169 (King papers), Stewart to King, October 10, 1929.
37. LAC, RG 84, Vol. 1767, PA155, Harkin to Cory, October 8, 1929.
38. LAC, RG 84, Vol. 483, F2, James McKenna to Harkin, October 25, 1927; Harkin to McKenna, October 31, 1927.
39. Ibid., Cory to Harkin, May 25, 1927; Cory to J.A. Glen, June 1, 1927.
40. Cited in Lothian, *A History of Canada's National Parks*, 1, 71.
41. *Winnipeg Free Press*, August [12], 1928.
42. Vol. 1841, J.A. McFadden to Stewart, March 20, 1929.
43. Vol. 483, Harkin to Cory, February 20, 1929.
44. Ibid., Harkin to Cory, February 28, 1929.
45. Ibid., Cory to Harkin, September 23, 1929.
46. Ibid., H. Albright to Harkin, February 25, 1929.
47. Vol. 1841, "Re: Riding Mountain Park," March 12, 1930.
48. *Debates*, May 26, 1930, 3959.

THIRTEEN

1. Vol. 2071, J.B. Harkin to R.A. Gibson, March 2, 1926.
2. Ibid., March 4, 1926.
3. Ibid., Gibson to Biggar, March 9 & 11, 1926.
4. Ibid., "Memorandum re: Proposed Amendments to Parks Act," January 27, 1927.
5. Ibid., "Memorandum re: Amendment of Dominion Forest Reserves and Parks Act," February 14, 1927.
6. Vol. 214, J.E. Brownlee to Charles Stewart, November 26, 1926; Stewart to Brownlee, December 2, 1926.
7. Ibid., G. Webster to Mayor Osborne, February 2, 1927.
8. Ibid., Memorandum by J.M. Wardle, January 20, 1927.
9. Ibid., Canadian National Parks Association *Bulletin*, February 15, 1927.

10. Vol. 1955, J.E. Brownlee to W.L. Mackenzie King, March 2, 1927.
11. Ibid., Brownlee to King, March 2, 1927. Brownlee was actually a strong supporter of continuing Dominion control of national parks lands, recognizing that the federal government was spending resources on them far in excess of what the province could. In a later interview about the natural resources transfer he described the province as being "very willing" to see the parks remain in federal hands. See John E. Brownlee, "The Transfer of Alberta's Natural Resources (interview with Una MacLean)," *Alberta History*, Vol. 53, No. 4, Autumn 2005, 21.
12. Vol. 1955, Harkin to Cory, March 3, 1927.
13. LAC, RG 84, Vol. 1956, Harkin to Gibson, May 13, 1927.
14. Ibid., Brownlee to Stewart, May 4, 1927.
15. Ibid., "Summary of a Report by R.W. Cautley, D.LS., on the Selection of Permanent Boundaries for Rocky Mountain and Jasper Parks," 1–3.
16. Ibid., Harkin to Cory, November 14, 1927; Gibson to Harkin, December 6, 1927.
17. Foster, *John E. Brownlee*, 143
18. Luxton family fonds, Harkin to Luxton, October 5, 1927.
19. Vol. 1956, Harkin to Cory, January 18, 1929.
20. Ibid., Harkin to Cory, January 18, 1929.
21. Ibid.
22. Ibid., Harkin to K.R. Daly, January 2, 1929.
23. Ibid.
24. Ibid., Cautley, "Summary," 7–10.
25. Ibid., Harkin to Cory, January 26, 1929; Gibson to Harkin, January 30, 1929.
26. Ibid., Harkin to Cory, April 29, 1929.
27. Cited in James Gray, *R.B. Bennett, The Calgary Years* (Toronto: University of Toronto Press, 1991), 284.
28. Vol. 2071, Stewart to Brownlee, December 14, 1929.
29. Foster, *John E. Brownlee*, 166–68.
30. Vol. 2071, "Agreement made on the Fourteenth Day of December, 1929 between the Dominion of Canada and the Province of Alberta on the Subject of the Transfer of the Natural Resources of Alberta," 7–8.
31. *Calgary Herald*, December 20, 1929.
32. Vol. 491, F.E. Osborne to Stewart, December 21, 1929.
33. Ibid., Harkin to Gibson, December 23, 1929.
34. Ibid., Stewart to Osborne, December 23, 1929.
35. Vol. 2071, J.H. Hanna to G.C. Siddall, President, Wainwright Board of Trade, February 12, 1930.
36. Ibid., "Support the Parks Bill," *Bulletin of the Canadian National Parks Association*, No. 8, January 1, 1930, 1.
37. "The Campaign Against The Parks," *Manitoba Free Press*, March 28, 1930.
38. "Conditions Within Park Boundaries Are Debated in the House," *Banff Crag and Canyon*, April 4, 1930.

39. Vol. 2071, "Memorandum re: Legislative Authority Clause (Parks) in Natural Resources Agreement," March 29, 1930.
40. *Calgary Albertan*, January 11, 1930; Vol. 491, Memorandum, April 23, 1930.
41. *Debates*, May 9, 1930, 1935; *Banff Crag and Canyon*, May 16, 1930.
42. Vol. 1956, J.O. Apps to Cory, March 1, 1930; Harkin to Cory, March 1, 1930.
43. Ibid., Explanatory Notes, Bill 135.
44. Ibid. See C.J. Taylor in "Legislating Nature: The National Parks Act of 1930" and *Negotiating the Past: The Making of Canada's National Historic Parks and Sites*. Taylor believes that the failure of the act to define game sanctuaries left the branch's wildlife program on the periphery and helps to explain the eventual splitting off of the Canadian Wildlife Service as a separate branch in 1947. Similarly, he holds that failure to give the Historic Sites and Monuments Board the legislative footing to act as an independent agency condemned it to a further period of uncertainty.
45. "Something Achieved," *Manitoba Free Press*, May 12, 1930; *Saskatoon Star-Phoenix*, May 15, 1930.
46. Vol. 1956, Harkin to H. Albright, June 21, 1930.
47. *Calgary Daily Herald* and *Calgary Albertan*, August 28, 1930.
48. "Lake Minnewanka Again," *Manitoba Free Press*, August 30, 1930.
49. Vol. 491, Cory to Thomas G. Murphy, September 11, 1930.
50. Ibid., Harkin to K.G. Chamberlain, September 17, 1930.
51. Ibid., E.J. Chambers to Murphy, September 16, 1930.
52. Ibid., J.T. Johnston to Deputy Minister, October 17, 1930.
53. "National Park Still Safe," *Manitoba Free Press*, October 31, 1930.
54. "The Minnewanka Dam Project," *Calgary Daily Herald*, November 1930.
55. Vol. 491, Harkin to Bennett, January 23, 1931.
56. Ibid., Johnston to Gibson, March 31, 1931.

FOURTEEN

1. LAC, RG 84, Vol. 212, J121–3, Harkin to Superintendent R.H. Knight, Jasper National Park, August 9, 1930.
2. See Waiser, *Park Prisoners*, in particular the chapters "Relief Workers" and "Transients," for a complete picture of national park depression relief projects.
3. WMCR, Banff Advisory Council Minutes, October 15 and November 5, 1930.
4. Vol. 212, Harkin to Cory, January 12, 1931.
5. P.C. 74, January 14, 1931.
6. Vol. 212, Harkin to Bennett, January 29, 1931. Harkin indicated the money had been allocated based on the number of unemployed in each park and consisted of $16,000 to Banff, $15,000 to Jasper and $2,000 to Waterton.
7. Ibid., [unknown] to Superintendent, Jasper Park, March 30, 1931.
8. *Debates*, July 3, 1931, 3368.
9. LAC, RG 84 Vol. 213, J121–3, Harkin to Superintendent, Jasper National Park, September 18, 1931. The official explanation for the change appeared in

Harkin's annual report for 1932: "As the majority of the works—consisting of the erection of buildings and bridges and repairs to existing structures, surveys, road construction, clearing right of way, and delineating park boundaries—were of an engineering character, responsibility for carrying on operations was placed in the hands of the Chief Engineer of the National Parks Service, who made Banff, Alberta, his temporary headquarters for the winter." Canada. Department of the Interior. *Annual Report for the Fiscal Year Ending March 31, 1932*, "National Parks of Canada, Report of the Commissioner, J.B. Harkin," 91.

10. Taylor, *Negotiating the Past*, footnote 12, 223. While perhaps an exaggeration, at least with respect to the regularity of Bennett's call for his resignation, the story does speak to the climate of the times and the pressure Harkin was working under. Bennett biographer P.B. Waite states, "He was a sublime egotist, clever, irascible, unsparing of himself or others. Forgiveness was one of the Christian virtues he found difficult to practise." P.B. Waite, "Richard Bedford Bennett, 1st Viscount Bennett," *Dictionary of Canadian Biography Online*, 3.
11. W.F. Lothian, *A History of Canada's National Parks*, 2 (Ottawa: Parks Canada, 1977), 17–18. Mabel Williams was among those who lost their position.
12. Vol. 213, G.D. Robertson to Murphy, October 10, 1931.
13. Provincial Archives of Alberta, 69.218, v. 12, f. B60–23 (120a), Wardle to Harkin, April 22, 1932.
14. LAC, RG 84, Vol. 210, GR60, Harkin to Cory, September 30, 1929; Harkin to Deputy Minister, November 19, 1929.
15. "National Parks of Canada, Report of the Commissioner, J.B. Harkin," 1932, 91.
16. Vol. 213, Harkin to Rowatt, December 22, 1931.
17. Waiser, *Park Prisoners*, 64–70.
18. Vol. 213, Wardle to Harkin, November 23, 1931.
19. Ibid., Harkin to Wardle, November 28, 1931.
20. Ibid., Wardle to Harkin, November 23, 1931.
21. Ibid., Harkin to Rowatt, November 30, 1931.
22. Ibid., Wardle to Harkin, December 2, 1931. After this affair, both Harkin and Wardle took a tough approach to those complaining about working conditions, the latter in particular letting it be known by his actions that those causing problems could expect to be dismissed in the belief that there were plenty more willing candidates to replace them.
23. "Report of the Deputy Minister," 1932, 7; "National Parks of Canada, Report of the Commissioner, J.B. Harkin," 1932, 68, 70. Total relief expenditures for the 1931–1932 fiscal year were $885,000, more than twice what Harkin had asked for in his original plan.
24. *Debates*, November 22, 1932, 1450.
25. Waiser, *Park Prisoners*, 87–98.
26. Vol. 212, Harkin to Wardle, May 4, 1933.
27. Ibid., General A. McNaughton to Harkin, May 10, 1933.

28. Ibid., Harkin to Rowatt, June 2, 1933. Despite his efforts, it would be difficult for Harkin to uphold branch interests and practices in the face of McNaughton's success at making the DND camps the most important in dealing with single homeless men, reaching 14,000 men at their height.
29. LAC, RG 84, Vol. 213, B60–23, Harkin to Rowatt, February 16, 1934.
30. Waiser, *Park Prisoners*, 110.
31. Vol. 213, Memorandum, "Unemployment Relief in National Parks," March 12, 1934.
32. Larry A. Glassford, *Reaction and Reform: The Politics of the Conservative Party under R.B. Bennett, 1927–1938* (Toronto: University of Toronto Press, 1990), 143.
33. Waiser, *Park Prisoners*, 114–15.
34. *Banff Crag and Canyon*, October 19, 1934.
35. For example, in the August 4, 1933 edition of the *Crag and Canyon* an article under the headline "Explains Why There Is Not a Landing Field Here," provided an extensive report on Harkin's answer to a question about the delay in getting a landing field and described to fellow Rotarians the success of the recent inauguration events at Riding Mountain Park, paying particular tribute to J.C. Campbell and the Publicity Division for their good work.
36. This idea was mentioned by several individuals interested in game management near the international boundary around 1910, including F.K. Vreeland of the Campfire Club of America and Commissioner Howard Douglas.
37. Ray Djuff, *High on a Windy Hill: The Story of the Prince of Wales Hotel* (Calgary: Rocky Mountain Books, 1999), 105 & endnote 51, 162.
38. Vol. 2167, "Programme at the Consummation and Dedication of the Waterton-Glacier International Peace Park, July 4, 1936."
39. Canada. Department of the Interior, *Annual Report for the Year Ending March 31, 1933*, "National Parks of Canada, Report of the Commissioner, J.B. Harkin," 76.
40. Vol. 219, Albright to Harkin, May 10, 1919.
41. Ibid., Albright to Harkin, December 30, 1931. Albright had to have co-operation of the Indian Service, the Bureau of Public Roads, and the Montana State Highway Commission to achieve his part of the proposal.
42. Ibid., Harkin to Albright, June 16, 1933; A.E. Demaray to Harkin, July 3, 1933. Albright would retire in August 1933 to pursue a career in private business.
43. *Lethbridge Herald*, July 16, 1933. The Going-to-the-Sun Highway was a significant new tourist route that the Parks Branch had to consider. After travel over it during an inspection trip to Waterton in August 1933, Wardle described it to Harkin as "the first road I have traveled in the United States National Parks that compares favourably with the best of our mountain highways" and recommended "completion of the Banff-Jasper Highway as quickly as possible to compete with it." Vol. 219, Wardle to Harkin, January 8, 1934.
44. Ibid., Middleton to Herbert Knight, January 7, 1936.
45. Ibid., Knight to Harkin, January 10, 1936.
46. Ibid., Middleton to Knight, May 19, 1936.

47. Vol. 2167, speech of Senator W.A. Buchanan, July 4, 1936.
48. Canada. Department of the Interior. *Annual Report for the Fiscal Year Ending March 31, 1936*, "National Parks of Canada, Report of the Commissioner, J.B. Harkin," 5, 9.

FIFTEEN

1. LAC MG 26 K, Vol. 381 (Bennett papers), R.B. Bennett to Philip C. Locke, n.d. 1935; Bennett to Wardle, August 19, 1935.
2. *Banff Crag and Canyon*, August 23, 1935. Bennett's friend Mary Schäffer Warren was one of many delighted with the appointment. She wrote, "You have done many great things in the past five years but nothing has come so close to my heart as your appointment of J.M. Wardle to the post to which he will soon succeed. Fifteen years at least I have known that man and his steady and consistent actions have endeared him to those who have watched him." Bennett responded, "I am satisfied he will bring to the discharge of his onerous duties a well-trained mind, integrity, character, and a desire to serve his country and not himself." Vol. 381, M.S. Warren to Bennett, August 18, 1935; Bennett to Warren, August 23, 1935.
3. Vol. 983, "Memorandum re: National Parks in Nova Scotia," June 27, 1931.
4. Ibid., Harkin to A. McCall, October 19, 1922.
5. LAC, RG 84, Vol. 1777, PE12, Harkin to Gibson, June 13, 1923.
6. Cited in MacEachern, *Natural Selections*, 38.
7. Vol. 1777, D.A. Mackinnon to Harkin, April 2, 1923.
8. Ibid., A. Newbury to Mackinnon, May 5, 1923.
9. Ibid., Mackinnon to Harkin, May 22, 1923; Harkin to Mackinnon, May 29, 1923.
10. Vol. 983, Resolutions passed by the National Park Committee at Amherst, January 22, 1925.
11. Ibid., Harkin to Cory, February 11, 1925.
12. Ibid., Harkin to R.D. Crawford, February 12, 1925.
13. P.C. 901, June 10, 1926.
14. Vol. 483, Harkin to C.D. Richards, June 13 & July 6, 1927.
15. Ibid., Harkin to Cory, May 30, 1930.
16. Ibid., Harkin to F.M. Sclanders, August 19, 1930.
17. LAC, RG 84, Vol. 1964, U2, R.W. Cautley report on New Brunswick park sites (1930). Cautley's description of his task is one of the clearest articulations on the combination of the standard with tourism in new parks creation.
18. Vol. 483, Harkin to Cautley, December 18, 1930. As mentioned, Harkin had contacted Horace Albright in February 1929 concerning U.S. practices for acquiring park lands. In his response, Albright advised that "Congress has never appropriated funds for the establishment of national parks," although it had appropriated funds to match a donation to acquire private lands containing "some of the finest existing Sequoia Trees" for Sequoia National Park and it had spent some $3 million to acquire privately held "inholdings" in several

national parks. This confirmed that the two country's policies were basically the same and undoubtedly strengthened both Harkin's and his minister's resolve that unencumbered lands must be transferred from the provinces for new parks. Vol. 483, Albright to Harkin, February 25, 1929.

19. Vol. 983, Harkin to Rowatt, October 19, 1931.
20. Ibid., Harkin to G.S. Harrington, September 22, 1933.
21. Canada. Department of the Interior. *Annual Report for the Year Ending March 31, 1933*, "Report of the Deputy Minister," 15.
22. Canada. Department of the Interior. *Annual Report for the Year Ending March 31, 1934*, "National Parks of Canada, Report of the Commissioner, J.B. Harkin," 79.
23. Ibid., pp. 90–93; Canada. Department of the Interior, *Annual Report for the Year Ending March 31, 1935*, "National Parks of Canada, Report of the Commissioner, J.B. Harkin," 105.
24. Canada. The Senate. *Report of the Proceedings of the Special Committee on Tourist Traffic*, 1934, "Testimony of J.B. Harkin," 79.
25. Ibid., "Order of Reference and Members of the Committee," v.
26. Ibid., "Testimony of J.B. Harkin," 3.
27. Ibid., 4–11.
28. Ibid., 12–14, 276. The Senate committee, in its final recommendations, was unable to agree with the island idea, but Harkin's ideas about retiring Canadians had staying power as BC did become a retirement mecca and the idea of Canada obtaining a holiday island has reappeared in public policy discussions from time to time.
29. Ibid., "Testimony of J. Murray Gibbon," 69–70. The Trail Riders of the Canadian Rockies and its sister organization The Sky Line Hikers of the Canadian Rockies were an important indicator of co-operation between the Parks Branch and the CPR, an extension of the symbiotic relationship between the two organizations that extended back to the founding of the national parks and which Harkin tried, within reason, to foster. He saw their value being much like that of the Alpine Club and sent a message to the Trail Rider's founding meeting pointing out it was "destined to be quite a live, enthusiastic institution, conscious of the urge of the mountains" and noted, "I will be glad to cooperate with your Association in any way possible." Both he and Wardle were charter council members of the organization. "Three Letters from the Secretary's Mailbag," *Trail Riders of the Canadian Rockies Bulletin No. 1*, October 15, 1924, 3.
30. Ibid., *Final Report*, viii-ix.
31. MacEachern, *Natural Selections*, 44.
32. *Report and Proceedings of the Special Committee on Tourist Traffic*, "Testimony of Leo Dolan," 31.
33. Ibid., "Testimony of W. Baldwin," 180–82.
34. Ibid., *Final Report*, x.
35. Vol. 983, Memorandum: "National Parks in Nova Scotia," June 27, 1931.

36. LAC, RG 84, Vol. 985, CBH2 Cape Rouge, "Extracts from the Report on Examination of Sites for National Park of Canada in the Province of Nova Scotia," by R.W. Cautley, D.L.S., December 1934, 9.
37. Vol. 983, Harkin to Gibson, December 14, 1934 & February 6, 1935.
38. Ibid., A.L. Macdonald to Murphy, February 14, 1935.
39. Vol. 985, Harkin to Wardle, January 10, 1936.
40. Ibid., Wardle to Harkin, March 18, 1936.
41. Ibid., draft of a letter from Minister to Hon. Angus L. Macdonald, March 18, 1936.
42. Ibid., Harkin to Wardle, March 27, 1936.
43. Ibid., Wardle to Harkin, March 27, 1936.
44. Ibid., Harkin to Wardle, April 6, 1936.
45. Ibid., draft of letter from Crerar to Macdonald, April 16, 1936.
46. Vol. 1777, T.A. Campbell to C.D. Howe, February 8, 1936.
47. Ibid., Campbell to Crerar, March 31, 1936.
48. MacEachern, *Natural Selections*, 77.
49. Vol. 1777, Harkin to Wardle, April 16, 1936.
50. Ibid.
51. Originally the Maritime parks were to be designated by an amendment to the *National Parks Act*, but because of concerns that "opening up" the existing act might lead to unwanted amendments it was decided to create a new act for the purpose.
52. Vol. 1777, Harkin to Wardle, May 22, 1936.
53. Ibid., Williamson to Harkin, March 23, 1936.
54. Ibid., Williamson and Cromary to Harkin, July 28, 1936
55. Ibid., Harkin to Wardle, June 2, 1936.

SIXTEEN

1. Mills, *Rustic Building Programs in Canada's National Parks*, 4. Between 1925 and 1929 Cromarty also served as acting superintendent in Waterton Park during the summer months.
2. Ibid., 48. Mills records that Cromarty's views were rarely mentioned in internal memoranda or instructions to builders. He also reports that it is unknown whether the adoption of Arts and Crafts motifs was due to Cromarty's personal preferences or was the result of a branch policy decision.
3. This building has been restored and is now used as the Town of Banff Firehall. The Upper Hot Springs, with many subsequent renovations, is also still in use.
4. Mills, *Rustic Building Programs*, 61.
5. Lewis, "Lively," 138, 165–67.
6. Canada. *Annual Report of the Department of the Interior for the Fiscal Year Ending March 31, 1930*, "National Parks of Canada, Report of the Commissioner, J.B. Harkin," 104.
7. Lothian, *A History of Canada's National Parks*, 4, 138.

8. Sheilagh Jameson, *W.J. Oliver: Life through a Master's Lens* (Calgary: Glenbow Museum, 1984), 51–54.
9. Ironically, while Harkin was agreeing to employ Grey Owl for his work with beaver at Riding Mountain, problems with too many beaver were occurring in Jasper's Cabin Lake, the local water supply, and two pair were eventually removed and donated to Vancouver's Stanley Park zoo. See Canada. *Annual Report of the Department of the Interior for the Year Ending March 31, 1932*, "National Parks of Canada, Report of the Commissioner J.B. Harkin," 77.
10. LAC, RG 84, Vol. 1768, PA174–18, Harkin to Rowatt, April 7, 1931. See Tina Loo, *States of Nature*, 111–17 for an interesting interpretation of Grey Owl. Loo believes that he adopted his Indian persona so that he would have the voice of authority in his message and that the message had more to do with sentimentality for past, simpler times rather than real conservation.
11. Vol. 1768, Harkin to Rowatt, April 17, 1931.
12. Ibid., Harkin to Gibson, September 24, 1931.
13. Ibid., Murphy to Robert Weir, Minister of Agriculture, May 22, 1931.
14. Ibid., Rowatt to Harkin, September 24, 1931.
15. Ibid., Harkin to Rowatt, February 3, 1932.
16. Cited in Donald B. Smith, *From the Land of Shadows: The Making of Grey Owl* (Saskatoon: Western Producer Books, 1990), 120.
17. Ibid., note 76, 272.
18. Vol. 1768, Harkin to Gibson, April 25, 1936.
19. Smith, note 76, 272.
20. Vol. 1768, Harkin to Rowatt, February 3, 1932.
21. Ibid., Harkin to Archie Grey Owl, June 24, 1936.
22. Ibid., J.A. Wood to Harkin, June 30, 1936.
23. Vol. 35, N. Biddle to Harkin, April 23, 1926.
24. Ibid., Harkin to W.A. Dowler, June 1, 1929.
25. Ibid., J.R. Dymond to Harkin, April 15, 1929; Harkin to Dymond, April 25, 1929.
26. Ibid., C.W. Hobley to Harkin, January 31, 1930; Harkin to Hobley, February 21, 1930.
27. LAC, RG 84, Vol. 14, J300, "Memorandum re: Predatory Animals in National Parks of Canada," January 16, 1933.
28. Vol. 35, Harkin to Supt., RMP, October 8, 1928.
29. Ibid., Harkin to Cory, January 18, 1929.
30. Vol. 7, Harkin to Supt., RMP, November 15, 1928.
31. LAC, RG 84, Vol. 15, KNP300, Sibbald to Harkin, November 20, 1928. Warden Bill Peyto's virtual disregard for a directive concerning the disposition of cougar skins is described in Chapter 7.
32. Vol. 14, Harkin to Acting Supt., JNP, February 7, 1929. It is unclear if the "no traps" restriction was affected by action in the U.S. parks. It was not until 1931 that the U.S. Park Service's official policy was published in the *Journal of*

Mammalogy, indicating that as predators were to be considered an integral part of the wildlife protected in national parks "no widespread campaigns of destruction are to be countenanced." The article also mentioned that use of steel traps had been banned by agreement of the superintendents some years previously. However, in an October 1933 letter to Selby Walker, Harkin stated, "The policy respecting predatory animals in the Canadian National Parks which has been in effect since 1928 has apparently been adopted for the United States Parks....This is apparently a case of the two administrations having independently reached similar decisions." Thomas Dunlap, who has studied both American and Canadian wildlife policies in this period, believes it is unlikely Canadian parks officials were unaware of U.S. action. Vol. 35, Harkin to Selby Walker (U.S. policy attached), October 4, 1933; Dunlap, "Ecology, Nature, and Canadian National Parks Policy," 140.

33. Vol. 36, Harkin to W.B. Conger, September 24, 1929.
34. Although Lloyd argued that wardens trapped an average of 2.5 coyotes each a year in Jasper, providing an average income of $30 each, other accounts indicate that it was far more lucrative. Robert Burns, in his history of the warden service, reports that some wardens earned up to $500 a year from the practice. See Ann Dixon, *Silent Partners: Wives of National Parks Wardens (Their Lives and History)* (Jasper: Dixon and Dixon Publishers, 1983), 43; Frank Camp, *Roots in the Rockies* (Jasper: Frank Camp Ventures, 1993), 46; Burns, *Guardians of the Wild*, 114–16.
35. See Alan MacEachern, "Rationality and Rationalization in Canadian National Parks Predator Policy," *Consuming Canada*, 198 for a description of predator control policies in Canada and for an interesting viewpoint on the branch's predator control policies in the 1930s. With respect to the situation in the United States at the time, Thomas Dunlap notes that the U.S. Biological Survey won the battle with ecologists in the American Society of Mammalogists on predator control because the emerging field of animal ecology did not yet have the science necessary to buttress their view and it would not be until the next decade that game managers formed a wildlife policy based on predators as a controlling element in the ecosystem. Dunlap, *Saving America's Wildlife*, 61.
36. Vol. 7, Lloyd to Harkin, October 10, 1930.
37. Vol. 14, Rogers to Harkin, January 16, 1932; Harkin to Rogers, January 27, 1932; Rogers to Harkin, February 2, 1932; Harkin to Rogers, March 12, 1932; Rogers to Harkin, March 19, 1932.
38. Ibid., "Memorandum Mr. Harkin Re: Predatory Animals in National Parks of Canada," January 16, 1933.
39. Ibid., Harkin to Dr. D.M. Kennedy, April 26, 1933.
40. Ibid., "Memorandum Mr. Harkin," March 8, 1933; Harkin to Superintendent, Jasper National Park, March 28, 1933.
41. Ibid., "Memorandum Mr. Harkin Re: Predatory Animals in National Parks of Canada," January 14, 1933.
42. Banff Advisory Council Minutes, December 7, 1932.

43. *Banff Crag and Canyon*, December 23, 1932.
44. Vol. 14, "Memorandum Mr. Harkin Re: Predatory Animals in National Parks of Canada," January 14, 1933.
45. Ibid., Harkin to D.M. Kennedy, February 10, 1933.
46. Ibid., Kennedy to Harkin, April 28, 1933.
47. Ibid.
48. Ibid., Harkin to Gibson, July 11, 1933.
49. Ibid., Rowatt to Murphy, July 12, 1933.
50. Vol. 7, Murphy to Bert Wilkins, July 13, 1933; Rowatt to Harkin, July 13, 1933.
51. Ibid., Rowatt to Harkin, August 30, 1933.
52. Ibid., Harkin to Rowatt, September 13, 1933.
53. Ibid., Rogers to Harkin, September 27, 1933; Harkin to The Superintendent, Jasper National Park, October 17, 1933; Rogers to Harkin, October 26, 1933; Rogers to Harkin, November 14, 1933; Harkin to The Superintendent, Jasper National Park, November 22, 1933; Rogers to Harkin, January 9, 1934.
54. Ibid., Harkin to Rowatt and notation, February 17, 1934.
55. Vol. 14, Harkin to Wardle, February 27, 1934.
56. Ibid., Supervising Warden to Acting Superintendent, Jasper National Park, November 17, 1934; Lloyd to Harkin, May 31, 1935; Harkin to Gibson and notation, June 25, 1935; Lloyd to Wardle, November 19, 1935.
57. Vol. 7, R.D. Barnetson and W.D. Neish to The Superintendent, Banff National Park, November 19, 1933.
58. Ibid., P.J. Jennings to Harkin, July 4, 1934. Jennings's report showed that eleven of the thirteen coyotes destroyed in June 1934 had been taken by Peyto but that "I would mention that the Supervising Warden advises me that he has no proof of this kill as Warden Peyto has not turned in either hides or tails."
59. Ibid., Harkin to The Superintendent, Banff National Park, March 1, 1935.
60. Ibid., Harkin to Jennings, May 29, 1935.
61. Ibid., Harkin to Jennings, July 23, 1935.
62. *Banff Crag and Canyon*, November 22, 1935.
63. Vol. 7, E.R. Lee to Jennings, December 19, 1935.
64. Vol. 7, Harkin to Selby Walker, December 16, 1935.
65. See Burnett, *A Passion for Wildlife*, 5–19 for a discussion of the role of scientists in wildlife management in national parks during this period.
66. Environmental historians have disagreed on Harkin's importance in wildlife conservation history during this key period. Thomas Dunlap believes that the "confusing mixture of protection and 'natural balance'" evident in his writings resulted from him having no certain model, and that "the scientists themselves were not calling for absolute protection, and had as little idea as the administrators about the actual impact of predator on prey populations." He concludes, "The transformation of park wildlife policy was an early step in one of the most important shifts in our ideas in the twentieth century. That it came in the interwar years, as part of scientific discussion and through the influence of scientists on public policy, is part of the early history of

environmental sensibility." On the other hand, Alan MacEachern posits, "I would argue that what Dunlap sees as a sweeping victory for rationalization is not so clearcut. Science was less an ultimate objective arbitrator in making of predator policy than it was a tactic, a language used to defend what were still quite human positions." MacEachern sees Harkin as intolerant of predators and less of a force in the support of the scientists' position, arguing, "Lloyd never did convince the commissioner to adopt a more tolerant attitude toward predators, but he supplied Harkin with ammunition to fight proponents of increased kills and in this way helped keep the policy stable despite the criticism of the early 1930s." In his view, change to parks predator policy only occurred after Williamson replaced Harkin, signalling "a period of sympathy for predator species." Obviously, I tend to favour Dunlap's assessment. Dunlap, "Ecology, Nature and Canadian National Parks Policy," 143–44; MacEachern, "Rationality and Rationalization,"199, 205.

SEVENTEEN

1. Lothian, A *History of Canada's National Parks*, 2, 18.
2. Vol. 484, Williamson to Sclanders, September 17, 1936.
3. *Banff Crag and Canyon*, April 9, 1937.
4. With respect to his statement about unfinished business, it is important to record that he did believe his career had been successful, reminiscing in his notes, "Looking back after 25 years in the National parks I think I can say that a good deal has been accomplished." Winks fonds, miscellaneous notes.
5. Luxton family fonds, Harkin to Luxton, December 15, 1938.
6. Granatstein, *The Ottawa Men*, 2.
7. Unfortunately, Harkin's personnel records from the time of his appointment as commissioner until his retirement, which would undoubtedly shed light on this and other important career matters, have not been found. However, while Lothian's comments make it appear that he had the option to take on the new comptroller's role if he wished, it may be that Harkin had reached full pension eligibility in 1936. The *Civil Service Superannuation Act* of 1924 called for a maximum of thirty-five years of service or age sixty-five but service was based on matching contributions to the plan over the employment period from employer and employee. It is possible that Harkin "bought back" his years of service between 1901 and the passing of the act in 1924 in order to be in a position to retire in 1936.
8. *Ottawa Journal*, January 28, 1955.
9. *Banff Crag and Canyon*, April 9, 1937.
10. Luxton family fonds, Luxton to J.A. Wood, September 6, 1928 and Luxton to H.C. Oliver, May 16, 1928.
11. Winks fonds, Luxton to Harkin, January 1, 1952.
12. In a letter written in 1960, Williams recorded, "After I left the National Parks Branch I spent some years in old London and while there, at the request of some people who were interested in starting a National Parks movement in

Great Britain, I wrote a little book which was published by Nelson's called 'Guardians of the Wild.' It told the story of the Canadian movement, its inception and growth, and showed—or at least tried to—that it was the outgrowth from the imagination and devoted service of one man." Ibid., Williams to Winks, January 9, 1960.

13. Ibid., Harkin to Williams, August 6–11, 1954.
14. Ibid., Miscellaneous notes.
15. Ibid., Harkin to Williams, August 6–11, 1954.
16. Ibid., Miscellaneous notes.
17. *Ottawa Journal*, January 28, 1955. Karsh's notes indicate that the portrait of Harkin, taken on February 24, 1947, was done for Rotary purposes. Jerry Fielder, Karsh Curator, personal communication.
18. M.H. Long, "The Historic Sites and Monuments Board of Canada," *Canadian Historical Association Report*, 1954, 3–4.
19. LAC, RG 84, Vol. 1424, HS 10–182, F. Landon to A.J.H. Richardson, January 31 & February 3, 1955.
20. Ibid., J.R.B. Coleman to J.A. Hutchison, February 11, 1955; Hutchison to Coleman, February 14, 1955.
21. Ibid., R.E. Edwards to Coleman, March 14, 1957.
22. Ibid., Coleman to B.I.M. Strong, December 16, 1957; Strong to G.H.L. Dempster, April 21, 1958.
23. Ibid., Edwards to Coleman, June 6, 1958; Strong to Dempster, June 12, 1958.
24. Ibid., Edwards to Coleman, September 6, 1958.
25. The inscription on the "official" Historic Sites plaque in Canada's two official languages reads, "Born in Vankleek Hill, Ontario, Harkin was named Commissioner of the recently created Dominion Parks Branch in 1911, and over a period of twenty-five years organized a nationwide system of national parks. A firm believer in the recreational and economic value of park land, he directed his efforts to ensure access to the system for the greatest possible number of Canadians. Harkin was an ardent conservationist who was responsible for important advances in the field of wildlife preservation. On his advice the Historic Sites and Monuments Board was created in 1919, and he was one of its original members" (1997 version).
26. Winks fonds, Harkin to Williams, August 6–11, 1954.
27. Ibid., Williams to Winks, January 9, 1960. Winks was a professor of history at Yale who had become aware of Harkin through research on his book *The Blacks in Canada*, which contained a reference to his employment of a black man in the branch, a most unusual circumstance in the period. Winks contacted Williams in 1960 with the intention of writing an article or a book on Harkin, a project he apparently never completed. However, he did provide a valuable service to Harkin's legacy by corresponding with Williams, leading her to provide important insights into the man. These letters, along with others from Dorothy Barber and the notes, were eventually turned over to Parks Canada and then to Library and Archives Canada. As they did not meet their collecting

criteria, they were offered to the Library and Archives of the Whyte Museum of the Canadian Rockies, my employer, in 2004.

28. Harkin, *The History and Meaning of the National Parks of Canada*, "Acknowledgement," p. 2.
29. Ibid., "Foreword," 3.
30. Paul Servos, "CPAWS...A Brief History," *Parks News*, Summer 1987, 2.
31. "The Hon. Jean Chrétien Awarded J.B. Harkin Medal," *Parks News*, October 1972, 3–4.
32. Harkin, *The History and Meaning of the National Parks of Canada*, 16.

Bibliography

ARCHIVAL SOURCES

Eleanor Luxton Historical Foundation Archives (maintained at the Whyte Museum of the Canadian Rockies, Library and Archives), Luxton family fonds.

Federal Records Centre (Edmonton), RG 84, E 1985.

Library and Archives Canada, MG 26 A (Macdonald papers), Vol. 39; MG 26 G (Laurier papers), Vol. 55; MG 26 H (Borden papers), Vol. 163; MG 26 I (Meighen papers), Vol. 29; MG 26 J1 (Mackenzie King papers), Vol. 169; MG 26 K (Bennett papers), Vol. 381; MG 30 E169 (Harkin papers); RG 6, Vol. 135; RG 10 (Indian Affairs), Vol. 3052; RG 76, Vol. 5; RG 84 (National Parks), Vol. 7, Vol. 15, Vol. 14, Vol. 35, Vol. 45, Vol. 52, Vol. 68, Vol. 69, Vol. 74, Vol. 102, Vol. 103, Vol. 104, Vol. 107, Vol. 169, Vol. 210, Vol. 212, Vol. 213, Vol. 214, Vol. 217, Vol. 219, Vol. 483, Vol. 484, Vol. 491, Vol. 631, Vol. 654, Vol. 718, Vol., 983, Vol. 985, Vol. 1041, Vol. 1424, Vol. 1631, Vol. 1699, Vol. 1700, Vol. 1726, Vol. 1767, Vol. 1768, Vol. 1777, Vol. 1841, Vol. 1955, Vol. 1956, Vol. 1960, Vol. 1964, Vol. 1965, Vol. 2071, Vol. 2165, Vol. 2166, Vol. 2167, Vol. 2226.

Provincial Archives of Alberta, 69.218, v. 12, f B60–23.

University of Alberta Archives, William Pearce papers.

Whyte Museum of the Canadian Rockies, Library and Archives, Winks fonds; Vaux fonds; Banff Citizens' Association Minutes; Banff Advisory Council Minutes.

NEWSPAPERS

Banff Crag and Canyon, July 13, 1910; July 20, 1910, August 10, 1912; June 21, 1913; June 27, 1914; May 29, 1915; July 24, 1915; January 15, 1916; October 7, 1916; November 10, 1917; February 2, 1918; June 18, 1918; June 29, 1918; September 17, 1918; October 28, 1918; September 4, 1920; July 8, 1922; July 5, 1923; April 4, 1930; May 16, 1930; December 23, 1932; October 19, 1934; November 22, 1935; April 9, 1937.

Calgary Albertan, January 11, 1930; August 28, 1930.

Calgary Daily Herald, July 28, 1922; August 28, 1930.

Calgary Herald, December 20, 1929.

Calgary Morning Albertan, July 29, 1923.

Edmonton Journal, June 10, 1914; May 5, 1925.

Lethbridge Herald, March 26, 1915; July 16, 1933.

Lethbridge Telegram, April 29, 1915.

Manitoba Free Press, March 28, 1930; May 12, 1930; August 30, 1930; October 31, 1930.

Ottawa Evening Journal, June 24, 1896.

Ottawa Journal, January 28, 1955.

Prince Albert Herald, September 3, 1929.

Revelstoke Mail Herald, July 17, 1915; July 31, 1915.

Toronto Globe, August 14, 1914.

Victoria Times, August 10, 1909.

Winnipeg Free Press, August [12], 1928.

PUBLISHED SOURCES

Adams, Charles C. "The Conservation of Predatory Animals." *Journal of Mammalogy*, Vol. 6, No. 2 (February 1925).

Altmeyer, George. "Three Ideas of Nature, 1893–1914." *Journal of Canadian Studies*, 11, 3 (1976)

Alpine Club of Canada *Gazette*, December 1922; June 1923.

Armstrong, Christopher and Nelles, H.V. "Competition vs. Convenience: Federal Administration of Bow River Waterpowers, 1906–1913." In *The Canadian West*, edited by Henry Klassen. Calgary: University of Calgary Press, 1976.

Artibise, A.J.F. and Stelter, G.A. "Conservation Planning and Urban Planning: The Canadian Commission of Conservation in Historical Perspective." In *Consuming Canada: Readings in Environmental History*, edited by Chad and Pam Gaffield. Toronto: Copp Clark Ltd., 1995.

Bella, Leslie, *Parks for Profit*. Montreal: Harvest House, 1987.

Binnema, Theodore. "'Let the Line Be Drawn Now:' Wilderness Conservation, and the Exclusion of Aboriginal People from Banff National Park." *Environmental History* (October 2006).

Brewster, F.O. *They Came West*. Banff: The Author, 1979.

Brown, R. Craig. "The Doctrine of Usefulness: Natural Resource and National Parks Policy in Canada, 1887–1914." In *Canadian Parks in Perspective*, edited by J.G. Nelson. Montreal: Harvest House, 1970.

Brownlee, John E. "The Transfer of Alberta's Natural Resources." *Alberta History*, Vol. 53, No. 4 (Autumn 2005).

Burnett, J. Alexander. *A Passion for Wildlife: The History of the Canadian Wildlife Service*. Vancouver: UBC Press, 2005.

Burns, Robert. *Guardians of the Wild: A History of the Warden Service in Canada's National Parks*. Ottawa: Parks Canada, 1999.

Canada. House of Commons *Debates*. May 3, 1887, April 23, 1902, March 20, 1908, April 28, 1911, April 10, 1924, May 9, 1930, May 26, 1930, July 3, 1931, November 22, 1932.

Canada. Department of the Interior *Annual Reports*. "Part V. Rocky Mountains Park," 1899; "Report of the Deputy Minister," 1908; "Report of Artistic Layout of Banff by Thos. H. Mawson," 1914; "Report of the Commissioner of Dominion Parks," 1911–1921; "Canadian National Parks, Report of the Commissioner, J.B. Harkin," 1922–1927; "National Parks of Canada, Report of the Commissioner, J.B. Harkin," 1928–1936.

Canada. *Dominion Forest Reserves and Parks Act*, 1–2 George V., c. 10 and amendment 3–4 George V., c. 18.

Canada. Commission of Conservation Reports. 1910, 1911, 1912, 1913, 1916; *National Conference on Conservation of Game, Fur-Bearing Animals and Other Wildlife, February* 18 & 19, 1919.

Canada. *The Canada Gazette*. September 9, 1911, October 31, 1914.

Canada. The Senate. *Report of the Proceedings of the Special Committee on Tourist Traffic*, 1934.

Canada. P.C. 1338, June 8, 1911; P.C. 646, March 27, 1913; P.C. 1264, May 29, 1918; P.C. 2594, September 18, 1917; P.C. 901, June 10, 1926; P.C. 74, January 14, 1931.

Camp, Frank. *Roots in the Rockies*. Jasper: Frank Camp Ventures, 1993.

Canadian Alpine Journal, 1912.

Clarke, C.H.D. "In Memoriam, Hoyes Lloyd." *Auk*, Vol. 96, No. 2 (1978).

Colpitts, George. *Game in the Garden: A Human History of Wildlife in Western Canada to 1940*. Vancouver, UBC Press, 2002.

Conan Doyle, Sir Arthur. *Memories and Adventures*. Boston: Little Brown, 1924.

Dawson, R.M. *The Civil Service of Canada*. London, 1929.

Dixon, Ann. *Silent Partners: Wives of National Parks Wardens (Their Lives and History)*. Jasper: Dixon and Dixon Publishers, 1983.

Djuff, Ray. *High on a Windy Hill: The Story of the Prince of Wales Hotel*. Calgary: Rocky Mountain Books, 1999.

Dilsaver, Lary M. *America's National Park System: The Critical Documents*. Baltimore: Rowman and Littlefield, 1993.

Diubaldo, R. "Wrangling over Wrangel Island." *Canadian Historical Review*, Vol. 48, No. 3 (September 1967).

Dunlap, Thomas R. "Ecology, Nature and Canadian National Parks Policy: Wolves, Elk and Bison as a Case Study." In *To See Ourselves/To Save Ourselves: Ecology and Culture in Canada*. Montreal: Association of Canadian Studies, 1991.

Dunlap, Thomas, R. *Saving America's Wildlife*. Princeton: Princeton University Press, 1988.

Findlay, Nora. *Jasper: A Backward Glance at People, Places and Progress*. Jasper: Parks and People, 1992.

Flader, Susan L. *Thinking Like a Mountain: Aldo Leopold and the Evolution of an Ecological Attitude toward Deer, Wolves and Forests*. Madison: University of Wisconsin Press, 1974.

Foster, Franklin L. *John E. Brownlee: A Biography*. Lloydminster: Foster's Learning, 1996.

Foster, Janet. *Working for Wildlife: The Beginning of Preservation in Canada*. Toronto and Buffalo: University of Toronto Press, 1978.

Francis, Daniel. *A Road for Canada: The Illustrated Story of the Trans-Canada Highway*. North Vancouver, BC: Stanton, Arthur & Dos, 2006.

Fraser, Esther. *Wheeler*. Banff: Summerthought, 1978.

Gaffield, Pam and Chad, ed. *Consuming Canada: Readings in Environmental History*. Toronto: Copp Clark, 1995.

Glassford, Larry A. *Reaction and Reform: The Politics of the Conservative Party under R.B. Bennett, 1927–1938*. Toronto: University of Toronto Press, 1990.

Granatstein, J.L. *The Ottawa Men: The Civil Service Mandarins, 1935–1957*. Toronto: Oxford University Press, 1982.

Gray, James. *R.B. Bennett: The Calgary Years*. Toronto: University of Toronto Press, 1991.

Great Plains Research, *Jasper National Park, 1792–1965: A History*. Ottawa: Parks Canada, 1984.

Hall, David. *Clifford Sifton, Vol. 2*. Vancouver: UBC Press, 1985.

Harkin, J.B. "Canadian National Parks and Playgrounds." *Annual Report of the Historic Landmarks Association of Canada*, 1921.

———. "Canada's National Parks." In *Handbook of Canada*. Toronto: University of Toronto Press, 1924.

———. *Just a Sprig of Mountain Heather*. Ottawa: Dominion Parks Branch, 1914.

———. "Our Need for National Parks." *Canadian Alpine Journal*, 1918.

———. *The History and Meaning of the National Parks of Canada*. Saskatoon: H.R. Larson, 1957.

———. "Wild Life Sanctuaries." *Rod and Gun*, Vol. XXI, No. 5 (October 1919).

Hart, E.J. *Golf on the Roof of the World*. Banff: EJH Literary Enterprises, 1999.

———. *The Brewster Story: From Packtrain to Tour Bus*. Banff: Brewster Transport, 1981.

Henderson, Gavin. "The Father of Canadian National Parks." *Borealis* (Fall, 1994).

Hewitt, C. Gordon. *The Conservation of the Wild Life of Canada*. New York: Charles Scribner's Sons, 1921.

Hornaday, William T. *Camp-Fires in the Canadian Rockies*. New York: Charles Scribner's Sons, 1906.

———. *Our Vanishing Wild Life*. New York: Charles Scribner's Sons, 1913.

Jacoby, Karl. *Crimes against Nature: Squatters, Poachers, Thieves, and the Hidden History of American Conservation*. Berkeley: University of California Press, 2001.

Jameson, Sheilagh. *W.J. Oliver: Life Through a Master's Lens*. Calgary: Glenbow Museum, 1984.

Long, M.H. "The Historic Sites and Monuments Board of Canada." *Canadian Historical Association Report*, 1954.

Loo, Tina. *States of Nature: Conserving Canada's Wildlife in the Twentieth Century*. Vancouver: UBC Press, 2006.

Lothian, W.F. *A History of Canada's National Parks*, *Vols*. 1, 2, 4. Ottawa: Parks Canada, 1976–1981.

MacEachern, Alan. *Natural Selections, National Parks in Atlantic Canada, 1935–1970*. Montreal and Kingston: McGill-Queen's University Press, 2001.

———. "Rationality and Rationalization in Canadian National Park Predator Policy." In *Consuming Canada: Readings in Environmental History*, edited by Chad and Pam Gaffield. Toronto: Copp Clark, 1995.

Millar, W.N. *Game Preservation in the Rocky Mountains Forest Reserve*. Ottawa: Dept. of the Interior, 1915.

Mills, Edward. *Rustic Building Programs in Canada's National Parks, 1887–1950*. Ottawa: National Historic Sites Directorate, Parks Canada, 1994.

Nash, Roderick. "Wilderness Man in North America." In *Canadian Parks in Perspective*, edited by J.G. Nelson. Montreal: Harvest House, 1970.

Reichwein, PearlAnn. "'Hands Off Our National Parks': The Alpine Club of Canada and Hydro-Development Controversies in the Canadian Rockies, 1922–1930." *Journal of the Canadian Historical Association*, Vol. 6 New series (1995).

Russell, William. "James Bernard Harkin (1875–1955)." National and Historic Parks Branch, Manuscript Report Number 216.

Sandlos, John. *Hunters at the Margin: Native People and Wildlife Conservation in the Northwest Territories*. Vancouver: UBC Press, 2007.

Sellars, Richard W. *Preserving Nature in the National Parks*. New Haven: Yale University Press, 1997.

Scott, Duncan Campbell. "Relation of Indians to Wild Life Conservation." In *Proceedings of National Conference on Conservation of Game, Fur-Bearing Animals and Other Wildlife*. Ottawa: Commission of Conservation, 1919.

Servos, Paul. "CPAWS...A Brief History." *Parks News* (Summer 1987).

Smith, Donald B. *From the Land of Shadows: The Making of Grey Owl*. Saskatoon: Western Producer Books, 1990.

Stefansson, Vilhjalmur. *Discovery: The Autobiography of Vilhjalmur Stefansson*. New York: McGraw-Hill, 1964.

Taylor, C.J. "Legislating Nature: The National Parks Act of 1930." In *To See Ourselves/To Save Ourselves: Ecology and Culture in Canada*, edited by Rowland Lorimer et al. Montreal: Association for Canadian Studies, 1991.

————. *Negotiating the Past: The Making of Canada's National Historic Parks and Sites*. Montreal and Kingston: McGill-Queen's University Press, 1990.

Thorpe, F.J. "Historical Perspective on the 'Resources for Tomorrow Conference'." Ottawa: Department of Northern Affairs and National Resources, [1961].

Trefethen, James B. *An American Crusade for Wildlife*. New York: Winchester Press and Boone and Crockett Club, 1975.

Waiser, W.A. *Park Prisoners: The Untold Story of Western Canada's National Parks, 1915–46*. Saskatoon: Fifth House, 1995.

————. *Saskatchewan's Playground*. Saskatoon: Fifth House, 1989.

Waite, P.B. "Richard Bedford Bennett." *Dictionary of Canadian Biography Online*.

Williams, M.B. *Through the Heart of the Canadian Rockies & Selkirks*. Ottawa: Minister of the Interior, 1921.

————. *Guardians of the Wild*. London: Thomas Nelson, 1939.

Williamson, F.H.H. "Game Preservation in Dominion Parks," *Proceedings at a Meeting of the Committee on Fisheries, Game and Fur-Bearing Animals, November 1 and 2, 1915*. Ottawa: Commission of Conservation, 1916.

————. "Good Roads for Canada." *Good Roads Canada*, Vol. 1, No. 10.

————. "Roads in the Parks of the Dominion," *Good Roads Canada*, Vol. II, No. 1.

Woodcock, George & Avakumovic, Ivan. *The Doukhobors*. Toronto: McClelland and Stewart, 1977.

Worster, Donald. "Doing Environmental History." In *Consuming Canada: Readings in Environmental History*, edited by Chad and Pam Gaffield. Toronto: Copp Clark, 1995.

————. *Nature's Economy: A History of Ecological Ideas*. Cambridge: Cambridge University Press, 1985.

Zaslow, Morris. *The Northern Expansion of Canada*. Toronto: McClelland and Stewart, 1988.

UNPUBLISHED SOURCES

Brower, Jennifer Lynn. "Buffalo National Park and the Second Demise of the Plains Buffalo in Canada, 1909–1940." Master's thesis, University of Alberta, 2004.

Getty, Ian L. "The History of Waterton Lakes National Park, 1800–1937." Research paper prepared for the National Historic Parks Branch, 1971.

Lewis, Harrison. "Lively: A History of the Canadian Wildlife Service." Unpublished ms, 1976.

Lothian, Fegus. "James Bernard Harkin, a brief biographical sketch." Unpublished ms (available at the Whyte Museum of the Canadian Rockies, Library and Archives).

Michener, E. Alyn. "The Development of Western Waters, 1885–1930." PhD thesis, University of Alberta, 1973.

Reichweinn, PearlAnn. "Beyond the Visionary Mountains." PhD thesis, Carleton University, 1995.

Taylor, C.J. "A History of National Parks Administration, Part One: The Harkin Era." Unpublished manuscript (available at the Whyte Museum of the Canadian Rockies, Library and Archives).

Van Kirk, Sylvia. "The Development of National Park Policy in Canada's National Parks, 1885 to 1930." Master's thesis, University of Alberta, 1969.

Index

Page numbers in bold refer to photographs.